T >90 *

80-89 "

70-79 /

60-69 —

50-59 /

40-49 :

30-39 #

<30 ⊗ forget it

AN MMPI HANDBOOK

Volume I: Clinical Interpretation

by

W. Grant Dahlstrom

George Schlager Welsh

Leona E. Dahlstrom

A revised edition

UNIVERSITY OF MINNESOTA PRESS Minneapolis

Printed in the United States of America at Lund Press, Minneapolis

Published in Great Britain and India by the Oxford
University Press, London and Bombay, and in
Canada by the Copp Clark Publishing Co. Limited, Toronto

Library of Congress Catalog Card Number: 74-172933

ISBN 0-8166-0589-0

TO Jeanne Sinnen

Foreword to First Edition

IT WAS difficult to persuade a publisher to accept the MMPI in 1941. Dr. McKinley and I had faith sufficient to carry us through several rejections before the University of Minnesota Press finally undertook publication. We had begun in the late 1930's to assemble items for a new kind of personality inventory or test because we were convinced that an objective instrument for the "multiphasic" assessment of personality by means of a profile of scales would be useful in research and clinical practice. With an approach related to the empirically developed Binet tests of intelligence and the Strong Vocational Interest Blank, we had built scales from the responses of groups of patients routinely classified into the current clinical nosology. Most of the other tests of the time derived scales from the rational construction of items having face validity for the variables to be measured; or if empirical scales were employed, they were derived from heterogeneous neurotic or other maladjusted groups. The available tests seemed deficient both in the popularity of their theoretical bases and in the clinical usefulness of what they were expected to measure.

Our most optimistic expectation was that the methodology of the new test would be so clearly effective that there would soon be better devices with refinements of scales and of general validity. We rather hoped that we ourselves might, with five years' experience, greatly increase its validity and clinical usefulness, and perhaps even develop more solidly based constructs or theoretical variables for a new inventory. I doubt now that it is possible to improve the MMPI enough to repay the effort. I am not even sure that we could hold to what validity and usefulness we have.

Work on the MMPI began at a time when the modernized Kraepelinian classification system was still functioning. The individual scales then derived their particular properties from whatever was peculiar to those groupings. There were obvious shortcomings to this system. More rational and more clinically useful groupings were needed; also, it was clear that the system was not dynamic enough. We anticipated that the development of these better systems would make possible superior scales constructed by the MMPI methodology, but our hopes were not realized. Although various rational systems emerged, each with some adherents, none has prevailed. The new theoretical structure which we supposed would suggest a nosology of dynamically coherent personality types suffered the same fate. No such types have become popular.

Progress has not been better in the unpretentious approach to classification of clinical description. We still have only a weak rationale for speaking of specific causation or treatment of the mentally ill. I doubt that today's psychiatrists and psychologists could agree in descriptively identifying more than two or three modestly discrete diagnostic groupings among patients. The ubiquitous schizophrenia has spread into nearly every syndrome to the point where we may need to base a clinical nosology upon a breakdown not of mental disorders but of schizophrenias. In the meantime, the new and better MMPI cannot be derived from such amorphous clinical types. The original test has partly preserved the old classifications and possibly, weak as they are, some of its code pattern types cannot be bettered by the practices of modern clinical diagnosis.

The persons who obtain a given type of profile among those the MMPI provides are indubitably alike in that they make item responses with item and scale communality. We can select similar groups of people with this often mysteriously meaningful objectivity and somewhat stabilize our experiments in therapy, prognosis, and psychologic manipulation. Using MMPI codes for description of these groups provides at least an interim communication method about personality until we develop better classes.

A justification for the MMPI can be suggested now that was unforeseen in 1941. The subsequent wide use and availability of the test permits easier replication and application of experimental results than is the case if unfamiliar items and tests are used. The latter require too much of us. Our inertia prevents a proper pyramiding of new data upon the findings of others. When new findings are presented using an unfamiliar test, we rarely even replicate the work and still more rarely build upon it. If an investigator uses the MMPI or another widely employed test, however, then more information is easily added to the substantial fund already accumulated and the tool to use in replication or further work is readily available.

That the MMPI will be a steppingstone to a higher level of validity I still sincerely hope; I hope too that the new level will soon loom in sight. In the meantime I see it as a steppingstone that permits useful communication at its own level even though the stone is rather wobbly.

As I have stated, the MMPI began with validity based upon the usefulness of the various diagnostic groups from which its scales were derived. Now the burden of its use rests upon construct validity. Only a small fraction of the published data relating clinical or experimental variables to its scales or profiles can be understood in terms of the original approach. If the validity views of 1941 were the only support for the inventory, it could not survive. What is happening is that the correlations being observed with other variables in normal and abnormal subjects are filling out personality constructs that emerge, to be in turn tested for their ability to survive. It is significant that constructs, in the general sense of construct validity, can be the forerunners of diagnostic classes.

I do not think that marked improvement in clinical validity can come now with merely different items, with modification of item weighting, or, in general, with revision of scales based upon our present diagnostic and statistical methods. No improvement that seems presently attainable is likely to remedy by much the deficiencies of the criterion groups we can provide from current clinical practice or personality theory. In developing some of the MMPI scales (Hathaway, 1956b) we tried a variety of item-weight systems. Nothing that we could find improved discrimination enough even to compensate for the increased complexity of scoring in contrast to the simplicity of unit weights. It seemed that a scale needed at least thirty separate responses and if a criterion group was not homogeneous, as with schizophrenic patients, then many more responses were required. We lost test power whenever we did anything but add empirically pertinent items. Further, adding "extra-good" items did not work appreciably better than adding items with only moderate reliability. We were eventually driven to the simple generalization which had provided our initial point of departure: the more differential items a person answered like some criterion group, the more like the group he appeared in other ways — without there being any requirement that the items belong together statistically, show a difference of extra-high reliability, or have a recognizable rational validity.

People who answer True to questions asking if they have red hair or large feet, like turnips, or read science fiction are alike. Every objective response like these has a group of implicit associated responses dispositionally suggested by the primary one. These implicit responses may be the real carriers of personality inventory validity. An example might be that people who say they like turnips are likely to be farmers or to play juke boxes or to smoke a pipe. Meehl has referred to this as the projective aspect of objective items. These associated implicit items probably relate to the syndromes we identify rather than to the primary item about turnips. At any rate, our early lesson was that the face content of the scale items did not well suggest the clinical construct that grew up with use of a scale. Preoccupation with item form and content misses the real nature of the item. This real nature can only be discovered by a process of searching through the indefinite multitude of other implicit items.

Once one is free of preoccupation with the item as a bit of language or a factual report, it is easier to see why the attempt to avoid distortion of scales by response sets or role playing or lying is unlikely to help us much. If certain of those persons who say they like turnips are lying, they are, of course, different from the others to some degree. We have to evaluate the validity implications of the fact that they tell this lie. I have asserted above that to say one likes turnips carries associated contingent implications. Some people would not even admit to liking turnips if pushed to lie about it; those who can be induced to lie to that effect do not consider it completely intolerable to be associated with the turnip eaters. The data on response sets, such as social desirability, nicely show that the seeming fact of an item is perhaps infrequently the real determiner of the subject's response in a test situation. Preoccupation with some kind of *real* meaning or truth about the turnip item could therefore have little to do with the scale validity of the item.

A kind of lying or role playing (if we must use a euphemism) is inevitably a part of personality. Role playing can be extended to include all personality facets, and overuse of the word *role* may be confusing us. It is obvious that we provide a physician, a bartender, an employer, and a spouse with different views of ourselves. One cannot say which of us is the *real* person. The *real* person we speak of is usually a vaguely described confidential self that we see in ourselves or others. But such confidential selves are roles too and much less useful ones for most purposes than are the routine ones of our daily encounters.

The problem of a salesman is to present his product. He may confidentially consider the product to be inferior; nevertheless he must know how to make it appear desirable to others. He also sells himself. He may see his *real* self to be different from the one he shows the prospective buyer, but he must know and express a self or role that is good for the sale. A personality test insensitive to the personality that a salesman produces in response to appropriate social situations would be a poor instrument to use for identifying salesmen. Similarly, a patient will be more responsive to treatment as a psychotic if his responses are like those of routine psychotic patients even if these are in some sense put on for the occasion. A personality test can be used as a communication method between clinicians, but it also permits clinicians to know which patients are prepared to play the game of diagnosis and therapy as we have learned it. A personality test would likewise be a poor instrument if it were not responsive to such a "clinically desirable" distortion by patients.

I still feel, as I have for some time, that no subject is more important for our work with personality measurement than is role playing or, perhaps better, multiple personality. We need to know the various personalities of an individual and the motivational factors influencing their appearance. To me, it seems naive to assume that the turnip item could be replaced by an associated one found to be the actual validity carrier, because the subject's implicit association will have a different response probability if it is made into an explicit item. Like earlier psychometricians, I believe that personality test data depend greatly upon the situation of testing, which is itself a function both of the particular items and of the more obvious environmental factors. Skilled manipulation of the environmental testing situation is crucial to elicit the personalities we wish to measure, and interpretation of test data can proceed validly only when we can have an idea which personality the testee has presented. It is clear that a test should be sensitive to these various personality aspects because the data we get are valid only for the proper role. If we want to select a salesman, we would not want a physician to obtain the MMPI profile unless we were more interested in the applicant's physical and mental health than in his ability to be a good salesman. We must not be dismayed by having to give the personality test twice if we want two valid assessments of a person. We may have to administer the test once under the auspices of a personnel department and once with the protection of professional confidence. Different persons, instructions, surroundings, and implied uses of the data are needed to elicit different personalities of the individual. Once again I want to emphasize that the various profiles are all valid. Our tests often appear weak because we have not evoked the appropriate profiles or properly extracted the available validity.

The "K" attitudes — those influencing lying or role playing — are a crucial area for progress with the problems of objective personality measurement. To understand and manipulate the "K" attitudes is more significant than expending energy on the undesirable, indeed impossible, effort to eradicate "K" from personality variable measurements.

Construct validities for personality test profiles, then, appear to be what we are working toward. These provide standardization as communication and suggest the stabilization of some of the constructs into diagnoses. Beyond this I cannot see. If we conclude that the methods we are using are not satisfactory, we seem to need something really novel. This could come in the discovery of a successful rational approach to personality analysis or in some difficult-to-imagine breakthrough in psychometric method.

First with their *Basic Readings on the MMPI in Psychology and Medicine* (1956) and now with their *Handbook*, Dahlstrom and Welsh are providing us with a basis for construct development of the MMPI as well as for present practical applications of the test in ways that will develop what validity we have. Because the need for tests is great, there is always a danger that research energy will be dissipated by wide and improper use of an instrument. To prevent this, it is necessary that the methods and promise of a test be sharply understood and ruthlessly evaluated. Dahlstrom and Welsh prepared the present volume to contribute to this understanding and evaluation of the MMPI.

The *Handbook* began as a small book and grew up. It was to have been made up of useful tables and other basic information and a brief survey of the literature. But the proliferation of publications bearing on the MMPI made the bibliography alone almost unmanageable; even a selective review of the research findings represented by the bibliography required a much lengthier discussion than had at first been anticipated. Yet if the volume was to be a handbook in the fullest sense of the word, such an analysis seemed imperative. The statistical and other tabular material, too, grew at a surprising rate as practical reference data were assembled. When the word *Multiphasic* (an etymological bastard) was chosen, we thought that numerous scales would be found among the items, but we surely never expected the number listed in Appendix I.

The authors have done a real service in this *Handbook*; it is factual and thorough. We could not tolerate a biased selection of data and empty statements of faith in the value of the MMPI. Dahlstrom and Welsh have organized and presented objectively an impressive array of materials from a wide variety of sources. They have permitted the data and the work in progress to speak for themselves. We who use the MMPI today and who are already trying to look into the future of this field are therefore lastingly in their debt.

Starke R. Hathaway

University of Minnesota
December 1959

Foreword to New Edition

THE Foreword for the first edition of the *MMPI Handbook* was signed "December 1959." These paragraphs are being written twelve years later.

I will not write of the excellence of this edition. It is good and will speak in its own favor. There are now a third author, two volumes, and an incredibly larger amount of useful and interesting data. The greatest compliment in my value system lies in the objectivity of reporting and comparatively unbiased representation of the MMPI and its history.

The MMPI was established by empirical methods; it is good that its most significant reporters exemplify a low-key review of the evidence that is appropriate. The MMPI atlases were a deliberately uncontaminated collection of typical case histories organized so that the user was left to find what validity he could in relating the accounts to MMPI codes. He was not instructed about reputed interpretive meanings of this and that quantitative or qualitative feature of MMPI profiles. Indeed, there were few convincingly valid coherences between case histories and code types that could have been documented at that time.

Now, in this new *Handbook* there are emerging correlates of code types and descriptive and predictive outcomes. The validities of these emerging syndromes are not bad. I do not think we are yet at the end of this empirical accumulation of personality correlates.

This *Handbook* is timely. I sincerely believe that it contains most of what we shall learn from the MMPI method about personality organization and measurement. We are long overdue for someone to put together a new system and method that will be distinctly better. Here are some fundamental data, and I cannot doubt their basic stability since they do not rest principally upon theoretical constructs or a current system of personality theory that, like most past ones, is temporally bound and will run a brief course in popularity.

The MMPI has always been handicapped by impoverished associative personological color. I and most others who have worked with the test have felt this. It has been critically reviewed a hundred times with objections to its lack of the validity we hope for. Most of the reviewers pause at some point to puzzle for a moment why the MMPI should not have faded away as so many more glamorous tests have done. The answer, I think, lies in the fact that whatever we hope for or even espouse as we write or teach about personality tends always to contain more promise than our present methods can fulfill. Meanwhile, most working psychologists and others who must make daily judgments and decisions that affect the lives of others find that the test, with all its faults, affords some independent security for insecure personal judgments. Working psychologists cannot yet afford the luxury of throwing away a tool for its lack of constructural quality. For practical decisions, the MMPI offers its modest validities with an occasional bonus in a few high-probability correlates. Perhaps conversion hysteria has gone out of style along with diagnosis and evaluative formulations, but even an amateur reader of MMPI profiles who sees a code 13′ . . . can for a moment feel professional identity in giving a little interpretive statement about the modal person who produces such a profile. He can usually enrich this description with some insightful item. He is, for example, rather safe if he asks what disablement the person developed when he encountered a period of psychological stress.

But I am not writing this to do what I have complimented the authors for not doing. If I have engaged in a brief polemic, it is an expression of satisfaction that the MMPI has aided us in spite of its shortcomings and of my sincere hope that we can move on with surer steps. If another twelve years were to go by without our having gone on to a better instrument or better procedure for the practical needs, I fear that the MMPI, like some other tests, might have changed from a hopeful innovation to an aged obstacle. Do not misunderstand me. I am not agreeing with a few critics who have already called for the funeral and written the epitaph. They have not yet identified what is better. We cannot lay down even a stone-age ax if we have no better one to hew with.

I am now retired from my professional role. The MMPI has been a line of communication between me and my contemporaries. Whatever else may be said of it, it has led me to a most satisfying accumulation of friends and associates. Perhaps there was a common pattern of thinking that, exemplified in the qualities of MMPI research and applications, has selected such rewardingly attractive people. But also many of my friends have been active critics. I cannot possibly express my esteem and warm feelings for many of those whose names appear in this *Handbook* – and among those most esteemed and loved are the authors.

Starke R. Hathaway

May 1971

Preface

In 1960 when the first edition of this volume was published it was, with some forethought, given the title of *An MMPI Handbook.* For lack of companions, it soon became known as The Handbook but, as we had hoped, this isolation did not last long. Now the title is particularly cogent: many MMPI handbooks and atlases are in existence; this revision is intended for use in close conjunction with these other MMPI references. The compilation of special scoring procedures included in Chapter 3 and the personological interpretive materials presented in Part Three frequently refer the user to these other works. Jointly, this small library of MMPI research data constitutes an impressive archive of personological lore which is unique in the psychological test field. No other test instrument operates from an empirical base of this size and quality, not even the historically prior and much more focused scales in the ability and aptitude areas. Perhaps its closest relative is the empirically based Strong Vocational Interest Blank. It is our sincere hope that the information presented here will enable MMPI users to apply these research findings with increased effectiveness in evaluating and alleviating the many forms of human misery described herein.

The decision to divide this work into two volumes was a difficult one. Although the MMPI has by now been used for a vast variety of clinical and research problems, any one application of a test like this may involve most or all of the knowledge gained from these different uses and investigations. Each user must be as fully informed as possible about the accumulated lore on the test if he is to capitalize on its validities and minimize its biases and inherent limitations. Thus, in this first volume, the reader will find frequent citations of the research literature bearing upon issues that arise in the process of evaluating a protocol from some client or patient. In that sense, this volume is not merely a how-to-do-it manual, nor is the second volume a simple compendium of research findings. Rather, the first volume contains the material that is especially pertinent to the interpretation of individual MMPI records and the second contains the discussions relevant to the use of the MMPI as a research instrument by means of which subjects for a study may be selected or the impact of some manipulation may be evaluated. Of necessity, there are frequent cross-references between the two volumes. The placement of various topics in one or the other of the volumes has often had to be quite arbitrary. This was particularly difficult in the allocation of materials to the two technical appendixes.

As was true for the first edition, there are different levels of presentation in the various sections of Volume I. The material in Part One, for example, is intended for individuals who are relatively unfamiliar with the MMPI and perhaps even quite uninformed about testing and psychometric procedures in general. We hope that Part One contains enough that is new to be worth going over by old MMPI hands, but we also hope that it is presented simply and clearly enough that it can be read with comprehension by the many nonpsychologists who are carrying the responsibility of administering, scoring, and monitoring the files of the MMPI in institutions, clinics, schools, and industries in the United States and abroad. We have tried to collate carefully the presentation here with the current MMPI test *Manual* to avoid contradictions or confusing instructions. We are grateful to the Psychological Corporation for its help, guidance, and kind permission to duplicate parts of the *Manual* here.

In Part Two a careful examination of the complex issues of protocol validity is attempted. The standard indices of acceptability of a given test for individual inferences and interpretation are presented in the context of the research material available for judging their strengths and weaknesses. In addition, a number of new scales and indices which have appeared over the years are cited and discussed. It should be clear from these chapters that MMPI interpretation is already well under way while the clinician is carefully scrutinizing and appraising this kind of validity of the protocol. It will also be clear that the level of presentation in these chapters presupposes some degree of familiarity with MMPI terminology and concepts. The new reader should know the contents of Part One and may also profit from a reading of Chapter 6 before attempting to digest what is covered in Chapters 4 and 5. Additional background material may be found in Section II of the *Basic Readings* volume (Welsh and Dahlstrom, 1956).

Part Three is the heart of the test interpretation material. It is organized a little differently from the way it appeared in the first edition. Originally, all the material pertinent, say, to scale 1 was given sequentially beginning with the nomothetic correlates and followed by the idiographic ones. Here, these two kinds of application of the component scales are taken up separately. That is, in Chapter 6 data on the scale correlates of subjects scoring absolutely high or low on each of the basic clinical scales are summarized. In Chapter 7 the correlates of the scales when they appear as prominent elevations in the total profile are presented. As indicated in Chapter 8, proper clinical interpretation of an MMPI protocol involves a synthesis of both kinds of information, nomothetic and idiographic, together with evidence about the testing context and the subject's life circumstances. Material pertaining to these latter problems is scattered throughout the two volumes of this revision.

The main body of Chapter 8 is made up of a special case study composed of the reports on the same man generated by each of the commercial MMPI interpretive services now available in the United States. These reports, of different lengths and levels of interpretation, are evaluated against a detailed psychiatric workup and more comprehensive psychological assessment battery carried out with this man. Although data from a single case cannot and should not be used as a basis for typifying any given MMPI interpretive service, this presentation serves as a vehicle for illustrating and discussing the strengths and weaknesses of this important new MMPI development. We are grateful to the following services for their kind permission to reprint here the reports generated on this case: Clinical Psychological Services, Inc.; the Finney-Auvenshine Project; Institute of Clinical Analysis; National Computer Systems, Inc.; the Psychological Corporation; and Roche Psychiatric Service Institute. It should also be noted that a few identifying data have been altered to maintain the anonymity of the person used as the basis for this cross-comparison; we hope the psychological fidelity of the presentation has not been reduced by these substitutions.

As indicated above, the material in the technical appendixes of this volume was selected for its relevance to the evaluation of a given test record, but in this division several compromises were necessary. The first appendix in this volume is a good case in point. Appendix A contains a listing of the scoring direction (X or O) for each item when employed in the card form of the test. These data are necessary for individual case interpretation when inspecting a card-form record sheet for answers to particular items; it is not immediately clear on the record form whether the subject answered True or False to any given item. Obviously, this list is crucial as well in preparing a scoring key on a new research scale for the card form and could just as appropriately have been placed in Volume II. In either of these applications, however, Appendix A would probably be used in conjunction with Appendix C, necessitating that they be in close proximity. In fact, all of the first five appendixes in this volume serve important needs in research applications of the MMPI as well as in interpretive processing of a test record.

Appendix B was retained without change from the first edition, but Appendix C, which lists the equivalent item numbers from the various test forms, had to be expanded to include the information on Form R. It was not possible to list all combinations of item conversion, however, so conversion between card form and Form R must proceed through the intermediate step of converting to the regular booklet form numbers. We are grateful to the Psychological Corporation for permission to reprint here the Form R conversion tables from the MMPI *Manual.*

In Appendix D the alphabetical listing of the component items of the MMPI has been retained, which greatly facilitates locating the item number of a given item if the precise wording is known. Often, however, the clinician or investigator has only an approximate recollection of the statement or is working from a list of items which may or may not be MMPI items. In this case it would be much easier to work from certain key words and use the listing developed by Aaronson and Rothman (1962) which reduces the search to a few alternatives. This list can also be used to locate all items in the test pool that relate to particular topics, although the reader must bear in mind that some thesaurus work may also be required to locate all the variations a given theme may take in the MMPI statements. Through the kind permission of the *Journal of Psychological Studies* and the authors this listing is reprinted in Appendix E.

Appendix F and Appendix H both contain normative tables. The data in Appendix F cover the T scores (male and female) for various frequently used special scales on the MMPI based upon the responses of the original normal sample of Minnesota men and women as reported by Hathaway and Briggs (1957). The selection is quite arbitrary and many other scales deserve comparable scaling.

A supplementary set of such norms are presented in Volume II. In addition, means and sigmas for each of the other research scales from the same Minnesota norm groups appear in Volume II; from these data individual investigators can generate comparable T scores on any published MMPI scale.

Appendix G lists the so-called critical items from the MMPI item pool. The list was compiled by Leon I. Hellman at the Veterans Administration Center in Los Angeles, California, and published in Grayson (1951). These test items are neither psychometrically nor psychodiagnostically more powerful in their discriminations than many other items in the test and should not be considered crucial or critical in this sense. The content of these statements, however, covers material which is of particular interest in mental health screening or medical in-take evaluations. Many clinicians employ procedures of item tallying which enable them to inspect the answers their test subjects give to these individual items for guidelines to follow-up interviews or for supplementing their general profile interpretations.

The T-score tables presented in Appendix H all pertain to the basic MMPI scales or to subscales derived from them. The Minnesota normative groups used in the original test derivational work provided the basis for the male and female adult norms, with and without K corrections. Although these subjects ranged in age from 16 to 65, most of them were between the ages of 25 and 45 at the time they were tested. They were also used to derive comparable T scores for the subtle and obvious subscales of these basic clinical scales generated by Wiener and Harmon (1946) and for the content subscales developed by Harris and Lingoes (1955, 1968). Special psychiatric norms for these latter subscales are available in their 1968 materials. Special composite samples of adolescent boys and girls were assembled by Marks and Briggs, based primarily on the ninth-grade Minnesota statewide samples of Hathaway and Monachesi (1963) but also including cases from Ohio, California, and North Carolina. Non-K-corrected T scores on each of the basic MMPI scales were derived from subsamples of these adolescents: 14-year-olds or under, 15-, 16-, and 17-year-old subgroups. Data from a normal, aged sample of men and women living in Minnesota that was collected by Swenson (1961) were used as the basis for the T scores on male and female subjects over the age of 60 included in Appendix H. These norms are K-corrected values. One other set of T scores is provided in this appendix for use with college or university undergraduates. The data come from a total testing of entering freshmen, male and female, carried out at the University of North Carolina in 1964 and are the same data as those tabulated for two-point high-point code combinations in Tables 7 and 8 in Appendix M.

The special scales listed by item numbers from the regular booklet form in Appendix I are only those which have been derived from the basic scales of the MMPI. A much more extensive listing of research scales on this instrument appears in Volume II. With each scale, in addition to the items scored True and False on the scale, are given the means and sigmas earned by the Minnesota normal men and women on that set of items. The reference samples are the same purified and refined groups employed by Hathaway and Briggs in deriving the special norms given in Appendix F. The means and sigmas in Appendix I have not been systematically corrected for age or marital status, however, as was true in the computations reported by Hathaway and Briggs (1957); the obtained values in Appendix

I will not correspond directly, therefore, to their results. One additional note on these values for the means and sigmas: occasionally, the scores are based on a subset of the items in a given scale because of the items missing from the original MMPI pool (see the explanation in Chapter 1).

In Appendix J, the Meehl-Dahlstrom rules have again been presented, but additional sets of rules provided by Henrichs for separating neurotic, psychotic, and character-disorder patterns, separately for men (1964) and women (1966), have also been included. The rules and flow chart for using Kleinmuntz's (1963) decision rules for determining emotional maladjustment are also summarized there, as well as the Buer (1959) rules for computing the index of somatization.

Material in Appendix K is new in this edition. It provides a rough guide to the prorating of component scale scores from an incomplete test record based on the regular booklet version of the test. Such abbreviated or abortive test administrations may be salvaged in some instances by use of these prorating weights.

Appendix L reproduces the standard booklet form of the MMPI test items. The original versions of the *Manual* incorporated a set of the item statements (in card-form order), but the items have been omitted from the latest revision of the *Manual* (1967). Often the test interpretation is carried out in a place where a test booklet may not be at hand. We are grateful to the Psychological Corporation for permission to reproduce these materials here.

The data on two-point high-point pairs in the profile patterns from selected groups have largely been retained from the first edition and appear in Appendix M. A few sets of data have been substituted when better samples were available from recent research, however, and additional data on new populations have been incorporated in this appendix.

Appendix N contains reproductions (slightly reduced in size) of various test forms, answer sheets, and profile materials available for use with the different versions of the MMPI. These materials are discussed in Part One and illustrate various specific features of the administering, scoring, and profiling of the test. Reproduction of these materials is made with the kind permission of the Psychological Corporation and of TESTSCOR and Mr. Elmer Hankes.

Appendix O contains a list of the test-scoring and interpretive services currently available in the United States. These various services are described and discussed in Chapters 1, 2, and 8 of this volume.

The references included here are a selected set of MMPI items covering the material cited in this volume. A comprehensive MMPI bibliography is to be found in Volume II.

The additional author and the multiple volumes of this revision attest to the magnitude of the job which is now involved in preparing a work of this kind. Further evidence is the number of people and agencies to whom we are indebted for help in this project. The first author (WGD) had a generous Senior Postdoctoral Research Fellowship from the National Institute of Mental Health in 1967–68 (1-F3-MH-35,376) which enabled him to serve as a research associate at the Menninger Foundation in Topeka, Kansas, for twelve months and a visiting scholar at the Institute of Personality Assessment and Research (IPAR) at the University of California, Berkeley, for an additional three months. Both of these periods of study enabled him to get the work on this manuscript well launched by bibliographic searches, leisurely reading, and cogent discussions with professional colleagues deeply involved in research and study of the MMPI and other assessment techniques. In addition, the National Institute of Mental Health funded a research grant to him (MH 17139) from their small grant program for 1969–70 which facilitated the project by underwriting bibliographic costs and summer salary for WGD. The University Research Council at the University of North Carolina at Chapel Hill has also underwritten various expenses in this project through grant number 324-ALU-3(34) in 1968.

The Alabama MEDLARS Service Center of the National Library of Medicine, Birmingham, Alabama, has provided us with comprehensive bibliographic searches of the recent literature which have been invaluable in completing our MMPI files on both English-language and foreign-language references. Additional help on special bibliographies has come from Drs. Earl S. Taulbee, Raymond D. Fowler, James N. Butcher, Julian J. Lasky, Leona Egan, Nathan Rosenberg, and Irving Gottesman. It should be noted that the support from these colleagues and friends has gone well beyond the mere supplying of information or checking of data. We also want to acknowledge our appreciation for the consistently efficient and supportive efforts of the staff members of the library at the Menninger Foundation, particularly the help from its director, Miss Vesta Walker, and the staff librarians, Miss Helen Carlyle and Miss Rebecca Breeden.

Assistance in collecting various MMPI scales and indices has been given by many colleagues, but we are particularly indebted to Dr. Jerry Wiggins, at the University of Illinois, Drs. Leonard Rorer and Lewis Goldberg, at the Oregon Research Institute, Dr. Douglas N. Jackson, at the University of Western Ontario, Dr. James Webb and Mr. Marvin Miller, at the Roche Psychiatric Service Institute, and Drs. Peter Briggs and Paul E. Meehl at the University of Minnesota, for their help in these efforts. Dr. Mark I. Appelbaum, in the L. L. Thurstone Psychometric Laboratory at the University of North Carolina in Chapel Hill has provided us with invaluable support in the scoring of the many extant MMPI scales on the Minnesota normative samples to generate the supplementary data provided in Appendix I. To all of these individuals and many more, we owe a debt for the accuracy and comprehensiveness of the scale tabulations in this volume and in Volume II.

A real debt must be acknowledged as well to several people who are both innovative investigators and what Hathaway in his Foreword has called "working psychologists," dealing with the MMPI in their daily professional activities. William J. Eichman, Robert H. Hickey, John R. Graham, Arnold D. Krugman, Carl M. Cochrane, and James H. Panton have all contributed generously of their data, their ideas, and their experience in this area, for which we are most grateful.

The staff members of the clinical services and research division of the Menninger Foundation were highly successful in creating the perfect atmosphere for scholarly work: peace and quiet when solitary work was under way, stimulation and critical discussion when desired. The continuing seminar on the MMPI that spontaneously formed during 1967–68 was a source of many insights and syntheses for WGD and LED. We are grateful to the participants: Drs. Philip S. Holzman, Rowe Mortimer, Henry Bachrach, Peter Bierkens, Siebolt Frieswyk, and Ronald

Lee. Dr. Gardner Murphy was a supportive and stimulating sponsor for our stay at the Foundation.

The staff of IPAR was uniformly helpful and facilitating in all of our efforts in library research, data organization, and writing. The opportunities for lengthy discussions with Drs. Donald MacKinnon, Harrison Gough, Frank Barron, Wallace Hall, Ravenna Helson, and Jack Block were most welcome, as were the lively lunch meetings at the International House. The excellent resources of the psychology library in Tolman Hall were greatly appreciated as well.

Preparation of the bibliographic materials and the typescripts has been a joint effort of many people too. Mrs. Hazel Bruce and Miss Nancy Domingues of the Menninger Foundation, and Mrs. Florence Cho, at IPAR, helped in early drafts. Mrs. Shirley Talley and Mrs. Blanche Critcher at the University of North Carolina have also provided needed and much appreciated help in various phases of the work. Mr. Donald Baucom prepared many of the tables and checked bibliographic citations as well as aiding in the proofing and manuscript preparation.

We wish to express our appreciation to Starke R. Hathaway for his contributions to the project, both explicit in his Foreword and implicit in the formulations and conceptualizations inherent in this manuscript. The influence of his thought, his philosophy, and his insights is indeed pervasive throughout our efforts.

Dr. James H. Ricks and his staff of the Test Division of the Psychological Corporation have been supportive and helpful in many ways in the course of preparing this revision. We have acknowledged their permissions and clearances at various places but also wish to express our appreciation for their interest and assistance in many other ways as well.

The editorial, design, and production staffs of the University of Minnesota Press have earned our respect, admiration, and gratitude for their conscientious care, artistic creativity, expeditious and accurate processing of the printing, and effective promotion of both editions of this volume. The whole staff has been wonderful to work with, but it is appropriate that we acknowledge at this time the special role which Miss Jeanne Sinnen, senior editor at the Press, has played in this work and in every other MMPI volume issuing from their presses. Her mastery of the technical detail on the test itself, her solicitude for the clarity and precision of the presentation, and her deep involvement in the preparation of these books have been impressive to all who know her and have worked with her in these ventures. The field owes her a great deal for her contributions to the MMPI effort. It is with particular pleasure that we dedicate this volume to her in small repayment for her support and friendship over the years.

Acknowledgments and Permissions

THE authors also wish to thank the companies and persons listed below for permission to use various other materials included in this volume:

Roche Psychiatric Service Institute and Mr. Marvin Miller for permission to reproduce the Patient Instructions from the booklet *Administering the MMPI*, Roche Laboratories, 1967, that appear in Chapter 1.

TESTSCOR and Mr. Elmer Hankes for permission to reproduce the Hankes answer sheet for the booklet form of the MMPI in Appendix N.

The *Journal of Psychological Studies* for permission to reproduce the key word index prepared by B. S. Aaronson and I. Rothman that appears in Appendix E.

The Williams and Wilkins Company, publishers of P. A. Marks and W. Seeman, *An Atlas for Use with the MMPI: Actuarial Description of Abnormal Personality*, 1963, for permission to reproduce the various sets of rules defining the MMPI code types summarized in Chapter 3.

W. B. Saunders Company, publishers of H. Gilberstadt and Jan Duker, *A Handbook for Clinical and Actuarial MMPI Interpretation*, 1965, for permission to reproduce the various sets of rules defining the MMPI profile types summarized in Chapter 3.

Perceptual and Motor Skills for permission to reproduce the material in the table in the article by C. O. Watson and R. W. Thomas, "MMPI Profiles of Brain-Damaged and Schizophrenic Patients," appearing in volume 27, 1968, which is summarized in Chapter 3.

Przeglad Psychologiczny, Poznan, Poland, for permission to reproduce the table of linear discriminant function weights from the article by M. Choynowski, "The Usefulness of the Fisher Linear Discriminant Function in Clinical Diagnosis with the MMPI," in Volume 11, 1966, appearing in Chapter 3.

The *Journal of Clinical Psychology* for permission to reproduce the following: Table 1 in Phyllis M. Reese, J. T. Webb, and J. D. Foulks, "A Comparison of Oral and Booklet Forms of the MMPI for Psychiatric Inpatients," *Journal of Clinical Psychology*, 1968, 24, 436–437, appearing in Chapter 1; Table 7 and pp. 22–25 in W. J. Eichman, "Factored Scales for the MMPI: A Clinical and

Statistical Manual," *Journal of Clinical Psychology,* 1962, 18, 363–395, appearing in Chapters 3 and 7; the novant correlates presented on pp. 46–47 in G. S. Welsh, "MMPI Profiles and Factor Scales A and R," *Journal of Clinical Psychology,* 1965, 21, 43–47, appearing in Chapters 3 and 7; Table 1 in J. S. Wiggins and Judith Vollmar, "The Content of the MMPI," *Journal of Clinical Psychology,* 1959, 15, 46–47, appearing in Chapter 7.

The American Psychological Association for permission to reproduce the following: The decision rules and flow chart from pp. 21–22 in B. Kleinmuntz, "MMPI Decision Rules for the Identification of College Maladjustment: A Digital Computer Approach," *Psychological Monographs,* 1963, 77, 14 (Whole No. 577), appearing in Appendix J; Table 1 in Jane K. Cooke, "MMPI in Actuarial Diagnosis of Psychological Disturbance among College Males," *Journal of Counseling Psychology,* 1967, 14, 474–477, appearing in Chapter 3; Table 4 in A. Rosen, "Test-Retest Stability of MMPI Scales for a Psychiatric Population," *Journal of Consulting Psychology,* 1953, 17, 217–221, appearing in Chapter 1; Table 2 in W. J. Eichman, "Discrimination of Female Schizophrenics with Configural Analysis of the MMPI Profile," *Journal of Consulting Psychology,* 1959, 23, 442–447, appearing in Chapter 3; Table 1 in E. S. Taulbee and B. D. Sisson, "Configurational Analysis of MMPI Profiles of Psychiatric Groups," *Journal of Consulting Psychology,* 1957, 21, 413–417, appearing in Chapter 3.

Dr. Jack Fox for permission to reproduce material from Table 16 and Figures 1A and 1B from his copyrighted manuscript, "Patterns of Stimulus-Avoidance on the MMPI," 1964, which appears in Chapter 4.

Dr. Carl F. Buer for permission to reproduce the rules for his somatization index developed in 1959 in his doctoral dissertation, which appear in Appendix J.

Contents

PART ONE: ADMINISTRATIVE PROBLEMS

CHAPTER 1. Administering the Test

THE Minnesota Multiphasic Personality Inventory (MMPI) is a standardized inventory designed to elicit a wide range of self-descriptions from each test subject and to provide in quantitative form a set of evaluations of his personality status and emotional adjustment. Each subject is asked to answer 550 different items either True or False as they apply to him, although he may also indicate that some of them do not apply. The items may be administered in any of several test formats with either booklets or boxes of cards; the responses are recorded by the subject himself on an answer sheet or by a clerical worker at a later time. Scoring of the inventory is objective and may be carried out by clerical workers, either by hand or with machine-scoring equipment, or by any one of several scoring services in different regions of the United States.

Standard scoring procedures generate a test profile, or psychogram, composed of four validity indicators and ten clinical or personality scales, which have come to be known both by abbreviations of the scale names and by code numbers, used interchangeably (see Table 1-1). Numerous special scales and indices are also available for scoring on the same test protocol. The basic norms for the component scales of the profile were derived from samples of normal Minnesota adults. The scale values have been derived separately for each sex. The raw-score means of Minnesota normal men and women on each scale serve as reference points; the standard deviations of their score distributions provide the unit for measuring degree of deviation above or below these means. The profile scores, termed T scores, provide comparable measures for each component scale in the psychogram, both validity and clinical scales. Detailed analyses of the patterns and configurations that they form, together with guidelines for personological and psychopathological inferences from them, are provided in this volume and in a number of other general publications on this instrument. (See Hathaway and Meehl, 1951a; Welsh and Dahlstrom, 1956; Drake and Oetting, 1959; Good and Brantner, 1961; Hathaway and Monachesi, 1961; Hathaway and Monachesi, 1963; Marks and Seeman, 1963; Gilberstadt and Duker, 1965; Lanyon, 1968; Butcher, 1969.)

Table 1-1. Basic Minnesota Multiphasic Personality Inventory Scales

Scale Name	Abbrev- iation	Code Number	No. of Items
	Validity Scales		
Cannot Say score	?		
Lie	L		15
Infrequency	F		64
Correction	K		30
	Clinical Scales		
Hypochondriasis	Hs	1	33
Depression	D	2	60
Conversion hysteria	Hy	3	60
Psychopathic deviate	Pd	4	50
Masculinity-femininity	Mf	5	60
Paranoia	Pa	6	40
Psychasthenia	Pt	7	48
Schizophrenia	Sc	8	78
Hypomania	Ma	9	46
Social introversion	Si	0	70

Brief History and Development

Starke R. Hathaway (who, in collaboration with J. Charnley McKinley, developed the MMPI) gives some historical perspective on the origins of this inventory in several publications (Hathaway, 1960, 1965, 1969). Beginning about 1939, Hathaway, a psychologist, and McKinley, a neuropsychiatrist, set out to construct an effective and practical instrument "as an objective aid in the routine psychiatric case work-up of adult patients and as a method for determining the severity of the conditions. As a corollary to this, the inventory was expected to provide an objective estimate of psychotherapeutic effect and other changes in the severity of their conditions over time" (Hathaway, 1965, p. 463). It was deemed necessary to make a radical departure from preexisting personality questionnaires, both in mode of derivation and in selection of criteria defining the component scales. These earlier instruments had turned out to be too transparent and undependable, and made relatively little contribution to psychiatric case study (Ellis, 1946; Dahlstrom, 1969). Embarking upon an empirical approach to scale construction, Hathaway and McKinley (1940a) first collected an item pool of over 1000 statements. These items came from a wide array of sources including scales of personal and social attitudes, clinical reports and case résumés, psychiatric interviewing manuals, forms, and guides, as well as their own clinical experience. Much of the derivational work was based upon a set of 504 items that survived early efforts to eliminate duplicates, simplify wording and readability, restate in personal declarative form, and balance positive and negative wording to avoid excessive correspondence between answering True and acknowledging pathological or socially stigmatized characteristics.

The range and balance of general topics covered by this original item set can be seen in the content categories listed in Table 1-2. This list uses

Table 1-2. An Arbitrary Classification of MMPI Items by Content

Category	Content Area	No. of Items	Box-Form Nos.
1	General health	9	A1–A9
2	General neurologic symptoms	19	A10–A28
3	Cranial nerves	11	A29–A39
4	Motility and coordination	6	A40–A45
5	Sensibility	5	A46–A50
6	Vasomotor, trophic, speech, secretory problems	10	A51–B5
7	Cardiorespiratory system	5	B6–B10
8	Gastrointestinal system	11	B11–B21
9	Genitourinary system	5	B22–B26
10	Habits	19	B27–B45
11	Family and marital relations	26	B46–C16
12	Occupational problems	18	C17–C34
13	Educational problems	12	C35–C46
14	Sexual attitudes	16	C47–D7
15	Religious attitudes	19	D8–D26
16	Political attitudes: law and order	46	D27–E17
17	Social attitudes	72	E18–F34
18	Affect, depressive	32	F35–G11
19	Affect, manic	24	G12–G35
20	Obsessive and compulsive states	15	G36–G50
21	Delusions, hallucinations, illusions, ideas of reference	31	G51–H26
22	Phobias	29	H27–H55
23	Sadistic, masochistic trends	7	I1–I7
24	Morale	33	I8–I40
25	Items primarily related to masculinity-femininity	55	I41–J40
26	Items to indicate whether the individual is trying to place himself in an improbably acceptable light	15	J41–J55

SOURCE: Hathaway and McKinley (1951).

the card-form item identification system based upon the placement of items on the record form (see Chapter 2 for an explanation of this system). Historically, the items were first used in a format in which the items were individually presented on cards in two small boxes and the subjects were asked to sort them into response categories. The content categories were organized on the record form as indicated in Table 1-2 for scoring purposes but were, of course, randomly distributed in the boxes. When the group test form was prepared, the items from these various content categories were disseminated widely throughout the test booklet. Appendix C provides a table of conversion by means of which the items making up each of these categories in the card form can be located in the standard booklet (reproduced in Appendix L).

The 504 items in the preliminary form of the MMPI included all the items listed in Table 1-2 except those in category 25. These items in the area of masculinity-femininity were added somewhat later, after being adapted and rewritten in MMPI format from items in sections 5, 6, and 7 of the Terman and Miles's Attitude-Interest Analysis Test (1938). Since they were not administered in the testing of the bulk of the Minnesota normal subjects, frequency of item endorsement for this category is not available from these samples (see the appended material in Volume II* of this *Handbook*). Most, but not all, of these items appear in scale 5 (Mf) in the basic clinical profile.

It should also be noted in this context that the items making up category 26 in Table 1-2 were introduced into the MMPI pool as a group, all being modeled on items that had been shown to be indicators of test faking in the studies of honesty and deceit by Hartshorne and May (1928, 1930). These fifteen items constitute the lie, or L, scale which is one of the validity indicators discussed in Part Two of this volume.

Although the content covered in the MMPI item pool included by far a larger array of personological topics than in any other instrument then available, subsequent studies have indicated that—while some areas of emotional maladjustment may be overrepresented (Block, 1965)—items referring to values, to primary group relationships, and to mood, temperament, and various special attitudes are probably too scarce to provide a well-balanced coverage of the domain of personality (see Schofield, 1966). As Stone (1965) has shown, items in these several content areas vary widely in the adverse implications that endorsing them may have for one's social acceptability or presentability. Also, as will be noted below, the inclusion in the MMPI item pool of even a few items in some of these areas of inquiry has occasioned concern about the test's suitability for certain kinds of personality assessment and its acceptability to some test subjects. Important issues in testing ethics arise directly from the basic content and orientation of an instrument like the MMPI.

The empirical method of scale derivation employed by Hathaway and McKinley (1940a) involves a basic distinction: the test subject is instructed to describe himself as accurately as he can by answering True or False to each of the MMPI statements but the test scorer and interpreter does not assume that the subject has in fact provided a veridical account of himself or of his own experiences by these item endorsements. Subsequent studies (e.g., Greene, 1954; Pinneau and Milton, 1958) have indicated that the trustworthiness of the factual content of these self-descriptions varies extensively over the different content areas of the test. This dual orientation has made it crucial that the items be on the one hand sufficiently readable and relevant to engender test acceptance and appropriate test-taking attitudes in the test subject and, simultaneously, sufficiently ambiguous in reference to permit differential interpretation by subjects and thus to provide the clinician with dependable personological discriminations. Studies of readability (e.g., Johnson and Bond, 1950; Hanes, 1953; Pierce-Jones, 1954) have generally substantiated the success of the test authors in getting items that are readable at a sixth-grade level of comprehension. (Below this level, special forms of the test must be considered; see the section later in this chapter on oral administration of the test.) Other aspects of the component items of the MMPI that affect its acceptance by a wide range of test subjects (plausibility of items for the test's stated purpose or face

An MMPI Handbook (revised edition): Volume II, *Research Developments and Applications* (Minneapolis: University of Minnesota Press, in preparation).

validity, ambiguity or difficulty in deciding upon a given answer, annoyance, irritation, or boredom aroused by individual items, etc.) have also been studied. The general results of these investigations (see the summary in Volume II of studies of the itemmetric and administrative variations in the MMPI) indicate that the personal referents in the items, the familiar idiom in which they are couched, their specificity and clarity, as well as the breadth of coverage, all serve to make the task a relatively easy and interesting one for most test subjects (see Mehlman and Rand, 1960; Hanley, 1962; Fiske, 1969). These features, combined with the built-in checks upon the occasional protocol that is faulted by noncompliance or poor comprehension, have undoubtedly helped to bring about both the wide acceptance and the diversity of application that the MMPI enjoys today (Hathaway, 1965).

Using the original 504-item pool, Hathaway and McKinley proceeded to gather samples of both normal men and women and selected adult patients in the clinics and wards of the University of Minnesota Hospitals. The normal subjects were friends and relatives of patients who were visiting them at the Hospitals and who were willing to complete the inventory while sitting in the waiting rooms. They were asked a few background questions to determine their comparability to the clinical cases in age, education, marital status, occupation, and area of residence and, in addition, were questioned about their current medical status. Any subject who indicated that he was under the care of a physician at the time that he was asked to take the MMPI was excluded from the normative sample; no other rule of exclusion was used. Table 1-3 lists the numbers of these normal subjects of each sex, single and married, who fell within the particular age ranges indicated. Hathaway and McKinley (1940a) found that this sample of adults corresponded well in age, sex, and marital status to the Minnesota population in the 1930 census. In Table 1-4 are given the age characteristics, educational levels, and socioeconomic levels (occupational classifications) of the subsamples of these normal men and women that Hathaway and Briggs (1957) used to extend the normative tables to several new MMPI scales. These subjects were essentially the same ones used in deriving the original scales and establishing the early norms; only cases with incomplete protocols or faulty background records were dropped from their retabulations. As will be explained in Part Three of this volume, the performance of these

Table 1-3. Age and Marital Status of the Minnesota Normative Group

Age Range (in Years)	Males		Females	
	Single	Married	Single	Married
16–25	70	28	62	45
26–43	26	123	39	194
44–54	5	38	8	61
55–65	0	9	2	14
Total	101	198	111	314

SOURCE: Hathaway and McKinley (1940a).

men and women on each of the component scales in the MMPI is used as the basis for the norms in the test profile. Each subject taking the MMPI, therefore, is being compared to the way a typical man or woman endorsed those items. In 1940, such a Minnesota normal adult was about thirty-five years old, was married, lived in a small town or rural area, had had eight years of general schooling, and worked at a skilled or semiskilled trade (or was married to a man with such an occupational level).

Table 1-4. Age and Educational and Socioeconomic Characteristics of the Minnesota Revised Male Sample and Age and Educational Characteristics of the Revised Female Sample

Item	Males (N=226)	Females (N=315)
Age in years		
Mean	33.1	33.9
Median	34.3	34.5
S.D.	10.9	12.0
School grades completed		
Mean	9.7	10.0
Median	8.0	10.5
Socioeconomic level[a]		
Mean	3.8	
Median	3.9	

SOURCE: Hathaway and Briggs (1957).

[a] The socioeconomic level is based on the Minnesota Occupational Rating Scales (Paterson, Schneidler, and Carlson, 1936), which classifies occupations on a scale from 1, high professional and executive occupations, to 6, unskilled occupations. The values in Table 1-4 correspond to skilled tradesmen and low-grade clerical workers.

The MMPI was originally copyrighted and published by the University of Minnesota Press in 1943 (although a mimeographed version of the *Manual* was made available in 1942). Arrangements were made to distribute the test through the Psychological Corporation, which has published the various manuals, forms, and scoring materials since 1947. The format for recording test profiles was also standardized by the Psychological Corporation, thus assuring comparability of scale sequence and score plotting in clinical installations around the country. Undoubtedly, the development of configural indices and pattern interpretation of the MMPI was enhanced by this early standardization of procedures and format. More recently, greater diversity has appeared in scoring and profiling (see the discussion in Chapter 3 of this volume) with the development of various automated scoring and interpretational services and with the spread of the MMPI both in English and in numerous translations around the world. Many special scales have also been devised on the same item pool (see the subsequent discussions in this volume and the appendix material in Volume II); some scoring services provide scores on these scales as supplements to the basic MMPI profile. Wherever possible the means and standard deviations of Minnesota normative groups on each of these special scales have been provided in this *Handbook.*

The Basic Test Forms

Since the time that the items were assembled into a pool in the late 1930's and early 1940's, the test has gone through several changes in format. The original test (provisionally called the "Medical and Psychiatric Inventory") was composed of 504 items typed individually on 3 by 5 cards and presented in two separate boxes. Simple instructions were attached to the tops of the boxes and file-card dividers labeled True, False, and Cannot Say were provided. Each subject was instructed to read the items in order and place them behind the appropriate divider. A record form was constructed for use by the test administrator so that the sorting or placement given each item by the test subject could be tallied. After tallying, the cards in each box were shuffled to be presented to the next test subject in a randomized order. The test authors knew they might add further items or omit some before the final form of the inventory was determined, so this procedure of mixing the item sequence was followed to obviate problems of item position and order effects. That is, by using the random order of presentation they felt they could minimize the systematic-position effects inherent in a printed booklet of test items. In addition, presenting the items on separate cards relieved the subject of the need for working with a pencil or keeping careful track of his place on an answer sheet. These latter points seemed particularly important both in administering the test to men and women long out of school or away from work settings in which writing and marking are commonplace and in testing patients suffering physical and mental distress in a ward or clinic.

The Individual (Box) Form. Most of the features of the experimental form of the MMPI described above are preserved in the present-day box form. The items have been increased to 550; the cards are smaller and of different stock, and they are now presented to the subject in a single box. The instructions are printed inside the cover and the same file dividers are provided. In addition to the item statement, each card bears a large number designating the column (letters A through J) and row (numbers 1 through 55) in which it is to be tallied on the standard record form and a smaller serial number by means of which replacement cards may be ordered from the Psychological Corporation. The printing of the items on each card is larger and more legible in this form of the test than in any of the available booklet versions, an important consideration in testing situations where lighting is marginal or when examining older subjects or patients with visual problems.

Perhaps the most significant change in the stimulus cards since the derivational work on the test is the introduction of corner cuts. After the direction in which the majority answered each item (True or False) was determined by tallying the endorsements from the samples of Minnesota normal men and women, an appreciable saving in clerical work was effected by requiring that only deviant answers be identified on the record sheet. The rationale and procedures for this kind of recording system will be presented below in Chapter 2, but it should be noted here that the statements for which the majority answer is True are printed on cards with the lower left corner cut off while those answered False by these normative subjects are on cards with the lower right corner cut. Generally, this feature of the card is unobtrusive and ignored by the test subject but on occasion it may serve as a source of test-taking distortion (see below and the discussion in Chapter 4). In some special scoring systems, other alterations or mutilations may be made on the item cards and these features may also produce special reactions or changes in the test subject's behavior. As will be noted in describing the booklet form of the test, sixteen items have been duplicated in that format, increasing the total number of answers to be given to 566. It has been suggested by Hathaway (in Buechley and Ball, 1952) that these same sixteen items could be added to the card deck but without corner cuts on the cards. Thus, the response-consistency measure made possible by this item duplication could be obtained without complicating routine recording and sorting of the box form.

Hathaway (1956a) has developed a system for machine scoring the individual or box form of the MMPI. The items are typed individually upon standard Hollerith cards that are prepunched for processing by IBM sorters and collators. A permanent record is made on a printed tape of the item numbers appearing in each of the three categories, True, False, and Cannot Say. The total of significant answers on each of the basic scales in the True and False response categories is also obtained to provide the basic raw scores for the profile. In this system the items are returned to a standard order of presentation for use with the next test subject. In addition, a check each time the set is scored assures that the deck of items is complete and that no items have been lost or mislaid. Visual inspection is still necessary, of course, to spot any mutilations or graffiti.

In some clinical settings special decks of cards have been prepared on which the statement is typed in the Braille alphabet for use with blind or visually handicapped subjects who have been trained in touch reading. Generally, however, the taped version of the test is serving as a better medium for these subjects, since many have not been trained in the Braille alphabet.

Early Group Forms. The first format of the MMPI prepared for large-scale group testing was a booklet made up for use with the standard box-version record form. The subject marked each item T for True or U for Untrue, or entered a dash for Cannot Say responses. The order of the items, however, did not conform to the order followed in recording responses to the box form, so special scoring stencils were needed.

A short time later the Adjutant General's Office in the War Department issued the technical manual TC-M3, *Multiphasic Personality Inventory* (1944), together with two group forms of the MMPI: TC-8a with 564 items and TC-8b with only 300 items. A great deal of work in testing servicemen with the MMPI during and after World War II was carried out with these two forms (Morton, 1948). Both forms included instructions to the subject for recording his replies on a standard IBM machine-scored answer sheet.

Current Group (Booklet) Forms. The group form of the MMPI now appears in two standard booklet versions, several special forms, and a tape-recorded version which can also be used for either individual or group administration.

The most familiar and widely used form of the MMPI is the standard booklet version (catalog no. 5F061) published in 1947 by the Psychological Corporation. It employs a sequence of items that is different from the original box and group forms and from each of the AGO versions. In addition, to facilitate scoring of the IBM answer sheet by machine, sixteen of the items on scales 6, 7, 8, and 0 are repeated in the booklet, increasing the number of answers required to 566. Various answer sheets are available for use with this booklet which differ among themselves in organization, ease of locating item numbers, legibility, and use of one or both sides of the sheet (see Chapter 2).

The booklet version was altered somewhat in producing Form R in a step-down, hardboard format. The total of 566 items (with the same item duplications) was retained but the order was changed from the standard booklet in order to present all scorable items on the basic validity and clinical scales within the first 399 statements in the booklet. (Form S, which was developed for the Peace Corps, is based on this reduced set of 399 items; see the next paragraph.)

Special booklets of the MMPI have been prepared for use with the assessment battery for Peace Corps trainees and for evaluation of Catholic seminarians. In each of these versions, it should be noted, some of the original MMPI items have been omitted. While these omissions are unlikely to change substantially the test-taking orientations of the test subjects (see the discussion below on scale separates), the range of research scales that may be applied is seriously restricted. There are also a growing number of foreign-language versions of the MMPI that have been carefully constructed and, in some instances, restandardized. Any clinic serving a population that includes a number of immigrants to the United States should have the appropriate foreign-language booklets and answer sheets on hand for use with these clients.

Note should be made of a special booklet used in the Mayo Clinic in Rochester, Minnesota. The test booklet is made up of a number of detachable Hollerith cards on which have been printed the MMPI statements (several to a card) and spaces for marking True or False for each. A special pencil is used to complete the test and after the subject is finished, the cards are torn out and scored by a mark-sensing scanner. This format eliminates the need for a separate answer sheet but it is still machine scorable. As will be noted in Chapter 2, this format has also been combined with an automated interpretive system so that once the subject is done with his booklet, machine operations take over and produce both a profile and a preliminary personality interpretation.

Taped (Oral) Form. Early experience with the MMPI indicated that many subjects with inadequate reading skills (Altus, 1945), marginal cooperation, limited intelligence (Glenn, 1949), or poor visual efficiency (Dean, 1957) could nevertheless be tested if the items were read to them orally and if some system was worked out to record their responses. This could be most easily achieved by means of the card form in an individual testing session; if the item card was read to the subject he could place it himself in the appropriate category. The booklet version, however, has also been used with considerable success. J. H. Panton (personal communication) has adapted the oral delivery to group testing in a prison classification center with incoming felons. Regular booklet-form answer sheets are employed with sufficient supervision to determine whether the test subjects are keeping their answers in the proper spaces on the answer sheet. Under Panton's method, the man with the most education and best reading competency is given the task of reading the test to the rest of the group. Butcher (1965) and Baughman and Dahlstrom (1968) employed this same method of group testing but read the items onto a tape which was then played to classes of eighth-grade students. Proctoring was sufficiently close to minimize misplaced answers and wandering attention. Missed items were read individually to the subjects after the taped presentation was completed.

The Psychological Corporation subsequently published a taped version (5F035) of the MMPI using the standard booklet order of item sequence and including all 566 item presentations. (It would obviously be desirable to have a tape with the somewhat different order of items on Form R for those clinics which have converted to that format and employ the routine scoring services by National Computer Systems.) Although the item presentation is the same, the taped version includes a few supplementary definitions of some words appearing in the MMPI item statements. Table 1-5 lists the items, the terms, and the definitions which have been added in the taped version of the test. (See the discussion below of the work of Glenn, 1949, on common sources of ambiguity.)

Table 1-5. Supplementary Definitions Given on the Standard MMPI Tape

Item No.	Definition
14	"Diarrhea" means loose bowel.
18	"Constipation" means difficulty moving one's bowels.
23	"Nausea" means dizzy, sick to the stomach.
126	"Dramatics" means playacting.
204	"Journalist" means a writer for newspapers or magazines.
236	"Brood" means to frown over, moodiness.

The taped version of the MMPI has several obvious advantages over an examiner's reading the items aloud: comparability across occasions and agencies, uniformity of pacing and inflection, elimination of distortions from fatigue, boredom, or voice strain on the part of the reader. The recorded version is slow compared to the usual self-pacing when reading the booklet; at least two hours is required exclusive of replays.

Some special problems remain, however, in testing blind or visually handicapped subjects with the taped version since there is no ready provision for recording their answers to the series of statements being presented. Dean (1957) chose to read and record the items in person but earlier Potter (1950) had worked out a combination of the recorded presentation (wire recording) and the individual card form of the test that preserved the privacy of the testing session. Subjects held each card while it was read out to them by the recorder and then placed it in one of three piles identified for them before the test began as True, False, and Cannot Say categories. To assure correspondence between the recorded item and the card being held, Potter provided a routine check: every fifty-one items was followed by a piece of sandpaper; the recorded message instructed the subject to place it in a particular category. If the next card was not actually a sandpaper section, the subject was instructed to summon the examiner to straighten out the confusion. Thus, the blind subject could take the test in privacy and if some trouble developed, the subject would have to resort at most a pack of only fifty-one items. Obviously, the Potter system could be modified to make use of the standard MMPI tape. Some other means of routinely recording item endorsements could also be developed. J. L. Mack (personal communication) has experimented with Braille answer sheets which the subject can complete without help. Simple lever-pressing manipulanda for True and False answers could also be adapted to provide an item-by-item record of the subject's responses.

One serious limitation remains in either method of administering the MMPI orally, by tape or by an individual reading aloud, when subjects of very limited comprehension are examined. In such a situation, confusion may arise about the person being described in the item statements: the test subject or the examiner who is delivering the statements. Some workers, therefore, are experimenting with an oral interrogative form of the test. Fowler (1968), Panton (1969), Jennings, Goldberg, and Powell (1969), and Graham, Schroeder, and Lilly (1971) have all explored various methods of rewording the items in such a way as to maintain stimulus equivalence but redirect the statement in the second person for delivery to test subjects orally. Often such a transposition involves adding a word or two to retain the sense of the original query. Thus, for a statement like "I cannot keep my mind on one thing," the reformulation may have to be stated "Do you have trouble keeping your mind on one thing?" rather than merely "Can you keep your mind on one thing?" If these preliminary developments are followed through, such forms of the MMPI may help extend the range of application of the instrument even further. Nevertheless, these adaptations are still likely to encounter a lower boundary posed by severe intellective retardation. Similarly, limitations in the subject's experience or maturity will further restrict their use.

There has been a little research devoted to some further variations in administering the MMPI statements. Bashaw (1967) compared standard administration and a paced presentation of each item projected on a screen by means of 35-millimeter slides. The paced-projected administration affected the validity-scale values to some slight extent but the two modes of presentation were essentially comparable, at least with college-level men and women. The same comparability may not be obtainable on subjects with less facility in taking tests or reading this kind of verbal material rapidly. Nevertheless, the results with this mode of presentation suggest that computer-based test presentation, by typewriter or by display scope, may be feasible (see Kleinmuntz, 1969).

Short Forms of the Test. Because the coverage of the MMPI item pool is extensive and the length of time it takes to administer the test is at times prohibitive, a number of workers have proposed various shortened versions, even single-scale administrations. In the special case of Kincannon's Mini-Mult (1968), both a shortening and a shift to the interrogative form have been introduced (see below). Parts of the MMPI have also been incorporated into other standard personality instruments either as they appeared in the original MMPI item pool or with slight modifications: the California Psychological Inventory (Gough, 1957, 1963); the Minnesota Counseling Inventory (Berdie and Layton, 1957); the Tennessee Self-Concept Scale (Fitts, 1965); and the Omnibus Personality Inventory (Heist et al., 1960).

In a large-scale program, Gough used all the original MMPI items in a combination of two group-form booklets prepared at the Institute for Personality Assessment and Research: the California Psychological Inventory (Gough, 1957, 1963) and the Special Composite Inventory (IPAR staff, 1952). In these tests the MMPI statements are presented along with many other items. Although the effect on the responses to the MMPI items produced by this different matrix has not been systematically studied, the general response patterns do not seem to be significantly changed.

Early efforts to abbreviate the MMPI have already been mentioned above in the discussion of oral methods of test administration. Thus, Altus and his colleagues (Altus, 1945, 1953; Altus and Bell, 1945, 1947; Clark, 1948, 1949a, 1949b) developed various brief scales for screening military recruits for emotional and behavioral disorders. Usually, these versions involved eliminating some items and rewording and simplifying MMPI statements into interrogative formats in addition to taking them out of the MMPI test context. Therefore the correspondence of these brief oral scales to the original MMPI measures was often minimal; serious questions arose about claims for comparability and validity without explicit tests of the generalizability of such adaptations. Other abbreviated forms have been proposed (including the one mentioned above that was designed for military programs, the AGO form TC-8b, 1944), which have, while reducing the item pool, usually retained all the items in the regular scales. However, Jorgensen (1958) has published a short form which involves a reduction in the number of items in the basic scales themselves.

Both cards and booklets have been used in abbreviated versions of the test. One of the main issues raised by the use of a short MMPI depends in part on which form, card or booklet, is being administered. This issue concerns the matrix of questions within which the subject is given a particular subset of items. The belief of Hathaway and McKinley (1940a) in proposing the card form for the MMPI that in this format items could be added to or removed from the test without any marked effect on replies to the other items has in general been borne out by subsequent empirical work. Ferguson (1946) reported finding that the removal of 200 items not at the time being scored on any scale had little effect. MacDonald (1952a, 1952b) tried a shortened version of the card form with the items randomized for part of the subjects and presented in the booklet order for others; there were no appreciable shifts in mean values on the scales. Holzberg and Alessi (1949) made a systematic study of a short version of the card form in a psychiatric setting. They administered the test twice to thirty patients, counterbalancing the order of the complete item set and a subset of the 350 items that were scored on some scale or other at that time. The two administrations were separated by not more than two days. The largest shift in mean value on any clinical scale was for scale 1 (Hs) on which the patients obtained a T score of 58.0 for the long form and only 53.8 for the short form. On the L scale, however, the long form produced a T score of 63.7 as compared with a short-form value of 57.3. (See Table 1-6.) The difference on scale 1 is statistically stable at the 5 percent level, and the difference on L at the 1 percent level. Holzberg and Alessi concluded that the differences between the two versions for psychiatric patients were not "clinically significant as judged by profile results."

Table 1-6. Means, Standard Deviations, and Differences between Weighted T Scores for Each MMPI Scale on the Long and Short Versions of the Card Form

	Long Form			Short Form			Mean Differences		
Scale	Mean	S.D.	$S.E._M$	Mean	S.D.	$S.E._M$	Diff	$S.E._{diff}$	Diff/ $S.E._{diff}$
?	55.2	9.3	1.70	53.0	5.5	.99	2.2	1.17	1.88
L	63.7	10.6	1.93	57.3	9.1	1.66	6.4	1.03	6.21
F	58.4	10.5	1.92	59.5	11.2	2.05	1.1	.77	1.43
1 (Hs)	58.0	12.6	2.30	53.8	11.5	2.09	4.2	1.80	2.33
2 (D)	58.3	14.2	2.59	61.1	15.4	2.81	2.8	1.71	1.64
3 (Hy)	54.8	16.4	3.00	53.4	15.0	2.74	1.4	1.46	.96
4 (Pd)	59.8	13.7	2.50	63.2	11.9	2.17	3.4	2.31	1.47
5 (Mf)	55.1	11.7	2.13	56.8	10.8	1.97	1.7	1.44	1.18
6 (Pa)	55.7	12.0	2.19	58.2	13.1	2.39	2.5	1.52	1.64
7 (Pt)	53.8	11.4	2.07	52.9	11.1	2.03	.9	1.53	.59
8 (Sc)	58.7	13.4	2.44	58.8	12.0	2.18	.1	1.11	.09
9 (Ma)	56.7	12.4	2.26	58.4	11.1	2.02	1.7	1.96	.87

SOURCE: Revised from Table II in Holzberg and Alessi (1949).

The comparability of the short and regular forms of the MMPI reported in Table 1-6 is very similar to the results which Rosen (1953) obtained in a retest study of the box form of the test on forty male psychiatric cases in a Veterans Administration hospital in Minnesota. The initial testing in Rosen's study was within two or three days of admission of these men to the psychiatric service of the hospital, while the retesting was carried out within three to four days of the first administration of the test. Table 1-7 shows the raw-score means and standard deviations on all the component scales obtained on each testing, as well as the product-moment correlations found between the scores on the two administrations. With a sample of this size, a correlation of .31 or larger is significantly different from zero beyond the 5 percent level of confidence. The means on all the scales give essentially identical psychological results on both occasions.

Table 1-7. Differences in Raw-Score Means on MMPI Scales from Test to Retest

Scale	Mean		Difference	S.D.		r
	First Test	Retest		First Test	Retest	
L	4.05	4.35	.30	2.17	2.09	.62
F	7.78	7.48	−.30	5.12	4.75	.81
K	13.08	14.58	1.50°	4.08	4.69	.65
Hs	13.00	11.90	−1.10	6.25	7.26	.85
Hs + .5 K	19.82	19.45	−.37	6.25	6.90	.86
D	29.20	29.55	.35	6.27	6.66	.80
Hy	28.50	27.62	−.88	6.38	7.71	.88
Pd	21.50	20.45	−1.05°	5.49	5.50	.88
Pd + .4 K	26.65	26.28	−.37	4.86	4.97	.87
Mf	25.48	24.75	−.73	4.20	4.21	.64
Pa	13.00	11.92	−1.08°	4.39	4.04	.75
Pt	23.12	21.02	−2.10°	9.45	9.57	.80
Pt + 1.0 K	36.20	35.50	−.70	7.98	8.05	.88
Sc	21.40	18.95	−2.45°	10.94	9.90	.83
Sc + 1.0 K	34.48	33.43	−1.05	9.49	8.49	.86
Ma	17.88	18.35	.47	4.30	5.28	.56
Ma + .2 K	20.52	21.25	.73	3.87	4.90	.55
Si	34.48	33.25	−1.23	11.00	11.08	.83

SOURCE: Rosen (1953).
° Difference significant at the 5 percent level.

Psychologically, a short group form presents different considerations. The order that Hathaway and McKinley used, in the revised booklet, places the items that appear on the main clinical and validity scales early in the test. When the subject takes this form, he is asked to answer the questions in a predictable and fixed matrix of items. If his responding is stopped somewhere along the way, his behavior up to that point is still comparable, in terms of the relevant stimuli operating for that period, to the samples of behavior drawn from any other group administration of the test. The evidence offered below on the general equivalence of the two basic forms of the MMPI (at least on the populations studied to date) suggests that slight variations in the item matrix for any *one* MMPI scale given in the setting of all the *other* clinical scales are not very important.

When a short form is used the Cannot Say score levels change meaning and some prorating must be done (see Hathaway and McKinley, 1967, and Appendix K). Other scales may also require prorating for scores when an abbreviated version of the test is used. For example, Olson (1954) has introduced the Hastings Short Form with 420 items of the booklet. This version loses two items from the K scale and twenty from scale 0 (Si). Olson suggests using a correction of one point on K if the score on K is equal to or higher than twelve of the twenty-eight available items, and provides a table for prorating scale 0. He reports empirical data on the accuracy of his prorating procedures with both patients and normals. If a shortened version must be used on some special occasion, the suggestions of Olson seem to be the soundest procedures to employ.

On the box form of the MMPI, of course, preparation of a short form is an easy task. The nonworking items are simply removed from the box and the test subject is asked to sort a substantially reduced deck of item statements. Such a procedure does not affect the recording or scoring of the test, except that any use of the Cannot Say category by the test subject has a particularly direct and important impact on the component scores in the test. The limits on the acceptable number of such item omissions are usually considerably reduced in this modification of the test, as will be made clear in Chapter 4.

Group forms of the test can be adapted to short-form administration but such modifications require careful preparations. In the regular booklet, all items through number 366 are working items (that is, they appear on one or more of the basic clinical or validity scales in the profile). Beyond that point, the items on the K scale and on scale 0 (Si) are scattered in among items which do not appear in these basic scales, the last one being numbered 547. Since they become increasingly less frequent through the remainder of the booklet, Olson (1954) recommended that the subject be asked to continue on through the booklet up to item number 420 and then stop, omitting only two K-scale items but twenty items from scale 0. If this procedure is used, a prorating scheme may be employed to get the estimated raw scores. From these estimated raw scores, regular T-score values can then be obtained. Olson's system will be described in Chapter 2. He found that 97 percent of the Si prorated scores in his 157 cases fell within five raw-score points of their actual scores on the full scale.

Other alternatives can be used, however, which save all relevant items and obviate the need for prorating. First, the items beyond number 366 used in scales K and 0 may be typed up on an extra sheet and numbered from 367 on. This page can then be pasted into the booklet covering over the regular items. Since the answers will appear at a new place on the answer sheet, special keys will have to be prepared to score this short-form modification. Care must be taken in transcribing the items so that their wording is precise and the statements are legible. A second method of adapting the regular booklet to a short-form administration involves changing the answer sheets rather than the booklets. By overprinting, the spaces where the subject would ordinarily enter his replies to the items which are to be discarded may be blacked out. The subject is then asked to answer all the items up to 366 but only the scorable ones beyond that point. This method has the advantage that the test booklets do not have to be marred (they are available for either the short form or the whole test as time may dictate on a particular testing occasion), and the standard scoring templates can be used to score either version, short or long. There is an obvious danger, however; the test subject may sometimes become confused about the particular items to be read and may answer the wrong ones.

If Form R of the MMPI is used, the shift from short form to complete test is considerably facilitated. The first 399 items in this form include all component items on the basic scales in the standard profile; a short-form administration involves merely having the subject stop at that point in the test. As noted below, special National Computer Systems answer sheets for the short form are available if large-scale use of a short form is contemplated. The answer sheet is similar in format to the regular NCS answer sheet for Form R, but the answer spaces are numbered consecutively and proceed from left to right across the page. (No space is provided for item numbering on the regular Form R answer sheet.) Hand-scoring keys for this NCS answer sheet are not available at this time.

In various research studies, each of the MMPI scales has been employed as a separate test. For example, Charen (1954) used the items from scale 1 (Hs) and Helen J. Anderson (1948) used scale 4 (Pd) items in separate administrations without the rest of the MMPI pool. On neither scale did the two groups of patients tested seem to show different central tendencies or variances. The earlier work of Grant (1946) on psychiatric screening and Manson (1948) on a scale for alcoholism did not preserve the original MMPI scales, and therefore the effect of change in the item matrix on the response consistency in their studies cannot be determined. Beaver (1953) used a nursing scale from the MMPI in separate administrations without appreciable loss in discriminability. Usually, however, the effects of administering the items of a single scale out of the context of the rest of the item pool have not been established or studied systematically. The few studies in which this question has been explored have generally been reassuring (Perkins and Goldberg, 1964). Occasionally the evidence has indicated that the scale as a separate test may be viewed as more evocative of defensiveness; that is, the separate test produces a lower mean and smaller variance than when the component items are encountered in the context of other (perhaps more threatening) MMPI items. A substantial part of the original MMPI has been used in the Iowa Biographical Inventory (Farber, 1952), although some of the items have been reworded in the revised form. The Taylor manifest anxiety scale (Taylor, 1953) is used extensively as a separately printed scale. Bechtoldt (1953) found statistically stable but numerically small differences in the means and variances for college students between two administrations of the Taylor manifest anxiety scale: one in the MMPI matrix and one in a separate booklet of the Biographical Inventory. Bendig (1956) failed to substantiate these findings on the Taylor scale. Heineman (1953), using triads of items, studied the effects of introducing the MMPI items of the Taylor scale into a forced-choice format; in this form of administration, the frequency of endorsement of the Taylor scale items shifted appreciably. The effect of MMPI context, therefore, may shift the frame of reference for the test subject so that items in particular scales may not appear to be as socially unfavorable as they do in isolation (see the discussion in Volume II).

In any case, however, the use of shortened versions of the MMPI means the loss of important data. Many of the early abbreviated versions (like TC-8b) were prepared before the K scale was developed and published. It is now impossible to return to those test protocols to investigate the role the K scale might have played in evaluating the cases. Obviously, much valuable material has been lost to psychology at a relatively small saving in time and money to the client or agency using a short form. Although recent abbreviated versions may now provide for the scoring of K, there is a chance that a similar problem will be encountered when new material is developed. In the three validity scales and the ten clinical scales (including 0), 357 of the 550 items are scored. The number of nonworking items in the test is rapidly shrinking, however, as new scales, developed for a wide variety of special problems, are continually introduced.

The recommendations made at various places in this volume cannot be fully carried out without the complete MMPI test protocol. Conscientious and responsible clinical practice makes it necessary to maintain an attitude of scientific inquiry toward psychodiagnostic methods and techniques. Continuing interest in and attention to new possibilities and developments are essential to this practice. With complete MMPI data available on a file of clients or patients, it is possible to check out immediately any new recommendations and to determine directly the importance of such revisions for improvement of clinical work. This alone would argue strongly for the use of the full versions not only of the MMPI but of many other clinical tests in use today.

Kincannon's Mini-Mult. In 1968, Kincannon proposed a seventy-one-item short form of the MMPI from which most component scores on the test could be estimated. To reproduce all the important scale-variance sources, he chose items from different clusters in each scale. In addition, inclusion was based primarily on the appearance of an item on several component scales of the test (see the discussion of item overlap in Part Three). He also proposed using this subset of items in an oral administration with the items restated as questions phrased in the second person. (This same set can be used in the original wording, of course, as a very brief version of the MMPI.) The items and scoring of these statements are provided by Kincannon (1968), together with tables for prorating raw scores on the Kincannon Mini-Mult version into raw-score equivalents for the regular MMPI scales. The usual T-score tables for the appropriate sex of the subject can then be consulted to construct an estimated MMPI profile.

Kincannon's preliminary analyses were directed primarily to the question of the scale-by-scale comparability in both wording and length of the standard MMPI and the Mini-Mult. He found that the seventy-one-item version gave mean-scale values corresponding quite closely to the standard-length test, but generated narrower score ranges and underestimated the extreme scores on most scales. In terms of rank ordering on the two sets of scales, the Mini-Mult scales were about as comparable to the standard-length scales as a readministration of the standard scales within the same brief interval. Correlations, for example, between initial Mini-Mult scores and retest scores with the standard MMPI on the comparable scales ranged from .60 (on F) to .89 (Pt), while the range of correlations on two testings with the standard test was from .62 to .91 (the same two scales being highest and lowest).

In clinical or research applications of the MMPI, however, of equal importance to the scale-by-scale comparability of the Mini-Mult is its ability to generate comparable configurations in the estimated profile. Kincannon offered evidence that the rank ordering of scales within the profile (specifically, the scales appearing within the three-point high-point codes) was a little less stable from Mini-Mult to standard format than from two administrations of the standard MMPI. Thus, 82 percent of the cases with standard administrations had the leading scale appear within the first three scales of the profile on retesting within a day or two, while 72 percent of the cases involving the Mini-Mult on one of the testings had profiles in which the leading scale was among the top three on retesting. The second high-point scale was among the top three scales on the retest in 89 percent of the cases reexamined with the full MMPI but in only 66 percent of the cases given the Mini-Mult on one of these occasions. Kincannon also had the comparability of the profiles on these cases rated by experienced clinicians without their knowing whether the records were generated by the Mini-Mult or by the complete test. Although these ratings varied somewhat among the judges, he found in general that the standard reexaminations generated profiles judged to be overlapping about 75 percent in clinical meaning and the standard and Mini-Mult profiles showed a little better than 60 percent equivalence. Additional studies of the comparability of the regular MMPI and Kincannon's version (Skovron, 1969; Armentrout and Rouzer, 1970) have indicated that the Mini-Mult gives satisfactory correspondence in cases with primarily neurotic configurations, while patterns involving the psychotic tetrad and some of the character-disorder configurations are less well identified. In addition, the validity indicators, particularly the F scale, seem to be seriously underestimated, suggesting that interpretive limits should be more stringent when using the Mini-Mult than in regular usage of the standard form of the MMPI.

General Administrative Considerations

The steps in administering and scoring the MMPI are described in Hathaway and McKinley's *Manual for the MMPI* (revised 1967), published by the Psychological Corporation. Anyone interested in using the test should be thoroughly familiar with the material presented in the *Manual.* Our discussion here may often duplicate material presented in the *Manual;** such overlapping seems justified in order to present a coherent picture of

*We gratefully acknowledge our indebtedness to Starke R. Hathaway and to the Psychological Corporation for permission to abstract large sections of the *Manual.*

the problems that arise in clinical or research use of the test. On some points the presentation here departs from the recommendations that were originally made by the test authors. In such instances, the reasons for offering these suggestions or alternative procedures will usually be clear.

We shall later in this chapter take up the specific procedures for administering different forms of the test. In this section will be presented a discussion of some of the important considerations involved in choosing the appropriate form.

Subjects Who Can Take the MMPI. Test subjects sixteen years of age or older with at least six years of successful schooling can be expected to complete the MMPI without difficulty. When an individual is specifically referred for testing it can generally be ascertained beforehand whether the MMPI is appropriate for him and the embarrassment that would arise from failure during the actual administration can be avoided. Where the MMPI is employed as a routine measure on a wide range of subjects, this prior evaluation is not always possible. In any case, it is generally wise to ask a few brief questions before beginning to explain the test procedures so that any obvious lack of comprehension can be detected; for example, the administrator can ask the subjects to fill out the answer sheet in the spaces provided for age, marital status, education, and occupation, or if a record blank is being filled in for the subject, can ask for this information. (This is also an excellent time to enter the date on the protocol.)

Hathaway and Monachesi (1957), as part of a series of studies on delinquency, tested about 15,000 ninth-grade students in Minnesota. Although the F-scale values on these test subjects, particularly on those from the rural areas, were somewhat higher than the adult norms, most of the protocols were valid and acceptable. The median age for these subjects was fifteen years. Baughman and Dahlstrom (1968) used a tape-recorded version in testing eighth-grade rural subjects with comparable success. On occasion the MMPI has been used successfully with bright children as young as twelve. Here the determining conditions are ability to read the items, willingness to stay at the task long enough to cover the material, and range of experience wide enough to make most of the content of the test items psychologically as well as semantically meaningful to the subject.

Some intellective or reading achievement measure may be efficiently combined with the MMPI for routine testing programs. Such brief devices as the Wide Range Achievement Test (Jastak, Bijou, and Jastak, 1965), the Ohio Literacy Test (Foster and Goddard, 1924), or the Kent EGY (Kent, 1946) are often worth the little extra time needed for their administration and scoring since they may reveal crippling educational deficiencies or emotional conditions that would make an MMPI administration difficult or impossible, or perhaps would suggest an alternate mode of presentation. Considerable experience has indicated that a Wechsler Adult Intelligence Scale (WAIS; Wechsler, 1958) IQ below 80 (either Verbal or Full-Scale) is evidence that the subject may not be able to handle the MMPI without special attention or extensive guidance. However, the MMPI should not be omitted simply because of apparently poor contact or cooperation in psychiatric patients. Experienced users of the MMPI have found that even severely depressed patients who are psychomotorically retarded and orally uncommunicative have been able and occasionally have even been pleased to convey their feelings and troubles by the simple mechanical means of sorting cards. Such patients have been known to express relief at finding that some of the experiences they had felt were their own unique miseries were common enough to be written on test cards or listed in a booklet!

If no pretest evidence is available in a doubtful case and the MMPI is given in a setting that permits conversation between the examiner and the test subject, the first few items in the box or booklet can be used to gauge to some extent the subject's competence. After explaining the general procedures and going over the instructions, the examiner can ask the subject to read aloud a few of the items and perhaps even to discuss the reasoning behind his replies. In the booklet, the first items are generally not psychologically disturbing and contain words such as "mechanics," "librarian," and "newspaper" that give an opportunity for judging the person's ability to read and respond to the rest of the test appropriately. The behavior of the subject at this point may be sufficiently marginal to make the examiner decide to shift over from the booklet to the card form, or to discontinue testing with the MMPI.

Some examiners have resorted to reading the items to a subject who is illiterate but for whom it is important to have a personality evaluation. Glenn (1949) provides evidence that even the procedure of reading items aloud is not successful for persons with an IQ below 65 or with less than three years of schooling. Krug (1967) reported similar difficulties in testing patients with extensive neurological involvements which limit attention span, reduce cognitive capacities, or cause memory losses.

With either form of the test, even though the examiner makes every effort to let the subject make his own choice, there will be some subjects who will seek advice, guidance, or clarification of items from the examiner. Since the basis for the success of the test in showing personality differences lies in the different ways that the test subjects interpret and answer the statements, it is clear that any help and information must be offered circumspectly and in moderation. The test subject must also be cautioned against seeking advice from others who are taking the test or who may be nearby.

Glenn (1949) found in his borderline and defective cases that during oral administration of the test items the subjects encountered trouble most frequently on these words: "tension," "constipation," "diarrhea," "nausea," "mixer," "confidence," "dramatics," "brood," and "journalist." The examiner may offer a standard dictionary definition for these terms when a subject needs help. (The standard tape version, as noted above, gives definitions for several of these words.) Glenn's subjects also had trouble with the following idioms: "strongly attracted to own sex," "never in trouble because of sex behavior," "never indulge in unusual sex practices," "mother was a good woman." The words in these phrases are not difficult and the subject must be allowed to interpret them himself. The last phrase deserves some special comment, however, since young subjects are frequently confused by the statements in the past tense which do not clearly imply continuation into the present. In these instances, it is best for the examiner to say that the test was made for all sorts of people and that for most people statements worded in this way would be most accurate. Younger subjects can be encouraged to answer them as they apply to the present time.

Another general question that many people ask about the test is whether they should answer the items as they apply to them now or as they did just before some special circumstance. The general instructions tell the subject to answer the item True if it is "mostly true." This is usually a sufficient guide to enable the test subject to overlook the special circumstances of hospital confinement or other temporary considerations. However, there are some situations that make an important difference in the set of replies the subject gives. If the subject has faced a trauma such as a parent's death, for example, he may be in doubt whether to answer the question "the way I feel now, or the way I did before mother died." In such a situation, the subject should be advised to give current feelings and reactions.

Because of the way in which the MMPI is scored, any item not answered either True or False is in effect eliminated from the test. Therefore the examiner should make every effort to keep the number of unanswered items at a minimum. Instructions to the subject before the test begins help in preventing this form of evasion. Every test should be examined before the subject is dismissed to see if an unusually large number of items have been left unanswered. Carefully phrased requests to reconsider the unanswered items are usually effective in getting the number of these items below ten or so.

Typically, an hour to an hour and a half is required to complete the test. Many college-level subjects finish in forty-five minutes. Some hospitalized psychiatric patients may continue sorting the card form over a period of several hours or even days. In most instances, the subject will proceed rapidly, sorting or marking each item in order. Some subjects, however, will form a "temporary Cannot Say" category for items felt to require special thought or consideration. Many of these slow administrations can be prevented if the subject is told at the beginning that he does not have to spend a great deal of time on any one question and that his first impression is generally desired. This may also help to reassure some who are initially dismayed at the number of questions in the test.

Patients with limited vision, poor reading competency, limited attention, or physical handicaps which limit their ability to manipulate the test materials may be examined with the oral form of the MMPI administered by tape recording and given any needed assistance in completing one of the regular group-form answer sheets. This version requires an adequate level of auditory acuity and sufficient familiarity with basic English to comprehend the component statements of the inventory. As noted above, some agencies have developed special test materials printed in both regular type and Braille so that they can use this format with the occasional visually handicapped subject who has learned touch reading. It would also seem highly desirable to prepare a booklet with extra-large type for use with partially sighted subjects in ophthamology clinics, geriatric centers, or rehabilitation programs.

One further characteristic of the test subjects for whom the MMPI is suitable involves mastery of the English language. Subjects with a native language which is not English may still be encountered with some frequency in our clinics and hospitals. If they have some general familiarity with American ways and culture and merely have an inadequate mastery of English for formal testing, one of the translations of the MMPI in their native language may be a more suitable means for evaluating their emotional status than the regular English-language version. Agencies in which these clients appear with considerable frequency may find it desirable to have copies of the Spanish, Italian, French, German, Japanese, or Chinese versions available for clinical use. These and other translations are discussed in Volume II.

Comparison of the Basic Forms. Generally, the card form of the MMPI is considered less demanding for the test subject. Therefore, this is the form of the test that is preferred whenever there is some doubt concerning the subject's educational background, his orientation or distractibility, or his level of comprehension. How sophisticated he may be about testing and how cooperative and sensitive about revealing his feelings and attitudes are other important considerations. Since the card form does not require the use of a pencil or the close matching of booklet number and answer-sheet space, it eliminates the possibility of the subject's making clerical errors in recording his responses. There also seems to be less feeling on the subject's part that he is making a permanent record and committing himself irrevocably. Of course in filing item cards the subject may confuse the True and False categories and mix his answers to an unknown extent. Also the sequence of the items within a given administration is uncontrolled and unpredictable, although, as indicated below, test users are advised to place a few simple, neutral items at the beginning to encourage an easy start on the sorting. Some of the IBM procedures described above do permit replacing all the cards in some standard order before the next administration; there is, however, no clear evidence that this makes any important difference in test results.

In the booklet forms although the test subject may make errors, either random or specially motivated, in recording his answers, once he has completed the answer sheet, one important source of clerical error by the test scorer has been eliminated. The well-educated test subject who is familiar with tests can complete a booklet form of the MMPI almost as quickly as he can the card form. P. N. Strong (personal communication) has indicated that subjects in a psychiatric setting with scores as low as the fourth-grade level on the Ohio Literacy Test (Foster and Goddard, 1924) can manage the booklet form with the IBM answer sheet.

A direct comparison between the box form and the booklet form of the MMPI is not possible. Studies based on the same subjects invariably invoke distortions from memory of earlier responses, familiarity, and test sophistication. By counterbalancing the order of presentation the systematic variance may be controlled, but any special interaction effects between familiarity and test format cannot be eliminated. However, some of the reports in the literature furnish indirect evidence about the equivalence of the forms.

In one of MacDonald's studies (1952a), shortened versions of both the group and the individual MMPI were administered to twenty-five nursing students at a single test session. He randomized the order and reported no statistically stable difference between the two forms on the means for any of the scales. He did not report the actual mean values that he obtained, however. In this administration, the card-form items were placed in the same order as those in the booklet. On a smaller group of ten nursing students he made the same comparison except that the items in the card form were randomly mixed. No differences between these two subgroups of nursing students reached a statistically stable level. It should be noted that in these populations, none of the conditions for which the card form is considered to be particularly advantageous were operating (i.e., low education, lack of test sophistication, etc.).

McQuary and Truax (1952) examined the results of retesting with the card form one hundred University of Wisconsin male freshmen who had initially been tested with the booklet form on admission to the university. They were retested after periods of 3 to 178 days when they appeared at the Student Counseling Center as clients. These men are probably not representative of university undergraduates as a whole, being perhaps more emotionally disturbed, although no means or variances were provided by which the extent of their deviation could be determined. The authors reported that the group form gave consistently higher scores than the individual form, but it should be noted that the group-form tests were always administered first. A number of retest studies have indicated that the initial means are generally higher than the retest means, even for normal populations (see Windle, 1954, 1955). McQuary and Truax also reported that 40 to 50 percent or more of the retest scores on the MMPI scales fell within ±5 T-score points of the original scores for all the scales, except scale 2 (D) and scale 7 (Pt), with 38 percent each. However, the T scores were rarely identical on the two testings; the most stable was L with 70 percent and F with 40 percent identical values.

In a more extensively reported study, Cottle (1950) found that his one hundred college students gave slightly higher scores on the booklet form than on the card form when these tests were administered in a counterbalanced order. The group also put fewer items in the Cannot Say category in the booklet form, which probably contributed to the higher scores on that form. He reported, in addition, a set of values for the standard error of estimate for each scale in predicting from one form of the MMPI to the other over a week's time. Scale 2 (D) had the largest $S.E._{est}$ with 7 T-score points; scale 6 (Pa) with 6 points and scales 3 (Hy), 4 (Pd), and 9 (Ma) each with 5 points were the next largest. All the other scales, including the validity scales, had values of either 3 or 4 T-score points.

Wiener (1947) studied a larger group of Veterans Administration clients at a guidance center. The two forms were given alternately to two hundred successive applicants for vocational and educational guidance. Any personality differences between the groups were presumably reduced by this randomization procedure. No statistically stable differences between the sets of means were obtained although the individual form gave numerically larger values on all the scales except 4 (Pd) and 9 (Ma). Since these clients were young, psychologically intact, and with a better than average education, the crucial psychological differences between the test formats were not necessarily sampled well in this investigation.

In the alternative booklet version of the MMPI, Form R, the answer sheet is inserted directly into the test folder which is made up of sturdy hardboard covers and a twenty-three-page booklet fastened together by a spiral binding. The answer sheet fits over two metal pegs which serve to align the spaces on the answer sheet with the printed test statements. The first page of the booklet is large and contains the specific test instructions for Form R as well as the first column of twenty-four MMPI items. This page covers all but the extreme right-hand column of spaces on the answer sheet. The test subject enters his responses to the items by filling in a designated oval space in either the True column or the False column adjacent to the end of each item statement. The second page of the booklet is slightly narrower, exposing the next column on the answer sheet which lines up with the next twenty-four items of the test. The pages continue in this step-down pattern progressively exposing columns across the answer sheet to within eight or nine centimeters of the left-hand edge of the answer sheet. The last few pages present items in a cramped and crowded space, further reducing the legibility of the light typeface. The final page covers a space on the answer sheet reserved for entering identifying data (last name, part or all of the first name, age, and sex), both in alphabetic and optical scanning code.

The omission of item numbers from the Form R answer sheet creates several problems. It is difficult to locate a given answer if the sheet is not in the booklet and in position. Even while inserted in the booklet the item and answer space do not invariably come into precise alignment. Slight distortions of the holes for the anchoring pegs or shifts of the page in the wire spiral binding (which increase with wear and tear on the booklet) permit significant mismatching of item and answer space. Small wedges (arrows) inserted in each column on the answer sheet must be kept in juxtaposition to corresponding wedges (arrows) printed on each of the step-down pages, as indicated in the test directions; this requires considerable care and patience on the part of the test subject during the examination. For pages early in the booklet, the alignment is facilitated by opening the booklet out flat on a large surface; later, the pages fit best if the front cover is folded around behind the back cover. The latter arrangement is, of course, better for using the Form R booklet as a lapboard when a desk or table is unavailable. When the booklet is used in this way, the test subject must constantly take pains to keep his marks properly placed on the answer sheet. Less sophisticated test subjects may find this task distracting and may work less efficiently or accurately than they would with a regular booklet and answer sheet, or with a box form of the test. However, there are no empirical studies in the literature assessing the actual importance of these considerations. Studies of the comparability, legibility, and practicality of Form R of the test are very much needed, especially in settings in which elderly, confused, or handicapped patients make up an appreciable segment of the clientele.

The standard tape-recorded version of the MMPI now available from the Psychological Corporation has been compared to the regular booklet administration in a number of studies (Urmer, Black, and Wendland, 1960; Dahlstrom and Butcher, 1964; Wolf, Freinek, and Shaffer, 1964; May, 1968; Reese, Webb, and Foulks, 1968; Simia and di Loreto, 1970). As was true in the research on the comparability of box and booklet forms, these studies have usually employed subjects who do not possess the crucial characteristics which pose a challenge to the routine modes of administration. With subjects who can easily comply with either mode of testing, then, oral administration by means of a recorded transcript gives essentially comparable results to silent reading in a test booklet. However, two of these studies provide data on the comparability of the forms when the subjects are sufficiently deviant to suggest some testing problems and one also is relevant to the second consideration, namely, does one form or the other give better results when some special clinical problem intervenes?

Reese, Webb, and Foulks (1968) studied a sample of forty male psychiatric inpatients at a Veterans Administration hospital in Alabama using a testing sequence in which booklet and tape-recorded presentations were counterbalanced. Short forms of both the booklet and tape were employed so that fatigue and boredom effects were probably not explored fully in this investigation. The general findings were reassuring as to the direct comparability of these two modes of administration. Means and standard deviations obtained from each version on the basic MMPI scales are reported in Table 1-8. The test-retest coefficients listed in Table 1-8 for each scale are closely comparable to those reported by Rosen (1953) for retests on psychiatric patients over a similar interval with the card form of the test.

Simia and di Loreto (1970) compared the booklet version and the oral administration in examining youthful inmates in an institution for delinquents. A number of these boys and girls were distractible and marginally cooperative, and had poor comprehension in reading. Judging the test protocol's acceptability by the usual validity indicators (see Chapter 4), the investigators found that the oral version administered by tape recording over earphones resulted in appreciably fewer invalid records than the booklet version. They noted fatigue, boredom, and irritation with both versions but indicated that these subjects were more attentive and persistent with the taped version, even though it extended over a longer period of testing. Occasional rest periods were necessary with both administrations.

Only limited test-retest data with the tape-recorded version are available at this time. Leath and Pricer (1968) examined a sample of elderly long-term residents of the former epileptic colony at Abilene, Texas, all of

Table 1-8. Means, Standard Deviations, t's, F's, and Correlation Coefficients on Scales for Oral and Booklet Forms of the MMPI (N=40)

MMPI Scales	Oral Form		Booklet Form				
	Mean	S.D.	Mean	S.D.	t	F	r
L	56.32	9.84	54.58	10.18	1.57	1.07	.76°°
F	68.90	22.28	71.08	25.92	1.24	1.35	.91°°
K	56.62	11.37	56.72	12.51	.10	1.21	.86°°
Hs	44.25	19.30	44.12	18.88	.06	1.04	.92°°
Hs + .5K	65.20	17.82	64.82	17.66	.23	1.02	.83°°
D	71.65	18.25	71.02	16.21	.42	1.27	.86°°
Hy	63.17	13.94	60.05	13.30	2.08°	1.10	.76°°
Pd	56.20	12.82	54.62	11.79	1.09	1.05	.73°°
Pd + .4K	70.68	13.10	69.88	11.34	.45	1.33	.59°°
Mf	57.82	8.27	58.85	10.29	.89	1.55	.72°°
Pa	63.68	16.27	61.72	14.94	1.43	1.18	.85°°
Pt	33.40	23.64	32.08	23.82	.90	1.02	.92°°
Pt + 1K	67.28	14.04	66.42	15.19	.55	1.17	.79°°
Sc	43.32	28.37	42.80	30.09	.29	1.13	.94°°
Sc + 1K	74.98	20.29	74.88	23.88	.04	1.38	.81°°
Ma	52.52	15.63	52.45	15.46	.05	1.02	.84°°
Ma + .2K	10.18	14.39	60.48	13.86	.21	1.08	.81°°

SOURCE: Reese, Webb, and Foulks (1968).
° Significant at the 5 percent level.
°° Significant at the 1 percent level.

whom earned full-scale IQ's of 85 or higher on the WAIS. Retest correlations obtained on this small group of subjects between repeated administrations of the taped version over intervals ranging from five to thirty-nine days were comparable to values obtained with readministrations of either the box or booklet versions of the MMPI.

There is one further consideration in the choice of test formats and modes of administration which affects to an important degree the kind of test record that can be obtained from the test subject. Whether the regular booklet form or the standard tape is employed to administer the items, one of several versions of the answer sheet will have to be used. The available answer sheets for these group forms of the test vary considerably in layout, marking procedures, legibility, and simplicity. With test subjects who are bright, adaptable, and knowledgeable about taking tests of all kinds, these variations among the available answer sheets are probably relatively unimportant. If the clientele to be tested includes, however, substantial numbers of elderly, rural, disadvantaged, visually or physically handicapped, foreign-born, or very young subjects, it will be well to pay close attention to the differences among answer sheets. (It should also be kept in mind that Form R takes special answer sheets and that some of the automated scoring and interpreting services employ answer sheets of their own devising.)

For many years there were only two answer sheets available for use with the regular MMPI test booklet: an IBM form (ITS 1100 A 2413) that was set up for either hand scoring or machine scoring, and the Hankes form (PC-47-230-AS 9-51) to be scored by the Testscor scoring service. The IBM form required the use of both sides of the sheet and presented spaces for the answers in columns arrayed vertically along the long dimension of a 21.5 by 28.0 centimeter (8 1/2 x 11 inch) sheet. The subject was asked to blacken a 5-millimeter slot opposite the item number under either the T (True) or the F (False) heading at the top of the column. Although the slot was rather faint, the item numbers were large and readable and the whole layout rather clear and uncluttered. In addition to blanks for basic identifying data on the test subject and the testing occasion, spaces were provided for recording raw scores on the basic scales. The instructions for using this answer sheet were printed on the front cover of the test booklet itself.

The Hankes form was the same-sized page but provided spaces for all the subject's answers on one side of the sheet. The instructions for completing this form were printed on the back of the answer sheet. Space for each item was provided by a series of 1.0 by 0.5 centimeter rectangles arrayed horizontally in rows across the short dimension of the page. Within each rectangle was printed the item number. The subject was asked to mark a large X above the item number for True answers and below the number for False responses. Although these item numbers were considerably smaller than the numbering on the IBM answer sheet, the format was simple, comprehensible, and free of distracting elements. Headings provided spaces for case identification but there was no provision for the recording of raw scores on the answer sheet itself.

Both of these answer sheets have been revised and there are several additional forms available for routine clinical use. There are now two IBM versions: one (catalog no. 5F255) for use with electrostatic scoring devices (the 805 IBM scoring machines) and one for optical scoring equipment (the IBM 1230 or 1232 scoring systems). The former is almost identical to the original IBM version, the changes primarily being a shift from blue to purple ink and more detailed headings for the identifying data. The response layout is sufficiently close to the original to permit use of the hand-scoring stencils distributed for the original form. This form of the group answer sheet is also currently employed by Clinical Psychological Services, Inc., of Los Angeles in their automated scoring and interpretation system.

The answer sheet for the IBM 1230 and 1232 systems differs in several respects from the form for electrostatic scoring. The response sequence now proceeds across the page in rows of eight answers rather than in columns of thirty answers each. Although the slots to be marked are similar to the spaces to be completed in the other IBM versions, each slot is individually identified as T or F rather than relying upon a designation for the whole column or row. Item numbers are smaller but only 284 answers appear on the front of the sheet instead of the original 300 answers. No examples of completed items are provided for use in giving the test subject his instructions on the test. The headings for the subject's identifying data cover only name, age, and date and place of testing; there is also provision for an identification number in arabic numerals and an optical scoring code. The rows are closely packed and it is difficult to keep track of the place where the next series of answers are to be recorded. The over-all layout is consequently quite cramped and rather difficult to read.

The Hankes answer sheet for use with the Testscor scoring service of Minneapolis has also been revised (catalog no. 5F310) but not as extensively as the second IBM form. The layout of the answer spaces is identical in size but its position on the page is a little lower, giving more room for the headings but complicating hand scoring by older keys. The headings are also precisely the same (there is still no place provided for the date of testing) but the printing is now in blue rather than black ink. The instructions (including sample answer markings) are presented on the back of the sheet. Instead of open rectangles in which the subject was asked to inscribe a large X, each box now contains a small oval area to be blackened by the subject, above the item number for True and below for False responses. (These ovals are then scanned optically in the Testscor scoring procedures.) These special spaces within the answer boxes, unfortunately, increase the clutter and distractions in marking the response decisions. There is now a source of confusion for some subjects when they interpret the instructions as requiring that they blacken the entire answer box. Since the item numbers are rather small and hard to read, these additional marking spaces serve to reduce the legibility of the answer sheet even more. The light blue color probably adds to the difficulties in reading this new form of the Hankes answer sheet.

The National Computer Systems of Minneapolis also provides routine scoring services (see Chapter 2) but requires the use of special answer sheets for both the regular booklet form and Form R test booklets. For the regular test booklet, catalog no. 5F282 is used. This is an optical scoring format which has numbered places for all the answers. Spaces are provided for supplying name, age, sex, and date and place of testing either by writing in this information or by completing the special coding system employed for these data. Instructions and examples of response completions are provided on the back of the page. The subject is asked to blacken a dot, one for True or one for False, beside each item number. The subject proceeds down the narrow dimension of the page in columns of forty answers each. Each dot contains the letter T or F; these letters are unfortunately printed in very small type. Since the item numbers themselves are also small, the legibility of this answer sheet is poor in spite of its neat and uncluttered general format. Green inking for the item numbers and response dots also contributes to the difficulty in reading these numbers and response alternatives.

Different IBM answer sheets similar to 1230 65-238 AS for optical scoring are employed by the Roche Psychiatric Service Institute (IBM H95935; adapted from Marks's version IBM H93010 1232-65) and by the Institute of Clinical Analysis (IBM H93819). They both use two sides of the page for answers with 240 and 232 responses, respectively, recorded on the front of the answer sheet. Both are quite legible but require the subjects to go down rather lengthy columns in marking their answers. In both forms, each answer space is clearly numbered and the place for indicating True and False responses is indicated periodically as a reminder to the subject. Both answer sheets have provision for identifying data in optical scoring codes.

Two answer sheets are employed in the Psychodiagnostic Consultation Service of the Finney Institute for the Study of Human Behavior, Inc., of Lexington, Kentucky. One is the Versatile Answer Sheet (DC 5135A) devised by Dr. Joseph Finney for the Optical Scanning Corporation; the other is the Special Answer Sheet (DC 5137A; Finney, 1969). Both are laid out along the long dimension of the page and provide spaces for 580 (or 566) True and False answers. The subject works down columns of twenty responses; the first column is placed at the far right of the page so the subject proceeds from the far right toward the left of the sheet. All answers are recorded on the front side of the page. (The back of the page contains only headings for the subject's name, the place of testing, and the referral source.) The headings on the front of the answer sheet cover a particularly broad range of identifying and background data; included are such items as Social Security number, marital history, religious preference, political preference, and occupational status. Unfortunately, the columns are not well delineated from one another (in fact, the sheet has guidelines which run horizontally) so that it takes careful attention to maintain one's place in recording the answers properly and accurately. Subjects must be clearly instructed and closely monitored to be certain that they are marking these sheets correctly.

The answer sheet available for use with Form R of the MMPI is set up for optical scoring procedures by National Computer Systems of Minneapolis or for use with hand-scoring stencils. Form S, developed for the Peace Corps, has an answer sheet that is more conventional since it has numbered answer spaces which are listed in thirty-five-item response columns arrayed from left to right up to item number 399. Instructions and spaces for some identifying data are on the back. The instructions include examples of response completions. The subject fills in his name and sex, however, on the front of the sheet in alphabetic and optical scoring code. Each response is recorded by filling in a circle, identified as either T or F, opposite each item number. The numbering and answer-space designations are clear and readable. The answer sheet is the usual page size and can be stored in a regular file folder without bending or folding.

The regular Form R answer sheet, however, is a rather unusual size (24 by 28.8 centimeters) and, as indicated above in discussing the Form R format, requires the subject to complete the answer sheet by proceeding from right to left in succeeding columns of twenty-four items each. There are no answer numbers by means of which the subject can verify his place on the answer sheet; instead, he has to rely upon the alignment of the step-down pages in the booklet with the markers in the columns of the answer sheet. Instructions for the completion of the Form R answer sheet appear on the first page of the test booklet. The back of the answer sheet provides the standard MMPI profiles for both men and women and the K-weight chart, as well as a full heading of case-identifying data. The answer patterns and the clinical profile are thus conveniently on the same sheet, although the size of the page used for this answer sheet does not fit easily into the regular file folders employed in most American service agencies.

Box-Form Administration

The test administrator should make himself thoroughly familiar with the instructions and procedures for the card form of the MMPI (preferably by taking this form of the test himself). The boxes of cards should be stored so that they are ready for the next administration, with the cards in each box randomly intermixed. As noted above, most users of the MMPI keep out a few items that are relatively neutral in content and place them in the box at the beginning of the deck. Such items are chosen for ease of vocabulary, shortness of statement, and freedom from content that is likely to arouse defensiveness, anxiety, or hostility. The first several items in the booklet form are examples of such relatively bland and noncontroversial items.

The small identification card on the front of the box should be filled out with at least the subject's name and the date of the testing. In this way, if the box is moved the test information will not be lost. If possible, the record form for the subject should be filled out and kept handy for notes about the subject's test behavior.

It is preferable that the subject work alone without close observation by the examiner, although the latter should be near enough for the test subject to call him for consultation, or he should inform the subject when he will return to provide any help needed. Some examiners tell the subject to put aside items about which he finds it necessary to ask a question. It other subjects are working nearby, they should be cautioned about communicating with one another.

The instructions on the inside of the cover of the box may then be read to the subject:

Take out the first card in front of the box.

Read the statement on it and decide whether or not it is true as applied to you.

If it is true, or mostly true, put it in the back of the box *directly behind* the card that says TRUE.

If it is not usually or not at all true, as applied to you, put it behind the card that says FALSE.

If the statement does not apply to you, or if it is something that you don't know about, put it behind the card that says CANNOT SAY.

Be sure to put less than 10 cards behind the CANNOT SAY.

Do this with every card in the box.

There are no right or wrong answers.

Remember to give your own opinion of yourself as you are now.

These instructions were the ones used in the derivational work on the MMPI, except for the caution about the number of omissions, which was added later. The method of filing the cards behind the dividers in the box makes the test practical in crowded waiting rooms or, in busy wards, at a bedside table or even in bed. The procedures work well also in the disturbed wards of a psychiatric service. Ideally, however, the test subject should be seated at a table with enough space to lay out the cards and form piles with his answers to the items. Therefore, where conditions permit, most test subjects find it easier and quicker to form piles of the cards in each category of response rather than taking the trouble to file items one at a time. When the test administrator is going to have his test subject use this latter method he should not read the instructions from the cover of the box but should show the subject how to sort the items into appropriate categories. As the True and False instructions are given, the examiner should place the divider cards on the table, one on each side of the box. Then the first few items should be removed and the subject asked to read and decide about them. This wide separation of the piles for True and False will help reduce errors from inadvertent confusion of the two sortings. After the subject has worked through the first few items, and begun to form the True and False piles, the examiner should mention that some items may not apply to the subject, and that although these are usually fewer than ten, if he finds any he should place them in a pile in the center, beyond the box of cards. The examiner should then place the Cannot Say divider on the table in that position. It is desirable to leave the directions handy in case the subject wishes to consult them during the test. After this the subject is left alone, except for periodic checks to see that he is making satisfactory progress.

It should be noted that at least one difficulty has arisen from this system. When the cards are sorted into piles the accumulation of cards bearing similar corner cuts comes to the attention of some subjects who would not have noticed the pattern if each set had been accumulating in the box. For the sensitive or highly defensive subject, this may provide a cue to the expected direction of reply (Hovey, 1948; Feldman, 1952). If a subject asks about the cuts, a general statement that the corner cuts are there to make the cards easier to arrange and set straight is acceptable to most subjects.

Some special problems may be encountered in testing the more disturbed patients in a psychiatric setting. A particular effort should be made to reassure the patient about the purpose of the test and about the way in which his answers will be protected and reported. If the MMPI is introduced into a battery of individually administered tests, rapport may have already been achieved and cooperation obtained. A special problem may arise with the MMPI since there is a change from an interview to a solitary setting. Also, since it is often left to the end of an individual testing series, fatigue, irritation, or confusion may become a problem. On the other hand, when the MMPI is used by itself as a routine admission test, it may be necessary for the nurse or attendant, the physician in charge, or the ward psychologist to start the patient on the test without knowing much about his problems, his possible limitations or handicaps. Under these conditions, administration of the MMPI may be difficult, and close supervision should be provided. Since the very disturbed patient may destroy cards or try to hide them rather than answer them, an attendant must be present while such a patient is working on the test. These attendants should be carefully briefed about the kind and amount of help they may give the patient. Patients in an open ward may seek or receive advice from other patients and this must obviously be discouraged.

During the test session, a patient may confuse the two piles of cards he is forming. One way of checking on these errors has been suggested by Potter (1950) in his description of MMPI testing of the blind. As an index of category consistency he introduced at various places in the pack three cards bearing the simple statement "Place this card in the True group" and three others for the False category. These cards may be of some special color, but this is not necessary since they can be easily spotted if they do not have corner cuts. Before the recording is begun these cards should be checked to see that they are placed in the correct category. At this time notation should be made of any discrepancy. If they are kept with the respective packs during the recording, they also provide additional safeguards against confusion of the Trues and Falses when the piles have been taken from the box.

When confusion or disorientation of the patient may be a complication, the additional check on test acceptability provided by the sixteen duplicated items (see the discussion above) should be used. At the time of recording, note should be made of the direction of answers given so that the extent of response consistency can be determined for this special subset of items.

When the subject has completed his sorting, the piles should be straightened and then, with the proper response-direction divider in front of each pack, returned to the box. It is often desirable to ask the subject how he feels about the test and to record any special features of his behavior noted during the testing.

Administration of the Booklet Form

Like administrators of the box form, administrators of the booklet form of the MMPI should thoroughly familiarize themselves with the test itself and with the test instructions and procedures before giving it. When several subjects are to be tested at the same time, the administrator should also study some general references on the problems of group testing (for example, Ligon, 1942; Lindquist, 1951; or Super, 1949). Although concern for standardized procedures is necessary, there are many other problems to be considered, especially if large numbers of subjects are being tested.

The examiner should be aware of the pretest activities of the subjects and know when tardiness, fatigue, or strain may interfere with effective testing. In the same way he should be alert to the possibility that apprehension, worry, or undue excitement in the subjects will influence the test results. The problems in a medical clinic and in a college admission testing program will be different, but no matter where the test is given, there is a chance that these conditions may interfere with a subject's interest and efficiency.

The place in which testing is to be conducted is important. Lighting and ventilation should be suitable, and the room should be as quiet as possible. The work space available should be adequate to allow each subject to manage the booklet and answer sheet without awkwardness or discomfort.

The materials should be checked carefully. The booklets must be clean and complete. Subjects occasionally write in comments on the items or record their answers directly on the booklet. These marks must be removed before the next test administration. If machine-scoring procedures are to be employed, the special electrographic pencils should be checked. (International P3B, Venus No. 1, or other appropriately soft lead may be used with machine-scored answer sheets.) Even if the responses are to be scored by hand the subjects should be supplied with pencils since marking with a pen does not permit easy erasures or changes.

Routine Testing in Outpatient Service. Since the MMPI is essentially self-administering and provides a wide variety of personality measures, there is an increasing trend among general physicians and internists as well as psychiatrists and clinical psychologists to administer the test routinely to all office patients. The articles by Houk (1946), Kamman (1947), Walch and Schneider (1947), and White (1951) give many indications of the practicality and utility of such a routine procedure. Kamman and Kram (1955) provide some excellent suggestions about how to set up this routine, while the report of Hastings et al. (1957) presents empirical evidence of the diagnostic effectiveness of the test on a series of 479 consecutive admissions to a medical outpatient department.

In addition to the suggestions given in the *Manual* and earlier in this chapter, there are several points about using the MMPI in this way that should be kept in mind. Most patients will be able to take a group form of the test. If no table space is available in the waiting room, however, the card form or Form R may be used instead since they require little more than a chair. The receptionist or office nurse can easily be placed in charge of giving the patient the booklet and answer sheet, after she has obtained the preliminary background information and presenting complaints. The time that the test requires is convenient to waiting periods in normal office practice and usually gives the patient additional confidence in the thoroughness and completeness of the doctor's examination.

If the booklet form is used and the patients return for follow-up visits, it would be practical to have the answer sheets mailed to a test-scoring service for rapid scoring and profiling. Only a few days are required for such service and the cost is nominal. However, the scoring and recording of the test can easily be taught to the receptionist or nurse, who can then provide the physician with a completed profile by the time he is finishing up his diagnostic examination of the patient. After appropriate training and experience with this test, a clinician will find the test data increasingly valuable in assessing somatization trends, extent of emotional disturbance, adequacy of control, and incipient psychotic conditions. Questions concerning the patient's emotional dependence upon physical symptoms, the likelihood of his becoming confused about medical prescriptions, or the need for direct referral to a psychiatric specialist or prompt hospitalization can be answered more directly and effectively with the additional psychometric information the MMPI provides. (See Guthrie, 1949.)

The MMPI data should be filed with the rest of the case record for reference at later dates, for comparison with retests obtained after various treatment regimes, and for surveys of similar patients in checking on clinical hunches gathered in working with the test over a period of time. The office receptionist or nurse can also maintain a code file (see the discussion in Chapter 3) to facilitate this cross-comparison of test records from similar patients.

Large-Scale Testing with the Booklet Form. For group testing the answer sheets can be inserted in the first page of the booklets to keep the distribution of materials down to one simple step. If younger subjects are being examined, however, it is easier to give out pencils and answer sheets first, so that they will not be distracted by the questions in the booklet while the headings on the answer sheet are being completed and the initial instructions are being given.

The session should be started with a brief statement about what will be done and the purpose of the testing. The subjects should be told approximately how long the session will last and whether they may leave when finished. It is advisable to indicate how the materials are to be turned in.

These instructions and the directions for the test proper should be given in a professional but comfortable manner. The attitudes, manner, and style of delivery of the examiner can markedly affect the success of the session. The examiner should practice his actions and attend to the considerations described by Super (1949, p. 81): "The examiner's *voice and attitude* . . . have considerable effect on the attitudes of examinees and therefore on the validity of the tests which they take. An examiner whose clear, confident, and friendly voice and interested alert manner are noted by the examinees gives them the feeling that the tests are important, interesting, and worth taking seriously; one who is lackadaisical in manner, fearful in front of a group, or careless in his speech is not likely to create in his subjects attitudes which make for serious application and genuine co-operation. When proctors assist in test administration, the manner in which they walk the aisles and watch examinees or stand with their minds obviously far away is equally important."

As noted above, several different answer sheets are available for use with the booklet form of the MMPI. The person giving the directions should make sure that he is thoroughly familiar with the headings on the answer sheet being used. He should tell the subjects clearly just what is to be filled in and what may be left blank. For large groups he should if possible demonstrate by putting an example on a blackboard. The information to be asked for includes name, date (supplied by the examiner), and any other data such as age, schooling, and home address that will be needed to identify the subject or group. (It should be kept in mind that there is no clearly specified place for the date on the Hankes answer sheet; the subject should be told where to write it in.)

When the IBM answer sheet is being used, the subject should be asked to follow along silently while the examiner reads the instructions aloud from the cover of the test booklet. Younger test subjects may profit from seeing briefly an actual completed answer sheet as a model; this helps get across to them the need for making clear pencil marks and for keeping the sheet clean so that machine scoring can be done. When the Hankes answer sheet is being used, the group must be told to ignore the instructions printed on the booklet and to follow instead the instructions printed on the back of the answer sheet itself. In this situation it is often easier to complete the test instructions with only the Hankes sheet available to the subjects. After the instructions have been completed, the booklets may then be distributed. With either form, proctors should watch carefully as the subjects mark the first few responses on the answer sheets. Many scoring difficulties can be prevented at this time. Some subjects may make marks that are acceptable for scoring purposes but are unnecessarily time consuming—for example, completely blacking in the squares on the Hankes form or drawing a continuous line through successive answers on the IBM answer sheet.

The subjects should be encouraged to answer every item possible. The instructions on the current booklet form include the statements "do not leave any blank spaces if you can avoid it. . . . Remember, try to make some answer to every statement." Several variations on this instruction have been used on other forms as a way of discouraging Cannot Say answers: "Do not make many 'cannot say' responses" (old group form); "Do not leave any blank spaces if you can make any judgment regarding your answers" (TC-8a); "Do not leave any blank spaces unless you really can't decide how to mark the statement" (TC-8b). All of these are ways in which the test subjects may be exhorted to deal with every item in the test.

In a small group, the examiner may be able to do his own proctoring. However, most examiners prefer to have at least one other person helping. Generally one additional proctor will be needed for each twenty to twenty-five subjects. Special conditions in the testing room may make additional help necessary. The proctors should conduct themselves in the same professionally mature manner recommended for the administrator. During a test like the MMPI, a sensitive subject may interpret even casual conversation between proctors as some discussion of his own test replies.

Proctors experienced in the close supervision required in timed and exacting ability testing should be explicitly instructed to be more circumspect and to avoid being too close and attentive during the administration of the MMPI. No proctor should stay near a subject long enough to suggest an interest in his specific responses. Only enough attention to detect marking errors, lack of persistence, or actual copying of answers should be given. Proctors should be informed about the kinds of questions that are likely to arise and advised clearly about the amount of help they should give on any item (see the discussion above).

In special testing programs when the tests are administered to a group by examiners unknown to the subjects, it is desirable to have one or more proctors in the room who know the subjects by name. The emotional reactions that a few subjects may have to some of the questions can on occasion be contagious. These reactions (giggling, for example) can be prevented easily if a proper businesslike atmosphere has been established by the administrator and proctors, or cut short by prompt attention from someone who knows the subjects. Separation of troublemakers helps prevent the spread of disruptive comments. These reactions may be difficult to control once they are well started, however. As Ligon (1942, p. 398) says: "Once group morale is lost, it is very hard to regain. Let there be a few sighs, whistles, groans, shufflings of feet, low-intensity grumblings, or catcalls and the situation for good group testing is almost hopelessly lost. The leadership of the examiner and the alertness of the proctors will play a large part in preventing this."

Although group reactions of this sort have not been frequent in the use of the MMPI, care must be exercised to maintain the appropriate test conditions. So long as the test is introduced as neither a threat nor a diversion, even adolescents, sophisticated military personnel, and hardened criminals can be expected to respond well to the group administration of the MMPI. The experience of Hathaway and Monachesi (1953) shows that large groups of ninth-grade children, sometimes several hundred at a time, can be given the MMPI without a single significant difficulty. They attribute a great deal of their success in testing thousands of children to careful preparatory work with responsible teachers and other school officials and to the professional and competent bearing of the examiners.

Oral Administration by Tape-Recorded MMPI

The standard tape-recorded version of the complete MMPI in booklet form order currently distributed by the Psychological Corporation (5F035) may be used with any of the regular-form answer sheets and given to single subjects or to large groups of subjects in a single session. The tape is recorded at 3¾ inches per second on dual tracks. Side one contains the first 300 items. When side one has been played it is turned over and the remaining 266 items may be presented. The total time to play the tape is slightly over two hours. It can be played on any machine which holds a seven-inch tape reel, has a speed setting for 3¾ inches per second, and a playback head for reading half-track recorded material.

Each item is read twice on the tape by a professional announcer. For a few items, supplementary definitions of some words are given on the tape (see the discussion above). The pacing of the item administration is adequate for most subjects to keep up with the tape but occasionally a subject fails to answer during the interval provided. The test administrator should indicate that there will be an opportunity after the testing is completed to go back over items that may have been missed. A test booklet should be on hand for such item reviewing since it is difficult to locate particular items quickly and efficiently on the tape for replay. As indicated earlier, research on the tape-recorded version indicates that the results from this mode of administration are in general comparable to those obtained by the booklet version, but the length of time taken to play the tape may cause special motivational problems. The general instructions and procedures for test administration with the booklet form given above should be consulted as guides for the administration of the tape-recorded version as well.

Individual Administration. If a single subject is to be examined with the tape-recorded version it may be played to him through earphones. He can then work on the test without disturbing others who may be working or resting nearby and the privacy of the presentation and the responding would be comparable to his taking the booklet version. If he possesses reasonable maturity and competency, he should be instructed in the controls of the tape recorder itself so that he can stop and replay any item which may require more time or thought than usual. If he is given such instruction, it is particularly important that the machine have a provision for locking out the recording switch so that the test subject does not inadvertently erase sections of the tape. In the unlikely eventuality of such an accidental loss of parts of the standard tape, it should be returned to the Psychological Corporation for retransmission. The subject should also know whom to call in case of difficulty (tape breakage, equipment failure, etc.).

Special provision must be made for a subject who is not able to see well enough to complete the usual answer sheet of the MMPI. Instructions with the tape-recorded form of the test suggest that a clerk may take down the answers given orally by the visually handicapped subject. This arrangement is satisfactory but is obviously expensive in time for the clerk and may significantly alter the test setting by reducing the privacy of the test subject. It is better if some method is worked out by which the blind or near-blind clients may record their own answers. As indicated above, Braille answer sheets or typewriters may be employed, the tape-recorded version and a box form of the test may be combined (see Potter, 1950), or some simple lever-pressing device may be arranged for recording serial True and False responses.

Whatever the means of recording answers that may be used, the administration of the tape form of the test takes a long time. Some rest periods should be planned to enable the subject to remove the earphones, stretch and relax, and shift his attention briefly from the concentration required to listen and evaluate the MMPI statements. A few brief rests are probably better than one long interval after which it may be difficult to get back into the proper test-taking set.

Group Testing with the Tape Form. It is unlikely that the physical facilities available will permit group administration of the MMPI by earphones and tape recorder. Therefore, the items will have to be played over loudspeakers. This mode of presentation is feasible if the subjects have been adequately prepared and the test properly introduced. Such a testing situation requires particular care be given to the general group-testing procedures and safeguards outlined above in discussing the administration of the booklet form of the test. Baughman and Dahlstrom (1968) report that this mode of administration was successfully carried out with several groups of rural junior high school subjects of both sexes in regular classroom testing by experienced female testers and proctors.

The test administrator must be certain that the reproduction equipment is adequate to the task (proper tape deck speed, playback heads clean and adjusted, amplification and speakers appropriate to the room size and audience) and that he understands the operation of the equipment to be used. He should also be familiar with the change in the tape reel required at the end of the first 300 items. He should make certain that he has extra take-up reels to be used in case a break occurs in the tape during the test, and that he has a tape repair kit on hand to carry out tape patching in order to play the second half of the test.

Subjects for whom the tape version is deemed appropriate in place of the usual booklet-form administration are likely to require especially careful instructions on the completion of the answer sheets. Care should be used in the selection of answer sheets (see the comparisons made above of those available) to be certain that these materials are as clear, uncluttered, and legible as possible. The administrator should develop procedures for demonstrating the way in which the headings are to be completed and illustrating the marking of True and False responses. He should spell out clearly how changing of answers can be effected. He should also tell the subjects in the group that if they miss an item in the regular playing of the tape, there will be an opportunity to go back over it later. The subjects should be urged, therefore, to keep up with the items as they are read and not get behind. Proctors who are helping with this administration should be alert to the occasional subject who is proceeding in the wrong direction down or across the answer sheet or who is working on the wrong section of the answer sheet.

As with individual administration of the taped version, opportunities for stopping to stretch and relax should be interpolated in the testing session, but they should be kept relatively brief. At the end of the tape, the test administrator should read any items that particular subjects wish to go over from the booklet (or from Appendix L of this volume). Generally, these items are few in number and the rest of the test subjects can be asked to take this opportunity to go back over the test headings to be certain that they have given all the information that is needed.

The tape should be returned to the box in shape to be readministered with all repairs completed and the tape rewound to the starting place. If the whole test has been played, it is ready for replay at the end of the playing of the second half of the test. The tape should be stored in a place that is away from excessive heat or cold and is free of magnetic fields. Spare reels should be stored with the test tape ready for the next use.

Special Administrative Considerations

A number of important aspects of giving the MMPI which arise from its format, its special ease of administration, and its coverage of item content are taken up in the following pages. The very success of this test has given rise to new problems and concerns. Many of these issues were already recognized at the time the test was developed but a number of them have come to view since the test was first published and introduced to the field. Any use of the test should take special cognizance of these important considerations.

Setting and Context. Evaluations of personality are currently being made in an ever-broadening array of settings and contexts (Hathaway, 1965). Simultaneously, the general public is growing increasingly knowledgeable and sophisticated about tests and inventories. Through public debates (Ridgeway, 1964; Braaten, 1965; Brayfield, 1965; Gordon, 1965), through a variety of popular books on tests, testing procedures, and testing ethics (e.g., Alex, 1965; Dustin, 1969; Engberg, 1967; Gross, 1962; Whyte, 1956), and through the increasing exposure being given to psychological instruments in general psychology texts and lectures, important segments of the public in America are becoming conversant with the methods of personality assessment. At the present time, therefore, an even greater range of test sophistication exists among potential test subjects than ever before. As a result, there is now a greater demand for proper execution of these assessment procedures and the utilization of sensitive indicators of the acceptability of any given test protocol (see the discussion in Part Two of this volume). Test examiners and interpreters must be constantly alert, as well, to the differential impact of the particular setting in which they carry out their assessment work upon the attitudes, expectations, apprehensions, and test-taking intentions of their clients.

In any administration of the MMPI, therefore, the test should be presented to the subject as a serious and important undertaking. Assurance should be given that the responses of the subject are to be used for his own benefit. This attitude, if effectively communicated, will help immeasurably in enlisting full cooperation from most subjects. A few people may require additional reassurance or clarification of the purposes for which the test results will be used. If possible, frank replies should be made; evasion and shifting of responsibility should be avoided. Although an invalid sorting of the MMPI can generally be detected, no measures can remedy an administration marred by poor cooperation from the subject.

A growing body of research has demonstrated that several aspects of the testing situation, including features of the MMPI test instrument itself, play an important role in determining the feelings and reactions that the subjects have about being examined. Thus, there is evidence that merely being asked to take the MMPI may itself be stressful through arousal of evaluative anxiety (Gocka and Burk, 1963; Kausler, Trapp, and Brewer, 1959; Miller, Bohn, Gilden, and Stevens, 1968; Voas, 1956, 1957). The effects are similar to those resulting from the stress of course failure (Jacobs and Leventer, 1955). In addition, reactions to being screened for the presence of a possible emotional disorder (Vaughan, 1963) or for the feasibility of release from a psychiatric hospital (Braginsky, Braginsky, and Ring, 1969; Wilcox and Krasnoff, 1967; R. C. Young, 1965) may alter MMPI scores. Subjects also are known to react to variations in the test instructions (Baldry and Sarason, 1968; Graham, 1963) and to different aspects of the test format and content (Butcher and Tellegen, 1966; Fiske, 1969; Rankin,

1968; Simmons, 1968; Stone and Margoshes, 1965; Walker, 1967; and Walker and Ward, 1968). In general, the MMPI is judged to be interesting, the content unambiguous, explicit, and easily evaluated and answered, but many of the items are seen as intrusive, objectionable, or perhaps even offensive, particularly when the situation itself involves close scrutiny of the subject's competency, emotional stability, or integration. Since the efficacy of the test depends in important ways upon the items that cover various sensitive areas of the subjects' lives (see the material in the following sections), it is impossible to omit such items and retain its validity. Instead of seriously altering the test itself, therefore, it is more appropriate to give much greater consideration than hitherto to evaluating the suitability of the MMPI for the given context and proposed applications and to preparing the test subjects properly for the examination. Test acceptance can be anticipated to be good if professional competence is high and ethical safeguards believable and trustworthy.

Administration by Nonprofessional Personnel. The administration of the MMPI does not require the presence of one who is specially trained in psychology. Although a psychometrist is of course best, in routine use in a hospital or clinic the examiner may be any willing and interested person who is able to obtain the required information and present the directions for the test. Attendants, receptionists, secretaries, and nurses have been shown to be very competent in enlisting the cooperation of clients and patients. They may offer the test as part of the regular clinic or hospital procedures by saying, for example, "This test is part of what you do here," or "The doctor wants this information on everyone; it will help him to understand your case." The lack of psychological training of such examiners is usually not a handicap in administering the MMPI, although they should be cautioned against being too officious, overly friendly, or gossipy.

Although in administration the MMPI is less demanding of professional skill than many other personality instruments, it should never be forgotten that the use of any personality test is a professional action to be carried out with all the maturity and finesse at one's disposal (Hathaway, 1964); this will be discussed further below. The MMPI has simple, straightforward instructions and is a self-administering test. Even in this situation, however, a subject easily senses a test administrator's attitude, especially as it may be reflected in superficiality or flippancy of manner, and he may respond with similar lightness or with an unwillingness to reveal personal feelings or socially unacceptable reactions to an apparently unsympathetic audience. The administrator's approach to the testing session, whether it is with a deeply disturbed patient in a hospital room or in an auditorium full of restless adolescents, can seriously affect the usefulness of the sample of behavior drawn by the MMPI. The same care must be exercised in handling the test materials after the subject is finished as is employed in setting up the situation originally. Every effort should be made to convince the test subject that his responses are important and will be treated as confidential and professional communications.

In using a group-form booklet for routine testing of single patients (or small groups of similar clients in office practice or ward testing) some clinicians have found it useful to employ a special set of test-orienting instructions which may be handed to the test subject while the person who is administering the test goes over it with him. The following detailed instructions have been suggested for such use by the Roche Psychiatric Service Institute to the clients who subscribe to their test-scoring and interpreting service.

INSTRUCTIONS TO TEST ADMINISTRATOR

In order to assure uniformity of test administration, the instructions which follow have been specified in considerable detail. It is suggested that they be read carefully each time and not memorized in whole or part. The instructions should be given exactly as written since a rewording could change the meaning for the patient.

Before the Test

1. Hand the patient the Patient Instructions [see below].
2. *Say*: "Please read the instructions as I read them aloud to you."
3. *Read*: "The questions you are about to answer are designed to help you tell about your attitudes, feelings, and problems. They will provide additional information for making decisions about your treatment. Some of the questions may seem puzzling or strange to you. They were designed to be used with a wide variety of people. If you are unsure about the meaning of any question try to answer it as best you can. Do not ask for help, since the important thing is how *you* answer the questions. Your results are of course confidential as are all of your other records. Your answer sheet, identified only by a code number, will be processed by an electronic computer. Do not write your name on the answer sheet. Be sure to answer the questions rapidly but carefully. Do not spend too much time on one question—your first impression is best. Now please read the instructions on the cover of the test booklet."
4. Hand the patient the test booklet and point to the instructions. *Say*: "Now follow on this booklet while I read these instructions to you."
5. *Read*: "This inventory consists of numbered statements. Read each statement and decide whether it is *true as applied to you* or *false as applied to you.* You are to mark your answers on the answer sheet you have. If a statement is *true* or *mostly true,* as applied to you, blacken between the lines in the column headed T. If a statement is *false* or *not usually true,* as applied to you, blacken between the lines in the column headed F. If a statement does not apply to you or if it is something that you don't know about, make no mark on the answer sheet. Remember to give *your own* opinion of yourself. Do not leave any blank spaces if you can avoid it. In marking your answers on the answer sheet, *be sure that the number of the statement agrees with the number of the answer sheet.* Make your marks heavy and black. Erase completely any answer you wish to change. Do not make any marks on this booklet. Remember, try to make *some* answer to every statement. Are there any questions?"
6. *Read*: "Now open the booklet and read the first question."
7. After the patient has read the question "I like mechanics magazines," *say*: "If the answer to that question is true, you should mark the

space on the answer sheet under T." (Point to the correct space.) "If it is false, mark the space under F." (Point to the correct space.)

8. When the patient has marked the first item correctly, *say*: "That's fine," and ask him to continue with the rest of the items in the same way.

9. After five minutes or so, it is wise to check to be sure that the patient is following instructions and is not having difficulty.

During the Test

1. If the patient has questions about the *mechanics* of the test, such as how to place the answer sheet or how to mark the answers, assistance may be given.

2. If the patient asks how to answer specific questions, he should be urged to answer them independently. Under no circumstances should the test questions be explained, defined or answered for the patient by the examiner or by anyone else since to do so might influence the patient's response and distort the test results. It is sometimes helpful to respond to such requests for help with remarks like the following: "Please answer the questions as best you can by yourself." "I am not permitted to help with any of the questions. Just give the answer that seems best to you."

3. The patient may, however, be reassured that other people sometimes ask questions about the test and that it has been found best for each person to answer entirely by himself.

4. If the circumstances permit, the patient may be allowed to take a short break during the test for coffee or a rest period. The test should not be discussed during the break, however.

5. If the patient is obviously in distress, he may be reassured and encouraged to complete the test.

6. If the patient should become too emotionally or physically upset, the test may be interrupted, but it should be completed as soon as possible—preferably by the next day.

7. The test should not be started unless sufficient time is available to complete it. However, if the patient is unusually slow and there is insufficient time, it can be interrupted and completed as soon as possible.

8. The test should always be administered under professional supervision; under no circumstances should the test be taken at home or otherwise removed from the designated location for the test administration.

After the Test

1. Before the patient leaves, quickly inspect the answer sheet for the following: (a) *Omissions*: If the patient has failed to complete the test or has omitted a large number of items (30 or more), he should be encouraged to make every attempt to complete the missing items. (b) *Errors*: If he has incorrectly followed instructions by giving two answers to some questions or making his marks in the wrong places, he should be asked to make corrections. If only a few errors have been made, however, this is not necessary.

2. Be sure the identification data on the answer sheet are complete (date of birth, sex, etc.).

PATIENT INSTRUCTIONS

The questions you are about to answer are designed to help you tell about your attitudes, feelings, and problems. They will provide additional information for making decisions about your treatment.

Some of the questions may seem puzzling or strange to you. They were designed to be used with a wide variety of people. If you are unsure about the meaning of any question try to answer it as best you can. Do not ask for help, since the important thing is how *you* answer the questions. Your results are of course confidential as are all of your other records. Your answer sheet, identified only by a code number, will be processed by an electronic computer. Do not write your name on the answer sheet.

Be sure to answer the questions rapidly but carefully. Do not spend too much time on one question—your first impression is best. Now please read the instructions on the cover of the test booklet.

Forced-Choice Responses. The task for each subject on the MMPI is to describe himself by placing each of the statements into one of the three categories of response: True, or mostly true; False, or not usually true; and Cannot Say. He is asked to admit or deny various actions, ascribe to various beliefs, express preferences, own up to physical symptoms, and endorse an assortment of personal and social values. He is not free to change the wording or emphasis in any of the statements, nor can he modify his endorsement by any qualification concerning intensity or frequency. He is to take the items as they stand and decide how they apply to himself.

These response categories were originally based upon two general considerations: first, the choices should be simple so as to extend as far as possible the range of subjects with whom the test could be employed; second, some option of not answering should be allowed since few items with universal applicability could be obtained. However, the subject was to be discouraged from using the Cannot Say category as much as possible. Only the response categories True and False have been used in the development and scoring of the scales.

There are wide variations among the items in the degree to which subjects are likely to classify them under Cannot Say. The list of response frequencies in the appendix materials of Volume II gives the proportions of Cannot Say responses made to each of the items by several of the normative groups. M. N. Brown (1950) has suggested that certain items, particularly those applying to family and childhood background, are legitimate points of ambiguity for adult subjects and may be impossible for them to answer. He indicated that items bearing on the present status of the subject, however, should not cause any difficulty; placing of these items in the Cannot Say category should be considered a form of falsification.

A few administrators of the MMPI have dispensed with the Cannot Say category altogether by removing the divider from the box form or by encouraging "guessing" on the booklet form. This makes the instrument a forced-choice test: True or False. Psychometrically this format has some clear advantages since all items function in describing each test subject. One of the more important implications of the empirical approach to scale construction, as noted above, is that the test does not actually involve the assumption that the person is describing himself in these responses. He may be describing himself as he wishes he were; or he may be meticulously and mercilessly laying bare his soul in his replies. The scoring procedure rests only on the fact that he did sort or mark the items in a given way. The forced-choice procedure assures that a response of some sort will be made to each of the test items.

From interviews with many subjects it seems clear that most of them assume that the person conducting the test is directly interested in the content of their self-descriptions. Although the scoring procedure does not take the content into account, the test subjects do. Therefore, the attitudes aroused during testing by the instructions, by the format, and by the categories are important influences on the test scores. The forced-choice variation in MMPI administration may raise special problems for some subjects and may affect their test-taking attitudes and motivations. Caution should be exercised in introducing variations of this sort into any standardized instrument without appropriate supporting research. Such research is needed to demonstrate the degree of equivalence of the original and modified procedures or to evaluate the magnitude and nature of any changes resulting from such alterations.

Ethical Considerations. A number of the features of the MMPI format which have contributed to its attractiveness for a variety of clinical and research problems and which have enhanced its objectivity and dependability for these uses have at the same time allowed a dulling of professional sensibilities about what it may mean to a test subject to take the test. That is, administering the test does not take extensive psychological training but instead only requires reasonable care and conscientiousness; hence, as already noted, the job of giving, scoring, or recording the MMPI is often delegated to a nonpsychologist or even a nonprofessional. Unless the persons charged with giving and processing the test materials are carefully briefed on the ethical and procedural niceties of sound psychological testing, needless intrusions upon the feelings and concerns of their clients may result.

It is imperative, therefore, that persons who administer and process the MMPI be aware of the requirements for protecting the client's feelings and preserving professional confidentiality and personal privacy. Any administration of the MMPI is a professional act; every effort should be devoted to keeping it proper, meaningful, and dignified. Every test answer sheet completed is a communication from the test subject to the professional worker, whether it is directly transmitted to him or mediated by auxiliary personnel or even by professional test-scoring services. Test responses must be elicited carefully, identified accurately, and treated confidentially. Unless there are clearly established reasons for doing so, the test profile, score levels, or personological inferences derived from the MMPI should not be shown to the client or patient himself. If for any reason the test findings or interpretations are reported back to the client, the professional must be certain that the client possesses the requisite knowledge, balance, and perspective needed to understand their import and accept their implications.

Some test subjects have serious reservations about taking a test like the MMPI (Dahlstrom, 1969a; Meehl, 1969). For some, the main worry is that the confidentiality of their answers will not be preserved. They may be afraid that some unauthorized person could examine their replies and learn some feelings or experiences which they have endeavored to keep secret. For others, however, the concern involves both confidentiality and invasion of privacy. (See Westin, 1967.) For them, the objection is that they are being asked to think about and express themselves on matters which they feel are entirely personal and private. Any inquiries into these areas of their lives, therefore, constitute intrusive and disturbing invasions which they resent and resist. It should also be noted, however, that there are many other individuals for whom the test is in no sense an intrusive disruption but a welcome opportunity to communicate a variety of feelings, fears, and special concerns which they have hitherto had difficulty talking about with anyone.

It is strongly recommended, therefore, that every administration of the MMPI, to a large group, small group, or single individual, be introduced by a frank statement about the test, the purpose of the testing, and the safeguards that have been introduced to preserve privacy and professional confidences, to assure proper use of the data, and to protect the interests of the test subjects in the ultimate disposition of the test materials and records. Any psychological test is a contract between the professional and the test subject. The subjects must be fully informed about the nature of the contract and must be fully aware of the voluntary nature of this agreement.

In routine psychological screening or assessment in which all or part of the testing is carried out by nonprofessionals, the psychologist must make sure that the following points are covered by the test examiner in his initial contact with the client or patient. The nature of the test, as a general personality inventory covering a broad range of topics and designed for use with a great variety of different people, must be made clear. The fact that there are no right or wrong answers but that the subject's own opinions are being solicited should also be conveyed. The purpose of the testing and the person or persons who will receive and apply the information should also be spelled out. The measures used to preserve the confidentiality and security of the test materials should be briefly outlined to the subjects. With this information it is possible for the client or patient to know in a general way how the test results may benefit him in obtaining more appropriate and effective treatment or in contributing to scientific research and study, if that is the purpose of the examination. He may also assess the dangers of revealing undesirable aspects of his own background or personality and weigh them against expected gains. In other words, with this kind of information he can make an informed decision to participate or not, as he sees fit. An introduction of the proper kind goes a long way in generating a professional atmosphere and a serious approach to the testing that are essential to good professional use of this instrument.

These assurances must, of course, be backed up with sound procedural controls and careful handling of case records and documents. Test answer sheets or record blanks must not be left lying around the receptionist's desk or on waiting-room tables. Answer sheets and profiles must be carefully labeled by name and date, or other identifying information, to avoid possible confusion or mismatching of case materials. If scoring services are used, answer sheets should be coded so that individuals cannot be identified by unauthorized personnel. Written interpretations or printouts from MMPI administrations must not be left in case folders which may be available to patients or clients as they wait in dressing rooms or interview cubicles. Idle gossip or comments about the patients, their test responses, or their test findings must be avoided. Physicians, psychiatrists, or psychologists who are to use the results of the test must get the results with reasonable promptness and high accuracy to enable them to provide the kind of service for which the testing was originally scheduled and carried out. All these features are essentials of ethical and professional case management and test administration.

CHAPTER 2. Scoring and Profiling the Test

In this chapter the steps involved in the process of recording and scoring the MMPI and preparing an individual's profile are described in detail. At various points along the way there are alternative procedures which can be used; their advantages and disadvantages will be discussed where appropriate. Also described are the routine data-processing and special research-scoring services offered by commercial scoring (and profile interpretive) organizations in the United States that may suit the needs of many clinics and hospitals as well as private clinicians in different parts of the country. Further data analyses and reductions that may be performed upon the profile after it has been plotted will be taken up in Chapter 3.

Recording and Scoring the Box Form

After the subject has sorted the cards, the administrator has three scoring steps to follow. He must, first, sort out the cards containing significant responses; second, enter these on the record blank; and third, apply the scoring-key templates to this blank. The record blank used with the card form is shown in Appendix N.

Since one of the most serious errors in recording the MMPI is the tendency to omit making a permanent record of the items left unanswered by the subject (Krise, 1949), it is recommended that this be the first step in the recording process. After these items have been tallied, they should be placed out of the way so that they cannot subsequently be confused with the True and False piles. In the first step, then, the Cannot Say items are recorded in their appropriate cells, designated by letter (A–J) for the columns and number (1–55) for the rows, on the record blank as *black* question marks or, more simply, as single, heavy, black diagonal lines. The Cannot Say items should be counted and this number entered in the space labeled "?" at the right-hand margin of the record blank.

The next step is to remove the True pack from the box and separate it into two packets of cards, one with the lower right-hand and the other with the lower left-hand corners cut off. This separation is easily effected by placing the thumbs on the lower (cut) corners and pressing outward as the fingers of both hands press against the tops of the cards. If the pack of True cards is large, it may be impossible to do this all at one time. One of these two True packets will consist of items frequently classified as True by normal persons; the other, usually much smaller, will be composed of items infrequently classified as True. Only the latter packet, representing the significant answers, is used in recording scores. For the cards filed as True items, this packet will be the one with the *lower right-hand corners* cut off. Each item in this group is recorded as a red X or + in the appropriate cell of the record blank as identified by code letter and number. *The True items in the other packet are not recorded.*

After the infrequent True items have been recorded, the pack of cards answered as False should be similarly divided into two piles according to the corner cuts. In this case the significant answers will be those with the *lower left-hand corners* clipped. These items are next entered in the appropriate cells on the record blank with exactly the same type of red X used for the True items, since it is not important to differentiate the items. Again, *the frequent False answers are not recorded.*

If the box contains supplementary cards as suggested by some of the special administrative procedures outlined in Chapter 1, these cards will not have either lower corner cut and will be readily detected at the time the significant items are being separated and tallied. These supplementary cards may be either of two kinds: direction cards to check on the subject's understanding of the instructions or duplicate item cards to check on the subject's response consistency. The direction cards merely instruct the subject to place the card in the True or the False category. The scorer should note whether the subject did in fact place these cards in the correct location. If not, special note of any misplacements should be entered on the profile side of the record form so they can be included in the clinical evaluation of the protocol.

Inclusion in the card form of the sixteen duplicate items found in the booklet form makes it more comparable to the booklet version and provides the clinician with the additional validation check from the TR score. The TR score is the total number of discrepancies in endorsement of the original item and the duplicate item. Thus, for example, if the duplicate item A15 was placed in the True category, there should be an X or a + already entered on the record form for item A15. If this is the case, the two answers are in agreement; if not, this discrepancy adds one point to the TR score. (One of the unmarked supplementary raw-score spaces in the right-hand margin may be designated for the TR score.) Each of the remaining duplicate items should be checked in the same way. The number of answers given to this supplementary set which do not agree with the answers to the original items constitutes the total TR score. Table 2-1 contains the information needed to determine the TR score if this supplementary set is being used.

These steps complete the recording. The system whereby the cards have been coded and corner-clipped makes the task of completely recording the responses to the 550 items both simple and reasonably economical of time. Only on very unusual records will there be a great many items to be recorded. It should be remembered that the X's do not necessarily indicate abnormal answers. Some of the scales have items that are abnormal when answered in the frequent direction (that is, items for which no red X's have been recorded).

Table 2-1. Card-Form Designation and Direction of Plus Response for the Sixteen Items Duplicated in the Booklet Form

Card No.	Item Statement	+ Direction
A15	I am troubled by attacks of nausea and vomiting	T
A22	At times I have fits of laughing and crying that I cannot control	T
C6	At times I have very much wanted to leave home	T
C47	My sex life is satisfactory	F
D32	During one period when I was a youngster I engaged in petty thievery	T
E17	I have never been in trouble because of my sex behavior	F
E37	No one seems to understand me	T
F10	I am more sensitive than most other people	T
F35	Even when I am with people I feel lonely much of the time	T
F39	My daily life is full of things that keep me interested	F
G53	If people had not had it in for me I would have been much more successful	T
G55	I am sure I get a raw deal from life	T
H12	I have had very peculiar and strange experiences	T
I27	I find it hard to keep my mind on a task or job	T
I34	I work under a great deal of tension	T
J41	Once in a while I think of things too bad to talk about	F

To prepare the box of cards for the next subject, shuffle the cards well, taking care that the True, False, and Cannot Say packs are intermixed. All cards can then be returned to the box and the guide cards placed in order at the back. As mentioned in Chapter 1, it is best to put several simply stated items in the front of the box so that the first items answered by the next subject will not be disturbing.

The scoring of the various scales in the MMPI is likewise very simple. It is best to obtain the validating scores first. The Cannot Say score, as indicated above, is simply the total number of question marks. The L items are the last fifteen items listed on the record blank. To obtain the raw L score one merely counts the red X's among these items (J41 to J55 inclusive). For the F score, the transparent scoring-key template marked F is used. The sixty-four items are printed on the template in proper position with X's so arranged that when the template is placed over the record blank and the anchoring points aligned, the X's will fall beside the red X's that are significant for the F scale. To obtain the raw score, count one point for every item having a *red X on the record blank beside an X on the template. Question marks are never counted.* The raw score is thus the sum of the number of agreements between the key and the record. It should be entered in the proper space on the right-hand margin of the blank.

The raw scores for the remaining scales are obtained from the appropriate keys in the manner just described for the F score. It should be noted that all the keys except Hs contain 0's in addition to X's. When *a blank cell on the record blank corresponds to a zero on the key,* score one point. In other words, the total score on each scale is the number of both kinds of agreement, X's and 0's. Question marks are not scored, whether opposite a 0 or opposite an X. Also note the change in the Mf scoring key when used for female rather than for male subjects.

The examiner should then transfer all raw scores to the profile side of the record blank, making sure that they are entered under the profile that is appropriate to the sex of the examinee.

Alternative Card-Scoring Methods. The card form of the MMPI was set up in such a way that the subject can record his answers merely by filing each card behind any one of three dividers. When the boxes are in heavy demand in a clinic or other testing center, there is the somewhat time-consuming task of making a permanent record of these replies before the set can be used on another case. This recording problem has been the subject of considerable research and discussion in the literature.

Several alternatives were open to the authors of the MMPI originally in setting up the handling of the item tallies. A record of every response and its direction of reply could have been made. However, this seemed wasteful of clerical time and energy. One obvious abridgement could have been the recording of only the Cannot Say responses and the responses in the smaller pile (the less frequent category)—True or False—used by that subject. All the items not so marked would have been known to be in the other class. However, the authors decided to use a somewhat different basis. Since the direction in which the majority of the Minnesota normative group replied was known for each item, all that had to be recorded were responses in which the subject did not answer with the majority. The examiner notes such deviations, easily identified by the corner cuts, by entering an X on the record sheet. The completed record sheet is therefore made up of a few items marked X and the remaining ones left unmarked. If the subject answered every item in the same way the majority of the Minnesota group did, there would be no items marked X on his record blank. If he chose the minority direction on each item, every space would have an X mark in it. The scoring stencils for the card form are based upon the matching of the subject's item record with the items and direction of answering indicated for each scale. Some of the scale stencils have only X items indicated (that is, significant answers occur only if the subject gives a minority answer to that item subset). However, on most of the scales, the subject also gets points for some items when he answers in the majority direction. The latter, indicated by open spaces on the record sheet, are marked as 0's on the stencil; this system of designation is the basis for the X or + (plus) item and 0 or zero item terminology that was first used by Meehl and Hathaway (1946) in their discussion of the K-scale derivation.

One difficulty in this recording system is the possibility of a serious clerical error if the True and False piles are confused while the cards are being separated by the corner cuts. As will be noted later, this error is usually reflected in an extreme F-scale elevation. Another difficulty in this system is that the response a subject actually made to a given item cannot be immediately determined at some later date. The record sheet will show that a subject agreed or differed with the majority of the reference group on an item, but the material in Appendix A in this volume must be consulted before one knows whether the answer was True or False. Although empirical study (Corsini, 1949) has indicated that the recommended system of recording leads to the greatest economy of time over the long run, occasionally the clerical task is very heavy, particularly in recording a psychotic case with many deviant replies. Unfortunately, the system has also led to confusion in the recording and reporting of data in the research literature. There is some difficulty in the preparation of new keys for research scales when the item lists are given by booklet numbers and the True/False direction of reply. (See the discussion below.)

In the face of such problems, some workers have suggested ways to get scale scores directly from the cards without the preparation of an answer record blank. These methods involve color coding the item cards (Davis, 1947; Mullen, 1948; Wilcox, 1958), the use of special markings on the cards (Gulde and Roy, 1947; Navran, 1950), and key-sort punching (Ferguson, 1946; Shneidman, 1946; Manson and Grayson, 1946; Krise, 1947). These procedures are generally not appreciably faster (see Corsini, 1949) and the subject's specific item replies are not preserved. This lack of an item record prevents subsequent scoring of other scales, either special or newly developed ones, and the development of new scoring methods through subsequent research. It is possible to employ one of these procedures to obtain a set of scores for immediate use without disrupting the order of the cards. The permanent record of the subject's replies can then be prepared later at a more convenient time. This delay in recording may tie up a box of cards for a longer period of time, but there would be the advantage of expediting the disposition of some particular case.

There have also been suggestions to revise the scoring of the card form while preserving a record of specific item replies as part of normal scoring operations. Drake (1947) proposed a way of marking a standard group-form IBM answer sheet with card-form information. An electrograph pencil is used to record the X item responses and the record is then processed by special keys in the IBM scoring machine. The main advantage this system offers is the use of the scoring machine for processing the record once it is prepared; Cannot Say and deviant responses must be tabulated by hand.

Burton and Bright (1946) proposed the use of IBM cards for the items themselves. By a system of prepunching the item cards, the subject's responses may be recorded and counted by the IBM tabulator. This method has been revised and extended by Hathaway (1956a), who has worked out the scoring procedures for IBM card-sorting and tabulating machines. The items are printed directly on individual IBM cards. Since the item numbers and corner cuts are preserved, hand scoring this set is still possible. The series of punches on each card provide for the accumulation of the separate scale scores and the printing of the number of the items answered Cannot Say and True by the subject. Thus, the score profile of the subject is available for immediate use and the item record is completely preserved. The sorter puts the cards back in a standard order after the record is completed and before the test is used on the next case. This system offers excellent possibilities for installations where the card form of the MMPI is used on a large scale. Routine hospital and clinic administrations are examples.

Preparation of Special Stencils for the Box Form. Appendix I contains the item-composition lists for a wide variety of special scales which may be scored for clinical or research use on the standard form of the MMPI. The items are designated by regular booklet-form numbers, however, which must be converted into box-form numbers. Similarly, the direction of scoring is indicated by True and False; these must be transformed into either X or 0 scoring direction before a key for this form of the test can be constructed. Three major steps are thus involved in preparing these special keys: the item-number conversion, the scoring-direction transformation, and the marking and punching of the stencil.

It is best to use a separate worksheet before marking the stencil itself. Note that for each scale listed in Appendix I, the items scored True and the items scored False are listed separately. On this worksheet list in appropriately designated columns all the item numbers given under the True heading, skipping the two adjacent columns to give adequate space for recording first the scoring direction and then the item numbering on the box form. Next, list separately the booklet item numbers of the items that are scored False. After these booklet numbers under the two headings have been listed and double-checked for accuracy, the entries in Appendix A should be consulted. Here, for each booklet-form number, is listed the box-form scoring designation, X or 0, for a True answer to that item. Thus, in the group of items to be scored for True answers on this special key, the designation X or 0 can be taken directly from the list in Appendix A and entered in the second column of the worksheet beside each booklet-form item number. These entries should be carefully checked for clerical errors. Then the items to be scored for a False answer may be identified. In these tallies, however, the designation *opposite* (X for 0, and 0 for X) to the entry in Appendix A must be entered on the worksheet. These entries must be *double-checked* since the chance for errors is very great in this clerical operation.

Second, each of the booklet-form items must be converted into the box-form numbering system. These item numbers are provided in Table 2 in Appendix C. In the third column of the worksheet, enter the letter (A–J) and number (1–55) which identifies the box-form location of each item in the special key. It is a good idea to double-check this step by reversing the operation in this item number identification; that is, each box-form number written in should be located in Table 1 of Appendix C and the original booklet-form item number verified.

The third step involves preparing an accurate stencil for scoring the record form of each test subject. For this purpose, an unused record form is most suitable since after proper punching it will fit precisely over the spaces on any other record form. (The preparation of transparencies may be justified if heavy usage is anticipated, but the next step is necessary in their preparation also.) Locate on this blank record form each item listed in the special key by column and row. Enter an X or an 0 in the white space to the right of the answer space, *not in the answer space itself,* close enough to make comparisons between the keyed answer and the recorded answer easy and accurate. This crucial step should be checked for accuracy in two ways: the total number of item tallies on the new stencil should be counted and verified against the total number of items in the special scale as listed in Appendix I and the specific item marking should be double-checked by proceeding back up the list of entries on the worksheet to be certain that each tally appears in the correct column and row. The last step in preparing the stencil involves punching or cutting out the designated answer space on the stencil for each item on the key. This kind of punching cannot easily be carried out with the usual short-nosed paper punch but IBM No. 171971 stencil punch will work on this size paper, or any paper drill can be used if the stencil is first placed over a soft cardboard surface to permit clean and complete perforations. A sharp razor blade or knife may also be used to slice out a square opening where the answers on the subject's record form will appear. It is helpful in lining up the stencil and record form if the letter A and the letter J at the top and bottom of the first and last column are punched out. When the A's and J's from the record form to be scored appear through these openings, the stencil is correctly placed for scoring the subject's protocol.

If the special stencil is going to be used heavily in routine scoring, it may be wise to mount the stencil on heavy cardboard (repunching the holes and placement markers) to make it more sturdy or, if plastic sheets of transparent material are available, a transparent scoring template may be prepared from the stencil. After placing the plastic sheet over the stencil, marker positions should be identified (at least four places, such as the letters A and J above and below the first and last columns) and each item number, response space, and scoring designation carefully traced in India ink. Both the stencil and the transparency should, of course, be labeled with the scale name, abbreviation, author, and total number of possible points.

For a scale that is described in some research publication the list of component items may not provide the regular booklet-form numbers needed to prepare the stencil. That is, the item content may be given seriatim in the research scale but omit the identifying numbers from the MMPI booklet. In such instances it will be necessary to consult the alphabetical listing of items presented in Appendix D of this volume. Both box-form and booklet-form numbers are given in Appendix D for each item. (If it is unclear in the research article whether or not the items are actually MMPI items, it may be necessary to use the key word list in Appendix E to locate likely MMPI items to compare in wording with the items in the publication.)

Scoring the Short Form of the Box Version. In the usual method of giving the short form of the MMPI by means of the box of cards, no special scoring problems are involved. That is, if the only change is the omission of the items that are not scored on any of the basic scales, then the recording of the significant answers and the Cannot Say items is carried out as described above. The raw scores for the basic scales are also obtained in the same way with the single exception of the Cannot Say raw score. Since the test is only about two-thirds the standard length, the importance of item omissions is considerably greater than their actual number. Use Table 2 in Appendix K to prorate the raw score obtained on Cannot Say into the predicted value for the full test. Enter the raw score in the side column of Table 2 and read off the predicted value from column E.

When the box form has been further shortened by leaving out some of the component items from the basic scales, special scoring problems occur if the standard record form is used. That is, if only the significant items are recorded for the short form, it may be difficult to tell whether a given item has been answered in the majority direction (and appropriately indicated by an open space on the record form) or has been removed from the test and not answered by the subject. In such a situation, it is necessary either to mark the regular record form routinely to show where the items that have been omitted would be recorded or to prepare special scoring stencils on which the omitted items have been marked so that they can be skipped in the scoring process. In addition, when the short-form raw scores have been tallied (either from the specially marked record forms or from the specially prepared scoring stencils) they must each be prorated to get the predicted raw scores if the standard test had been administered. To carry out this prorating step, the tables in Appendix K must be consulted for all the scales which have been abbreviated. Table 1 in Appendix K gives the information necessary to determine the prorating method that has to be used with the given short form that has been adopted. These same tables can be used to rescue a standard-length test that has been abandoned by the test subject before he has been able to complete it.

Scoring the Booklet Form

Several possibilities are open to the user of the MMPI for the scoring of the answer sheets from his test subjects. He can send his materials to a scoring service, where each protocol is scored, the raw scores entered, and the profile plotted. If an IBM test-scoring machine is available he can have the MMPI answer sheets scored and the raw scores totaled on it, and then prepare his own profiles. Hand-scoring stencils are also available for the IBM and NCS answer sheets or can be made for use with the others.

Scoring Services. There are two scoring services for the MMPI. Testscor (see Appendix O) provides a rapid scoring service for both the Hankes group-form answer sheets and the IBM answer sheets, the latter at a slightly higher cost. The service scores all the standard clinical and validity scales, including Si. Arrangements can be made for scoring special scales. For each case a profile is drawn; the profile bears the numbers and signs for the Hathaway code (see Chapter 3). National Computer Systems (see Appendix O) also provides a scoring service for the various NCS answer sheets that are available for group forms of the MMPI. Routine scoring by NCS for either the regular booklet or Form R provides both raw and T scores on the validity and clinical scales and on 11 special supplementary scales (the scales listed in Appendix F). The profile sheet contains plots for all three sets of scales and basic case identification data. Either of these scoring services offers special research scoring services upon request from individual investigators, as well as custom-tailored answer sheets and profile forms for large-scale clinical applications.

It should also be noted that scoring and profiling of group-form answer sheets are included in routine services of several computer-based MMPI interpretive concerns. These printouts include raw and T scores on the basic scales and usually several supplementary scales as well, together with the coding and many special indices that are described in the next chapter. These agencies do not, however, provide this scoring service separate from the total interpretive service given their clients. (See the material on these computer systems in Chapter 8.)

There are also available procedures and programs by means of which local scoring and profiling can be automated on existing computing systems (e.g., Goldstein, Linden, and Baker, 1967; Gravitz, 1967b; Gravitz and Davis, 1965a, 1965b) in combination with optical or electrostatic readers.

It should be noted in the use of all these automatic scoring and data-processing procedures that recently some serious concern about their accuracy and reliability has been expressed (Weigel and Phillips, 1967; Fowler and Coyle, 1968c). As Fowler and Coyle point out, some of the scoring discrepancy revealed by empirical study of the comparability of hand scoring and machine scoring appears to have arisen because of the use of different items on scoring keys for the basic scales in the MMPI. This kind of difference arises from the fact that sixteen items are duplicated in the test booklet; a key on which these duplicated items occur can score the items the way that the subject answers them the first time they appear or the way the subject answers them the second time they are given. The IBM scoring stencils available through the Psychological Corporation often use one item number, say the earlier one, for the scoring of an item when it appears on one scale and the other later placement for that same item when it is scored on another scale. The item lists that are presented in Appendix I, however, always list the item composition in terms of the earlier appearance in the test booklet. Scoring services and computer interpretive systems which have derived their scoring formats from the *Handbook* lists will differ an indeterminant amount from scoring of the same protocols by published hand-scoring keys on this basis alone. These differences in keying are unfortunate and should be eliminated in future published scoring materials. They do not account for all the discrepancies, however, since Fowler and Coyle also found appreciable diurnal variation in the printouts of scores from the scoring services and errors even in the identifying codes and data on the cases resubmitted for repeat scoring. The raw-score variations were rarely large enough to make a serious difference in the clinical interpretation of the resulting profiles but these variations would obviously affect the application of profile rules and categorizing schemas, as well as some of the interpretive programs. Errors on case-identifying data are potentially very serious, too, in large-scale test programs and surveys. Both studies cited above recommend repeat hand-scoring procedures in research and clinical applications in which high accuracy is mandatory.

The answer sheets discussed below are reproduced in Appendix N.

Machine Scoring the IBM Electrostatic Answer Sheet. The *Manual* describes the steps for scoring the MMPI by means of the IBM 805 scoring machine. This material should be read carefully before attempting to use this scoring method. The following discussion is offered to clarify some possible sources of error or confusion.

The first step in scoring the IBM answer sheet is to separate the papers of males and females. At this time the answer sheets should be carefully inspected for faulty response completions or extraneous marks. Any inappropriate marks should be erased thoroughly before processing. Doubly marked items should be erased and treated as Cannot Say responses. Blacken in any weak completions.

Next carefully mark each omitted item with a red pencil line across both the True and False spaces. The total number of these red marks is the raw score for the Cannot Say score. This total should be entered in the space marked "?" at the top of the sheet.

Seventeen keys are used for machine scoring. With the exception of Sc on the back of the answer sheet, all keys are used in pairs, with one of the pair read with the switch at "Rights" and the other with the switch at "Wrongs."

For the preliminary checking of the machine it is advisable to use an answer sheet with both possible responses (True and False) for each item blackened. Insert each pair of keys as listed in Table 2-2 with the master control switch at A; with "B" and "C" formula switches at A read R and W, using the "A" formula switch. The "plus" rheostat should be adjusted so that the indicated item numbers correspond to the "A total" indicated on each of the keys. Next, the "B" formula switch should be shifted to any position other than A. The scores obtained for Rights and Wrongs should now correspond to the numbers called "C part" on the keys being checked. Finally, the "B" formula switch should be put at A and the "C" formula switch moved to some position other than A or B. The Rights and Wrongs scores should now correspond to the numbers called "B part" on the two keys.

Table 2-2 shows the general plan of running the keys, which is designed to permit the scoring of answer sheets with the smallest possible number of machine runs. In all but one of the nine runs through the machine, two scores are obtained. Seven of these scores are total scores, and ten are part scores which must be added together in pairs to form five more total scores. In each run, the first scale in Table 2-2 (Rights) is read with the "A" formula switch at R ("B" and "C" formula switches at A) and the corresponding scale in the Wrongs column is read with the "A" formula switch at W. The master control switch remains at A. Note that for the first run the appropriate Mf key (male or female) must be used.

Item 296, which is on the front of the answer sheet, occurs in both the K scale and the Si scale when answered False. In order to score the front of the answer sheets for the K scale and the Si scale in the same machine run, item 296 has been omitted from the Si scale *machine-scoring* key. The item has *not* been omitted from the Si scale hand-scoring key, or from the Si scale scoring template used with the individual (card) form. This means that *with machine scoring* there will be a loss of one raw-score point in the Si score of some examinees, but because this loss will occur for fewer than half the examinees (False is less frequently marked than True) and because there are a large number of items in the Si scale (70), this difference is not serious. No correction need be made for this scale either in raw-score points or in the T scores listed for Si in Appendix H of the present volume and on the profile form.

Table 2-2. Master Plan for Runs in Machine Scoring on IBM 805

Machine Run	Side of Answer Sheet	Scale on Rights [a]	Score Maximum [c]	Scale on Wrongs [a]	Score Maximum
1[b]........	Front	Mf (m), Mf (f)	60	Hs	33
2........	Front	Ma	46	D	60
3........	Front	Hy	60	F	64
4........	Front	Sc (front)	41	Pd	50
5........	Front	Pa (front)	26	Pt (front)	25
6........	Front	K (front)	21	Si (front)	31
7........	Back	Pa (back)	14	Pt (back)	23
8........	Back	Sc (back)	37		
9........	Back	K (back)	9	Si (back)	38

[a] Setting for the "A" formula switch (master control switch and "B" and "C" formula switches at A).

[b] Two scales are scored on each machine pass except run 8.

[c] Maximal scores for the run; these values may be partial scores to be added to get total raw scores.

After the nine runs are completed, the five part scores from the back should be transferred to the front of the answer sheet and the total obtained. Finally, the raw scores are transferred to the side of the profile form that is appropriate to the sex of the examinee.

Machine Scoring the IBM Optical Answer Sheet. The IBM answer sheet for use with either the 1230 or 1232 scoring systems (which is also compatible with the requirements of the IBM 1231 scoring machine) contains spaces for answers to the entire inventory of 566 items: 284 items on the front of the sheet and 282 items on the reverse side. Space for a nine-digit identification number is provided on each side, and space for the indication of sex is provided on the front. Before processing, these answer sheets should be separated by sex, since the Mf scale requires different master answer sheets for males and females. At this time double-marked items should be erased and treated as Cannot Say responses.

Since the items scored for any particular scale may be scattered throughout the test, the most practical way to use this answer sheet is to transfer item responses to punched cards for subsequent scoring on a computer. If this is done on the IBM 1230, it will be necessary to modify the machine configuration of the 1230 and associated punch (e.g., Model 534), in order that four punches can be made in one card column. When there are four punches in a column, only one card need be punched for each answer-sheet side (seventy-one columns for item responses and nine columns for identification, with sex included in the identification block). The computer in which these punched cards are used must have a column binary feature, i.e., the ability to accept the otherwise nonvalid characters thus produced.

If an IBM 1232 machine which has not been modified in a manner similar to that mentioned for the 1230 is used to transmit item responses to punched cards, the machine must be equipped with two special features: a *segmented-word feature* and a *multiple-spread-card feature*. The first of these will punch the responses from a half-word on the answer sheet into one column of a tabulating card. This permits the punching of responses for two items in one card column. The multiple-spread-card feature allows up to four cards to be punched per side during one pass of the answer sheet; without this feature only one card per side could be punched. Since the front of the sheet contains 284 items, 142 columns must be assigned for the responses to these items. If the complete identification field of nine digits is to be punched into each of two cards, 160 columns would be needed. In order to identify the cards, a column is needed for card number. This leads to the requirement of three cards for the front. If, however, fewer than nine digits of identification are used, two cards will be sufficient for the responses on the front of the answer sheet, the identification number, and a card number. If the user wishes to punch sex, one digit of the identification number can be used to code sex. The data from side 2 of the answer sheet can be punched into two cards.

Although the most practical method for scoring this answer sheet is by computer, users of the IBM 1230 can score it in standard fashion. To print out the basic validity and clinical scales (plus Es), a separate pass of the answer sheet is required for each scale on each side. This will result in a tightly packed array of printed scores on the front side of the answer sheet, using both inside and outside margin print positions. Thirteen of the fourteen printed scores on the front will be part scores to which must be added the scores printed on the back in order to obtain the total scores for the scales. Table 2-3 shows the location on the program control sheet of readout and end-of-part signals for the printout of scores on successive passes. (The shaded area at the bottom of the answer sheet is provided to facilitate the location of some of these signals on a program control sheet.) The margin print locations (outside or inside lines) are also indicated in the table. Appendix I contains a list of the item numbers and the scored responses for the fourteen scales shown in Table 2-3. These lists may be used in the preparation of master answer sheets. A separate master answer sheet and a program control sheet for each side are required to score each scale. To avoid improper identification of the printed scores the user should mark one answer sheet with the scale identifications in the appropriate printout positions. Each master answer sheet should be carefully checked to ensure that the response positions have been marked correctly. To determine whether all marks have been made dark enough, use the master answer sheet and the appropriate program control sheet to set the scoring machine, then score the master answer sheet. The number printed in the margin should equal the number of scored item responses for that scale (see Appendix I). The scored master answer sheet also shows the print position for that scale, and this can be used for identification of the printed scores.

Table 2-3. Information for Preparation of Program Control Sheet for IBM 1230 Answer Sheet

Scale	End of Part Signal	Read Out Signal	Margin Print Position
	Front of Answer Sheet		
L	T of item 255	F of item 255	Outside
Pt	T of item 271	F of item 271	Outside
Es	T of item 271	F of item 271	Inside
K	T of item 279	F of item 279	Outside
D	T of item 279	F of item 279	Inside
Hy	A (shaded area)	B (shaded area)	Outside
F	A (shaded area)	B (shaded area)	Inside
Hs	F (shaded area)	G (shaded area)	Outside
Ma	F (shaded area)	G (shaded area)	Inside
Sc	K (shaded area)	L (shaded area)	Outside
Si	K (shaded area)	L (shaded area)	Inside
Pd	P (shaded area)	Q (shaded area)	Outside
Mf	P (shaded area)	Q (shaded area)	Inside
Pa	U (shaded area)	V (shaded area)	Outside
	Back of Answer Sheet		
L	T of item 299	F of item 299	Inside
Hy	T of item 323	F of item 323	Inside
F	T of item 347	F of item 347	Inside
D	T of item 371	F of item 371	Inside
Pd	T of item 395	F of item 395	Inside
Ma	T of item 419	F of item 419	Inside
Mf	T of item 443	F of item 443	Inside
Pt	T of item 467	F of item 467	Inside
Sc	T of item 491	F of item 491	Inside
Pa	T of item 515	F ot item 515	Inside
K	T of item 539	F of item 539	Inside
Es	T of item 563	F of item 563	Inside
Si	K (shaded area)	L (shaded area)	Inside

Hand Scoring the IBM 805 Answer Sheets. In hand scoring the IBM answer sheets, the preliminary examination of the papers is the same as that described above under machine scoring. The answer sheets should be separated by sex and cleaned up carefully. The omitted and double answers should be marked with a red pencil and the raw value for the Cannot Say score entered in the appropriate space at the top of the answer sheet. If the shortened version (e.g., 366 items) has been used, the raw score should be prorated in order to make it equivalent to a similar count for the regular version of 550 items. Table 1 in Appendix K gives the Cannot Say raw scores which would be predicted for 550 items when a given Cannot Say raw score has been obtained for 366 items (or in the case of Form R, 399 items). It is this *predicted* raw score which will be converted to a T score later.

The L score should be obtained next. No key is necessary. This raw score is simply the number of statements marked False among the following: 15; 45; 75; 105; 135; 165; 195; 225; 255; 285; 30; 60; 90; 120; 150. These fifteen items of the L scale are located in an easily remembered pattern. The number of False responses among them should be recorded in the proper space as the L raw score.

For all the remaining raw scores the key is laid over the answer sheet and the blackened spots appearing through holes in the key are counted. The raw score for each scale is entered in its appropriate place at the top of the answer sheet. Note especially that for some of the scales two keys are necessary and that the part score on the back of the answer sheet must be transferred to the space for it on the front and the two part scores added to obtain the final raw score. Also note that there are separate Mf keys for men and women. After the raw scores have been obtained they should be transferred to the side of the profile form that is appropriate to the sex of the examinee. If, through some oversight or disruption of the test session, only the front page of the answer sheet has been completed by the test subject, proceed in the scoring as instructed below in the section on scoring short forms of the test.

Hand Scoring the Form R Answer Sheets. Thirteen overlay keys are used to score by hand the NCS answer sheet for Form R of the MMPI. No key is needed to obtain the Cannot Say score. Raw scores are recorded at the top of the answer sheet, then transferred to the appropriate profile chart on the reverse side. Use Table 3 in Appendix K for prorating if only 399 items have been completed.

The scoring materials include a card called the Score Identification Chart which indicates where and the order in which the raw scores should be recorded and identifies each raw score by its scale title. This card may be used to check that all scales have been scored, and to determine where to record the Cannot Say score.

Before scoring, the answer sheets should be separated by sex, since the Mf scale has separate keys for men and women. All omitted or double-answered items should be marked with a colored pencil across both spaces. The total number of these marks is the Cannot Say score. Refer to the Score Identification Chart to determine where to record this score.

To obtain the other raw scores, each key is laid over the answer sheet and the number of marks appearing through the squares on the key are counted. Use the following procedure: First, turn the answer sheet so that the black timing marks on the edge of the answer sheet are at the top. Place each key on the answer sheet so that the row of black marks on the edge of the key coincides with the row of black timing marks on the answer sheet. The blue area of the answer sheet should appear just below the bottom edge of the key. Second, count the number of marks showing through the squares on the key and record the number in the blue area directly below the arrow printed on the bottom edge of the key. Third, to transfer the scores to the profile side of the answer sheet, fold the answer sheet along the edge of the blue area. The scores appear in the same order (Cannot Say to Si) as the columns of the profile. Be sure to use the profile (male or female) that matches the sex of the subject. One further word of warning: Do not place these scoring transparencies where they may be exposed to excessive heat. The plastic sheets expand under heat and become so deformed that they no longer fit properly over the spaces on the answer sheets.

When the Form R answer sheet (or any other answer sheet with the Form R booklet) is to be scored for any of the supplementary scales listed in Appendix I, special procedures are required to convert the item numbers given in the appendix to the appropriate numbering for the Form R booklet order. Most *but not all* of the item numbers in the two group-form booklets are identical. It is therefore recommended that a worksheet be used as an intermediate step between the item list for a particular scale in Appendix I and the preparation of the scoring stencil. First, list in appropriately marked columns the regular booklet-form number of each item scored True, leaving an empty column for recording the equivalent Form R item numbers for each of these items. Then, in a second set of vertical columns list the items to be scored False; space should be left beside each of these columns, too, for the Form R number. Then, consult Appendix C, Table 3, for the Form R number corresponding to each item in the True and False lists and write it next to the regular booklet-form number. Third, insert a blank answer sheet into the back of a Form R booklet and locate each item marked True by its Form R number in the step-down pages; blacken the oval on the answer sheet in the designated place, the True (T) or left-hand position. Check off each item on the worksheet as it is located and marked in the stencil. Do the same thing with the items to be scored for False, locating them by their Form R number in the booklet and blackening the right-hand oval, marked F on the answer sheet. Double-check to be sure that all the items have been entered on the stencil and that the total agrees with the total number of items for that particular scale given in Appendix I. Lastly, remove the marked answer sheet from the back of the booklet, identify the scale by name, abbreviation, author, and total number of items, and punch out the answers that have been marked with a long-nosed paper punch or a paper drill. It is also a good idea to punch or cut out some convenient positioning landmarks to supplement the two holes already present on the top of the Form R answer sheet. A few of the black timing bars at the bottom of the answer sheet may be cut out halfway along, so that the subject's answer sheet can be lined up, bar for bar. Another possibility is to punch out the two sex-identifying circles which can then be centered over the subject's sheet so that one or the other mark always appears through the stencil. After these stencils have been constructed, they may be applied in the same way that the transparent overlays are used, the total raw score on each special supplementary scale being the total number of marks that show through the stencil.

If heavy usage of these supplementary scoring stencils is contemplated in routine scoring tasks, the answer sheet should be mounted on heavy cardboard and the holes repunched. Transparencies may also be constructed by tracing the scoring pattern on plastic sheets with india ink.

Hand Scoring the Hankes Answer Sheet. If the Hankes answer sheets are used and hand scoring is desired, it is necessary to prepare one's own scoring stencils since none are commercially available. The same problem confronts the user of any of the other group-form answer sheets if scores are needed on any of the special supplementary scales for the MMPI; special scoring stencils will have to be prepared for these scales as well. Blank answer sheets, preferably mounted on heavy paper, can be appropriately perforated. The material presented in Appendix I may be used to locate the items in each of the basic MMPI scales. Extreme care must be used in the preparation of any stencil. The work must be carefully checked and rechecked at each step of the way to guarantee accurate templates. It should also be noted that there are no spaces on the Hankes answer sheet for recording the raw scores for each of the scales as they are determined. These raw scores should be recorded directly on the profile sheet as the scoring procedure is being carried out. Once the stencils have been made up and punched, scoring of the subject's answer sheet proceeds as outlined above for the IBM 805 hand-scoring operations.

Use of Normative and Corrective Data

The T-score tables published with the MMPI provide a basis for comparing a given test subject with a group of midwestern American adults before World War II. Questions have been raised in the literature about the defensibility of using these norms for all clinical populations. For example, on scale 5 (Mf) male college students average about one standard deviation above the general mean for males (Goodstein, 1954). Are they, as a group, that much more feminine than the MMPI sample of men in general used in deriving this scale? Or is there some variable not connected with femininity that is operating specially within this college subgroup to distort their verbal behavior in this way? Should an appropriate change be introduced in the mean value used to compute the T scores for college students on this collection of items? Such questions require empirical data for their final resolution. The answers do not lie in cavalierly altering the norms for any group that happens to show a bias in central tendency or variance on some scale. The between-group differences may turn out to be just as valid variance as the within-group differences. The differences between college males on scale 5 cannot be taken as a reflection of valid differences in psychological femininity while at the same time, and with no additional research evidence, the differences between college students and men in general are obliterated by the adoption of new special norms for the college-educated males.

Normative data provide a basis both for quantitative description and for explicit inferences (see Aumack, 1954). In some ways these two aspects of norms are independent of one another although for the general run of test subjects, the two functions may be coextensive. Given a certain number of raw-score points on a scale, this score can be precisely described, compared, and collated in terms of its being, say, two and one-half standard deviations from the mean of general normals; inferences can be drawn from the same descriptive characterizations (see Bauernfeind, 1956). When research indicates that certain subgroups possess appreciably different means or variances on the scale under consideration from those of the general population, then the possibility of a split in these functions arises. It may be desirable to shift the bases of reference in the quantitative description of a given score when a subject comes from that subgroup in order to preserve some rule of inference. On the other hand, the same descriptive comparisons may be employed, but the transformed scores are no longer considered to mean the same thing. Goodstein (1954) has suggested the need for special norms for college subjects, and Weisgerber (1954) has made a similar point for nursing students. Underlying these proposals is the premise that the usual norms provide an erroneous basis for inferences about subjects from these special groups.

A related point bears on a long-standing issue in psychometrics. It appears in the intellective area as the difference between the mental-age scale and the intelligence quotient. That is, is there a need for both a relative measure and an absolute scale? The answer is that separate and equally important predictions can be made from a validly determined mental-age value of eight years and an IQ of 135 earned by a given child. Similarly, a T score of 75 on scale 5 may have certain predictive utilities no matter who the male is that validly obtained it, while at the same time the score may have some special vocational or social implications when the man is living and interacting within a college setting. Appropriately designed research may well illuminate these latter considerations without necessarily forcing the adoption of a multitude of specialized norms. The loss of the communicative clarity that accompanies use of commonly agreed-upon reference groups may not be offset by the greater precision of rules of inference about personality that these recommended changes might permit.

In the use of the K-scale corrections, the question of communicative clarity is certainly a relevant point. Already there is a great deal of confusion in the research literature about whether or not the correction was employed in a given study. There was, then, considerable justification for the decision to introduce the corrections routinely into all profiles by revising the test profiles at the point of distribution. For all intents and purposes, a corrected scale like scale 1 (Hs) is now defined as one with thirty-three body-complaint items and 0.5 of the K score.

The K factor, however, is known to be relatively independent of the clinical personality variables and relates most closely to personality characteristics like defensiveness and psychologic exhibitionism. These characteristics will be present in different degrees and frequencies in the populations sampled by different service agencies. Consequently, the K factor will be subject to fluctuations in base rates (see the discussion in Part Two) and must be adjusted to the characteristics of the local agency employing the MMPI. In some settings the K corrections may actually be deleterious to diagnostic appraisal. For this reason it is recommended that the slight extra effort of drawing two profiles, one with and one without the K correction, be made until it can be decided which set of scores is more dependable for the particular clinical setting. For convenience in preparing these profiles, both noncorrected and K-corrected T-score values have been tabled in Appendix H.

Appendix H also provides special normative tables for age corrections in the profiles of adolescent test subjects. These norms were prepared by Marks (1967) primarily from data provided by Hathaway and Monachesi (1963) which they collected from their large-scale survey of the schools in Minnesota. In any particular application, it is recommended that two profiles for adolescent subjects be drawn: the regular profile based on adult norms (using the values printed on the standard profile sheet) and the age-corrected profile from the norms in Appendix H for the particular age group within which the subject falls. These two patterns should be carefully evaluated over a series of cases in a given agency to determine the relative merits of the two norm standards in that setting.

Drawing the Profile

For both the individual and group forms of the MMPI, the directions given so far have led the examiner to record the raw scores in the appropriate spaces on a profile form (see Appendix N). This section now describes how these raw scores are converted to T scores and how profiles are made; the next chapter will indicate how these profiles may be coded for analysis and reference.

The T scores on which the profile and code are based are standard-score equivalents for the raw scores on each of the scales. With the exception of the Cannot Say, L, and F scales, these T scores were determined by taking the nearest integral value of T in the following formula:

$$T_i = 50 + \frac{10(X_i - M)}{S.D.}$$

X_i is the raw score earned by a particular subject, and M and S.D. the mean and standard deviation of the raw scores on the particular scale for the Minnesota normative group. These were determined separately for each sex when necessary. In Appendix H the T scores for all raw-score values on each of the regular MMPI scales have been provided in tabular form.

The original meaning of T score as introduced by McCall (cf. Lindquist, 1951) included a normalizing transformation of these values to more closely approximate the Gaussian distribution. This step has not been carried out in deriving and tabulating the T-score values for the component scales in the MMPI. Weisgerber (1965) made a careful comparison of the skewed distributions usually encountered in the MMPI normative data with the normalized values. He reported that the frequency of extreme scores was slightly reduced by the normalizing steps but that the advantage gained appeared to be negligible. Some MMPI investigators, however, do report their findings in normalized T scores rather than the standard tabled values (see Finney, 1968).

The Validity Indicators. The standard profile sheet for the MMPI contains four validity indicators to be plotted separately to the left of the clinical profile: the Cannot Say score (?), the lie (L) scale, the infrequency (F) scale, and the correction (K) scale. Although T-score conversions have been established for each of these individual measures, the scaling has sometimes been a priori and arbitrary (rather than empirically based as in the case of the clinical scales), is the same for males and females, and on the standard profile sheet has been arbitrarily curtailed at a T-score value of 80. Some usages of these indicators are based upon raw-score values rather than these T-score scales, as will be made clear below. In addition to these basic measures, recent research has led to the appearance of a number of special validational indices and scales. These special measures, as well as the interpretive implications of configurations among the basic validity indicators, are taken up later in Chapter 4.

The total number of items left unanswered by the subject is tallied and constitutes the raw score for the Cannot Say score. On the card form this is the total number of cards placed in the Cannot Say category; on group forms employing an answer sheet, this score is the number of items left unmarked or double marked. In the T-score conversion any score of less than thirty unanswered items is set at a value of 50 or marked "OK" to indicate that the test protocol has probably not been unduly affected by these omissions. Plotting T-score values less than 50 would not make psychological sense because there is no continuum of test evasiveness that is presumed to be operative with an average, a below-average, or an above-average level of test responding comparable to some of the other validity indicators. Rather, from the earliest work on this instrument, the omission of item responses has been a legitimate alternative available to subjects taking the MMPI. The test authors envisioned the Cannot Say response as serving to accommodate the rigid testing format with its narrow response constrictions to the diversity of subjects to whom the test is administered and thus allowing subjects to decline to answer either way those items which are inapplicable, unanswerable, or too intrusive. Consistent with this belief, a Cannot Say endorsement to a given item in the MMPI is not considered a scorable datum in any derivational work on the basic scales of this instrument.

After entering the Cannot Say value in the profile, the value for L should be entered next. Proceed up the values in the column marked L until the number corresponding to the raw score obtained for L is found. Draw a small circle around this value or blacken a small dot on the line. The value in the T-score scale at the far left (or right of the profile) opposite this mark is the T-score equivalent of the raw score on L. Similarly, for F and K locate the corresponding values in these columns for the raw scores obtained on these scales. Connect these four points together by straight lines; this graph constitutes the validity-scale profile. The next step involves preparing either a K-corrected or an uncorrected clinical profile (or both).

In plotting the profile, several things should be kept in mind. First, make certain that the profile appropriate to the sex of the examinee is used. Second, be sure to circle *raw scores* on the profile form, since the left-hand or right-hand column will give T scores. Third, be careful to plot the *corrected* raw scores for those scales which are K-modified.

Having placed dots, circles, or other small marks at the raw-score points for each scale on the profile form, connect these marks with a plain red line broken between the validity scales (at the left of the profile) and the clinical scales (which begin with Hs). This completes the plotting of the corrected profile.

The K-Corrected Profile. The standard profile forms currently distributed by the Psychological Corporation for use with the card and booklet versions have been prepared to facilitate drawing the K-corrected profile. (The steps to obtain a noncorrected profile are outlined below.) If a profile form is employed that does not have the raw-score conversions printed on it, the tables in Appendix H may be used to obtain either set of T scores.

After the raw scores for each scale have been listed on the profile form, the next step is to obtain the actual amount of K correction to be added to five of the ten scales: Hs, Pd, Pt, Sc, and Ma. On the profile form, there are spaces provided beneath the row of raw scores for these fractions of K score. The raw scores are always used in making these corrections. With the raw-score value obtained for K on the subject for whom the profile is being drawn, consult the K-fraction table printed on the profile form. (For convenience this material has also been reproduced here in Table 1 in Appendix H.) The values from this table are entered beneath the raw scores on the five scales to be corrected as follows: for Hs, .5 K; for Pd, .4 K; Pt, 1.0 K; Sc, 1.0 K; and for Ma, .2 K. These values are added to the original raw scores on these scales and the sums entered in the spaces on the next line below. These totals are the new corrected raw scores to be used in determining the T-score values for these five scales.

Next, locate the raw score listed for each scale in the column for that scale in the profile. Circle or otherwise mark each value precisely. The T-score equivalent for each raw score is given at either side of the profile form.

In Tables 2 and 3 of Appendix H the range of some of the T scores has been extended beyond the values tabled on the profile sheets or in the *Manual*. Recent clinical work has indicated that there is a need for these additional discriminations on some scales. If the tables in Appendix H are being used, note that the male and female T-score values are listed separately and be sure that the values obtained are appropriate to the sex of the test subject. In the conversions listed on the profile form and in Table 2 of Appendix H, the T scores for the K-corrected scales are actually based upon the standard deviations of the distributions of the sums, e.g., Hs + .5 K. (See the discussion of the various scales in Part Three.)

The Noncorrected Profile. The K scale was not one of the original MMPI scales. Examiners who use some shortened versions of the group form cannot correct for K. Some workers may prefer not to use the K corrections when local considerations or some specific research findings suggest that the K modifications do not improve the diagnostic accuracy of the profile. The current profile forms distributed by the Psychological Corporation do not permit easy determination of the noncorrected profile. This noncorrected profile *cannot* be obtained by simply entering the original raw-score totals in the raw-score columns of the profile. A separate set of T-score tables must be consulted; the raw-score columns on the profile must be ignored if the K corrections are not being made.

Table 3 in Appendix H presents the T scores for all the scales with scores for scales Hs, Pd, Pt, Sc, and Ma based on original raw scores to which the K fractions have not been added. Workers who do not wish to use any K corrections in their work may consult this table to find the uncorrected T-score equivalents for the five scales mentioned above. A mark should be entered at the appropriate T-score elevation for each of these scales on the profile form; *the raw-score values on the profile are disregarded.* If the K-corrected values have also been entered on this same profile, the new points for noncorrected scale values should be connected by means of a black line. Both the corrected and noncorrected profiles will then be complete. The two profiles should be coded separately; the discussion in Part Three of this volume should be consulted for the differences in interpretative significance of each profile.

Plotting Supplementary Scale Values. If additional scales have been scored on the test protocol, these raw scores may be entered in the extra spaces to the right of the clinical scale profile. For several of these special scales, T-score values have been provided in Appendix F. These values may be read off for the raw scores obtained and written below the raw-score values. Then in the supplementary profile columns above these spaces the T score for each supplementary scale should be located and marked with a small dot or X. If more than one supplementary scale is plotted, a third profile (in addition to the validity- and clinical-scale profiles) may be constructed by connecting the T-score markers.

CHAPTER 3. Procedures for Coding and Configural Analysis

THE previous chapter covered the procedures for obtaining the raw scores, T scores, and basic psychogram for a test subject from any one of the several test forms and answer sheets in use for the MMPI. This chapter takes up the various ways in which the interrelationships among the basic (and many of the supplementary) scales have been analyzed. These include coding of the profile pattern and elevation, computing various indices from either the raw scores or the T scores of different combinations of scales, applying sequentially sets of special interpretive rules, and carrying out item analyses and tallies. The steps involved in these various special procedures will be described here along with the application of particular cutting scores when they are appropriate. The interpretive significance of the various measures, however, will be taken up in the appropriate places in Part Three. It should be made clear that routine scoring and interpretive procedures do not by any means require all the pattern-analytic methods summarized in this chapter. Many of these procedures have only very limited applicability or no relevance in some clinical settings.

Coding the Profile

In clinical use of the MMPI it has continually been emphasized that the individual scale in a profile is not to be evaluated on its own, but rather the pattern afforded by the whole group of scales, including the validity indicators. There is an indefinitely large number of patterns possible; and, although one may often feel he has seen some given pattern a number of times before, there are in reality almost no exact duplicates. To make patterns usable, a coding system is applied that reduces the possible number of different profiles to a more practicable size. Much of the interpretative material in Part Three is based upon profile codes.

In coding, each clinical scale is assigned a number, so that Hs becomes 1, D becomes 2, Hy 3, Pd 4, Mf 5. Pa 6, Pt 7, Sc 8, and Ma 9; the Si scale, when coded, is given a 0 (zero) designation. These numbers are the basis for coding profile patterns; many clinicians consider it wise to use them rather than scale names or abbreviations even as routine symbols, since numbers avoid many of the psychiatric implications which may be misleading in a nonclinical setting.

Any statistical reduction, such as the coding procedures about to be described, involves the problem of reducing the amount of data to a workable size while retaining enough information to serve the purposes described. Two different systems have been employed in MMPI work, the original coding method of Hathaway (1947) and the extended or total coding procedure of Welsh (1948, 1951). The respective merits of the two systems have been compared by Welsh (1956a) and will be summarized a little later. A great deal of material has now been published in both systems, however, and the reader is advised to become familiar with the notation of each. The material in Part Three will be presented in the Welsh notation, but frequent references to such important publications as the *atlases* (Hathaway and Meehl, 1951a; Hathaway and Monachesi, 1961) will presume familiarity with the Hathaway coding schema.

The Hathaway Code. To code a profile by the Hathaway method, the following steps are carried out. First, write down the number of that scale having the largest T score. Second, write after this in descending order of T-score value the numbers of any other scales having T values greater than 54. Third, insert a prime (′) after the last number in the code which represents a T score of 70 or higher. Thus, if the highest point were Pd (scale 4), and this were at 70 or greater T score, no other score being so large as 70, the prime would be written after the 4 and ahead of any scales with T-score values between 70 and 54. Some workers now use two primes to mark the 80 level and three primes for 90. Fourth, underline all adjacent scale numbers for which the T scores are equal or within one point of each other. As in the Welsh coding system (see below), the underlining simply indicates that the scales are negligibly, or not at all, different in value. It is obvious that such scales have no absolute order in the code; but conventionally, if one is a point higher than the other, the number of that scale is placed first. If two or more scales are of absolutely equal T-score value, then the numbers of those scales are written in their usual ordinal sequence. The symbols now written represent what is called the high-point code of the profile. The numbers show approximately the magnitude and order of all scales having T scores larger than 54. Those numbers to the left of the prime indicate scales that reach T score 70 and over; those to the right of the prime indicate the scales between 70 and 54 T score. Fifth, after a dash write the number of the lowest scale on the profile if that scale has a T-score value less than 46. Following the number of this scale, write the numbers of any other scales whose T scores lie between this lowest one and 46. Sixth, follow the same rule for underlining as is given above. Some workers now insert a prime in this part of the code to separate the values below 40. The code as now written to the right of the dash (which signifies the region around the mean value) is called the low-point code. Seventh, to the right of the code, write the *raw scores* for L, F, and K in that order, and separate them by colons. If the raw score of L is equal to or greater than 10 or if the raw score of F is equal to or greater than 16, a capital X is placed immediately after the code for the clinical scales, which indicates that there is a possibility the profile may be invalid (see Chapter 4).

The coding system used in the first *Atlas* (Hathaway and Meehl, 1951a) is identical to that described above except that scale 5 and scale 0 are not coded (where T scores for scale 5 were available, however, they are listed in this *Atlas* in parentheses following the code for the clinical scales). In the second *Atlas* (Hathaway and Monachesi, 1961) the more complete coding system described above is used.

The Total (Welsh) Code. A hypothetical profile may be used to exemplify this method:

Example 1

Scale	Hs	D	Hy	Pd	Mf	Pa	Pt	Sc	Ma
Code	1	2	3	4	5	6	7	8	9
T score	64	92	53	44	58	35	85	79	29

The first step in coding the profile is to write down the digits representing the scales in order of T-score elevation, from highest to lowest. The highest scale is D with a T score of 92 so the digit 2 will be the first number in the code. The second highest scale is Pt at 85; the code is now 2 7. The third highest is Sc and the code becomes 2 7 8. The fourth highest is Hs–2 7 8 1. This procedure is followed until all the scales are listed by digit in descending order of T scores. The digit sequence for the example above is 2 7 8 1 5 3 4 6 9. Many workers find it convenient to place a small mark on the profile sheet near the T score for a scale as the code digit is written down; this helps to ensure that all scales will be included. Another check consists in reading through the completed code series in numerical order, that is, one, two, three, and so on through the nine (or ten if scale 0 is included). Of course, no digit should appear more than once in this series. If a scale has been repeated or omitted it can easily be detected and a correction made at this time.

The second step in coding is to enter the appropriate elevation symbols. All digits representing scales whose T scores are 90 or over will be followed by *, 80 to 89 by ″, 70 to 79 by ′, 60 to 69 by –, 50 to 59 by /, 40 to 49 by :, 30 to 39 by #; all scores 29 or lower will appear to the right of #. These particular symbols were selected because they appear on standard typewriters and can also easily be made by hand. In the hypothetical example above, the D scale has a T score of 92; thus the scale digit 2 will be followed by *, that is, 2*. The Pt scale at 85 will be followed by ″ and hence will read 2*7″. Sc is in the 70's so the code becomes 2*7″8′. Hs at 64 will be followed by –, and the code will now read 2*7″8′1–. When two or more scales fall in the same range of ten T-score points, the elevation symbol follows the digit for the lowest scale. Thus, since both Mf and Hy are in the range from 50 to 59 their appropriate code digits will be followed by /. Pd is the only scale falling in the 40's so it is followed by a colon. The code now reads 2*7″8′1–53/4:. Since Pa is in the 30's and Ma falls at 29, the symbol # will follow 6 and precede 9. The complete clinical code is 2*7″8′1–53/4:6 # 9.

In addition to the clinical scales, the validating scales should be coded and placed separately to the *right* of the clinical scale code. Suppose the scores on the validating scales for the hypothetical example considered above are as follows:

Scale	?	L	F	K
T score	50	61	72	41

The code for these scales will appear as F′L–?/ K and the complete code is now 2*7″8′1–53/ 4:6 # 9F′ L –?/ K.

When two or more scales are within one T-score point of each other both symbols are underlined: D = 75 and Pt = 74 will be coded as 27′. When two or more scales have the *same* T score they are placed in the usual ordinal sequence and underlined: if Pd and Ma are both 65, the code will be 49– rather than 94–. If scales fall into two different ranges but are still within one T-score point, they and the elevation symbol will all be underlined: D = 70 and Pt = 69 will be 2′7. These coding features may be illustrated by another hypothetical example:

Example 2

Scale	Hs	D	Hy	Pd	Mf	Pa	Pt	Sc	Ma
Code	1	2	3	4	5	6	7	8	9
T score	72	56	59	60	55	56	69	68	54

This code is 1′78 4–3 2659. In this example, it should be noted that the digits for the D scale (2) and the Ma scale (9) are bound together by the same underlining even though they are actually two T-score points apart because they are each within one T-score point of a common scale, Mf (5). No elevation symbol is placed after scale 9 since it is clear from the code that the T-score value of the Ma scale is less than 60 and above 50.

This use of underlining to indicate essential equivalence of T-score values is somewhat arbitrary and may prove to be overly precise. In many studies, comparison of code types has indicated that codes with the same two high points fall into an essentially equivalent psychological group regardless of the order of the two high points. In Part Three, material will be offered supporting the interchangeability of two-point code combinations, e.g., 49's and 94's. These values may actually be separated by several T-score points and still show essential interchangeability.

Some workers use additional elevation symbols; scores from 100 to 109 are followed by **, 110 to 119 by !, and 120 by !!. Whether or not it is necessary and useful to preserve this information in the code will depend on the number of cases seen with such extreme elevations and the diagnostic importance found for scores within these ranges.

Some workers employ another refinement. They begin and end each code with an elevation symbol. The example just given above would be ″1′78 4–3 2659 /. While the initial and terminal symbols are actually redundant, it may be somewhat easier to locate cases by the highest (or lowest) score if they are used.

Sometimes a ten-point T-score range does not contain any scale; for example D may be 80 and the next highest scale, say Pt, may be 67. The appropriate elevation symbol for the missing range must be included, 2‴7. If a twenty-point range is skipped all three symbols may be included although the middle symbol is actually redundant. If D = 90 and Pt = 67, the code could be either 2*‴7 or 2*′7. In other words, the symbols adjacent to the digit indicate the ten-point range in which it falls; it would be apparent from the second code sequence that no scale fell in the 80 to 89 T-score range.

Some of the reasons for the utility of the code are obvious. For example, the finding of similar profiles is expedited. It is easy to see in the code for Example 1 that the highest scale in the profile is D and the T score is 90 or greater, that Ma lies below 30 and is the lowest scale. When a collection of cases has been coded and filed in sequence it is possible to locate very quickly all the cases that begin with 2 and end with 9. If a code type is specified by the three highest scores, it is easy to identify all the 278 profiles. The degree of similarity desired between profiles can be specified as to both scale order and absolute elevation. When profile matching is the objective, a set of rules can easily be set up that depend on the stringency of the requirements. It may be that only the first digit is to be considered, or the first two. On the other hand we may require that the first four be alike and that they be within ten T-score points. Naturally the greater the degree of similarity that is required between two profiles, the less chance there will be of finding a match.

It is always possible to reconstruct a profile from the total code itself with a reasonable degree of accuracy. As an example, Schiele and Brozek (1948) report the testing of a case (No. 234) after ten weeks on experimental semistarvation. His code is given as $8''\underline{235}79'4\underline{16}$. The highest scale is Sc and it lies alone in the 80 to 89 range; the best guess then would be somewhere near or below the midpoint, say 84. There are five scales in the 70 to 79 range and D, Hy, and Mf are within one T-score point of each other. Pt must be two points from Mf and Ma two points from Pt. The estimates then might be 76 for D, Hy, and Mf, 74 for Pt, and 72 for Ma. The last three scales are in the 60 to 69 range so one might place Pd at 66 and Hs and Pa at 64. The basic strategy in attempting to estimate the T scores is to assume that the midpoint of the interval is the most likely position unless there is some other clue afforded by another scale or by underlining. In the upper T-score ranges, however, the most likely estimate is somewhat below the midpoint of the T-score interval. That is, when the deviations are extreme and the distribution is tapering off, then, for example, a score of 92 may be more likely for some scale code beyond the * than one of 95. However, even if a midpoint guess is always used there can never be more than a five-point discrepancy. When a scale actually has a T score of 89 and a guess is made of 85, the error will be four points; if the score were in fact 80, the guess would be off five points.

Compare in the accompanying tabulation the estimates as deduced from the code with the actual T scores of the Schiele and Brozek case. It can be seen that the differences between the two sets of T scores are not great, all except Sc are within one or two points. Naturally it is better to refer to the original T scores for complete accuracy but sometimes they may not be available or may not be conveniently located. In using a file of coded cases, to match profiles, for example, it is helpful to be able to reconstruct from the code alone an approximation of the actual T scores.

Scale	*Actual T Score*	*Estimated T Score*	*Discrepancy*
1 (Hs)	62	64	2
2 (D)	78	76	2
3 (Hy)	77	76	1
4 (Pd)	68	66	2
5 (Mf)	77	76	1
6 (Pa)	62	64	2
7 (Pt)	74	74	0
8 (Sc)	80	84	4
9 (Ma)	70	72	2

Comparison of Coding Methods. The original coding system developed by Hathaway differs from the extended method in three ways. First, the scales lying in the T-score range from 46 to 54 are not coded; that is, if any scale or scales are in this range, their code digits will not be written down. Second, for those scales above 55 which are coded in order from the highest to lowest only one elevation symbol is regularly used, namely a prime to indicate the 70 T-score mark, although, as noted above, two primes are sometimes used to indicate the 80 level, three for 90. Third, scales lying below 46 are written in the *reverse* order from lowest to highest. A comparison of the two methods is given in Table 3-1.

Table 3-2 provides some examples of codes in the two different systems. It should be noted that profiles coded in the extended method can be converted easily to the system of Hathaway with only a minor ambiguity for scores in the 46–54 range. This conversion is not possible from the Hathaway code to the extended system; therefore, the more detailed code is to be preferred for general coding use.

Preparation of a Code File. Coding permits filing of MMPI profiles according to their dominant features as expressed in high or low points. The code for each profile is put on a file card along with identifying information and diagnostic data. These cards are then filed by code numbers to permit easy reference to all profiles in the file that have specified high points. A comparable low-point code file may also be prepared on cards with the low points written first; such a file would facilitate the location of profiles with similar low-point characteristics. In using the extended coding system it is possible to follow one of two alternatives in preparing a low-point code file. A separate card may be prepared as suggested above, with the whole code merely written in reverse order. On the other hand there would not be much chance of error if a copy of the high-point code card is made and filed in a separate container in the order of the digits from right to left in the code.

Hathaway (1947) has given an excellent description of the procedures to follow in constructing and maintaining such a code file. His instructions should be consulted in setting up a new file. A sample code file card is shown

Table 3-1. Summary and Comparison of Original (Hathaway) and Extended (Welsh) Coding Methods

Item	Original Hathaway Method	Extended Welsh Method
Code length	Variable: From none up to ten digits.	Constant: Always ten digits (if all scales are used).
Code without all scales	It may be impossible to tell whether a given scale has been used or whether it is merely in the uncoded range from T score 46 to 54.	If a scale (such as 5 which was not used in the *Atlas* or 0 which is not routinely scored by all workers) is not in the profile, this is immediately apparent from the code.
Code order	Variable and inconsistent: 1. From highest to lowest for scores above T=54. 2. Scores between T=46 and T=54 not coded. 3. From *lowest* to *highest* for scores below T=46.	Constant: Always from highest to lowest in a natural sequence throughout the range of scores.
Position of highest scale	Variable or indeterminate: 1. Will be the first digit if the T score is over 54. 2. If it falls in the T-score range from 46 to 54 and any other scale also falls in this range, the high scale cannot be determined. 3. If the highest scale is below 46, it will be the *last* digit in the code.	Constant: Always the first digit in the code.
Position of lowest scale	Variable or indeterminate: 1. Will be the last digit if all T scores in the profile are over 54. 2. Will be the first digit if all T scores in the profile are under 46. 3. If it falls in the T-score range from 46 to 54 and any other scale also falls in this range, the low scale cannot be determined. 4. It will be the last digit if it is the only scale below 46. 5. It will be the next to last digit if two scales are below 46; etc.	Constant: Always the last digit in the code (increasingly important since work on low points has begun—e.g., Cantor, 1952, and Sutton, 1952).
Elevation indication	Four unequal classes: 1. ⩾70 2. 55–69 3. 46–54 4. <46	Eight standard classes: 1. ⩾90 2. 80–89 3. 70–79 4. 60–69 5. 50–59 6. 40–49 7. 30–39 8. <30

Table 3-1—continued

Item	Original Hathaway Method	Extended Welsh Method
Reproducibility of profile from code	Only crude reconstruction is possible for most profiles; some cannot be reproduced at all.	All profiles with scores between 20 and 99 can be reproduced absolutely to an accuracy of five T-score points; usually an accuracy of two to three points is obtained.

SOURCE: Welsh and Dahlstrom (1956).

Table 3-2. Hypothetical T Scores for MMPI Profiles and Corresponding Welsh and Hathaway Codes

Case	?	L	F	K	1 (Hs)	2 (D)	3 (Hy)	4 (Pd)	5 (Mf)	6 (Pa)	7 (Pt)	8 (Sc)	9 (Ma)	0 (Si)
A ...	50	60	48	55	70	62	75	59	50	48	52	53	55	42
Welsh Code: 31′2–49875/60 L–K?/F														
Hathaway Code: 31′249–0 7:2:15[a]														
B ...	53	70	53	66	45	55	54	72	52	56	46	48	69	50
Welsh Code: 4′9–62350/871 L′K–?F														
Hathaway Code: 4′962–1X 10:4:21														
C ...	50	40	73	46	40	91	49	39	35	68	75	72	61	70
Welsh Code: 2*″780′69–/31:45 F′–?/KL														
Hathaway Code: 2780′69–541 1:13:10														

[a]The numbers in the validity scale code in the Hathaway system are based on the original raw scores for these scales.

in Figure 3-1. The code number should be prominent and unambiguous since this will be the basis for filing the cards. Obviously any alternative codes available on the case should be entered at the time the card is being prepared. It should also be obvious that the utility of such an MMPI code file will be determined by the range and accuracy of the information entered on the data card.

Codebook Groupings

One of the most significant derivatives from the MMPI coding methods has been the development of various codebooks and atlases based upon clinical correlates discovered to recur with various code combinations. Many of these codebooks simply use the two-point high-point designations that are provided by the Hathaway or Welsh code described above or, perhaps, a combination of the two-point high-point and the low-point designation (Angers, 1963; Carkhuff, Barnett, and McCall, 1965; Carson, 1969; Cuadra and Reed, 1954; Drake and Oetting, 1959; Good and Brantner, 1961; Hathaway and Meehl, 1951a, 1951b; Hathaway and Monachesi, 1961; Hovey and Lewis, 1967; Wilson, 1965). Some of the recent codebooks, however, specify rather precisely the pattern in the MMPI profile which must be present before the particular sets of descriptors that they provide may be

MMPI Code				
Name			Date of Test	Case Number
Age	Sex	Education	Occupation	
Referral				
Diagnosis				
Disposition of Case				
Other MMPI Codes or Special Scales				

Figure 3-1. Sample code file card.

applied to a given case. Often these distinctions require more data than are available in either the Hathaway or Welsh code; the decision whether or not a profile falls into one or another of these profile groups must be made on the basis of the original profile.

Gilberstadt-Duker Profile Prototypes. In 1965, Gilberstadt and Duker brought together and summarized nineteen basic MMPI configural patterns, some of which they had described previously (Gilberstadt, 1952, 1962; Duker, 1958; Gilberstadt and Duker, 1960). They were developed on male patients in a Veterans Administration hospital setting but have been applied with some success to female cases as well. Profiles with suspicious validity-scale elevations (either L or K with T scores over 70) were excluded. Gilberstadt and Duker mainly studied cases who were under sixty years of age and had verbal IQ levels (Wechsler-Bellevue or WAIS) above 105; this latter specification may be somewhat relaxed however, particularly for the 8-1-2-3 prototype.

The rules for determining membership in one of the Gilberstadt-Duker prototypes are presented in Table 3-3. These rules have been summarized from Gilberstadt (1970) where they were presented in a format for computer application. The scores are all specified in terms of T-score values. If a test profile fits one of the prototypes in Table 3-3, the expected personality correlates may be noted in the relevant sections of the Gilberstadt-Duker *Handbook* (1965). In some clinics and hospitals, a majority of the MMPI profiles obtained fall in one or another of these groupings but in other settings only a fourth or a fifth of them may match a given prototype (Fowler and Coyle, 1968a; Payne and Wiggins, 1968; Shultz, Gibeau, and Barry, 1968; Vestre and Klett, 1969). This percentage of matching may be improved somewhat by appropriate relaxation of the rules but this adjustment involves clinical judgment. (See Gilberstadt and Duker, 1965; Payne and Wiggins, 1968; Gilberstadt, 1969.) The Gilberstadt and Duker prototypes can be useful in clinical interpretation of profiles which strongly resemble these basic patterns but do not precisely fit into one or another of the categories.

Table 3-3. Rules of Membership in the Gilberstadt-Duker MMPI Prototypes

Prototype	Rules for Admission
A. 1-2-3	(a) 1, 2, and 3>70 (b) 1>2>3 (c) No other scales>70 (d) L≤65, F≤85, K≤70
B. 1-2-3-4	(a) 1, 2, 3, and 4>70 and higher than all other scales (b) 0<70 (c) L, F, and K<70 unless two or more scales>100, in which case F<80
C. 1-2-3-7	(a) 1, 2, 3, and 7>70 (b) 1 and 2>3 (c) 1, 2, and 3>7 (d) 9<60 (e) 0<70
D. 1-3-2	(a) 1, 2, and 3>70 (b) 1 and 3>2 (c) No other scales>70 (d) 2>7 by 5 or more points (e) 9≤60
E. 1-3-7	(a) 1, 3, and 7 highest scales (b) 1 and 3>70 (c) 7>65 (d) 1 minus 2≥10 points (e) K, 4, and 0<70
F. 1-3-8 (2)	(a) 1, 3, and 8 highest scales (b) 8>70 (c) 5>60 (d) 4<80
G. 1-3-9	(a) 1, 3, and 9 highest scales (b) Either 1, 3, or 9>70 (c) 3>2 by 8 or more points (d) 0<60 (e) If 9>70, 8<9 by 18 or more points (f) If 9<70, 8<9 by 7 or more points
H. 2-7 (3)	(a) 2 and 7>70 (b) 2>7 (c) 7>8 by at least 15 points (d) 0<70 (e) 4 and 6<80 unless 2 and/or 7≤85, in which case 4 and 6<70
I. 2-7-4 (3)	(a) 2, 4, and 7>70 (b) 7 minus 8≥5 points (c) 7 minus 2≤10 points (d) 2 minus 4≤20 points (e) Among 2, 4, and 7, two scores<100 (f) If 4 is peak, include only if 4 minus 2≤10 points, or 4 minus 7≤10 points (g) 0<70 (h) 9>8 (i) 9>40 (j) If 9<50, include only if 0 minus 9≤15 points
J. 2-7-8 (4-0-1-3-5-6)	(a) 2, 7, and 8>70 (b) 2 minus 8<15 points (c) 7 minus 8<20 points (unless 2 or 7 or 8>100) (d) If 7 is peak, include only if all other scales<90 and 7 minus 2≤5 points

Table 3-3—continued

Prototype	Rules for Admission
	(e) 0>9
	(f) 9<70
	(g) 2 minus 1>10 points
	(h) 6<80
K. 4	(a) 4>70
	(b) No other scales>70
L. 4-3	(a) 3 and 4>70
	(b) No other scales (except 1)>70
M. 4-9	(a) 4 and 9>70
	(b) No other scale>70
	(c) L<60
	(d) 9 minus 8≥15 points
	(e) 4 minus 5≥7 points
N. 7-8	(a) 7 and 8>70
(2-1-3-4)	(b) 7 and 8 highest scales
	(c) 7 within 10 points or less of 8
O. 8-1-2-3	(a) 1, 2, and 8>80
(7-4-6-0)	(b) 1>2>3
	(c) 8>7
	(d) F<85
	(e) L may be>70
	(f) IQ may be below average
P. 8-2-4	(a) 2, 4, and 8>70
(7)	(b) 2 or 8>4
	(c) 0<70
	(d) 6<70
	(e) L and K<70
	(f) 4 minus 3≥10 points
	(g) 8 minus 2≤13 points
Q. 8-6 (7-2)	(a) 8 and 6>70
	(b) 8 and 6>any other scales
	(c) F>70 does not invalidate profile
R. 8-9	(a) 8 and 9>70
	(b) 8 and 9>any other scales
	(c) 8 within 15 points or less of 9
S. 9	(a) 9>70
	(b) No other scales>70
	(c) 2<50

SOURCE: Gilberstadt (1970).

Marks-Seeman Code Types. The rules for identifying a given profile as one of the Marks and Seeman (1963) code types are presented in Table 3-4. These procedures were developed on female cases but have been recommended for use with both sexes. The rules have been adapted and modified from the Marks-Seeman *Atlas* to reduce ambiguities and potential double classifications as noted by Rosman, Barry, and Gibeau (1966), Fowler and Coyle (1968b), and Payne and Wiggins (1968). The percentage of cases which fit into some one category in the Marks-Seeman system will vary ex-

Table 3-4. Rules of Membership in the Marks-Seeman MMPI Code Types

Code Type[a]	Rules for Admission
A. 2-3-1/2-1-3	(a) 2, 3, and 1≥70
	(b) 2 minus 1≥5 points
	(c) 2 minus 3≥5 points
	(d) 7 and 0<2, 3, and 1
	(e) 8 minus 7≤5 points
	(f) 9 and 0≤70
	(g) 0≥9
	(h) L, F, and K≤70
B. 2-7	(a) 2 and 7≥70
	(b) 2 minus 8≥15 points
	(c) 7>1 and 3
	(d) 7 minus 4≥10 points
	(e) 7 minus 6≥10 points
	(f) 7 minus 8≥10 points
	(g) 9≤60
	(h) L, F, and K≤70
C. 2-7-4/2-4-7/4-7-2	(a) 2, 7, and 4≥70
	(b) 2 within 15 points of 4
	(c) 2 within 10 points of 7
	(d) 7>1 and 3
	(e) 7 within 10 points of 4
	(f) 7 minus 8≥5 points
	(g) 8≥9
	(h) 9≥40
	(i) L and K≤70, F≤80
D. 2-7-8/2-8-7	(a) 2, 7, 8≥70
	(b) 2 minus 1≥15 points
	(c) 2 minus 8≤15 points
	(d) 7 minus 4≥10 points
	(e) 7 minus 6≥10 points
	(f) 8 minus 7<5 points
	(g) 7 and 8>1 and 3
	(h) 9≤70
	(i) 0≥70
	(j) L and K≤70, F≤80
E. 2-8/8-2	(a) 2 and 8≥70
	(b) 2 within 15 points of 8
	(c) 7≥4 and 6
	(d) 8≥1 and 3
	(e) 8 minus 7≥5 points
	(f) 9≤70
	(g) 0≥9
	(h) L and K≤F
F. 3-1/1-3	(a) 3 and 1≥70
	(b) 1 minus 2≥10 points
	(c) 3 minus 2≥10 points
	(d) 3 minus 4≥10 points
	(e) 5≥45
	(f) 8 minus 7≤5 points
	(g) 9 and 0≤70
	(h) K≥F, F≤60
G. 3-2-1/3-1-2	(a) 3, 2, and 1≥70
	(b) 1 minus 2≤5 points

Table 3-4—continued

Code Type[a]	Rules for Admission
	(c) 3 minus 1 ≤ 15 points (d) 3 minus 2 ≤ 10 points (e) 8 minus 7 ≤ 5 points (f) 7 and 0 < 3, 2, and 1 (g) 9 and 0 ≤ 70 (h) L, F, and K ≤ 70
H. 4-6/6-4[b]	(a) 4 and 6 ≥ 70 (b) 4 minus 2 ≥ 15 points (c) 4 minus 5 ≥ 25 points and/or 6 minus 5 ≥ 25 points (d) 4 and 6 > 8 (e) 6 minus 2 ≥ 10 points (f) 8 ≥ 7 and 9 (g) 9 and 0 ≤ 70 (h) L, F, and K ≤ 70
I. 4-6-2/6-4-2	(a) 4, 6, and 2 ≥ 70 (b) 4 minus 2 < 15 points (c) 4 and 6 > 8 (d) 4 > 7 (e) 6 minus 2 ≤ 10 points (f) 8 minus 7 ≤ 5 points (g) 9 ≤ 70 (h) L and K ≤ F, F ≤ 80
J. 4-8-2/8-4-2/8-2-4	(a) 4, 8, and 2 ≥ 70 (b) 4 within 15 points of 2 (c) 4 > 7 (d) 8 minus 2 ≤ 15 points (e) 8 minus 7 > 5 points (f) 8 minus 9 ≥ 10 points (g) 9 ≤ 70 (h) L and K ≤ F, F ≤ 80
K. 4-9/9-4	(a) 4 and 9 ≥ 70 (b) 4 > 8 (c) 9 minus 4 ≤ 5 points (d) 6 ≤ 8 (e) 9 minus 8 > 5 points (f) 2 and 7 ≤ 70 (g) 0 ≤ 60 (h) F ≥ L and K, F ≤ 70
L. 8-3/3-8	(a) 8, 3, and 1 ≥ 70 (b) 3 minus 1 ≤ 10 points (c) 3 minus 2 > 5 points (d) 3 minus 8 ≤ 5 points (e) 8 minus 7 > 5 points (f) 8 minus 9 ≥ 10 points (g) 9 ≥ 0 (h) 0 ≤ 70 (i) 3 > 4
M. 8-6/6-8[b]	(a) 8, 6, 4, and 2 ≥ 70 (b) 1 and 3 < 2, 6, 7, and 8 (c) 2 minus 1 ≥ 10 points (d) 6 minus 5 ≥ 25 points (e) 6 > 7 (f) 8 minus 7 ≥ 10 points

Table 3-4—continued

Code Type[a]	Rules for Admission
	(g) 8 minus 9 ≥ 10 points (h) F ≥ L and K, L and K ≤ 60
N. 8-9/9-8	(a) 8 and 9 ≥ 70 (b) 5 ≥ 40 (c) 8 minus 7 > 5 points (d) 9 minus 8 ≤ 5 points (e) 0 ≤ 70 (f) F ≥ L and K
O. 9-6/6-9	(a) 9 and 6 ≥ 70 (b) 1, 2, and 3 < 70 (c) 6 > 4 (d) 9 minus 2 ≥ 15 points (e) 9 minus 4 > 5 points (f) 9 minus 8 > 10 points (g) 0 ≤ 70 (h) L and K ≤ 70, F ≤ 80
P. K+	(a) Psychiatric inpatients only (b) All clinical scale scores < 70 (c) Six or more clinical scale scores ≤ 60 (d) L ≥ F (e) K minus F ≥ 5 points (f) F ≤ 60

SOURCE: Marks and Seeman (1963, revised 1969).

[a]The first fifteen code types are designated by mnemonic names. These designations consist of several scale numbers in sequence. The order indicates that these scales are higher than any of the other clinical scales. For example, in checking for code type A. 2-3-1/2-1-3, at least one of the following two conditions must be met: (1) 2 ≥ 3 ≥ 1 > 4, 5, 6, 7, 8, 9, 0; or (2) 2 ≥ 1 ≥ 3 > 4, 5, 6, 7, 8, 9, 0. If neither of these sequences fits, a profile does not belong in this type.

[b]Apply this set of rules to female cases only.

tensively from one setting to another (Marks and Seeman, 1963; Huff, 1965; Pauker, 1965, 1966a, 1966b; Cone, 1966; J. Sines, 1966; Payne and Wiggins, 1968). This range of applicability may be extended by relaxation of a rule (Shultz, Gibeau, and Barry, 1968; Payne and Wiggins, 1968) in some of the categories. As is the case when the rules in the Gilberstadt-Duker system are selectively relaxed, this procedure in the Marks-Seeman system also involves skillful clinical judgment. Data from Payne and Wiggins (1968) and from Fowler and Coyle (1968a) indicate that when the systems of Gilberstadt-Duker and Marks-Seeman are employed conjointly a greater percentage of profiles get classified. When the two systems are employed together, some profiles may fit a category in both systems; in these instances the clinical interpretive material is generally in accord.

Basic Scale Indices and Interpretive Rules

A large number of special indices, configural patterns, and sequential rules for combinations of the basic validity and clinical scales of the MMPI have been advanced in the research literature. In this section are listed the various procedures which employ with only an occasional exception the standard scales in either raw-score or T-score form in their formulas and rules. In the next section the procedures are listed which require some special supplementary scale values before they may be applied to the test protocol. In each instance the appropriate cutting scores are given whenever they are available. Most of these indices have been advanced as single measures of some attribute or clinical feature but occasionally these procedures have been put forth in sets and cutting scores proposed in terms of numbers of signs that are significant. Some of these sets have also been formalized into sequential rules in which multiple cutting scores and decision points are employed.

Index of Psychopathology. L. K. Sines and Silver (1963) published a simple formula for combining the T scores from the Pa (6) and Sc (8) scales to derive an index of the degree of psychopathology being shown. This index ranges from a low of 1.0 to a high of 10.0 for most psychopathology. A separate formula is used for each sex:

$$\text{Males: } I_p = .10\text{ Pa} + .06\text{ Sc} - 6.26$$
$$\text{Females: } I_p = .08\text{ Pa} + .10\text{ Sc} - 7.36$$

No cutting score was recommended for determining when clinically significant degrees of psychopathology are present.

Disturbance Index. The combined clinical judgment of five experienced MMPI judges was used by Cooke (1967a, 1967b) as a criterion against which to derive a measure of psychological disturbance from the standard MMPI profile scores plus three commonly scored supplementary scales: Welsh A, Welsh R, and Barron Es scales. (See Volume II for the item composition of these scales.) All the scale weights are based upon *raw-score* values. In addition, the raw scores on L and F are adjusted according to these formulas: $L_a = 10(L - 5)$; $F_a = 10(F - 10)$. Use L_a and F_a values along with the raw scores on the other basic and supplementary scales to determine the weighted combination for the disturbance index (DsI). These sixteen weights are presented in Table 3-5. All are positive except the weight for the Hs (1) scale which is to be subtracted from the combination of the others. Cooke recommended that a cutting score of 550 and above be used to determine that significant degrees of disturbance are present; values of 549 and below are called normal adjustment.

Delinquency Index. Rempel (1958, 1960) published a weighted combination of T-score values on five basic MMPI scales which was predictive of subsequent delinquency patterns among Minnesota boys. The linear discriminant function derived for MMPI variables was as follows:

$$\text{DeI} = .0695\text{ F} + .0116\text{ Hs} + .0578\text{ Pd} - .0782\text{ Mf} + .0256\text{ Sc} - 2.0169$$

The values for DeI which are above zero are predictive of delinquency; values below zero are predictive of nondelinquency.

Schizophrenic Signs Score. Eichman (1959) developed a set of signs for discriminating female schizophrenic cases from other psychiatric groups in an inpatient setting. These signs are then tallied to produce five simple scores

Table 3-5. Raw-Score Form of the Beta Weights Which Optimally Predict Judges' Ratings

Scale	Beta Weight
L	.14
F	.36
K	7.76
1 (Hs)	−1.14
2 (D)	2.69
3 (Hy)	.74
4 (Pd)	5.35
5 (Mf)	1.57
6 (Pa)	2.54
7 (Pt)	.92
8 (Sc)	3.58
9 (Ma)	2.93
0 (Si)	.34
Welsh R	.14
Welsh A	2.87
Barron Es	.68

SOURCE: Cooke (1967a, 1967b).

which are combined in a linear discriminant function. The signs which make up the five component scores are shown in Table 3-6. Each sign is counted as one point if present, so the score for each set is the number of schizophrenic signs in the category that are significant. Thus, if three of the seven L signs are significant in the test profile, the L-sign component score, L_c, would be three. The score totals from each of the five sign components listed in Table 3-6 are then weighted and combined according to the formula

$$ScI = 6\ L_c - 2\ K_c + 1\ F_c + 1\ Mf_c + 7\ NP$$

ScI values of 46 or higher are identified as schizophrenic, while 45 and below are called nonschizophrenic.

Schizophrenic Weighted Index. A simple linear discriminant function of the standard clinical scales plus the Taylor manifest anxiety scale, At (see Appendix I in Volume II), was devised by Dahlstrom and Wahler (1955) to separate male schizophrenic profiles from other abnormal patterns in an inpatient setting. The function was based upon T-score values weighted according to the following formula:

$$SwI = -.01\ Hs - .09\ D - .01\ Hy + .01\ Mf + .04\ Pa + .01\ Pt + .07\ Sc - .06\ Ma - .06\ At$$

No general cutting score was advanced for clinical use.

Choynowski Diagnostic Functions. In a systematic comparison of three general categories of male psychiatric cases seen in a hospital setting with each other and with a sample of adult normals, Choynowski (1966) devised a set of linear weights to be used to separate each group from each of the others. These weights are applied to the T-score values obtained in a given profile. The weights have been adjusted so that the best cut-off score is zero for each discrimination. The weights to be used in each comparison are shown

Table 3-6. Significant Signs for Differentiating Female Schizophrenics from Controls, Arranged in Categories Used for Discriminant Function Analysis[a]

Sign	Score
L Component	
L	⩾ 53
D	⩽ 62
Hy	⩽ 62
Hs−L	⩽ 2
D−L	⩽ 7
Hy−L	⩽ 7
Pd−L	⩽ 12
K Component	
Hs−K	⩽ 2
Hy−K	⩽ 7
Pd−K	⩽ 12
F Component	
Hs−F	⩽ 2
D−F	⩽ 7
Hy−F	⩽ 2
Pd−F	⩽ 7
Mf Component	
Mf	⩾ 48
Hs−Mf	⩽ 12
D−Mf	⩽ 12
Hy−Mf	⩽ 12
Pd−Mf	⩽ 17
NP Component	
Pa−D	⩾ −2
Pt−D	⩾ −2
Pt−Hy	⩾ 3
Sc−Hs	⩾ 8
Sc−D	⩾ 3
Sc−Hy	⩾ 3
Sc−Pd	⩾ −2
Sc−Pt	⩾ 3

SOURCE: Eichman (1959).

[a] For scoring individual profiles, add the number of significant signs in each component to obtain five scores.

in Table 3-7. In each comparison, positive scores (above zero value) indicate membership in the second category while negative scores indicate membership in the first category. Values close to zero are more ambiguous than large positive or large negative values. (These weights were devised upon samples of Polish patients and normals; they should be validated upon samples of local cases in each clinical setting.)

Interpersonal Diagnostic Indices. There are two major dimensions in the circumplex of Leary's (1957) interpersonal diagnostic schema: dominance-submission and love-hate. Separate indices based on T scores from the standard MMPI scales (with appropriate K corrections) were provided for these two dimensions along with standard-score norms from a Kaiser Foun-

Table 3-7. Six Final Functions for Discrimination between Four Diagnostic Groups[a]

Comparison	Weight
Normals-neurotics	$Y_1 = .341x_1 + .582x_2 - .170x_3 + .085x_4 - .106x_5 + .032x_6 + .215x_7 - .034x_8 + .082x_9 - .304x_{10} + .560x_{11} - .245x_{12} - .378x_{13} - 50.601$
Normals-schizophrenics	$Y_2 = -.383x_1 - .357x_2 + .501x_3 - .184x_4 + .397x_5 - .260x_6 + .148x_7 - .081x_8 - .144x_9 + .183x_{10} - .538x_{11} - .220x_{12} + .112x_{13} + 53.945$
Normals-psychopaths	$Y_3 = -.462x_1 - .653x_2 + .578x_3 - .709x_4 + .261x_5 - .181x_6 + .279x_7 + .225x_8 - .161x_9 + .294x_{10} - .480x_{11} + .194x_{12} + .105x_{13} + 48.709$
Neurotics-schizophrenics	$Y_4 = .057x_1 + .343x_2 + .279x_3 - .390x_4 + .398x_5 - .001x_6 + .346x_7 - .022x_8 - .228x_9 - .317x_{10} + .006x_{11} - .248x_{12} - .086x_{13} - 18.064$
Neurotics-psychopaths	$Y_5 = .118x_1 - .083x_2 + .373x_3 - .517x_4 + .341x_5 - .298x_6 + .577x_7 + .091x_8 - .064x_9 - .010x_{10} + .117x_{11} + .025x_{12} - .222x_{13} - 30.786$
Schizophrenics-psychopaths	$Y_6 = -.055x_1 - .493x_2 + .425x_3 - .524x_4 - .073x_5 - .143x_6 + .135x_7 + .354x_8 + .030x_9 + .226x_{10} + .167x_{11} + .455x_{12} - .090x_{13} - 20.457$

SOURCE: Choynowski (1966).

[a] x_1 = Hs; x_2 = D; x_3 = Hy; x_4 = Pd; x_5 = Mf; x_6 = Pa; x_7 = Pt; x_8 = Sc; x_9 = Ma; x_{10} = Si; x_{11} = L; x_{12} = F; x_{13} = K.

dation (Oakland, California) research sample of normal adults. These indices are shown in Table 3-8 with the means and standard deviations that were used to develop the norms. Scores on DOM above −25 (smaller negative values and all positive values) indicate increasing dominance levels on Leary's vertical axis in the Interpersonal Profile Chart; values below −25 (larger negative values) indicate increasing submission levels. Similarly, values above −6 on LOV indicate greater love orientation along the horizontal axis while values below −6 signify greater hate orientation. The joint plotting of these two indices locates the subject in the circumplex. Leary also indicated that the special indicators listed for each of the octants served to clarify degrees of deviation or extremity of manifestation of the particular interpersonal style.

Deviant Life-Style Patterns. L. D. Smith (1969) published a set of profile indicators used to group individual MMPI patterns according to type of bohemian life styles. Most of the patterns applied to profiles from young male subjects but some can be applied to either sex group. Among the validity scales, only F-scale values enter into the defining patterns. All the patterns are based upon standard T scores with K corrections where appropriate. The six groupings and their respective profile indicators are listed in Table 3-9.

Peterson Psychotic Profile Signs. In Table 3-10 are listed the six diagnostic signs Peterson (1954) adapted from the differential diagnostic study of Meehl (1946) in which he described some general profile attributes characteristic of psychotic as opposed to neurotic MMPI patterns. The presence of any three or more signs indicates a psychotic configuration in the profile.

Taulbee-Sisson Psychotic-Neurotic Signs. Sixteen pairs of scales form the basis for the Taulbee-Sisson signs for differentiation of neurotic from

Table 3-8. MMPI Indices in Leary's Interpersonal Diagnostic System

Attribute	MMPI Index
	Major Dimensions
Dominance-submission[a]	DOM = (Ma − D) + (Hs − Pt)
Love-hate[b]	LOV = (K − F) + (Hy − Sc)
	Circumplex Octants
Autocratic (power)	(K + Ma) − (D + Pt)
Responsible (hypernormal)	$\frac{(K + Hs + Hy)}{3} - \frac{(F + D + Pt + Sc)}{4}$
Overconventional (cooperation)	(K + Hy) − (F + Sc)
Dependent (docility)	D + Hy + Pt
Masochistic (self-effacement)	D + Pt
Rebellious (distrust)	F + D + Pd + Sc
Sadistic (aggressiveness)	F + Pd + Ma; Sc > Pt; low Mf (males)
Narcissistic (competition)	(Hs + Ma) − (D +Pt)

SOURCE: Leary (1957).
[a]Mean = −24.4; S.D. = 24.1.
[b]Mean = −6.1; S.D. = 27.1.

Table 3-9. MMPI Indices of Deviant Life Styles

Life Style	MMPI Indicators
Tormented Rebels	(a) F ≥ 65 (b) 2 ≤ 59 (c) 4, 5, and 8 > 70 (d) 9 ≥ 65 (e) Only one (1, 3, 6, or 7) > 70
Lonely Ones	(a) F, 2, 4, 5, 7, and 8 > 70 (b) 1, 3, 6, and 9 may vary
Earnest Artists	(a) 5 ≥ 65 (b) 1, 3, and 6 > 70 (c) 2, 4, 7, and 8 > 65 (d) 9 any value
Passive Prophets	(a) 4 and 5 > 65 (b) F, 1, 2, 3, 6, 7, and 8 < 65 (c) 9 any value
Beat Madonnas	(a) 9 ≥ 65 (b) 1 and 3 < 70 (c) 2, 6, 7, and 8 < 65 (d) 5 < 50
Angry Young Women	(a) F, 4, 6, and 8 > 70 (b) 1, 2, 3, 4 and 9 > 60 (c) 5 < 50

SOURCE: Smith (1969).

psychotic MMPI patterns. Each sign is scored as present or absent. The presence of thirteen or more signs is considered strongly suggestive of a neurotic pattern; the presence of six or less is suggestive of a schizophrenic profile. These signs are listed in Table 3-11. Taulbee and Sisson (1957) used

Table 3-10. Peterson's Signs of a Psychotic MMPI Profile

Sign	MMPI Indicators
Elevation	Four or more clinical scales > 70
F level	F ≥ 65
Psychotic triad	6, 8, or 9 > 1, 2, and 3
Neurotic triad	2 > 1 and 3
8 versus 7	8 > 7
Elevation of 6 and 9	6 or 9 > 70

SOURCE: Peterson (1954).

Table 3-11. Scale Pairs in Taulbee-Sisson Signs for Neurotic Patterns[a]

Hs > Hy	Hs > Pt	D > Pa	Hy > Ma
Hs > Pd	Hs > Sc	Hy > Pd	Pt > Mf
Hs > Mf	Hs > Ma	Hy > Mf	Pt > Pa
Hs > Pa	D > Pd	Hy > Pa	Pt > Sc

SOURCE: Taulbee-Sisson (1957).
[a]13–16 = neurotic; 0–6 = schizophrenic.

the profile analysis method of Sullivan and Welsh (1952) in deriving these patterns.

Various MMPI Profile Indices. Table 3-12 lists a variety of additional MMPI indicators and signs. These patterning indices have been advanced individually as a means of identifying various clinical features not adequately reflected in single MMPI scales. The formulas for computing these indices are based upon the usual T scores of standard MMPI scales unless otherwise indicated, the exceptions being either the use of raw-score values or non-K-corrected T scores. Occasionally the same index is designated by different names or one index will incorporate some other index in its computing formula. Some of the indices listed in Table 3-12 are employed in the applications of the formal rules described in the next section.

Special Diagnostic Rules

In Appendix J are presented several sets of special interpretive rules which may be applied to the standard MMPI profile pattern as a means of evaluating various diagnostic implications of the test scores. After the basic scale scores have been obtained, two further scores and several special index values must be computed before consulting the rules. It is also important to limit the application of these rules to those cases which meet the prior screening standards established for the derivational samples.

Maladjustment Rules. Kleinmuntz (1963) programmed a sequence of steps in the inspection and categorization of MMPI profiles from college-level subjects employed by an experienced clinician to determine whether the pattern indicated serious emotional maladjustment or not. He also made internal analyses of the various steps in this decision schema to improve upon the hit rate of these decision rules. The resulting set of profile interpretive rules is given in Appendix J.

Table 3-12. MMPI Configural Indices Based upon Standard Scale Scores

Index	Computational Formula	Source
Active hostility index . . . . AHI	$=(Pd+Ma)$	Welsh and Sullivan (1952b)
Aging index . . . . AgI	$=(1.5\,Pd+Sc+0.5\,Pt)-(Hs+D)$	Franks (1965)
Anxiety index. . . . . . . AI	$=(1.33\,D+1.00\,Pt)-(.66\,Hs+.66\,Hy)$	Welsh (1952a)
Anxiety sign . . . . AxS	$=(L+Hs+Pa)-(D+Pt)$	Gough (1965)
Anxiety score . . . . AS	$=(Hs+D+Hy)$[a]	Modlin (1947)
Average elevation score . . . AV	$=\frac{(Hs+D+Hy+Pd+Mf+Pa+Pt+Sc+Ma)}{9}$	Modlin (1947)
Beta . . . . B	$=(Pt+Sc)-(Hs+D)$	Meehl and Dahlstrom (1960)
Character-disorder sign. . . . . CdS	$=Pd-\frac{(Pa+Sc)}{2}$	Gough (1965)
Composite moderator. . . . . CM	$=(D+Pd+Sc)-(F+Hs+Pa)$	Goldberg (1969)
Delta . . . . Δ	$=(Pd+Pa)-(Hs+Hy)$	Meehl and Dahlstrom (1960)
Dissimulation index DFK	$=(F_{rs}-K_{rs})$[b]	Gough (1950)
Expression of anger AnE	$=\frac{(Pd+Pa+Ma)}{(Hs+Hy)+(D+Pt)}$[c]	Cochrane, Prange, and Abse (1963)
Expressive-repressive index. . ERI	$=(L+K+Hy)-(Pd+Ma)$	Sanford, Webster, and Freedman (1957)
Frustration tolerance index . . . FTI	$=\frac{(Ma+Pd)}{(Hy+D)}$	Beall and Panton (1957)
Internalization ratio . . . . IR	$=\frac{(Hs+D+Pt)}{(Hy+Pd+Ma)}$	Welsh (1952a)
Masculinity index. . . MfI	$=50+(Hs+Pt)-(1.5\,Hy+0.5\,Pa)$	Franks (1965)
Neurotic score . . . . . . NS	$=(Hs+D+Hy)$[d]	Ruesch and Bowman (1945)
Organic sign index . . OSI	$=(D+Mf+Sc)-(Pd+Ma)$[e]	Watson and Thomas (1968)
Passive-aggressive index . . . . PAI	$=(Hy+100)-(Pd+2\,Pa)$	Welsh and Sullivan (1952)
Psychotic index. . . . . PsI	$=(L+Pa+Sc)-(Hy+Pt)$	Goldberg (1965)
Psychotic score . . . . . PS	$=(Pa+Pt+Sc)$	Ruesch and Bowman (1945)
Repressor-sensitizer index . . . . RSI	$=Hy-Pt$[c]	Eriksen and Davids (1955)
Scatter index . . . . SI	$=\text{Sum}\left[\lvert Hs-50\rvert+\lvert D-50\rvert+\ldots+\lvert Si-50\rvert\right]$	L'Abate (1962)
Triad elevation index . . . . TI	$=\frac{(Hs+D+Hy)}{3}-\frac{(Pa+Pt+Sc)}{3}$	Lovell (1965)

[a] See NS.
[b] Raw scores.
[c] No K corrections.
[d] See AS.
[e] Raw scores with K.

After the profile has been coded (the Hathaway code is sufficient), score the protocol for the Barron Es scale and the Kleinmuntz Mt scale (see Appendix I in Volume II for the item composition and direction of scoring of these two scales). Then, compute the beta, delta, anxiety index, and internalization ratio values according to the formulas in Table 3-12. Enter the sequence of rules given in Appendix J and apply each rule in the specified order, keeping a record of each outcome. Then enter the flow chart provided and proceed until a firm decision is reached: to call the pattern adjusted, to call it maladjusted, or to call it unclassified. The last category is also considered a firm decision, one in which it is decided that the present MMPI configuration does not provide enough useful information to make either of the other two decisions.

Psychotic-Neurotic Discrimination Rules. In 1960, Meehl and Dahlstrom published a special set of rules to be applied to profiles of cases on which the decision had been narrowed down to either a neurotic or a psychotic categorization. The sequential order of inspection of the profile was worked out on male psychiatric cases but has also been applied to profiles from female patients. The Meehl-Dahlstrom rules have been programmed for computer application by Kleinmuntz and Alexander (1962).

After the standard scales in the MMPI profile have been scored and plotted in T-score form, the profile must be coded (the Hathaway code is sufficient), and the values for beta, delta, and the internalization ratio must be computed according to the formulas in Table 3-12. The rules in Appendix J indicate the levels of acceptability of the validity indicators: L must be below 70 and F below 80; the Cannot Say level is specially treated in Appendix J. In these procedures, the rules are applied in order but only until some decision is reached. In each instance, the instruction is clear whether to make a firm decision at that point or proceed to apply the next rule. The decision will finally be to call the pattern psychotic, to call it neurotic, or to call it indeterminate. The last category is considered a firm decision, one in which it is decided that the present MMPI configuration does not provide enough useful information to make either of the other two decisions. Record the number of the rule on which the decision was finally made as well as the decision.

Psychotic–Neurotic–Character-Disorder Rules. Henrichs (1964, 1966) has expanded the Meehl-Dahlstrom rules to include a third category in the discrimination: psychotic profiles, neurotic profiles, and profiles from character-disorder or behavior-disorder cases. He referred to the latter category as the Pd type. The rules are applied to profiles from cases on which the decision has already been made that there is some definite psychopathological condition present which is not an organic disorder but the discrimination into one of these broad categories has not yet been made. Separate rules are provided in Appendix J for profiles from men and women.

After the standard profile scales have been scored and plotted in T-score form, the pattern of clinical and validity scores must be coded in the Welsh or extended code and the values for beta, delta, and the internalization ratio computed according to the formulas provided in Table 3-12. Then enter the set of rules in Appendix J appropriate to the sex of the test subject and apply each rule in order until a firm decision is reached. If any given rule in the sequence does not apply, proceed to the next. If the rule applies it may give either a firm decision or instruct one to proceed to the next rule. The firm decision will be to call the pattern psychotic, to call it neurotic, to call it character disorder, or to call it indeterminate. The last call is a firm decision and means that the present MMPI profile does not provide sufficient information to make one of the other decisions. Record the number of the rule on which a firm decision was reached as well as the final decision.

Organic-Schizophrenic Reaction Signs. These rules were developed by Watson and Thomas (1968) on cases in which the only remaining diagnostic discrimination was between a schizophrenic disorder and some cerebral lesion (see Table 3-13). They are based upon the T scores from the standard scales plus the value of the organic sign index which must be computed according to the formula provided in Table 3-12 from the raw scores (with K values added) of five of the basic scales.

Table 3-13. MMPI Signs for Differentiation of Males with Organic Brain Disorder from Those Showing Schizophrenic Reaction

MMPI Sign	Direction: Schizophrenic	Direction: Organic Brain Damage
Profile peak sign	Code: 2, 5, or 8	Code: 4 or 9
Elevation sign[a]	Code is starred	Code is double-primed or lower
Organic sign index[b]	OSI ≥ 40	OSI < 40

SOURCE: Watson and Thomas (1968).

[a]Apply the first two signs sequentially; the third sign is applied independently of the first two.

[b]See Table 3-12; values are based upon raw scores with K weights included.

Apply the first two signs in order. That is, the second sign is applied to cases on which no decision was reached on the first sign. The final sign applies to all cases. A decision is made on each profile to call the disorder schizophrenic or to call it organic. The rules were developed on male cases. They have also been applied to profiles from females but the accuracy is substantially lower for them.

Special Supplementary Scale Patterns

Several procedures have been developed for summarizing MMPI patterns that are based in whole or part upon special scales not routinely included in the standard profile. These procedures require the preparation of special scoring stencils and occasionally the utilization of special norms. (See the appendix materials in Volume II.) A number of these procedures are included in routine scoring by national scoring services or by computerized interpretive services.

Welsh A and R Novants. The factor scales which Welsh (1956b) developed to reflect the first two major sources of variance common to the scales in the clinical profile of the MMPI are used in a two-dimensional grid to form a set of interpretive categories (Welsh, 1965). Each scale value is converted into the T score appropriate for the sex of the subject (see Appendix F); the combination of the A and R values is used to assign a subject to one of the nine categories or novants in the grid. The A-scale values are plotted along the vertical axis (ordinate) and the R-scale values along the horizontal axis (abscissa). Each score distribution is divided into thirds by cutting one-half standard deviation above and below the mean or at a T score of 45 and below and 55 and above. The resulting grid produces nine categories numbered from the upper left-hand to the lower right-hand novants. Table 3-14 shows the range of values for A and R scales for each novant. The profile is designated by the number of the novant in which it falls.

Table 3-14. A and R Levels for Each Novant

Novant	A Score	R Score
I	55+	45−
II	55+	46–54
III	55+	55+
IV	46–54	45−
V	46–54	46–54
VI	46–54	55+
VII	45−	45−
VIII	45−	46–54
IX	45−	55+

SOURCE: Welsh (1965).

Eichman Factor-Scale Patterns. The factor scales developed by Eichman (1962) have close correspondence to the Welsh scales but extend the dimensional system to four and generate a short coding schema rather than a simple grid. The scales are designated by number (1, 2, 3, and 4) and plotted on the basis of psychiatric norms. Table 3-15 provides these values for each sex on the four Eichman factor scales. After the special T-score values have been determined for each scale they are listed in order of highest to lowest. Then the

Table 3-15. Special T-Score Tables for the Eichman Factor Scales

Raw Score	I		II		III		IV	
	Males	Females	Males	Females	Males	Females	Males	Females
20	73	71	84	78	81	84	92	99
19	71	69	82	76	78	82	89	96
18	69	67	79	73	76	79	86	93
17	66	65	76	70	74	77	83	90
16	64	63	73	67	72	75	80	86
15	62	61	71	65	69	72	77	83
14	59	58	68	62	67	70	74	80
13	57	56	65	59	65	67	72	77
12	55	54	62	56	63	65	69	74
11	52	52	59	54	60	63	66	71
10	50	50	57	51	58	60	63	68
9	48	48	54	48	56	58	60	65
8	45	45	51	46	54	55	57	62
7	43	43	48	43	51	53	54	59
6	41	41	46	40	49	51	51	56
5	38	39	43	37	47	48	48	53
4	36	37	40	35	45	46	45	50
3	34	35	37	32	42	43	42	47
2	31	33	34	29	40	41	39	43
1	29	30	32	26	38	39	37	40
0	27	28	29	24	36	36	34	37

SOURCE: Eichman (1962).

scales which fall above a value of 55 on the psychiatric norms are designated as high values; those with values of 54 or below are considered to be not high. The interpretive configurations provided are based upon both coding order and number of high values (see Table 7-5). Eichman (1970) has also found that intellective level should be combined with the factor-scale pattern for most accurate interpretation.

Expression and Sensitization Indices. Altrocchi and his colleagues (Altrocchi, 1961; Altrocchi and Perlitsh, 1963; Altrocchi, Parsons, and Dickoff, 1960; Altrocchi, Shrauger, and McLeod, 1964) have devised a set of indices which have been used to characterize the extent to which an individual expresses or inhibits his (unacceptable) impulses and the extent to which an individual is aware of (sensitizer) or blocks from awareness (repressor) knowledge of these unacceptable impulses. The two indices, together with cutting scores for forming the various categories, are given in Table 3-16. The expressor index, ExI, involves Pd-scale values which are in T scores without K corrections and Welsh R-scale and Little and Fisher Dn-scale T-score values. The repressor-sensitizer index, R-SI, is based upon Pt-scale values which are in T scores without K correction. The Welsh A-scale and Little and Fisher Dn-scale values are used in this index as well. These two indices are used conjointly to form the three groups, with the cutting scores designated in Table 3-16. McDonald (1965) has devised a similar set of categories but has substituted Byrne's repression-sensitization scale (1961) for the R-S index of Altrocchi.

Table 3-16. Altrocchi Indices of Expression and Sensitization

Item	Expressor Index	Repressor-Sensitizer Index
MMPI formula	ExI = 2 Pd − (R + Dn)[a]	R-SI = (L + K + Dn) − (D + Pt + A)[a]
Expressors	above 30	below 23 but above −10
Expressor-sensitizers	above 30	below −22
Repressors	below 14	above 50

SOURCE: Altrocchi, Parsons, and Dickoff (1960).
[a]Without K corrections.

Item-Analytic Procedures

Some clinical users of the MMPI have devised techniques for inspecting the content of all the items that make up the significant answers to the validity- and clinical-scale scores in the test profile (see Clark and Allen, 1951). Such procedures are time consuming and largely judgmental. Somewhat more objective and systematic procedures have been advanced for this general purpose, however, which have been introduced in routine application in many different clinical settings and adopted by some of the computer-based interpretive services as well. These procedures will be briefly described here.

The TR Index. As noted in Chapter 1, the booklet version of the MMPI contains sixteen duplicated items (listed in Appendix C) which may be scored for consistency of item endorsement. It was also noted in discussing the box form of the test that these items may be added to the cards in such a way that this same index may be derived for this version of the test. A scoring template may be prepared for the particular answer sheets being used, enabling the scorer to compare the initial endorsement and second endorsement of each item. This is easiest for those answer sheets which have all the answers on one side of the sheet. It is a little more complicated to inspect the answers which occur on opposite sides of the sheet (see Buechley and Ball, 1952) but the task is not difficult. The TR index is the total number of items answered oppositely on the two occasions (early and late in the booklet or box).

Critical Items. Appendix G lists a special set of items suggested by Grayson (1951) to serve as stop items or indicators of special clinical difficulties which may require special inquiry or exploration. Many installations have prepared tally sheets of these items, together with their item numbers and direction of scoring. Each answer sheet is then checked for these items and any item found to be answered in the designated direction is marked for the clinician's special attention. In addition, some clinicians have grouped these items by content to highlight certain problem areas (e.g., sexual, aggressive, suicidal). Gravitz (1968) has published frequency data on these items which indicate the extent to which each is endorsed in the significant direction by a sample of general normal adults.

Harris-Lingoes Subscales. A similar clinical function is provided by the subscales devised by Harris and Lingoes (1955) from several of the basic clinical scales in the profile. These subscale values enable the clinician to better determine the kinds of item endorsements which have led to the particular scale elevation in question. These subscale groups are listed in Appendix I and the norms for their use are given in Appendix H.

Maladjustment Score. Gallagher (1953) recommended a simple count of the number of items answered in the statistically rare direction (deviant responses) by the test subject as an index of severity of maladjustment. On the box-form record blanks, this MS value is simply the number of X's or + marks recorded on the form. For the group-form answer sheet, the information provided in Appendix A must be consulted. For routine scoring of MS, this can best be done by preparing a stencil with the deviant direction of response noted for each booklet item. The MS value is simply the total number of these deviant answers.

PART TWO: EVALUATION OF TEST VALIDITY

CHAPTER 4. The Validity Indicators

VALIDITY is a complex concept. In current psychometric discussions many other terms are being offered as refinements of or substitutes for one aspect or another of validity. These include such alternatives as utility for some particular application, dependability as a basis for some specific inference, and factorial saturation in covariations with other measures. There are strong arguments in favor of retiring from current scientific usage all terms which become so burdened with diverse meanings and qualifications that they lose their original precision and denotational accuracy. Many would so argue in regard to such terms as "validity" and "reliability" as applied to psychological tests. In practical usage, however, the practitioner must be concerned about the adequacy and suitability of his test data for making the kinds of decisions being posed for him about a particular person. For him, therefore, the question of test validity is basic and omnipresent. Until present-day practice is drastically changed there are strong reasons to retain such concepts. It is necessary at the outset, therefore, to clarify the particular meanings of validity that are being employed in discussions of the validity indicators of the MMPI.

Two Meanings of Validity

In designating MMPI indicators as "validity scales," "validity checks," or "validity signs," there arises an additional risk of ambiguity and of potential misunderstanding. In psychometric theory, the term "validity" has been largely reserved to designate the property of a scale or instrument which legitimizes the particular substantive psychological inferences that may be drawn from score values generated by appropriate administration of that scale. Thus, a musical aptitude scale of high validity when properly given to subjects provides a basis for anticipating their ultimate musical proficiency, high or low, even though they may never before have turned their hand to playing a musical instrument. A scale of low validity will not provide any dependable basis for predicting these subjects' later standing in musical accomplishment. Validity, for a wide array of different personological and psychopathological inferences and as a property of particular MMPI scales or of sets of scales in various configurations, is a major concern to users of this test. Validity in this sense enters recurrently into the discussions throughout the two volumes of this *Handbook*. Validity in the special sense of the MMPI validity indicators, however, pertains to the appropriateness or the acceptability of any one administration of the test. In the example above, even when a particular scale of musical aptitude which has been shown to possess high predictive validity is used, it is possible that on any one occasion it may be improperly given to a subject, it may fail to enlist the appropriate motivation or orientation from him, or it may be tallied or scored ineptly or carelessly. If so, the resulting score is less likely to provide its usual dependable basis for predicting that person's musical accomplishments. These various factors that may vitiate particular test administrations are ubiquitous and it is surprising how few of our current psychological test instruments provide any built-in checks on the many sources of invalidity that arise in routine applications to heterogeneous populations of test subjects.

Each administration of a test raises anew the question of its validity in this second sense, a question that is often difficult to pose properly and complex to answer adequately. From one point of view, perhaps, it would be better to employ two different terms for these two kinds of evaluations of validity: determination of the utility of the test in general for particular assessment issues versus determination of the acceptability of a particular set of data from a given subject by means of that test. From another point of view, however, it may be well to retain a single term to cover both aspects of validity since it is imperative that the practicing psychologist bear in mind the admonition that the most valid psychological scale available for any given assessment decision can be invalidly applied on any particular occasion. (The obverse of this dictum is also worth bearing in mind: no matter how carefully the administration of an invalid instrument may be monitored or how much concern is devoted to the reduction of random errors in its tallying and scoring, the scores obtained will not be worth the effort needed to obtain them.)

The remainder of this chapter will be devoted to a description of the various validity indicators that have been advanced for use with the MMPI, together with the kinds of implications that they each provide about various sources of invalidity of the test protocol. In addition, the alternatives open to the practitioner and the procedures he may wish to follow to rectify some flawed test administration will also be outlined. In the following chapter, the ways that the information from the validity indicators, and the various patterns appearing among them, may be used to generate inferences from the MMPI will be presented. Inevitably, some of these discussions will anticipate information to be presented in later chapters on the clinical scales and their configurations.

The Cannot Say (?) Score

As described in Part One on test administration, the standard instructions to the subject make it explicit that if some item does not apply to him or if he does not know about the question he should omit it. The Cannot Say or ? score is simply the total number of items that he has placed in that category for the card form or has omitted or double-marked in completing his answer sheet on one of the group forms of the test. In the usual way of giving this test, the option of skipping items that seem inappropriate is considered to be one important way in which the restrictive confines of objective test procedures can be accommodated to the great variations among potential test subjects and examination settings. Thus, subjects orphaned at an early age may interpret test items pertaining to their relationships with their parents as actually applying to their foster parents and be able to report on any relevant parental experiences covered in the test, or they may interpret these items as referring to their biological parents and be in no position to answer any of them. Similarly, hospitalized subjects may answer items about their activity patterns in terms of their usual patterns of involvement before their confinement, or they may, particularly when the institutionalization has involved many years in a sanatorium, find themselves unable to answer whole sets of such items in any meaningful way. It is difficult to anticipate the different ways in which a subject's life situation or his idiosyncrasy of semantic interpretation may render various items in the MMPI item pool inapplicable to himself. Brown (1950) has offered some suggestions on how particular case-history material and MMPI item omissions may be collated to identify those items which clearly and legitimately do not apply to a particular test subject, but this always remains a question of individual judgment.

A second general consideration in evaluating those items which a person may have left unanswered is the extent to which he finds the content of the items intrusive upon his privacy and deliberately withholds his answers to them because he feels that they should be neither asked nor answered in that particular setting. Although the findings of Mosher's research (1966) seem to indicate that most of the items which the various normative groups at Minnesota most frequently left unanswered (see the tabulations of item omissions in the appendix of Volume II) are not considered to be particularly intrusive or too highly personal, other studies (Butcher and Tellegen, 1966; Gravitz, 1967; Walker, 1967) have indicated that many people feel that large numbers of the items in the MMPI are too personal or too private to answer in those settings in which they feel themselves under close critical scrutiny. Thus, when a person is asked to answer the test items without giving his own name, the MMPI items omitted are largely those which are difficult to interpret or understand clearly; but in some selection contexts this tendency to leave out answers is extended to items that bear upon sexual and religious practices or beliefs, family interrelationships, and experiences with various intimate bodily functions. It should be pointed out that these studies also show that merely giving the subject a clear option to leave objectionable items unanswered does not fully meet the objections that some people raise to the MMPI. For these persons, just being asked to take a test in which such content as listed above is encountered is in itself a distressing experience, one which they resent bitterly and protest about vigorously. For most test subjects, however, the explicit instructions to leave out such items are sufficient to reconcile them to an examination of this sort. That is, they do not feel that the fact that they have chosen to omit particular items constitutes any serious reflection upon them or the adequacy of their adjustment. The importance of this consideration as it bears upon the ethical and professional trust involved in all psychological evaluations should be borne clearly in mind in the subsequent discussions on ways that various practitioners have tried to resolve the problem of excessive numbers of item omissions.

Levels of Cannot Say Scores. Most subjects, with or without personological difficulties, find that they are able to answer all the items of the MMPI. For example, in a group of 126 consecutive male neuropsychiatric admissions Tamkin and Scherer (1957) found that the modal number of items omitted was zero. They also reported a few (twelve) cases with excessive Cannot Say scores, ranging upwards to 145 items left unanswered.

In routine practice, as already noted, these item counts are treated as a scale and plotted in T-score form on the profile sheet. The user should be aware of the limitations that these scores have as a basis for a psychometric scale. Any item can be included in this score if it is left unanswered or if it is double-marked. No hypothetical continuum of test evasiveness can be assumed to underlie this set of scores. That is, one cannot assume that there is some typical level to be represented by a mean of 50 on the T scale or that various degrees of evasiveness or explicitness are to be represented by scores above or below that point. Rather, the concern in setting up the a priori T-scale values for the Cannot Say score has been to scale the extent to which such omissions may or may not weaken scores on the other component scales of the test. Thus, raw scores below 30 are entered on the profile as equal to a T score of 50, or simply as "OK," to indicate that the test administration has probably not been unduly affected by the number of items found unanswered. This assumption, of course, is only tenable when the items that were left unanswered fall rather haphazardly among the various scales. As indicated below, inspection of the item distribution may occasionally reveal highly selective item omissions so that sometimes a relatively small number of items omitted may have a drastic effect on one or two scales. In the same way that the T-score value of 50 was established arbitrarily (rather than empirically, as was true for the MMPI clinical scales), T-score values above 50 were also scaled judgmentally. The value of 70 was set equal to 110 items. In other words the practitioner should become seriously concerned about the weakening effect of item omissions when they reach a ratio of about one in five. (If a short form of the test is being used, the tolerance limits for the Cannot Say score must be lowered or appropriately adjusted according to this same ratio.) It should be noted that, in terms of present scoring practices and the standard-test profile forms, the score ranges on Cannot Say described by Blazer (1965a) are somewhat in error.

In addition to being rather rare, high scores on the Cannot Say scale seem to be complexly determined. As suggested by the research summarized in Volume II on these scores, there are several different kinds of cognitive or personological processes that may lead to an excessive number of items being left unanswered (or being answered both ways). Some of these trends are more likely to appear in certain testing situations or under special circumstances.

The most likely cause of an excessive number of Cannot Say responses is that the person completing the test has been unable to comprehend the content of many of the MMPI statements. As noted in Chapter 1, although the authors tried to set the reading level of the items at approximately the fifth grade (and such studies as those of Johnson and Bond, 1950, and Pierce-Jones, 1954, indicate that these efforts were generally successful), nevertheless there are a number of items in the pool which are ambiguous, contain double negatives, involve special terminology or knowledge of special idioms, or refer to experiences which some people cannot readily identify or recognize. On these items it may be that the subject literally cannot say for sure how the statement applies to him. If the test subjects have marginal literacy, are so young that they have not mastered the requisite vocabulary, have yet to encounter the life experiences needed to comprehend the statements (see Ball and Carroll, 1960), have led markedly constricted lives through physical or sensory handicapping conditions or environmental deprivations, or, most importantly, have marginal levels of intellective competence, they may find large numbers of MMPI items hard to read, difficult to comprehend, or otherwise unanswerable. Similar difficulties in comprehending the MMPI procedures may lead some of these subjects to mark some items both True and False, rendering the items unscorable.

A second important basis for large numbers of unanswered items is failure to enlist the full cooperation of the test subject before administration of this test. Through anger, alienation, or hostility, the subject may decide to go through the motions of test compliance but leave out so many answers as to vitiate the results. Opposition to authority, represented in various institutions by professional staff, test administrators, secretaries, nurses, or attendants, may be manifested indirectly in this form of submarginal compliance with routine procedures, short of full defiance but effectively blocking diagnostic or remedial efforts by the staff. As noted above, just being asked to complete a test like the MMPI may arouse this kind of opposition in some people. In these circumstances, the otherwise quite legitimate option of omitting an occasional item on the test is seized upon and used in an extreme way as a means of expressing their resentments, irritations, and gripes. Obviously, these reactions may appear in any test setting but are more frequently encountered in testing programs in prisons, in training schools, or on wards of committed patients in state hospitals. It also follows that the items omitted are often quite randomly chosen or haphazardly selected, more a function of momentary whim than of calculated response to the item's content, although on occasion these subjects will focus their rebellion and refuse to answer any item that is even mildly intrusive.

A related problem but one which is likely to take a somewhat different form of expression is the tendency to omit items defensively. The subject in this instance is not fully cooperating to express himself or his true feelings about the material cited in the MMPI items but is deliberately tailoring his responses to create some particular image of himself. In these efforts, he may find it convenient to omit a number of items rather than to answer them definitively one way or the other. Brown (1950) has discussed this form of lying in which the subject says he cannot answer when in fact he knows quite well how the item should be answered. Tamkin and Scherer (1957) tried to verify this kind of process in the patients they identified with high Cannot Say scores by examining the relationship between the Cannot Say scores and elevations on the L and K scores on these protocols. Their results did not lend support to a general defensive basis for Cannot Say scores. There is a difficulty inherent in this kind of study, however, since the item omissions on the MMPI attenuate scores on all the other scales, including L and K, thus making it difficult to carry out such intratest comparisons. There is some indirect evidence that bears upon this question. In a sample of general mental-hygiene-clinic cases, for example, Welsh (1956) found that the Cannot Say scores correlated negatively with all other basic scales on the MMPI except the L scale. Resorting to item omissions as a defensive procedure, therefore, appears to be one significant cause of elevated Cannot Say scores, but by no means the only source of item omissions.

Several other bases for high Cannot Say scores have been identified. Sensitive and suspicious subjects may omit a series of items that they are wary of marking in such a way as to expose or reveal themselves. Often, then, the items that they omit all bear upon the same topic. For depressed persons, the task of weighing alternatives and making decisions about a long series of items in the test may prove to be particularly burdensome. In addition to taking a long time in completing the answer sheet, these subjects may leave out many answers. Contributing to their difficulties in taking the MMPI is their often expressed feeling that they and their problems cannot be helped anyway so it is not worth all the effort involved (on their part or by the staff members) to complete the test answer sheet. In a similar way the process of completing the test may become enmeshed in the obsessional systems of some patients so that either an undue amount of time is taken to decide each answer or many items are omitted because the person is so indecisive. Brown (1950) refers to this difficulty as "pathological irresoluteness" in taking the test. Many of the items that are left unanswered are ones which are interpreted in rather unusual ways, with many peculiar semantic implications being read into the idioms or modifiers in these statements.

Correction Measures for High Cannot Say Scores. Because an excessive number of Cannot Say responses has such widespread effect upon the rest of the MMPI profile the test authors have generally recommended that a subject who has omitted large numbers of items should be reminded about the instructions for the test, especially the fact that a True or False answer means *generally* true or *generally* false, and be requested to go back over those unanswered items to make certain that he cannot answer them one way or the other. Although some clinicians, such as Brown (1950), have raised questions about the logic of such a request to reexamine Cannot Say responses, it has generally proved to be effective in keeping such omissions within tolerable limits. Seemingly, some items early in the test box or booklet are left unanswered because the subject has approached them with some special momentary set or while he is still trying to make up his mind about the kind of test that the MMPI is actually going to be. Later, after encountering a wide range of different items, he finds that he can after all make decisions about these different content matters expeditiously and comfortably. With this new perspective, when he goes back to the items that he had previously found difficult to answer, he often finds that his mixed feelings have disappeared and he can readily answer most of them. The same phenomenon has also been demonstrated experimentally in such studies as that of Walker (1967) involving retesting the same subjects after an interval of several weeks: item omissions are appreciably reduced upon retesting. Nevertheless, Brown's point is well taken and the test administrator is advised to be alert to the subject's feelings about a request to reduce his item omissions. He may rightfully resent being asked to answer unanswerable test items.

A rather different approach to the administration of the MMPI that is calculated either to reduce markedly or to irradicate the problem of omitted items has been advanced by some workers. These clinicians recommend that the MMPI be given as a forced-choice test. This approach has already been mentioned briefly but further discussion is warranted here. The instructions are modified to indicate that the subject should answer each item, guessing the answer to those items that he is uncertain about. As Good and Brantner (1961) have cogently pointed out, this change in administration involves a significant departure from the way the test was originally standardized; there is a risk of vitiating the norms and scales of the MMPI derived on data from the traditional mode of administration. This alteration in MMPI administration has several implications that should be borne in mind.

First of all, the forced-choice procedure only reduces but does not eliminate item omissions. Since the instructions indicate that a subject is to make an answer to every item, failure to comply with these directions seems to be psychologically rather different from failure to answer items in the usual format. For example, using test materials similar to MMPI statements, Edwards and Walsh (1964) found that Cannot Say scores on regular true-false test blanks had a different factor-analytic composition than item-omission scores on forced-choice tasks. Similarly, Eaddy (1962) found that indeterminate answers on the Strong Vocational Interest Blank were independent of MMPI Cannot Say scores, although ? scores on the SVIB did show a relationship to item omissions on the MMPI answer sheet. Thus, it would appear that the change in mode of administration merely changes the nature of the phenomenon but does not eliminate the problem. The problem is still present in a forced-choice presentation and requires appropriate understanding and comparable methods of coping with it.

With the forced-choice mode of presentation it is difficult to maintain the pretense that the examiner is interested in the subject's actual experiences, factual background, or other material covered by the test items. In the usual administration, the MMPI is introduced as a psychological examination devoted to elicitation of these kinds of data. Apparently most subjects interpret the test instructions accordingly. If then the subject is also told to guess on ambiguous items, he may come to feel that the examination is in some respects fraudulent. If the subject is instructed to guess about his feelings concerning a father whom he never knew (his having been a casualty of war before the subject's own birth, say), he may be both puzzled about what meaning such a guess may have on this particular item and correspondingly skeptical about what may be desired in response to the more appropriate items concerning which he would not otherwise have had any particular doubts. Thus, one impression may be given through the test instructions and another through the response alternatives presented to the test subject. The problems created by such a forced-choice administration of the MMPI may not be quite as intense as those created by forced-choice tests in which the subject is confronted with item couplets or triplets. Nevertheless, the shift in mode of administration is likely to generate a number of special attitudes and reactions in the test subject which are not fully understood or appropriately recognized now.

Some clinicians, rather than asking their subjects to redo the Cannot Say items, or instructing them to guess on any questionable items, have resorted to various arbitrary scoring procedures to try to get around the weakening effect that these item omissions can have upon the rest of the test. One approach, by Brown (1950), will be taken up in detail together with some special considerations that are involved in his approach.

First, it should be noted that Brown's work was based on the card form (which was more popular at that time than it is currently). Since specific placement of cards involves a discrete and identifiable response, rather than merely skipping over a blank on an answer sheet, the card-form Cannot Say response may have a firmer psychological rationale than is true of ways of getting an elevated Cannot Say score on some group form of the MMPI. This is certainly true in regard to items, for example, that are double-marked on the group answer sheet; there is no behavior comparable to this on the card form of the test.

Second, Brown indicated that all the items in the Cannot Say category should first be examined and those items that the clinician knows to be inapplicable should be removed and not even tallied on the record form. This part of Brown's recommendations is particularly difficult to defend. On the card form, some mark for an item that is to be given special treatment must be entered or the scoring procedures will be in error. On scoring stencils for the card form any unmarked item is treated as if it were definitively answered in the majority (or zero) direction. Thus, merely ignoring an item is not sufficient if in fact the clinician wishes to have the item removed from consideration in subsequent scoring procedures. Even if the clinician does make some special notation on the record form to have certain items inoperative in the subsequent scoring steps, there are reservations about doing this sort of thing on an objective and standardized test. An important consideration in this practice is that such decisions about these items in terms of their relevance or irrelevance to a particular test subject made by a given clinician are quite likely to be undependable and nonreproducible. The practice is analogous to that carried out by some investigators of personality characteristics among seminarians who have eliminated subsets of items from the MMPI item pool as inappropriate to ask seminarians (see Bier, 1948). Any one investigator is quite unlikely to arrive at the same subset to be eliminated as that selected by another investigator. Compare this approach with recent work on a special Catholic version of the MMPI in which the items to be dropped from the MMPI as inapplicable were selected on the basis of a detailed, empirical item analysis of responses from several seminarian groups (Bier, 1965).

Brown's proposal amounts to having each clinician carry out this kind of item purification for each of his subjects separately, probably for each separate testing occasion as well. It is highly presumptuous to believe that even an experienced and conscientious clinician can make dependable judgments about how his client has actually interpreted the content of the item or how it bears upon various special circumstances in his background and experience. Obviously, in many routine applications of the MMPI, the person responsible for MMPI administration and processing is in no position to know these circumstances about each of the test subjects. In such situations, the most defensible decision to make in the presence of large numbers of item omissions may be to discard the test protocol as an inadequate basis for making further personological inferences or judgments about that individual. In many other applications, however, this decision would be wasteful and inappropriate, since useful information can still be gained from the MMPI. It is unlikely, however, that very many clinicians will be able to make the kind of detailed judgments about item applicability required by the recommendations of Brown. Therefore, it does not seem wise to carry out this part of Brown's recommendations in the routine processing of MMPI data. This kind of practice would be risky and unproductive at best; at worst, it would vitiate the advantages inherent in objective psychological examinations.

The second part of Brown's proposal on Cannot Say responses involves giving the remaining unanswered items some weight in the scoring of scales on which they fall. He suggested that one-half credit be given for any item which was left unanswered but which the clinician felt the subject could have been expected to answer. On any scale on which a Cannot Say response falls, no matter which way the item would be scored, one-half point would be counted toward the raw score. Obviously, then, a subject could get some credit for a False answer to the item on one scale and some credit for a True answer on another, even though he did not answer the item either way. Brown did not offer any empiricial evidence that this treatment of the Cannot Say responses would provide more dependable clinical profiles than those generated solely from the answered items. Hovey (1958), however, has carried out a small-scale study of the impact of a similar correction procedure. He contrasted profiles from test scores generated both ways, either by leaving the Cannot Say responses out or by scoring them all with full credit on the scales in which they fall, as if they were answered in the scorable direction. He has also contrasted profiles generated by regular scoring procedures with those obtained by instructing the subject to guess on items that he was uncertain about. In general, Hovey found that the profiles with scores augmented by either the arbitrary scoring procedures or the forced-choice instructions were more in accord with nontest evaluations of these subjects than were the untreated profiles in which the component scores were weakened by large numbers of item omissions. He also noted that the primary effect of either of these augmenting procedures was upon profile elevation rather than upon profile configuration. Therefore the augmented profile, being higher, seemed to correspond more closely to clinically determined degrees of severity of emotional disorder without altering as greatly the determinations of the form of the disorder. Using either Brown's or Hovey's scoring supplement is not likely to enable the clinician to get an unflawed test protocol but does give him an estimate of the outer limits of scores that could have been obtained had all items been endorsed.

A more defensible recourse, perhaps, than any of those described above when the administration of the MMPI results in an elevated Cannot Say score is to seek an opportunity to interview the subject directly about his reasons for leaving particular items unanswered. If rapport is satisfactory and time permits, a detailed discussion of each of the omitted items can perhaps clarify many of the questions raised by such excessive omissions. Within this context, too, it may be appropriate to ask the subject to go back over the items and make decisions about them that he was unable to make before. By having the person himself read the items aloud to the examiner, by listening to the inflections and emphases which he places upon particular phrases or modifiers, by asking for synonyms from him for particular words, or by noting his explanations concerning his interpretive difficulties, the examiner may gain the information needed to understand why large segments of the MMPI were left unanswered. Care must be taken, of course, so that his defensiveness which may already be high is not raised still further by these inquiries; efforts must be made to see that the subject understands the reasons for these additional questions and does not feel the confidentiality of his responses is being violated.

It is quite possible that the efforts a clinician makes to reduce the number of item omissions on the MMPI may in fact result in an even larger number of items being left unanswered. That is, with the booklet form, not only may the subject go back over the items originally omitted without resolving them but he may also find that in the course of redoing the test there are other items that he should not have answered the way he did. With the card form of the test, the examiner may circumvent this possibility by returning to him only the items left in the Cannot Say category; with the booklet form of necessity the whole inventory is back in the subject's hands. With the tape version, also, where it may be more convenient to have a booklet on hand for this kind of special inquiry rather than trying to locate specific items along the tape, the problem may arise as well.

Psychometrically, there is a clear advantage to be gained by any effort to reduce the number of unanswered items on the MMPI. This gain, however, must be carefully weighed against potential loss in test rapport, trust, or open cooperation of the subject with the purposes of the examination and the ultimate goals of the current assessment.

L Scale

The second validity indicator in the regular MMPI profile is the fifteen-item scale designed to identify deliberate or intentional efforts to evade answering the test frankly and honestly. This scale is called the lie scale or simply the L scale. Hathaway and McKinley tailored this scale after a similar scale devised by Hartshorne and May (1928) in their studies of deceit among school-age children. In their work, Hartshorne and May found that there were a number of common foibles or personal faults which their subjects indicated were generally bad but also acknowledged as true about themselves. They found that some subjects, however, would systematically try to make themselves look better by denying these negative attributes even though it was quite likely that these characteristics were just as true for them as for anyone else. Using this general approach, Hathaway and McKinley reworked some of the same content and wrote new statements in the same vein to produce fifteen items that were consistent with the rest of the MMPI item pool in format and wording. These items were introduced as a set into the pool and arbitrarily scored as an index of a falsifying tendency in taking the test. The items in the L scale are presented in Table 4-1, together with item overlap designations and direction of scoring.

Inspection of the items listed in Table 4-1 will show that the content refers to denial of aggression, bad thoughts, weakness of character or resolve, poor self-control, prejudices, and even minor dishonesties. The data in that table also reveal that all the items are scored significantly if answered False. This latter feature of the scale has led to the criticism that it is unduly susceptible to a general acquiescence set in answering the items of the test. (See the discussion on acquiescence below.) Most of these items are scored only on the L scale but some of them also appear on one or more of the other scales in

Table 4-1. The L Scale: Item Composition, Direction of Scoring, and Overlap with Other Basic Scales

False: L

45. I do not always tell the truth.
60. I do not read every editorial in the newspaper every day.
90. Once in a while I put off until tomorrow what I ought to do today.
135. If I could get into a movie without paying and be sure I was not seen I would probably do it.
150. I would rather win than lose in a game.
165. I like to know some important people because it makes me feel important.
195. I do not like everyone I know.
225. I gossip a little at times.
255. Sometimes at elections I vote for men about whom I know very little.

False: LF

75. I get angry sometimes.

False: L2

285. Once in a while I laugh at a dirty joke.

False: LK23

*30. At times I feel like swearing.

False: L59

120. My table manners are not quite as good at home as when I am out in company.

False: L. True: (678)

15 (314). Once in a while I think of things too bad to talk about.

False: L9

105. Sometimes when I am not feeling well I am cross.

NOTE: In this and subsequent tables showing item composition of scales, an asterisk (*) before an item indicates that it is a correction item on the K scale; a dagger (†) before an item indicates that it is a correction item on scale 2; and a double dagger (‡) before an item indicates that on scale 5 the item is scored in the opposite direction for females. The code number of a scale is given in parentheses if the item is scored as a zero item on that scale.

the profile, usually scored in the same direction. The largest overlap, however, is only of two items each with scale 2 and scale 9 which does not limit score ranges or covariations to any important degree.

The research studies on the L scale have generally indicated that the assumptions made in assembling the items on the L scale were essentially correct. Data from the Minnesota normative groups (see the technical appendixes in Volume II) and from such studies as that of Gravitz (1970) have shown that most of the items on the L scale are answered in the nondefensive direction by at least 50 percent of the normals. The personal faults listed in items 15, 135, 165, and 255, however, were not acknowledged by a majority of the Minnesota college students or by the adults in Gravitz's sample of job applicants. Some of these items focus upon behavioral attributes which may be just emerging in younger adults and thus be less appropriate to their current self-descriptions, e.g., voting or self-monitoring of conversational topics. These studies also indicate that items 60, 75, 90, and (for males) 285 were rarely answered in the scorable direction. These items do not contribute appreciably to the useful variance on the L scale and technically qualify for inclusion on the F scale (only item 75 now appears on the F scale), as will be made clear in the next section of this chapter. One other trend is also noteworthy in studies of the item characteristics of the L scale: few adults omit answering these items. This is not true, however, of college males. For perhaps the same reasons suggested above concerning their failure to answer defensively on some of these items, college men also seem to find many of these items difficult or impossible to answer in either direction. It is quite likely that the patterns of responsibilities and involvements are sufficiently different for students who are still single, not yet legally able in most states to participate fully in citizenship, and not yet working at their professional careers from what they are for married men and women in this country to generate important differences in the frame of reference with which they approach a test like the MMPI. Among the items of the L scale can be found many aspects of behavior which have a bearing upon experiences or life patterns of the post-adolescent in our culture quite different from the way such behavior affects the involvements, concerns, and problems faced by mature adults.

L-Scale Elevation and Profile Characteristics. Some of the pervasive effects of the test-taking attitude that is embodied in the L scale can be demonstrated by tabulating certain of the characteristics of the clinical profile at each score level on L. In Table 4-2, for example, are shown the relationships between elevation on L and the absolute number of scales in the clinical profile which reach or exceed a T-score value of 70 (i.e., the number of primed scales in the profile code) among a sample of patients that was collected by Hathaway and Meehl (1951a) and published in coded form as *An Atlas for the Clinical Use of the MMPI.* Since the early Hathaway coding system was used to report these profile patterns, only eight of the clinical scales were included in the codes of the *Atlas.* The number of primed scales, therefore, ranged from zero to eight. Although high scores on L are quite rare and profiles with large numbers of primed scales are also rare, there is evidence with-

Table 4-2. The Relation between L-Scale Value and Number of Clinical Scales Exceeding a T-Score Level of 70 in Codes from the *Atlas*, as Shown by the Number of Codes with Each Combination of Characteristics

L Raw Score	Number of Scales over 70									
	0	1	2	3	4	5	6	7	8	Total
15	2									2
14	1									1
13	1	1								2
12	6	1	1	2		1				11
11	6	4	3	2	2	2				19
10	6	3	3	5	4	3	1			25
9	14	9	7	3	3	7	4	3		50
8	15	11	7	21	6	7	4	7		78
7	28	15	17	26	11	12	9	8	1	127
6	19	27	29	15	9	11	6	6	0	122
5	48	28	30	27	17	13	15	6	3	187
4	40	46	25	33	23	24	11	12	2	216
3	41	46	26	18	18	22	17	11	5	204
2	30	31	13	11	25	26	20	11	3	170
1	18	11	13	10	12	9	6	6	4	89
0	5	3	3	3	1	4	3	2		24
Total	280	236	177	176	131	141	96	72	18	1,327

SOURCE: Hathaway and Meehl (1951a).

in the table of a special dearth of higher ranging profiles (those which have a majority of their scale values above a T score of 70) in records with very high L scores. As noted by Marks and Seeman (1963), the number of profiles with any primed scale in it drops off appreciably at and beyond a raw-score value on L of 9 or a T-score value of 66.

This suppressive effect of L on profile elevation is not restricted to MMPI records obtained from adult psychiatric cases, as is shown in Table 4-3. In this table is presented an identical tabulation of the relationships between L scores and number of primed scales in profiles obtained from adolescent Minnesota schoolchildren and published by Hathaway and Monachesi (1961) as *An Atlas of Juvenile MMPI Profiles*, familiarly called the *Juvenile Atlas*. In this second collection of MMPI codes, the case selection was carried out on a somewhat different basis. A deliberate effort was made to include among the 1088 boys and girls chosen "several representatives of every code type that [could] be encountered" (Hathaway and Monachesi, 1961, p. vi) among the 11,000 or so completed ninth-grade records available to them. Among these codes, too, the higher the L-scale elevations in the MMPI, the lower the overall elevation of the clinical profile tends to be. A similar discontinuity about a raw score of 9 on L can also be seen.

A second way of demonstrating this effect of L on the clinical profile is presented in Table 4-4. At each score level on L the codes were separated into subgroups on the basis of the highest scale value in the profile (scale 1, 2, etc.) and each of these subgroups was further divided into primed and non-primed codes. Thus, at a raw-score level of 12 on L there were four cases in the *Atlas* that had scale 1 (Hs) as the highest score; in two of these four re-

Table 4-3. The Relation between L-Scale Value and Number of Clinical Scales Exceeding a T-Score Level of 70 in Codes from the *Juvenile Atlas,* as Shown by the Number of Codes with Each Combination of Characteristics

L Raw Score	Number of Scales over 70									Total
	0	1	2	3	4	5	6	7	8	
15										0
14	1									1
13	2			1						3
12										0
11	2	1								3
10	2	1								3
9	14	6	5	2	1					28
8	28	8	3		1	2				42
7	38	17	11	2	1	1	2			72
6	53	26	11	3	2	5	2	1		103
5	81	35	18	5	3	4	2			148
4	98	42	15	1	3				1	160
3	115	56	17	7	7	2	2	2		208
2	81	41	15	6	3	2	1	1		150
1	50	37	21	3	3	3	2			119
0	18	11	14	2	3					48
Total	583	281	130	32	27	19	11	4	1	1,088

SOURCE: Hathaway and Monachesi (1961).

cords the value of scale 1 reached or exceeded a T score of 70 while the other two had values below the primed level. In the lower half of Table 4-4, the frequencies of these various high-point elevations (primed and nonprimed) are grouped into three score ranges on L; the percentages of records at each level with each high-point code are also given. Two general trends are particularly noteworthy. At the higher levels of L, there is a shift from primed to nonprimed codes, showing the same trend noted in Table 4-2 within each high-point subgroup. Even more important, perhaps, the relative frequency of codes with high points on the lower numbered scales (scales 1, 2, 3, and 4) tends to rise with score elevations on L while the relative frequencies of the higher numbered scales (scales 6, 7, 8, and 9) falls off. A similar point has been documented by Marks and Seeman (1963) in a further analysis of these data. The data from the *Juvenile Atlas* that are plotted in Table 4-5 lend further support to this relationship between L and clinical-scale configuration. In these records, too, there are data on scales 5 and 0 which were not always reported for the adults in the original *Atlas*. These two scales do not show this general shift in relative frequencies over levels on the L scale. As will be made clearer in the discussions in Part Three of this volume, L-scale elevations accompany neurotic configurations on the clinical profile but are relatively absent among records with psychotic configurations.

F Scale

The third validity indicator routinely plotted on the standard MMPI profile sheet is the F scale. This scale has variously been designated as the frequency (or infrequency) scale, the confusión scale, and sometimes merely as

Table 4-4. The Relation of High Point and Elevation to L-Scale Value in Codes from the *Atlas*, as Shown by the Number of Codes with Each Combination of High Point (Primed and Unprimed) and Raw L Score

L Raw Score	High Point and Elevation of Code																No High Point	Total	
	1′	′1	2′	′2	3′	′3	4′	′4	6′	′6	7′	′7	8′	′8	9′	′9		Primed	Unprimed
15				1				1		1									3
14												1							1
13						1								1	1			1	2
12	2	2	1	1	3	2		3						1	1			7	9
11	5	1	2	1	6	2	2		1					1			1	16	6
10	5		5	2	4	1	3	2	1	2			1	1	1			20	8
9	7	1	12	2	6	1	7	8	2	3	1		2		3		1	40	16
8	14	3	20	3	9	4	9	6	3	1	6		8	1	3	3		72	21
7	18	6	35	5	10	5	12	11	5	2	8	5	12	2	2	3		102	39
6	19	2	42	3	15	5	16	3	6	5	5	2	5	4	11	6	2	119	32
5	15	5	48	10	19	8	31	13	13	5	12	1	19	5	9	5	3	166	55
4	17	1	63	8	19	6	34	17	9	7	19	5	25	8	16	9	2	202	63
3	10	5	48	15	23	6	17	9	11	5	19	6	23	5	30	6	1	181	58
2	8	1	43	8	10	5	25	10	8	5	24	2	35	3	17	7	1	170	42
1	4	2	12	2	3	5	12	6	10	1	9	5	28	1	12	2		90	24
0	1		2				1	3			3	1	10		4	1		21	5
7–15																			
No.	51	13	75	15	38	16	33	31	12	9	15	6	23	7	11	6	2	258	105
%	17.6		24.8		14.9		17.6		5.8		5.8		8.3		4.7		.6	71.1	28.9
4–6																			
No.	51	8	153	21	53	19	81	33	28	17	36	8	49	17	36	20	7	487	150
%	9.3		27.3		11.3		17.9		7.1		6.9		10.4		8.8		1.1	76.5	23.5
0–3																			
No.	23	8	105	25	36	16	55	28	29	11	55	14	96	9	63	16	2	462	129
%	5.2		22.0		8.8		14.0		6.8		11.7		17.8		13.4		.3	78.2	21.8
Total																			
No.	125	29	333	61	127	51	169	92	69	37	106	28	168	33	110	42	11	1,207	384
%	9.7		24.8		11.2		16.4		6.7		8.4		12.6		9.6		.7	75.9	24.1

SOURCE: Hathaway and Meehl (1951a).

the validity scale. It was designed to detect unusual responding or atypical ways of answering the test items. Recent research stemming from the deviation hypothesis of Berg (see the discussion later in this chapter) and related lines of investigation of deviant test behavior have confirmed the presence of many different psychological factors leading to unusual modes of item endorsement. The early insights of Hathaway and McKinley into the diverse sources of invalidity of inventory scores have largely been borne out. These studies have also helped to clarify the many different personological implications of high scores on the F scale.

Hathaway and McKinley chose the sixty-four items making up the F scale simply on the basis of the skewed distribution of their endorsements by men and women in the Minnesota normative samples: those items which no more than 10 percent of these adult subjects (and often less than 5 percent) answered in a particular direction. A significant answer to these items is an endorsement in the infrequent direction. With the exception of responses to item 112, there is an extreme consistency among the Minnesota normative adults in the beliefs, attitudes, feelings, and experiences expressed in these items. Generally, the content is unambiguous in its reference and pertinence (Harris and Baxter, 1965). As can be seen in the F items listed in Table 4-6, the content is also extremely diverse, ranging from bizarre sensations, strange thoughts, and peculiar experiences to feelings of alienation and isolation from family members, from others, or from social institutions, or to atypical attitudes toward laws, religion, or authority and to a number of unlikely or

Table 4-5. The Relation of High Point and Elevation to L-Scale Value in Codes from the *Juvenile Atlas*, as Shown by the Number of Codes with Each Combination of High Point (Primed and Unprimed) and Raw L Score

L Raw Score	High Point and Elevation of Code																				No High Point	Total	
	1′	′1	2′	′2	3′	′3	4′	′4	5′	′5	6′	′6	7′	′7	8′	′8	9′	′9	0′	′0		Primed	Unprimed
15																							
14																				1			1
13						2	1															1	2
12																							
11							1	1		1												1	2
10								1			1							1				1	2
9	1	1	1	1	2	2	3	3	1	4					5	1	1	2				14	14
8	2	1	1	3	1	3	2	6	1	4		3	1	1	3		3	2		3	2	14	28
7	4	1	4	2	2	9	5	1	4	6	4	1		7	9	3	2	2		3	3	34	38
6	2	1	5	7	2	7	12	10	4	4	3	4	3	2	11	6	5	5	2	6	2	49	54
5	4	3	6	5	3	12	9	11	5	8	8	6	4	8	15	5	11	4	1	16	4	66	82
4		3	3	6	3	7	12	15	6	10	2	11	4	7	12	6	12	10	8	14	9	62	98
3		2	6	8	2	10	21	17	6	11	13	11	8	16	14	13	17	6	5	16	6	92	116
2	3	2	3			8	8	6	4	7	2	10	4	12	21	9	21	10	6	7	7	72	78
1	2		3	3	1	1	9	8	4	4	2	4	5	5	16	6	24	8	3	6	5	69	50
0	2	1		1			3	2	3	2	4		1	2	10	2	6	4	1	1	3	30	18
7–15																							
No.	7	3	6	6	5	16	12	12	6	15	5	4	1	8	17	4	6	7	0	7	5	65	87
%	6.6		7.9		13.8		15.8		13.8		5.9		5.9		13.8		8.6		4.6		3.3	42.8	57.2
4–6																							
No.	6	7	14	18	8	26	33	36	15	22	13	21	11	17	38	17	28	19	11	36	15	177	234
%	3.2		7.8		8.3		16.8		9.0		8.3		6.8		13.4		11.4		11.4		3.6	43.1	56.9
0–3																							
No.	7	5	12	12	3	19	41	33	17	24	21	25	18	35	61	30	68	28	15	30	21	263	262
%	2.3		4.6		4.2		14.1		7.8		8.7		10.1		17.3		18.3		8.6		4.0	50.1	49.9
Total																							
No.	20	15	32	36	16	61	86	81	38	61	39	50	30	60	116	51	102	54	26	73	41	505	583
%	3.2		6.3		7.1		15.3		9.1		8.2		8.3		15.3		14.3		9.1		3.8	46.4	53.6

SOURCE: Hathaway and Monachesi (1961).

contradictory beliefs, expectations, and self-descriptions. Low scores on this set of items, therefore, signify a general conformity to the response patterns of the standardization population over a wide range of experiential content. Conversely, answering a large number of these items in the scored direction reflects a deviation from the normative group in a number of different content areas (see Comrey, 1958a).

Endorsing any one F-scale item in the deviant direction, of course, may be quite expected and understandable if the item bears upon some special aspect of the person's life or some particular problem that he has encountered. Twenty-one of the F-scale items appear in Grayson's Critical Items List (see Appendix G), a collection of thirty-eight statements which may have some special pathological meaning in a person's life circumstances. Gravitz (1968) has offered additional evidence that these items are rarely answered in the significant direction by men and women in a general normal sample of test subjects. Yet answers to one or a few of these items may validly reflect some important problem in the person's situation to which special attention should be directed (seizures, alcoholism, fugues, temporal lobe tumors, etc.). In the utilization of the F-scale items as a set of rare answers, the clinician should not lose sight of the possibility that one or all of the answers to these items from some test subjects may be quite literally true, clinically relevant, and worthy of special investigation.

Table 4-6. The F Scale: Item Composition, Direction of Scoring, and Overlap with Other Basic Scales

True: F

14. I have diarrhea once a month or more.
31. I have nightmares every few nights.
34. I have a cough most of the time.
42. When I am with people I am bothered by hearing very queer things.
49. It would be better if almost all laws were thrown away.
50. My soul sometimes leaves my body.
53. A minister can cure disease by praying and putting his hand on your head.
56. As a youngster I was suspended from school one or more times for cutting up.
66. I see things or animals or people around me that others do not see.
85. Sometimes I am strongly attracted by the personal articles of others such as shoes, gloves, etc., so that I want to handle or steal them though I have no use for them.
139. Sometimes I feel as if I must injure either myself or someone else.
146. I have the wanderlust and am never happy unless I am roaming or traveling about.
184. I commonly hear voices without knowing where they come from.
197. Someone has been trying to rob me.
200. There are persons who are trying to steal my thoughts and ideas.
205. At times it has been impossible for me to keep from stealing or shoplifting something.
206. I am very religious (more than most people).
209. I believe my sins are unpardonable.
211. I can sleep during the day but not at night.
218. It does not bother me particularly to see animals suffer.
227. I have been told that I walk during sleep.
246. My neck spots with red often.
247. I have reason for feeling jealous of one or more members of my family.
252. No one cares much what happens to you.
256. The only interesting part of newspapers is the "funnies."
269. I can easily make other people afraid of me, and sometimes do for the fun of it.
286. I am never happier than when alone.

False: F

54. I am liked by most people who know me.
83. Any man who is able and willing to work hard has a good chance of succeeding.
113. I believe in law enforcement.
169. I am not afraid to handle money.

Table 4-6—continued

185. My hearing is apparently as good as that of most people.
199. Children should be taught all the main facts of sex.
257. I usually expect to succeed in things I do.
258. I believe there is a God.

False: LF

75. I get angry sometimes.

False: KF2

272. At times I am all full of energy.

True: F123

23 (288). I am troubled by attacks of nausea and vomiting.

True: F4

42. My family does not like the work I have chosen (or the work I intend to choose for my life work).
215. I have used alcohol excessively.
245. My parents and family find more fault with me than they should.

True: F468

35 (331). If people had not had it in for me I would have been much more successful.

False: F48

20 (310). My sex life is satisfactory.

False: F5

112. I frequently find it necessary to stand up for what I think is right.
115. I believe in a life hereafter.

True: F6

27. Evil spirits possess me at times.
123. I believe I am being followed.
151. Someone has been trying to poison me.
275. Someone has control over my mind.
293. Someone has been trying to influence my mind.

False: F7

164. I like to study and read about things that I am working at.

True: F68

121. I believe I am being plotted against.
202. I believe I am a condemned person.
291. At one or more times in my life I felt that someone was making me do things by hypnotizing me.

True: F8

40. Most of the time I would rather sit and daydream than to do anything else.
168. There is something wrong with my mind.
210. Everything tastes the same.

False: F8

17. My father was a good man.
65. I loved my father.
177. My mother was a good woman.
196. I like to visit places where I have never been before.
220. I loved my mother.
276. I enjoy children.

True: F89

156. I have had periods in which I carried on activities without knowing later what I had been doing.

The utility of the F scale as a validity sign lies in the number of factors which may be operating in a given test setting that can lead to both unusual clinical-scale scores and high frequencies of endorsement of the items on the F scale. As a consequence, sound MMPI interpretation requires that F-scale elevations be examined first for their implications about the acceptability of each test protocol before examining any additional implications that they may possess for the clinical status or personological characteristics of the test subject. This admonition is particularly important in clinical settings in which a wide range of clients are served and when usual procedures require that the MMPI be used to get preliminary synopses of the clients before very much else is known about them. The more that is already known about the current status of a given client, the more the interpretation of F-scale elevations can shift from protocol validity to personological concerns.

A large number of factors may interfere with a test subject's attention and careful response to the individual items on a personality questionnaire. He may be unable to see the items clearly enough to read them accurately either because he has serious limitations in his visual acuity or because the physical conditions in the work area provided are inadequate for sustained reading and marking (lighting, type format and printing of the booklet or answer sheet, glare, noise, or distractions). Some of these problems, which were discussed in Part One of this volume, may seriously affect the subject's test performance. In particular, these factors may lead to an elevation of the F score because the subject is not perceiving the test items with sufficient clarity to interpret them in the way that he otherwise would.

Even if his perceptions of the test items are clear and unambiguous, however, it is possible that a test subject may not be able to read or comprehend the content of the statements to the degree necessary to answer them meaningfully. Subjects with marginal reading skills, persons falling within the borderline or mentally deficient intellective ranges, or those who stopped at the elementary school level in their education (sixth grade or below) may not understand some of the MMPI statements. Thus, they may mark them on the basis of inadequate grasp of what they may be saying about themselves or what attitudes they are actually endorsing. Since a number of the more difficult items in the MMPI appear in the F scale (see Costa, London, and Levita, 1963), a subject's marginal reading proficiency is particularly likely to result in an elevation of his score on this scale.

Research has also indicated that an adequate level of reading comprehension, although necessary, may not be sufficient for the proper interpretation of MMPI test items. A highly literate subject with a bilingual background in which English was acquired as his second language may be able to read these statements without necessarily having the requisite familiarity with the idioms or enough understanding of the emotional connotations of the test phrases or modifiers to interpret the statements in the same way that the normative subjects did. An important part of interpreting test items seems to be an ability to share the common cultural framework of the derivational samples studied by the test authors. Many subjects lacking this essential experiential core will show their atypical attributions and self-labeling by endorsing F-scale items in an unusual way; some persons, however, do not seem to be identified in this way. That is, although their verbal response patterns are sufficiently deviant to affect scores on other scales in the test, they do not endorse enough F-scale items to reveal this special orientation to the MMPI. Special validity checks are needed for this purpose. (See the discussion of moderator scales below.)

Another source of difficulty in answering test items is the pervasive personality disorganization stemming from acute psychotic reactions. Although patients with this problem may generally have been able to read and interpret such test statements before their behavioral disruption and may regain such competencies after some degree of remission, during the acute phase they are so out of contact with stimuli in their surroundings that the instructions are misunderstood, the statements are meaningless, or the answer sheets so confusing to them that they are unable to organize their answers into a scorable protocol. As a result they may confuse Trues and Falses, double-mark items, lose their place and mark wrong items, or otherwise produce an unscorable test record. As noted in Part One, these confused patients may be able to manage a card form of the MMPI or may even find a tape-recorded administration within their competencies. Patients suffering from toxic reactions, those in heavily drugged states or in the acute stages of an undifferentiated schizophrenic reaction, a hypermanic or delirious manic reaction, or a markedly depressed reaction, or those who are tested shortly after shock treatments may be unable to give interpretable test records. High scores on the F scale may document their inability to discern the content or meaning of the test items and the fact that they were not responding differentially to the statements in the test. It is noteworthy that their ability to respond to the MMPI items may be regained well before they are able to show effective interpersonal skills or sufficient self-management to herald a clear move toward clinical remission. Many of these patients are able to give valid MMPI sortings while still socially unresponsive and withdrawn or while their spontaneous speech may still be incoherent and inarticulate. With a test like the MMPI, these gross behavioral indicators may not be dependable guides to their testability.

Another way in which the clinical status of the subject may generate difficulties in the testing situation is through the introduction of special test-taking orientations or sets which are at variance with the general test instructions. Marks and Seeman (1963), for example, have documented how a patient may impose special meanings on the test session and employ the MMPI, not as an opportunity for careful self-description of this current situation and outlook, but rather as a cry for help or pleading for special attention. This is particularly likely in a screening situation in which the patient may come to feel that unless he dramatizes his condition he will not be given appropriate attention. Then, too, when he is being considered for discharge, the patient may not otherwise be free to indicate how unready he feels to make this decision. The resulting profile may be high-ranging and almost uniformly grossly elevated, with a markedly elevated F scale as well. There may be other response sets operating in a comparable way during the test, such as answering everything True, or False, or some cyclical alternations of these answers, giving a socially unfavorable or socially deviant response to every item, acquiescing to every suggested symptom or difficulty, or giving a highly stereotyped picture of social competence and effectiveness. Most of these test-taking approaches generate recognizable patterns of scale scores, often involving the scores on the F scale. (See Fox, 1964.) They will be discussed more systematically in the next part of this chapter.

One other general difficulty in obtaining a valid and usable test record from a subject may also appear as an elevation on the F scale. Persons who approach the test with hostility, resentment, or only superficial compliance with the task may be so careless that they make frequent clerical errors in placing their cards or entering their marks on an answer sheet. Since the F scale is long and the items extend well through the test, poor cooperation and inattention may be detected by a tendency to mark the F-scale items in the deviant direction. In the card form, it should also be noted, some of the clerical work in generating the test protocol is taken over by the test administrator or test scorer. Clerical errors on the part of the scorer thus may distort the test record, and F-scale elevations may reflect this kind of error as well (e.g., when the True cards and the False cards are inadvertently reversed). Not all these instances, however, may be fully identifiable by dramatic F-scale elevations. Sometimes the subject begins the test with reasonable attention and adequate care, only to become bored and distractible after he is well into the task (see Harris and Baxter, 1965). If the booklet form is used, one way to check on this possibility is to examine the proportion of F-scale items marked deviantly on the first forty (among the first two hundred items in the booklet) and the last twenty-four (those appearing in the next one hundred items). There are also three items on the F scale that are repeated (early as 20, 23, and 35 and later as 310, 288, and 331); these items may be inspected to see whether the subject endorsed them the same way on each occasion. In addition, it would be even more helpful to examine all the repeated items in the test (see Appendix C and the TR index later in this chapter) as a check on this source of error, rather than restricting attention merely to that subset in the F scale alone.

F-Scale Elevation and Profile Characteristics. When the cases from the *Atlas* and the *Juvenile Atlas* are plotted against elevation on the F scale (as explained above in the discussion on L), it is clear that the F scale bears a different relationship to MMPI profile pattern and elevation from what was true for L. In Table 4-7 are shown the number of records at each F-scale level with various numbers of primed scales from the Hathaway and Meehl *Atlas* (1951a) (adult psychiatric cases), while Table 4-8 presents the same data from the adolescent cases in the *Juvenile Atlas* of Hathaway and Monachesi (1961). As noted by Marks and Seeman (1963), profile elevations in cases from a psychiatric setting are significantly positively related to score levels on F. Interestingly, the same strong trend is obvious in the MMPI profiles from the adolescents as well.

The relationship between F-score elevation and the particular clinical scales which appear most prominently in the clinical profile is shown in Table 4-9 for the adult psychiatric cases and Table 4-10 for the adolescents. On most of the scales, higher F scores are accompanied by a shift from nonprimed leading scores to primed scores. Among the various clinical scales, high points on scales 1, 2, 3, 4, 7, and 9 become relatively less frequent as the F score rises, while codes with peak scores on scales 6 and 8 become much more frequent relative to their general occurrence in the *Atlas* sample. In the *Juvenile Atlas* sample, these trends are not quite so consistent (note the inversion of the trend on scale 4 peaks) but seem to follow this pattern in a general way. Data on scales 5 and 0 that are available on the adolescents indicate that while peaks on scale 5 appear to follow the trend of the lower code-number scales, those on scale 0 are not strongly influenced by F-scale level.

Table 4-7. The Relation between F-Scale Value and Number of Clinical Scales Exceeding a T-Score Level of 70 in Codes from the *Atlas*, as Shown by the Number of Codes with Each Combination of Characteristics

F Raw Score	Number of Scales over 70									
	0	1	2	3	4	5	6	7	8	Total
25+				1		1	1	1		4
24		1		1		1				3
23		1		1			1	1		4
22			1				1			2
21					2			1	2	5
20			1	1		1			1	4
19			1	1	2	3	3	1		11
18				1	1	1	1	3	2	9
17			1		1	3	4		1	10
16		1		2			3		1	7
15	1	1	3	2	5	5	4	5		26
14		1	3	1	2	6	2	3		18
13	4	2	3	6	5	6	9	6	2	43
12	2	4		8	6	6	5	4		35
11	4		3	4	12	7	7	4	1	42
10	2	9	9	6	7	13	5	5	2	58
9	2	8	6	10	2	10	4	11	1	54
8	11	16	15	15	9	18	9	8	2	103
7	6	18	13	9	12	13	10	6	1	88
6	16	27	15	16	13	14	7	4		112
5	26	24	19	22	12	16	9	5	1	134
4	33	35	24	23	19	8	1	2	1	146
3	54	31	20	27	6	5	4	1		148
2	60	32	21	12	11	3	3	1		143
1	41	19	14	3	3		2			82
0	18	6	5	4	1	1	1			36
Total	280	236	177	176	131	141	96	72	18	1,327

SOURCE: Hathaway and Meehl (1951a).

K Scale

While the three validity indices discussed previously were all introduced as a set at the time the MMPI was published, a fourth measure, the K scale, was added later after experience with the initial complement of validity checks in a number of different clinical settings. This experience indicated that the existing validity indicators (?, L, and F) operated primarily to detect gross instances of protocol invalidation while permitting some important kinds of test distortion to go unrecognized. In addition to this growing body of clinical experience with the MMPI, a number of empirical studies of test faking and test slanting had also been conducted at Minnesota and elsewhere (see the discussions in Volume II) which served to highlight both the strengths and the weaknesses of the available validity measures. The research leading to the development of the K scale was devoted to increasing the sensitivity of the validity indices on the test, to identifying the impact of more subtle score-enhancing or score-diminishing factors, and to providing a means of statistically correcting the values of the clinical scales themselves to offset the effects of these factors on the clinical profile.

Table 4-8. The Relation between F-Scale Value and Number of Clinical Scales Exceeding a T-Score Level of 70 in Codes from the *Juvenile Atlas,* as Shown by the Number of Codes with Each Combination of Characteristics

F Raw Score	Number of Scales over 70									
	0	1	2	3	4	5	6	7	8	Total
25+					2	2	4			8
24					1	1				2
23					1			1		2
22					1	2	1			4
21	1	1						1		3
20		1	1			1				3
19							1			1
18			2			2				4
17				1		1				2
16	1	1	3	1		2				8
15	1	4	6	1	2	2	1	1	1	19
14		3	4		3					10
13		1	5	1	1		1			9
12	4	7	10	3	2	1				27
11	4	8	11	3	1	2	1			30
10	11	16	13	4	1		2	1		48
9	16	9	16	5	3					49
8	21	20	4	1	2	1				49
7	40	29	11	4	2	1				87
6	39	39	13	1	3	1				96
5	78	46	14	3	1					142
4	75	23	5	2						105
3	90	27	6	2	1					126
2	102	24	3							129
1	72	15	1							88
0	28	7	2							37
Total	583	281	130	32	27	19	11	4	1	1,088

SOURCE: Hathaway and Monachesi (1961).

The scheme below shows the two kinds of test misses with which the test authors were concerned in the clinical application of the MMPI in various diagnostic settings. Taking the profile as a whole, the scores can be considered to show sufficient elevation (on one or more component scales) to determine that the individual is showing significant psychopathology or the profile can be considered to be within normal limits. If this dichotomy of a set of profiles into normal and abnormal patterns is then evaluated against nontest evidence of the actual clinical status of each person tested, that is, currently demonstrating significant psychopathology or presently functioning in a normal way, the fourfold classification shown is generated. The general intention

	Clinical Status	
MMPI Profile	*Normal*	*Abnormal*
Abnormal	False Positive	True Positive
Normal	True Negative	False Negative

in the derivation and application of the K scale was to minimize both kinds of test misses, false-negative and false-positive test records, without reducing the number of either kind of test hits, true positives and true negatives. The

Table 4-9. The Relation of High Point and Elevation to F-Scale Value in Codes from the *Atlas*, as Shown by the Number of Codes with Each Combination of High Point (Primed and Unprimed) and Raw F Score

F Raw Score	High Point and Elevation of Code																No High Point	Total	
	1′	′1	2′	′2	3′	′3	4′	′4	6′	′6	7′	′7	8′	′8	9′	′9		Primed	Unprimed
25+									1				3					4	
24					1				2									3	
23													3		1			4	
22									1				1					2	
21													5					5	
20									1				4					5	
19			2				2		1				6		1			12	
18	1		1				1		2		1		5					11	
17	2		2				1		1				6		1			13	
16			2				1				1		4		2			10	
15			6		1		2	1	4		3		12		3			31	1
14			1						3		3		11		5			23	
13	4	1	7			1	2		2	1	3		19	2	5			42	5
12	2	1	12		2		5		5		2		7	1	1			36	2
11	2		12				9	2	5		4		13	2	4	2		49	6
10	2		20	1	2		12	1	5	1	4		18	1	4			67	4
9	5		17	1	7		6		5		11		7	1	4			62	2
8	9	1	29		4		14	5	12	2	11	1	14	5	10	2		103	16
7	6		29	2	9	1	18	2	2		12		9	1	10	1		95	7
6	11		39	3	12	1	20	7	4	3	4	3	5	3	11	2	3	106	25
5	20	2	34	4	16	5	21	7	3	6	17	5	6	3	12	4	1	129	37
4	14	6	37	10	21	3	19	13	3	6	13	5	3	2	19	5	1	129	51
3	19	7	33	16	21	14	13	15	2	5	9	3	4	5	5	12		106	77
2	15	4	27	9	16	15	19	18	3	7	5	8	2	3	8	8	3	95	75
1	6	4	18	13	7	5	3	14	1	5	2	3	1	2	4	4	2	42	52
0	7	3	5	2	8	6	1	7	1	1	1			2		2	1	23	24
17–25+																			
No.	3	0	5	0	1	0	4	0	9	0	1	0	33	0	3	0	0	59	0
%	5.1		8.5		1.7		6.8		15.3		1.7		55.9		5.1		0.0	100.0	0.0
10–16																			
No.	10	2	60	1	5	1	31	4	24	2	20	0	84	6	24	2	0	258	18
%	4.3		22.1		2.2		12.9		9.4		7.2		32.6		9.4		0.0	93.5	6.5
5–9																			
No.	51	3	148	10	48	7	79	21	26	11	55	9	41	13	47	9	4	495	87
%	9.3		27.1		9.4		17.2		6.4		11.0		9.3		9.6		0.7	85.0	15.0
0–4																			
No.	61	24	120	50	73	43	55	67	10	24	30	19	10	14	36	31	7	395	279
%	12.6		25.2		17.2		18.1		5.0		7.3		3.6		9.9		1.0	58.6	41.4
Total																			
No.	125	29	333	61	127	51	169	92	69	37	106	28	168	33	110	42	11	1,207	384
%	9.7		24.8		11.2		16.4		6.7		8.4		12.6		9.6		0.7	75.9	24.1

SOURCE: Hathaway and Meehl (1951a).

approach involved defining the hits and misses in terms of the whole profile (rather than particular diagnostic subgroups identified by separate scales) and searching for a general corrective factor or measure. This kind of variable has since been termed a suppressor factor (Meehl and Hathaway, 1946).

Table 4-10. The Relation of High Point and Elevation to F-Scale Value in Codes from the *Juvenile Atlas,* as Shown by the Number of Codes with Each Combination of High Point (Primed and Unprimed) and Raw F Score

F Raw Score	High Point and Elevation of Code: 1′	′1	2′	′2	3′	′3	4′	′4	5′	′5	6′	′6	7′	′7	8′	′8	9′	′9	0′	′0	No High Point	Total: Primed	Total: Unprimed
25+							1								7							8	
24..															2							2	
23..															2							2	
22..															4							4	
21..								1			1				1							2	1
20..									1						1		1					3	
19..															1							1	
18..							2								2							4	
17..															2							2	
16..											2	1			3		2					7	1
15..	2		3				1				1				11	1						18	1
14..	2		1								1				6							10	
13..							1		1		2				3		1		1			9	
12..			1				5				2	1	1	1	12	1	2	1				23	4
11..	1		2	1			4		1		2	1			11	1	4	1	1			26	4
10..	1		4				2		1		3	1	3	2	10	1	11	1	2	5	1	37	11
9..	2		2			2	5	3	2	1	1	1	2	2	10	2	8	3	1	2		33	16
8..	2	1	1	5		1	4	1	1	1	3	1	3	2	7	3	5	4	2	2		28	21
7..	3	2	3	3	3	1	11	3	2	6	4	3	3	6	6	4	11	2	1	9	1	47	40
6..	2	4	2		2	1	12	5	5	4	7	5	5	4	6	2	10	4	6	8	2	57	39
5..	2	2	4	2	4	5	13	5	8	7	7	9	5	13	2	8	15	7	4	16	4	64	78
4..	1	1	3	9	2	4	6	7	1	12		10	2	2	3	7	8	7	4	9	7	30	75
3..	1	4	2	5	4	12	8	18	3	8	3	6	2	9		7	11	8	2	11	2	36	90
2..		1	3	6	1	16	5	22	4	10		7	2	12	2	6	10	7		5	10	27	102
1..	1			3		11	5	14	4	8		3	1	5	1	7	3	6	1	6	9	16	72
0..			1	2		8	1	2	4	4		1	1	2	1	1		3	1		5	9	28
17–25+																							
No.							3	1	1		1				22		1					28	1
%							13.8		3.4		3.4				75.9		3.4					96.6	3.4
10–16																							
No.	6		11	1			13		3		13	4	4	3	56	4	20	3	4	5	1	130	21
%	4.0		7.9				8.6		2.0		11.3		4.6		39.7		15.2		6.0		.7	86.1	13.9
5–9																							
No.	11	9	12	10	9	10	45	17	18	19	22	19	18	27	31	19	49	20	14	37	7	229	194
%	4.7		5.2		4.5		14.7		8.7		9.7		10.6		11.8		16.3		12.1		1.7	54.1	45.9
0–4																							
No.	3	6	9	25	7	51	25	63	16	42	3	27	8	30	7	28	32	31	8	31	33	118	367
%	1.9		7.0		12.0		18.1		12.0		6.2		7.8		7.2		13.0		8.0		6.8	24.3	75.7
Total																							
No.	20	15	32	36	16	61	86	81	38	61	39	50	30	60	116	51	102	54	26	73	41	505	583
%	3.2		6.3		7.1		15.3		9.1		8.2		8.3		15.3		14.3		9.1		3.8	46.4	53.6

SOURCE: Hathaway and Monachesi (1961).

As the scheme suggests, this search could proceed in several ways. For example, sets of significantly elevated MMPI profiles could be collected from known patients and known normals and contrasted to try to isolate some indicator of when such a profile elevation is suspect and when it is bona fide. This approach was used by Meehl (1945) in deriving the N scale (see the discussion below), which was one of the forerunners of the K scale. The work on the N scale was encouraging, but it seemed to identify only certain kinds of false positives (i.e., those with misleading elevations on the neurotic triad but not those with psychotic tetrad elevations). In contrast to the N-scale approach, work on the K scale began with groups of *normal* records drawn from known abnormals and presumed normals (some of the Minnesota normative cases). Equal numbers of cases of each sex were used and efforts were made to exclude sex differences in the resulting scale. As it turned out, the development of the K-suppressor scale involved two stages in its derivation.

Twenty-five male and twenty-five female records from patients in an inpatient psychiatric setting were found in which the profile was within normal limits (no score over 70) and there was evidence of test-taking defensiveness (an L score of at least 60). Psychiatric evaluations of these fifty men and women indicated that they were manifesting a variety of different disorders, primarily behavioral or characterological problems (like alcoholism) rather than neurotic or psychotic disorders. Judging by their clinical status they should show deviant profiles on the test but from the nature of their problems it might not be surprising if they were in fact quite defensive about them in such a situation. The elevations on the L scale added credence to the belief that they had failed to get appropriately elevated MMPI profiles because of a general defensiveness in describing themselves.

No additional efforts were made to match in either pattern or elevation the profiles of these false-negative psychiatric cases with normal subjects' profiles. Obviously, with profiles showing variations only within normal limits from either group, both the range and the configurational variations were quite restricted. In addition, as subsequent discussions of the clinical-scale configurations will make clear, it should be noted that the most frequently occurring patterns on the MMPI in samples of normals are those involving characterological rather than neurotic or psychotic patternings. Therefore, except for the added stipulation in the false-negative sample that the L scale be appreciably elevated, in both elevation and patterning the true-negative and false-negative cases used to derive the K scale were probably quite comparable.

Systematic item analyses within each sex group led to the identification of twenty-two items common to both sexes which separated the true- and false-negative profiles in their item endorsements by at least 30 percent. Any item already on the L scale was excluded from this set. This set of items was designated L_6 and is shown (without the asterisks) in Table 4-11. The items were scored in such a way that higher scores indicated greater defensiveness and greater likelihood that a normal test record was the product of test slanting rather than conscientious self-evaluation and self-description.

Inspection of the items making up L_6 shows that the content is quite heterogeneous, covering descriptions of one's mental health, stability and con-

Table 4-11. The K Scale: Item Composition, Direction of Scoring, and Overlap with Other Basic Scales

False: (K)

374. At periods my mind seems to work more slowly than usual.

397. I have sometimes felt that difficulties were piling up so high that I could not overcome them.

False: K

406. I have often met people who were supposed to be experts who were no better than I.

°461. I find it hard to set aside a task that I have undertaken, even for a short time.

°502. I like to let people know where I stand on things.

False: LK23

°30. At times I feel like swearing.

False: KF2

°272. At times I am all full of energy.

False: (K2)

39. At times I feel like smashing things.

False: (K23)

°160. I have never felt better in my life than I do now.

False: (K235)

89. It takes a lot of argument to convince most people of the truth.

False: K240

296. I have periods in which I feel unusually cheerful without any special reason.

True: 27. False:(K)

142. I certainly feel useless at times.

True: 20. False: (K)

138. Criticism or scolding hurts me terribly.

False: K3

°71. I think a great many people exaggerate their misfortunes in order to gain the sympathy and help of others.

False: (K3)

129. Often I can't understand why I have been so cross and grouchy.

234. I get mad easily and then get over it soon.

False: K34

°170. What others think of me does not bother me.

False: 4. True: (K)

96. I have very few quarrels with members of my family.

False: (K4)

°183. I am against giving money to beggers.

False: K4. True: (59)

134. At times my thoughts have raced ahead faster than I could speak them.

True: 57. False: (K)

217. I frequently find myself worrying about something.

False: (K8)

322. I worry over money and business.

False: (K9)

148. It makes me impatient to have people ask my advice or otherwise interrupt me when I am working on something important.

True: 0. False: (K)

383. People often disappoint me.

398. I often think, "I wish I were a child again."

True: 0. False: (K349)

180. I find it hard to make talk when I meet new people.

267. When in a group of people I have trouble thinking of the right things to talk about.

True: 0. False: (K36)

124. Most people will use somewhat unfair means to gain profit or an advantage rather than to lose it.

True: 0. False: (K49)

171. It makes me uncomfortable to put on a stunt at a party even when others are doing the same sort of things.

True: 0. False: (K6)

316. I think nearly anyone would tell a lie to keep out of trouble.

trol, feelings and expectations about others, and various family relationships. It is interesting that Comrey (1958b) did not find any particular coherence in item intercorrelations of the K scale; even the correction subset (to be discussed below) did not emerge from his factor-analytic plots as a unit. This lack of unity led Comrey to disparage the use of this scale as a test-taking measure. An alternative interpretation is that only a pervasive defensiveness leads to these items of such diversity of content being answered consistently in a defensive (or exhibitionistic) direction. Among a sample of individuals who are dealing with the test in an open and forthright manner, then, there would be little reason to expect that these items would be answered with any uniformity. Thus Comrey's diverse factor loadings could well result.

From the mode of deriving L_6 the expectation would have been that subjects who are defensive would get normal MMPI profiles and high scores on L_6 while normal subjects with appropriately normal test profiles would get low scores on this special defensiveness measure. In their preliminary studies of the characteristics of the L_6 scale, Meehl and Hathaway (1946) found that most normals from the Minnesota derivational sample did not fall at the low end of this scale but rather scored in the middle range, neither very high nor very low. Exploration of the psychological characteristics of low L_6 scorers led to the discovery that the scale was bipolar in its psychological implications. While high scores identified some kinds of defensiveness in answering the MMPI, scores at the opposite end seemed to reveal what Florence Goodenough later described as "a peculiar kind of exhibitionism which takes the form of an urge to display one's troubles and confess one's weaknesses" (1949, p. 408). Subjects answering the test with candor and appropriate degrees of self-disclosure avoid either of these extremes and earn scores in the middle range of L_6. Later studies of response acquiescence have extended our understanding of this process.

These same explorations revealed an additional feature of the L_6 scale which the authors felt to be a serious flaw: low scores not only were found among normal subjects who seemed to be exaggerating their psychopathology (false positives) but were also earned by some psychotic patients, primarily those showing marked depressive or schizophrenic reactions. Since these patients typically got elevated MMPI profiles, they should be considered true positives; it would be misleading to discount their clinical scores on the basis of their simultaneously obtaining very low L_6 scores. In an effort to offset this special problem, Meehl and Hathaway carried out additional item analyses to find a subset of items which would identify this psychoticism trend that was affecting the L_6 scores. Since one kind of low L_6 score seemed to be a tendency to fake "bad" or fake "abnormal" on the test, they reasoned that a good correction for psychoticism would be made up of items that are not affected by deliberate efforts to fake abnormality on the MMPI. Previous work on the faking of abnormal MMPI patterns by ostensibly normal subjects carried out by investigators like Gough (1947), Hunt (1948), and Bird (1948) provided data about which items were likely to be endorsed in a different way when the subject was trying to create a picture of psychopathology and which ones were relatively unaffected by this special test-taking set but were answered about the same way as on regular administrations of the MMPI by these same subjects. For example, within the subset of change items, Gough (1947) had identified those items which do not actually match the way that real patients describe themselves. From them, Gough derived his dissimulation scale, Ds (see the discussion later in this chapter). Within the stable items from these faking studies, Meehl and Hathaway sought the items that differentiate normals and psychotic patients. Eight such items were identified and added to the L_6 scale, the total thirty-item set being designated the K (correction) scale. These items are also listed in Table 4-10, marked with an asterisk. The psychoticism correction subset is scored in such a way that true psychotic subjects get high scores on this scale, bringing their scores back up into the middle ranges on the composite K scale with the nonexaggerating normals and away from the score levels of false-positive subjects. These latter subjects presumably get low scores on the whole K scale because they end up at the low end of L_6 and do not say the really pathological things needed to get a high score on the psychoticism subset. The resulting makeup of the K scale is complex. (It is obvious that some later MMPI investigators carrying out item analyses on the K scale have tended to misunderstand this special "correction" of the correction scale, e.g., Hanley, 1956.)

In deriving L_6, the authors deliberately had to exclude items already identified on the standard L scale from consideration since one of the criteria for case selection for L_6 was a high score on L. One L item was added to the K scale in the second step, however, as part of the correction for psychoticism. On a third of the items, the K scoring is either in the opposite direction from its clinical scoring or unrelated to scoring on any of the other component scales of the basic profile. The majority of items in K, however, also appear in some clinical scale, scored the same way as they are in K. The implications of these overlapping items will be discussed later in the context of the clinical-scale derivations and profile configurations but it can be noted here that a number of efforts to correct individual scales by subsets of correction items have generally led to the identification of kinds of items that are very similar to those that make up the K scale.

Correction of Clinical Scales by K Weights. Although the authors of the K scale suggested that the scores on this new validity indicator be used as the preexisting validity measures had been employed, that is, applied judgmentally in altering clinical inferences to be drawn from the basic profile, they soon advanced a formal psychometric set of procedures to be routinely applied to all MMPI profiles. McKinley, Hathaway, and Meehl (1948) established a means by which explicit corrective weights from the K score were to be added to the raw scores on selected scales in the profile before the determination of their T-score values. In 1947, Hathaway and Meehl brought out a supplement to the test *Manual* incorporating these procedures. The Psychological Corporation subsequently modified its printed profile forms to provide for routine K corrections and integrated the material on K-correction procedures and weights into the later revisions of the *Manual*. As noted in Part One of this volume, to determine T-score values without K corrections for these selected scales (or to use different sets of weights) special tables must be consulted (see Appendix H in this volume). It should be emphasized that it is *not* possible to obtain non-K-corrected T scores simply by using the raw scores without their K-fractional increments in the columns of scores in the regular profile.

Since the K scale was intended to improve the discrimination of normal from abnormal profiles, the crucial range of score variation on any component scale was considered to be about a sigma above and below the 70 T-score value, and at most two sigmas above and below this value (see the discussion of borderline elevations in the next section of this volume). Thus, the region of concern in determining the specific K weights for each scale was defined by McKinley, Hathaway, and Meehl (1948) to be the T scores from 50 to 80. Scores below this range were arbitrarily set at 50 while scores beyond this range were set at 80. This decision was quite consistent with the initial purposes of the K scale but the authors urged others to try alternative ranges, weights, and methods of discrimination for their own areas of application. To date, their decisions have not received the theoretical examination or empirical investigation which they deserve and need. The rationale for the arbitrary limits which they imposed upon their data was a straightforward one: scores below this range are so low that simple statistical correction cannot bring them up to the range of clinical interpretation while scores above this range are so high that no statistical reduction can bring them within normal limits. Since the K weights are in fact applied to the whole array of possible raw-score values, however, and since T-score values are interpreted quite differently within different regions along the whole scale and not merely within this arbitrary "borderline" region, it remains an unresolved question whether the weights suggested by the early Minnesota studies are actually optimal for all routine applications. A second important issue also remains unresolved: are the changes in the profile patterning among the clinical scales introduced by the scale-by-scale corrections of these five scales enhancing or detrimental to the accuracy of clinical inferences and judgments which hinge upon these configurations? On the face of it, the expectation would certainly be that these adjustments to the component scales, each of which enhances the discriminative power of that particular scale, would thereby improve the fit of the total configuration. On the other hand, score variance is being added to several scales, thereby serving to reduce, perhaps, the independent information provided by these component scales and possibly blurring some crucial discriminations. Further comparisons of the patterns of MMPI profiles with and without K corrections together with information about the direct empirical ties that each set can provide to crucial nontest characteristics of test subjects are urgently needed.

A simple cut-and-try method was devised to determine the optimal value of the K weights for each scale in separating criterion cases of neurotic and psychotic reactions from the Minnesota reference normals. No sex differences were maintained in these determinations; the resulting weights are the same for both sex groups. Increments of tenths of the K raw-score value were systematically added to the original raw-score values on each scale earned by the criterion patients and by Minnesota normal adults. New T scores were derived for each and the resulting scores of each group were compared in terms of a differential ratio of what the authors termed the "half sums of squares" remaining after curtailing the distribution to T scores from 50 to 80. The weight which generated the maximal value of this differential ratio over several samples of criterion cases was chosen as the standard weight for that scale. For scales 7 and 8, the whole raw score of value K proved to be best in separating normals from diagnosed obsessive-compulsive neurotic and schizophrenic cases, respectively. On scales 1, 4, and 9, however, fractional values (0.5, 0.4, and 0.2, respectively) were found to be best, larger and smaller fractions of K raw score providing poorer separations between the Minnesota reference group and the criterion cases of hypochondriasis, psychopathic personality, and hypomanic reaction. McKinley, Hathaway, and Meehl (1948) studied the effects of K corrections on scales 2, 3, 5, and 6 but found that any correction at all tended to reduce the discriminations provided by the original scale values. These scales are not corrected in routine application of the MMPI although Heilbrun (1963) has recommended corrections for some of them in college counseling contexts.

McKinley, Hathaway, and Meehl (1948) also provided evidence that upon cross-validation on cases from the same clinical setting the particular clinical scales that they corrected by means of K weights were both statistically and pragmatically improved in their ability to identify designated patients and presumed normals. New mean and standard-deviation values were computed to generate K-corrected T-score values and the clinical and normal groups were found to show significantly less overlapping in their score distributions. Whether this overlapping was evaluated by means of an arbitrary cutting score on the T scale (i.e., 70) or a fixed percentage of normal subjects (e.g., the 95th percentile), it was clear that each K-corrected clinical scale gave better separation between normals and appropriate criterion abnormals than the uncorrected version (see Chapter 6 on the basic clinical scales). Their tabulations showed that this decrease in overlapping of the distributions was sometimes achieved by reducing the number of low scores among the new samples of clinical cases, sometimes by reducing in the Minnesota reference group of normals the number of subjects with elevated scores on that scale, and sometimes by both effects operating simultaneously. These findings and subsequent experience with the K corrections in profiles from various clinical services at the University of Minnesota Hospitals led the authors to recommend that the clinical scales with K corrections be considered the basic versions of those component scales in the inventory. At the same time, they strongly urged MMPI users, whenever possible, to carry out direct comparisons of K-corrected and noncorrected scores in the identification of patients and clients in their own clinical settings and also to try other weighting values of the K scores.

The published research on these efforts to cross-validate K applications and variations on K weighting is scanty and inconclusive. Obviously, many agencies within which the MMPI is used cannot provide ideal criterion information for this kind of cross-validational work: dependable clinical criteria that are completely independent of the test-based information or decisions.

But far too little attention has been paid to these questions in research settings where this kind of investigation could have been carried out many times over in the more than twenty years since the K-scale weights were published.

The available research has been devoted to several related questions concerning the use of K corrections: would it be better to subtract K fractions rather than add them to the raw scores of the clinical scales; do K corrections offset deliberately faked clinical scores; and can K corrections be used to improve the clinical discriminations of some of the other component scales in the MMPI profile not now corrected? Less attention has been paid to the more central question: does a given improvement in the efficacy of each component scale in the profile by means of K corrections yield corresponding improvement in the differential diagnostic accuracy of the patterns appearing among the scales in the total profile?

To date it appears that the suppressor effect of a correction scale like K is not enhanced by changing the algebraic sign given to its weightings. The prime consideration is that the suppressor scale reflect important amounts of the variance in the clinical scale that is not related to the attribute for which the clinical scale was devised. If this relationship holds, then part scores on the suppressor scale can be weighted and combined with the clinical scale in such a way that the resulting distribution of scores will more clearly reflect the proper variations in the attribute which serves as the criterion for that scale. Neither the efforts of Fricke (1956) nor those of Heilbrun (1963) to work out procedures for subtracting K weights from the Hy scale, for example, have yielded appreciable improvement in hit rates for this scale.

Similarly, the few studies devoted to the question of how to offset the effects of deliberate faking in either the positive or negative direction have not indicated that the K-correction weights employed in the standard MMPI profile can serve this function. In an early study of this problem in a clinical setting, Schmidt (1948) asked eleven men with severe psychoneurotic reactions whom he had studied in a military hospital to retake the MMPI as though they were normal healthy people. Under these instructions, their scores shifted appreciably toward the average level of Minnesota normals, especially on scales 1, 2, 3, 4, 7, and 8. When the scores on scales 1, 4, 7, and 8 were K corrected, the shifts on scales 4 and 8 had been effectively offset but those on scale 7 only partially, while those on scale 1 were almost unaffected by the statistical correction. (Scale 9 values were not altered by the faking or the statistical corrections.) On the related problem of separating faked protocols from nonfaked or presumably bona fide records, Schmidt noted that the K scale was affected by the faking instructions to about the same extent as the scores on the L scale. The way in which these soldiers completed the MMPI under faking instructions—their attempts to put themselves into a favorable light psychologically—was most clearly revealed by elevated L and K scores but not by appreciably lowered F-scale values. (These results will be discussed in more detail in the following chapter, along with later studies like those of Grayson and Olinger, 1957, Rapaport, 1958, and Marks and Seeman, 1963.)

Since the derivation of L and the composite K scale was based upon general comparisons of groups with normal and deviant profiles, it was a little surprising to find that the K-suppressor effect could be pragmatically demonstrated only upon selected scales in the profile. Hathaway and Meehl (1946) attributed this patterning of K effect to particular characteristics of the scales, either the prior existence of corrective components in the scale (e.g., scale 2) or the inclusion of subtle items in the scales arising directly from the criterion-based item tallies (e.g., scales 3 or 6; see Wiener and Harmon, 1946, or Seeman, 1952, 1953). The work of Heilbrun (1963), mentioned above, was devoted to a scale-by-scale search for new K-correction weights, either positive or negative, which might improve the separation of college normals and known abnormals. He expected both that some zero weights might be raised to appreciable weightings and that some large weightings might be lowered or eliminated. His criterion cases were defined in terms of over-all normality or abnormality, rather than in terms of specific subgroupings by clinical diagnosis. In this way the criterion was like the contrasting groups employed by Meehl and Hathaway (1946) in the original scale derivation, rather than the subgroup-by-subgroup derivation of the specific weightings. Heilbrun recommended weighting the scores for males and females differently, suggesting that weights be used on scale 3 (negatively) for the first time (for both men and women), that weights for scales 1, 4, and 9 be reduced to zero, and that weights for scales 7 and 8 be variously reduced for each sex group separately. Although he made new T-score tables available for use with college populations, Heilbrun also advised caution in their use until more cross-validational work could be carried out. There does not seem to have been any further work published on this question, however, since his original efforts in 1963.

The research on the over-all impact of K corrections upon the MMPI configurations themselves is also of disappointing quantity and precision. The two main studies were both based upon the way in which clinical records of the MMPI were read blindly and sorted by clinicians, while a third (Wiener, 1948) used a crude psychometric index (any score in the profile over a T score of 70) on samples of Veterans Administration hospital patients but did not employ a corresponding normative comparison group. Wiener found that there were more significantly elevated profiles in his two clinical groups when their profiles were plotted with K-corrected than with noncorrected T scores, reducing false negatives by 8 percent. No basis for estimating the effect upon the hits among true negatives was available in his study.

Hunt et al. (1948) plotted the MMPI's from 114 Veterans Administration hospital neuropsychiatric cases both without and with K corrections on the appropriate scales and evaluated the accuracy with which each set of records was sorted into one of three categories: psychotic, psychoneurotic, or conduct disorder. Sorting was carried out by a panel of three clinical judges and any case upon which they could not agree was eliminated from the tabulations. It also turned out that there were too few cases in the conduct-disorder category so their final analysis was based upon the dichotomy psychotic versus nonpsychotic. Only 89 of the 114 cases plotted with noncorrected profiles gained the requisite unanimous judgments from the panel and only 53 (or 58 percent) of these placements were in agreement with the wholly independent psychiatric diagnosis on these cases. When these cases were plotted with K corrections, the accuracy rose slightly (to 61 percent) but not to a statistically stable degree. These investigators also explored the effects of K corrections on these samples with the small number of conduct-disorder cases excluded and found that the accuracy on the psychotic versus neurotic dichotomy was essentially the same as that achieved on the whole sample. They also studied the forty cases with borderline elevations (at least one scale above a T score of 65 but no scale value above 80) upon which the K corrections might be most suitable (see the discussion of the K weights above) with essentially the same results again. Hunt et al. concluded that the K corrections did not improve the differential diagnostic utility of the over-all profile information in the MMPI. If there was any more useful information in the set of K-corrected patterns as opposed to the more usual MMPI profile configurations, this panel of judges, at least, was unable to capitalize upon it.

Silver and Sines (1962) carried out a similar study on a sample of psychiatric cases from a state hospital inpatient population. Although their panel was made up of only two judges, they studied a wider range of diagnostic categories (known numbers of affective psychotics, schizophrenics, neurotics, and personality disorders) with more variations in the way that the MMPI data were presented. While the judges in the Hunt et al. study were not informed about the presence or absence of the K corrections, Silver and Sines systematically varied this kind of information. The MMPI profiles were presented both with and without the actual T-score values of the K scale itself and with and without the K corrections in the clinical profile, each appropriately labeled. Thus, if the particular judge had developed different ways of interpreting MMPI's with or without corrections he could utilize such interpretive "rules" for any particular profile. Their results, however, indicated that there was little advantage to their judges from this information: either with or without K scores or K corrections on these profiles, the judges performed about equally well. The hit rate was about 50 percent in their placements among these four categories, which was well above a chance level on both the 100 males and the 110 females for whom tests were available but which was a rather disappointing level of over-all accuracy in this task. Thus, for their judges too any increase (or decrease) in the utility of MMPI profile data introduced by K corrections to the five component scales could not be demonstrated against these particular external criteria.

It should be noted that the vast majority of profile correlates and general interpretive data available in the literature and summarized in the next section of this volume are based upon K-corrected MMPI records. In order to capitalize upon these findings and interpretive guidelines a clinician must score and K correct the MMPI in accordance with the standard procedures outlined in the *Manual* and in Part One of this volume. Whenever possible, however, each clinician is also urged to investigate the value of K corrections in the MMPI records that he obtains in his agency or practice as well as the suitability of the particular weights that have been recommended for the K-score additions.

K-Scale Elevation and Profile Characteristics. As was true in the presentations for the L and F scales above, it is profitable to examine the relationship between general pattern or elevation characteristics of the clinical profile and level of K-scale elevation. In these analyses, however, it must be borne in mind that the K score itself has entered into the determination of the absolute level of the T score on five of the component scales (scales 1, 4, 7, 8, and 9). The raw scores on these scales, of course, make important contributions to these values, too, and the scores on the other scales (variously from three to five uncorrected clinical scales) are not directly contaminated. Therefore, the empirical tabulations on the relation of K score to these profile features are still of considerable interest.

Table 4-12 presents an analysis of data from the Hathaway and Meehl (1951a) *Atlas* and Table 4-13 shows the corresponding plots from the MMPI records of the Minnesota adolescents presented by Hathaway and Monachesi (1961). High scores on K are associated with lower profile elevations generally, in spite of the increasing amounts of raw-score increments that these scale elevations contribute to the selected clinical scales, while low K-scale values are accompanied by more frequent primed-scale values in the profile (see Marks and Seeman, 1963). Both of the *Atlas* samples document this general relationship which emphasizes the bipolarity of the K-scale continuum.

The relationship between K-score level and high-point pattern in these two sets of records is presented in Tables 4-14 and 4-15. It can be seen that two of the K-corrected scales (1 and 4) demonstrate an increasing rise in relative frequency of occurrence as high points in the profile with rises in K-scale level (as does the noncorrected scale 3) but the other three corrected scales drop in high-point frequency as K goes up (as does the noncorrected scale 6). Data on scales 5 and 0 from the adolescent sample indicate that high points on scale 0 follow the general trend of scales 6, 7, 8, and 9 while peaks on scale 5 seem to have about the same independence of K-scale level as scale 2 does in both sets of records. Thus, low K values are accompanied by peaks on the psychotic tetrad and on scale 5 as well, while high K-scale elevations are associated with neurotic triad peaks, particularly scales 1 and 3, and with high points on scale 4.

Special Response Measures on the MMPI

Continuing research on the MMPI has provided a number of additional ways of assessing the acceptability of a given protocol for personological interpretations. Some of these pertain to particular scales, or to very special differential diagnostic problems or settings; they will be discussed in the appropriate context later in these volumes. There are a number, however, that have the same kind of generality as the traditional indices of protocol validity routinely included in the basic test profile. The most useful of these scales and indices will be briefly noted here. Whenever possible, data will be provided about the way in which these can be applied in general clinical practice.

Table 4-12. The Relation between K-Scale Value and Number of Clinical Scales Exceeding a T-Score Level of 70 in Codes from the *Atlas,* as Shown by the Number of Codes with Each Combination of Characteristics

K Raw Score	Number of Scales over 70									Total
	0	1	2	3	4	5	6	7	8	
30										
29					1			1		2
28	1									1
27	1			2						3
26	3	1		3	1	1				9
25	7	3	3	4	1	1				19
24	9	8	4	4	1					26
23	13	8	6	3	1	1		2		34
22	10	9	9	5	2		1			36
21	13	9	10	8	1	4	1	1		47
20	13	8	6	2	3	4	5	5		46
19	11	11	6	4	9	7	3	7		58
18	25	11	11	5	7	7	10	5		81
17	17	14	7	9	4	12	3	3	1	70
16	18	16	16	10	9	10	6	4	2	91
15	19	14	9	5	11	9	11	3		81
14	19	21	15	12	13	7	5	7	2	101
13	19	17	14	18	4	6	6	9	1	94
12	16	22	7	16	4	11	8	7	2	93
11	20	16	16	13	12	13	8	2	1	101
10	11	11	11	13	12	10	6	4	1	79
9	11	8	9	10	9	10	6	6	3	72
8	9	8	7	10	10	6	4	4	1	59
7	7	8	2	7	6	10	6	1	1	48
6	4	4	4	2	5	2	3	1	1	26
5	3	5	4	6	1	6			1	26
4	1	1	1	3	1	2	1		1	11
3		1		2	1	1				5
2		1				1	1			3
1		1								1
?[a]					2		2			4
Total	280	236	177	176	131	141	96	72	18	1,327

SOURCE: Hathaway and Meehl (1951a).
[a] ? = K score not reported.

A large body of research is now available on the role of various identifiable response sets in mediating the answers of test subjects to the items of the MMPI. Various special scales have been devised to identify subjects who appear to be employing a particular mode of response to an extreme degree and to evaluate the relationship between various scores on the MMPI and these special response-set scales. Although the evidence has often suggested that valid components of variance on the MMPI scales are mediated through particular self-descriptive styles or identifiable modes of item endorsement (see the discussion of response-set studies in Volume II), it is clear that on some occasions such response sets may also serve to reduce scale discriminations and attenuate score validities. For this reason, clinicians have found it helpful to use special scales on the MMPI to evaluate possible contribution of such test approaches to the profile obtained from a given subject. The

Table 4-13. The Relation between K-Scale Value and Number of Clinical Scales Exceeding a T-Score Level of 70 in Codes from the *Juvenile Atlas*, as Shown by the Number of Codes with Each Combination of Characteristics

K Raw Score	Number of Scales over 70									Total
	0	1	2	3	4	5	6	7	8	
30										
29										
28										
27		1								1
26	1			1						2
25	2	5								7
24	5	5		1						11
23	5	2	3				1			11
22	16	8	2	1						27
21	24	5	4	1	1	1				36
20	20	10	2	2		2	1			37
19	24	10	5		1	1				41
18	41	18			1	1				61
17	48	16	5	2						71
16	65	20	11		2	2		1		101
15	59	23	11	4	3	1				101
14	49	16	8	4	3	3				83
13	41	17	8	2	2		1	1		72
12	40	11	13	2	1		1			68
11	30	25	12	2	2			1		72
10	32	23	17	4	2	3	2			83
9	23	18	6	1		2	1			51
8	24	18	7	2	3	1	1		1	57
7	14	11	4		2	2	2	1		36
6	12	7	7		2		1			29
5	4	7	1	1						13
4	1	4	2	2	1					10
3	3	1	1		1					6
2			1							1
1										
0										
Total	583	281	130	32	27	19	11	4	1	1,088

SOURCE: Hathaway and Monachesi (1961).

response sets which have gotten the greatest amount of attention in the literature are measures of response deviation or conformity, response bias (true or false), general acquiescence or willingness to acknowledge psychopathology, and social favorability or desirability. Before examining these various special response-set measures it is appropriate to explore the effects on the MMPI profile of answering the items without any systematic mode of item response at all, so-called random responding. The various ways in which this may be accomplished have been termed by Fox (1964) patterns of stimulus avoidance.

Random Responding. If the answer sheet for a group form of the MMPI is filled out, or if the cards on the MMPI are placed into sets for True and False endorsements, but no attention is paid to the particular items being answered, it can be assumed that any given mark or card placement will be in the scorable direction on a particular scale one-half the time and in the

Table 4-14. The Relation of High Point and Elevation to K-Scale Value in Codes from the *Atlas*, as Shown by the Number of Codes with Each Combination of High Point (Primed and Unprimed) and Raw K Score

K Raw Score	High Point and Elevation of Code																No High Point	Total	
	1′	′1	2′	′2	3′	′3	4′	′4	6′	′6	7′	′7	8′	′8	9′	′9		Primed	Unprimed
30																			
29									1				1					2	
28														1					1
27	2					1												2	1
26	2		1		1		3	2			1			2				8	4
25	3	2			4	1	5	1		2		1		2				12	9
24	5	3	3	4	4	1	6	5		1			1	2	1			20	16
23	5		2		4	4	10	9			2	2	1	1				24	16
22	4		2	1	7	4	10	7			1		2	1	1	1		27	14
21	9	1	7	2	7	5	14	7		1	2	1	1	1	1			41	18
20	8	2	7	4	7	3	8	7	1	1	3	1	1	1	2			37	19
19	9		17	1	6	2	5	4	2	1	5	3	6	2	5	1		55	14
18	9	3	10	5	8	4	15	6	5	3	9	4	6	6	3	5		65	36
17	7	2	21	3	7	3	11	5	1	2	4	1	6	1	5	2	2	62	21
16	9	1	27	6	16	2	17	4	2	1	7	1	6	3	7	6		91	24
15	4	2	27	4	8	4	5	8	4	3	9	5	6	1	5	2		68	29
14	11	1	25	8	15	6	8	5	6	3	6	2	10	2	12	4		93	31
13	6	2	29	7	9	3	11	5	3	3	6		13		7	4		84	24
12	3	2	33	1	3	1	9	3	5	7	11		16	1	10	1	2	90	18
11	7	3	28	6	4	3	8	5	9	3	8		12	2	12	4	1	88	27
10	6	1	29		4	2	7	3	4		6		11	1	10	2	4	77	13
9	8		18	2	6	1	6	2	6	1	9	2	18	3	5	3		76	14
8	2	1	17	4	1	1	3	1	6	2	2	3	19		5	3	2	55	17
7	3	1	13		3		4	2	4	2	6		11		5	3		49	8
6		1	6	1	2		2	1	4	1	5	2	5		5			29	6
5	1		5	2			1		2		2		8		5	1		24	3
4		1	2				1		4		1		5		1			14	1
3	1		1										1		2			5	
2			1										1		1			3	
1					1													1	
?[a]	1		2								1		1					5	
21–30																			
No. ...	30	6	15	7	27	16	48	31	1	4	6	4	6	10	3	1		136	79
% ...	16.7		10.2		20.0		36.7		2.3		4.7		7.4		1.9			63.3	36.7
17–20																			
No. ...	33	7	55	13	28	12	39	22	9	7	21	9	19	10	15	8	2	219	90
% ...	12.9		22.0		12.9		19.7		5.2		9.7		9.4		7.4		0.6	70.9	29.1
13–16																			
No. ...	30	6	108	25	48	15	41	22	15	10	28	8	35	6	31	16	0	336	108
% ...	8.1		30.0		14.2		14.2		5.6		8.1		9.2		10.6		0.0	75.7	24.3
9–12																			
No. ...	24	6	108	9	17	7	30	13	24	11	34	2	57	7	37	10	7	331	72
% ...	7.4		29.0		6.0		10.7		8.7		8.9		15.9		11.7		1.7	82.1	17.9
0–8																			
No. ...	7	4	45	7	7	1	11	4	20	5	16	5	50	0	24	7	2	180	35
% ...	5.1		24.2		3.7		7.0		11.6		9.8		23.3		14.4		0.9	83.7	16.3
Total																			
No. ...	125	29	333	61	127	51	169	92	69	37	106	28	168	33	110	42	11	1,207	384
% ...	9.7		24.8		11.2		16.4		6.7		8.4		12.6		9.6		0.7	75.9	24.1

SOURCE: Hathaway and Meehl (1951a).

[a] ? = K score not reported.

Table 4-15. The Relation of High Point and Elevation to K-Scale Value in Codes from the *Juvenile Atlas*, as Shown by the Number of Codes with Each Combination of High Point (Primed and Unprimed) and Raw K Score

K Raw Score	High Point and Elevation of Code																				No High Point	Total	
	1′	′1	2′	′2	3′	′3	4′	′4	5′	′5	6′	′6	7′	′7	8′	′8	9′	′9	0′	′0		Primed	Unprimed
30																							
29																							
28																							
27							1															1	
26					1	1																1	1
25					1	1	3	1	1													5	2
24	1			1		1	3	1					2			1	1					6	5
23	1					2	3	1		1				1	2							6	5
22			1		1	5	8	8		1				1	1	1						11	16
21		1	3	1	2	4	5	11	1	3				1	1	1		1			1	12	24
20	1				1	3	5	7	1	1		2	2	5	5	2	2					17	20
19	1				1	5	5	5	3	3	4	1		1	3	5		2		1	1	17	24
18	2	3	2	4	1	7	5	8		8	1	1		3	5	2	4	1		1	3	20	41
17	2	2	2	3	2	8	1	6	3	8	1	5	4	4	4	5	5	2		2	2	24	47
16	4	2	2	1		9	3	6	2	5	2	2	6	9	11	9	5	12		6	5	35	66
15	2	3	4	8	1	3	9	8	5	3	4	7	1	6	4	3	11	7	1	5	6	42	59
14		2	4		2	3	5	6	5	4	1	8	1	3	7	3	9	6		6	8	34	49
13	1		1	5	1	1	4	6	4	6	1	3	1	6	5	2	10	4	3	6	2	31	41
12		1	2	4		3	3	2	1	1	1	2	2	3	10	5	8	4	1	11	4	28	40
11	2	1	2	1	1	4	8	1		1	5	3		3	8	4	11	3	5	7	2	42	30
10	1		2				7	2	3	8	5	7	3	8	12		14	3	4	3	1	51	32
9			2	2			2			5	3	4	2	2	11	3	5	1	3	5	1	28	23
8	1		2	5			3	1	3	2	6	1	2	1	9	1	4	4	3	6	3	33	24
7			2	1		1			2		2	2	1	1	8	2	5	2	2	5		22	14
6	1		1		1		1		1	1	2	1	1	1	5	2	2	1	2	5	1	17	12
5									1				1	1	3		4			3		9	4
4							1		1		1				2		2		2	1		9	1
3							1	1				1	1				1				1	3	3
2									1													1	
1																							
0																							
21–30																							
No. ...	2	1	4	2	5	14	23	22	2	5	0	0	2	3	4	3	0	2	0	0	1	42	53
% ...	3.2		6.3		20.0		47.4		7.4				5.3		7.4		2.1				1.1	44.2	55.8
17–20																							
No. ...	6	5	4	7	5	23	16	26	7	20	6	9	6	13	17	14	11	5	0	4	6	78	132
% ...	5.2		5.2		13.3		20.0		12.9		7.1		9.0		14.8		7.6		1.9		2.9	37.1	62.9
13–16																							
No. ...	7	7	11	14	4	16	21	26	16	18	8	20	9	24	27	17	35	29	4	23	21	142	215
% ...	3.9		7.0		5.6		13.2		9.5		7.8		9.2		12.3		17.9		7.6		5.9	39.8	60.2
9–12																							
No. ...	3	2	8	7	1	7	20	5	4	15	14	16	7	16	41	12	38	11	13	26	8	149	125
% ...	1.8		5.5		2.9		9.1		6.9		10.9		8.4		19.3		17.9		14.2		2.9	54.4	45.6
0–8																							
No. ...	2	0	5	6	1	1	6	2	9	3	11	5	6	4	27	5	18	7	9	20	5	94	58
% ...	1.3		7.2		1.3		5.3		7.9		10.5		6.6		21.1		16.4		19.1		3.3	61.8	38.2
Total																							
No. ...	20	15	32	36	16	61	86	81	38	61	39	50	30	60	116	51	102	54	26	73	41	505	583
% ...	3.2		6.3		7.1		15.3		9.1		8.2		8.3		15.3		14.3		9.1		3.8	46.4	53.6

SOURCE: Hathaway and Monachesi (1961).

nonscorable direction the other half. Thus, theoretically, a set of random completions of the MMPI should give a distribution of scores on the various component scales which will average around the value of one-half the number of items in each particular scale. These theoretical or expected values for the raw-score means and standard deviations for random responding are given in Table 4-15, together with the corresponding T-score values of each raw-score mean as if it were earned by an adult male and an adult female subject. These T scores have been given for both K-corrected and noncorrected MMPI norms. (Finney, 1968, provides such T values for a normalized T-score distribution.) In Figures 4-1 and 4-2 are plotted graphically the profile patterns generated by these expected mean T-score values, as listed in Table 4-16 for male and female subjects, including both K-corrected and noncorrected values for scales 1, 4, 7, 8, and 9. Profiles encountered in actual practice with these configurations should be carefully scrutinized.

Various empirically derived random records closely resemble these theoretically expected values. For example, Cottle and Powell (1951) produced twenty-four records by rolling a die to decide how to mark each successive item in the MMPI, marking it True if an even number appeared, False if an odd one came up. For twenty-six additional records they employed a table of random numbers, again assigning True answers for even numbers, False for odd. Their results are included in Table 4-16 for all fifty artificial records. The means and standard deviations that they found correspond well with the theoretical expectations for each scale; no mean or sigma value differed from the expected value by as much as one raw-score point.

In a more ambitious venture, Fox (1964) repeated the work of Cottle and Powell, generating twenty-two artificial records by means of a table of random numbers, and added several new methods, including a completion based on a coin toss in which heads determined a True answer and tails a False, various intratest patterns, and sixteen records generated by the actual guessing patterns given by normal adults. Fox's intratest patterns were records in which the response was tied to a feature of the test booklet or the answer sheet in some systematic fashion but independent of the item content. Thus, a True answer to each odd-numbered item and a False for each even-numbered item was one manner in which Fox believed a test subject could complete the MMPI and avoid the stimuli provided by the test items. He used this method for one artificial record and its obverse for another. He also produced records with odd-numbered columns marked True and even-numbered columns False, and vice versa. Some of the other patterns or systems of response that he employed included various-sized blocks of True responses, followed by a block of Falses; sets of Trues and Falses of unequal size alternating with an appropriate switch in the sizes of the sets so that equal numbers of True and False answers are given for the total booklet; all upper rows answered False, all bottom rows True. In all, thirty records based upon some orderly system were produced. (Fox also included records generated by answering all the items either True or False; see the discussion of the special sets below.) He included the profiles generated by all these procedures in his

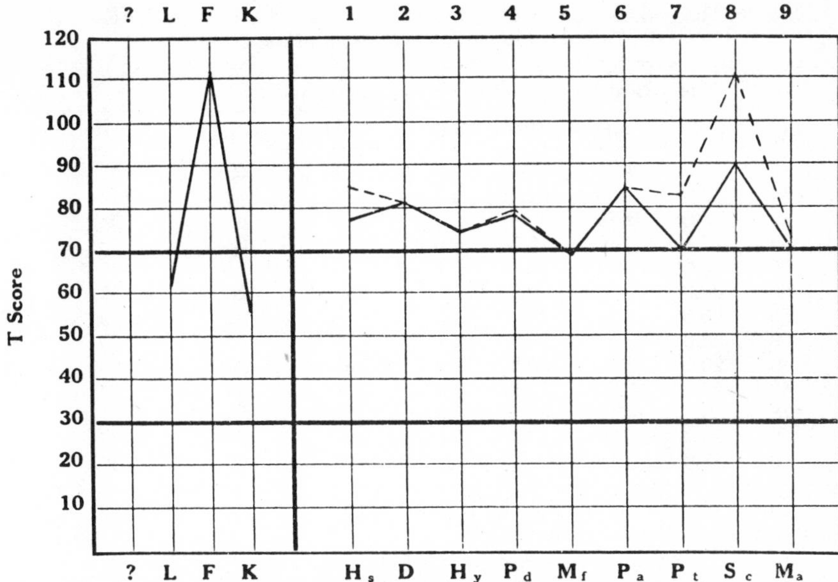

Figure 4-1. The uncorrected (solid line) and K-corrected (broken line) T-score values expected theoretically for male subjects from a random sorting of the test items. Uncorrected code = 8*62″41379′5 F*′L. K-corrected code = 8*16 72″439′5 F*′L–K.

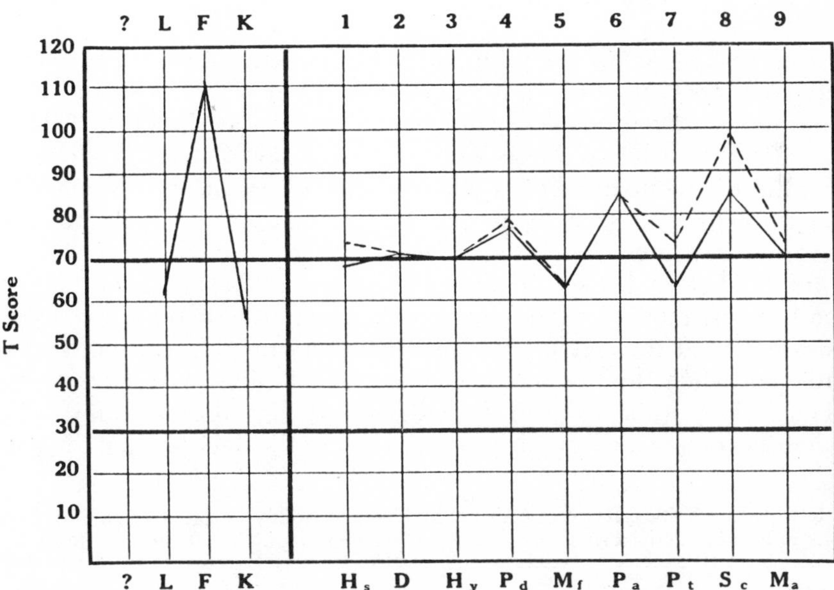

Figure 4-2. The uncorrected (solid line) and K-corrected (broken line) T-score values expected theoretically for female subjects from a random sorting of the test items. Uncorrected code = 86″4239′175 F*′L. K-corrected code = 8*6″479123′5 F*′L–K.

Table 4-16. Theoretical and Empirical Means and Standard Deviations for Each of the Basic Scales from Random Sortings of the MMPI

Scale	No. of Items	Theoretical [a] Mean	Theoretical [a] S.D.	Empirical [b] Mean	Empirical [b] S.D.	Uncorrected T Scores [c] Male	Uncorrected T Scores [c] Female	Corrected T Scores [c] Male	Corrected T Scores [c] Female
L	15	7.5	1.94	7.8	2.3	62	62	62	62
F	64	32.0	4.00	32.4	4.3	112	112	112	112
K	30	15.0	2.74	14.4	2.9	55	55	55	55
1	33	16.5	2.87	16.5	3.0	77	68	85	74
2	60	30.0	3.87	29.4	3.7	82	71	82	71
3	60	30.0	3.87	30.1	3.1	75	70	75	70
4	50	25.0	3.54	24.7	3.5	78	77	79	79
5	60	30.0	3.87	29.8	4.1	69	63	69	63
6	40	20.0	3.16	20.4	3.0	85	85	85	85
7	48	24.0	3.56	23.6	3.1	70	64	83	73
8	78	39.0	4.42	38.5	3.6	90	86	111	98
9	46	23.0	3.39	23.3	3.6	70	70	73	73
0	70	35.0	4.18	...	...	62	62	62	62

SOURCE: Adapted from Cottle and Powell (1951).

[a] Based on the following formulas:

$$\text{Mean}_x = n_x p \qquad SD_x = \sqrt{n_x pq}$$

where n_x = number of items in scale x; p = probability of a significant answer equal to 0.5; q = (1 − p) = 0.5.

[b] The scores are based on fifty randomly sorted records, twenty-four using dice, the rest from a table of random numbers.

[c] Based on theoretical raw-score means.

report, plotted both as if a male had given these answers and as if a female had produced them.

From these data, and the information from Cottle and Powell (1951), Fox generated expectancy ranges for deviations from true or theoretically expected random values on each component scale for the MMPI. In Table 4-17 are presented for each of the scales the rounded raw-score values derived by Fox for the 1 percent and the 0.1 percent levels of significance. Some of these values are so low that they do not provide useful discriminations, but a number of these raw-score levels are sufficiently high to enable the clinician to determine whether his set of raw-score values is likely to have been generated by some method of stimulus avoidance on the MMPI. Obviously, the F score provided the single best basis for discriminating random and valid records, but when the raw score on F exceeds 20, appeal to the score variations on various other scales in the validity and clinical profile may facilitate the identification of a randomly produced test or the decision that the pattern

Table 4-17. Low Critical Raw-Score Values for Two Probability Levels on Each MMPI Scale in Records Derived from Systematic and Random Responding to the Test Items

Significance Level	F	K	1	2	3	4	5 m	5 f	6	7	8	9
1 percent	21	5	8	17	18	15	21	39	11	10	21	10
0.1 percent	16	1	6	13	14	12	18	42	8	6	15	6

SOURCE: Table 16 and Figures 1A and 1B in Fox (1964).

is not likely to have been produced in this way. Given a record with an F score larger than 20 raw score, if two or more other raw-score values fall beyond the critical value for the 1 percent level, or if one falls beyond the 0.1 percent level, Fox suggests that the record be accepted as bona fide rather than as a product of some form of random responding.

A further check on the possibility that the test subject may not be responding meaningfully or consistently to the content of the MMPI items is provided by the next index, the repeated items in the MMPI test booklet.

The TR Index. In the group form of the MMPI (regular test booklet, Form R, or the taped version) an opportunity exists to determine how consistently a given test subject has endorsed sixteen items that are repeated identically in the inventory (they are primarily found among the first forty items and repeated about the middle of the test; see appendix C). The reason for this duplication was explained in Part One in describing the use of the IBM answer sheet; namely, that machine scoring of that answer sheet was greatly facilitated by having some item answers appear on both the front and the back of the sheet.

Buechley and Ball (1952) first pointed out how this duplication could be employed systematically to furnish a check on the subject's consistency within one test session in item interpretation and marking. Scoring this index, as indicated in Part One, is somewhat more demanding than scoring other indexes since mere notation of True or False responses is not sufficient; a careful matching of answers to paired items must be carried out. The total raw score on the TR index is the number of items answered inconsistently. Because of these scoring difficulties, particularly on the two-sided IBM answer sheet, Buechley and Ball employed only fourteen of the sixteen pairs. Using a score of three or less as an acceptable level of response consistency and four or more to indicate questionable response reliability, these authors offered evidence that an occasional record with a middle-range score on F may in fact be subject to serious vagaries of item endorsement and that at least 15 percent of the test records with moderately high or higher F scores (in their population of institutionalized delinquent boys) did not show this kind of response inconsistency. Thus, they argued that this TR index can help to clarify questions about the acceptability of a given protocol that may be raised by unusual scores on the traditional validity indicators.

A similar index, the carelessness (Ca) scale, was introduced into the Addiction Research Center Inventory (Haertzen and Hill, 1963), which is based upon both identical items that are repeated (fifteen items) and items that are psychological opposites (eight items). These authors also found that a cutting score between three and four mismatched items was optimal for identifying records in which drugs may have led the subject to be too inattentive or uncoordinated to complete the inventory appropriately. Since the work of Haertzen and Hill on their Ca measure indicated that the opposite subscore was even more sensitive than the set of items simply duplicated in the inventory, perhaps some of the work of Rorer (1963) and Goldberg and Rorer (1963, 1964) could be utilized to generate an additional set of items for this TR index to be made up of psychological opposites.

Response Deviations. Following the lead of Berg (1955, 1957), a number of psychologists (see Dahlstrom, 1969b) have investigated general tendencies to deviate or depart from a social norm or pattern as a basis for understanding some sources of test validity and invalidity. Before this "deviation hypothesis" was formulated by Berg and his students, however, considerable work had already been carried out by Hathaway and McKinley on the implications of this kind of response as it appeared in both the clinical scales and the validity indicators of the MMPI. The basic mechanics of recording and scoring the card form of the test (on which most of the original derivational research was carried out) greatly facilitated this particular line of investigation. As described in Part One, each subject's performance on the card form of the MMPI is recorded on the form by means of either a blank space or a mark, such as "X" or "+," opposite each item number. The blank space indicates that the subject answered the particular item the way that the majority of Minnesota normative subjects had answered it, either True or False; a plus indicates that the subject deviated from the majority direction on that particular item. Scores on particular scales come from correspondences (zero for zero and plus for plus) between the record form and the scoring template, not merely from deviant or plus answers alone. When one looked over these record forms, it was obvious that some subjects had many more X's or +'s than others and that this feature could provide some potentially useful information about the test subject. It was also easy to determine by inspection that some subjects showed fewer than usual plus responses, thus deviating in their lack of "deviations" or showing what Wiggins (1962) has termed "hypercommunality."

The most direct measure of the tendency to deviate, therefore, in Berg's sense of the term is the total number of plus responses on a test subject's record form. On the card form of the MMPI this score is easily determined. On answer sheets for the group form, however, the total number of deviant responses is difficult to ascertain. (A special stencil is required listing the deviant direction of response on each item as indicated in Appendix A; this total number of agreements with the deviant direction of response will then correspond to the total number of plus responses on the card form.) On the Minnesota normals, a mean of 122.9 plus responses for men and 131.5 for women was obtained, with standard deviations of 40.3 and 39.1, respectively.

It is also enlightening to examine the role of conforming and deviating responses in generating scores on each of the scales in the MMPI profile. The data presented in Table 4-18 show the number of items in each scale which earn credit when answered in the same direction as the majority of Minnesota normals (0 items) and when answered in a deviating direction (X items). Also included in Table 4-18 is a separate breakdown of 0 and X items for True and for False answers in these scales. Totals for all 0 or all X answers for each scale, as well as for all True and all False responses, are also provided. Thus, on the L scale, all scorable answers are False answers; on all these items a False response deviates from the majority of Minnesota men and women, most of whom tended to answer them True. If a subject answered all items of the MMPI in a deviant direction, he would thereby earn

Table 4-18. Number of Items Answered in Each Direction and in Conformity with or Deviation from the Normal Group in Each of the Basic Scales

Scale	No. of Items	X Items True	X Items False	O Items True	O Items False	Total X	Total O	Total True	Total False
L	15	0	15	0	0	15	0	0	15
F	64	44	20	0	0	64	0	44	20
K	30	0	9	1	20	9	21	1	29
1	33	11	22	0	0	33	0	11	22
2	60	18	26	2	14	44	16	20	40
3	60	12	28	1	19	40	20	13	47
4	50	24	18	0	8	42	8	24	26
5[a]	60	25	18	3	14	43	17	28	32
6	40	24	8	1	7	32	8	25	15
7	48	38	8	1	1	46	2	39	9
8	78	58	18	1	1	76	2	59	19
9	46	32	6	3	5	38	8	35	11
0	70	32	24	2	12	56	14	34	36
Scored items .	357							124	233
Nonscored items .	193							82	111
All items.	550							206	344

[a] Male key.

a score of 15 raw-score points on L; if he answered in the conforming direction throughout the test, he would earn a raw score of zero on L. The results of adopting extreme conforming or extreme deviating response sets to the test are shown in the profiles drawn in Figure 4-3. The all-X pattern is a dramatically deviant pattern, both in validity-scale and clinical-scale configurations. It can be seen that the scores on each of the clinical scales in the all-0 pattern fall around the mean on the Minnesota T-score norms, or a little below. This is particularly the case when K corrections are applied. The validity-scale values do not center about their mean values, however, which indicates that they can be used to help identify this particular kind of response distortion on the test.

It should also be mentioned that this pattern, the all-0, or zero-response, pattern corresponds to the kind of test circumvention noted by Hovey (1948) in early work with the card form of the MMPI. He found that several of his psychiatric cases had discerned the significance of the corner cuts on the test item cards. They used this cue to categorize the cards into True and False piles, instead of answering the specific content of the items, thereby generating an all-zero sorting. Hovey found that they usually did not leave the test in this division but went through the cards to find twenty or thirty of the relatively innocuous items which they then placed in the opposite piles to produce a more believable test sorting. The signs in the profile that Hovey advanced as usually suggesting that this possibility may have occurred can be seen in Table 4-18 and Figure 4-3. The lowest value that K is likely to take with this sorting is 21 raw-score points while the raw-score value of L will be near zero. Very low raw scores (before K correction) on scales 1, 7, and 8

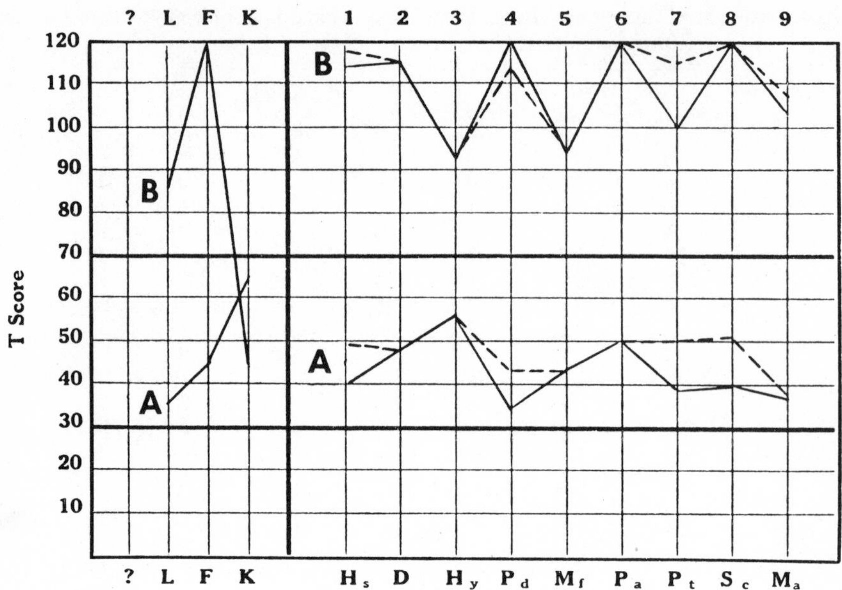

Figure 4-3. A. The uncorrected (solid line) and K-corrected (broken line) T-score values expected for male subjects answering each item in the direction of the majority of normals (all zero response pattern). Uncorrected code = 36/2518:794 F:L. K-corrected code = 3867/12 45:9 K–/F:L. B. The uncorrected (solid line) and K-corrected (broken line) T-score values expected for male subjects answering each item in the direction opposite to that of the majority of normals (all X response pattern). Uncorrected code = 486219753* F*L. K-corrected code = 861274953* F*L″/K.

are also to be expected. On the booklet form, where there are no direct cues to guide the test subject in generating such a record, some subjects seem to try to discern the "right" direction of response in an effort to second-guess the psychologist in this kind of personality appraisal.

It can be seen in the data for endorsement frequencies on the various items in the MMPI (provided in the technical appendixes in Volume II) that many items are endorsed True or False by only a bare majority of men and women in the Minnesota normative samples while others show a nearly unanimous consensus. Thus, a subject may be deviating relatively little or a great deal when he scores a plus response. Correspondingly, then, not all of the plus responses on his record form carry the same implication for this tendency to respond deviantly from the Minnesota reference group. Hathaway (Meehl and Hathaway, 1946) tried to devise a more direct measure of this tendency to get plus responses on the MMPI. Working with subjects in the Minnesota normative group, Hathaway found groups of subjects very high and very low in the number of plus entries they had on their record forms. He then carried out an item analysis to try to locate the items that most consistently separated high and low plus-getters. The fifty-six items in the plus scale proved to give the best separation between these two groups. As would be expected, most of these items are scored in the deviant direction, but six of the items are actually scored in the conforming direction in this empirical separation. While most of these items are scored significant when answered True, thirteen are scored False on this scale. Minnesota men obtained a mean of 19.7 on the plus scale while women scored a mean of 22.3. The standard deviations were 8.3 and 9.0, respectively, with women showing the greater tendency to deviate in their endorsements of MMPI items. It is interesting to note that men and women do not differ in their endorsement of the extremely deviant responses which constitute the standard F scale (see above). The plus scale of Hathaway seems to provide the best general measure of response deviation (or, conversely, response conformity) as a general test approach to MMPI items. Although it is appreciably correlated with the F scale, it is clearly measuring some different aspect of self-description on this inventory task. Few direct personological correlates of this scale have as yet been identified.

Acquiescence Response Set. Another response style that has been studied extensively on the MMPI and related tests is the tendency a subject may have to give one or the other of the response alternatives available to him on the answer sheet (for the MMPI, True or False), with little regard to the content of the items so marked. Here too a variety of measures have been advanced for this style of approach to the task of self-description.

The most direct empirical study of this kind of behavior was made by Weiss and Moos (1965), who carried out a search for serial dependencies in sequences of answers to the MMPI given by psychiatric patients in a Veterans Administration hospital at Palo Alto, California. While they reported finding ample evidence for such sequential dependencies in a content-free psychomotor task, they reported little support for the hypothesis that any of these patients completed the MMPI by assigning one or another response category to the test items without regard to the content of the item statements. Their conclusion was that this response style could not be discerned in the item pool as a whole. It was still possible, however, that certain specific kinds of items may provide this kind of opportunity or are particularly susceptible to this kind of responding. This possibility has been the basis for a number of scale-construction efforts to get a measure of such response acquiescence.

Another means of evaluating the potential impact of tendencies to answer MMPI items more in one direction than the other can be gained from the data presented above in Table 4-18 on the number of items scored when answered True and when answered False in each component scale. These data are also plotted in T-score form (for a male subject) in Figures 4-4 and 4-5. An all-False responding would thus produce a generally neurotic configuration while an all-True response set would generate a psychotic pattern. In both profiles, however, the validity-scale values are markedly elevated and atypical for the clinical patterns which they accompany. Fox (1964) also included these extreme response tendencies in his study of patterns of stimulus avoidance on the MMPI (see the discussion above under the F scale).

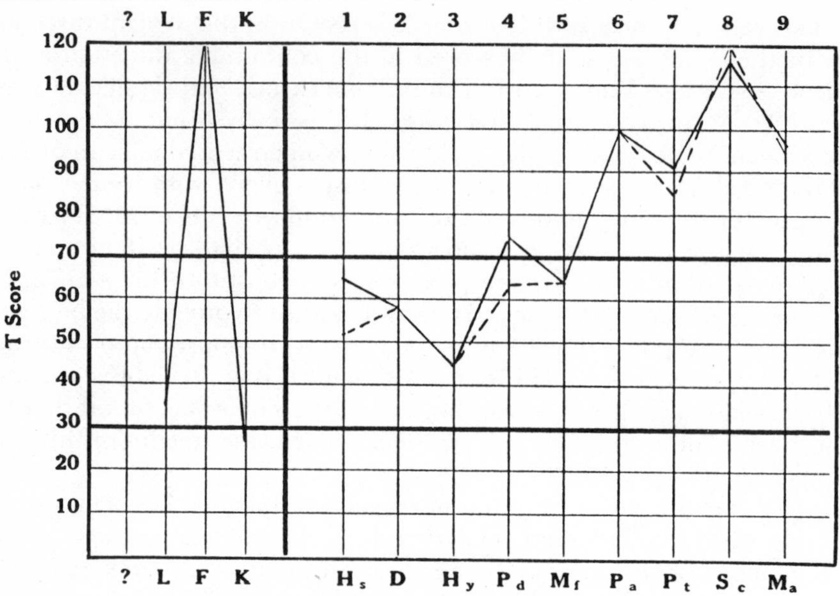

Figure 4-4. The uncorrected (solid line) and K-corrected (broken line) T-score values expected for male subjects answering each item True. Uncorrected code = 8697*″4′15–2/3 F*:L. K-corrected code = 869*7″′54–21/3 F*:L#K.

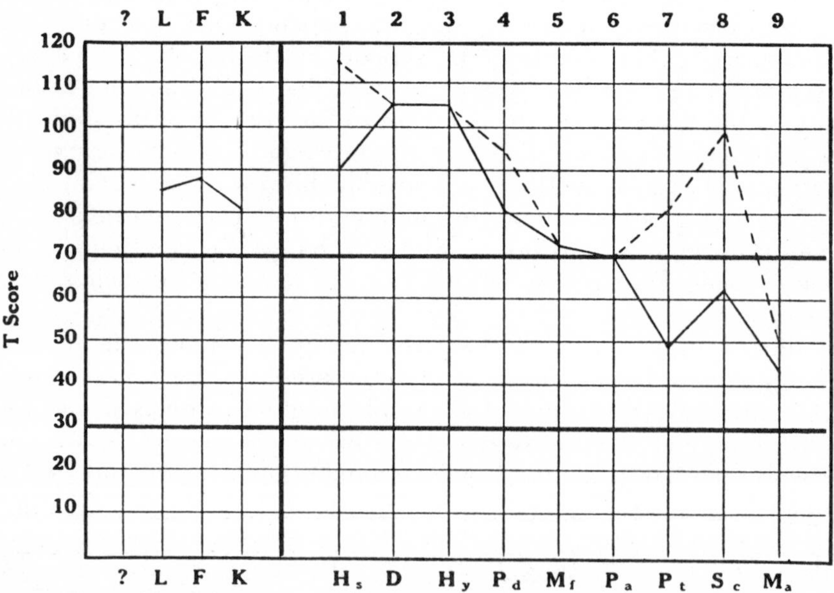

Figure 4-5. The uncorrected (solid line) and K-corrected (broken line) T-score values expected for male subjects answering each item False. Uncorrected code = 231*4″56′8–/79 FL″. K-corrected code = 12384*7″56′–9 FLK″.

Recent research of Morf and Jackson (1969) has indicated that the tendency to endorse items of psychopathological import may be separate and distinct from a tendency to say True or to say False on subsets of inventory items. If so, then a general measure of True-response marking, such as the one used by Wiggins (1962) in some of his studies of the total number of True answers given on the MMPI answer sheet, would be some unanalyzable composite of both such tendencies with rather unclear psychological significance. Experience has shown that simple counts of this kind, such as the total number of No responses on the Humm-Wadsworth Temperament Schedule, provide only crude checks upon protocol validity (see Meehl and Hathaway, 1946). Instead, investigators of response acquiescence have usually followed the lead provided by Cronbach (1950) in searching for the locus of impact of this response style among sets of items for which the answer may be difficult to determine for reasons arising from the items themselves or from the test subject and his interpretation of the task, the setting, and the purpose of the assessment.

The most carefully constructed and extensively studied measure of this tendency of a subject to answer either True or False when confronted with an item that is unclear, ambiguous, inapplicable, or otherwise difficult to make a decision about was devised by Fricke (1957) and called a response-bias, or B, scale. It reflects the tendency at the upper end of the scale to give True answers to MMPI items, and at the lower end of the distribution the tendency to give False answers. As noted above, the composition of the scales in the MMPI is such that a consistent response of False yields a generally neurotic configuration of clinical scores while a consistent endorsement of True yields a psychotic pattern. If a response bias toward one or the other of the alternatives provided in the answer sheet is operating in a subject's completion of the MMPI booklet, one or the other of these effects could be erroneously generated in the person's test profile. To construct his B scale, Fricke identified items with maximum controversiality in the item pool. That is, by averaging response frequencies from the men and women in the Minnesota normative samples (Hathaway and Briggs, 1957) as well as from a sample of University of Minnesota undergraduates (see the technical appendixes in Volume II), he identified those items that were answered True by from 40 percent to 60 percent of these normal subjects. Since normal subjects seemed to be split about half and half in the way they endorsed these items, these statements constituted the most controversial ones in the test. People, young or old, single or married, men or women, would disagree with each other most about how they should be answered. These sixty-three items in the B scale are accordingly all scored in the True direction. As is indicated in Volume II, Minnesota normal men and women answer about half of these items in the True direction earning a mean of about 30 raw-score points; unusually high (45 or more) or unusually low (15 or less) scores reflect important tendencies to give True or False answers, respectively, on this kind of test item. Fricke reports that B-scale scores are positively related to F-scale values (on Minnesota normal samples, .43 for men and .40 for women) but negatively correlated with L (−.28 for men, −.30 for women) and even more strongly with K as well (–.67 for men and –.68 for women). Thus, the B scale may be useful in identifying additional ways in which special response slanting may have interfered with getting appropriate score patterns on the clinical scales. Fricke (1956, 1957) has tried employing the B scale as a psychometric suppressor in a way comparable to the K scale in the identification of women with conversion reactions but with very limited success.

Several other measures of acquiescence on the MMPI have been advanced, most of them taking off from the same basis employed by Fricke in selecting his potential items for the B scale, namely the controversiality of the item as interpreted by normal subjects. The Bn scale of Hanley (1957), the Rb scale of Wiggins (1962), and the Ars scale of Shaffer (1963) are quite similar in derivation to the B scale with the additional provision that the items also must be neutral in their social favorability implications (see below). The AT scale of Hanley (1961) approached the measurement of response acquiescence the other way; that is, eighteen maximally controversial items selected for their extreme social favorability (high or low) were combined in the Ex scale with half True answers and half False. The AT scale is the Ex scale with the False items rekeyed to give an eighteen-item all-True response scale. The Acq scale of Fulkerson (1958) added the requirement that the component items be both maximally controversial and unrelated to rated psychopathology in the endorsers (samples of airmen in his derivational work).

The research literature offers little evidence to guide the clinician in his use of these more recently derived scales of response acquiescence. More attention will be given to them in the second volume in discussing the implications of Block's (1965) scales for ego resiliency and ego control which he concludes are better designations for these various response styles.

Social Favorability or Desirability Responding. As mentioned above, scales to detect and evaluate the tendency to answer MMPI items primarily to make a favorable impression on the test interpreter rather than give an honest and accurate view of oneself have been advanced by several investigators. The earliest work on this kind of test-taking bias in the MMPI has already been described above in the sections on the L scale and K scale. In a rather different approach to this problem, Heineman (1952) obtained ratings from State University of Iowa undergraduates of all the statements in the MMPI item pool on the social favorability that an answer of True would convey about one's personality. (These values are provided in the technical appendixes in Volume II.) Heineman himself did not use his ratings to derive a separate scale for social favorability slanting on the MMPI but instead constructed a forced-choice form of the Taylor manifest anxiety scale. These ratings, however, provided the basis for Wiggins's subsequent derivation of two social favorability scales (1962): Tsd, which was made up of all items that fell outside the neutral range (less than 2.5 or greater than 3.5 on a five-point scale), and Esd, items that were very extremely rated (less than 1.5 or beyond 4.5). (See the item lists for these scales in Volume II.)

Hanley (1961) developed a measure of test-taking defensiveness, the Tt scale, and Jackson and Messick (1958, 1961, 1962a, 1962b) generated a set of desirability scales, Dy_1 to Dy_5, with different degrees of average rated favorability (from Heineman's data) in the item composition. These scales have only recently been examined for their sensitivity to known protocol invalidity (Dies, 1968); instead, they have usually been used in a variety of factor-analytic work on the MMPI (see the discussion in Volume II).

The scale which has received the greatest amount of attention in the psychometric area of MMPI research was derived in a similar way by Edwards (1953, 1957); it was based upon ratings for social desirability of 149 items from the MMPI L, F, and K scales and the Taylor anxiety scale. The seventy-nine items receiving unanimous ratings by the ten judges in his panel formed the social desirability scale (called SD by Edwards; see the So scale in the appendix material of Volume II). This long form was employed in the early studies (see Fordyce, 1956) but was subsequently reduced to a short form of thirty-nine items (So-r) by internal-consistency analyses.

In the short form, the social desirability scale has been widely studied and scrutinized. As the discussion in Volume II makes clear, however, most of these studies have been carried out without external criteria of protocol validity so that there is little firm evidence to support the application of this scale in clinical practice as a way to examine the extent to which a given subject has actually been deliberately slanting his MMPI answers. The available data indicate that this scale has more relevance for personological interpretation than for estimation of protocol validity. (See Block, 1965.) In contrast to the scale to be discussed next, Wiggins's Sd scale, the So-r scale of Edwards appears to be quite ineffectual in detecting deliberate test slanting.

An empirical approach to the evaluation of favorability slanting on the MMPI, comparable to the work by Cofer, Chance, and Judson (1949) on the Mp scale (see below), was carried out by Wiggins (1959) on faked and bona fide records obtained from Stanford University undergraduates. By item analyses, Wiggins found forty items that identified the role-playing protocols and keyed these items in such a way that higher scores indicated greater likelihood of faking good or trying to create socially favorable impressions. He found that most of his college students scored between 10 and 15 raw-score points on this scale while most of the subjects who were trying to create favorable impressions in their answers fell beyond 20 raw-score points. In this comparison, the two groups of students, bona fide and role-playing alike, were almost indistinguishable on the Edwards So-r scale; both groups fell at the very desirable end of the scale range (25 to 39 raw-score points). The Sd scale would seem to warrant greater empirical study as an additional validity check, especially in clinical situations involving sophisticated college-level clients who may be motivated to slant or distort their answers or may seek to minimize psychopathology and other unfavorable personological characteristics.

Moderator Variables

In the discussion earlier in this chapter, the use of the standard validity indicators as a means of discarding the protocol as "uninterpretable" was discussed. Also noted there was the use of a cutting score on L in the Meehl-

Dahlstrom rules to decide how the basic clinical scale information is to be employed in determining whether the test configuration is characteristic of some neurotic or psychotic pattern (see Rule 4, the Fake Good Rule). That is, a test record with an L score above a value of 60 on the T scale is interpreted differently from the way it would be if the L score fell below that level. Such uses of the validity indicators are based upon the assumption that the validity scale operates as a moderator variable (see Saunders, 1956) or serves to increase what Ghiselli (1960) calls the prediction of predictability.

A moderator variable serves to indicate the kind of subject (or test record) for whom the rest of the test profile is particularly applicable or inapplicable or for whom the patterns will have different personological implications. Scores on a moderator variable, therefore, may identify relatively useless test protocols or signal which alternative interpretive approach is most suitable for a given record. A number of MMPI scales have been developed to serve the clinician in making this kind of decision about test-protocol utility.

Meehl's N Scale. As noted earlier, one of the forerunners of the K scale in the research program at the University of Minnesota on test-taking attitudes was the N scale. Meehl (1945) developed this scale to evaluate what Rosanoff (1938) had termed a control factor in a person's personality. That is, some characteristic was hypothesized which would enable an individual to maintain his effectiveness in spite of serious maladaptive tendencies in his personality. Meehl contrasted subjects who showed bona fide psychological disorder with subjects who were apparently functioning normally but who produced general MMPI profiles that were similar to those from patients in both pattern and elevation. By item analysis he identified seventy-eight items that separated the true-positive from the false-positive cases. He scored these items in the direction of lower scores for subjects who are normal in spite of having elevated clinical profiles. Since the K scale was based upon the separation of false negatives from true negatives in the same kind of item analysis, it was expected that the two scales would be mirror images. Although they were appreciably correlated (.73 between L_6 and N, according to Meehl and Hathaway, 1946), the N scale seems to be sufficiently independent to provide additional information to supplement that already provided by the standard validity indicators. The N scale is not as effective in ruling out false negatives as it is in identifying false-positive cases, particularly those who show elevations on the neurotic triad (scales 1, 2, and 3) despite evidence that they are functioning adequately. Minnesota normal males score about 30 raw-score points (35 for females) on the N scale, with each sex group showing a standard deviation of about 10 raw-score points. College-level subjects score about a standard deviation from the normals of their respective sex group, in the direction of lower raw scores (greater likelihood of pathology if the clinical scores are elevated). From the data provided by Meehl, if the N scale value falls below 20 raw-score points (or a T score of 60 or more), then the clinical profile elevation is likely to be a bona fide reflection of psychopathology, particularly if the elevation is indicative of a neurotic reaction. Deviations in the opposite direction on N, higher raw scores or lower T scores, suggest that a given clinical-profile elevation is not so likely to indicate actual maladaptation. These latter discriminations are less dependable, however, and the clinician should perhaps put less reliance upon this kind of decision.

On the basis of evidence available to him at the time that he carried out these analyses for his doctoral dissertation, Meehl specifically precluded the use of the N scale as a measure of ego strength or some kind of emotional control factor in personality organization. In the light of the subsequent research findings on both the K scale and Barron's ego strength scale (1953), it may have been premature to rule out this kind of interpretation of the N scale since it is clearly related to both of these other MMPI measures. Further studies to determine what kinds of clinical interpretations the N scale may have over and above its significance in determining the validity of a given MMPI test protocol would be well worth while.

Gough's Ds Scale. The research that led to the development of the dissimulation scale (Ds) was the pioneering effort of Gough (1954), who studied the stereotypes held by professionals and laymen alike about the self-perceptions and inner experiences of neurotic patients. Using the items in the MMPI pool as a basis for sampling these various misconceptions, Gough asked samples of college undergraduates in a course on abnormal psychology and a group of professional staff members (psychologists, psychiatrists, and social workers) of an army hospital to answer the test the way that a person would who was "experiencing a psychoneurotic reaction." Gough included both male and female subjects in the group of dissemblers that he studied. He contrasted their MMPI answers with groups of male and female patients who were tested in the midst of various forms of psychoneurotic reaction and identified seventy-four items (see the Ds scale in Appendix I of Volume II) that separated male and female dissemblers from patients. The content of these items ranged rather widely over the alleged self-views of neurotic patients, namely, that they suffer from various physical dysfunctions, social ostracism, lack of self-sufficiency, sexual conflicts and preoccupations, or feelings of irritability, tenseness, and anxiety. Gough also demonstrated that these answers were not characteristic of normal subjects either but were better interpreted as a product of the stereotypic views that normal subjects have about how psychoneurotic patients will answer the MMPI. That is, when the average normal subject is asked to answer the test as neurotics do, he endorses about fifty of these items in the significant direction while known neurotics and normal subjects answering under standard test instructions endorse only about fifteen items in the set. Using an essentially cross-validational sample of both dissembling and standard administrations, Gough found that a score of 35 raw-score points and above identified 93 percent of the faked neurotic records while mislabeling only 6 percent of the records from either known neurotics or normals taking the test under standard conditions. These findings are in accord with the values obtained from Minnesota adult men and women on the Ds scale. Thus, in clinical practice, any record with a Ds raw score of 35 or higher should be considered suspect, particularly if it has a generally neurotic configuration in the clinical-scale scores. Similarly, a Ds score of 15 or fewer raw-score points from a record with a neurotic clinical configuration should be considered reassuring; the subject probably did not deliberately create a neurotic profile in an attempt to dissemble or malinger such an emotional disturbance. Even from fairly extensive contact with severely neurotic patients it appears to be very difficult to reconstruct with any fidelity how such individuals view themselves, see the world, or experience their relationships with others. The professionals in Gough's study did not achieve any more accuracy in this kind of test slanting than his undergraduate psychology students in spite of their more extensive reading, their training in therapeutic empathy, and their many hours of direct observation and interviewing of patients in the midst of neurotic difficulties.

Cofer, Chance, and Judson's Mp Scale. Another promising but less well studied validity indicator was derived from an investigation by Cofer, Chance, and Judson (1949) of malingering in both directions, greater adjustment as well as very poor adjustment, by college students. These investigators used both male and female undergraduates but did not report analyses carried out on the sexes separately. Nor did they gather additional data for cross-validational evaluations of shrinkage from the separations achieved on their original groups of subjects.

The general procedures used in this faking study were, briefly, that three groups of undergraduate students in psychology were requested, in a counterbalanced order, to complete the MMPI under standard instructions and under one of three retest conditions: standard retest, fake emotional disturbance (negative malingering), or making the best possible impression (positive malingering). The two administrations were given a week or two apart and the results were similar in either testing order. A little over a hundred items in the test showed statistically stable changes in endorsements from standard to positive malingering instructions, while over 450 items were changed from standard to negative malingered conditions. The authors then searched for items which were unchanged under negative malingering instructions but which were shifted under positive malingering instructions. These thirty-three items provide a check on the tendency to answer the MMPI in such a way as to create a very favorable impression. On the original groups, Cofer, Chance, and Judson found that 86 percent of the positively malingered records from these college students fell above the cutting score of 20 raw-score points, while only 4 percent of the bona fide records obtained under standard instructions scored above that point. (No negatively faked record had an Mp score as high as 20 points.) Minnesota men and women score within the same range as the college students on the Mp scale. The suggested cutting score is probably a good basis for judging either that the person has been sufficiently free and open in his answers to the test to provide a dependable protocol for personological interpretation or that he has been slanting the answers to create a particularly favorable impression. When a test with a normal clinical profile is obtained with an Mp score below 20, greater credence can probably be given the test inferences about the adequacy of the subject's adjustment.

Moderator (Mo) Scale. A different approach to this problem was used by Osborne (1969) who derived a special validity indicator which he called the moderator scale, Mo, to identify MMPI records from which clinical judgments were found to be undependable. The clinical interpretations of the MMPI profile which he studied were provided by two experienced MMPI judges on the staff of the University of Minnesota Department of Psychiatry. They were given sets of profiles which were carefully screened for acceptability on the usual validity-scale criteria (no more than 10 Cannot Say answers; raw scores on L, F, and K less than 10, 21, and 23, respectively) as well as an F minus K index (see Chapter 5) of no greater than 11 T-score points. Their test interpretations consisted of tallies on a standard checklist of thirty-one symptoms commonly appearing in male and female inpatients as observed at intake on the psychiatric wards of the University of Minnesota Medical Center. Their MMPI interpretations were restricted to five or fewer features expected to appear on each case as judged by their interpretation of the MMPI.

Osborne divided the cases into those patients on whom the MMPI interpretations were most accurate (hits) and those on whom the MMPI judges were in greatest error (misses). He derived by item analysis a list of thirty-eight items for the Mo scale which separated hits from misses and evaluated the effectiveness of this scale on a cross-validational sample of similarly classified hits and misses from the same psychiatric setting. The Mo scale stood up well on this new sample. Osborne cited the need for more extensive cross-validational work, both in similar settings and in new contexts.

On his population, a score of 21 raw-score points or higher identified about 50 percent of the new misses while misidentifying around 7 percent of the dependable records. There is little indication in the work so far about the base rate of such undependable records in the usual run of acceptable MMPI protocols in such a setting. Osborne reports that the main feature of the records which were consistently misinterpreted was their lower than usual clinical-scale elevations. Consistent with this finding was the fact that the Mo scale correlated strongly negatively with the F scale and all the clinical scales except scale 9. Mo was positively related at a moderate level with both L and K, but it seems to be reflecting variance that is independent of these standard validity indicators. It is not clear either why Osborne's approach was generally successful when the effort of Smith and Lanyon (1968) to develop a moderator scale intended to improve MMPI-based predictions of probation violations by juvenile offenders was so completely unsuccessful. The approach used in the study by Kanun and Monachesi (1960) also resembles these two investigations; they were quite successful in deriving a special scale to be employed on cases which are declared invalid by the usual validity-scale standards.

One further line of research would seem to bear upon this general approach. Pepper (1964) derived two scales, which he called the item change scale, Ic, and the T-score change, Tc, to identify normal test subjects who showed the greatest shifts in their item endorsements and profile elevations over a three-week test-retest interval. Subjects low on the Ic or Tc scales possess high MMPI stability or predictability, while subjects high on these scales are likely to change their answers extensively within this short interval (during which relatively little has changed in either their life circumstances or their emotional adjustment). Goldberg and Jones (1969) found that Pepper's Ic scale was dependable in identifying subjects with short-term test-retest instability in a sample of undergraduates at the University of Oregon, thus generally substantiating Pepper's findings with this measure. These scales may provide a means of identifying subjects whose answers to the MMPI are either enduring self-views or transitory and unstable reports of their momentary perceptions and experiences. This scale may also provide moderator information about the utility of a given MMPI record as a basis for inferences about stable or enduring personality attributes.

CHAPTER 5. Validity-Scale Configurations

THE VALIDITY indicators that are available for use with the MMPI were generally developed one by one, without regard for the role or contribution of the other indices. Interpretation of them usually involves some attention to their patterning as well. The growing body of research bearing upon the significance of each scale and the various patterns or combinations will be reviewed in this chapter. Here, too, it will be necessary to anticipate some of the concepts and findings on the clinical scales proper that will be more systematically presented in Part Three of this volume. Some of the scale designations and coding procedures which have already been introduced in Part One on the scoring, coding, and determination of various special indices and scores should be reviewed at this time if the reader is not already familiar with them.

Although the original validity indicators (?, L, and F) were scaled on an a priori basis in deriving the T-score transformations for them, it can be seen from the actual means and standard deviations obtained by Hathaway and Briggs (1957) on carefully refined subsamples of Minnesota men and women (selected from the original derivational groups) that the standard profile sheets are quite appropriately tabled. Table 5-1 gives the values for the standard validity indicators and for the rest of the basic scales in the MMPI profile as well. Therefore, the various interpretative ranges given below for each of the standard validity indicators, both in raw scores and T scores, correspond closely to the familiar values employed by clinicians since the final format of the MMPI profile sheet was agreed upon in 1950. The qualitative labels supplied largely agree with the usage in various standard interpretive works on this instrument, e.g., Hathaway and Meehl (1951a, 1951b), Good and Brantner (1961), Marks and Seeman (1963), Gilberstadt and Duker (1965), but where necessary some arbitrary divisions have been introduced for the sake of clarity and uniformity.

Single-Scale Interpretive Implications

Each of the standard validity indicators on the MMPI will be taken up separately to summarize the general meaning that each has at various levels or within particular score ranges. In this section it should be assumed that

Table 5-1. Raw-Score Means and Standard Deviations on Each MMPI Scale for the Minnesota Male and Female Normals

	Males			Females		
Scale	No.[a]	Mean	S.D.	No.[a]	Mean	S.D.
L	294	4.05	2.89	397	4.27	2.63
F	111	3.88	4.24	118	3.49	3.13
K	274	13.45	5.66	373	12.08	5.07
1 (Hs)	294	4.53	4.37	397	6.86	5.28
1 (Hs) + .5 K	274	11.34	3.90	373	13.14	4.88
2 (D)	294	16.63	4.18	396	19.26	5.18
3 (Hy)	345	16.49	5.51	475	18.80	5.66
4 (Pd)	294	13.99	3.93	397	13.44	4.23
4 (Pd) + .4 K	274	19.30	4.11	373	18.41	4.40
5 (Mf)	117	20.44	5.13	108	36.51	4.83
6 (Pa)	293	8.06	3.56	397	7.98	3.32
7 (Pt)	293	9.86	7.19	397	13.06	7.78
7 (Pt) + 1 K	274	22.95	4.88	373	25.21	6.06
8 (Sc)	294	9.57	7.43	397	10.73	7.96
8 (Sc) + 1 K	274	22.26	5.21	373	22.65	6.50
9 (Ma)	294	14.51	4.42	397	13.65	4.50
9 (Ma) + .2 K	274	17.00	3.87	373	16.12	4.11
0 (Si)	193	25.00	9.58	350	25.00	9.58

SOURCE: Hathaway and Briggs (1957).

[a] These figures are merely the total number of men and women used in the derivation of the statistics. In the actual calculation, data from smaller numbers of subjects were combined in various ways to balance the effects of age or sex.

the other validity indicators in the profile are somewhere within their middle ranges and that attention is focused on the deviations (or lack of deviation) on the scale under discussion. In the next portions of the chapter, the deviations on two or more scales in combination will be taken up and their special interpretive significance noted.

Range of Scores on the L Scale. When the MMPI was first published (Hathaway and McKinley, 1943), none of the validity scales were tabled for values below 50. The mean for both male and female normal adults on L was set at four raw-score points and the standard deviation rounded to three raw-score points. Current profile sheets from the Psychological Corporation give values down to a T score of 36 for a raw score of zero and up to 80 for a raw score of 13. (Some of the automated scoring services use profile forms in which the L-scale values have been tabled for the whole range from zero to fifteen items.) These T-score values for L conform well to the results of the reanalyses carried out by Hathaway and Briggs (1957) as shown in Table 5-1. Clinical practice has generally shown that somewhat narrower limits of interpretation should be employed for L-scale T-score levels than those recommended initially in the early test manuals. Such practice would also be consistent with the findings of Rosen (1952) when he analyzed the records of a representative sample of psychiatric patients. He found that the standard deviation on L for these cases was closer to two than to three. (This restriction in range, for example, meant that a raw score of 10 was equal to three standard deviations or a T-score equivalent of 80 rather than 70 on the regular profile.) Therefore, the general interpre-

Raw-Score Range	*T-Score Range*	*Interpretive Levels*
0–2	36–43	Low range
3–5	46–53	Middle range
6–7	56–60	Moderate elevation
8–9	63–66	High elevation
10+	70+	Marked elevation

tive ranges shown in the accompanying list are suggested for use with the L scale. These designations do not correspond precisely with Blazer's (1965b) ranges but are in good accord with the recommendations and descriptions provided by Gilberstadt and Duker (1965) and Marks and Seeman (1963). The interpretive guidelines provided by Good and Brantner (1961) are also consistent with these cutting-score levels.

Low-range scores have not been studied very extensively but available evidence indicates that all or most of the L-scale items may be answered True by persons attempting to create an extremely pathological picture of themselves on the test. Scores in the low range, however, are also earned by normal persons who are relatively unconventional, independent, and self-reliant and are merely unusually free in acknowledging such social foibles or faults. As will be made clearer later, these normal subjects may answer the items on the K scale in a defensive way while freely acknowledging the negative attributes cited in the L-scale items.

Scores in the middle range, of course, occur most frequently and indicate some care and discrimination in answering the items in this scale (and in the remainder of the test). Scores in this range are generally earned by denying tendencies to gossip, or to think bad thoughts, or wanting to avoid paying for a movie by sneaking into a theater, or seeking to become friends of important people to increase the subject's own sense of importance. (See Table 4-1.) That is, most persons when taking the MMPI selectively defend themselves against some specific faults while candidly acknowledging a number of others. Extreme adoptions of either a self-excoriative or self-enhancing set are the exception rather than the rule in responding to this test. Similarly, extreme acquiescence in acknowledging that the items pertain to them (all True) and extreme rejection of all items (all False) as not having any applicability to themselves are both atypical modes of approach to this task of self-description.

As scores on L approach the level where half of the items or more are endorsed in the defensive direction, the interpretation becomes more complicated. It is quite possible, for example, that a score in this general range (7 or 8 raw score) may be the result of an indiscriminate pattern of marking the items without any regard for the content of the items endorsed. If a subject answers the test essentially at random (see Chapter 4), about half of the L items would end up marked False and the T score of the L scale would fall in the moderate or the high range. It would be inappropriate to interpret such a score as reflecting any particular personological attribute, be it defensiveness or whatever.

Valid elevations in the high to markedly elevated ranges are most likely to be generated by subjects who are honestly describing themselves as they see themselves. They tend, therefore, to be overly conventional, socially conforming, and prosaic. Some of the descriptions actually correspond to their habitual patterns of behavior while other features of their test answers reflect their poor insight and limited self-knowledge. That is, they may be highly religious and moralistic individuals who rigidly control any overt expression of antisocial or unethical impulses. At the same time, studies of these test subjects also indicate that they may be expressing some of these tendencies without being aware of the impact that their behavior may have upon others or without recognizing their own motives and purposes. Thus, elevated L-scale values are likely in test subjects who are ministers, reformers, social activists, or evangelical missionaries. Persons with borderline paranoid reactions may answer many L items in the defensive direction (Good and Brantner, 1961; Coyle and Heap, 1965) through their grandiose views of themselves and the perfectionism that they must ascribe to themselves. Other conditions which generate serious limitations in self-insight are also related to elevations on the L scale, particularly hysteroid defensive mechanisms and elaborate hypochondriacal reactions.

Less frequently, an elevated L scale indicates that the subject has deliberately slanted his test answers to create a special impression of freedom from any psychological problem or characterological fault. This kind of test distortion is employed by persons with limited sophistication or proficiency in dealing with psychological tests, however, and L-scale elevations of this kind are most frequently encountered in tests from people with only elementary school education, with intellective levels below average, or with histories of socioeconomic or cultural deprivation (rural, urban ghetto, or ethnic minority backgrounds). Both clinical studies and experimental investigations of faking on the MMPI have indicated that brighter, more highly educated, and more knowledgeable subjects avoid L-scale items in their efforts to create both a favorable and a believable image on this test. Scores on L, therefore, are only likely to reflect the more crude and brazen attempts at test distortion. Correspondingly, however, the test-slanting approach is likely to have a very pervasive impact upon scores on the rest of the MMPI. For example, Meehl and Dahlstrom (1960) found it necessary to have a separate rule to cover the neurotic and psychotic cases with even moderately elevated L-scale values (Rule 4 in Table 1 in Appendix J). Occasionally, the lack of psychological insight which leads to excessive L-scale values may result in a test subject's generating some uncharacteristically high elevations on the clinical scales through a failure to comprehend the implications of his answers. Thus, elevations on scale 9 may result from a pervasive denial of psychopathology that simultaneously generates high L-scale values and low scores on most of the remainder of the clinical profile.

Levels of F-Scale Elevation. General clinical usage of the F scale has led to the system of designating levels of F scores shown below. These levels conform to most of the interpetive guides advanced by Good and Brantner (1961); Marks and Seeman (1963); Gilberstadt and Duker (1965); Carkhuff,

Barnette, and McCall (1965); and Hovey and Lewis (1967). It should be noted that they are at variance with some of the designations by Blazer (1965c) in which raw-score and T-score levels appear to have been confused.

Raw-Score Range	*T-Score Range*	*Interpretive Levels*
0– 2	44–48	Low range
3–10	50–66	Middle range
11–16	68–80	Moderately high range
17–20	82–88	Very high range
21–25	90–98	Markedly high range
26–38	100+	Random range
39+		Atypical range

Scores in the low range, as mentioned above, indicate that the test subject has agreed with the normative subjects on almost all these items, showing a marked degree of response conformity. Since the average subject gets a raw score of 4 significant items on this scale, those falling in the low range show fewer than the typical number of deviant beliefs, attitudes, or unusual experiences. These low scores may reflect a systematic tendency to avoid endorsement of socially unacceptable, threatening, or disturbing content among the test items; this possibility should be checked out by examination of the other validity indicators and the pattern generated by the clinical scales (see below). Efforts to hide serious psychopathology and deliberately fake a good test record may lead to very low F-scale scores.

There is evidence from the IPAR studies (Gough, McKee, and Yandell, 1955) that such low F scores may also be given by well-adjusted persons who are described by interviewers as unassuming and unpretentious, simple and sincere, moderate, honest, slow, calm, and dependable. The F-scale levels that they show on their MMPI profiles appear to be consistent with their life style and temperament, reflecting few protestations, little social friction, and general compatibility with and accommodation to their present situation.

Middle-range F scores are generally obtained on most administrations of the MMPI in normative studies and in applications in most typical clinical settings. Scores toward the upper end of this range may reflect some special area of concern which leads to the atypical endorsement of several items as a subset of the F scale. For example, there are several items dealing with a person's relationship with his family on this scale (see Table 4-2). If a subject is currently going through a period of mild rebellion against his family's religion, standard of living, or other basic values, he may answer such items in the significant direction as a reflection of this special alienation. McKegney (1965) has pointed out that some of the F-scale items bear upon delinquent acts or experiences encountered when one is treated as a juvenile delinquent in current police and court procedures. Scores on the F scale may reflect these special circumstances in the person's present situation. Similarly, elevations may also reflect involvement in radical or extremist political movements, participation in deviant religious sects, or experience with special health problems. Although these rebellious or socially deviant involvements may affect the subject's answers to some MMPI items, these special circumstances, in themselves, do not generate markedly high F-scale elevations or spuriously high clinical-scale values. Whenever these effects are noted on the MMPI, it is likely that the MMPI patterns and the special social involvements are jointly reflecting more pervasive psychopathology. As noted below, it requires an extensive basis of special circumstance to generate both high-ranging F scores and corresponding profile configurations.

Moderately high F-scale elevations may, therefore, reflect the same special circumstances noted above but in extreme form. Social protest or emotional commitment to religious or political movements may lead to occasional elevations in this range on the F scale. More likely sources of these elevations, however, are difficulties in reading and interpreting the test statements or comprehending the test instructions, severe neurotic or moderate psychotic reactions which lead the test subjects to report these unusual feelings and experiences, or behavioral disturbances that affect test cooperation. In early applications of the MMPI, scores on F within this range were usually considered to be invalidating and the records therefore were not interpreted clinically. Studies by Kazan and Sheinberg (1945), Gough (1946), Modlin (1947), and Schneck (1948), however, soon documented the fact that many of these records were being needlessly discarded. Although some of the cases which they studied had produced random or grossly confused MMPI protocols, the majority of the tests they obtained among their patients with moderately high or even very high F-scale values showed profiles which corresponded well with the clinical status of these persons, as judged by independent observations. The data published by Brozek and Schiele (1948) were particularly cogent in documenting this broader interpretation of elevated F-scale values since they were able to plot changes in endorsements of F-scale items that matched closely the alterations in clinical status during a period of experimentally induced emotional and physical stress. Both deterioration and amelioration in this experimental neurosis were accurately reflected in the shifts in self-descriptions on the F scale as well as on the neurotic triad in the clinical profile. A number of other studies (see Volume II) have indicated that the F scale mirrors extent and severity of psychopathological involvement.

Among persons relatively free of serious psychopathology, the IPAR studies (Gough, McKee, and Yandell, 1955) characterize those with moderately high F-scale scores as moody, restive, curious, changeable, dissatisfied, restless, talkative, complex, unstable, opinionated, affected, and opportunistic. These findings appear to be in close agreement with the contentions above that F-scale elevations in this general range may reflect valid content pertaining to special involvements in deviant social and political movements. The temperamental attributes found to correlate with F-scale values in groups of subjects who are above average in intellective ability and fully cooperating with the test instructions are consistent with this kind of participation and commitment.

Very high F-scale values are rare among neurotic or intact psychotic patients but are given by more severely disorganized psychotic patients, severely disturbed alcoholics on the brink of delirium tremens, very uncooperative subjects with behavior problems, or persons with marginal reading comprehension. Before clinical or personological inferences can be drawn from F scores within this range, therefore, it is necessary to attempt to rule out the possibility that the test subject was either so out of contact or so far beyond his reading comprehension level in taking the MMPI that he was not responding to the content of the test items in many if not most instances. If such determinations can be made, research studies indicate that even with F scores in this very high range the MMPI protocol may yield dependable clinical information.

One line of evidence comes from the work of Kanun and Monachesi (1960) on the identification of delinquency-prone adolescent boys and girls from MMPI data obtained while these youngsters were in the ninth grade. These investigators identified samples of ninth graders who had given invalid MMPI profiles; the judgment of invalidity was based primarily on elevated F-scale values (above 15 raw score) but also on elevated L scores (above 9 raw score). From such records they were successful in deriving a special delinquency scale, with separate norms for boys and girls, which stood up well on cross-validation with other similarly invalid protocols but which did not discriminate boys or girls with delinquency proneness from nondelinquents when applied to MMPI protocols with lower L and F scores. The verbal behavior of subjects with high F scores (or L scores) is thus demonstrably different on many other items in the MMPI item pool besides those constituting these validity indices but is not therefore necessarily random or unpredictable. Other studies (Gynther, 1961; Gauron, Severson, and Englehart, 1962; Gynther and Shimkunas, 1965a, 1965b; Blumberg, 1967; Gynther and Petzel, 1967; and F. W. King, 1967) have reinforced and extended the original findings that on occasion the F-scale items may directly pertain to special experiences, beliefs, or attitudes that derive from the psychopathological processes also being sampled by the MMPI clinical scales. In these instances, then, elevated F-scale scores are part and parcel of the behavioral disorder generating the clinical-scale configuration, documenting its range and severity but not reflecting adversely upon the dependability of the MMPI protocol itself. Furthermore, there is reason to believe that this same overlap in what is being reflected both in high-ranging clinical-scale configurations and in F-score elevations can generate F scores well beyond this very high level into what we generally call the random range. In some rare instances these F-scale scores will even fall beyond this random range with raw-score values of 40 or more. The interpretation seems to be essentially the same: the person's psychopathology is sufficiently extensive and severe to give him a long list of bizarre, peculiar, and atypical experiences which he then describes and relates at length in the items in the F scale and elsewhere in the MMPI and which affect scores on a number of clinical and validity scales (see Shaffer, Ota, and Hanlon, 1964).

A study by Rice (1968) also throws additional light on the clinical correlates of very high F-scale elevations. He identified two groups of patients at the University of Wisconsin Medical Center who were hospitalized for psychiatric disorders. One group all showed F-scale elevations on their admission MMPI protocols beyond 16 raw-score points; the other scored between 3 and 13 points. He found the very high F scores correlated with a variety of acting-out patterns, primarily involving aggression directed toward the environment or toward themselves. This relationship between F-scale elevation and aggressive characteristics was particularly clear in the male patients. Among females, there were fewer instances of lack of control or explicit acting upon these impulses and greater evidence of hostility in their projections on the Rorschach.

When the F-scale values fall in the random-score range a distinct possibility exists that the record was generated by some approach to the test that did not in fact involve reading the statements or making any attempt to apply them to oneself. As previous research has indicated (Cottle and Powell, 1951; Dahlstrom and Welsh, 1960; Fox, 1964; and Finney, 1965b), whether the answers are merely guessed, marked haphazardly, determined by the roll of a die or the flip of a coin, completed alternately as True, False, True, False, etc., or marked True or False by odd and even rows or columns on the answer sheet, the average score on the F scale falls close to the theoretical mean for a sixty-four-item scale, namely, 32 raw-score points. In addition, the standard deviations of the F scores obtained on such sets of test records range from 3.5 to 5.1. While the actual ranges of the raw scores on F from these empirical studies may extend from 20 to 44, most of these scores fall within the limits established for the random range (26–38). A score falling within this range, therefore, should prompt careful examination of the answer sheet and the test configuration for evidence of the operation of some kind of random-response approach to the MMPI (see configurations of L, F, and K below).

Scores beyond the random-score range have already been discussed (see the material above for very high F-scale values) as most likely reflecting severity of psychopathology or highly special and atypical experiences in the individual's behavioral disorder. When the card form of the MMPI is used, however, there is another possible reason for F-scale values falling within this atypical range. Occasionally the card piles may become inadvertently exchanged so that the zero items from each set are recorded as plus items (see Part One of this volume on administration and scoring the card form of the test). As a result the set of raw scores obtained will be complements of the true raw scores on each component scale. Such an accidental mixup in recording would usually generate an unfamiliar test pattern but if the subject answers many items in the significant direction, the pattern would be less easily detected as an artifact. The best check, however, is the score on F which would probably be at a suspicious level in almost any protocol on which such a mixup had occurred. Recovery of the original scores is possible if the confusion occurred on both the subject's

True and False answers. The raw score can merely be subtracted from the total number of items in that scale, and this difference entered on the test profile instead. This is not possible, unfortunately, if only the True answers (or the False answers) were involved in the scoring mixup. The test would then have to be readministered to the subject to get a useful set of MMPI scores. It should also be noted that the same kind of protocol may result if the subject who is given one of the group forms should misunderstand, for one reason or another, where he is to mark his True and his False endorsements on the answer sheet. Most subjects who can read the MMPI statements well enough to produce an otherwise valid test protocol are not likely, of course, to misunderstand the T and F rows or columns, but it does happen occasionally. It is more likely, however, that a subject who is being given a tape-recorded version because of his marginal literacy may fail to understand where to record True and False answers on the answer sheet that is placed before him for his use while listening to the recording. Similarly, a blind subject who is using numbered cards to record his answers to the tape recording may also reverse the placement for True and False answers, thus producing the same artifactual protocol that would result from a confusion at the time of recording and scoring.

Levels of K-Scale Elevation. In general test usage, the values of the K scale have not been a basis for discarding a protocol as invalid or excluding it from a research sample in the way that values of ?, L, and F have been employed. There are no cutting-score levels on K, then, in this sense. Nevertheless, there are general interpretive levels on this scale which can be used as guidelines for inferences about both specific test-taking orientations and more general personological attributes of a particular subject. MMPI practice follows the general format shown in the accompanying list.

Raw-Score Range	*T-Score Range*	*Interpretive Levels*
0– 4	27–35	Markedly low
5– 9	36–44	Low range
10–15	46–55	Middle range
16–20	57–64	High average
21–25	65–74	Moderately elevated
26–30	75–83	Markedly elevated

As in the interpretation of the other validity indicators, first consideration should be given to the implications of a given K score for the way that the person has approached the MMPI task, secondarily to the clues it may provide about the kind of person he is. Obviously, these two kinds of test inference are not independent; he may approach the task of self-description in a given way because he is a certain kind of person, as well as for reasons stemming from the behavior of the examiner, the status that he may currently possess, the situation in which he finds himself, or the purposes for which he believes these examinations are being carried out. Since the primary personological inferences are to be drawn from the clinical profile, higher priority in any implications of the K-scale values goes to test-taking considerations that may set limits or put special conditions on the utility of the remainder of the test protocol.

Markedly low T scores on K raise the immediate concern that the subject has fabricated his answers on the test or exaggerated his problems to create an impression that he is undergoing a serious emotional disturbance. Obviously, the motivation for such test slanting may arise from deliberate malingering, from special pleading for help or attention, or from a general state of panic in which the subject believes for the moment that his world or his control over his destiny is rapidly disintegrating. Whatever the source, the subject readily acquiesces in every adverse implication of the test statements, freely acknowledging every horrifying experience, every undesirable attribute, every forbidden impulse. Such indiscriminate endorsement of all these diverse items usually affects other validity indicators as well, as will be discussed in detail below. The effect upon the clinical profile is usually to generate very high elevations on most or all of the scales, weakening the discriminatory power of individual scales and of the interscale configurations alike. Occasionally, in spite of the masking effect of this general approach to the test, some insight may be provided by the clinical profile into the psychological basis for the general acquiescence set; often the explanation must be sought elsewhere. These problems will be taken up in the next section of this volume. At this point, however, it should be noted that markedly low K scores may be part of an acute undifferentiated schizophrenic reaction, may reflect the (often masked) confusional state of an alcoholic on the verge of delirium tremens, may merely be the way a patient with limited intellective capacities and naive comprehension of the operations of a modern medical center tries to make sure that he will be listened to and considered for assistance in competition for limited medical and psychiatric services, or may stem from an unskillful effort to create an image of a psychiatric casualty for financial gain, for reduction of responsibilities, or for discharge from military service.

Scores within the low range on K may, of course, stem from the same processes that generate markedly low scores, except that the subject may be a little less naive in his faking, a little more discriminating in his endorsements, or a little less confused or disorganized. Less frequently, however, will scores within this range reflect these special motivations or problems in taking the MMPI or in communicating with the test examiner. Rather, these scores are more likely to be the product of the general way in which the person sees himself and manages his daily affairs. Such subjects often have limited educational experience, a deprived family background, small-town or rural origins, low occupational status, and limited incomes. As part and parcel of this life situation they have many problems—financial, interpersonal, occupational—to which they also are quite willing to admit and which they delineate at length on a test like the MMPI. They are often quite self-critical and overly candid in their self-disclosures. They are also often quite unaware of the unfavorable impression that they thereby may create on higher status persons with whom they come into contact.

Even within the limited range of subjects which Block and Bailey (1955) and Gough, McKee, and Yandell (1955) studied at IPAR in samples of air force officers many of these personological characteristics could be discerned. The men in their groups who scored low on K were described as conforming, submissive and compliant with authority, slow in personal tempo, cautious, awkward, inhibited, peaceable, retiring, shallow, dissatisfied, high-strung, cynical, and individualistic. While not all these descriptors are fully consistent with one another, the general picture that emerges is a person with a poor self-concept, strongly self-dissatisfied, but lacking either the self-managing techniques or the interpersonal skills required to deal effectively with his situation in such a way as to improve his lot in the world. Consistent with these interpretations of low-ranging K scores are the findings of Berger (1953, 1955), Sweetland and Quay (1953), Gowan (1955), E. E. Smith (1959), King and Schiller (1959), Heilbrun (1961), and Yonge (1966) that K scores are positively related to self-management, personal effectiveness, and healthy personal insight and self-understanding. Many of these findings support the early interpretive hypotheses about K advanced by Collier (1946), Snoke and Ziesner (1946), and Wiener (1951) that this scale reflected positive characteristics of control, personality integration, and insight. There is evidence from the work of Nakamura (1960) and Himelstein and Lubin (1966) that these implications about personality integration from the K-scale values hold more dependably for women than they do for men; for male subjects they suggest that the test-taking orientations are the more appropriate kind of inference. The findings of Rogers and Walsh (1959) in their studies of self-ratings of college women suggest that the K scores may be complexly determined even for female subjects, reflecting efforts to maintain self-esteem and block personal insights.

Scores in the typical range on K indicate a balance in self-disclosure and self-protection in answering the items of the MMPI (Blazer, 1966). Adult subjects with elementary school levels of education and lower-middle-class socioeconomic status will generally earn scores within this range. Occasionally clients with higher status backgrounds may score at this level and the implications of such lower-than-expected scores are generally that these persons are undergoing some decrement in their self-maintenance or personal control. Accompanying this lowered defensiveness one generally finds a readiness to confide and to disclose problems, concerns, and undesirable personal actions or attitudes in interviews and tests alike. While such accessibility greatly facilitates initial assessments or early treatment efforts, these self-attitudes may later prove to be stumbling blocks to long-range psychotherapeutic efforts.

Scores in the high average range on K are generally earned by subjects with upper-middle-class or lower-upper-class status and background. College-level subjects typically score within this range. Most frequently in these instances the subject is well adjusted, self-reliant, and easily capable of dealing with his day-to-day problems. The generally favorable view of himself which these answers convey is, therefore, correct and appropriate. Contrary to some of the conclusions of many of the response-set studies summarized in Volume II, the subject is not merely describing himself favorably to curry social acceptance; his life *is* under control and his affairs *are* well managed. There seem to be few emotional disturbances or threats to self-esteem or self-control and little interpersonal wrangling. These subjects show restraint, prudence, and circumspection in their everyday conduct and behavior.

The IPAR studies of Block and Bailey (1955) and Gough, McKee, and Yandell (1955) identified several characteristics of the subjects among the air force officers who scored at this level on the K scale: reasonable, clear-thinking, showing initiative, readily ego-involved, enterprising, resourceful, versatile, having high intellective ability, ingenious, enthusiastic, verbal, sociable, taking an ascendant role, being a good mixer, having wide interests, and fluent. As seen by psychological judges, then, these men were competent, effective, and well balanced. There is no implication that they are not concerned about their own personal or social status, rather they are quite content with the way they find themselves.

If such persons get into psychological difficulties, however, they try to maintain a façade of adequacy by working to make a favorable impression upon others, particularly those with whom they have only superficial contacts, and by denying to themselves, Pollyanna fashion, that they are having difficulties. Block and Bailey noted that these subjects were often taciturn and reserved in their interviews and that their vocabulary was often perceived as overreaching.

Moderately elevated and markedly elevated K scores, therefore, are generally indicative of consistent efforts on the part of these test subjects to maintain an appearance of adequacy, control, and effectiveness. On each occasion where there is some feature which may be rationalized away, they give themselves the benefit of the doubt and endorse the item in the more acceptable direction. Studies of the kinds of items which tap these concerns about the way in which society views misbehavior, personality defects, or social ineptitudes (see Volume II for résumés of research on social favorability) have demonstrated that the K scale covers several such concerns. Interestingly, there are important limits to these rationalizing tendencies so that the facade of adequacy that may be erected does not usually include the frankly unfavorable kinds of attributes included in the L scale. Thus, extremely high elevations on the K scale may be accompanied by low or average scores on L. (Note also the criteria of Hovey, 1948, for identifying special circumvention tricks on the card form of the test, as described in Chapter 4.)

Elevations in the upper ranges of K in patients with already recognized and acknowledged psychological difficulties indicate serious limitations in personal insight and understanding. Unless there are some special problems in the situation, such as uncertainties about the confidentiality of the test records, which create artificial barriers to communication on the test, extremely high elevations on K in psychiatric patients indicate rigidity and inflexibility which are distinct liabilities in any program to restore them to adequate and effective adjustment. Glasscock (1954), for example, found that K scores within this range from psychiatric inpatients signaled slower recovery and less likelihood of remission and release from the hospital than scores in the middle ranges on this scale.

When the K scale is markedly elevated, large portions of the raw scores on the K-corrected scales in the clinical profile will be composed of the K fractions. The clinician should always be alert to two distinct possibilities: either that these corrections may not be sufficient so that there are important trends that are effectively masked or that the corrections are inappropriate on one or more of the corrected scales. As an example of the latter problem, the corrections for scales 7 and 8 may be appropriate, raising the scores on those scales into the range where the clinician accurately discerns the extent of the patient's self-doubts and his questions about his own identity, but the correction for scale 1 inappropriately suggests important somatic preoccupations which do not in fact characterize the patient's current adjustive efforts. In other words, when the K score is very high, it is very likely that the subject is being defensive about some kind of psychological inadequacies, but just which ones may not always be determinable from the MMPI scores or patterns.

Validity-Scale Combinations

The discussions just preceding this portion of the chapter can be considered to be devoted to special combinations of the standard validity indicators in which all but one of the scales fall within the middle range of values. Each deviating scale was then considered either to be submerged, forming a valley, or to be elevated, forming an increasingly prominent spike in the validity-scale configuration. In the remainder of the chapter, the various patterns formed by two or more scales deviating upwards or downwards will be noted and some of their interpretive implications discussed in terms of both the protocol validity and the more general personological correlates that have been found for them.

Combinations with Elevated Cannot Say Scores. The factors which may operate to elevate the Cannot Say score have been discussed at length in Chapter 4. The most usual combination of validity-scale values with such an elevation would, for obvious reasons, be a set of submerged values on each of the other three validity indicators in the profile. The attenuating effect of removing a large number of items from the test in this fashion shows up as a reduction in raw scores across all scales, and a corresponding reduction in T-score values for all scales in the standard profile, except for scale 5 for females. (When the Es scale is used in a routine way, it suffers from the same effect on either male or female records; lower raw-score values reduce the T scores, suggesting erroneously greater "ego weakness" in protocols with large numbers of unanswered items.)

When contrary to this general trend the validity scales show an appreciable elevation along with a rise on the Cannot Say score, they provide some help in distinguishing among alternative interpretations of the Cannot Say score itself. Thus, high Cannot Say and L-scale values lend additional support to the interpretation that the subject is trying to place himself in a highly favorable light but using rather crude methods to distort the test record. That is, the subject appears to be avoiding self-critical answers whenever possible and avoiding answering altogether when he cannot determine the way to cast his answer to make himself look good. These combinations are characteristic of the efforts of subjects lacking in general intelligence, or with limited socioeconomic, educational, or experiential background so that their test sophistication is quite limited.

When an elevated F-scale value accompanies a rise on the Cannot Say score the best explanation seems to be that some important degree of emotional disturbance or confusion is operating to make the task particularly difficult for the test subject. If the basis lies in some intellective limitation, it would appear to be more pervasive and severe than the difficulties leading to the ? and L combination noted above. That is, as Hovey and Lewis (1967) point out, the basis for a joint rise on ? and F seems to be a serious difficulty in comprehending the items so that either the subject answers them haphazardly and rings up a number of F-scale deviations or he acknowledges his difficulties by leaving them blank. Both of these kinds of response to the test serve to limit the usefulness of the final set of clinical-scale values. This validity-scale combination should raise suspicions about the dependability of the clinical profile and instigate efforts to clarify the basis for the difficulties encountered in taking the MMPI. Intelligence testing, reading comprehension batteries, and direct examination of the subject's gross mental status by interview are all fruitful ways of evaluating these possibilities.

Hovey and Lewis (1967) have offered an interpretation of elevated ? and K combinations similar to that advanced for the ? and L pattern above; namely, the test subject was overly defensive in completing the MMPI. Since elevations on the K scale can be obtained by a large number of conforming (zero) responses, a person who seeks to give the conforming answer each time, but who systematically omits answering the items that he cannot decipher, would give this combination of validity indicators and produce a rather submerged profile on the clinical scales at the same time. Since it is impossible to tell specifically what has been omitted in his fairly skillful circumvention of the test instructions, the only recourse in this instance is to make a direct appeal to him to take the test again and answer the items more openly and frankly. Occasionally a more unstructured projective instrument may lead to the clinical insights needed when the MMPI has been unhelpful but even the Rorschach test is susceptible to this kind of guardedness and skillful avoidance of unfavorable material.

Elevations on L and F. There is a basic contradiction in simultaneous elevations of a significant degree on both L and F. While denying socially disapproved actions and thoughts and producing the L-scale elevation, the subject is also acknowledging a number of unusual, bizarre, or atypical experiences, feelings, and reactions to get the F score up as well. As Wilson (1965) has noted, these two trends can often be noted as contrasting behavior in different contexts. That is, the defensiveness that is reflected in the L-scale elevation may characterize the patient in an interview or other face-to-face encounters; the disclosures appearing in the F scale may also show up on the rest of the MMPI and in the results of projective testing. This dissociation may arise from a lack of full appreciation about what is being revealed, as when a person has rather atypical attitudes and valuations about various behavioral deviations, or from poor integration of the diverse behavioral trends that characterize some psychotic processes. In this connection, it is interesting to note that one of the places in which this combination of L- and F-scale elevations has been reported is the simulated psychotic pattern shown by Gough's (1947) normal test subjects.

When the elevations on L and F are extremely high, but K is still low or in the middle range, the pattern is suggestive of the all-plus (or all-X) response pattern that was discussed in Chapter 4. Since the configuration tends toward a psychotic pattern but is too elevated and floating, care should be taken to try to evaluate the likelihood that the subject was responding to the MMPI with this special test orientation. On the card form, this check is quite easy: the total number of X or plus marks on the record form would be obviously excessive. On the booklet answer sheet, a special key for deviant answers would have to be used (see Chapter 4).

Elevations on L and K. As indicated in Chapter 4, the L and K scales are both indices of the process of self-enhancement. Various studies of faking and test distortion (see the section on response biases in Volume II), however, have strongly suggested that this process is a complex and many-faceted one, as yet only partially understood. Generally it has been found that the two kinds of self-presentation reflected in L and in K are mutually exclusive when test subjects are completing the MMPI under the usual kinds of motivation that operate in a clinical setting in which the client is seeking some kind of help and the assessment is being carried out to further those client-centered ends. Test subjects who are naive and relatively less complicated psychologically will, when trying to present themselves favorably to someone in authority, usually endorse the more blatant item content of the L-scale statements but will somehow fail to grasp the more subtle self-denigrations embodied in the K-scale items. With greater knowledge of themselves and with greater worldliness about human foibles, the sophisticated test subject avoids the unbelievable and homely virtues of the L scale and readily acknowledges commonplace character defects; but when presented with the opportunity for more subtle and perhaps more cogent self-enhancements that are provided by the K-scale items, he is able to rationalize and equivocate in such a way as to give himself the benefit of the doubt, thus earning an elevated K score. As indicated above, too, it is not clear from the K-scale value alone, whether he is fully aware of this kind of self-inflation and is waging a conscious conflict over the response alternatives all the way along or is merely giving his own typical self-view quite automatically and comfortably, with or without adequate insight into his own emotional status or psychological health. Since there is a well-known tendency for women to describe themselves more harshly on this kind of test instrument, the evidence suggests that when the elevated K value is earned by a woman it is more likely to reflect psychological effectiveness rather than self-defense; with men, the probability seems higher that the K elevation is a product of skillful evasion.

With this background, then, it is clear that a record that shows a simultaneous rise at a significant level on both L and K raises some special interpretive problems. One possibility that should be considered (although there is little research evidence on this point) is that the two validity indicators are both appropriately reflecting psychological processes characteristic of the person. That is, the clinician should examine the subject's background to check on the possibility that he has recently gone through some move upward in his social level. If the transition is still rather recent and the shift in self-presentation remains incomplete, the L scale may be reflecting his prior modes of defense while the K scale is now mirroring his newly acquired sensitivities and social concerns. Since this kind of mobility can in itself arouse serious conflicts of a more pervasive kind than those centering upon the completion of a personality inventory, the new status may also help account for the emotional difficulties that the subject is experiencing and that have brought him into the agency for study and help.

Joint elevations on L and K have also been frequently found in studies of deliberate faking on the MMPI. These subjects (usually fairly bright and reasonably knowledgeable college undergraduates) were usually instructed to create the most favorable impression of their psychological health that they could (e.g., Hunt, 1948; Cofer, Chance, and Judson, 1949; Gough, 1950; Wiggins, 1959). Since this kind of combination has also been noted in records of bona fide patients who have been instructed either to complete the test the way they think a well-adjusted person would (Rapaport, 1958; Boe and Kogan, 1964; Lanyon, 1967; but not so clearly in Grayson and Olinger, 1957), or the way they hope to be upon discharge (Marks and Seeman, 1963), it must be considered a distinct possibility that the occasional record encountered in clinical practice with this combination of validity indicators is a result of this same kind of deliberate falsification. Marks and Seeman (1963) also note the occurrences of this L and K elevation in combination with two of their clinical-scale configurations; the 13, 31 code and the K+ pattern (see the next section). Their findings on this L and K combination are also in general agreement with the validity-scale V pattern reported by Gross (1959) on samples of Veterans Administration male and female psychiatric inpatients. In his study, Gross did not relate the validity-scale configurations to other MMPI characteristics or evaluate the validity of the particular test protocols but rather collated validity-scale configuration with levels of prior social adjustment and current behavioral disturbance as evaluated from the clinical records of these men and women. The validity-scale V pattern (moderately and equally elevated L and K scores with an F-scale value generally at least a half sigma below them) was associated with rather mild disturbances in behavior but poor pre-hospital social adjustments, particularly in the records from men.

The K+ record, as reported by Marks and Seeman (1963), has an additional elevation on L which brings it into this discussion also. This pattern is characterized by a relatively low general profile elevation for a clinical setting. The personological implications of this pattern are discussed in the next section. Note here should be made of the reservations about the universality of these clinical implications of the K+ record reported by Gynther and Brilliant (1968).

Elevations on F and K. This combination obviously involves the same kind of internal contradiction implied in joint elevations of L and F: the subject is apparently self-enhancing and self-deprecatory at one and the same time. The origins of this pattern seem to be the same kinds of processes as well: pervasive lack of self-insight, confusional states, or difficulties in grasping the nature of the task or the instructions and procedures. Special circumstances should also be considered on rare occasions. For example, Goldman (1961) reports an instance of a college student who shifted his attitude toward the MMPI in mid-testing when he found the time growing short before his scheduled participation in a varsity baseball game; he completed the test by random marking of the remaining items.

Glasscock (1954) has documented the poor treatment prognosis for subjects who give records with elevated F and K scores in a study of psychiatric inpatients. He found that their treatment course was longer in the hospital before they were released and their likelihood of eventual remission significantly lower than was true of patients not having elevated F and K scores. These findings appear to be in accord with the interpretive implications noted above for this validity-scale combination.

Configurations of L, F, and K. Several special combinations of the L, F, and K scales should be noted initially. With very low values of L and F but high K elevations, the likelihood that an all-zero response set was operating should be considered. If the L and K scales occupy the low ranges but F is highly elevated, then an all-True response pattern is suggested. This is also the configuration generated by some patients who are making a blatant appeal for psychological help.

If all three scales are elevated, L and K moderately but F markedly high, then the random-marking pattern is strongly indicated. If all three are extremely elevated, however, the all-False response pattern would appear to be a more likely source of the pattern. Checks for all these special test biases have been described in Chapter 4.

Gross (1959) found that the combination of all three validity scales appreciably above the mean had important implications about the social adjustment and behavioral disturbance of Veterans Administration psychiatric inpatients. Both men and women with this pattern (the inverted V or caret shape) tended to manifest poor interpersonal relationships and show severe disorganization of their behavior both preceding admission and after hospitalization while on the psychiatric wards. Thus, this simultaneous rise on L, F, and K seems to accompany severe psychotic disorders characterized by agitation, disintegration, and poor self-maintenance.

It is also noteworthy that the small group of military subjects with a severe psychoneurotic reaction studied by Schmidt (1948) produced a simultaneous elevation on all three scales, L, F, and K, when they were asked to take the MMPI a second time answering it the way a normal, healthy person would mark it. Although the clinical profile was appreciably lowered under these instructions, the configuration was largely retained, particularly with K-corrected values for the relevant scales.

The F minus K Index

In 1947, Gough advanced a special validity-scale index for the evaluation of a subject's attitude toward the MMPI when completing the test protocol. His studies of faking or deliberate distortions of the test in both self-enhancing and self-depreciating directions (1947; see also Gough, 1950, 1952, 1954) had provided a basis for detection of the effects of these test sets upon both the validity-scale values and the clinical-scale patterns. This index was the difference between the raw score on F and the raw score on K, the F−K index. (Note that this difference uses *raw scores*, not T scores.)

Gough found that the differences between F and K raw scores ranged from −28 to +25, with the median value about −9. Most normals in the Minnesota samples fell between −2 and −19. Subjects who completed the test to create an impression of significant psychopathology, however, had considerably larger F scores than K scores so that the F − K differences generally showed positive values. In his initial report, Gough recommended that any score with an F − K difference of +9 or larger should be considered a malingered record rather than a bona fide product of a psychiatric patient who is giving an accurate self-description on the test. He would have recommended lowering that cutting point to +7, which would have identified even more of the dissembled records, except that he found that many of the MMPI records obtained from military cases who were diagnosed as having some form of psychopathic or character disorder would have been labeled dissembled as well. In his discussion he suggested, however, that this may in fact have been the case since these patients often exaggerated or overemphasized their difficulties in the course of their clinical workup in a military hospital. (See the discussion of the Anthony, 1971, study below.)

Gough (1950) indicated that for some purposes a cutoff of +5 on the F−K raw-score difference would be optimal for identifying malingered or deliberately feigned psychopathology. Branca and Podolnick (1961) found that this cutting point identified all but one of the MMPI records in which a subject was asked to deliberately fake an anxiety state, or respond as "a person suffering great anxiety." The records obtained when the subjects were hynotized and an anxiety state induced by suggestion were not characterized by this kind of validity-scale configuration.

Encouraging results with the F − K index have also been reported by Anthony (1971) in his investigation of air force enlisted men seen in a psychiatric setting who were asked to deliberately exaggerate or enhance their problems on the MMPI. The F − K index separated in a dependable way these "inflated" records both from bona fide test completions by these same subjects and from actual test records of other patients showing the same configural and elevation characteristics as these exaggerated ones. In separating the bona fide original tests from their exaggerated retest counterparts, Anthony found that an F – K raw-score difference of zero was optimal. Comparing exaggerated profiles to presumably bona fide records from other patients with the same profile patterns, Anthony indicates that a cutoff at +19 was best. He also found that the F scale alone, the Ds scale (see Chapter 4), and various tallies of deviant or obvious and zero or subtle items were also useful in this discrimination. He apparently did not attempt any method of compounding probabilities from these various validity indicators in the way reported by Fox (1964) to capitalize upon the accumulative benefits of these converging lines of evidence.

Gough (1950) also explored the utility of the F – K index as a means of identifying records that have been slanted toward extremely sound psychological health. He found that these records generally gave negative values for this index but overlapped so much with the distribution of records from Minnesota normals and particularly from college students' records obtained under standard instructions that he could not establish an efficient cutting-score level.

The difficulty in using the F – K index with college students was also noted by Hunt (1948) in his faking studies with Army Student Training Program enrollees during World War II and by MacLean, Tait, and Catterall (1953) with records from nursing school applicants. Drasgow and Barnette (1957) found the same problem in using the F – K index in their industrial-screening program. MacLean et al. provided a set of transformations for the raw-score differences on F – K by means of sten scores on their student sample; the range of negative values that they report is even greater than the distribution of this index that Gough (1950) found for Minnesota reference normals. The difficulty posed by these college populations, of course, arises from the fact that although they generally get F-score distributions comparable to those obtained from more representative groups, the range of K scores is shifted upward by almost a sigma. That is, the typical record from a college-level subject falls well within the positively malingered range on the F – K index as judged by adult noncollege norms. The same results have also been noted by Exner et al. (1963) in their study of positive and negative malingering by college subjects.

Nelson (1952) noted the effect on the F – K index of different levels on a measure of socioeconomic status. His data help clarify the shift in K values in college samples and the difficulties encountered in using the F – K index on such populations. Table 5-2 shows the relationship between his measure of actual socioeconomic status earned by the subject (as opposed to status gained from his family of origin) and Gough's F – K index on a sample of Veterans Administration psychiatric cases. The socioeconomic levels used in forming his groups were based on a combination of educational and occupational criteria. The high-status group had an average of sixteen years of education and fell within the upper two levels of the Warner occupational scale (Warner, Meeker, and Eells, 1949), while the lower status group averaged a little more than seven years of education and fell within the seventh, or lowest, level on the Warner occupational scale. The F – K

Table 5-2. The Relation between Socioeconomic Level and the F − K Index,[a] as Shown by the Number and Percentage of Psychiatric Inpatients Rated as Having Low or High Status Who Obtained Given F − K Values

F − K Value	Low Status		High Status		Total	
	No.	%	No.	%	No.	%
Low negative or positive (−6 and above) ..	28	65.1	12	29.3	40	47.6
High negative (−7 and below)	15	34.9	29	70.7	44	52.4
Total	43	100.0	41	100.0	84	100.0

SOURCE: Data collected by S. E. Nelson (1952) on eighty-four Veterans Administration psychiatric inpatients.

[a] $\chi^2 = 10.81$; significant at the .1 percent level.

index is significantly affected by the status level of the subject taking the MMPI (a tetrachoric correlation of .55). Different cutting scores should be employed in the application of this index for the various socioeconomic levels being evaluated.

PART THREE: INTERPRETATION OF THE MMPI

CHAPTER 6. Basic Clinical Scales

IN A SERIES of papers (Hathaway, 1956b; Hathaway and McKinley, 1940a, 1942; McKinley and Hathaway, 1940,,1942, 1944) the test authors described the construction of the item pool and the derivation of the scales that make up the standard MMPI clinical profile. Since five of these scales are now routinely plotted in the profile with K corrections, the publication by McKinley, Hathaway, and Meehl (1948) in which the K component of these scales is described should also be considered a part of the basic research material on the clinical scales. All these papers were reprinted in the *Basic Readings* (Welsh and Dahlstrom, 1956) with only slight abridgement and editing. The standard profile that was developed by the Psychological Corporation for the test in 1947 also included Drake's social introversion (Si) scale as the tenth scale in the clinical profile. The derivational research on this scale was described in Drake (1946) and Drake and Thiede (1948); these papers are also reprinted in slightly condensed form in the *Basic Readings*. All of these original publications should be consulted for details of the basic research on these scales; the discussion in this chapter will review the major features of the empirical investigations leading to these scales and some of the important considerations that stem from the choice of criteria, the setting of the research, and the refinements which Hathaway and McKinley introduced in their derivational work.

In Chapter 1, the MMPI item pool and the Minnesota normal reference population were described. The general procedures for constructing each clinical scale involved an item-by-item contrast of the endorsements (True or False) given by a selected group of psychiatric patients and the answers provided by these normal adult men and women. Items which showed appreciably different distributions of endorsements by the criterion and normative groups were selected for membership in that scale, whether the content of the item appeared to bear upon the psychiatric condition or seemed quite irrelevant. Hathaway and McKinley also introduced additional checks to make certain that the empirical differences found in item endorsements were not directly attributable to systematic but irrelevant differences between criterion cases and normals in age, marital status, education, area of residence, or work history. Often the derivational work involved many different samples of criterion patients and it always included cross-validational samples to evaluate the stability of the obtained separations and generality of the scale findings. The derivation of each scale in the clinical profile will be discussed separately below.

Each of the scales has been studied in terms of the personality characteristics associated with subjects who earn high or low scores on that scale. These findings will be summarized for each scale separately in the appropriate places in the remainder of this chapter. It should be remembered that groups formed on the basis of the elevation on a single scale may still be quite heterogeneous and the stable correlates may be rather different in this kind of analysis from those resulting when the groups are formed on the basis of common test *patterns*. The personality correlates of the various basic clinical scales when these scales both are elevated and constitute the highest or second highest scale values in the profile will be summarized in Chapter 7.

Scale 1 (Hs)

The first scale published on the MMPI was an attempt to measure the personality characteristics related to the neurotic pattern of hypochondriasis (McKinley and Hathaway, 1940). Persons diagnosed to have this disorder show an abnormal concern for their bodily functions. Their worries and preoccupations with physical symptoms typically persist in the face of strong evidence against any valid physical infirmity or defect. This worry over their health dominates their life and often seriously restricts the range of their activities and interpersonal relations. The classic picture of hypochondriacs also includes egocentricity, immaturity, and lack of insight into the emotional basis for their preoccupations with somatic processes.

This scale went through several revisions including an attempt to correct for the large number of psychiatric cases who obtained high hypochondriasis scores without having major hypochondriacal features in their clinical picture. (See the H scale and C_H scale in the appendix material of Volume II.) The version now used is the result of a selective elimination of many of the original items and the addition of a few new ones (Hathaway, 1956b). The final list of thirty-three items is shown in Table 6-1. From this list, it can be seen that the items that differentiate hypochondriacs from normal subjects range over a variety of bodily complaints. They are not restricted to any particular part of the body or kind of function. They include generalized aches and pains, specific complaints about digestion, breathing, thinking, vision, and sleep, as well as peculiarities of sensation. A few of the items relate to general health or competence.

There are only eight items which do not overlap with any other scale. According to the work of J. W. Little (1949), based on records from college students seeking vocational guidance, the highest biserial correlation between any of these singly scored items and the total Hs scale is .69 for the item "I have a great deal of stomach trouble." Likewise, the item "I am troubled by discomfort in the pit of my stomach every few days or oftener" is correlated .63 with scale 1. It is interesting to note from Little's work, however, that the items with the highest coefficients in the scale are not the

Table 6-1. Scale 1 (Hypochondriasis): Item Composition, Direction of Scoring, and Overlap with Other Basic Scales

True: 1

29. I am bothered by acid stomach several times a week.
62. Parts of my body often have feelings like burning, tingling, crawling, or like "going to sleep."
72. I am troubled by discomfort in the pit of my stomach every few days or oftener.
108. There seems to be a fullness in my head or nose most of the time.
125. I have a great deal of stomach trouble.
161. The top of my head sometimes feels tender.

False: 1

63. I have had no difficulty in starting or holding my bowel movement.
68. I hardly ever feel pain in the back of the neck.

True: F123

23 (288). I am troubled by attacks of nausea and vomiting.

False: 1. True: (2)

†130. I have never vomited blood or coughed up blood.

False: 12

18. I am very seldom troubled by constipation.

False: 123

2. I have a good appetite.
9. I am about as able to work as I ever was.
51. I am in just as good physical health as most of my friends.
153. During the past few years I have been well most of the time.

True: 123

43. My sleep is fitful and disturbed.

True: 1237

189. I feel weak all over much of the time.

False: 124

155. I am neither gaining nor losing weight.

True: 13

114. Often I feel as if there were a tight band about my head.

False: 13

7. My hands and feet are usually warm enough.
55. I am almost never bothered by pains over the heart or in my chest.
163. I do not tire quickly.
175. I seldom or never have dizzy spells.
188. I can read a long while without tiring my eyes.
190. I have very few headaches.
230. I hardly ever notice my heart pounding and I am seldom short of breath.
243. I have few or no pains.
274. My eyesight is as good as it has been for years.

False: 137

3. I wake up fresh and rested most mornings.

False: 138

103. I have little or no trouble with my muscles twitching or jumping.
192. I have had no difficulty in keeping my balance in walking.

False: 1680

281. I do not often notice my ears ringing or buzzing.

True: 18

273. I have numbness in one or more regions of my skin.

NOTE: In this and subsequent tables showing item composition of scales, an asterisk (*) before an item indicates that it is a correction item on the K scale; a dagger (†) before an item indicates that it is a correction item on scale 2; and a double dagger (‡) before an item indicates that on scale 5 the item is scored in the opposite direction for females. The code number of a scale is given in parentheses if the item is scored as a zero item on that scale.

pure items but ones which overlap with the other scales in the neurotic triad. Thus, Little found that the item "I am troubled by attacks of nausea and vomiting" has a biserial value of .92 with scale 1. Two general body items, "During the past few years I have been well most of the time" (.90) and "I am about as able to work as I ever was" (.82), together with the item "Often I feel as if there were a tight band about my head" (.86), have considerably more discriminating power in scale 1 than any of the pure items even though the items also are scored on scales 2 and 3.

The amount of item overlap with the other scales is large for scale 1. For example, twenty of the thirty-three items in scale 1 also appear on scale 3 (Hy); all are scored in identically the same way. It is interesting to note that except for one item (a correction item on scale 2) there are no items on the hypochondriasis scale for which the scoring direction is reversed on some other clinical scale. This reflects the obviousness and lack of subtlety of the content of the items on scale 1. It also can be noted from Table 6-1 that the items that scale 1 has in common with the other scales are restricted primarily to the neurotic scales; only four items overlap with schizophrenia and one with paranoia. These latter items are more bizarre in content than the others, involving muscle-twitching, balance, ringing and buzzing, and numbness. In contrast, the characteristically hypochondriacal items refer to straightforward internal disorders or to common symptoms of illness. Hathaway, in his chapter in the *Readings* (Welsh and Dahlstrom, 1956), indicated that the current combination of scale 1 plus .5 K can be considered a compromise, a straightforward symptom scale corrected by an index of unwillingness to verbalize such obvious symptomatology. (See the means and standard deviations for Minnesota normal males and females on scale 1, with and without the K corrections, given in Table 5-1.)

Although scale 1 in many instances is interpreted as a symptom scale, it is one of the most stable measures in the MMPI even on clinical groups. The test-retest correlations range between .80 and .90 as reported from various sources in the appendix material in Volume II.

These reliability studies have typically involved retesting over relatively brief periods of a few days. Endicott and Endicott (1963) found an appreciably lower test-retest correlation, however, in a sample of eighty-four military personnel and their dependents over a six-month interval during which most of their cases received some kind of treatment for their psychiatric condition. The correlation between the first testing and the second on scale 1 was .43 indicating considerable shift in Hs scores over this period of time. Of particular interest in their study was the relationship of the Hs scores on these two occasions to ratings of somatic preoccupations at those times. These authors found (personal communication) that the scale 1 level was significantly but only minimally correlated with the degree of somatic preoccupation that these men and women showed in an independent interview at the time of their initial psychiatric workup (.31) but on retesting the Hs level was appreciably more in line with their later levels of somatic concern (.62). Both of the concurrent correlations, however, were higher than the relationship shown between early Hs scores and later ratings (.26) or between later Hs scores and earlier ratings (.13). In other words, when the Hs scores shifted on some of these cases, the changes were in accord with behavior noted in the psychiatric studies. The rather low correlation between manifested somatic preoccupation and scale 1 scores at intake was also reported by Endicott and Jortner (1967) on new samples of psychiatric cases from a civilian hospital and from Endicott's private psychiatric practice, .23 and .37 respectively. This modest level of correspondence between inventory scale and demonstrable somatic concerns in an acutely disturbed psychiatric population has been a persistent difficulty in developing a hypochondriasis measure since the original work reported by McKinley and Hathaway (1940). The stronger relationship between these two measures in the six-month follow-up seems to be attributable to the fact that it is the more traditional and chronically stable hypochondriacal concern that is reflected in the later interviews, and the scale 1 scores appropriately reflect this kind of somatic preoccupation. At the acute phase, scale 1 scores seem to be sensitive to somatic concerns in depressive, anxious, and even schizoid reactions which do not stand out in the interview as blatant or severe somatic concerns and do not get rated as strongly as the typical hypochondriacal complaints.

Although patients with bona fide somatic problems (Greene, 1954; Pinneau and Milton, 1958; Aaronson, 1959; Lair and Trapp, 1962; Stone, Rowley, and MacQueen, 1966) earn somewhat elevated scores on the Hs scale in contrast to physically normal subjects, they do not get scores as high as psychiatric cases with somatization reactions. Rather, the neurotic with somatic concerns and preoccupations will endorse a wide variety of different symptoms and worries while the somatically ill patient without neurotic complications will tend to restrict his answers to the specific manifestations of his disorder. The difference would appear to be that the specific symptoms involving a particular anatomical or physiological system which a physically ill patient may legitimately claim are not sufficiently concentrated either in the MMPI item pool or in the Hs scale to give a markedly elevated score on scale 1.

Consistent with the clinical findings noted above, studies of the factor-analytic complexity of the Hs scale (Comrey, 1957a; O'Connor and Stefic, 1959; Eichman, 1962; Lushene, 1967; Stein, 1968; Barker, Fowler, and Peterson, 1971) have indicated that the pervasive pattern of self-description in this scale is a general tendency to deny good health, both by endorsing explicit statements of that sort and by acknowledging a large variety of rather vague somatic complaints. Thus, Eichman's factor scale III (denial of good health) or the Tryon-Stein-Chu cluster scale II (body symptoms versus lack of physical complaints) both appear to capture the essential features of the score variance in scale 1. This same kind of feature emerged as a second-order factor in O'Connor and Stefic's analysis of the Hs scale, their health concern factor.

There have been some studies of the correlates of high or low scores on scale 1 observed in relatively normal subjects. These cross-validational investigations have furnished evidence on the generality of the findings on psychiatric cases and the usefulness of this scale (as well as the other clinical scales) in evaluating personality processes and characteristics in nonpsychiatric settings. These findings will be summarized here for scale 1 and for the other clinical scales in the remainder of this chapter. The correlates of scale 1 when it is the highest scale in the whole clinical profile, however, are summarized in appropriate sections of Chapter 7.

High Scale 1 Scores. In their analysis of the ratings provided by friends and acquaintances of normal men with high scores on scale 1, Hathaway and Meehl (1952) found that the group was described rather favorably. The terms related to this MMPI variable included sociable, in both senses of mixing well and being forward, enthusiastic, kind, grateful, versatile, courageous, and having wide interests. The contrast between this set of descriptions and findings on psychiatric cases with high scores on scale 1 is attributable in some degree to the fact that these men had only moderately high elevations on scale 1. More important, perhaps, is the fact that the other elevations that this group showed on the MMPI were not taken into consideration. The tabulations in Appendix M indicate that scale 1 occurs most frequently in combination with scale 3 and to a lesser extent with scales 5 and 6. If most of the high scale 1 cases in the group studied by Hathaway and Meehl had even higher scores on one of these three other scales, then the adjectives that were used to describe them would be consistent with the findings in the rest of the literature. (See the descriptions of these other scale correlates below.)

The women in Hathaway and Meehl's normal group who scored high on scale 1 were described as good-tempered, responsive, modest, frank, verbal, and orderly.

In the IPAR study (Gough, McKee, and Yandell, 1955), the staff reported that the assessees who got a high score on scale 1 in part as a function of the K correction were judged to be dull, unambitious, and stubborn. They also showed a dutiful attitude toward their parents and a general looseness in their posture and demeanor. The dullness in speech that the judges perceived in this group corresponds to the observation of the supervisors of student nurses in Hovey's (1953) study that high scale 1 subjects lack ease in oral expression. Hovey's observers also found these girls slow to adjust and lacking in alertness.

When the IPAR staff examined the characteristics of those subjects who got scores at the top of the group distribution of scale 1 without the K correction being used, they found that a slightly different set of adjectives was applied to them. The subjects were still described as stubborn but were now characterized as being aloof, apathetic, awkward, cool, and silent as well. They were judged to show a slowness of personal tempo, a rigidity in thought and action, and a tendency to be easily upset in social situations that differentiated them from the other assessees. The subjects in this group, formed on the basis of their greater tendency to endorse the frankly somatic items in scale 1, seem to be merely psychologically attenuated versions of the more clear-cut hypochondriacal patients on whom the scale was derived.

The derivation of scale 1 involved some consideration of the responses to MMPI items of psychiatrically adequate but physically or medically incapacitated patients in a general hospital. Although physically ill patients may get a raised score on the scale, their illness does not very often lead them to get scores above a T score of 70. (See the discussion above.) Therefore, as Hathaway and Meehl (1951b) pointed out, when a medical patient shows a significant elevation on scale 1, it is an indication of the patient's need for at least some therapeutic reassurance about his physical condition and perhaps for more direct psychotherapeutic attention to his emotional difficulties. Hathaway (1946) and Hastings et al. (1957) have offered evidence of the relationship between high scale 1 scores and overemphasis on existing physical disorders.

Within the psychiatric patient population, a high score on scale 1 is likely to reflect what Gough (1953) characterized as a "crabbed, dissatisfied and demanding demeanor." It frequently indicates a selfish, narcissistic view of the world on the patient's part. Cuadra and Reed (1954) have noted the whiney, sour, and pessimistic approach to their problems that these patients show; they are cynical and defeatist about treatment and unwilling to stick with any therapy or to give a therapist credit for helping them. Diagnostically, a high score on scale 1 minimizes the likelihood of psychosis, although there is an important subgroup of schizophrenic patients who show elevations on scale 1 early in their illness, before the more frankly psychotic behavior is evident either clinically or on the rest of the profile. The more frequent diagnostic implications of high scale 1 scores are (a) various somatic reactions like hypochondriasis and neurasthenia, (b) depressive reactions with important anxiety features like reactive depression, involutional melancholia, and agitated depression, (c) hysterias, both anxiety hysteria and conversion hysteria, and (d) anxiety state, anxiety condition, and the like.

The men in the Hathaway and Meehl normal group who had high scores on scale 1 described themselves as conscientious, frank, and disorderly, and as having home and family interests. There was only one term significant in the self-ratings of the group of high 1 women: affectionate.

Low Scale 1 Scores. The normal men and women studied by Hathaway and Meehl (1952) who scored low on scale 1 were not very clearly typified. Their friends described the men as having narrow interests and the women as being balanced and conventional. Perhaps these persons have behavior patterns that prevent their friends from achieving close familiarity with them, since a better picture came out of the ratings of judges who had to scrutinize these subjects carefully as part of their professional function, for example, as members of an assessment staff or as training supervisors.

Hovey (1953) found the nursing student subjects with low scores on scale 1 to be alert, quick to adjust, and at ease in oral expression. These features were polar opposites of those for high 1's. Gough, McKee, and Yandell (1955) reported rather similar characteristics for low scorers among their assessees at IPAR whether scale 1 was corrected by K or not. When K was used the adjectives typifying the low 1's were these: alert, cheerful, capable, good-looking, responsible, and warm. The judges described those who scored lowest when the scale was not K corrected as alert, ambitious, argumentative, intelligent, and outgoing, and as having initiative. These latter subjects were also seen to be persuasive and to be competitive with their peers. The general picture seems to be one of freedom from hampering, neurotic inhibitions, from overvaluation of oneself and one's own problems, and from undue concern about the adverse reactions of others. These persons are also characterized by an energetic and spontaneous pursuit of the goals and aims in which they have a sincere interest and investment.

Hathaway and Meehl (1952) found the differentiation on self-ratings for their group of low 1's no better than that for the peer ratings. No adjective was significantly used by the low scale 1 women, while in the self-reports of the men only the descriptions sensitive, emotional, and softhearted appeared in the analysis.

Scale 2 (D)

The second scale in the clinical profile was established empirically to measure the degree or depth of the clinical symptom pattern of depression. This mood state is characterized generally by pessimism of outlook on life and the future, feelings of hopelessness or worthlessness, slowing of thought and action, and frequently by preoccupation with death and suicide. The clinical group on which the scale was developed showed relatively uncomplicated depressive patterns, but depression may also accompany a variety of other psychiatric disorders or may complicate personality patterns of almost any kind. Later discussions in this volume will point out how important the elevations on this scale are in a wide variety of personality reactions.

The majority of the sixty items included in the depression scale were selected directly by comparison of this psychiatric group and normals. However, a subset of these items, indicated by a dagger (†) in Table 6-2, was introduced into the scale in an attempt to minimize the elevations on psychiatric cases whose primary diagnosis was not depression. Through these empirical corrections, the final version of scale 2 included items similar to the K scale. (McKinley, Hathaway, and Meehl, 1948, found that the addition of K weights to scale 2 did not improve the differentiation of depressed from normal cases.) In spite of the length of scale 2, there are only thirteen nonoverlapping depression items (six of them are correction items). J. W. Little (1949) reported that on scale 2, as on scale 1, the pure items are not the most differentiating items in the scale. Only the item "I do not worry about catching diseases" has a correlation with the rest of the scale as high as .61. It could be expected from the college groups on which Little performed his analysis that the correction items would show only a very small correlation with the main scale. Some of these items are negatively related to the main item cluster. The best differentiating items are "I feel weak all over much of the time," .78; "I have a good appetite," .71; "My sleep is fitful and disturbed," .66; "I am afraid of losing my mind," .66; "My memory seems to be all right," .65.

Examination of Table 6-2 indicates that the items are in many ways in accord with general expectations about the clinical manifestation of psychiatric depression. The items deal with a lack of interest in things, expressed in a general apathy, in a rejection of base impulses, and in a distinct denial of happiness or personal worth. They describe a feeling of being incapable of performing work satisfactorily or controlling one's thought processes. Another cluster of items, indicating physical symptoms, sleep disturbance,

Table 6-2. Scale 2 (Depression): Item Composition, Direction of Scoring, and Overlap with Other Basic Scales

True: 2

5. I am easily awakened by noise.

False: 2

46. My judgment is better than it ever was.
88. I usually feel that life is worth while.
†95. I go to church almost every week.
†98. I believe in the second coming of Christ.
131. I do not worry about catching diseases.
†154. I have never had a fit or convulsion.
207. I enjoy many different kinds of play and recreation.
242. I believe I am no more nervous than most others.
†270. When I leave home I do not worry about whether the door is locked and the windows closed.

False: (2)

†58. Everything is turning out just like the prophets of the Bible said it would.
145. At times I feel like picking a fist fight with someone.
†191. Sometimes, when embarrassed, I break out in a sweat which annoys me greatly.

False: L2

285. Once in a while I laugh at a dirty joke.

False: FK2

°272. At times I am all full of energy.

False: LK23

°30. At times I feel like swearing.

True: F123

23 (288). I am troubled by attacks of nausea and vomiting.

False: (K2)

39. At times I feel like smashing things.

False: (K23)

°160. I have never felt better in my life than I do now.

False: (K235)

89. It takes a lot of argument to convince most people of the truth.

False: K240

296. I have periods in which I feel unusually cheerful without any special reason.

False: 12

18. I am very seldom troubled by constipation.

True: 123

43. My sleep is fitful and disturbed.

False: 123

2. I have a good appetite.
9. I am about as able to work as I ever was.
51. I am in just as good physical health as most of my friends.
153. During the past few years I have been well most of the time.

True: 1237

189. I feel weak all over much of the time.

False: 124

155. I am neither gaining nor losing weight.

False: 1. True: (2)

†130. I have never vomited blood or coughed up blood.

False: 2346

107. I am happy most of the time.

False: 23478

8 (318). My daily life is full of things that keep me interested.

True: 234780

32 (328). I find it hard to keep my mind on a task or job.

False: (24)

248. Sometimes without any reason or even when things are going wrong I feel excitedly happy, "on top of the world."

True: 2470

67. I wish I could be as happy as others seem to be.

False: (25)

†80. I sometimes tease animals.

True: 26

158. I cry easily.

True: 27

86. I am certainly lacking in self-confidence.

Table 6-2—continued

True: 27. False: (K)

142. I certainly feel useless at times.

False: 27

36. I seldom worry about my health.
122. I seem to be about as capable and smart as most others around me.
152. Most nights I go to sleep without thoughts or ideas bothering me.

True: 278

41. I have had periods of days, weeks, or months when I couldn't take care of things because I couldn't "get going."
159. I cannot understand what I read as well as I used to.
182. I am afraid of losing my mind.

False: 278

178. My memory seems to be all right.

True: 28

52. I prefer to pass by school friends, or people I know but have not seen for a long time, unless they speak to me first.
104. I don't seem to care what happens to me.
259. I have difficulty in starting to do things.

True: 29

13 (290). I work under a great deal of tension.

True: 20

236. I brood a great deal.

True: 20. False: (K)

138. Criticism or scolding hurts me terribly.

False: 20

57. I am a good mixer.

False: (20)

208. I like to flirt.

True: 8. False: (2)

241. I dream frequently about things that are best kept to myself.

True: 9. False: (2)

†64. I sometimes keep on at a thing until others lose their patience with me.
233. I have at times stood in the way of people who were trying to do something, not because it amounted to much but because of the principle of the thing.
†263. I sweat very easily even on a cool day.
271. I do not blame a person for taking advantage of someone who lays himself open to it.

False: 0. True: (2)

†193. I do not have spells of hay fever or asthma.

and gastrointestinal complaints, is not generally considered part of the depression syndrome, but these features can very frequently be observed in markedly depressed psychiatric patients. The excessive sensitivity and lack of sociability shown in these items can also be seen in their behavior. Appendix I lists the items as grouped by Harris and Lingoes (1955) in their judgmental separation of the clinical scales into subscales. For scale 2 they list five clusters: subjective depression, psychomotor retardation, complaints about physical malfunctioning, mental dullness, and brooding.

O'Connor, Stefic, and Gresock (1957) intercorrelated the items from the D scale and identified five sources of variance common to these items: hypochondriacal trends, cycloid tendencies, hostility, inferiority, and depression, with a general second-order factor of depression appearing common to these subgroupings. Comrey (1957b) identified a longer list of factors which included the health concern, hostility, mood swings, and frank depression labeled by O'Connor et al. but also neuroticism, cynicism, religious fervor, and tearfulness not described by these investigators. Comrey felt that the common concern in this scale was neuroticism rather than depression. Tuthill, Overall, and Hollister (1967) carried out an item study of the D scale but in the context of ratings for different components of the depression syndromes: anxiety, psychomotor retardation, and subjective depression. They found that different items within scale 2 correlated with each of the subparts of the depression pattern but also noted that the total scale related most clearly to an over-all rating of degree of depression (.61 in their psychiatric sample). Thus, scale 2 appears to be heterogeneous in item composition but shows a greater degree of communality than would be expected from the content when completed by patients with high levels of clinical depression. Among normal subjects, the scale coherence breaks down into relatively specific kinds of experiences and concerns.

There have been several shortened or abbreviated scales advanced in the literature to use as substitutes (or improvements) for the D scale. Canter (1960) suggested using items from scale 2 and scale 7 as a brief index of morale loss while Dempsey (1964, 1965) recommended a thirty-item subscale made up primarily of the obvious items in scale 2 as a measure of pure depression. Shipman (1963) proposed the use of a shortened depression scale (along with a brief anxiety scale) as a practical clinical and research instrument. Overall et al. (1962) contrived a manifest depression scale based upon expert judgments of scale 2 items. There is little evidence that these variations on scale 2 have any clear advantages over the D scale in clinical applications. (These scales may be found in Appendix I in Volume II.)

Wiener and Harmon (1946) made a simple division of the items on scale 2 into two subscales, a twenty-item subscale of subtle depression content and a forty-item obvious subscale (see Appendixes H and I). In general, those subjects who are showing more severe forms of psychopathology tend to endorse the obvious items more than they do the subtle ones, while persons with milder forms of maladjustment will endorse primarily subtle items in describing their feelings and reactions.

In the light of the description of this scale's content it is not surprising to find that the scores on it serve as sensitive reflectors of current mood. The test scale was devised as a symptom measure and the low test-retest stability on clinical groups (see the appendix materials in volume II) bears out the general expectation. Such a measure has obvious utility in evaluating the effects of various therapeutic regimes as well as in plotting the course of a particular difficulty. Although the scale was devised on a largely psychotic group of patients, it became clear in the early research that the items reflected depressive mood changes on a neurotic basis—in fact, any depressive reaction, no matter what the underlying character structure or adjustment status of a patient might be. It can be seen in Table 6-2 that the item overlap of scale 2 is about equal for the neurotic scales and the psychotic scales. Scale 2 is listed in the neurotic triad, but it is frequently found to be important in evaluating the psychotic picture as well. This will be discussed in the next chapter.

In two different clinical samples of psychiatric patients, Endicott and Jortner (1966) reported finding a correlation of .51 between level of rated depression and scale 2 scores. In the study of Zuckerman et al. (1967) scale 2 correlated with rated depression a little higher (.59), but showed an even higher correlation with ratings of manifest anxiety (.66). (Their findings indicated that it was difficult to differentiate anxiety and depression in several modalities—scales, checklist self-descriptions, as well as clinical ratings by psychiatric judges.) Self-descriptions on mood checklist items for depression correlated with scale 2 scores somewhat higher than did the judges' ratings (.69). Zung (1967) and Zung, Richards, and Short (1965) have also noted a substantial correlation between scale 2 scores and a short list of self-descriptive items in Zung's self-rating depression (SDS) scale, typically about .70. Morgan (1968) found a value of .72 in his correlation of the Zung SDS and scale 2 scores.

High Scale 2 Scores. The characteristics noted about normal test subjects with elevated scores on scale 2 depend more than usual upon the degree of acquaintance the rater has with the subject. The personality processes correlated with scale 2 seem to act against familiarity and closeness between the high 2 normal and his peers. In Hovey's (1953) study (and in Black's work discussed below), the adjectives shy and nonaggressive were the sum and substance of the description of the high 2 women.

The high 2 males studied by Hathaway and Meehl (1952) were somewhat more completely described by their acquaintances, but within the set of descriptions can be seen the same social distance and reserve. That is, these men were said to be modest, sensitive, and individualistic and to have general aesthetic interests. They also seemed to be dissatisfied generally, but particularly self-dissatisfied, as well as emotional, high-strung, and prone to worry. Although serious, they liked drinking, and seemed verbal. They were considered generous and sentimental. The women with high 2 scores were, like the men, described as high-strung and modest, and as frank and intuitive as well.

Further evidence about the personality makeup of normal subjects with elevated scores on scale 2, and further insight into their social alienation, come from the IPAR data (Gough, McKee, and Yandell, 1955) on men who scored relatively high on scale 2. The following adjectives were applied to these subjects by the professional assessment staff: aloof, apathetic, cautious, conventional, dull, evasive, indifferent, leisurely, modest, moody, painstaking, patient, peaceable, quiet, retiring, silent, simple, slow, submissive, timid, unassuming, unexcitable, and withdrawn. In other observations on these high 2 subjects, the judges noted their typical overcontrol, slow personal tempo, and inability to make decisions without hesitation and vacillation. They were seen as conforming, conscientious, and responsible men, but with a lack of confidence in their own ability and a pessimism about their own professional advancement and careers. Although they respected others, and were permissive and accepting, they tended to avoid becoming involved in things and to maintain a coldness and distance in their relationships with others. In difficult situations, these subjects tended to sidestep troubles and make concessions to avoid unpleasantness.

Within psychiatric populations, scale 2 generally reflects disturbance and discomfiture about failure to achieve satisfactions and adjustment. As Hathaway and Meehl (1951b) pointed out, almost any psychiatric patient who is clinically ill and who recognizes his illness is depressed, whatever else he may be suffering. Thus, scale 2 appears in a variety of combinations with other scales in the profile; the behavioral, characterological, and prognostic implications of elevations on scale 2 depend upon the other features of the MMPI curve. The interpretations of scale 2 also depend upon the current observable behavior of the patient, particularly in the case of "smiling" depressions. In this syndrome, the patient achieves a significant elevation on scale 2 but does not cry or show moroseness, psychomotor retardation, or other depressive mannerisms and may, on questioning, even deny depressive content. In these instances, when the profile appears acceptable under the usual criteria (see the discussion in Chapter 3), the scale 2 elevation should be given serious consideration. Suicidal risk appears to be greater in these cases than when the depression is more dramatically demonstrable in clinical behavior. For further material on this point, see the discussion of suicide in Volume II.

The normal men with high 2 scores in the Hathaway and Meehl study did not differ from the general group of subjects on many terms in their self-descriptions. Each of the adjectives they used, however, was included in the list of terms applied to them by their friends: individualistic, high-strung, and likes drinking. This same sort of insight was shown by the self-descriptions of the women in the group. Their self-ratings included the terms frank, modest, and high-strung. They also endorsed several other adjectives, many of which agreed in theme if not in identical terminology with the descriptions of them provided by others. That is, they said they were sensitive, shy, naive, self-dissatisfied, and prone to worry.

Low Scale 2 Scores. To judge by the initial findings reported in the literature, scale 2 is a unipolar scale in which low scores merely reflect the absence of the characteristics of high scorers. The score levels of the typical normals, therefore, seem to indicate moderate levels of depression. Younger subjects score below the typical adult level on this scale (Hathaway and Monachesi, 1963; Black, 1954); older subjects range upward on scale 2, presumably because of increasing serious responsibilities, an attitude of pessimism about themselves and the world, and a common lack of energy and forcefulness in meeting demands and challenges (Hathaway and McKinley, 1942; Brozek, 1952, 1955; Swenson, 1961). Lower scores on scale 2 seem to reflect a naturalness, buoyancy, and freedom of thought and action that lead to easy social relations, confidence in taking on tasks, and effectiveness in a variety of activities. The lack of inhibition in low 2's may in certain contexts lead to negative reactions from others, however, as a result of hurt feelings, slighted friendships, and threatened confidences. Many of these characteristics can be seen running through the descriptions given below.

Hathaway and Meehl (1952) report that the normal men they studied with relatively low scores on scale 2 were seen by their peers as balanced, reasonable, self-controlled, and self-confident. The women were said to be adaptable, practical, cooperative, easygoing, and reasonable; they were also described as cheerful, good-tempered, talkative, and energetically spirited. Similarly, the normal women studied by Hovey were reported by their supervisors to be efficient, emotionally stable, good socializers, poised and at ease in social situations, able to adjust rapidly, desirous of responsibility, and easy in oral expression; to have initiative; and to participate in group discussions.

Gough, McKee, and Yandell also found a long list of adjectives characteristic of low scorers on scale 2 among IPAR assessees: active, adventurous, affected, aggressive, alert, autocratic, cheerful, egotistical, emotional, energetic, enthusiastic, excitable, generous, good-natured, hardheaded, humorous, impulsive, informal, intelligent, outgoing, outspoken, quick, responsible, restless, self-seeking, prone to show off, spontaneous, talkative, witty, and having initiative. This set of terms has many internal contradictions. Since all the variations of scale 2 patterns are combined in this analysis, there may well be some as yet unspecified basis within the remainder of any given profile to separate certain of the more socially unacceptable characteristics from the rest of this cluster of personality attributes for low 2 normals.

The personality descriptions of the low 2 subjects on the Q-sort items in the IPAR study strengthen the picture formed by the adjectives found characteristic of them. One of the dominant themes is the undercontrol that these subjects show; they were described as expressive and ebullient people, colorful, active, and vigorous. Within acceptable limits this leads them to take the initiative in social relations, to take ascendant roles, to be persuasive and verbally facile and fluent. They become ego-involved in a variety of activities, are competitive with their peers, and emphasize success and productive achievement. However, the low 2 person who is less carefully controlled tends to be ostentatious and exhibitionistic, sarcastic and cynical, and strongly counteractive in frustrating situations. He frequently is unable to delay gratifications, is rebellious toward authority figures or toward other constraints, and easily arouses hostility and resentment in other people.

In their self-descriptions, the low 2 men and women in the Hathaway and Meehl study were more explicit than the high 2 subjects. The men said that they were sociable (in the sense of mixing well), cooperative, and practical. They also said they were natural and balanced, affectionate, and enthusiastic, had interests in home and family, and faced life. The low 2 women, like the men, admitted to home and family interests; they claimed physical strength and endurance, and said they were enterprising and adventurous. They seemingly denied deep inner tensions in describing themselves as placid and relaxed, natural and balanced, trustful and self-confident. They also said that they were alert, responsive, adaptable, reasonable, clear-thinking, cheerful, laughterful, enthusiastic, loyal, and grateful.

Brown and Goodstein (1962) contrasted the self-descriptive checklist items endorsed by college women who scored high and low on scale 2 in terms of the need variables of Gough and Heilbrun (1965). High D scorers were significantly higher than low scorers on deference, succorance, and abasement. They were significantly lower than the low scale 2 girls on achievement, exhibition, autonomy, dominance, change, and heterosexual needs. Brown and Goodstein interpreted these findings as being consistent with the levels of scale 2 serving as a general index of maladjustment within this relatively normal group of college women.

Scale 3 (Hy)

This scale was developed to aid in the identification of patients using the neurotic defenses of the conversion form of hysteria. These patients appear to use physical symptoms as a means of solving difficult conflicts or avoiding mature responsibilities. This resort to physical disorder may appear only under stress, while in ordinary circumstances no clear personality inadequacy is readily demonstrable. The need for a personality measure to reflect such predisposition before breakdown was partly the motivation behind the development of this scale.

The items in this scale were selected on the basis of their differentiation from general normals of a group of patients demonstrating conversion reactions. The authors (McKinley and Hathaway, 1944) reported considerable difficulty in working with this criterion. There was usually little doubt concerning a case showing a single, dramatic conversion symptom such as aphonia; but there were varying degrees of ambiguity in cases that might have a covert physical basis, such as incipient multiple sclerosis, and in cases that might be an early manifestation of hypochondriasis or schizophrenia. Later discussions will point up the utility of this scale in pattern analyses for the identification of these various disorders and for differentiation of them from conversion reactions.

The items in scale 3 are listed in Table 6-3. In terms of its content, this scale is one of the most interesting of the clinical scales. Many of the items seem to be mutually contradictory. Broadly, it can be seen that the items fall into two categories: somatic items and social facility items (see Ad and Dn subscales in Appendix I). For normal subjects, the work of K. B. Little and Fisher (1958) showed that these items were actually negatively correlated, although the items in each subset correlated positively among themselves. The somatic items from scale 1 (Hs) that appear on this scale as well are the more specific in bodily reference, such as head, eyes, chest. There are also a few describing tensions, fears, and worries. In contrast, there are also a number of items in scale 3 that involve the denial of any kind of troubles. These may be denials of inadequacies, of base impulses, and of any sensitivity in social situations. Many items demonstrate a protest that other people are trustworthy, responsible, and likable.

J. W. Little's analysis (1949) of the relation of each item in scale 3 to the total score on the scale showed this same lack of homogeneity for the relatively normal subjects in his group of counselees. The highest single correlation with the total score was .75 on the item "I am troubled by attacks of nausea and vomiting." This same item correlated .92 with the total score on scale 1, for which it is also scored. Other highly discriminating items include "During the past few years I have been well most of the time," which gave

Table 6-3. Scale 3 (Hysteria): Item Composition, Direction of Scoring, and Overlap with Other Basic Scales

True: 3

44. Much of the time my head seems to hurt all over.
186. I frequently notice my hand shakes when I try to do something.

True: (3)

253. I can be friendly with people who do things which I consider wrong.

False: 3

12. I enjoy detective or mystery stories.
128. The sight of blood neither frightens me nor makes me sick.
174. I have never had a fainting spell.

False: (3)

6. I like to read newspaper articles on crime.
136. I commonly wonder what hidden reason another person may have for doing something nice for me.
162. I resent having anyone take me in so cleverly that I have had to admit that it was one on me.
265. It is safer to trust nobody.

False: LK23

°30. At times I feel like swearing.

True: F123

23 (288). I am troubled by attacks of nausea and vomiting.

False: (K23)

°160. I have never felt better in my life than I do now.

False: (K235)

89. It takes a lot of argument to convince most people of the truth.

False: K3

°71. I think a great many people exaggerate their misfortunes in order to gain the sympathy and help of others.

False: (K3)

129. Often I can't understand why I have been so cross and grouchy.
234. I get mad easily and then get over it soon.

False: K34

°170. What others think of me does not bother me.

True: 123

43. My sleep is fitful and disturbed.

False: 123

2. I have a good appetite.
9. I am about as able to work as I ever was.
51. I am in just as good physical health as most of my friends.
153. During the past few years I have been well most of the time.

True: 1237

189. I feel weak all over much of the time.

True: 13

114. Often I feel as if there were a tight band about my head.

False: 13

7. My hands and feet are usually warm enough.
55. I am almost never bothered by pains over the heart or in my chest.
163. I do not tire quickly.
175. I seldom or never have dizzy spells.
188. I can read a long while without tiring my eyes.
190. I have very few headaches.
230. I hardly ever notice my heart pounding and I am seldom short of breath.
243. I have few or no pains.
274. My eyesight is as good as it has been for years.

False: 137

3. I wake up fresh and rested most mornings.

False: 138

103. I have little or no trouble with my muscles twitching or jumping.
192. I have had no difficulty in keeping my balance in walking.

False: 2346

107. I am happy most of the time.

False: 23478

8 (318). My daily life is full of things that keep me interested.

True: 234780

32 (328). I find it hard to keep my mind on a task or job.

False: 34

137. I believe that my home life is as pleasant as that of most people I know.
141. My conduct is largely controlled by the customs of those about me.

Table 6-3—continued

False: 349

289. I am always disgusted with the law when a criminal is freed through the arguments of a smart lawyer.

False: 35

26. I feel that it is certainly best to keep my mouth shut when I'm in trouble.

False: (35)

213. In walking I am very careful to step over sidewalk cracks.

True: 358

‡179. I am worried about sex matters.

False: (36)

93. I think most people would lie to get ahead.

True: 37

10. There seems to be a lump in my throat much of the time.

True: 378

76. Most of the time I feel blue.

True: 3789

238. I have periods of such great restlessness that I cannot sit long in a chair.

True: 38

47. Once a week or oftener I feel suddenly hot all over, without apparent cause.

True: 9. False: (3)

279. I drink an unusually large amount of water every day.

True: 9. False: (36)

109. Some people are so bossy that I feel like doing the opposite of what they request, even though I know that they are right.

True: 0. False: (3)

147. I have often lost out on things because I couldn't make up my mind soon enough.

172. I frequently have to fight against showing that I am bashful.

292. I am likely not to speak to people until they speak to me.

True: 0. False: (34)

201. I wish I were not so shy.

True: 0. False: (K349)

180. I find it hard to make talk when I meet new people.

267. When in a group of people I have trouble thinking of the right things to talk about.

True: 0. False: (K36)

124. Most people will use somewhat unfair means to gain profit or an advantage rather than to lose it.

a biserial value of .70; "I seldom or never have dizzy spells," .60; and "My sleep is fitful and disturbed," .57. It can be seen that these items showing the closest relationship to the total variance in the scale for this group were all of the somatic type. The values of the coefficients are not large.

The items in this scale were also grouped judgmentally by Wiener and Harmon (1946) into subtle and obvious subscales. They found just about as many subtle items in this scale as obvious ones. They also provided a basis for transforming each of these two Hy scores into T-score units. The correlations they report among the subtle and obvious subscales of the five clinical scales they worked on furnish additional evidence on the point made earlier about the negative relationships between the patterns of response to the various subsets of items in this scale by normal subjects. At the scale level of analysis, the shift from a strong negative correlation in normals to a significant positive correlation in patients is an example of what Meehl (1950) has described at the item level as "configural scoring." Wiener and Harmon offered evidence concerning the utility of the subscales used separately, with each serving a different function. The clinical utility of the total scale 3 indicates that the configural combination of these two contradictory response trends in a single score is equally justifiable. Table 5-1 shows the means and standard deviations of the Minnesota normals of each sex on scale 3.

From the work of Schofield (1950) on item stability it can be seen that scale 3 is made up of the sort of items that are likely to be variable over time in the responses they elicit, especially among patient groups. The items are phrased in the present tense, contain ambiguous adverbial modifiers that are subject to different interpretations, and frequently refer to experiences that are also ambiguous and open to individual interpretation. Therefore, the scale would be expected to show relatively less test-retest agreement than other of the scales (see appendix materials in Volume II). The evidence given above indicates why, for this scale and several others, the split-half estimates of reliability are inappropriate, or at least misleading. A fortuitous combination of items into the two half scales could easily lead to a negative correlation, suggesting to the psychometrically naive that the scale possesses "negative" reliability.

It should also be noted that the item composition of scale 3 largely constitutes the low end of Byrne's repression-sensitization scale (1961) which reflects the repression component; the sensitization end is largely made up of the items from scale 7 (see below). The Byrne scale has been employed in several experimental investigations as well as some clinical contexts. This research is discussed in Volume II.

High Scale 3 Scores. According to Hathaway and Meehl (1952), there were some sex differences in the way persons with elevated scores on scale 3 were perceived by their friends and acquaintances. Peers described the women as prone to worry, frank, enthusiastic, poised, responsive, softhearted. For the males, however, a much longer set of characteristics was endorsed by friends and acquaintances, reflecting possibly the greater accessibility of these men and the more intimate friendships that they readily form. The adjectives reported to characterize high 3 males were fair-minded, persevering, prone to worry, enterprising, alert, generous, mature, clear-thinking, talkative, kind, energetic, enthusiastic, assertive, socially forward, adventurous, affectionate, sentimental, cooperative, good-tempered, grateful, verbal, courageous, and individualistic; they were also said to mix well socially and to have wide interests. The lack of any appreciable number of adverse characteristics in this list is noteworthy.

On the more selected group of males studied at IPAR (Gough, McKee, and Yandell, 1955) high 3 males were rated by professional judges to be clever, enterprising, enthusiastic, imaginative, impatient, thankless, infantile, inhibited, both irresponsible and responsible, and spunky. The judges were also impressed by the high degree of intellective ability of these particular subjects and thought they were independent in judgment and demonstrated ability to think for themselves.

In Hovey's (1953) group of nursing students, the supervisors described the girls with high 3 scores as cheerful, enthusiastic, friendly, and cooperative, but immature and quite careless in their personal appearance.

The subjects in the Hathaway and Meehl group who scored high on scale 3 rated themselves as favorably as did their friends and acquaintances, although they were not well differentiated on the checklist generally.

The males listed only three characteristics that were significantly related to this scale level: alert, talkative, and enthusiastic. By way of contrast, the high 3 females described themselves in this study as fair-minded, sociable, generous, talkative, friendly, enthusiastic, high-strung, and emotional. It is quite clear, therefore, that for the high 3 normals, both male and female, and as seen both by themselves and by others, the psychological picture is one of social participation and easy accessibility, ready involvement in activities, and participation in social activities.

Low Scale 3 Scores. Hathaway and Meehl found that the normal subjects with low scores on scale 3 were not well delineated. In their study, the peers of low 3 females described them as facing life, balanced, conventional and having general aesthetic interests. The low 3 male was described only as having narrow interests. These findings are in particularly sharp contrast to the wide number of attributes ascribed to the high 3 male. Similarly, Hovey found that the low 3 girls were characterized briefly as self-confident but lacking in industriousness.

In the IPAR study, the judges applied the following terms to the low 3 scorer: changeable, cold, commonplace, considerate, conventional, demanding, masculine, mischievous, peaceable, and sincere. Even in this highly selected group the low 3 subjects were seen as rather constricted, conventional, and controlled.

In their self-descriptions, the low 3 male and female subjects were modal; only a few characteristics appeared to distinguish this subgroup. Hathaway and Meehl found that only the terms inflexible and deliberate were statistically significant in the self-descriptions of low 3 females. Similarly only the terms modest and willing to settle down stood out in the analysis of the male adult ratings. The nature of these characteristics, however, is compatible with the conforming, relatively unadventurous, and socially nonparticipating pattern appearing in the clinical reports of low 3 scorers.

Scale 4 (Pd)

This scale was developed to measure the personality characteristics of the amoral and asocial subgroup of persons with psychopathic personality disorders, termed in this setting psychopathic deviates (McKinley and Hathaway, 1944). The major features of this personality pattern include a repeated and flagrant disregard for social customs and mores, an inability to profit from punishing experiences as shown in repeated difficulties of the same kind, and an emotional shallowness in relation to others, particularly in sexual and affectional display. Since he is relatively free of conflicts and does not show anxiety until actually in serious difficulty, the psychopathic deviate may go undetected by friends and acquaintances until the situation demands evidence of a sense of responsibility, appreciation of social patterns, or personal and emotional loyalties. As in the case of the conversion hysteric between stress situations, it may be difficult to identify the psychopathic deviate between one outbreak and another without some personality measure. The need for such a scale as this one is therefore clear and compelling.

The criterion group for this scale was made up largely of cases in a psychiatric setting that were being studied at the request of the courts because of delinquent actions. The pattern of delinquency took the form of stealing, lying, truancy, sexual promiscuity, alcoholic overindulgence, forgery; but no capital offenses were included. Probably because of selective biases shown by police authorities and courts in determining those sent to the hospital for study, these cases were fairly young people, with more girls in the group than boys. Each one had a long history of minor delinquency. When these criterion cases were contrasted with the Minnesota normals, they were being compared to older persons who for the most part were married and rural residents. The use of the college controls was particularly valuable here, therefore, in minimizing certain biases in the items selected that might have stemmed from important differences other than asocial and amoral psychopathic tendencies. Other biases in this particular criterion group were probably less easily eliminated, such as those special personality reactions arising from the fact that these young people had been caught in wrongdoing, had been incarcerated, and were being scrutinized in a psychiatric setting. Although subjects in this criterion group were characterized by a lack of concern and anxiety about *potential* dangers and punishments, they were not necessarily insensitive to the actualities of capture, or more particularly the frustration, boredom, uneasiness, depression, and irritation resulting from detention. The implications of some of these considerations will be discussed more fully later in dealing with the prediction of future characteristics as contrasted with the evaluation of current manifestations of both conduct and personality disorders.

Table 5-1 provides the means and standard deviations on this scale of males and females from the Minnesota normative group. It also gives the values of these statistics when .4 K is added to scale 4. It should be noted that this is the only scale showing an increase in the absolute value of the standard deviation when the K correction is made. Data presented by Murphree, Karabelas, and Bryan (1962) raise some doubts concerning the suitability of the usual K corrections applied to scale 4 in evaluating records from Negro subjects.

The available evidence on the reliability of scale 4 is summarized in the appendix material in Volume II. The lowest values reported for retest studies appear on the groups of patients undergoing psychiatric treatment. In studies of corresponding psychiatric groups that were tested a second time before therapeutic measures or milieu could be expected to have important effects (e.g., Rosen, 1953), scale 4 scores generally appear to be very stable. Another retest study showing low stability, that of Capwell (1945a; 1945b), was based upon the scores at the beginning and end of a school year for a group of young girls. Findings from the longitudinal studies of Hathaway and Monachesi (1963) suggest that important maturational changes in the personality attributes of the group may be reflected in their data.

Table 6-4 lists the items on scale 4. The content ranges widely, reflecting the alienation of the person from his family and the extension of difficulties to school and to authorities generally. Some of the items involve

Table 6-4. Scale 4 (Psychopathic Deviate): Item Composition, Direction of Scoring, and Overlap with Other Basic Scales

True: 4

61. I have not lived the right kind of life.
84. These days I find it hard not to give up hope of amounting to something.
118. In school I was sometimes sent to the principal for cutting up.
216. There is very little love and companionship in my family as compared to other homes.
224. My parents have often objected to the kind of people I went around with.
244. My way of doing things is apt to be misunderstood by others.

False: 4

173. I liked school.
235. I have been quite independent and free from family rule.
237. My relatives are nearly all in sympathy with me.
287. I have very few fears compared to my friends.

False: 4. True: K

96. I have very few quarrels with members of my family.

True: F4

42. My family does not like the work I have chosen (or the work I intend to choose for my life work).
215. I have used alcohol excessively.
245. My parents and family find more fault with me than they should.

True: F468

35 (331). If people had not had it in for me I would have been much more successful.

False: F48

20 (310). My sex life is satisfactory.

False: K240

296. I have periods in which I feel unusually cheerful without any special reason.

False: K34

°170. What others think of me does not bother me.

False: K4. True: (59)

134. At times my thoughts have raced ahead faster than I could speak them.

False: (K4)

°183. I am against giving money to beggars.

False: 124

155. I am neither gaining nor losing weight.

False: 2346

107. I am happy most of the time.

False: 23478

8 (318). My daily life is full of things that keep me interested.

True: 234780

32 (328). I find it hard to keep my mind on a task or job.

False: (24)

248. Sometimes without any reason or even when things are going wrong I feel excitedly happy, "on top of the world."

True: 2470

67. I wish I could be as happy as others seem to be.

False: 34

137. I believe that my home life is as pleasant as that of most people I know.
141. My conduct is largely controlled by the customs of those about me.

False: 349

289. I am always disgusted with the law when a criminal is freed through the arguments of a smart lawyer.

True: 45

239. I have been disappointed in love.

True: 46

110. Someone has it in for me.
284. I am sure I am being talked about.

Table 6-4—continued

False: 46

294. I have never been in trouble with the law.

True: 468

16 (315). I am sure I get a raw deal from life.
24 (333). No one seems to understand me.

True: 469

127. I know who is responsible for most of my troubles.

True: 47

94. I do many things which I regret afterwards (I regret things more or more often than others seem to do).
102. My hardest battles are with myself.
106. Much of the time I feel as if I have done something wrong or evil.

True: 48

38 (311). During one period when I was a youngster I engaged in petty thievery.

True: 48. False: (0)

33 (323). I have had very peculiar and strange experiences.

False: 48

37 (302). I have never been in trouble because of my sex behavior.

True: 489

21 (308). At times I have very much wanted to leave home.

False: 40

91. I do not mind being made fun of.

True: 5. False: (40)

‡ 231. I like to talk about sex.

True: 0. False: (34)

201. I wish I were not so shy.

True: 0. False: (K349)

180. I find it hard to make talk when I meet new people.
267. When in a group of people I have trouble thinking of the right things to talk about.

True: 0. False: (4)

82. I am easily downed in an argument.

True: 0. False: (K49)

171. It makes me uncomfortable to put on a stunt at a party even when others are doing the same sort of things.

frank admission of personal limitations, poor morale, and sexual troubles. At the same time, reminiscent of some of the contradictions in scale 3, there are also items involving denial of social shyness and assertion of social poise and confidence. A similar way of describing the type of items working on this scale is furnished by the judgmental subscales of Harris and Lingoes (1955). Using the preliminary Pd scale, they formed clusters relating to family discord, authority problems, social imperturbability, and alienation, the latter with both a social alienation and a self-alienation subgroup. (See Appendixes H and I.)

Wiener and Harmon (1946) also formed subtle and obvious subscales for scale 4 (see Appendixes H and I), with the obvious items somewhat predominating. It is interesting to note in their data that although the obvious items on scale 4 correlate highly positive with the obvious items on scale 3 and strongly negative with the subtle items on scale 3, the subtle items on scale 4 positively relate to both the subtle and the obvious subscales of scale 3.

Another similarity between scales 3 and 4 appears in J. W. Little's study (1949) of the internal relations of the items on scale 4 to the total score on that scale. He found that the items on scale 4 were also only moderately correlated with the total scale variance, the largest biserial value being .59

for the item "I believe that my home life is as pleasant as that of most people I know." The item "In school I was sometimes sent to the principal for cutting up" was a close second with a value of .58. The items "No one seems to understand me" (.52), "At times I have very much wanted to leave home" (.51), and "My parents have often objected to the kind of people I went around with" (.50) were the next highest in their correlation with the scores on scale 4. It is interesting to note the uniform reference to parental and home difficulties in these most discriminating items for college-level subjects. It is some of these same items which Murray, Munley, and Gilbart (1965) contend are inappropriate to scale 4 when used on college students; they propose the use of separate norms for such test subjects.

On a mixed group of normal subjects and psychiatric cases, Comrey (1958c) found eight factors which he considered meaningful in the intercorrelations among the items from scale 4: neuroticism, paranoia, psychopathic personality, shyness, delinquency, euphoria, antisocial, and family dissension sources of variance. Astin (1959, 1961) independently identified five such factors in scale 4 in the records from narcotic addicts studied in the USPHS hospital in Lexington, Kentucky. His first factor, self-esteem, seemed to correspond to Comrey's shyness factor while his second, a hypersensitivity factor, matched fairly well with Comrey's paranoia group. Both studies also reported a factor dealing directly with reports of psychopathic attributes, which Astin called social maladaptation. Astin also reported a factor dealing with problems of impulse control as well as one describing emotional deprivation. He noted that contrary to expectations, the family discord items did not form a unit, which does not accord with Comrey's results on a more heterogeneous subject group. Two of Lushene's (1967) factors from college male MMPI records correspond to these sources of variance in scale 4: 10, asocial psychopathic trends, and 11, control of hostile impulses. Neither of these factors appeared in the inter-item correlations of college females.

High Scale 4 Scores. Hathaway and Meehl (1952) found a large number of adjectives characteristic of high scorers on scale 4 among the normal adults who were described by friends and acquaintances. The number of attributes in itself is indicative of the social visibility of the high 4 normal, in some contrast to the low 4 person described below.

The adjectives singled out for the high 4 males in the Hathaway and Meehl study include adventurous and courageous, sociable in both senses of the word (socially forward and mixing well), talkative and verbal, enthusiastic, good-tempered, frank, generous, fair-minded, and individualistic; these men were also said to have wide interests and to like drinking. They were, in addition, characterized as sensitive and prone to worry, although these adjectives do not seem to be consistent with the rest of the list.

The high 4 males in the selected group of assessees at IPAR (Gough, McKee, and Yandell, 1955) were described by the raters as hostile and aggressive in their interpersonal relationships, sarcastic and cynical, as well as ostentatious and exhibitionistic. These descriptions appear to resemble the sociability and activity features of the peer ratings in the Hathaway and Meehl data, but they carry a devaluative quality not found in the terms chosen by the Minnesota raters. The adjectives appearing significantly more frequently in the descriptions of the high 4 assessees at IPAR that bear out this distinction include aggressive, immature, irritable, leisurely, and unemotional. The men were also described as tense, moody, nervous, and resentful.

Like the high 4 male, the high 4 female in the Minnesota study was seen by her acquaintances as frank and enthusiastic, but in addition she was described as assertive, emotional, and high-strung. This cluster does not suggest the picture of easy and spontaneous involvement with others and ready energy and interest given in the ratings of the high 4 male, but implies that these women are instead more tense and striving.

Hovey (1953) reported findings on high 4 girls evaluated by nursing training supervisors, in which the girls were judged against a standard of conformity and professional responsibility. There seems to be a mixture of two characteristics in the data from these special judges: mobilization of energy and lack of control. Thus these girls showed themselves to be participating actively in the program, to have initiative and to adjust rapidly, to desire responsibilities, to be enthusiastic, and to be unafraid of mental patients. However, they also were judged to be not industrious and not working persistently. They were seen as aggressive, self-confident, and not shy.

In marked contrast to the full descriptions from others, the high 4 male differs little in his self-descriptions from the general group of subjects in Hathaway and Meehl's study. On only two descriptive terms, talkative and mixing well socially, does he show a statistically stable difference. The high 4 females provide a few more adjectives than the male group in their self-descriptions. These include adventurous and enterprising, frank and deliberate, facing life, idealistic, and talkative.

Low Scale 4 Scores. Normal males who score relatively low on scale 4 do not appear to be as accessible or socially active as the high scorers on this scale. Hathaway and Meehl found only two adjectives characteristic of the peer ratings of these males in their group: conventional and having narrow interests.

The same picture of lack of assertiveness, particularly in its self-seeking forms, comes from the descriptions furnished on low 4 males in the IPAR studies. These men were described as submissive, compliant, overly accepting of authority, and conforming, and as doing things that are prescribed. They were also seen to be cheerful and good-tempered and persistent in working toward goals. In the long list of adjectives found to be characteristic of them this same theme appears recurrently: good-natured, reliable, attractive, mild, obliging, persistent, pleasant, shy, sincere, and trusting. They were also described as cheerful, conservative, dependable, enthusiastic, gentle, idealistic, inventive, meek, reasonable, and unassuming.

Hathaway and Meehl noted that the low 4 females too were described by their acquaintances as conventional, but the terms balanced, modest, good-tempered, and temperate were also applied significantly frequently.

These terms themselves perhaps indicate why the characterizations of these women are not more elaborate.

The supervisors of student nurses in the study by Hovey found low 4 girls to be persevering and willing to accept suggestions, but they were not rated as having stimulating personalities.

Thus, even within the narrow range of scores on this scale for normal groups, the high and low 4's show marked differences in drive, energy, and spontaneity. The enthusiasm and ready involvement of the high 4 subject, however, frequently lead to disapproval and condemnation by others, particularly when these others are in a position of responsibility or are in some way depending upon the high 4 subjects. The drive of the high 4 person can also appear readily in the form of aggression or retaliation, without effective control or direction.

In self-descriptions Hathaway and Meehl found that low 4 males added further evidence that is consistent with the summary above. These men described themselves as affectionate, balanced, cheerful, facing life, serious, natural, courageous, reverent, willing to settle down, and with home and family interests. The low 4 female differed from other women only in endorsing the term sensitive about herself.

Scale 5 (Mf)

Scale 5 was designed to identify the personality features related to the disorder of male sexual inversion. This syndrome is another homogeneous subgroup in the general category of psychopathic personality, sometimes called pathological sexuality. This group, like the psychopathic deviate group, shows considerably more uniformity than is found in the psychopathic personality category as a whole. Persons with this personality pattern often engage in homoerotic practices as part of their feminine emotional makeup; however, many of these men are too inhibited or full of conflicts to make any overt expression of their sexual preferences. The feminism of these men appears in their values, attitudes and interests, and styles of expression and speech, as well as in sexual relationships.

The description of the derivation of this scale by Hathaway (1956b) indicates that the usual empirical selection procedures for the items against a single criterion were not adhered to. As was noted in Chapter 1 some of the items in the pool were added late; these new items were particularly selected for their promise in identifying sexual inversion as shown in the studies of Terman and Miles (1936). However, basic response frequencies from the Minnesota normals were not available on these items. Special groups of normals had to be gathered for this scale construction work. The men were fifty-four soldiers and the women were sixty-seven airline employees. The initial comparisons were based upon the normal men and a small group of carefully selected male sexual inverts. These latter cases were selected for their relative freedom from neurosis, a difficult contamination to remove because there is little opportunity to study sexual inverts in a psychiatric setting unless the cases have important conflicts that motivate them to seek professional help. The cases were also carefully screened for psychotic disorders, since a few seriously disturbed patients may show homoerotic problems as an early or presenting complaint. Finally, the cases in the criterion group were judged to be relatively free of psychopathic tendencies. This contamination is an important one also since these personality characteristics often lead to rather chaotic sexuality that includes homoeroticism; they may also lead to deliberate homosexual activities for profit or possible blackmail, without serving necessarily as an expression of basic sexual preferences.

This careful pruning of the criterion cases left a rather homogeneous but disturbingly small number (thirteen) of cases. Therefore, items in the preliminary scale were also studied to investigate the way in which they separated males from females, since the dimension of inversion being evaluated had appeared to be psychologically very similar to the differences in personality between men and women in the studies by Terman and Miles (1936). A third set of comparisons on these items involved identifying feminine males on the Attitude-Interest Analysis Test of Terman and Miles (1938) and contrasting the item replies of this group of otherwise normal men with the rest of the group of men. An unsuccessful attempt was made to develop a corresponding scale (Fm) to identify female inversion by contrasting female patients and normal women.

The items in scale 5 are listed in Table 6-5. By no means all the items borrowed from Terman and Miles survived the selection (only twenty-three); many of the items already in the MMPI pool proved to be valuable differentiators (thirty-seven altogether). The content is heterogeneous on this scale, ranging over interests in kinds of work, hobbies and pastimes, social activities, religious preferences, and family relationships. There are also items on fears, worries, and personal sensitivities. One important feature of this scale is the amount of frankly sexual material in the items.

Table 6-5. Scale 5 (Masculinity-Femininity): Item Composition, Direction of Scoring, and Overlap with Other Basic Scales

True: 5

4. I think I would like the work of a librarian.
70. I used to like drop-the-handkerchief.
74. I have often wished I were a girl. (Or if you are a girl) I have never been sorry that I am a girl.
78. I like poetry.
87. I would like to be a florist.
92. I would like to be a nurse.
132. I like collecting flowers or growing house plants.
140. I like to cook.
149. I used to keep a diary.
203. If I were a reporter I would very much like to report news of the theater.
204. I would like to be a journalist.
261. If I were an artist I would like to draw flowers.
295. I like "Alice in Wonderland" by Lewis Carroll.
‡69. I am very strongly attracted by members of my own sex.

True: (5)

77. I enjoy reading love stories.

False: 5

1. I like mechanics magazines.
79. My feelings are not easily hurt.
176. I do not have a great fear of snakes.
198. I daydream very little.
214. I have never had any breaking out on my skin that has worried me.
221. I like science.
249. I believe there is a Devil and a Hell in afterlife.

Table 6-5—continued

264. I am entirely self-confident.
300. There never was a time in my life when I liked to play with dolls.
‡133. I have never indulged in any unusual sex practices.

False: (5)

19. When I take a new job, I like to be tipped off on who should be gotten next to.
28. When someone does me a wrong I feel I should pay him back if I can, just for the principle of the thing.
81. I think I would like the kind of work a forest ranger does.
116. I enjoy a race or game better when I bet on it.
144. I would like to be a soldier.
219. I think I would like the work of a building contractor.
223. I very much like hunting.
260. I was a slow learner in school.
280. Most people make friends because friends are likely to be useful to them.
283. If I were a reporter I would very much like to report sporting news.

False: L59

120. My table manners are not quite as good at home as when I am out in company.

False: F5

112. I frequently find it necessary to stand up for what I think is right.
115. I believe in a life hereafter.

False: (K235)

89. It takes a lot of argument to convince most people of the truth.

False: K4. True: (59)

134. At times my thoughts have raced ahead faster than I could speak them.

False: (25)

†80. I sometimes tease animals.

False: 35

26. I feel that it is certainly best to keep my mouth shut when I'm in trouble.

False: (35)

213. In walking I am very careful to step over sidewalk cracks.

True: 358

‡179. I am worried about sex matters.

True: 45

239. I have been disappointed in love.

True: 5. False: (40)

‡231. I like to talk about sex.

True: 5. False: (0)

25. I would like to be a singer.
126. I like dramatics.

True: 56

299. I think that I feel more intensely than most people do.

True: 57. False: (K)

217. I frequently find myself worrying about something.

True: 58

282. Once in a while I feel hate toward members of my family whom I usually love.
‡297. I wish I were not bothered by thoughts about sex.

True: 59

226. Some of my family have habits that bother and annoy me very much.

True: 50

278. I have often felt that strangers were looking at me critically.

False: 50

99. I like to go to parties and other affairs where there is lots of loud fun.
229. I should like to belong to several clubs or lodges.
254. I like to be with a crowd who play jokes on one another.
262. It does not bother me that I am not better looking.

False: 8. True: (5)

187. My hands have not become clumsy or awkward.

True: 0. False: (56)

117. Most people are honest chiefly through fear of being caught.

J. W. Little (1949) found the item "I like to be with a crowd who play jokes on one another" was the highest correlated item with the total score on scale 5, but its biserial value was only .50. Close to this value were the items "If I were a reporter I would very much like to report news of the theater" with .49 and "I am worried about sex matters" with .48. The next two largest values obtained were for "I very much like hunting (.46) and "I like mechanics magazines" (.45). For college students, therefore, this scale appears to be very heterogeneous. The interest items are the most differentiating, although one of the sexual items does appear in this list of the five highest items.

Pepper and Strong (1958) have formed judgmentally five subscales on Mf which also serve to characterize the content areas on this scale. They divided the items into clusters dealing with ego sensitivity, sexual identification, altruism, endorsement of culturally feminine occupations, and denial of culturally masculine occupations. In all these characterizations, it is clear that most of the items are psychologically obvious. The importance of this lack of subtlety will be made clear in later discussions of faking and dissimulation.

As can be seen in the means and standard deviations given in Table 5-1 above, the separation of the sexes is large on this scale. It should also be noted that the T scores on the profile sheets for female subjects are tabulated in such a way that high raw-score values correspond to low T scores. This provides for a uniform direction of interpretation of the profile elevation for both sexes of test subjects, but creates dangers of clerical error in profile plotting and in interpreting protocols with large numbers of unanswered items.

The appendix material in Volume II lists the available material on the test-retest stability of scores on scale 5. This scale seems to be quite stable, although appreciable shifts can be noted in some of Schofield's (1950, 1953) data on treated groups. The items in this scale have the content, the statement format, and the response direction that Schofield found to be related most clearly to response stability; only a few of the more variable MMPI items are included in the scale.

A factor analysis carried out on scale 5 item intercorrelations by Graham, Schroeder, and Lilly (1971) indicated that there were several rather independent identifiable sources of variance in the endorsements of a mixed sample of normal and psychiatrically involved male and female adults: narcissistic sensitivity, feminine interests, denial of masculine interests, homosexual concerns, denial of social extroversion and denial of exhibitionism. These components resemble the judgmental groupings of the items worked out by Pepper and Strong (1958) that were noted above. Manosevitz (1971) has carried out a new item analysis of the component items in scale 5 on two sets of homosexual versus heterosexual control males. Only a small subset of the items in this scale consistently separated both sets of criterion cases at an acceptable level of statistical significance. Both sets of contrasts, however, involved groups of men with unusually high educational and socioeconomic standing. He reported that the differentiating items came from several different subgroups in the Pepper-Strong schema. Murray (1963) noted that only forty of the sixty items in scale 5 separated college-level men and women with statistical reliability. He recommended that these items not be included in the application of this scale to college subjects; it is not clear from his data alone, however, that these items are not reflecting important personality attributes of men who go to college.

Two special scales have been advanced in the area of sexual deviation which serve to complement the role of scale 5. Poor sexual control leading to legal difficulties and imprisonment for sexual deviation (rape, sexual exhibitionism, pedophilia, etc.) served as the criterion for the Marsh, Hilliard, and Liechti (1955) sexual deviate scale (see Appendix I in Volume II) while homoerotic sexual activities in a prison setting served as the criterion for Panton's (1960) prison homosexual scale. Studies by Krippner (1964), Friberg (1967), and Singer (1970) indicate that the two supplementary scales may occasionally add important information to the identification or assessment of sexual deviations over that provided by the information in scale 5 and the rest of the basic MMPI scales but that the setting and context are important determiners of this diagnostic utility. Some homoerotic involvements among college males are more a function of the institutional setting, perhaps, than of feminine personality makeup or inversion.

High Scale 5 Scores. Hathaway and Meehl (1952) found that the high 5 males in the normal population were characterized by their peers as sensitive and prone to worry, idealistic and peaceable, sociable and curious, and as having general aesthetic interests. On this scale, high scores for women do not correspond psychologically to similar scores for men. Quite in keeping with the nature of the scale, the female group was described by the term adventurous.

The high 5 males evaluated by the judges at IPAR (Gough, McKee, and Yandell, 1955) were characterized as psychologically complex and inner-directed. These men were described as both intellectually able and interested. They were seen to value cognitive pursuits and to derive important satisfactions from such work and achievements. They showed a concern with philosophical problems, but not necessarily in only an abstract, disinterested way. Rather, they frequently took stands on moral issues and at times showed a great deal of self-awareness and self-concern that was neither neurotic nor immature. They were also seen as socially perceptive and responsive to interpersonal nuances, and as able to draw dependable and practical inferences; these attributes showed up as good judgment and common sense. They were frequently fluent verbally, with an ability to communicate ideas clearly and effectively and to win other people over to their point of view.

Gough, McKee, and Yandell reported a long list of adjectives typical of the high 5 males, including ambitious, capable, cautious, clear-thinking, clever, curious, effeminate, fair-minded, foresighted, fussy, imaginative, insightful, intelligent, logical, mature, nervous, organized, persevering, planful, precise, self-controlled, sensitive, serious, sharp-witted, submissive, and tolerant; they were also said to have wide interests. Many of these terms are consistent with the descriptions summarized above and help fill out the personality picture of this group.

This scale also correlates positively with ratings on personal scope and breadth (Woodworth, Barron, and MacKinnon, 1957).

According to the data from Hathaway and Meehl, the high 5 male sees himself, as do his peers, as being sensitive and prone to worry and as having general aesthetic interests, but in addition he regards himself as individualistic.

The women see themselves as adventurous (the only adjective appearing on the peer rating); they also endorsed several more terms: having physical strength and endurance, poised, easygoing and relaxed, balanced and logical, and facing life.

Low Scale 5 Scores. Males with low scores on scale 5 in the study of Hathaway and Meehl were judged by their friends to be practical, balanced, cheerful, self-confident, and independent. The low 5 female in this study was judged by others to be sensitive and responsive as well as modest, grateful, and wise.

The men in the IPAR study who scored low on scale 5 were not as clearly distinguishable as the men at the other end of the scale. The judges saw these men as preferring action to contemplation, lacking originality in their approach to problems, and showing stereotyped patterns of approach. Consistent with this view, perhaps, was the observation that these men lacked self-insight into their own motives and were unaware of their own social stimulus value. They also were seen to have a narrow range of interests and to be self-indulgent and unwilling to face unpleasant or troublesome situations. The adjectives applied to them are quite in keeping with this description: coarse, commonplace, contented, hasty, humorous, jolly, leisurely, reckless, and unaffected.

The low 5 men in the Hathaway and Meehl study agreed with their peers in seeing themselves as cheerful and independent. In addition they rated themselves as relaxed and easygoing, orderly and clear-thinking, contented and willing to settle down, kind and natural; they said they had physical strength and endurance, and were adventurous. In their self-descriptions the low 5 women endorsed only sensitive and idealistic.

From the material summarized above it can be seen that scale 5, within the normal limits imposed by these samples, plays a markedly different role in male and female subjects. The MMPI items used on the two groups are identical, with the scoring almost completely reversed for the sexes, but no simple reversible interpretation appears adequate. It is apparent that considerably more research work is needed if the nature of the sex differences is to be understood.

Scale 6 (Pa)

This scale was developed to evaluate the clinical pattern of paranoia, a diagnostic evaluation that is seldom used by itself but is frequently applied as a modifier of some other personality reaction. The concept of paranoia involves a set of delusional beliefs, frequently including delusions of reference, influence, and grandeur. Although the persons showing these personality features may appear to be well oriented to reality and integrated in the relation of one delusion with another in their belief structure, they may show misperceptions or misinterpretations of their life situations that are markedly out of keeping with their ability and intelligence. These paranoid characteristics may appear in schizophrenics or those with depressive reactions, more rarely in otherwise intact persons, and may be either temporary and reversible or long-standing and progressively more convoluted and involved.

The specific groups of patients used in deriving scale 6 were not reported on in any detail (Hathaway, 1956b). The present collection of items was the best of several versions but has generally been considered a preliminary scale. The criterion groups contained very few cases diagnosed as pure paranoia, but all had such diagnoses as paranoid state, paranoid condition, or paranoid schizophrenia in which ideas of reference, persecutory delusions, and grandiosity were prominent. The very nature of the disorder, with its pervasive suspiciousness and interpersonal sensitivity, involves the sort of attitudes toward tests and diagnostic appraisals that frustrate most of the conventional methods of personality study.

The items in scale 6 listed in Table 6-6 provide further insight into these difficulties with evasion and defensiveness. Some of the items that work to separate the criterion cases from normals are frankly psychotic items that

Table 6-6. Scale 6 (Paranoia): Item Composition, Direction of Scoring, and Overlap with Other Basic Scales

True: 6	True: F468
338. I have certainly had more than my share of things to worry about.	35 (331). If people had not had it in for me I would have been much more successful.
365. I feel uneasy indoors.	True: F6
False: 6	27. Evil spirits possess me at times.
327. My mother or father often made me obey even when I thought that it was unreasonable.	123. I believe I am being followed.
347. I have no enemies who really wish to harm me.	151. Someone has been trying to poison me.
348. I tend to be on my guard with people who are somewhat more friendly than I had expected.	275. Someone has control over my mind.
False: (6)	293. Someone has been trying to influence my mind.
313. The man who provides temptation by leaving valuable property unprotected is about as much to blame for its theft as the one who steals it.	True: F68
319. Most people inwardly dislike putting themselves out to help other people.	121. I believe I am being plotted against.
False: L. True: (678)	202. I believe I am a condemned person.
15 (314). Once in a while I think of things too bad to talk about.	291. At one or more times in my life I felt that someone was making me do things by hypnotizing me.
	False: 1680
	281. I do not often notice my ears ringing or buzzing.
	False: 2346
	107. I am happy most of the time.

Table 6-6—continued

True: 26	True: 6789
158. I cry easily.	22 (326). At times I have fits of laughing and crying that I cannot control.
False: (36)	True: 68
93. I think most people would lie to get ahead.	341. At times I hear so well it bothers me. 364. People say insulting and vulgar things about me.
True: 46	True: 689
110. Someone has it in for me. 284. I am sure I am being talked about.	157. I feel that I have often been punished without cause.
False: 46	False: 69. True: (0)
294. I have never been in trouble with the law.	111. I have never done anything dangerous for the thrill of it.
True: 468	True: 9. False: (36)
16 (315). I am sure I get a raw deal from life. 24 (333). No one seems to understand me.	109. Some people are so bossy that I feel like doing the opposite of what they request, even though I know they are right.
True: 469	True: 0. False: (K36)
127. I know who is responsible for most of my troubles.	124. Most people will use somewhat unfair means to gain profit or an advantage rather than to lose it.
True: 56	True: 0. False: (K6)
299. I think that I feel more intensely than most people do.	316. I think nearly anyone would tell a lie to keep out of trouble.
False: 6. True: (9)	True: 0. False: (56)
268. Something exciting will almost always pull me out of it when I am feeling low.	117. Most people are honest chiefly through fear of being caught.
True: 67	
317 (362). I am more sensitive than most other people.	
True: 678	
305 (366). Even when I am with people I feel lonely much of the time.	

are consistent with the textbook descriptions of this disorder: mental peculiarities, delusional and referential material, and the belief that unwarranted pressure has been placed upon them. However, some of the items are less clearly a part of this syndrome. Such items involve the admission of a psychological fragility that seems out of keeping with the façade of perfection these persons so often assume. In addition, there are some items that could be expected to have significance in differentiating the paranoid personality but which are answered in the unexpected direction, such as the item "Most people will use somewhat unfair means to gain profit or an advantage rather than lose it" (False).

In his correlations between component items and the total score on scale 6, J. W. Little (1949) found that a very frankly paranoid item, "I believe I am being plotted against," was the most differentiating item for his college-level subjects, with a biserial correlation of .77. Most items were not so highly related to total scale scores, however. The next highest items were "I think most people would lie to get ahead," .55; "I am happy most of the time," .51; "Most people are honest chiefly through fear of being caught," .49; "The man who provides temptation by leaving valuable property unprotected is about as much to blame for its theft as the one who steals it," .46; and "I do not often notice my ears ringing or buzzing," .46. These latter items are all significant when answered False and operate in a much more subtle manner in identifying paranoid characteristics.

Wiener and Harmon (1946) were able to form subtle and obvious subscales for scale 6, but in their judgment the obvious items predominated. They found that Minnesota normal males endorsed the Pa-obvious items much less frequently than they did on the other obvious subscales. Harris and Lingoes (1955) formed three subscales for scale 6: ideas of external influence, poignancy, and moral virtue. The item composition for all these subscales is listed in Appendix I of Volume II.

Table 5-1 above provides the means and standard deviations for scale 6 from men and women of the Minnesota normative group. The reliability estimates for this scale are listed in the appendix material in Volume II. The difference in operation of this scale on normals and on psychiatric groups is clear; it seems to be quite sensitive to fluctuations in degree and intensity of delusional material in psychiatric cases.

The negative value listed for the split-half reliability of scale 6 from the study of Gilliland and Colgin (1951) is a dramatic illustration of the inappropriateness of this index as a basis for judging the dependability of scores from complex scales. This problem is discussed in greater detail in Volume II, but it should be pointed out here how widely a split-half correlation coefficient may vary depending upon the way the scale is partitioned. Scales like the basic ones in the MMPI may have items in them with very small, or even negative, intercorrelations. There is no rational basis for grouping the items into half-scales. Any number of ways of combining the component items may be devised for any MMPI scale; each separation would generate some split-half correlational value. For example, Wiener (1948b) reported a correlation of only .10 between two parts of scale 6, the Pa-obvious and Pa-subtle subscales. The value of the split-half correlation that Gilliland and Colgin reported for scale 6 would be fully expected if they happened to place an undue number of either subtle or obvious items in one of their halves. This correlation, however, would not reveal very much about the way that the total scale relates to some complex external criterion like the paranoid personality syndrome. Actually, it has been found that scales like the ones in the MMPI work best against complex criteria when they contain items that have a high correlation with the criterion measure and *low* correlations with one another. Such items then are each bringing to the total scale quite independent but valid variance contributions.

In his factor analysis for the items on scale 6, Comrey (1958d) specified a large number of seemingly independent sources of variance: four subforms of paranoia (real, imagined, abnormal, and defeated forms), neuroticism, cynicism, antisocial behavior, hysteria, and rigidity. He felt that some of these item endorsements may pertain to actual persecutions which different subjects react to in a variety of ways. Some of the other factors were shared with other scales in the basic profile. Endicott, Jortner, and Abramoff (1969) offer some evidence that while the scale reflects a complex of attributes making up the paranoid syndrome the scores on scale 6 may not accurately mirror one of the main features, suspiciousness, in all of its manifestations. On one sample of patients, ratings between scale 6 scores and level of suspiciousness covaried monotonically (.29 correlation on forty outpatient cases) while on the other, a group of eighty-four hospitalized adults, the correlation of rated suspiciousness was only .19 and took on an inflection at a moderate level on the rating scale with mild and extreme suspiciousness giving essentially identical scale 6 values (about 60 T-score level). They offered a subset of items for suspiciousness (see Appendix I in Volume II) rather than the full scale 6, the suspiciousness scale correlating with these independent ratings on these two cross-validational samples .44 and .36 respectively.

High Scale 6 Scores. Hathaway and Meehl (1952) found that males with high scores on scale 6 were rated by their peers as sensitive, emotional, and prone to worry. They were seen to be kind, affectionate, generous, and grateful. In addition, these men were characterized as sentimental and softhearted, peaceable, cooperative, and courageous, and as having wide interests. This picture of the person with a high scale 6 score in the normal range contrasts sharply with the characteristics of the criterion group against which this scale was derived. These findings add strength to the contention made by Gough (1953) that the correlates of scale 6 change markedly in character as the elevation shifts from moderate values to the higher ranges. The high 6 female was described as being emotional, softhearted, and sensitive. In addition she was seen by her peers as frank and high-strung.

The IPAR raters (Gough, McKee, and Yandell, 1955) found the high 6 males to be more resistant than most groups to easy separation and characterization. They saw the 6's as readily becoming ego-involved in various activities and tending to make these pursuits personally relevant and important. The men were described as energetic and industrious, and as showing high initiative. In their expenditures of energy, however, these men were poised, rational, and clear-thinking. They were judged to be intelligent and insightful, with wide interests and progressive approaches.

Hovey (1953) reported that high 6 nursing students were judged by their supervisors to be dependent and submissive, lacking in self-confidence, and not outgoing.

The high scale 6 male is less clearly identified in his self-descriptions since only three terms—trustful, amorous, and worldly—appeared in the Hathaway and Meehl analysis. Similarly, the high 6 females used only two terms consistently in their self-descriptions: fair-minded and emotional.

Low Scale 6 Scores. Hathaway and Meehl did not find many features identifying the men who scored low on scale 6. Their acquaintances described them as cheerful, balanced, and decisive, but also, in some contradiction, as being self-distrusting and conscienceless. These men described themselves with the terms orderly and able to mix well socially.

The women with low scores on scale 6 were better summarized. The terms used by others to describe them included conventional and balanced, serious, mature and facing life, peaceable, reasonable, and trustful. The women described themselves with some of the same terms: balanced, peaceable, and facing life. In the same vein, the low 6 women also characterized themselves as being self-controlled, persevering, and wise. In addition they said that they were cheerful, loyal, and modest.

The low 6 males in the IPAR study were sketchily described as mild, self-centered, and wary, with narrow interests. Hovey found the low 6 girls in his nursing student group were perceived as adjusting rapidly, poised, and at ease around others, but not dependable.

W. Anderson (1956) studied 106 college counselees who had scale 6 scores below a T score of 40 and contrasted them with a randomly selected sample from the files of the counseling service. In addition to the low scale 6 score on which the experimental group had been selected, all the validating scales and all the clinical scales fell lower than the control group and closer to T score 50 except for scale 9. This latter scale averaged about a T score of 60, which was a few points higher than the controls. The low 6 group contained a significantly greater number of clients who had problems relating to underachievement or nonachievement, that is, they were obtaining poor grades. Those in the one group were achieving much below their tested intellectual ability; those in the second group had low tested ability as well as low grades. In addition, the low 6 group more often were having difficulty with their parents.

Scale 7 (Pt)

This scale was derived to help in the evaluation of the neurotic pattern of psychasthenia, or the obsessive-compulsive syndrome. The personality features included, in addition to the obsessive ruminations and the compulsive behavioral rituals, are some forms of abnormal fears, worrying, difficulties in concentrating, guilt feelings, and excessive vacillation in making decisions. Other frequently noted features include excessively high standards on morality or intellectual performance, self-critical or even self-debasing feelings and attitudes, and assumption of rather remote and unemotional aloofness from some personal conflicts. Although the term *psychasthenia* is no longer in wide use, the pattern of neurotic reaction is an important and persistent feature of many psychiatric disorders.

In the derivation of this scale (Hathaway and McKinley, 1942), two bases for item selection were used: the usual empirical separation from normals of a group of criterion cases, in this instance a very small group; and, in addition, the degree of correlation of each item in the pool with the total score on the preliminary scale derived from the empirical separation. The correlations for this second step were based upon two equal-sized groups, one of normals and the other of general psychiatric cases. The implications of this use of an internal consistency approach in deriving scale 7 will be discussed more fully in Volume II, but it seems clear that the variance of this scale is more saturated with general maladjustment variance than would have been the case in a scale formed by direct derivation on a select criterion group.

From the list of items in Table 6-7 it can be seen that the combined selection procedures did not often lead to the inclusion of specific obsessions, compulsive rituals, or phobias. Rather, the content appears to reflect a characterological basis for a vast variety of specific psychasthenic symp-

Table 6-7. Scale 7 (Psychasthenia): Item Composition, Direction of Scoring, and Overlap with Other Basic Scales

True: 7

337. I feel anxiety about something or someone almost all the time.
340. Sometimes I become so excited that I find it hard to get to sleep.
343. I usually have to stop and think before I act even in trifling matters.
344. Often I cross the street in order not to meet someone I see.
346. I have a habit of counting things that are not important such as bulbs on electric signs, and so forth.
351. I get anxious and upset when I have to make a short trip away from home.
358. Bad words, often terrible words, come into my mind and I cannot get rid of them.
361. I am inclined to take things hard.

False: (7)

329. I almost never dream.

False: L. True: (678)

15 (314). Once in a while I think of things too bad to talk about.

False: F7

164. I like to study and read about things that I am working at.

True: 1237

189. I feel weak all over much of the time.

False: 137

3. I wake up fresh and rested most mornings.

False: 23478

8 (318). My daily life is full of things that keep me interested.

True: 234780

32 (328). I find it hard to keep my mind on a task or job.

True: 2470

67. I wish I could be as happy as others seem to be.

True: 27

86. I am certainly lacking in self-confidence.

True: 27. False: (K)

142. I certainly feel useless at times.

False: 27

36. I seldom worry about my health.
122. I seem to be about as capable and smart as most others around me.
152. Most nights I go to sleep without thoughts or ideas bothering me.

True: 278

41. I have had periods of days, weeks, or months when I couldn't take care of things because I couldn't "get going."
159. I cannot understand what I read as well as I used to.
182. I am afraid of losing my mind.

False: 278

178. My memory seems to be all right.

True: 37

10. There seems to be a lump in my throat much of the time.

True: 378

76. Most of the time I feel blue.

True: 3789

238. I have periods of such great restlessness that I cannot sit long in a chair.

True: 47

94. I do many things which I regret afterwards (I regret things more or more often than others seem to).
102. My hardest battles are with myself.

Table 6-7—continued

106. Much of the time I feel as if I have done something wrong or evil.	360. Almost every day something happens to frighten me.
True: 57. False: (K)	True: 789
217. I frequently find myself worrying about something.	266. Once a week or oftener I become very excited.
True: 67	True: 70
317 (362). I am more sensitive than most other people.	304. In school I found it very hard to talk before the class. 321. I am easily embarrassed. 336. I easily become impatient with people. 342. I forget right away what people say to me. 357. I have several times given up doing a thing because I thought too little of my ability.
True: 678	True: 7. False: (0)
305 (366). Even when I am with people I feel lonely much of the time.	359. Sometimes some unimportant thought will run through my mind and bother me for days.
True: 6789	False: 70
22 (326). At times I have fits of laughing and crying that I cannot control.	353. I have no dread of going into a room by myself where other people have already gathered and are talking.
True: 78	
301. Life is a strain for me much of the time. 349. I have strange and peculiar thoughts. 352. I have been afraid of things or people that I knew could not hurt me. 356. I have more trouble concentrating than others seem to have.	

toms. The items cover such things as anxiety and dread, low self-confidence, doubts about one's competence, undue sensitivity, moodiness, and immobilization.

Although the values are not the highest obtained in the various scales he studied, J. W. Little (1949) found rather strong correlations between many of the items on scale 7 and the total score on the scale. Two items, "I frequently find myself worrying about something" and "Almost every day something happens to frighten me," were tied for the highest biserial correlation with a value of .73. About the same value (.71) was obtained for two other items in this scale: "I am certainly lacking in self-confidence" and "Even when I am with people I feel lonely much of the time." The item "Much of the time I feel as if I have done something wrong or evil" was the next highest with a biserial value of .67. These items reflect the scale homogeneity both in the values of their correlations with the scale and in the content they cover.

The normative group means and standard deviations on scale 7 listed in Table 5-1 above are given with and without K corrections. The reliability estimates listed in Volume II for scale 7 tend to be among the largest values for the scales. The split-half values that are listed are nearly as high as the test-retest values on this scale. These findings are consistent with the expectations for a scale derived in part on internal consistency criteria.

When Comrey (1958e) factored the intercorrelations among the items on scale 7 he identified no single source of variance which he could label psychasthenia; rather, he reported a variety of components of maladjustment: neuroticism, anxiety, withdrawal, poor concentration, agitation, psychotic tendencies, denial of antisocial behavior and poor physical health. Some but not all of these sources of variance, however, can be noted in the general obsessive-compulsive syndrome described above.

High Scale 7 Scores. In the peer ratings reported by Hathaway and Meehl (1952), the high 7 men were described as sentimental, peaceable, and good-tempered. They were also rated as verbal, individualistic, and dissatisfied. The women with high 7 scores were perceived rather differently; the neurotic components seem more heavily weighted for this group. Thus, their peers described these women as sensitive, prone to worry, emotional, and high-strung. They were seen to be conscientious and intuitive, with general aesthetic interests.

The selected men at IPAR (Gough, McKee, and Yandell, 1955) who scored high on scale 7 did not stand out very clearly, but the few adjectives found characteristic of them provide a rather consistent set. They were judged to be dull, formal, and unemotional. Although they were rated as idealistic and insightful, they also appeared to be immature and quarrelsome.

Hovey (1953) reported rather similar findings on the high 7 girls in his nursing student group. Their supervisors judged these girls to be neat in personal appearance, but shy, poor socializers, lacking in ingenuity, and tending to participate little in the group discussions.

The self-descriptions of the men and women in Hathaway and Meehl's group have more in common than the peer ratings of the two groups. The men endorsed the terms sentimental and high-strung, and said they had general aesthetic interests and national, political interests. The women in the high 7 group described themselves as prone to worry, high-strung, and emotional. They also said that they were frank and fair-minded, as well as both self-dissastisfied and dissatisfied generally.

Low Scale 7 Scores. In the analyses of Hathaway and Meehl, the low 7 males seem not to be very well perceived. The descriptions provided by their peers include only the terms balanced, self-controlled, and independent. For the low 7 women, only the term cheerful was singled out.

In their self-descriptions, the low 7 males characterized themselves as rather warm and effective. The terms endorsed included friendly and affectionate, balanced and natural, courageous, temperate, wise, and relaxed, as well as willing to settle down. The low 7 women also described themselves as balanced and relaxed, and as alert, having wide interests, self-confident, placid, and trustful.

Among the IPAR candidates, the low 7 men appeared to emphasize success and productive achievement as a means of gaining status or recognition and to be persistent in working toward such goals, with relatively little work inhibition. That is, they apparently were efficient, capable, and able to mobilize their resources easily and effectively. Although they seemed somewhat timid and wary, they nevertheless gave the judges the impression that they were organized, adaptable, and polished. They were judged to be self-seeking, but realistic and responsible.

Scale 8 (Sc)

The psychotic pattern of schizophrenia for which this scale was derived is very heterogeneous and contains many contradictory behavioral features. This may be in part a result of the way that the pattern is identified in terms of bizarre or unusual thoughts or behavior. Most commonly persons showing this psychiatric reaction are characterized as constrained, cold, and apathetic or indifferent. Other people see them as remote and inaccessible, often seemingly sufficient unto themselves. Delusions with varying degrees of organization, hallucinations, either fleeting or persistent and compelling, and disorientation may appear in various combinations. Inactivity, or endless stereotypy, may accompany the withdrawal of interest from other people or external objects and relationships. These persons frequently perform below the levels expected of them on the basis of their training and ability.

Hathaway (1956b) reports that more work went into the derivation of this scale than into the development of any other of the MMPI measures. The difficulty in getting a definitive scale did not lie in any lack of items that separated normals and diagnosed schizophrenic patients, but rather in the fact that the preliminary scales also reflected depression, hypochondriasis, and the like. The reason for this sort of contamination will be made clearer in later discussions of differential diagnosis, but the difficulties were persistent and important. The application of the K scale helped to resolve some of these problems. The present scale 8, originally labeled Sc4, proved to be slightly better than the other versions (especially with the correction of the total K score) in separating schizophrenic patients from normals.

The scale is the longest one in the regular group (see Table 6-8). Many of the items reflect the bizarre mentation, the social alienation, the peculiarities of perception, and the feelings of persecution included in the classic description of schizophrenia. There are also items which reflect the poor family relationships and the lack of deep interests which are part of the basic syndrome. The scale includes one of the largest subsets of items dealing with sexual matters. There are also items dealing with difficulties in concentration and impulse control. A little out of keeping with general clinical expectations are some of the items concerning fears and worries, and those that show the degree to which life is a strain.

The item that J. W. Little (1949) found to be highest in its biserial correlation with the total scale is a classic schizophrenic item: "I hear strange things when I am alone." The value of this correlation was .70, only a moderate magnitude in the set of values Little obtained. The next highest value (.67) was obtained on the item "I cannot keep my mind on one thing." The item "Even when I am with people I feel lonely much of the time" was next highest, with a value of .64. This item was also one of the most differentiating for scale 7, on which it obtained a biserial correlation of .71. The others among the five highest items were "My memory seems to be all

Table 6-8. Scale 8 (Schizophrenia): Item Composition, Direction of Scoring, and Overlap with Other Basic Scales

True: 8

303. I am so touchy on some subjects that I can't talk about them.
307. I refuse to play some games because I am not good at them.
312. I dislike having people about me.
320. Many of my dreams are about sex matters.
324. I have never been in love with anyone.
325. The things that some of my family have done have frightened me.
334. Peculiar odors come to me at times.
335. I cannot keep my mind on one thing.
339. Most of the time I wish I were dead.
345. I often feel as if things were not real.
350. I hear strange things when I am alone.
354. I am afraid of using a knife or anything very sharp or pointed.
355. Sometimes I enjoy hurting persons I love.
363. At times I have enjoyed being hurt by someone I loved.

False: 8

306. I get all the sympathy I should.
330. I have never been paralyzed or had any unusual weakness of any of my muscles.

False: L. True: (678)

15 (314). Once in a while I think of things too bad to talk about.

True: F468

35 (331). If people had not had it in for me I would have been much more successful.

False: F48

20 (310). My sex life is satisfactory.

True: F68

121. I believe I am being plotted against.
202. I believe I am a condemned person.
291. At one or more times in my life I felt that someone was making me do things by hypnotizing me.

True: F8

40. Most any time I would rather sit and daydream than to do anything else.
168. There is something wrong with my mind.
210. Everything tastes the same.

False: F8

17. My father was a good man.
65. I loved my father.
177. My mother was a good woman.
196. I like to visit places where I have never been before.
220. I loved my mother.
276. I enjoy children.

True: F89

156. I have had periods in which I carried on activities without knowing later what I had been doing.

False: (K8)

322. I worry over money and business.

True: 18

273. I have numbness in one or more regions of my skin.

False: 138

103. I have little or no trouble with my muscles twitching or jumping.
192. I have had no difficulty in keeping my balance in walking.

False: 1680

281. I do not often notice my ears ringing or buzzing.

False: 23478

8 (318). My daily life is full of things that keep me interested.

True: 234780

32 (328). I find it hard to keep my mind on a task or job.

True: 278

41. I have had periods of days, weeks, or months when I couldn't take care of things because I couldn't "get going."
159. I cannot understand what I read as well as I used to.
182. I am afraid of losing my mind.

False: 278

178. My memory seems to be all right.

True: 28

52. I prefer to pass by school friends, or people I know but have not seen for a long time, unless they speak to me first.
104. I don't seem to care what happens to me.
259. I have difficulty in starting to do things.

True: 358

‡179. I am worried about sex matters.

Table 6-8—continued

True: 378

76. Most of the time I feel blue.

True: 3789

238. I have periods of such great restlessness that I cannot sit long in a chair.

True: 38

47. Once a week or oftener I feel suddenly hot all over, without apparent cause.

True: 468

16 (315). I am sure I get a raw deal from life.
24 (333). No one seems to understand me.

True: 48

38 (311). During one period when I was a youngster I engaged in petty thievery.

True: 48. False (0)

33 (323). I have had very peculiar and strange experiences.

False: 48

37 (302). I have never been in trouble because of my sex behavior.

True: 489

21 (308). At times I have very much wanted to leave home.

True: 58

282. Once in a while I feel hate toward members of my family whom I usually love.
‡297. I wish I were not bothered by thoughts about sex.

True: 678

305 (366). Even when I am with people I feel lonely much of the time.

True: 6789

22 (326). At times I have fits of laughing and crying that I cannot control.

True: 68

341. At times I hear so well it bothers me.
364. People say insulting and vulgar things about me.

True: 689

157. I feel that I have often been punished without cause.

True: 78

301. Life is a strain for me much of the time.
349. I have strange and peculiar thoughts.
352. I have been afraid of things or people that I knew could not hurt me.
356. I have more trouble concentrating than others seem to have.
360. Almost every day something happens to frighten me.

True: 789

266. Once a week or oftener I become very excited.

True: 8. False: (2)

241. I dream frequently about things that are best kept to myself.

False: 8. True: (5)

187. My hands have not become clumsy or awkward.

True: 89

97. At times I have a strong urge to do something harmful or shocking.
194. I have had attacks in which I could not control my movements or speech but in which I knew what was going on around me.
212. My people treat me more like a child than a grown-up.
251. I have had blank spells in which my activities were interrupted and I did not know what was going on around me.

False: 890

119. My speech is the same as always (not faster or slower, or slurring; no hoarseness).

False: 80

332. Sometimes my voice leaves me or changes even though I have no cold.

False: 80

309. I seem to make friends about as quickly as others do.

right" (.62) and "I am worried about sex matters" (.61). This last item was also one of the most differentiating on scale 5, although its biserial correlation with the score on that scale was only .48. The items that Little found to be the most highly correlated with scale 8 for college-level subjects do not contain the most extremely bizarre content, therefore, but rather reflect more covert and subtle forms of mental disturbance and loss of efficiency.

Harris and Lingoes (1955) formed three general clusters of items from the scale, two of which were further broken down to facilitate comparison with similar subscales from other clinical scales. The first is an object-loss scale that includes a social alienation and an emotional alienation subscale. The second scale covers lack of ego mastery in three areas: cognitive functioning, conative functioning, and defect of inhibition and control. The third scale covers sensorimotor dissociation. (See Appendix I.)

Table 5-1 provides the means and standard deviations from the normative group. The length of this scale helps to generate large values for the test-retest and split-half coefficients, although the lack of stability over time on patients receiving psychiatric help in the interval reflects the role this scale may play in symptomatic assessment. (See the appendix materials in Volume II.)

When Comrey factored the interitem correlations on scale 8 (Comrey and Marggraff, 1958), he had to reduce the number of items to be included because of limitations in the computer capacity. He arbitrarily excluded items overlapping with scale 7, thereby reducing the set to fifty-eight items. He identified sources of variance which he labeled paranoia, poor concentration, poor physical health, psychotic tendencies, rejection, withdrawal, father identification, sex concern, repression, mother identification, and possibly another psychotic tendency factor. He felt that the psychotic tendency variance identified here was like that found in scale 7 and accounted for the high correlations found over and above item overlap.

Several correction efforts have been carried out to reduce the extent of high scores on scale 8 from other psychotic subjects (Benarick, Guthrie, and Snyder, 1951), from persons with brain injuries (Watson, 1968; Watson and Thomas, 1968), and from individuals manifesting conduct disorders (Harding, Holz, and Kawakami, 1958). Additional scales have been advanced for brief screening purposes (Clark and Danielson, 1956), for prognostic purposes (Pearson, 1950; Jenkins, 1952), and to identify various subgroups of schizophrenic patients (Johnson and Holmes, 1967; Watson, 1969). These various scales are listed in the appendix materials of Volume II.

High Scale 8 Scores. Hathaway and Meehl (1952) found that the normal males in their study who had high scores on this scale were not perceived by their peers as particularly deviant or withdrawn. Although they were rated as prone to worry, self-dissatisfied, and conscientious, there was little evidence of social or emotional disarticulation. Rather they were described as good-tempered, versatile, verbal, and enthusiastic, with wide interests and general aesthetic interests. They were also seen as frank, fair-minded, and courageous. Emotionally, they appeared to be kind and sentimental, as well as peaceable.

Rather similarly, the high 8 women in Hathaway and Meehl's study were judged to be sensitive and high-strung. They too were seen as frank and courageous, as well as kind and modest. Hovey (1953) also offered evidence that the high 8 female is socially active, since the nursing supervisors in his study rated these girls as showing initiative and participating actively in the group discussions. However, the girls were not viewed as enthusiastic, and although they were ingenious, they often showed poor judgment.

The men in the IPAR group (Gough, McKee, and Yandell, 1955) were described by the staff raters as being effective in communicating their ideas clearly, but as showing evidence of being at odds with themselves and of having major internal conflicts. The adjectives chosen to describe these men were generally less favorable than the peer ratings that Hathaway and Meehl obtained. Only the terms dissatisfied, having wide interests, and perhaps inventive (as compared to versatile given above) overlap between the two sets. The term hostile, and many similar terms like blustery, irritable, resentful, and touchy, suggest the problems in handling aggression that these men display. They were also judged to be moody, stubborn, opinionated, autocratic, deceitful, disorderly, and impulsive. However, they displayed imaginative, mischievous, and sharp-witted behavior. Perhaps the term immature summarizes the ratings best. These general findings provide support for the contention of Hathaway and Meehl (1951b) that most persons with scale 8 scores over a T score of 75 show schizoid mentation although not necessarily so severe as to constitute definite illness.

In their self-descriptions, the high 8 males in Hathaway and Meehl's group characterized themselves as high-strung, conscientious, worrying, and individualistic. They seemed to describe themselves as readily getting involved in activities, too, since they endorsed such terms as enterprising, adventurous, curious, and amorous. They also felt they were frank and talkative, as well as kind, sentimental, and grateful.

The women with high 8 scores were less clearly summarized by their self-descriptions; they endorsed only shy, dissatisfied, peaceable, and courageous.

Low Scale 8 Scores. The low 8 males in Hathaway and Meehl's study were described by their peers with the single term balanced. The females did not show up as significantly different from women in general on any of the checklist items. Hovey's girls with low 8 scores were described as friendly and alert.

The IPAR judges found the low 8 men in their group to be submissive and compliant, and in many ways overly accepting of authority. However, these men also tended to emphasize success and productive achievement as a means of achieving status, power, or recognition. The adjectives chosen to describe the low 8's strengthen this picture and emphasize the control and restraint in their behavior. They were characterized as mild, timid, cautious, conservative, conventional, responsible and self-controlled, dependable, steady, mannerly, and obliging. Although they were described as moderate, precise, and peaceable, the picture is not one of extreme overcontrol. Rather they were regarded as friendly, adaptable, cheerful, and good-natured. They also impressed the judges as being honest and thrifty.

In their self-descriptions, the low 8 men in the group studied by Hathaway and Meehl did not differ from the rest of the men in a statistically stable way. Several terms used by the women correspond quite well with the general picture for low 8 subjects coming from the IPAR data. That is, these women described themselves as contented and trustful, sensitive and reverent, with home and family interests. They also said they were cheerful and had wide interests.

Scale 9 (Ma)

The personality pattern for which this scale was derived is the affective disorder hypomania. Three features characterize this pattern: overactivity, emotional excitement, and flight of ideas. The activity may lead to a great deal of accomplishment but is frequently inefficient and unproductive. The mood may be good-humored euphoria but may on occasion be irritable, and temper outbursts are frequent. The enthusiasm and overoptimism characteristic of persons with this pattern may lead them into undertaking more than they can handle, although the milder forms of hypomania may be difficult to distinguish from the behavior of ambitious, vigorous, and energetic normals. Some of the behavior resulting from hypomania may be easily confused with psychopathic patterns and there are some important instances of combinations of both patterns in the same persons. The transitory nature of the hypomanic pattern makes it difficult to devise personality scales to measure and evaluate it.

The criterion cases for the development of this scale were difficult to obtain, partly because of the nature of the psychiatric setting in which the research was conducted and partly because of the untestability of these patients in the midst of their emotional upset (McKinley and Hathaway, 1944). Only a small group of cases was used in the selection of the items for scale 9, but subsequent research has indicated that the items chosen were differentiating and that the scale is a dependable one.

The items in scale 9, as shown by the list provided in Table 6-9, cover a wide range of content. Many of the classic features of the hypomanic patient are apparent in the self-descriptions appearing in these items: the grandiosity, the excitement, and the activity level. Many of the items bearing on moral attitudes and on home and family relationships, and some of those referring to physical and bodily matters, are less obviously related to the general syndrome. In their subscales, Wiener and Harmon (1946) placed an equal number of items in the subtle and obvious categories.

J. W. Little (1949) found that the items on scale 9 were typically only moderately correlated with the total scores on the scale. The highest biserial correlation for any item was .48 on the item "At times I have very much wanted to leave home." Two other items were tied at .45: "I don't blame anyone for trying to grab everything he can get in this world" and "I do not blame a person for taking advantage of someone who lays himself open to it." The items "I have often had to take orders from someone who did not know as much as I did" and "At times my thoughts have raced ahead faster than I could speak them" both correlated .43 with the total score on scale 9. These low correlations reflect the heterogeneity of the scale, while the content of these items that proved to be the most differentiating for college

Table 6-9. Scale 9 (Hypomania): Item Composition, Direction of Scoring, and Overlap with Other Basic Scales

True: 9

11. A person should try to understand his dreams and be guided by or take warning from them.
59. I have often had to take orders from someone who did not know as much as I did.
73. I am an important person.
100. I have met problems so full of possibilities that I have been unable to make up my mind about them.
167. It wouldn't make me nervous if any members of my family got into trouble with the law.
181. When I get bored I like to stir up some excitement.
222. It is not hard for me to ask help from my friends even though I cannot return the favor.
232. I have been inspired to a program of life based on duty which I have since carefully followed.
240. I never worry about my looks.
250. I don't blame anyone for trying to grab everything he can get in this world.
277. At times I have been so entertained by the cleverness of a crook that I have hoped he would get by with it.
298. If several people find themselves in trouble, the best thing for them to do is to agree upon a story and stick to it.

True: (9)

228. At times I feel that I can make up my mind with unusually great ease.

False: 9

101. I believe women ought to have as much sexual freedom as men.

False: (9)

166. I am afraid when I look down from a high place.

False: L59

120. My table manners are not quite as good at home as when I am out in company.

False: L9

105. Sometimes when I am not feeling well I am cross.

True: F89

156. I have had periods in which I carried on activities without knowing later what I had been doing.

False: K4. True: (59)

134. At times my thoughts have raced ahead faster than I could speak them.

False: (K9)

148. It makes me impatient to have people ask my advice or otherwise interrupt me when I am working on something important.

True: 29

13 (290). I work under a great deal of tension.

False: 349

289. I am always disgusted with the law when a criminal is freed through the arguments of a smart lawyer.

True: 3789

238. I have periods of such great restlessness that I cannot sit long in a chair.

True: 469

127. I know who is responsible for most of my troubles.

True: 489

21 (308). At times I have very much wanted to leave home.

True: 59

226. Some of my family have habits that bother and annoy me very much.

True: 6789

22 (326). At times I have fits of laughing and crying that I cannot control.

True: 689

157. I feel that I have often been punished without cause.

False: 6. True: (9)

268. Something exciting will almost always pull me out of it when I am feeling low.

False: 69. True: (0)

111. I have never done anything dangerous for the thrill of it.

True: 789

266. Once a week or oftener I become very excited.

True: 89

97. At times I have a strong urge to do something harmful or shocking.

Table 6-9—continued

194. I have had attacks in which I could not control my movements or speech but in which I knew what was going on around me.
212. My people treat me more like a child than a grown-up.
251. I have had blank spells in which my activities were interrupted and I did not know what was going on around me.

False: 890

119. My speech is the same as always (not faster nor slower, or slurring; no hoarseness).

True: 9. False: (2)

†64. I sometimes keep on at a thing until others lose their patience with me.
233. I have at times stood in the way of people who were trying to do something, not because it amounted to much but because of the principle of the thing.
†263. I sweat very easily even on cool days.
271. I do not blame a person for taking advantage of someone who lays himself open to it.

True: 9. False: (3)

279. I drink an unusually large amount of water every day.

True: 9. False: (36)

109. Some people are so bossy that I feel like doing the opposite of what they request, even though I know they are right.

True: 9. False: (0)

143. When I was a child, I belonged to a crowd or gang that tried to stick together through thick and thin.

True: 0. False: (K349)

180. I find it hard to make talk when I meet new people.
267. When in a group of people I have trouble thinking of the right things to talk about.

True: 0. False: (K49)

171. It makes me uncomfortable to put on a stunt at a party even when others are doing the same sort of things.

students reflects the emotional alienation of the underlying character rather than the symptomatic manifestations of the hypomanic state.

The normative group means and standard deviations on scale 9 are given in Table 5-1, the reliability estimates in the appendix material in Volume II. As might be expected on a symptomatic scale, the test-retest values run rather low. The internal consistency checks also are rather low, reflecting the heterogeneity of the items described above.

Comrey (1958f) also concluded that this scale was quite heterogeneous after factoring the interitem correlations, finding fourteen sources of variance among these forty-six items: shyness, bitterness, acceptance of taboos, poor reality contact, thrill-seeking, age, social dependency, psychopathic personality, high water consumption, hospitalization, sex membership, hypomania, agitation, and defensiveness. Most of these sources of variance seemed to be restricted to this scale rather than appearing in other clinical scales of the MMPI.

High Scale 9 Scores. These persons in the group studied by Hathaway and Meehl (1952) were apparently well known to their peers. The list of terms showing significant relationships to this scale is long and descriptive. One major theme running through the adjectives characteristic of normal males with high 9 scores centers about their sociability, energy, and openness. They were described as sociable in the sense of forward, talkative and verbal, individualistic, impulsive, enthusiastic, adventurous, and curious, with interests in national, political matters. They also were described as liking drinking. Another theme is reflected in the description of them as generous, softhearted, affectionate, and sentimental. Their acquaintances also described the high 9 males as prone to worry, self-dissatisfied, and conventional.

A rather similar but smaller subset of terms was applied to the high 9 females in Hathaway and Meehl's group. They were described as frank, courageous, and idealistic. The high energy level of this group is also shown in the common use of the terms talkative, enthusiastic, and versatile.

The high 9 girls in Hovey's (1953) group were described by their superiors as poised and at ease around others, not reserved or shy, but self-confident, with ease in oral expression. They were seen as likely to show initiative and ingenuity, and to be efficient and responsible, although they were not characterized as conscientious. They were seen as effective in dealing with mental patients and showing leadership qualities, but they also impressed the judges as being immature.

The high 9 men in the IPAR group (Gough, McKee, and Yandell, 1955) were viewed in a somewhat less favorable light by the psychological staff than those in this personality group that were described above. Like the high 9's in the other studies, they were seen as expressive, ebullient persons. However, they were also characterized as guileful and potentially deceitful. Their actions appeared to be importantly influenced by intangible subjective feelings that were diffuse and highly personal in nature. They sought and enjoyed aesthetic and sensuous impressions. The adjectives characteristic of this group strengthen this view of the high 9 male. They were described as sensitive, thoughtful, and imaginative, as anxious and nervous, and as deceitful and unfriendly.

In describing themselves, the high 9 males in the group of normals studied by Hathaway and Meehl matched to some extent the descriptions given them by their peers, but there are some notable disagreements. While they concurred in describing themselves as impulsive, talkative, adventurous, and liking to drink, and even added to this list the term frank, the high 9 males also described themselves as seclusive. There was agreement in the endorsement of the term worrying, to which these men added high-strung. The high 9 women described themselves as enterprising and sociable, in the sense of mixing well. They also said that they were grateful and idealistic.

Low Scale 9 Scores. The friends of the low 9 men in Hathaway and Meehl's group described them as reliable, practical, balanced, and mature, with home and family interests. A very similar but somewhat longer list of terms was applied to the low 9 female group. These women were perceived as mature, balanced, temperate, alert, natural, adaptable, clear-thinking, and reasonable, as well as orderly and practical. The low 9 girls in Hovey's study did not appear very clearly, but the supervisors characterized them as persevering, adjusting slowly, and participating very little in group discussions.

The IPAR judges described the low 9 men in their group as conscientious, responsible, and dependable persons who tended to take clear stands on moral issues. They were seen to show good judgment and common sense.

IPAR data also indicate that scores at the lower end of scale 9 are related to stability of emotional adjustment (Woodworth, Barron, and MacKinnon, 1957). In addition, the judges saw these men as somewhat self-indulgent and tending to emphasize oral pleasures. The adjectives found significantly related to this level of scale 9 were simple, unassuming, cool, and sincere.

Little material emerged from the analyses Hathaway and Meehl made of the self-descriptions of this group. The men endorsed the terms balanced and willing to settle down while the women described themselves as sensitive.

Scale 0 (Si)

The concept of introversion has had a long and varied course of development in personality formulations. Introduced originally in a typological form (Jung, 1923), it has been modified to trait conceptions and even to dynamic theories. The immediate theoretical antecedent of the adaptation of the concept for the MMPI was a tripartite analysis by Evans and McConnell (1941) of the general personality characteristics of introversion-extroversion into features of thinking, social participation, and emotional expression. In this formulation, a particular person need not be generally introverted in all aspects of his personality. For example, he could be introverted only in his emotional patterns, while at the same time his social preferences could be extroverted and his thinking patterns occupy some middle range, neither markedly introverted nor extroverted. Basing their approach on the work of Guilford and Guilford (1936; 1939), Evans and McConnell devised separate measures for the three features and offered a single test to evaluate the relative degrees of introversion-extroversion in each. In their terms social introversion is characterized by withdrawal from social contacts and responsibilities. Little real interest in people is displayed. In contrast, social extroversion involves the seeking of social contacts and a sincere interest in people. Many satisfactions stem from social contacts for the social extrovert.

As Eisenberg (1949) and French (1949) have pointed out, an a priori and judgmental basis for selecting items and forming scales for a personality test raises many doubts concerning its dependability. Since scale 0 was derived on the basis of separations provided by the social introversion key of such an instrument, the Minnesota T-S-E Inventory, many of its biases may appear in the present scale of the MMPI. Later discussions, however, will clarify some of the features of this scale and its personological correlates which are independent of the way in which it was derived.

Scale 0 was first published under the designation Social I-E by L. E. Drake (1946). The scale items were chosen by contrasting groups of students in the guidance program at the University of Wisconsin who scored above the 65th centile rank and below the 35th centile rank on the subscale for social introversion-extroversion in the Minnesota T-S-E Inventory. This use of a psychological test to form criterion groups for a new MMPI scale was employed in developing only one other regular scale (scale 5). The final scale includes the items which separated these groups and were endorsed by the test subjects with sufficient frequency to be useful in the differentiation.

The items in this scale are listed in Table 6-10. In addition to items with face validity that describe the person's uneasiness in social situations or in dealings with others, there are items covering a variety of special sensitivities, insecurities, and worries. The high scorer on scale 0 also denies many impulses, temptations, and mental aberrations. The conservative nature of many of the replies is striking, and a strong self-depreciatory trend is evident.

Table 6-10. Scale 0 (Social Introversion): Item Composition, Direction of Scoring, and Overlap with Other Basic Scales

True: 0

377. At parties I am more likely to sit by myself or with just one other person than to join in with the crowd.
411. It makes me feel like a failure when I hear of the success of someone I know well.
427. I am embarrassed by dirty stories.
455. I am quite often not in on the gossip and talk of the group I belong to.
473. Whenever possible I avoid being in a crowd.
487. I feel like giving up quickly when things go wrong.
549. I shrink from facing a crisis or difficulty.
564. I am apt to pass up something I want to do when others feel that it isn't worth doing.

True: (0)

436. People generally demand more respect for their own rights than they are willing to allow for others.

False: 0

371. I am not unusually self-conscious.
391. I love to go to dances.
415. If given the chance I would make a good leader of people.
440. I try to remember good stories to pass them on to other people.
449. I enjoy social gatherings just to be with people.
450. I enjoy the excitement of a crowd.
451. My worries seem to disappear when I get into a crowd of lively friends.
462. I have had no difficulty starting or holding my urine.
479. I do not mind meeting strangers.
482. While in trains, busses, etc., I often talk to strangers.
521. In a group of people I would not be embarrassed to be called upon to start a discussion or give an opinion about something I know well.
547. I like parties and socials.

False: (0)

400. If given the chance I could do some things that would be of great benefit to the world.
446. I enjoy gambling for small stakes.
469. I have often found people jealous of my good ideas, just because they had not thought of them first.
481. I can remember "playing sick" to get out of something.
505. I have had periods when I felt so full of pep that sleep did not seem necessary for days at a time.

False: K240

296. I have periods in which I feel unusually cheerful without any special reason.

False: 1680

281. I do not often notice my ears ringing or buzzing.

True: 234780

32 (328). I find it hard to keep my mind on a task or job.

True: 2470

67. I wish I could be as happy as others seem to be.

True: 20

236. I brood a great deal.

True: 20. False: (K)

138. Criticism or scolding hurts me terribly.

False: 20

57. I am a good mixer.

False: (20)

208. I like to flirt.

Table 6-10—continued

True: 48. False: (0)

33 (323). I have had very peculiar and strange experiences.

False: 40

91. I do not mind being made fun of.

True: 50

278. I have often felt that strangers were looking at me critically.

False: 50

99. I like to go to parties and other affairs where there is lots of loud fun.
229. I should like to belong to several clubs or lodges.
254. I like to be with a crowd who play jokes on one another.
262. It does not bother me that I am not better looking.

True: 5. False: (40)

‡231. I like to talk about sex.

True: 5. False: (0)

25. I would like to be a singer.
126. I like dramatics.

False: 69. True: (0)

111. I have never done anything dangerous for the thrill of it.

True: 70

304. In school I found it very hard to talk before the class.
321. I am easily embarrassed.
336. I easily become impatient with people.
342. I forget right away what people say to me.
357. I have several times given up doing a thing because I thought too little of my ability.

False: 70

353. I have no dread of going into a room by myself where other people have already gathered and are talking.

True: 7. False: (0)

359. Sometimes some unimportant thought will run through my mind and bother me for days.

False: 890

119. My speech is the same as always (not faster or slower, or slurring; no hoarseness).

True: 80

332. Sometimes my voice leaves me or changes even though I have no cold.

False: 80

309. I seem to make friends about as quickly as others do.

True: 9. False: (0)

143. When I was a child, I belonged to a crowd or gang that tried to stick together through thick and thin.

True: 0. False: (K)

383. People often disappoint me.
398. I often think, "I wish I were a child again."

True: 0. False: (K349)

180. I find it hard to make talk when I meet new people.
267. When in a group of people I have trouble thinking of the right things to talk about.

True: 0. False: (K36)

124. Most people will use somewhat unfair means to gain profit or an advantage rather than to lose it.

True: 0. False: (K49)

71. It makes me uncomfortable to put on a stunt at a party even when others are doing the same sort of things.

True: 0. False: (K6)

316. I think nearly anyone would tell a lie to keep out of trouble.

False: 0. True: (2)

†193. I do not have spells of hay fever or asthma.

True: 0. False: (3)

147. I have often lost out on things because I couldn't make up my mind soon enough.
172. I frequently have to fight against showing that I am bashful.
292. I am likely not to speak to people until they speak to me.

True: 0. False: (34)

201. I wish I were not so shy.

True: 0. False: (4)

82. I am easily downed in an argument.

True: 0. False: (56)

117. Most people are honest chiefly through fear of being caught.

Table 5-1 gives the means and standard deviations obtained from scoring a subgroup of the men and women of the Minnesota normative sample on this scale. The mean seems to be about the same as that reported for University of Wisconsin undergraduates, but the standard deviation runs a point or two larger. The available reliability estimates for scale 0 are given in the appendix material in Volume II. More evidence is needed, but the length of this scale seems to provide stability over time for these scores on normal subjects.

In their factor analysis of the interitem correlations of scale 0, Graham, Schroeder, and Lilly (1971) identified six factor sources: inferiority-discomfort, lack of affiliation, low social excitement, sensitivity, interpersonal trust, and physical somatic concern. These components appear to be consistent with the social facet of introversion with which Drake was working in his scale derivation and with the personological correlates that have been identified for scale 0 (see below). High scores on this scale can be composed of largely the social isolation components or the maladjustment and self-depreciation components (or both).

Briggs and Tellegen (1967) have proposed an abbreviated Si scale for use with the regular test booklet when only the first 366 items are administered. Giedt and Downing (1961) published a measure of extroversion in their Ex scale which is intended to be less related to maladjustment or psychopathology. Gocka and Holloway (1962) have devised a composite extroversion-introversion scale based in part on earlier work by Rozynko (1959) as well as Block's ego overcontrol scale, Welsh's second factor, R, scale, the Giedt and Downing Ex scale, and Mees's (1959) second factor scale. All these scales are presented in Appendix I in Volume II.

High Scale 0 Scores. Hathaway and Meehl (1952) found that there was an important sex difference in the degree to which peers were able to characterize normal persons with this scale elevated. The acquaintances of the men gave only one characteristic adjective, modest. The women, on the other hand, were described more fully. In addition to modest, these women were called shy, self-effacing, and sensitive. Over and above this social submissiveness, there was evidence of emotional warmth—kind, affectionate, softhearted, and sentimental were adjectives used. Although some maladjustive implications may be suggested by the term high-strung, these women were also described as natural, as serious, and as having home and family interests. This does not appear to be a group of persons who strive for social contacts and satisfactions but are blocked and thwarted in these efforts. Rather the ratings suggest a basic preference for a certain style of life and a social pattern in keeping with emotional needs. It is interesting to note how little came out of these analyses for the male group. The personality pattern may have served to keep the raters of these men from knowing their subjects well enough to characterize them on this checklist.

The judges at IPAR (Gough, McKee, and Yandell, 1955) provide a more complete picture of high 0 males. Although the findings are in harmony with those of the Minnesota study, there is in addition a quality of ineffectiveness or maladjustment in the IPAR pattern. The high 0 men were described as slow in personal tempo, stereotyped, lacking originality in approach to problems. The implication seems to be that these men showed such qualities as part of a general insecurity. They were also described as unable to make decisions without vacillation, hesitation, or delay. They were seen as rigid and inflexible in thought and action, as overly controlled and inhibited, and as lacking confidence in their own abilities. They were conforming and followed prescribed methods in the things they did. They became fussy and pedantic in even minor matters.

In their relations with others, they were seen as lacking poise and social presence, as becoming rattled and upset in a social situation. Perhaps as a consequence, these men were rated as cold and distant. They were not affected in this aloofness, however, but appeared free of pretense and conscientious and dependable in their responsibilities. They seemed to derive personal reward and pleasure from their work and placed a high value on productive achievement for its own sake.

Toward authority, these men were submissive, compliant, and overly accepting. They tended to sidestep as a way of handling troublesome situations. They either made concessions to avoid unpleasantness or passively resisted pressures by not getting involved in things. They were generally permissive and accepting, however, in their relations with others, respecting other people and not making judgments. As a result these high 0 men kept out of trouble and showed socially appropriate behavior. They get along well in the world as it is.

The adjectives associated with high 0 scores are quite similar: apathetic, slow, dull, retiring, unambitious, silent, simple, and conventional.

Hathaway and Meehl found only one term in their analysis of the self-ratings of the high 0 males that characterized this group: sensitive. As with the ratings by others, they found more terms typical of the high 0 females. These women described themselves as shy, sensitive, modest, sentimental, prone to worry, and self-dissatisfied.

Low Scale 0 Scores. Two terms typified the low 0 men in the normal group studied by Hathaway and Meehl: versatile and sociable in the sense of mixing well. The women were described by their acquaintances as sociable (also in the sense of mixing well), enthusiastic, talkative, assertive, and adventurous.

In the terms and phrases applied by the IPAR judges to men low on scale 0, the same picture is revealed and developed. These men were seen as expressive, ebullient, colorful persons. They tended to be ostentatious and exhibitionistic. They were active and vigorous and competitive with their peers. They showed strong initiative and took the ascendant role in relations with others. They appeared to possess high intellectual ability and were verbally fluent and facile. They were persuasive and often won others over to their viewpoint. They also manipulated others in attempting to gain their own ends, seeing things rather opportunistically rather than being sensitive to the meaning and value of these persons as individuals. These men were seen as potentially guileful and deceitful. They emphasized oral pleasure in a self-indulgent way, seeking aesthetic and sensuous impressions. They appeared unable to delay gratification and often acted with insufficient thought and deliberation. This undercontrol of their impulses, combined with their tendencies to get ego-involved in many different things, led to a characteristic aggressiveness or hostility in their personal relations. These men emphasized success and productive achievement as a means for achieving status, recognition, and power. They readily became counteractive in the face of frustration and easily aroused hostility and resentment in those with whom they dealt.

The adjectives found related to low 0 scores at IPAR were active, ambitious, and blustery. The men were also described as immature, hasty, quick, ingenious, witty, and having initiative.

Both the male and female groups of subjects with low 0 scores were more adequately characterized in their self-ratings in the Hathaway and Meehl study than were the high 0 subjects. The men described themselves as sociable in the sense of both being forward and mixing well. They also said they were enterprising and enthusiastic, affectionate and responsive, courageous and cheerful. In addition, they described themselves as hard-headed, facing life, temperate, and adaptable.

The women gave an even longer list of terms that included many of the same adjectives the men endorsed. The women also described themselves as sociable in both meanings of the word, enterprising and enthusiastic, cheerful, adaptable, and affectionate. To the sociability, they added such descriptions as talkative, friendly, frank, and verbal. They said they were energetic (spirited), versatile, assertive, and adventurous, with wide interests and good physical strength and endurance. They characterized themselves as quite responsible in such terms as reliable, conscientious, balanced, and reasonable. These women also endorsed terms descriptive of personal comfort, such as relaxed, trustful, poised, self-confident, and independent.

Norms for the Basic Scales

The basic scales contain different numbers of items and give rise to different endorsement patterns and frequencies. In order to compare relative position or degree of deviation on these component scales it is necessary to transform them to some common scale. In the standard profile this is accomplished by setting the mean value of the Minnesota normative male and female groups on each scale at a value of 50 and assigning each raw-score deviation the size of a standard deviation a value of 10 points. These scores have been called T-score values even though the usual normalizing step is not employed in this transformation. A careful comparison by Weisgerber (1965) of the usual MMPI T-score values and the results of a normalization of these values has indicated relatively little practical change since the basic distribution is quite markedly skewed in the raw-score form of each component scale.

Table 5-1 lists the raw-score means and standard deviations of each MMPI scale (with and without K correction when applicable) for each sex reported by Hathaway and Briggs (1957) on a somewhat purified sample of

Minnesota normals. These K-corrected values are equivalent to the T-score transformations provided for the male and female profile forms distributed by the Psychological Corporation. (See Chapter 3.) These values in Table 5-1 do not necessarily correspond, however, to the means and standard deviations given in Appendix I since no special age corrections have been made on the Appendix I values comparable to those devised by Hathaway and Briggs. The Hathaway-Briggs values are preferable in each instance for normative purposes.

The non-K-corrected values are used in the norms provided in Table 3 in Appendix H for plotting the standard adult profile for either men or women without K weights. (As noted in Chapter 3, the standard-profile raw-score values cannot be used to obtain non-K-corrected profiles.) Either K-corrected or noncorrected adult profile values for T scores are used in the vast majority of the profile patterning procedures, such as coding, special index computations, or discriminant functions, as described in Chapter 3. These values should be employed for purposes of comparison and interpretation when using the patterning findings summarized in Chapter 7. However, a number of special normative tables are reproduced in Appendix H to provide a basis for comparing a given test record with special age groups, etc. Norms for some of the more frequently used special scales have been prepared and will be found in Appendix F. Additional data for preparing Minnesota-based norms for each sex on any of the special MMPI scales are presented with the item composition and direction of scoring data on each scale in Appendix I of Volume II.

CHAPTER 7. Clinical Scale Configurations

THE CLINICAL implications of each of the basic scales taken as a separate personality measure have been summarized in Chapter 6. Even before these individual scales had all been devised, refined, and published, Hathaway and McKinley had discovered the utility of employing various combinations of scores in simple arrangements or patterns. After publication of the instrument, together with its standard profile of validity and clinical scales, clinical usage and related clinical research studies rapidly developed a general lore on configural analyses of the profile patterns. Thus, it was soon learned that the basic MMPI measures would yield both nomothetic (absolute scale level) and idiographic (intra-individual relative level) meanings. As the summaries of these developments provided in Volume II show, some methods of analyzing the MMPI rely primarily upon nomothetic approaches, even for patterned information, e.g., Gilberstadt's (1970) or Guthrie's (1949) scales for various code combinations, while others rely upon methods which preserve the idiographic configurations (at times even eliminating such nomothetic information as scale elevation). Both approaches are based upon the interrelationships that have been found among the basic clinical scales. These relationships will be briefly reviewed here, followed by a résumé of the dimensional approaches to MMPI configurations and ending with a summary of the configurational approaches.

Interrelationships among the Basic Scales

Even from the brief descriptions given in Chapter 6 of the clinical criteria used in deriving the basic scales it can be seen that they are by no means homogeneous, internally consistent groupings of behavioral features. Rather, they are pragmatically formed clusters of symptoms which overlap and interrelate in a variety of ways. Scales developed on the basis of these criteria, therefore, can be expected to have similar although not necessarily identical relationships, one to another. That is, if the syndrome used in developing a given scale is relatively complex and is characterized by a wide variety of symptoms, then the scale, reflecting this behavioral heterogeneity, is likely to show important relationships with some other scales in the profile.

As Hathaway (1956b) has pointed out, the appearance of certain patterns of MMPI scores again and again in clinical practice is in part dependent upon the relationships existing among the component scales. Without this recurrence of a limited number of configurations, the effort involved in building up research data on the various patterns would be many times more taxing than it is now and it would be extremely difficult to establish empirical foundations for any clinical inferences to be drawn from these patterns. It is important, therefore, to gain some insight into the nature and extent of these relationships among the basic scales in the test before attempting to deal with the profile patterns themselves.

Item Overlap. The method of item selection employed in deriving most of the scales led to the identification of the most discriminating items in the research pool for each separate diagnostic problem. As has already been noted, this method resulted in many items being included in more than one scale. That is, some items proved to be useful in differentiating several different clinical groups from a normal reference group.

The extent of item overlapping on the validity and clinical scales is summarized in Table 7-1. Since some items may appear on as many as six different scales and may be scored one way on some and oppositely on others, the values in Table 7-1 list the similarly scored and oppositely scored items separately, below and above the main diagonal, respectively. The values in the cells of the main diagonal of Table 7-1 are the numbers of items scored only on the particular basic scale and on no other in this set of scales. Thus, it can be seen that the F scale is tied with scale 5 (Mf) for the largest number of uniquely scored items. As to be expected from the way the F scale was derived, any item that was answered rarely enough to meet the defining characteristics of an F item had to be very highly discriminating to be in-

Table 7-1. Summary of Amount and Direction of the Item Overlap on the Basic Scales of the MMPI

Basic Scales	No. of Items	L	F	K	1 (Hs)	2 (D)	3 (Hy)	4 (Pd)	5-m (Mf)	5-f (Mf)	6 (Pa)	7 (Pt)	8 (Sc)	9 (Ma)	0 (Si)
L	15	*9*	...	...	...	...	...	...	...	...	1	1	1	...	...
F	64	1	*35*	...	...	...	...	...	...	...	...	...	...	...	...
K	30	1	1	*5*	...	2	...	1	2	2	...	2	...	1	8
1	33	...	1	...	*8*	1	...	...	...	...	...	...	...	...	...
2	60	2	2	6	9	*13*	...	...	...	...	...	...	1	4	1
3	60	1	1	10	20	13	*10*	...	...	1	...	...	...	2	7
4	50	...	5	7	1	7	10	*10*	2	1	...	...	...	1	6
5-m[a] ..	60	1	2	1	...	2	4	1	*35*[b]	5	...	...	1	...	4
5-f[a] ...	60	1	2	1	...	2	3	2	55	*35*[b]	...	...	3	...	3
6	40	...	9	2	1	2	4	8	2	2	*7*	...	...	2	4
7	48	...	1	...	2	13	7	6	1	1	4	*9*	...	...	1
8	78	...	15	1	4	9	8	10	3	1	13	17	*16*	...	1
9	46	2	1	4	...	1	4	6	3	3	4	3	11	*15*	5
0	70	...	...	1	1	7	1	5	5	6	1	8	5	1	*26*

[a] 5-m means male key for scale 5; 5-f means female key for scale 5.

[b] There are thirty-five items scored uniquely on scale 5 as a whole; there are no unique items on either 5-m or 5-f if they are considered as separate scales.

cluded in any clinical scale. The scale overlapping to the greatest extent with F is scale 8. There was no overlapping with the F scale in the opposite direction for any of the basic scales.

The data listed for scale 5 in Table 7-1 reflect the special circumstance of separate keys for each sex. Strictly speaking, there is no item on scale 5 for males that is not scored for females as well, although five of the sixty items are scored in the opposite direction. The entries in the main diagonal for scale 5, therefore, mean that thirty-five items in scale 5 (male or female) are not scored on any of the other basic scales. Thus, scale 5 has the largest number of uniquely scored items of any of the clinical scales. The K scale has the fewest number of singly scored items of any of the basic scales. As already noted in the discussions above, scales 1 and 3 have the largest number of items in common, all scored in the same direction. Scales 7 and 8 overlap nearly as much, with seventeen items in common all scored the same way. Scale 0 has the largest number of items scored oppositely from the other basic scales in the MMPI. It is not known at this time how much of this item overlap is attributable to similar psychological characteristics appearing in the complex symptom clusters used as scale criteria and how much is a function of different interpretations of an item by subjects showing each of the personality features involved.

Because of this overlap in the component items, the basic scales possess varying amounts of experimental dependence. Only seven pairs of scales have no common items, although the actual amount of overlap is frequently reduced by cancellation of positive and negative overlap. Wheeler, Little, and Lehner (1951) published a set of correlations among the basic scales based solely on this actual amount of item overlap. Table 7-2 presents their findings, with some additions and corrections. In the main diagonal of the table are listed the number of items in each scale. In the cells below the main

Table 7-2. Absolute Amount of Item Overlap among the Basic Scales and the Intercorrelations Resulting from This Overlap

Basic Scales	L	F	K	1 (Hs)	2 (D)	3 (Hy)	4 (Pd)	5 [a] (Mf)	6 (Pa)	7 (Pt)	8 (Sc)	9 (Ma)	0 (Si)
L	*15*	.03	.05	.00	.08	.03	.00	.03	−.04	−.04	−.03	.04	.00
F	1	*64*	.02	.02	.03	.01	.09	.03	.18	.02	.21	.01	.00
K	1	1	*30*	.00	.09	.24	.16	−.02	.06	−.05	.02	.08	−.15
1	0	1	0	33	.18	.46	.02	.00	.03	.05	.08	.00	.02
2	2	2	4	8	*60*	.22	.14	.03	.04	.26	.10	−.05	.09
3	1	1	10	20	13	*60*	.18	.06	.08	.13	.12	.06	−.09
4	0	5	6	1	7	10	*50*	−.02	.18	.12	.16	.10	−.02
5 [a] ...	1	2	−1	0	2	4	−1	*60*	.04	.02	.03	.05	.02
6	−1	9	2	1	2	4	8	2	*40*	.09	.23	.05	−.06
7	−1	1	−2	2	13	7	6	1	4	*48*	.27	.06	.12
8	−1	15	1	4	8	8	10	2	13	17	*78*	.18	.05
9	2	1	3	0	−3	3	5	3	2	3	11	*46*	−.07
0	0	0	−7	1	6	−6	−1	1	−3	7	4	−4	*70*

SOURCE: Adapted from Wheeler, Little, and Lehner (1951), with the use of Guilford's (1936) correlation.

[a] Scale 5 key for males only.

diagonal are given the actual number of overlapping items between each pair of scales (items scored in the same direction minus those scored oppositely). Above the main diagonal, the cells contain the corresponding correlations between the scale pairs arising from the actual number of common items and the number of items in the respective scales. These coefficients were computed by the formula

$$r = \frac{n_c}{\sqrt{n_a + n_c}\,\sqrt{n_b + n_c}}$$

in which n_a = number of items in scale A not in scale B; n_b = number of items in scale B not in scale A; and n_c = number of items in common between scale A and scale B (Guilford, 1936). These correlations show the degree to which each of the scales will covary with the other basic scales as a result of the experimental dependence arising from shared items. The values in Table 7-2 range from −.15 to .46. All sets of intercorrelations among the basic scales should be interpreted with these data in mind, although it is rare for empirically based correlations to show only the covariation attributable to item overlap.

The empirical method of deriving the basic scales resulted in some surprises in terms of the content that was expected to appear on the various clinical scales. Thus, the somatic complaints and references appearing on scale 1 do not represent by any means all the bodily complaint items in the item pool. On the other hand, some of these body reference items did appear on scale 2 although hypochondriacal preoccupations are not particularly salient features of most clinical depressive reactions. The extent to which items of this kind appear on the various scales making up the MMPI pool can be seen in Table 7-3 which has been adapted from Wiggins and Vollmar (1959). The content categories used in the tabulations are those employed by Hathaway and McKinley (1940a) in checking for item duplications and content coverage during the construction of the instrument (see Chapter 1). This table gives additional perspective on the nature of the interrelationships existing among the basic sales in the MMPI.

Dimensional Approaches to MMPI Patterning

A large number of analyses have been carried out on the MMPI in an effort to isolate more homogeneous and presumably psychologically more univocal dimensions or scales than the complex and interconnected empirical scales derived by the test authors. These investigations are reviewed in Volume II, where there is also a careful delineation of the different kinds of dimensions resulting from analyses carried out on interitem as opposed to interscale correlations. Some of the findings have been summarized in Chapter 6 in discussions of the factor analyses of the items making up each of the clinical scales but the results of this kind of investigation which have led to systems of clinical interpretation will be taken up in this section.

Welsh's A and R Scales and the Novant System. Welsh (1956b, 1965) has pioneered in the factor analysis of the variances in common among the

Table 7-3. Percentage of Items in Each Content Category Appearing in Each of the Basic Validity and Clinical Scales

Content Category	L (15)	F (64)	K (30)	Hs (33)	D (60)	Hy (60)	Pd (50)	Mf (60)	Pa (40)	Pt (48)	Sc (78)	Ma (46)	Si (70)
General health (9)			3	12	10	7	2	2	2	2			
General neurologic (19)		5		18	8	10			2	6	9	9	
Cranial nerves (11)		2		9		3			2		5	2	4
Motility and coordination (6)				9	2	7		2		2	5		
Sensibility (5)				12		2					1		
Vasomotor, etc. (10)		2		3	5	3				2	3	2	
Cardiorespiratory (5)		2		9	3	3							1
Gastrointestinal (11)		2		18	3	3				2			
Genitourinary (5)								2					1
Habits (19)		6		6	7	5	2			6	1	4	
Family and marital (26)		11	3			2	20	5	2		12	7	
Occupational (18)		2	13	3	5	5		2			1	7	3
Educational (12)		3				3	2	3		2			
Sexual attitudes (16)		3			2	2	4	8			5	2	4
Religious attitudes (19)		8			5			3				2	
Political attitudes (46)		6	13		2	10	14	12	22		4	20	10
Social attitudes (72)		6	27		7	17	16	8	5	10	12	13	43
Affect, depressive (32)		5	7		13	3	8	3	10	17	12		4
Affect, manic (24)		3	17		10	5	8	2	8	8	4	13	4
Obsessive-compulsive (15)		3			3	3		2	2	10	1	7	1
Delusions, etc. (31)		20				2	12	2	38	2	12	4	4
Phobias (29)		3			3	2	2	2	2	10	6	2	3
Sadistic, etc. (7)		5			2			2			3		
Morale (33)		3	13		7	2	10	2		17	4	2	10
Masculinity-femininity (55)								38					6
Lie items (15)	100	2	3		3	2		2	2	2	1	4	

SOURCE: Wiggins and Vollmar (1959).

basic scales of the MMPI. His initial efforts led to the derivation of two special scales, the A scale for the first common factor and the R scale for the second factor, which have been employed in a number of clinical settings as routinely scored supplementary scales (see Appendix F). Early studies revealed consistent personality correlates of high or low values on each of these scales separately. These will be summarized first.

The first factor scale, A, developed by Welsh (1956b; see the discussion in Volume II), which reflects the largest component of common variance among the basic scales in the MMPI profile, has been studied in relation to the assessment ratings made at IPAR (Block and Bailey, 1955). Although these men earned a low average score on the A scale (5.9 raw score points, with a standard deviation of 5.5 points), separation into high and low groups led to a fairly extensive list of differentiating attributes ascribed to these subjects by the staff judges.

High A men were described as lacking confidence in their own abilities and unable to make decisions without hesitation, vacillation, or delay. They were inhibited and overcontrolled their impulses. This even appeared in their personal tempo—they were characterized as slow in response, in speech, and in movement.

Socially, these men lacked poise and easy presence, becoming rattled and upset in social situations. With respect to authority they were submissive, compliant, and overly accepting. They were suggestible and responded more to the evaluations others made of them than they did to their own self-evaluations. They also appeared effeminate in both style and manner of behavior. They were conforming and followed prescribed ways of doing things. They appeared cold and distant, tending not to get involved in things but remaining passively resistant.

The high A men appeared strongly influenced in their behavior by diffuse personal feelings and intangible subjective impressions. They were self-defensive, constantly seeking to rationalize, excuse, and defend themselves while blaming others for difficulties. They were usually pessimistic about their own professional future and advancement. The judges at IPAR believed that these men would readily become confused, disorganized, and unadaptive under stress.

The adjectives associated with high A scale values for these subjects are generally in accord with this picture (Gough, McKee, and Yandell, 1955), although the emotionality was not noted. The men were described as unemotional and unexcitable, apathetic and retiring, silent and quiet. They were also described as cautious, fussy, painstaking, formal and awkward, meek, mild, simple, commonplace, and peaceable.

The low A men were seen to be much more active and vigorous persons than the high A men. They were said to be expressive, ebullient, and colorful, tending even to be ostentatious and exhibitionistic. They preferred action to contemplation and were efficient and capable. They easily mobilized their resources and did not appear bothered by work inhibitions. They were fluent and conversationally facile, taking the initiative in social relations and easily assuming ascendant roles in relation to others. They were also persuasive, readily winning others over to their point of view. All these latter characteristics facilitated their effectiveness as leaders.

The low A men were competitive with their peers, getting a great deal out of winning or being ahead. They emphasized success and productive achievement as a way of gaining status, power, or recognition. If they failed in this striving, they became counteractive under the frustration. In their dealings with others they seemed to manipulate people as a means to their own personal ends without regard for others as individuals. The low A men also seemed unable to delay gratification, often acting without sufficient thought or deliberation.

The adjectives checked for the low A men support the picture given above. The activity level is indicated in such terms as active, energetic, enterprising, ambitious, adventurous, high initiative, enthusiastic, forceful, spontaneous. Their relations with others were described as outgoing, sociable, friendly, informal. Although they were described as versatile, resourceful, and ingenious, their lack of control led the judges to use hasty, loud, impulsive, careless, and immature in characterizing them. In social situations they were regarded as frank, outspoken, self-confident, and excitable. In addition they were said to be quick, efficient, hardheaded, spunky, and clear-thinking.

In the IPAR analysis, the high R scoring men were not clearly differentiated. The distribution of scores that these men earned on R was more symmetrically formed than were their A scale scores, with a raw score mean of 13.2 and a standard deviation of 4.3, but they were less effectively separated, one from another. The judges saw the high R subjects as submissive, unexcitable persons who readily made concessions rather than face unpleasantness of any sort, sidestepping troubles or disagreeable situations. They appeared highly civilized, formal, and conventional. They seemed clear-thinking, but were rated slow, painstaking, and thorough.

The low R men at IPAR were described in greater detail. Some of the terms appearing for this group overlap with the list for low A: outspoken, enthusiastic, outgoing, spunky, and informal. Although this set implies a high activity level in this group as well as in the low A group, the general tone of this activity is quite different. Here the quality seems to be more an uninhibited zest for living. This is conveyed in such terms as robust, healthy, jolly, and daring. The low R's were also described as aggressive, bossy, dominant, courageous, and impulsive. This group appeared to be excitable and emotional, generous, talkative, sarcastic, and argumentative. Another trend running through the descriptions of the low R men is one of subterfuge or pretense. They were described as shrewd and wary, guileful and potentially deceitful, affected and showing off, self-seeking and self-indulgent. They also impressed the judges as intelligent.

These two scales of Welsh's are quite similar to the alpha and beta dimensions identified by Block (1965) using a rather different method of analysis (see the ER and EC scales in Appendix I of Volume II). Block offered these scales as close approximations to the social desirability and acquiescence dimensions which have been interpreted as major sources of invalid variance in personality inventories (see the discussion in Chapter 4). Many of the correlates of the alpha and beta dimensions reported by Block (1965) are quite consistent with the personological implications of the A and R scales summarized above.

More recently, Welsh (1965) has proposed that the two scales be employed conjointly to form a grid of nine categories, or novants. The cutting scores that determine the range of values on A and R within each novant are presented in Chapter 3. Table 7-4 summarizes a number of clinical correlates of these positions in the novant grid. As Welsh notes: "It should be emphasized that these descriptions are not to be taken literally and should not be used for 'cook-book' interpretations of profiles. Rather, the summaries are intended as general concepts that can lead to hypotheses for further investigation" (1965, p. 41).

By means of these A and R scale combinations, Welsh has also shown that groups can be formed with considerable homogeneity in code and profile patterns. This homogeneity reflects the amount of variance in the basic scales themselves that is summarized in these two scales. However, there re-

Table 7-4. Summary of Clinical Descriptors for Each Novant in Welsh's A and R Scale Schema

I. High A–Low R

Subjects falling into this novant may be expected to be introspective, ruminative and overideational, with complaints of worrying and nervousness. There may be chronic feelings of inadequacy, inferiority, and insecurity which are often accompanied by rich fantasies with sexual content. Emotional difficulties may interfere with judgment so that they are seen as lacking common sense. Patients in this novant do not use somatic defenses and although they seem able to admit problems readily the prognosis is poor.

II. High A–Medium R

Severe personality difficulties may be expected with loss of efficiency in carrying out duties. There may be periods of confusion, inability to concentrate, and other evidence of psychological deficit. Symptoms of depression, anxiety and agitation predominate although hysterical disorders sometimes appear. Subjects are often described as unsociable.

III. High A–High R

Depression is often encountered with accompanying tenseness and nervousness as well as complaints of anxiety, insomnia, and undue sensitiveness. Generalized neurasthenic features of fatigue, chronic tiredness, or exhaustion may be seen. These subjects are seen as rigid and worrying in a psychasthenic way and suffer from feelings of inadequacy and a brooding preoccupation with their personal difficulties.

IV. Medium A–Low R

This novant profile respresents a heterogenous group of subjects but often there are headaches and upper gastrointestinal tract symptoms following periods of tension and restlessness. Symptoms are often noted in response to frustration and situational difficulties although subjects are reluctant to accept the psychogenic nature of their complaints. Patients tend to drop out of treatment quickly so that a superficial approach is frequently all that is possible. Ambition is often noted but the level of adjustment may be poor with excessive use of alcohol.

V. Medium A–Medium R

Somatic symptomatology in this group tends to be specific rather than generalized, with epigastric and upper gastrointestinal pain predominating. In some cases there may be an active ulcer. Patients not showing somatic symptoms may complain of tension and depression. Frequently noted is the ability of these patients to tolerate discomfort rather than acting out.

VI. Medium A–High R

Subjects are often described as inadequate or immature and tend to use illness as an excuse for not accomplishing more. Lack of insight is often noted with mechanisms of repression and denial prominent in adjustment attempts. Patients give a chronic hypochondriacal history with somatic overconcern particularly in the alimentary system; abdominal pain is common. Response to treatment is not often favorable since they seem to have learned to use somatic complaints to solve emotional problems.

VII. Low A–Low R

Aggression and hostility may be noted in many subjects and they are often described as arrogant, boastful, and self-centered; some are seen as dishonest and suspicious. Patients may show episodic attacks of acute distress in various organ systems but these physical problems are not severe and generally yield to superficial treatment.

VIII. Low A–Medium R

Although subjects in this novant are characterized by attempts at self-enhancement they are not viewed favorably by others; they tend to be seen as irritable, immature, and insecure. Under stress they are prone to develop symptoms which are usually localized rather than diffuse. Patients suffer from complaints arrived at after protracted periods of mild tension but these are rarely incapacitating although there is an indifferent response to treatment and marginal adjustment is often noted.

Table 7-4—continued

IX. Low A–High R
Lack of self-criticism with impunitive behavior may be found in subjects in this novant and they are often self-centered with many physical complaints. Occasionally there is mild anxiety and tension but little depression occurs. Patients more often have pain in the extremities and the head rather than the trunk but precordial and chest pain may be noted. They profit from reassurance although insight is lacking into the nature of their symptoms.

SOURCE: Welsh (1965).

mains a large amount of important variation in each of the clinical scales that is common to some but not all of the other scales in the test. These sources of variation cannot be ignored in the utilization and interpretation of the regular MMPI profile. Some preliminary work on these additional sources of variance has been carried out by Welsh in the derivation of the factor scales C and P (see Appendix I in Volume II). Further investigation of the nature of these sources of variation requires the addition to the factor matrix of carefully selected variables that relate to particular criterion characteristics of the scale but bear little relationship to other components of the basic MMPI scales. Some of the possibilities inherent in these additional dimensions can be seen in the findings from Eichman's studies reported next in which at least one of the additional dimensions that Welsh was trying to isolate appears to have been identified and scaled.

Eichman's Factor-Scale Patterns. Following the general approach of Welsh in deriving special scales for the various dimensions which he identified in the correlations among the basic scales of the MMPI, Eichman (1961, 1962) has developed four short special scales for the main sources of variance found in a neuropsychiatric population. (See Appendix I in Volume II for these scales I, II, III, IV and their item composition.) In his research, Eichman felt that his first two factor scales were comparable to Welsh's longer scales for the same two main dimensions, A and R. The third scale, however, appeared to be primarily somatic preoccupation rather than either psychoticism or control as reported by Welsh in his P and C scales. Eichman's fourth factor did appear to be comparable to some composite of these two dimensions, perhaps, and the resulting scale was designated as a measure of acting out of impulses.

As summarized in Chapter 3, Eichman (1962) proposed a coding system (substituting arabic numerals for the roman numerals designating these scales) based upon both scale sequence and absolute elevation. The various ratings on clinical cases with each of these various code patterns are summarized in Table 7-5. Eichman has prepared a supplement to this résumé in which the code groupings are also divided on the basis of intellective characteristics (Eichman, 1970).

Other Dimensional Approaches. A number of special indices have been derived which generate additional dimensional schemata for general interpretive or diagnostic purposes. Welsh's (1952) anxiety index, AI, and internalization ratio, IR, were forerunners of the A and R scale novant system. Leary (1957) offered special indices for the two fundamental dimensions,

Table 7-5. Factor-Scale Codes based upon Eichman's Special Scales and Correlates of Each Based upon Psychiatric Male Cases

High 1234. MMPI 218°743"6'9–F'L/ K:

High ratings: disability 86%, somatic 71%, depression 57%, severe anxiety 36%, confusion 36%, arrests 29%, hallucinations 21%, mania 21%, chronicity 62%, failure to gain privileges 44%.

Low ratings: impulsivity 0%.

High 123. MMPI 21° 3" ' 7486–9/F–LK/

High ratings: anxiety 78%, confusion 44%, somatic 67%, severe somatic 33%, chronicity 78%, and suicidal acts 22%.

Low ratings: length of hospitalization 0%, arrests 0%, sexual deviance 0%, delusions 0%, suspiciousness 0%, mania 0%, impulsivity 11%, disability 33%, alcohol 33%.

High 124. MMPI 28"476'31–9/ F–L/K:

High ratings: depression 86%, hallucinations 44%, severe anxiety 29%, hostility 29%, mania 29%, failure to gain privileges 40%, arrests 43%, suicidal acts 57%, disability 71%.

Low ratings: irregular discharge 0%, confusion 0%, impulsivity 14%.

High 134. MMPI 1°8247"369' F'L/K:

High ratings: anxiety 86%, severe anxiety 43%, withdrawal 71%, severe withdrawal 29%, confusion 29%, hostility 29%, somatic 86%, severe somatic 43%, disability 71%, failure to gain privileges 50%, alcohol 86%.

Low ratings: suicidal acts 0%.

High 234. MMPI 21"348"'679– F"L–K/

High ratings: severe anxiety 43%, depression 57%, severe withdrawal 43%, delusions 43%, suspiciousness 43%, hallucinations 29%, confusion 43%, hostility 29%, disability 71%, failure to gain privileges 60%, length of hospitalization 50%, chronicity 86%, sexual deviance 29%, suicidal acts 29%.

Low ratings: irregular discharge 0%.

High 12. MMPI 2"47'3681–9/ F–KL/

High ratings: severe anxiety 25%, withdrawal 88%, severe withdrawal 38%, mania 25%, obsessive-compulsive 38%, disability 75%, failure to gain privileges 43%, length of hospitalization 38%, sexual deviance 25%, suicidal acts 50%.

Low ratings: delusions 0%, suspiciousness 12%, hostility 12%, somatic 25%, severe somatic 0%, chronicity 25%, alcohol 38%, arrests 0%.

High 13. MMPI 12"3478'69– F–LK/

High ratings: anxiety 82%, depression 64%, somatic 91%, irregular discharge 27%, chronicity 73%, arrests 27%.

Low ratings: severe withdrawal 0%, delusions 0%, hostility 0%, mania 0%, impulsivity 9%, failure to gain privileges 0%, length of hospitalization 0%.

High 14. MMPI 4897'62–13/ F'L/ K:

High ratings: severe anxiety 33%, delusions 44%, hallucinations 22%, confusion 56%, impulsivity 44%, disability 67%, failure to gain privileges 50%, length of hospitalization 44%, religiosity 44%.

Low ratings: suspiciousness 11%, hostility 11%, severe somatic 0%, chronicity 33%, suicidal acts 11%.

High 23. MMPI 3"21'46–87/9: KLF–

High ratings: somatic 92%, severe somatic 46%.

Low ratings: suspiciousness 8%, confusion 0%, mania 0%, length of hospitalization 8%, alcohol 38%, sexual deviance 0%.

High 24. MMPI 4'2139–678/ K–FL/

High ratings: withdrawal 75%, severe withdrawal 25%, delusions 50%, impulsivity 38%, obsessive-compulsive 25%, length of hospitalization 50%, sexual deviance 25%.

Low ratings: anxiety 50%, somatic 25%, irregular discharge 0%, alcohol 38%.

Table 7-5—continued

High 34. MMPI 21'48963-7/ F-KL/

High ratings: anxiety 86%, hostility 29%, somatic 86%, impulsivity 43%, failure to gain privileges 40%, arrests 29%.

Low ratings: hallucinations 0%, confusion 0%, severe somatic 0%, sexual deviance 0%.

High 1. MMPI 2'47891-36/ FL/K:

High ratings: alcohol 60%, irregular discharge 25%.

Low ratings: anxiety 40%, withdrawal 30%, severe withdrawal 0%, hallucinations 0%, hostility 0%, somatic 10%, severe somatic 0%, impulsivity 10%, failure to gain privileges 0%, length of hospitalization 0%, arrests 0%, suicidal acts 0%.

High 2 (Code 21). MMPI 2436-7918/ K-FL/

High ratings: anxiety 80%, depression 60%, withdrawal 60%, suspiciousness 40%, impulsivity 40%, alcohol 80%, sexual deviance 20%, mania 20%.

Low ratings: severe withdrawal 0%, delusions 0%, hallucinations 0%, confusion 0%, somatic 20%, severe somatic 0%, disability 20%, length of hospitalization 0%, irregular discharge 0%, chronicity 11%, arrests 0%.

High 2 (Code 23). MMPI 2'34-169/78: K'L-F/

High ratings: suspiciousness 36%, hostility 55%, length of hospitalization 36%, irregular discharge 27%, religiosity 27%.

Low ratings: withdrawal 27%, confusion 0%, mania 0%.

High 2 (Code 24). MMPI 234-691/78: K'L-F/

High ratings: suspiciousness 50%.

Low ratings: severe anxiety 0%, severe withdrawal 0%, delusions 0%, hallucinations 0%, severe somatic 0%, disability 17%, failure to gain privileges 0%, irregular discharge 0%, chronicity 17%, sexual deviance 0%.

High 3 (Code 31). MMPI 31'294-678/ LKF/

High ratings: anxiety 80%, depression 60%, sexual deviance 20%.

Low ratings: severe anxiety 0%, withdrawal 30%, severe withdrawal 0%, delusions 0%, confusion 0%, severe somatic 0%, disability 20%, irregular discharge 0%, alcohol 20%, arrests 0%, suicidal acts 0%.

High 3 (Code 32). MMPI 3"12' 46798/ KLF/

High ratings: suspiciousness 33%, somatic 67%, severe somatic 50%, mania 33%, chronicity 67%.

Low ratings: anxiety 17%, severe anxiety 0%, depression 17%, withdrawal 17%, delusions 0%, hallucinations 0%, impulsivity 0%, failure to gain privileges 0%, alcohol 33%, arrests 0%.

High 3 (Code 34). MMPI 1"324'98-67/ F-KL/

High ratings: anxiety 78%, withdrawal 67%, severe withdrawal 22%, severe somatic 33%, chronicity 78%, alcohol 67%, suicidal acts 22%.

Low ratings: suspiciousness 11%, arrests 0%.

High 4 (Code 41). MMPI 49'68 27/13: F-LK/

High ratings: hallucinations 25%, length of hospitalization 57%, chronicity 62%, alcohol 75%, arrests 38%.

Low ratings: anxiety 12%, severe anxiety 0%, depression 25%, delusions 0%, suspiciousness 0%, hostility 0%, somatic 25%, severe somatic 0%, disability 25%, irregular discharge 0%, sexual deviance 0%.

High 4 (Code 42). MMPI 24'689-137/ F'LK/

High ratings: delusions 33%, suspiciousness 33%, hallucinations 17%, confusion 33%, impulsivity 33%, disability 67%, arrests 50%.

Low ratings: anxiety 50%, withdrawal 17%, severe withdrawal 0%, hostility 0%, severe somatic 0%, mania 0%, failure to gain privileges 0%, alcohol 33%, sexual deviance 0%, suicidal acts 0%.

Table 7-5—continued

High 4 (Code 43). MMPI 9468-1723/ F-KL/

High ratings: delusions 38%, hostility 38%, mania 25%, religiosity 25%.

Low ratings: anxiety 25%, severe anxiety 0%, depression 25%, hallucinations 0%, confusion 0%, somatic 12%, severe somatic 0%, irregular discharge 0%, chronicity 25%, arrests 0%, sexual deviance 0%.

No High Score (Code 1). MMPI 4-92367/18: K-LF/

High ratings: delusions 24%, hostility 33%, impulsivity 33%, irregular discharge 24%, suicidal acts 29%.

Low ratings: severe anxiety 0%, severe somatic 0%, failure to gain privileges 6%, arrests 0%.

No High Score (Code 2). MMPI 234-69/178: K-LF/

High ratings: severe withdrawal 31%, severe somatic 31%, impulsivity 35%, religiosity 31%, suicidal acts 23%.

Low ratings: depression 19%.

No High Score (Code 3). MMPI 342-1697/8: K-LF/

High ratings: severe anxiety 25%, alcohol 62%.

Low ratings: anxiety 50%, depression 12%, withdrawal 25%, severe withdrawal 0%, delusions 0%, suspiciousness 12%, hallucinations 0%, hostility 12%, somatic 25%, irregular discharge 0%, chronicity 25%, suicidal acts 0%.

No High Score (Code 4). MMPI 4-92316/87: K-LF/

High ratings: irregular discharge 25%.

Low ratings: anxiety 33%, depression 17%, severe withdrawal 0%, severe somatic 0%, disability 25%, length of hospitalization 12%, sexual deviance 0%.

SOURCE: Eichman (1962).

LOV and DOM, in his octant compass which is basic to the interpersonal diagnostic schema which he proposed. In addition, he suggested various individual indices for each octant to determine degree of radial deviation within each sector. Although there have been many applications of this system in research on both the individual level (Klopfer, 1961; LaForge, 1963; Hurwitz and Lelos, 1968; and McDonald, 1968) and the interactional level (Phillips, 1967) of analysis, the original Leary indices have not been extensively utilized. Rather, a number of special ad hoc measures have been advanced or the MMPI has been combined with other instruments to produce the assignments to octants. The original indices of Leary, as well as the Welsh indices, are summarized in Chapter 3.

Recently a set of scales has been proposed to represent each of the major patterns identified by Tryon (1966, 1967) in his cluster analyses of MMPI scale interrelationships. Stein (1968) refers to these seven scales as the TSC scales (reflecting the contributions of Tryon, Stein, and Chu to their derivation). The first three scales (I, introversion, B, body symptoms, and S, suspicion) are proposed as the more fundamental measures since a subject's standing on the remaining four (D, depression, R, resentment, A, autism, and T, tension) can be approximated quite well from his scores on the first three. Stein also provides preliminary interpretive material and normative data based upon California samples of normal men and women. (The appendix material in Volume II provides normative data on these scales based upon the Minnesota normal samples.) Lorr (1968) has reported the degree of correspondence between the TSC scale values and his groupings of patients on the basis of factors appearing in their psychiatric symptoms. Five of the TSC dimensions seemed to be replicated by Lorr, but among his patients the depression and tension dimensions collapsed into a single source of variance and the body complaint measure seemed to be made up of two important dimensions. These TSC scales are a promising set for summarizing clinical status attributes but it is puzzling that the masculinity-femininity dimension is not represented in this set.

Configural Approaches to MMPI Patterns

Several major methodological problems must be recognized in any effort to review the implications for personality assessment of research on the major MMPI profile configurations. Each of these issues will be discussed here briefly to help the reader understand the strengths and weaknesses of the material that is now available on objective MMPI interpretation.

MMPI Cookbook Interpretations. Meehl (1956) has taken the position that there is an important need currently for a "cookbook" of personality interpretations. The advantages of such a tool are clear: it would stress representativeness of behavioral sampling, accuracy in recording and cataloguing data from research studies, and optimal weighting of relevant variables, and it would permit professional time and talent to be used economically. Important difficulties are posed in the handling of statistically rare observations on this basis—but indeed this would be true in any system of personality interpretation. The material in this chapter cannot be considered a cookbook in Meehl's terms, but some of the value of carrying out such a project can be seen in the characterizations that follow. For additional work on this general problem, see Halbower (1955), L. E. Drake and Oetting (1959), Marks and Seeman (1963), Gilberstadt and Duker (1965), as well as the computer-based interpretive systems described in Chapter 8.

Choice of Subjects. Any empirical study involves only a finite group of subjects who take the test and furnish the personality characteristics for analysis. The particular features of their behavior that are noted by the judges, reported by the subjects themselves in self-ratings, or otherwise made available for collation with the test results are often seriously restricted in these samples. The relationships that are found vary widely depending upon the range of behavior the subjects demonstrate and the degree to which they differ one from another, as well as the variations in MMPI patterns that they provide. Different characteristics are found for adolescents, for adults, for college students, and for medical patients. The relationships shift with sex, age, test sophistication, educational exposure, and personality complexity. Any of the ways of analyzing results that are discussed below are markedly affected by the degree of homogeneity or heterogeneity of the groups studied in respect to both test score ranges and personality trait distribution. Yet, any of the ways by which subjects are made available for traditional psychological study (e.g., college classes or programs, school systems, clinic rosters, physicians' clienteles) introduce biases through intraclass correlations and the elimination of deviant instances. Note will be made of these points when their effects seem particularly distorting in some study, but this general source of attenuation should be kept in mind throughout the following discussion.

Raters. Available studies also differ to an important degree in the personnel used to furnish the criterion ratings of personality. Judges range in training and sophistication from the friends and acquaintances of a general run of adult normals that were used by Hathaway and Meehl (1952) to the selected assessment staff of psychologists, psychiatrists, and social scientists employed at the Institute for Personality Assessment and Research (Gough, McKee, and Yandell, 1955; Block and Bailey, 1955). In between lie the college roommates and dormitory mates that served as judges for each other in Black's (1953) study, the nursing supervisors who furnished Hovey (1953) with material on the students they were instructing, the physician who made notes on the cases in his practice of internal medicine reported by Guthrie (1949), and the counselors, diagnosticians, and therapists who described patients' behavior in the course of their work as summarized in studies like those of Halbower (1955), L. E. Drake (1954, 1956), Mello and Guthrie (1958), Marks and Seeman (1963), and Gilberstadt and Duker (1965).

In such studies as these, there are clear opportunities for judges to differ in the sincerity with which they approach the task, in the conscientiousness or precision with which they complete the forms, and in their objectivity and candor. In addition, the judges differ widely in the degree of acquaintanceship that they have had with the subjects, in the opportunities they have had for making the relevant observations, and in the range of judgments they are willing to venture. Serious biases of many kinds may enter the data, therefore, when some of the rater characteristics are not carefully specified and controlled.

It should also be noted that although this wide range in raters' training and professional standing is by no means always a limitation, the different judges may provide qualitatively different kinds of observations. That is, it may be very worthwhile to know that a college girl with a peak score on scale 3 generates certain typical reactions in others her own age. Even though such a peer-rating procedure may not provide any direct evidence about the nature of personality conflicts or the depth of sexual identification that such a girl may have, the data on social stimulus are valuable, per se. But it would be misleading to combine these data with others from sources that differ widely in level of observation or in amount of inferential abstraction from basic response patterns.

Similarly, the ratings obtained from the test subjects themselves furnish valuable criterial data for these studies but at the same time present special problems in interpretation. Self-ratings and self-descriptions suffer from many of the same difficulties noted above: possible insincerity or lack of self-knowledge, limitations on comprehension and cooperation, and special biases and motivations.

For example, the comparison of what a person says about himself on the set of MMPI items making up scale 3 and what he says about himself on a checklist appears at first glance to be circular and noninformative. However, since the personality scale was derived on quite different grounds from an adjective checklist, it may be useful to turn attention to the way a person presents himself on the list and see if it bears some relationship to the way the MMPI scale characterizes him. Obviously, it would also be informative to compare his self-descriptions on the checklist with similar ratings by others and determine whether the discrepancies between the two descriptions bear any relationship to his performance on the MMPI. In none of these analyses would there necessarily have to be any face validity imputed to any of the measures, although presumably the outcome of such studies would be a better understanding of the construct validity of the personality scale.

Language of the Ratings. As might be expected from the wide variations in the qualifications of the judges noted above, the ratings themselves differ in terminology, systematization, and semantic clarity. Although this problem is most clearly demonstrated in the use of diagnostic or nosological labels, it complicates analyses based upon case-history material, symptom descriptions, or treatment notes. In any of these records, the observational material may be biased by errors of memory, selective or limited observation, personal predilections for certain labels or terms, lack of time to make consistent records, or individual differences among the clinicians in fluency, style, or legibility of notes.

Two important refinements in procedures have helped to introduce some degree of comparability in sets of personality descriptions from various judges and from widely differing subjects: adjective checklists and Q-sort decks. From a large number of sources Hathaway and Meehl developed at Minnesota a standard list of adjectives that they used with normal subjects as a basis for both peer ratings and self-ratings. Since such a list has the advantages of systematic coverage, direct comparability, and convenience in contrast to data from clinical records, the method offers excellent possibilities for assessment research. It has some limitations as well. One of the most important is that the lack of clear specification of how the terms are to be interpreted and applied may allow different judges to use them in different ways. Nor does the marking of terms allow for either fine gradations in endorsement or special reservations. In the summaries below, the data from the Hathaway-Meehl list will be noted as well as the findings from Black based on a list that is only a slight modification of the Minnesota material. Gough (1955) and Gough and Heilbrun (1965) have also developed a standard checklist for this work, based in part on the schedule of Hathaway and Meehl; it too will frequently be mentioned below.

The Q-sort deck typically contains upwards of seventy-five statements descriptive of behavior patterns, attitudes, feelings, symptoms, or problems. No standard set of statements has as yet been adopted for uniform research application. The set used at IPAR by Block and Bailey bears directly on observable behavior, while the items that Halbower furnished a group of therapists to describe their patients range more widely over symptomatology and inferences about personality dynamics. The advantages that the Q procedures have over a checklist lie in the way the judgments are made and recorded. The judge is asked to distribute the statements in a prearranged set of categories from a "most descriptive" category through middle categories to a "least descriptive" category. The number of items to be placed in each category is specified as well, in order to assure a symmetrical pattern of descriptions and to force each judge to make extreme statements. Thus, a rater using the Q-sort procedure can qualify his endorsement of any description by moving it from one category to another, although he may not alter the wording of the item itself. The Q-sort method provides a common language for all descriptions, on all subjects and from all judges, even self-judges. There are some drawbacks to this procedure, too; for example, one is unable to tell for sure where along the set of categories the person making the sorting stops saying that the items apply to the subject and begins describing increasing degrees of dissimilarity. Also, in complex items, the judge may have to endorse a part of the statement that he would not otherwise apply to the subject in order to use some pertinent description that is included on the card and is applicable to the subject (see Block, 1961).

All these methods involve small sets of personality characterizations. They must necessarily be small to be workable and practical in a limited research study, but this restricts the kinds of observations against which the MMPI scales are to be evaluated. There is a need for care, therefore, in interpreting findings based on such procedures; many important personality attributes may not have been included in the criterion ratings and therefore cannot show up in these summaries.

Idiographic Method of Data Analysis. In the nomothetic method of investigating personality correlates of the basic MMPI scales (such as those summarized in Chapter 6), there is a persistent problem of personality heterogeneity in the groups formed by contrasting high and low scores on only one scale at a time. That is, subjects who are high on a given scale may be very heterogeneous in regard to important attributes other than those reflected in a particular scale, and similarly for low scorers. Some correlates may be isolated by such statistical analyses which are more consistently related to other component scales (or to other dimensions not relevant to MMPI measures) but are listed as attributes of the particular scale under study at that moment. If there are other scales which are closely related to the scale under study in the particular sample being investigated, they may give rise to similar contaminations in the scale correlate set isolated from contrasts of high-low scorers. A method of analysis of MMPI data which preserves the relative elevation of scores in each subject's profile, that is, a method based upon ipsative data, will tend to reduce such complications. The configural correlates that emerge from studying coding groups which are reported here appear to be less affected by this kind of contamination.

Analysis by relative elevation helps to overcome some of these difficulties, although it does not eliminate them entirely. In this procedure, cases are selected on the basis of the highest score or, sometimes, the highest pair of scores in their profiles. All cases with peak scores on, say, scale 1 are put together and the personality attributes typifying the group are identified. When additional selective standards are imposed, such as both first and second high points in common, the group is made even more homogeneous.

The studies of Black, Guthrie, Drake, Mello and Guthrie, and Halbower employed variations on this method of configural analysis. L. E. Drake and Oetting (1959) have in addition routinely included the low point in the profile for selection of their cases in combination with various high-point pairs.

This general method gives considerably greater MMPI homogeneity to the criterion groups than the method of extreme scores, but there is still the possibility that important contaminations will affect the results. If the peak score is not reliably higher than the scores on some other scales in the profile (see the discussion on profile stability below) then the basis of grouping may be so undependable that no consistent findings are possible. In addition there may be in the same group cases differing in absolute level of peak score by three or four standard deviations. This spread may mean too large a degree of heterogeneity in a group (Gough, 1953) and thus stable correlates of MMPI profile types cannot appear. An obvious remedy would be to form the criterion groups on the basis of both code sequence and absolute elevation. This refinement requires a very large sample of subjects, however, which has not been available to date for this kind of work.

Additional problems arise from the use of varying numbers of scales in forming the categorizations (see the discussion of code patterning below). If some studies do not employ scales 5 or 0, for example, not only are the data on these two scales unavailable to other research workers, but the cases that would have been placed in these peak score groups are distributed into the remaining categories and may serve to attenuate the findings from those analyses as well.

In one of these two methods of MMPI analyses, then, the comparison is between two extremes on a single dimension, in the other the comparison is between one selected subgroup and the remainder of the population under study. In this latter procedure, particularly, the results of the study will depend upon the nature of the reference group and its predominant characteristics. If some feature is fairly generally represented in members of the reference group, this feature may not be distinguished in such comparisons.

Code Patterning. By no means all of the possible combinations of even the ninety high-point pairs from the ten basic scales can be summarized here. For one thing, some of these pairs are extremely rare. The fact that the code combinations are not distributed randomly has been one of the clearest and most important empirical findings in the analysis of MMPI profile patterns. As pointed out at the beginning of this chapter, this is in part attributable to the scale intercorrelations and in part to the overlapping of personality features in particular cases (Hathaway, 1956b). The score combinations discussed here form the familiar, recurrent patterns which are the bases for MMPI personality interpretations.

The extent of this departure from randomness can be judged from the following figures. In the *Atlas* (Hathaway and Meehl, 1951a), which was not intended to be a representative sample of the general psychiatric population but was rather aimed at a wide coverage of clinical material, over 60 percent of the cases fall into nine of the fifty-six two-digit code classes (with

5 and 0 omitted). Similarly, in Guthrie's 1104 cases examined by a general medical practitioner, more than 60 percent can be described by a different subset of nine two-digit codes. The codes on the Minnesota normals reported in the *Atlas* cannot be as readily tabulated since second high points are frequently unavailable, but the marked departure from randomness in the distributions can be seen in the tables of Appendix M in the present volume.

In the following discussion only the "popular" two-digit code groupings will be used to summarize the wide array of personality assessment data now available and to furnish a guide to the interpretation of MMPI profiles. The other scales in a particular code should not be ignored, of course. Where it is possible, findings from the literature will be reported as they bear upon the role of subordinate peaks and scores in the protocol in modifying or directing the effect of the prominent scale elevations, and code combinations that do not appear with sufficient frequency to generate stable samples for study and analysis will be mentioned from time to time in the appropriate sections. But the clinician will all too often be faced with atypical score combinations in his day-to-day work; interpretation of these cases will be facilitated by a thorough understanding of the derivation of the MMPI scales and a familiarity with the general interpretative principles discussed here.

Pattern Stability. An important consideration in the utilization of a code summary for a given profile is the stability or dependability of the given pattern. (The problem will be treated in more detail in Volume II, where changes of MMPI profiles in the course of therapy are discussed.) If a given profile is a highly transitory product that will shift markedly after change of a few points in raw score on some scale or scales, can this code be used to characterize the subject adequately? Some changes are large, of course, and reflect a valid change in the behavioral status of the test subject. Some changes are not great and leave the basic pattern and hence the basic code designation unaltered. However, clinical experience has indicated that certain changes in basic pattern, although altering the code designation, do not correspond to important personological changes, but rather constitute roughly equivalent patterns. Thus, a subject with a code of 13'26... may later show a code of 3'16–2... While much empirical research needs to be done to determine the degree of equivalence in these code groups, frequent mention in the following sections will be made of such psychological uniformities as 13-31 (see Hathaway and Meehl, 1951a). Empiricial data on some of these questions are available in the work of Layton (1954), D. R. Stone and West (1955), Mills (1954), Sivanich (1960), and Pauker (1965).

Descriptive Summaries. The personality descriptions that survive the methods of analyses outlined above are primarily sets of *differences*. That is, those features of behavior that are common to all, or nearly all, the subjects in a study are not recorded. The items that either are absent in all subjects in the sample or were never in the pool for consideration cannot be included in any final summary as clearly *not* typical. Only those features which serve to differentiate subgroups of various sorts appear in the résumés. Thus if practically all college men strive to move upward in socioeconomic level, this feature will not appear as one of the attributes of, say, high 3 undergraduates, since it does not serve to differentiate high 3's from other college males. This striving may, nevertheless, be an important attribute of this high 3 group in a variety of situations.

One approach, introduced by Halbower, circumvents this problem quite effectively. Rather than simply contrasting groups to find differentiating personality features, he sought to find a core of common features that would optimally epitomize the whole group. Since he worked with Q-sort items, he was able to use the average category assigned to each item by the judges as a means of summarizing the descriptions given the group of cases with each particular MMPI profile type. From this set of weights he was able to produce a modal Q-sorting for each of four important MMPI code types. The phrases included describe the common attributes (at the upper end of the distribution) as well as indicate the features of behavior not representative of the code type (at the lower end of the distribution). A summary of each of the descriptions isolated by Halbower has been made below under the appropriate codes, although the Q-sort structure could not be preserved. For a more complete discussion, his original dissertation should be consulted.

In the following sections the personality findings from profile patterns will be presented. The first material from patterning studies to be described will be the correlates of peak scores on each scale. Thus, the results on scale 1 patterning will start off with the findings obtained when cases are grouped together because they all have peak scores on scale 1. In this tabulation, the height of other scales is not taken into account. Each high-point summary will be followed by data on various high-point pairs, in which the attributes found among cases who have both first and second highest scores in the profile in common will be reported. Where available, material on profiles with some one scale as the common low point will also be included.

Within each of these sections, the data supplied by judges or observers will be reported first, followed by available findings from self-reports of the subjects with a given MMPI feature. Whenever there is a choice, the findings from general normal subjects will be reported first, followed by the data from more selected groups, normal and deviant.

High-Point 1's

When scale 5 is omitted in the coding system and when K corrections are routinely applied, scale 1 is one of the most frequent high points in the profiles of both normal and psychiatric groups. The data in Appendix M and in the *Atlas* also indicate that scale 1 is typically prominent in the code and is infrequently a low point in the code except in those with a leading 9. Scale 1 peaks increase in frequency with age and are especially prominent in patients consulting a physician (see Appendix M). This scale plays an important role in the patterning of the neurotic triad and furnishes useful interpretative data, either to characterize the current adjustment of the subject or to qualify the inferences drawn from other profile characteristics. The K correction applied to this scale can make important differences not only in the absolute level of the score on scale 1, but also in the configuration of the profile. Gough, McKee, and Yandell, as reported in Chapter 6, found different correlates of this scale with and without the correction. This scale is more frequently the low point in the profile when K corrections are not employed.

Guthrie found that medical patients with peak scores on scale 1 presented a wide variety of symptoms and complaints. Although many of the men presented epigastric symptoms, neither respiratory nor circulatory difficulties were well represented. There was typically little manifest anxiety in their initial behavior, but when present it indicated a better response to treatment than would otherwise be the case. The group did not typically show any evidence of incapacity of major proportions, even though many of the MMPI profiles were markedly elevated. Rather, these patients appeared to be carrying on with reduced efficiency. Their symptoms appeared to be part of a long-standing inadequacy and ineffectualness rather than a solution to some pressing problem of the moment. There was little evidence of psychopathic acting out in this group. They usually responded well on a short-term basis; but they made many return visits, usually with the same symptoms, or with new problems of equal severity.

In college groups peaks on 1 are quite rare. Neither Black nor Mello and Guthrie found enough cases to develop any stable basis for descriptions. Drake noted that counselees with "home conflicts" were found when either scale 4 or scale 5 was coded low in conjunction with a peak on scale 1.

12's

Codes with a leading 12 pattern, although not very frequent in either normative or clinical populations, constitute one of the more important clinical configurations. As can be seen in Appendix M (see Tables 1-4) only 2-3 percent of the normals show this pattern, and men are more likely to give this combination than women. The pattern is very rare in the young group studied by Hathaway and Monachesi (1963; see Appendix M, Tables 5 and 6). Sundberg (1952; see Appendix M, Tables 11 and 12) reported a higher percentage of cases with this pattern in outpatient groups than among hospitalized psychiatric cases; the same sex difference persisted among these abnormals.

In the *Atlas* the cases with this code fall roughly into two diagnostic groupings: somatic overconcern and schizophrenia. In the former group, constituting about two-thirds of the cases, the subordinate role of scales 3 and 7 is very important, comparing with the role of scale 8 in the latter group. The somatic group showed physical complaints, with the content centering on the alimentary system, particularly abdominal pain. These cases also were characterized by irritability and some suspiciousness. They presented a chronic and unabating hypochondriacal history.

The other third of the cases were younger, with more bizarre physical complaints concerning primarily the trunk, although ranging widely over the whole trunk. They also complained of weakness and tiredness. This group was composed of schizophrenic patients who had their delusional system centered about hypochondriacal problems. Their beliefs did not seem to be any more amenable to treatment or to suggest any better prognosis than delusions reflecting other content, such as mental or interpersonal problems.

L. E. Drake and Oetting (1959) indicated that the college men who came to them for counseling with 12 patterns showed tension, insomnia, and insecurity in social situations, but did not manifest gross bodily preoccupations as a typical pattern. These men were unhappy, worried a great deal, were introverted, and lacked skills in dealing with the opposite sex.

The female counselees that Drake and Oetting studied presented a greater variety of problems, with physical complaints like headaches appearing, particularly when the low point in the profile was on scale 5. These girls appeared depressed, worried, and anxious. Socially they seemed insecure, shy, and self-conscious. They too lacked skills in dealing with the opposite sex. They were indecisive, lacked self-confidence, and frequently sought reassurance about the findings of any tests that they had taken. One of the prominent problems with which these women came to the counseling center was a difficulty in examinations; they tended to tighten up and block.

Meehl (1951) has characterized psychiatric patients with this code pattern as persons who show irritability, depression, shyness, and even seclusiveness. The most prominent feature of the clinical picture these cases present is pain. Their complaints of pain center around the viscera in contrast with the pains singled out by the 13's who report difficulties in the peripheral organs and central nervious system. Running through all these manifestations is a pervasive emphasis on physical symptoms and physiological processes.

Guthrie found that a large subgroup of patients seen by his urban internist had MMPI's with the 12 pattern. In his analyses, he combined the 12's and the 13's since the differences were slight. The importance of the scale 1 peak in the profile of a patient seeking medical help can here be seen; the secondary scale does not make a great deal of difference in this situation. Each patient presented numerous complaints, mainly abdominal distress and backaches, with little demonstrable physical pathology. Sullivan and Welsh (1952) reported that this pattern and the 21 pattern were associated with ulcers in their group of Veterans Administration patients. Guthrie noted only one well-demonstrated case of ulcers in his group of medical patients. Guthrie also found that 12's returned time and again with only short-lived, symptomatic relief after each visit. It seemed clear that they had learned to use their complaints to help solve their emotional problems, although it was difficult for the internist to gain any insight into the nature of their problems. This kind of scrutiny was blocked by the patient's concentration upon his physical difficulties and his lack of self-understanding. In this sample, the cases with the 12 pattern on the MMPI did not show significant changes in medical status, for either better or worse, over a period of years. As noted, the changes were slight and transitory when obtained.

Guthrie found the same sex difference in his group as was described above, with men showing greater concern over physical problems and admitting fewer emotional difficulties than the women. Within his group, the 12's showed more anxiety and tension than the 13's. The twenty-two items (see the Co_{12} scale in Appendix I of Volume II) that differentiated this group from the other medical patients were almost entirely the frankly somatic items from the neurotic triad, with a few of the items bearing on personal inadequacy and interpersonal sensitivities from scale 7 included.

Halbower's Group I. In deciding on his basic groupings, Halbower surveyed 113 Veterans Administration mental-hygiene cases undergoing treatment. He found over 16 percent of these cases had either the 12 or the closely related 21 pattern on the MMPI. On a group of 336 cases tested consecutively in the same VA installation, he found an even higher percentage showing this code pattern. He therefore decided to use this code as one of his four MMPI groups. In his derivational case selection, he imposed a rigorous set of criteria for inclusion: a 123 slope, with all three above 70; scale 7 above 70; scales 4, 6, and 9 below 70, preferably with scale 9 a low point; scale 8 less than 7 by three points, preferably below 70; F between 55 and 70 and equal to or greater than ?, L, and K; the subtle score on scale 3 less than 65. Cases meeting these criteria were placed in Code Group I. He asked the therapists on these cases to make Q sorts on them, and then determined the characteristics that differentiated Code I cases from the other groups and a patient-in-general group. From these analyses he found that, according to their therapists, these particular cases had presented themselves initially as organically sick. They were manifesting either a somatization reaction or some psychophysiological reaction. Complaints of pain, weakness, and easy fatiguability were prominent features of a general hypochondriacal picture. They tended to be hypersensitive and to overevaluate minor dysfunctions.

Halbower also found that these patients were described as lacking insight into their own behavior, with repression as one of the important defense mechanisms they used. They had difficulty "labeling cause and effect relationships in psychological behavior" and resisted any implication that their symptoms were related to emotional causes or conflicts. The group also showed passive dependence and dealt with anxiety and conflict in a generally "internalized" fashion.

As a group these patients were relatively free of feelings of depersonalization, bizarre mentation, confusion, feelings of unreality, and suicidal thoughts. They were not characterized by reality distortions or other psychotic tendencies and were relatively free of obsessive and compulsive ruminations and self-depreciation. It should be noted that these characteristics were the ones that differentiated this group from others because of the rarity with which they were applied by the therapist-judges. The whole list of Q-sort items would have to be available to provide the reader with a basis for determining the kind of items which failed to separate this group from the other code patterns being studied.

In his cross-validational study, Halbower found that the Q array provided by the analyses of the criterion groups described new samples of cases with the various MMPI code patterns better, when compared to therapist descriptions of the new cases, than did rule-of-thumb interpretations by skilled judges. Thus, the pattern of descriptions given above seems to possess some appreciable validity although none of the items in the description has been individually substantiated by cross-validational analyses.

Further data on various 12 patterns are reported in the profile groupings for the 123, 1234, and 1237 types in Gilberstadt and Duker (see Chapter 3 for the defining characteristics of these MMPI patterns). Fowler and Athey (1970) have carried out a replication study of the 1234 type in Gilberstadt and Duker's schema. They reported finding in the patients seen in Alabama the same common core of general physical discomfort, depression, hostility, and heavy drinking which had emerged in the cases at the VA hospital in Minnesota where Gilberstadt and Duker obtained their samples. However, the Alabama cases were more characterized by headaches, abdominal pain, cardiac complaints, and chest pains than the Minnesota veterans and less by the direct expression of aggression in conflicts with a spouse, assaultiveness, or combativeness when drunk. Digestive difficulties, including ulcer, anorexia, nausea, and vomiting, together with tension, nervousness, and insomnia were reported for this pattern by both sets of investigators. Gilberstadt and Jancis (1967) also included further findings on the 12 code type in their analyses of the functional versus organic implications of the 13 code (see below).

13's

The 13 code results from an elevated neurotic triad in which the "conversion valley" pattern is present. It is one of the most frequent two-point combinations, in both normal groups and psychiatric populations. It is more frequent in women; the men who show this pattern often appear clinically feminine. Hathaway and Meehl (1951b) attribute this appearance to the characteristic reliance of these men upon passive methods of handling anxiety and conflicts and to their dependency. The MMPI pattern is often useful in differentiating these men from those in whom feminine personality inversion is a more central problem. Although some of the behavioral characteristics may be similar, the character structure, dynamics, and prognoses for the two groups are psychologically distinct and separate.

From the data presented above on elevation effects and in Chapter 4 on the L-scale effects on code type, it can be deduced that this pattern of MMPI scores is not usually obtained in high-ranging profiles. Rather, it occurs in moderate elevations or in the normal score range. The 13 score combination results from a selective endorsement of somatic items (Hs and Hy-obvious) and denial of social anxiety (Hy-subtle) without endorsement of the depressive and anxiety items that are concentrated primarily in the D and Pt scales. Although there is some psychological contradiction in the admission of some symptoms and problems and the protestation of emotional stability, the pattern of replies basic to this code type does involve a denial of the possibility of mental troubles. The 13's are differentiable from the normal reference group by the frequency and extremity of their denial of troubles or inadequacies. It seems clear, too, that many of the subjects scoring this pattern who do not show manifest emotional difficulties at the time are remaining symptom-free at some considerable effort and cost in emotional control and repression.

Black studied a small but homogeneous group of normal college girls showing either the 13 code or the closely related pattern, 31. These girls were judged by their peers on Black's version of the adjective checklist; they also filled out the same checklist on themselves. The 13-31 group of college women described themselves more frequently as partial, affectionate, and thoughtful than college women in general described themselves. They less frequently labeled themselves orderly, serious, conventional, aggressive, or contented. By and large, these descriptions are safe and innocuous, and form a sharp contrast to the kinds of characteristics their peers ascribed to them. This lack of self-criticism seems consistent with a general impunitive attitude in the way these girls view others, the world, and themselves.

Other college women described the 13 girl as selfish and self-centered, with many physical complaints. They said 13's were neurotic, dependent, indecisive, high-strung, and emotional. These girls were also seen as apathetic, eccentric, and secretive, even self-distrusting. In areas of aggression they were seen as hostile, irritable, and lacking in self-control. Although they were termed by their peers serious and idealistic, they were described very infrequently as energetic, enterprising, adaptable, conscientious, or versatile. The 13 girls were also seen as relying upon flattery more frequently than college women generally. Thus, although these girls could not be described as clear-cut psychoneurotics, the personality picture they presented to their acquaintances had many of the features of this psychiatric syndrome.

At the college level, Drake reported finding a significant number of 13 codes among his group of counselees who were called aggressive in the interviews held with them when they sought counseling and guidance. Such subjects showed behavior described as defiant, argumentative, cocky, snobbish, aggressive, resistant, opinionated, or belligerent. However, by no means all the subjects showing such behavior had the 13 code on the MMPI, since scales 4 and 9 played an even more important part in the MMPI profiles for this group.

L. E. Drake and Oetting (1959) found that men with this code not only showed aggressiveness in their initial counseling interview, but insisted on knowing the results of their tests and sought definitive answers from the counselors for their problems. They typically appeared free of tensions, restlessness, nervousness, and other signs of acute disturbance. They appeared socially skillful and confident, were fluent and expressive in the interview, and related well to the counselor. In spite of this easy initial relationship, men with this pattern were frequently seen only once, without returns to the center.

The women with high 13 profiles who were studied by Drake and Oetting were extroverted, socially outgoing persons, able to verbalize their troubles easily. They reported many conflicts centering around both parents and showed poor academic motivation. They had trouble in examinations from blocking and tightening up. A frequent consideration in such problems was the strong orientation of these women toward marriage.

As indicated above, patients showing the 13 pattern are similar in many respects to 12's, Guthrie actually considering them together in his analyses.

Hypertension, obesity, and vasomotor instability as well as gastrointestinal distress were the most common presenting complaints of Guthrie's 13 subjects. He found that the 13 subgroup showed less anxiety and tension in their clinical picture than the 12's, depression being virtually absent. However, the 13's did manifest the same general somatic concern common to the whole group. The twenty-three items characteristic of this group (see the Co_{13} scale in Appendix I in Volume II) were almost entirely somatic items on scales 1 and 3.

Within the psychiatric population, the patients with 13 patterns present problems concerning a variety of physical complaints, but most frequently involving pain. As mentioned above, the 13 patients tend to localize their pains in different parts of the body from the 12 patients. The pains are more frequently in the extremities or the head, rather than in the trunk. If the pain is in the trunk, it tends to be in the upper part, precordial or chest, rather than in the viscera or bowels. These patients complain more frequently of dysfunction of the muscular or central nervous system than of pain in the abdominal region. However, there is also a strong theme in their complaint picture of problems with eating. This may take the form of actual anorexia, or difficulties in appetite, but may also be reflected in nausea or vomiting, or may merely involve overeating. Other complaints that appear frequently are weakness, fatigue, and atypical spells.

Conversion hysteria is the modal diagnosis, as reported by Hathaway and Meehl (1951b), for patients with this pattern. Some receive one of several other neurotic diagnoses, and there are a few atypical psychopathic or schizoid cases. Consistent with this diagnostic trend are the findings of Hovey (1949) on somatization reactions, Hanvik (1951) on the functional cases of low back pain, and Sullivan and Welsh (1952) on the psychosomatic ulcer cases they studied. Fricke (1956) reported a mean profile of $\underline{31}$ $\underline{8247}$-5$\underline{69}$ K-LF? for sixty-three carefully selected female conversion-hysteria cases.

These patients are characteristically lacking in insight, difficult to get motivated in treatment, and, in marked contrast to most psychiatric patients, frequently extroverted and sociable. In a medical setting, these patients are more typically first seen because of their physical complaints and often resist psychological study or any intimation that their difficulties may stem from emotional problems. They find physical or organic explanations more acceptable and compatible with their self-concepts than any psychodynamic causes.

Halbower's Group III. In the tabulation of 113 cases carried out by Halbower on Veterans Administration cases undergoing treatment in a mental-hygiene clinic, the single largest group of codes was the 13-31's (19 percent). The specific criteria Halbower used in selecting criterion cases for his Code Group III included these: code beginning 13 or 31, with both scales over 70; scale 2 less than scale 3 by at least 10 T-score points; either L or K the highest validity scale, with F no higher than 65; no scales in the code except 1 and 3 over 70.

The items which the therapist indicated were characteristic of Code

Group III on their Q sorts described this group, like Group I (code 123), as manifesting somatization or psychophysiological reactions. This group was seen as gaining in other ways from these symptoms, however—by getting out of painful or stressful situations. They were characterized as very self-centered and selfish, dependent and demanding in their personal relations, and feeling that they did not get enough consideration from their families. Possibly as a result of this dependency and the resulting frustrations, these patients also seemed to the therapists to be passively aggressive and deficient in heterosexual drive and aggressiveness. The controls the patients employed were externalized ones that tended to involve other people or situations, such as rationalization, blaming others, projection, and acting out. Their self-control was unpredictable, however, and they appeared emotionally labile, easily stimulated, and poorly controlled emotionally. They tended to lose their tempers and blow up under slight provocation.

Halbower also found that these patients were relatively free of such psychotic tendencies as depersonalization, strange verbalizations or bizarre mentation, confusions in thought, and feelings of unreality, and of self-criticisms, ruminative introspections, and serious suicidal thoughts. Probably because of these characterological features, in part, and also because they appeared lacking in the ability to develop stable or mature interpersonal relations, these patients were not very frequently considered to be well motivated for intensive psychotherapy.

Further analyses of the 13 code groups are reported by Marks and Seeman in their 31-13 pattern and by Gilberstadt and Duker in their 132, 137, 138, and 139 profile types. The defining features of all these patterns are provided in Chapter 3. Carr, Brownsberger, and Rutherford (1966) and Gilberstadt and Jancis (1967) have compared 13 patterns in psychiatric and in medical settings. Their contention is that the higher the elevations on scales 1 and 3 the more likely the case is to be a psychiatric (or functional) problem rather than an organically based difficulty, although the dynamics in the two kinds of manifestations may be quite similar psychologically.

High-Point 2's

Black found only one term significantly related to an MMPI peak score on 2 in the descriptions of this group of college women furnished by others: shy. In these descriptions, there were also several terms that were omitted significantly from the checklists. These adjectives included cheerful and flattering, curious, energetic and courageous, kind, laughterful, peaceable, relaxed and frank, self-confident and independent, self-denying, sociable, and cooperative.

When Black tabulated the adjectives that the high 2 subjects checked about themselves, however, he found a more adequate basis for characterizing their self-concepts. The picture was one of self-depreciation and inadequacy. Included in the self-descriptions were these terms: affected, aloof, indecisive, moody, neurotic, quiet, secretive, self-dissatisfied, self-distrusting, shy, unself-controlled, and worrying. In addition, these high 2 girls omitted (at a statistically stable level) a number of adjectives in their self-descriptions: aggressive, cheerful, contented, courageous, decisive, energetic, friendly, independent, laughterful, lively, poised, practical, self-confident, and talkative.

Mello and Guthrie found that counselees from a college population frequently presented a profile with scale 2 as the peak. In this age group, high points on 2 seem to reflect disturbance over situational problems in the college setting. That is, these young people did not show the typical tearful depression associated with this pattern in adult groups, but rather were troubled by problems involving relations with the opposite sex, studying, or vocational choice. While in therapy these young people resisted efforts of the therapist to go deeply into the origins of their problems; they used intellectualized statements or often-repeated descriptions of their problems to keep the therapy superficial. When the situational pressures let up, these counselees discontinued treatment quickly, nearly half of them having only between one and three contacts with the center. They regarded the counseling situation as an opportunity to seek advice from a parent surrogate at a time when they were faced with insurmountable problems. They did not readily form dependent relationships with the therapist, however, doing so only if they had several contacts.

The medical patients in Guthrie's group who had peak scores on scale 2 showed, as might be expected, a high incidence of depression with some physical symptoms, but these were not prominent or varied. A mixture of depression and severe physical distress was found in some patients and was related to certain subordinate peaks in the profile, as noted below. This total group of patients showed rather poor response to treatment. It is difficult to tell whether this prognostic picture reflects primarily the fact that these patients are of a somewhat different sort from the cases of depression seen in a psychiatric setting or whether it reflects the ineffectuality of regular medical procedures used by an internist as contrasted with traditional psychiatric measures. Guthrie found that when scale 2 was the only codable scale (in the Hathaway coding system) and the low point was on scale 9, the depression was mild and the physical complaints were rather typically centered around fatigue and loss of energy. These moderate physical complaints yielded rather easily to reassurance and symptomatic treatment. Occasionally a period of mild overactivity was reported to have occurred before the depressive symptoms appeared. Drake has noted that college counselees characterized as unhappy or depressed tend to have peak scores on scale 2 and that these features appear intensified when scales 0, 7, and 8 are also elevated. Significantly absent from the peak 2 group were students judged to be lacking in academic motivation.

21's

Among male psychiatric groups, this code pattern is the second most frequent combination of high points, and in the outpatient data reported by Sundberg (1952; see Appendix M, Tables 11 and 12), this is the most frequent male pattern. Among normals, however, the pattern seems to be more frequent in women, although it is not a prominent one in any of the normal groups. From what is now known about the role of scale 1, the prevalence of this pattern in Guthrie's (see Appendix M, Tables 15 and 16) groups of medical patients is quite understandable. Empirical data on this particular code come largely from Guthrie's findings.

In his analysis of the MMPI configurations, Guthrie found that the 21's and the 23's were very similar. He pointed out, however, that the males in the 21 code group presented a somewhat different clinical picture from that of the females. The males showed either depression and tension or a very delimited physical complaint, generally concentrated in the upper gastrointestinal tract. Few had the multiple complaints of the 12's, and for few was there any physical basis for their problems. Sullivan and Welsh (1952), it may be noted, found this pattern and the 12 pattern related to an ulcer condition in male Veterans Administration patients, but only two cases in Guthrie's group had active ulcers at the time they were seen by the internist. His male subjects were described as immature and generally inadequate, although not clearly hypochondriacal like the 21 females. They showed varied responses to treatment that appeared less related to their symptom pictures than to the length of time they had experienced their difficulties.

The high 21 women in Guthrie's study, although having some tendency to concentrate on epigastric pains, showed hypochondriacal patterns with a wide range of physical symptoms and an even greater concentration upon tension and depression. Their depression was accompanied by restlessness rather than apathy. They described themselves as suffering from a loss of initiative, from dysphoria, and even occasionally from dizziness and from fear. No alcoholism or acting out appeared in their backgrounds. Guthrie also characterized these women as able or willing to tolerate high levels of discomfort and therefore rather poor therapeutic prospects.

These descriptions are consistent with the finding of Hovey (1949) that this pattern on the MMPI was the typical configuration of anxiety reactions. The items that Guthrie found characteristic of the 21 group were largely somatic and mood items from scales 1 and 2 (see the Co_{21} scale in Appendix I in Volume II). A significant number of them were ruminative and dysphoric items from scales 7 and 8 as well as personal sensitivity items (scored oppositely on scale 4).

Note that further data on the 21 pattern are reported in Marks and Seeman's 231-213 code type (see Chapter 3 for the defining characteristics).

23's

Guthrie described the 23's in the same terms as the 21's above. In the item analyses, however, he found a somewhat different set of items, with the somatic items inoperative in differentiating this group, and with a concentration upon inefficiency and inadequacy (see the Co_{23} scale in Appendix I in Volume II). Seemingly, the overcontrol noted above for the normals with high 2's appears in an extreme form in persons in this subgroup. As they describe themselves, they are unable to do things or even to start them. They have difficulty expressing their feelings, are "bottled-up," and feel filled with self-doubts and insecurities. They lack interest or involvement in things and feel constantly fatigued and exhausted, nervous and inadequate much of the time. Marked anxiety or episodes of tension and anxiety are infrequent. Their troubles are typically of long standing. Response to treatment is poor. In behavior, men with 23 codes seem driven, competitive, and industrious, but not wholeheartedly so. They are also dependent and immature, so that the increasing responsibilities that they strive for, and get, are, at the same time, dreaded as sources of additional stress and insecurity. They may suffer because of what they feel is lack of recognition in their jobs, or because they are not promoted as they feel they should be. Despite their conflicts, these men are usually able to maintain an adequate level of efficiency. About half of them failed to return to the internist after being informed that there were no clear-cut physical foundations for their disorders.

The women with 23 profiles in Guthrie's group also were termed inadequate and immature. They frequently showed family or marital maladjustment but divorce was rarely reported in the background of these women. Their unhappiness was so chronic and prolonged that it is surprising that alcoholism was not reported more frequently in this group. They showed little pressure to seek help, apparently tolerating unhappiness more than other persons and operating at a lowered level of efficiency for long periods of time.

All these characteristics appear consistent with the description of 23 women furnished by Hathaway and Meehl (1951b). Psychiatric patients with this code show depression prominently and also weakness, apathy, agitation, and tenseness. Diagnostically, these cases are either neurotics of various forms (conversion hysteria being quite rare) or psychotic depressions —manic-depressive, depressed, or involutional. Psychopathic disorders are unlikely to appear in this group.

Additional clinical data on the 23 pattern are reported in Marks and Seeman's 231-213 code type (see Chapter 3 for the defining characteristics of this pattern).

24's

This code group has not been reported very extensively in the literature. Guthrie found a small subgroup of medical patients with this profile type. They showed depressive patterns, usually associated with agitation and restlessness. Some men with this pattern reported severe epigastric distress, with positive evidence on X ray of ulcerative conditions. Some of these patients, particularly with scale 2 and several other scales at a primed level, were clearly psychotic. Only one case had a well-established history of alcoholism and drug addiction. There were some other indications of psychopathic backgrounds in the group, however. At the time of testing, these patients appeared to be seriously seeking help from the physician and treatment was moderately successful.

In psychiatric populations this pattern is likely to be found in a psychopatic person who is in trouble and appears at a medical center. Alcoholism, addiction, and legal difficulties are frequent in the patterns of these cases. Although the distress of these persons seems genuine it does not reflect internal conflicts that they may be suffering so much as situational pressures from legal confinement, psychiatric commitment, or close supervision and scrutiny. While the insight these persons show at this time may be good and their verbal protestations of resolve to do better may seem genuine, long-range prognosis is poor. Recurrences of acting out and subsequent exaggerated guilt are common.

Note the inclusion of 247 pattern in Marks and Seeman's 274-247 code type. Chapter 3 lists the defining characteristics for this pattern.

26's

Even among the medical patients studied by Guthrie, the personality problems of this group stand out more prominently than physical distress. A subgroup of his subjects with this code showed allergies or obesity, or complained of diffuse pains. More importantly, however, these patients showed strong evidence of paranoid trends; some of them were in early phases of a psychosis. In the profiles of these latter cases, there were several primed scales. Sensitivity, resentfulness, and aggressiveness were marked. These patients as a group were typically fatigued, resentful, hostile, and depressed. Their conditions were chronic and stabilized; they showed little change from one visit to another.

27's

This is the single most frequent high-point pair in hospitalized psychiatric groups, male and female, and is a prominent pattern among outpatient psychiatric cases and medical patients; as such, the 27 code is largely a manifestation of abnormality. Together with the similar pattern of 72, this code makes up about 15 percent of the male inpatient profiles (if scale 5 is not coded). For females, these codes make up around 11 percent of the total patterns of inpatients (again omitting 5).

The prominent feature of this group in presenting complaints, according to Hathaway and Meehl (1951b), is depression, with tenseness and nervousness as frequent accompaniments. Many of these patients also suffer from anxiety, insomnia, and undue sensitiveness. For both sexes, these authors reported a modal diagnosis of reactive depression, with obsessive-compulsive neurosis a close second, but mixed psychoneuroses and conversion reactions are unlikely. However, the psychotic diagnoses were more frequent by a small margin than the neurotic diagnoses, with manic-depressive and depressed types and involutional depressions predominating.

Guthrie considered the 27 group in his sample of medical patients to be unusual in two respects: first, they were the most homogeneous group of cases among his code types and, second, they presented surprisingly few medical complaints even though they were consulting an internist. Instead, these patients complained of easy fatiguability, chronic tiredness, or exhaustion, or even more frankly of depression. The men in this group also showed rigidity and excessive worrying of the obsessive-compulsive sort. They suffered from feelings of inadequacy and from sexual conflicts. Within this group of patients, the depressed condition did not seem to be easily reversible, but remained stable over a long period. The forty items that Guthrie found to be characteristic of the cases with this code (see the Co_{27} scale in Appendix I in Volume II) are almost all from scales 2 and 7, particularly the items on those scales that also appear on Welsh's (1956b) A scale. The items are concerned with loss of efficiency, initiative, and self-confidence, brooding preoccupation with personal deficiencies, and discomfort in relationships with others.

Drake has found that the total profile of the 27 group tends to be elevated among college counselees; these subjects frequently present various types of problems relating to home conflict.

Halbower's Group II. Since Halbower found that the 27-72 combination of codes was tied for second in frequency of occurrence in his Veterans Administration mental-hygiene sample, he used this pattern as one of his criterion groups. The bases of case selection that he employed were these: the code either 27 or 72, if 7 was within 10 T-score points of 2; the third scale in the code at least 10 points lower than 2; scales 4, 6, and 8 all below 70, preferably, but he allowed 6 between 70 and 80, if Pa-subtle was higher than Pa-obvious, and 8 between 70 and 80, if 7 was at least 10 points higher than 8.

As may be anticipated, Halbower's judges did not differentiate this group as clearly from the patients-in-general and from the other MMPI code groups as they did some of the other code types. From the Q-sort items chosen they identified this group as appearing intelligent, as manifesting feelings of inadequacy, inferiority, and insecurity, and as characterized by a strong motivation for personal achievement and recognition. These subjects also were described as relying heavily upon mechanisms of the internalized sort, like somatization, self-blame, withdrawal, and obsessive-compulsive behavior. In their descriptions of these patients, the therapists used some items significantly infrequently, and in these omissions there are some interesting discrepancies with the findings of Hathaway and Meehl mentioned above for this code type. Some of these differences involved the *lack* of psychotic manifestations in Halbower's group, such as strange verbalizations, feelings of depersonalization, bizarre mentation, confusion, feelings of unreality, ideational poverty or inappropriate affect, or other reality distortions. The fact that these patients were selected from an outpatient treatment center may account in part for the absence of the more frankly psychotic correlates of this code type. Also, Halbower placed stringent restrictions on the range of scale 8 in forming this code group. The other omissions are consistent with the general clinical picture of these patients reported above, in that these patients do *not* rely upon somatic complaints to reduce anxiety, do *not* tend to gloss over and rationalize their problems, do *not* minimize their hostile feelings. These patients were also not described as either euphoric or hypomanic by the observers.

Several additional subgroups within the 27 pattern have been reported in various codebooks. Marks and Seeman provide data on the 27 pattern and on 274 and 278 as well. Gilberstadt and Duker include data on these same prototype groups although the defining characteristics for their categories differ somewhat from the Marks and Seeman specifications (see Chapter 3 for the listings of these defining attributes). Forsyth and Smith (1967) included a 278 code type in their analysis of personality ratings made by group dynamics leaders on nursing school students during their group sessions. These girls were found to be readily distinguishable from other common code patterns, primarily in terms of the absence of various interpersonal styles and relationships. They were judged to be more able than other students to understand the feelings of others and having more problems with authority figures. On the other hand they were judged to be less likely to make tangential remarks or odd comments, to need to be liked, to want everyone's friendship, to be overpowering, to invite hostility, to be self-confident, stubborn, angry, busy rebelling, sarcastic, emotional, naive, anxious verbally and nonverbally, independent, outgoing, apologetic, to admire and imitate others, to be able to be indifferent to others, to be manipulative, to manage others, to ask questions continually, to monopolize group discussion, to deflate others' status, to be angry or sarcastic toward the leader, to communicate with the leader, to question the leader directly, to change the topic being discussed, to be oversympathetic, to confide in the group, to allow anger to be expressed, to be uncomplicated, to be absent.

28's

This pattern is quite infrequent in psychiatric groups and even rarer in normals. Hathaway and Meehl (1951b) found that depression, anxiety, and agitation predominated in the clinical picture that such patients present, although an important minority showed a variety of hysterical disorders. This relationship between hysteroid mechanisms and some forms of the schizophrenic process is an interesting and important one for careful research. Just as some hypochondriacal pictures are prodromal manifestations for a developing schizophrenic reaction, so hysterical symptoms or atypical spells may presage a more serious psychotic upset. The differentiation of serious upsets from the more benign and tractable hysterical disorders may be aided in part by evidence about the premorbid personality of the patient. For example, Hathaway and Meehl found that the patients with 28 codes were described as unsociable in contrast to the sociability of cases with 13 or 31 patterns, in whom a hysterical syndrome would be psychologically more consistent. As the illness reflected in this profile develops, the patients seem to suffer some form of psychological deficit, appearing as an inability to concentrate, a period of confusion, or a loss of efficiency in carrying out usual duties. These cases also develop sensitiveness or even suspiciousness and some show hypochondriacal behavior.

Diagnostically, persons with the 28 codes were most frequently labeled psychotic, generally psychotic depression (manic-depressive, depressed, or involutional), although many were described as having some form of schizophrenia. Among the neurotic diagnoses, psychoneurosis, mixed, was more frequent than reactive depression, while a final diagnosis of either hypochondriasis or hysteria was rarely made. Guthrie also noted schizoid features in the patients he studied with 28 codes, but seldom was a clear schizophrenic break reported. Confusion and apathetic indifference were the most frequent manifestations. The severity of the personality difficulties corresponded well with the elevations of profiles in this group.

It should also be noted that Marks and Seeman include data on the 28 code type (see Chapter 3 for the defining characteristics of this pattern).

29's

In spite of the apparent psychological contradiction in this high-point pairing, the 29 pattern appears with sufficient frequency in both normals and psychiatric populations to cast doubt on the unidimensionality of this set of personality characteristics. Often the manic features are most prominent, serving to hide the depressive upset from outside observers and even from the subject himself. Guthrie noted that the medical patients showing this code type were not described as depressed. Rather they showed a picture of tension and anxiety, the tenseness at times related to upper gastrointestinal complaints or to fatigue. Alcoholic histories appeared for the men with this pattern. None of these patients was in serious difficulties and none visited the physician frequently. They responded quite well to the physical therapies used by the internist. Drake found aggressive or antagonistic behavior in college counselees with the 29 pattern.

20's

The outstanding characteristics of this group in Drake's college counselees were problems relating to social introversion.

High-Point 3's

The data in the tables in Appendix M indicate that there is a large sex difference in respect to the frequency of scale 3 peaks. In women scale 3 peaks are exceeded in frequency only by the other two scales in the neurotic triad, 1 and 2; in the psychiatric subgroup only scale 2 has more frequent peaks for women. But in male profiles scale 3 occurs rather infrequently among normals and only scale 6 has less frequent peaks in the psychiatric groups.

In Guthrie's data, however, gathered on patients of a general physician, scale 3 peaks were the most frequently obtained among all MMPI profiles. Particularly dramatic is the frequent occurrence of spikes, that is, elevations on 3 combined with no other MMPI scale within Hathaway's codable range. The selective effect of this personality variable in a medical practice and, possibly, the special circumstances under which these patients were tested may have led to this highly biased sample in comparison with male and female normals.

The normal college women in this code group were described by their acquaintances, in Black's study, in rather uncomplimentary terms. This contrasted with the ways in which these college women described themselves on the same checklist. The adjectives found characteristic by peers of women with scale 3 peaks were these: flattering, irritable, religious, and having many physical complaints. They did not, however, apply the terms partial, undependable, energetic, and clever to the high 3 females. In their self-descriptions these high 3 college women described themselves as trustful, alert, friendly, and loyal. They avoided, to a significant degree, using the terms emotional, boastful, suspicious, unrealistic, shy, and conceited. The self-descriptions of these college women seemed to be as self-enhancing as those reported by Hathaway and Meehl for high 3's. However, the peer ratings of these girls were not as favorable to them, perhaps because the judges in this instance lived with the girls being rated and had a great deal more day-to-day contact with them than the judges in the Hathaway-Meehl study had with the subjects they were rating.

When high-point 3 persons in a college setting seek counseling help, Mello and Guthrie reported, they present problems rooted in an unhappy home situation. The prominent pattern involves a father described as rejecting of them, to which the women react with somatic complaints and the men with rebellion or covert hostility. Their specific worries are concerned with scholastic failure, difficulties with authority figures, and lack of acceptance by their social group. These young people, in some contrast to high-point 2's, develop dependency within the therapeutic situation and stay in therapy longer. Taulbee (1958) also noted a relationship between scale 3 elevations in the code and continuation with treatment in a Veterans Administration mental-hygiene population. Although these cases show cathartic release during treatment to a considerable degree, Mello and Guthrie did not find that they achieved much insight.

As noted above, Guthrie found in the records of his internist a large number of patients who had this scale as their peak score. These patients presented a clinical picture of anxiety attacks to a greater extent than any other general MMPI type. They suffered from sudden occurrences of tachycardia, palpitation, and headaches. In their backgrounds, home and marital maladjustments appeared prominently, but they did not often show acting-out behavior or psychotic disturbances. Their response to treatment was often good and they profited readily from advice and reassurance. However, many of these patients resented the imputation of personality difficulties and failed to come back for scheduled follow-up visits.

When the peak on scale 3 was the only scale in Hathaway's codable range, Guthrie found the symptoms of subjects to be mild, generally involving the circulatory system, the upper gastrointestinal tract, or headaches. There was no evidence of conversion formation in this subgroup of cases. They sometimes complained of feeling nervous and tense but, as could be expected from the pervasive denial shown on the profile itself, did not show or complain about any other neurotic problems. These persons were infrequently referred, either by themselves or other physicians, as being ill or in distress; more often they were seen for a general physical checkup.

Drake has noted that college counselees with scale 3 high and scale 0 coded low show aggressiveness and generally extroverted behavior.

31's

The psychological similarity between the 31's and 13's has been noted by Meehl and Hathaway (1951b) and by Black. The reader should refer back to the section on 13 codes, where the adjectives which the female subjects in Black's study ascribed to themselves and received from their peer ratings were summarized.

The similarities between the 13 and 31 patterns were also noted in the medical patient study by Guthrie; the only noteworthy differences were that the complaints of the 31 patients were of the sort "that arrive secondary to protracted periods of mild tension." Conversion hysteria itself in its classic manifestation was rare in this group; the symptoms that these patients showed ranged from headaches, backaches, pain in the chest, and abdominal distress to fatigue that was clearly out of keeping with their recent exertions. It is interesting to note how rarely these patients were fully incapacitated by their symptoms. Note also the similarity of this group to Hanvik's (1951) functional low back pain group. The long-standing tension states of the 31's are associated with insecurity, immaturity, and a proneness to develop symptoms under stress. When the symptoms appear they are relatively restricted and specific both in location and in nature, in contrast to the 13 patients. Their attention in the medical examination is usually focused on these symptoms and is concerned relatively little with their life situation or general emotional disturbance. Their response to treatment is indifferent; they seem stabilized at a marginal level of adjustment. The items that Guthrie found particularly characteristic of this group (see the Co_{31} scale in Appendix I in Volume II) are mainly characterized by physical symptomatology, but there are a few which deal with social poise and lack of disturbance in relating to others.

Cuadra and Reed (1954) note particularly in patients with 31 profiles the appearance of basic features of a hysterical character, exhibitionism, and repression, together with frank manipulation and exploitation of social relationships. Commenting on the relationships between scales 1 and 3, these authors also note that in those profiles in which scale 1 approaches the height of scale 3 the appearance of conversion reactions is more likely. This latter observation fits in well with the finding of Fricke (1956) on a very carefully selected set of sixty-three female conversion-hysteria cases from the University of Minnesota Hospital files. Hovey (1949) also obtained this pattern for his dissociative-conversion subgroup of cases.

The 31 pattern is also included in the Marks and Seeman *Atlas* as the 31-13 code type (see Chapter 3 for the defining characteristics of this pattern).

32's

The most direct information on the 32 pattern comes from the observations of Guthrie on patients seen by a general practitioner. These patients showed a wide variety of complaints, usually rather mild and rather clearly related to anxiety. Epigastric distress was the most frequent symptom. The complaints of several of these patients shifted to headaches a few months later. Guthrie reported that the usual contact with these patients was a single interview without follow-up or further treatment. The patients that returned typically continued to visit the physician very frequently. They showed a change in the nature of their symptoms with relatively little shift in the severity of their difficulties.

The women in this group had a history of marital difficulties but no divorces were reported in their records. They were frequently sexually frigid and were lacking in any desire for sexual relations with their husbands. They complained about the infidelity or drinking of their husbands. This profile pattern, more than other code types, seems to be related to menopausal difficulties. Hysterical attacks were also frequent in this group, characterized by episodes of fear, palpitation, sweating, insomnia, and abdominal pain. The women showed signs of fatigue and exhaustion as well. They were apparently very conscientious in their work, easily hurt by any criticism or rebuff. In the MMPI profile, the values of the neurotic triad ranged high, with elevations on L and markedly low scores on scale 5.

Men with 32 profiles were frequently diagnosed as being in a state of anxiety, and they showed the physical effects of prolonged tension and worry even more clearly than did the women. Their concerns centered around business problems: they were both ambitious and conscientious, taking their responsibilities very seriously. They had episodes of palpitation, dizziness, and being unable to concentrate. Gastric distress was frequent and several gave evidence of having ulcers. They profited from the reassurance given about their physical condition and did not very often return.

In his item analysis, Guthrie found (see the Co_{32} scale in Appendix I in Volume II) that some of the statements characteristic of this subgroup bore upon specific physical complaints, while many of the others dealt with social conformity and denial of either social insecurity or unacceptable impulses. These patients seem to lack insight, to be resistant to psychodynamic formulations of their problems, and to manifest little motivation in seeking psychological help for their problems.

The Marks and Seeman *Atlas* includes data on the 321 code type (see Chapter 3 for the defining characteristics of this pattern).

34's

Enough college women appeared in Black's group with 34 patterns to provide him with a basis for analyzing this code group separately. The peers of these college girls described them only as impatient. They did not apply the terms conventional, dependent, peaceable, and relaxed. In their self-descriptions the 34 women described themselves as energetic, frivolous, incoherent, talkative, and reasonable. They significantly avoided applying the terms affectionate, sensitive, shy, irritable, or dreamy, and did not say they had aesthetic interests. The role of scale 4 can be seen here as it works in changing the social stimulus value of the 34 women.

In this profile, where scale 4 is prominently elevated but exceeded by the level of scale 3, Welsh and Sullivan (1952b) noted a preponderance of passive-aggressive, passive type, problems among patients in a sample of Veterans Administration psychiatric cases. The magnitude of scale 4 seems to reflect the aggressive or hostile feelings and impulses that are present to a significant degree, while the scale 3 height in turn shows that repressive and suppressive controls are even stronger than the impulse. Consequently the aggressions these persons would otherwise be expected to show intensely are kept from direct expression, appearing only obliquely, ineffectually, or sporadically. When aggressive actions toward others do appear, these persons often deny hostile intent, showing lack of insight into either the origins or the manifestations of their behavior.

Renaud's (1950) data indicate that the combination of these two scales also bears a direct relationship to the manifestation and personal acceptance of homoerotic sexual feelings stemming from personality inversion. Men who had elevated scores on scale 5 (Mf) and whose scores on scale 3 were higher than their scale 4 scores showed fears of being homosexual but generally were less likely to have acted upon their sexual impulses than men with similar scale 5 values but with the heights of scales 3 and 4 reversed. The latter group had typically formed a number of extended homosexual liaisons and rather freely acknowledged homoerotic preferences and practices. Thus, scale 3 in its relationship to scale 4 appears to serve as a measure of control and inhibition of socially unacceptable impulses.

Guthrie's observations of the 34 group were also consistent with those above in that problems of impulse control appeared. He found the presenting complaints among these patients to be largely centered on the upper gastrointestinal tract and of a variety neither acute nor very incapacitating. They were unable to recognize their own limitations. They seemed particularly to be sexually maladjusted. Marital difficulties were numerous and divorces appeared more frequently in this code group than was typical in the population under study. The women did not show in their histories markedly psychopathic features but appeared to be overly controlled and rather perfectionistic in their self-attitudes. Consistent with this picture of control and guardedness is the fact that treatment had relatively little effect on these patients.

36's

Guthrie noted the similarity of the histories of medical patients with this code to those for the group described above under 34. That is, these patients were also mainly women with gastrointestinal symptoms. However, headaches, notably absent in the 34 group, did occur among the 36 women. These patients showed a single complaint, rather than an array of symptoms, but like the 34 group their conditions tended not to be serious, acute, or incapacitating. About half of the cases had histories of previous abdominal surgery.

Most of these patients were moderately tense and anxious. There was no evidence of paranoid delusions or even prepsychotic conditions. Rather, the paranoid element appeared as deep and often unrecognized feelings of hostility toward members of the subject's immediate family. Where there was awareness of these hostilities toward a parent or marriage partner, the feelings were clearly rationalized. Although their symptoms were well established and fixed, these patients continued to seek medical help.

Forsyth and Smith (1967) reported rating data on code 36 patterns appearing among nursing students who were rated by the leaders during a series of group dynamics sessions. These girls differed from other patterns in being more emotional, well thought of, continually asking questions, oversympathetic, not allowing anger to be expressed, and uncomplicated. They were perceived as less manipulative and having fewer problems with authority.

38's

Data on the 38 pattern are included in Marks and Seeman's 83-38 code type (see Chapter 3 for the defining characteristics of this pattern).

39's

Medical patients with a 39 pattern in Guthrie's study presented histories of episodic attacks of acute distress. The attacks were marked by anxiety, palpitations, and tachycardia. The presenting complaints of 39 patients seemed to center about the lower gastrointestinal tract, the back, and the extremities. When they had intestinal cramps or headaches, the pains came on suddenly and intensely. On the other hand, ulcers, hypertension, and respiratory difficulties were virtually absent. Occasionally the medical problems showed a classic hysterical pattern, being both dramatic and medically atypical or impossible. The 39 patients were frequently described as aggressive and as directing considerable hostility toward a domineering mother. While none of these patients had periods of severe depression in their histories, most of them were depressed and fatigued at the time they were seen. The physical problems of this group were not of a severe nature and readily yielded to superficial treatment.

Low-Point 3's

The occurrence of very low scale 3 scores among normals is not as frequent as would be expected by chance alone. The content of the scale items apparently is sufficiently socially desirable to lead to some degree of elevation on this scale for most groups. Consequently, data on low 3 scores are rather meager. There is the additional possibility that the personality characteristics of these people are actually of a kind that would not be well known and understood by the subject's peers. Preliminary work on this group has been reported by Cantor (1952).

High-Point 4's

Scale 4 appears prominently in many profiles from both normal and psychiatric populations. It is one of the frequent peak scores, particularly in males, and appears very often in a variety of high-point pairs. The preponderance of scale 4 elevations increases markedly in prison groups (see Appendix M), where the sex difference becomes negligible. The usual sex difference is actually reversed in the data Sundberg (1952) collected on outpatient psychiatric cases.

Early in the development of MMPI patterns, it was discovered that peak scores on scale 4, almost without regard to the absolute elevation of the profile, provided evidence of lack of social conformity or self-control and a persistent tendency to get into scrapes (Schiele, Baker, and Hathaway, 1943). This finding is clearly reflected in the way Meehl (1946) defined the profile characteristics of his conduct-disorder cases. When Hathaway and Monachesi (1953, 1957, 1963) studied the records of delinquent boys, they found a high frequency of peak scores on scale 4. The special effects of combinations with other scales as second high points and of differences in absolute elevation, however, can be seen in their data on two-point high points. Thus, when scale 4 as peak is paired with scales 1, 7, or particularly 2, the delinquency rate is reduced below the level expected for boys in general. When scale 4 is found in combination with scales 3, 8, and particularly 9, the delinquency rate is greatly elevated. In the 49 combination, for example, the eighty-five boys with this pattern (Hathaway and Monachesi, 1953) have a delinquency rate of 38 percent as compared with the 22 percent found for all boys in the study without regard to MMPI scores. In this group the effect of higher elevations of the pattern is also dramatically shown. The forty boys with 49 patterns that were at a primed level had a delinquency rate of 51 percent! Similar trends can be seen in the data from the girls, although the over-all delinquency rates were lower for the female group.

The college women in the study carried out by Black described the high 4 girls as sociable, arrogant, frivolous, incoherent, moody, and partial. These terms are quite unflattering on the whole, as are the significant omissions (by implication) that Black found in his analysis: practical, cheerful, self-controlled, and conventional were not used to describe high 4's. This unprepossessing set of terms may stem in part from the fact that the peer judges were living closely with the girls they rated and depended heavily upon their cooperation and willingness to share domestic responsibilities.

In their self-descriptions, the high 4 girls in Black's study were quite insensitive to the social favorability of the items. They rated themselves as apathetic, cynical, dishonest, clever, lively, and worldly. They left out of their self-descriptions to a significant extent the terms adaptable, practical, kind, easily bored, friendly, peaceable, and natural.

Mello and Guthrie reported that few of the cases with peaks on scale 4 seen in a university counseling center showed the classic asocial, amoral psychopathic pattern. This finding is understandable in the light of the referral policies of the center, most of the cases being self-referred. The role of scale 4 appeared to be an index of rebelliousness rather than an indication of the acting out of base impulses. These subjects resented authority and were hostile toward their parents, whom they blamed for all their problems. Their immediate concerns centered about vocational choices. The indecisive states of these college students were complicated by unstable relationships with the opposite sex and, at times, by a rejecting father. They continued to return to the center for their scheduled interviews, but were generally quite resistant to therapy. Since they resorted to intellectualization and stereotyped repetition of their problems, their response to therapy was minimal.

Medical patients with peak scores on scale 4 were described by Guthrie as having psychopathic features in their histories, particularly when their second high score fell on scale 2, 3, 6, or 9. That is, men with this profile tended to be alcoholic, to gamble excessively, or to show poor work records. For the women there were comparable indications that they had gone against social mores; they had histories of recurrent marital difficulties, illegitimate pregnancies, and the like. Their symptoms were episodic in nature, mild in degree, and overshadowed by their behavioral difficulties. Since they were unreliable patients, their response to treatment was difficult to assess. Deeper personality conflicts appeared in the groups with scale 7 or 8 in second place in the profile.

Gilberstadt and Duker reported a 4 pattern in their code groups also (see Chapter 3 for the defining characteristics of this pattern).

As can be seen in the summaries in Volume II on various special problems, scale 4 peaks appear prominently among alcoholic samples (Goss and Morosko, 1969), homeless vagabonds (Brantner, 1958), delinquent subgroups (Stone and Rowley, 1963; Shinohara and Jenkins, 1967; Tsubouchi and Jenkins, 1969; Mack, 1969), disciplinary and sexual offenders within a prison system (Stanton, 1956; Panton, 1958, 1960; Miller and Hannum, 1963; Oliver and Mosher, 1968), drivers with high frequencies of traffic violations and accidents (Buttiglieri, 1969; Waller et al., 1969), and various drug abuse groups (Gilbert and Lombardi, 1967; Ungerleider et al., 1968; McAree, Steffenhagen and Zheutlin, 1969; Smart and Fejer, 1969; and Smart and Jones, 1970). Mack (1969) noted that a 4 spike at the primed level was more frequently associated with recidivism among state training school inmates than those without further legal difficulties, while scale 3 also at a primed level in the profiles of these boys was related to lower likelihood of recidivistic difficulties.

41's

Guthrie noted briefly that for a small group within the population of medical patients he studied the role of scale 4 was obscured by the contributions of scale 1. That is, the 41 patients were clearly hypochondriacal with severe symptoms, there being little clear evidence of asocial behavior. They presented problems that were very resistant to treatment.

42's

The psychopathic features of this code type, like those of the 24 group, are prominent and correspond to long-standing behavioral patterns such as alcoholism; on the other hand, the depressive features appear to be situationally produced and short-lived. While guilt and self-depreciation may be part of the presenting picture of these persons, such manifestations are not usually very convincing or sincere. When both scales in this high-point pair are grossly elevated, the pattern is associated with psychotic or prepsychotic behavior, and suicide is a serious possibility.

Guthrie reported that medical patients with this profile type showed physical symptoms in only half of the cases. They impressed the internist as being severely psychoneurotic with psychopathic features, although some of the women with gross elevations were considered prepsychotic. Alcoholism and peptic ulcers were noteworthy in the small group of 42 men. There was little evidence of any response to treatment on the part of these patients.

Sheppard et al. (1969) included a 42 code pattern group in their analysis of subgroups of heroin addicts at a New York narcotic addiction center. Patterns of self-description in Plutchik's (1962) emotional model were reported on this group which characterized them as higher than other addicts on the incorporation, reproduction, exploration, and protection dimensions, all relatively positive features.

43's

Like 34, this pattern reflects problems in impulse control and social conformity. However, the relatively greater rise on scale 4 indicates that the controls are even less adequate than for the 34 group. Therefore, as noted by Welsh and Sullivan (1952b), persons with this configuration (particularly when scale 6 is also elevated), although inhibited and moderate, episodically express their aggressive feelings directly and intensely. They are characterized by chronic hostility and aggressive feelings.

In the medical patients he studied, Guthrie found the physical complaints to be mild, episodic, and with little basis in physical pathology. Their psychopathic tendencies were evident, including alcoholism, marital disharmony, and sexual promiscuity. Many cases showed an alternation in their histories between periods of acting out and hysterically determined illnesses. Thus, these persons have a strong impulse toward socially disapproved behavior, with rather ineffectual controls, but nevertheless suffer from conflicts and anxieties about their actions.

This 43 pattern also was represented in the code groups reported by Gilberstadt and Duker (see Chapter 3 for the defining characteristics of this pattern). J. Sines (1966) noted the high prevalence in 43 code patterns found among male prisoners in the Missouri prison system of a history of violent crimes. Persons and Marks (1971) verified and extended this relationship on male cases with 43 codes found in an Ohio reformatory.

46's

A small group of medical patients showed this pattern in Guthrie's study. Their physical complaints were varied, both among the patients as a group and for any given patient from one visit to another. Their physical and emotional difficulties were only vaguely described but some cases showed marked anxiety. When the profile was grossly elevated with a 46 pattern, the cases appeared clearly prepsychotic. There was a high incidence of asthma, hay fever, and hypertension, such symptoms in these cases being apparently related to instances of repressed hostility.

The social maladjustments of the patients in Guthrie's study are noteworthy. In almost every case there was a report of seriously disrupted relations with the opposite sex, half of the women being divorced or in the process of getting a divorce. When the score on scale 4 was in the primed range, there was also evidence of poor work histories. Both of the men included in this group were alcoholics.

In psychiatric cases, the 46 pattern is related to irritability and suspiciousness combined with depression, nervousness, and introversion. Alcoholism may be associated with this pattern as well as defects of judgment. Some form of conduct disorder characterizes the majority of patients, although schizophrenia of the paranoid form and paranoid states may also appear. Neurotic conditions associated with this pattern seem to have neither somatization features nor anxieties or obsessions stemming from deep inner conflicts. Rather neuroticism seems to be related to situational conditions or to circumstances arising out of judgmental defects or other psychopathic difficulties.

The 46 pattern is represented in two of the subgroups reported by Marks and Seeman, a 46 pattern and a 462 pattern (see Chapter 3 for the definitions of these patterns). Sheppard, Fiorentino, and Merlis (1968) also reported emotional profiles for various subgroups of heroin addicts, including the 468 pattern which was characterized as higher on the Plutchik (1962) dimensions of protection, exploration, deprivation, and rejection.

47's

This code group shows an interesting internal contradiction in self-description; 47's indicate both excessive insensitivity in scale 4 and excessive concern about the effects of their actions in scale 7. This psychological contradiction frequently appears behaviorally as an alternation of phases or cyclical variations. For a period these persons may act with little control or forethought, violating social and legal restrictions and trampling on the feelings and wishes of others heedlessly. Following such a period of acting out, however, they may show guilt, remorse, and deep regret over their actions and for a while seem overly controlled and contrite. Excessive alcoholic indulgence may be a part of these activity swings, as well as other amoral activities. While their conscience pangs may be severe, even out of proportion to the actual behavior deviations, the controls of these subjects do not appear to be effective in preventing further outbreaks.

Guthrie described a small group of women with this code pattern who consulted an internist. When seen by the physician they were tense and suffering from fatigue and a number of vague symptoms like headache, loss of pep, or pains in the stomach. They appeared to be dependent and insecure, requiring a great deal of reassurance. They had histories of family rejection or overindulgence. Although the number of visits made to the physician was above average, they obtained very little benefit from the simple reassurance or physical treatment given.

Data on the 472 pattern are reported by Marks and Seeman (see Chapter 3 for the defining characteristics of the 247-472 pattern).

48's

Persons with this profile pattern are frequently described by acquaintances as odd, peculiar, or queer. They are unpredictable, impulsive, and nonconforming and the term schizoid personality is frequently applied to them. Their educational and occupational histories are characterized by underachievement, marginal adjustment, and uneven performance. Nomadism, social isolation, or underworld membership is often present. Delinquency is closely associated with the 48 profile (Hathaway and Monachesi, 1953) and the prognosis for improvement under a rehabilitation program for delinquents is poor (Lauber and Dahlstrom, 1953). Crimes committed by persons with this profile (Pothast, 1956) are often senseless, poorly planned, and poorly executed, and may include some of the most savage and vicious forms of sexual and homicidal assault.

The small group of medical patients (mostly women) with this profile pattern in Guthrie's study did not show frankly bizarre behavior. However, the degree of personality involvement in these patients may be inferred from the vague physical complaints that characterized them, the recurring history of changes from doctor to doctor, and the lack of follow-up visits; the impression of the internist supported the picture of deep involvement. Over half of the group were considered early psychotic reactions. In addition to their vague, multiple complaints, they showed considerable anxiety at the time they were seen. Only one patient returned for a second visit in spite of encouragement to do so.

The combination of high 482 codes is included in the Marks and Seeman *Atlas* (see Chapter 3 for the defining characteristics of this pattern).

49's

Persons with this profile pattern show clear manifestations of psychopathic behavior, the hypomania seemingly energizing or activating the pattern related to scale 4. That is, these people tend to be overactive and impulsive, irresponsible and untrustworthy, shallow and superficial in their relationships. They are characterized by easy morals, readily circumvented consciences, and fluctuating ethical values. To satisfy their own desires and ambitions, they may expend great amounts of energy and effort, but they find it difficult to stick to duties and responsibilities imposed by others. In superficial contacts and social situations they create favorable impressions because of their freedom from inhibiting anxieties and insecurities. They are lively, conversational, fluent, and forthright; they enter wholeheartedly into games, outings, and parties, without being self-conscious or diffident. However, their lack of judgment and control may lead them to excesses of drinking, merrymaking, or teasing. They may be prone to continue activities so long that they exceed the proprieties, neglect other obligations, or alienate others.

Crook (1944) reported that women with this pattern made good prospects for the WAC. Wiener (1948b) indicated that this pattern was conducive to successful life insurance sales work. Drake reported that 49 patterns in college counselees were related to aggressiveness in the interview situation. Hovey found that these persons participated actively in group discussions. In another study Hovey (1954) suggested that a moderate elevation on scales 4 and 9 is an asset in impressing supervisors and winning social acceptance and approval.

The patients with 49 patterns who sought help from an internist were reported by Guthrie to be suffering from episodic periods of tension, sweating and dizziness, and anxious distress. They had histories of acting-out behavior covering a wide range of troubles including marital problems, divorce, alcoholism, and illegitimate pregnancies. These considerations far outweighed their medical problems.

According to Hathaway and Meehl (1951b), psychiatric patients with this pattern are primarily diagnosed as psychotic with manic disorders predominating. A significant subgroup were described as conduct disorders, but neurotic disorders were almost entirely excluded from this group. These patients were typically overactive; they were reported as extroverted, talkative, ambitious, and energetic, frequently irritable, and occasionally violent.

Drake found aggressive behavior to be particularly characteristic of college counselees with a 49 pattern when scale 2 was coded low.

Both Marks and Seeman and Gilberstadt and Duker have 49 code types included in their subgroups (see Chapter 3 for the defining characteristics of this pattern in each system).

Forsyth and Smith (1967) included a 49 group in their analyses of nursing students with various MMPI patterns who were rated by leaders after a series of group dynamics meetings. These girls were characterized as chatty, needing to be liked, anxious verbally and nonverbally, outgoing, distrustful, suspicious, manipulative, monopolizing group discussion, expressing personal problems, not allowing anger to be expressed, and intellectualizing. Watman (1966) examined the acting-out histories of 49 code prisoners and failed to find any particular proclivity for disruptions in prison routines for these prisoners. Sheppard, Fiorentino, and Merlis (1968) contrasted heroin addicts with 49 patterns with other subgroups of addicts in a narcotic addiction center in New York. These cases were characterized in Plutchik's (1962) schema as higher on the dimensions of incorporative, reproductive, orientative, and destructive emotionality. They were also appreciably lower on explorative and protective dimensions.

Low-Point 4's

Meehl (1951) has indicated that when scale 4 is the low point of the profile, the subjects appear to be characterized by a lack of heterosexual interest. Although this characteristic may appear in a variety of ways. the lack of effective expression of normal sexual interests seems pervasive. Other data on these cases are summarized in Cantor's (1952) dissertation.

High-Point 5's

Because of the special circumstances surrounding the derivation of scale 5 (see Chapters 1 and 6), a great many of the data from the Minnesota studies do not include material pertinent to scale 5. Thus, in the high-point-pair data summarized in Appendix M, the tabulations from Minnesota normal adults (Tables 1 and 2) and from the various patient populations omit scale 5. The effect of this enforced omission can be judged in part from the Iowa data provided in Tables 3 and 4 of Appendix M in which scale 5 has been included. The subjects in these latter groups are roughly comparable to the Minnesota normals. It can be seen that over 40 percent of these married men have scale 5 either as the peak score or as the second highest score in the profile. Were scale 5 to be ignored, these cases would be assigned to other cells, inflating the latter values correspondingly. On the other hand, the Iowa tabulations suggest that scale 5 is not a frequent peak score for normal female subjects; the Minnesota trends are probably not affected greatly by ignoring scale 5 in the high-point-pair data for females. It is interesting to note in the data from Hathaway and Monachesi (1963) in Tables 5 and 6 of Appendix M that the relative prominence of scale 5 in the profiles of ninth-grade boys and girls is reversed: more girls have scale 5 peaks than do boys at this age level. In the North Carolina college groups shown in Appendix M (Tables 7 and 8), the sex difference in the relative frequency of peaks on scale 5 is equally striking, while the prison groups (Tables 17, 18, 19, and 20) strongly resemble the adolescent population in the role played by scale 5.

The college women with high scores on scale 5 in Black's tabulations were seen by their peers as indecisive, rebellious, natural, and unrealistic. The group was infrequently characterized by their peers as dreamy, poised, polished, or sensitive. In their self-descriptions, these girls saw themselves as rough, incoherent, shiftless, and unemotional. They omitted from their self-descriptions the terms popular, good-tempered, polished, peaceable, kind, lively, alert, sentimental, and emotional, and they did not claim to have wide interests or aesthetic interests.

The various combinations of scale 5 with other clinical scales have not been extensively studied or reported. The importance of some of those patterns can be judged from the observations of Hathaway and Monachesi (1953, 1963) on the role of scale 5 (as well as scales 2 and 0) as an inhibitor of manifest delinquent behavior. As an example, the combination 59 in the profiles of ninth-grade boys was associated with a delinquency rate of only 11 percent, as contrasted with an over-all rate of 22 percent for the whole sample of boys in the study. The characteristics inhibited by scale 5, however, may be quite different from those related to other inhibitors; scale 5 should not necessarily be considered as a suppressor of all undersirable forms of behavior.

Drake found that college counselees with a 59 pattern presented problems relating to a mother conflict when scale 0 was coded low. He noted also that the 50 group showed introverted behavior, while in the group with a peak 5 and 0 coded low such behavior, as might be expected, was conspicuously absent.

Dean and Richardson (1964, 1966) and Zucker and Manosevitz (1966) report data on the role of high 5 patterns in identifying personality inversion in homosexual male samples. They also provide data on additional two-point high-point code combinations.

Low-Point 5's

Black reported that the women in his college group with 5 as the low point in their profiles were described by their peers as worldly, popular, decisive, and versatile. They were not seen as energetic, undependable, shy, rough, unrealistic, or disorderly. In their self-descriptions the low 5 girls gave a less flattering picture of themselves: self-distrusting, self-dissatisfied, moody, polished, shy, sensitive, neurotic, unrealistic, talkative, sentimental, and having aesthetic interests were the descriptions they checked. They did not endorse balanced, independent, decisive, good-tempered, practical, relaxed, or modest.

Although little definitive research has been directed to the occurrence and correlates of low 5 profiles in psychiatric groups, it should be noted that these patterns are common in women. It is observed clinically that the higher the elevation of the neurotic triad, the lower the value of scale 5 will be in this group. This configuration frequently accompanies a masochistic trend in the adjustive efforts of the woman, with self-depreciation, long-suffering sacrifice, and unnecessary assumption of burdens and responsibilities. The precise role of scale 5 in this configuration is poorly understood but specific difficulties in sexual adjustment appear frequently, especially when a low value of 5 is combined with at least moderate elevations on scales 4 and 6.

High-Point 6's

Profiles with peak scores on scale 6 are relatively rare, scale 6 often being lowest in rank of the various clinical scales among normal and clinical samples (see Appendix M). However, scale 6 peaks almost invariably appear more frequently in female groups than they do in male samples. According to Black, high-point 6's for women show a relative rise in the late adolescent period.

In his analysis of college girls with peak scores on scale 6, Black found that they were perceived by their peers as shrewd, hardhearted, and clever. They also appeared to be affected and poised, high-strung and submissive. In addition the girls in this group were rated as either mature or infantile —depending on the subordinate peak paired with scale 6. If either scale 3 or 7 was paired as a high point with a scale 6 peak, the girl tended to be judged mature. If the second high point was scale 1, 8, or 9, on the other hand, the girl was rated infantile. Black also found that high-point 6 girls were infrequently described as either grateful or rebellious.

The manner in which this group's self-descriptions differed from those of college girls in general was more clear-cut. The high-point 6 girls included two of the same terms applied to them by their peers: affected and submissive. They added several other rather derogatory terms: arrogant, fickle, boastful, ruthless, and unrealistic. They further described themselves as being shy, timid, and naive, but nevertheless sociable, and as being contented, conventional, unemotional, and persevering. They avoided endorsing either practical or easily bored.

Mello and Guthrie reported that there were too few cases in their college counselee sample to establish any pattern for peak 6 profiles.

Guthrie found that medical patients with peak scores on scale 6 typically presented complaints centering around the gastrointestinal tract, with epigastric distress most common. They established poor rapport with the physician, disliked talking about their emotional problems, and frequently did not return for follow-up visits. They had long-standing problems centering around hostility and resentment toward members of their family. Their response to treatment was poor. Characteristics associated with special configurations in this group are summarized below.

62's

Guthrie found that this group of patients showed serious emotional difficulties, overshadowing any particular medical problem that they may have presented initially, even though they were typically very worried and concerned about their physical difficulty. They were depressed, with a strong underlying trend of hostility. They had long histories of interpersonal difficulties and rejection of close associations, their hostilities seemingly handicapping them significantly in social skills. When seen such patients were severely psychoneurotic, a small subgroup of them appearing actually prepsychotic. Guthrie also noted that they tended to be more disturbed than their moderate elevations on the MMPI profiles would indicate. The height of the F scale, however, did seem to be proportional to the severity of their disturbance.

63's

Medical patients with this pattern were described by Guthrie as rigid, worrying, defensive, and uncooperative. They resented any implication that their difficulties were psychogenically determined, and usually failed to return when this was suggested. They had histories of medical shopping from one physician to another. Paranoid features were frequently apparent on the first contact; several subjects were considered to be clearly prepsychotic.

64's

Data on 64 and 642 patterns are included in the 46-64 and the 462-642 code types presented in the Marks and Seeman *Atlas* (see Chapter 3 for the defining characteristics of these patterns).

68's

Guthrie described the group of medical patients with this profile pattern as prepsychotic with schizoid personality patterns. They were, however, making a marginal adjustment without hospitalization; physical complaints and preoccupation with health may have served to stabilize their precarious adjustment. They presented a wide variety of complaints which shifted from visit to visit. They also had many food fads and depended upon patent treatments and medicines. Their relationships with others were unstable and characterized by resentment.

In the psychiatric population that they studied, Hathaway and Meehl (1951b) found the 68 group largely composed of psychotics, the majority being frankly schizophrenic, with a smaller portion in paranoid states. The most common feature of the behavior of these patients was the presence of paranoid delusions, but many of them also showed depression, apathy, irritability, and social withdrawal. Although they had conduct or behavior problems, their difficulties were not the classic scrapes of the amoral, asocial psychopathic group. The few neurotics seen in a psychiatric setting with this pattern were not of the somatic sort, but could be better characterized as dysphoric.

Information on the 68 pattern is also reported by Marks and Seeman in their 86-68 code type (see Chapter 3 for the defining characteristics of this pattern).

69's

This pattern is included in the 96-69 pattern reported in the Marks and Seeman *Atlas* (see Chapter 3 for the defining characteristics of this pattern).

Low-Point 6's

Black was able to identify a sizable group of college women with codes in which scale 6 was the lowest value. As a group these women were perceived by their peers as socially withdrawn and in poor rapport with others. The terms that they used to describe the low 6 girl include shy, timid, and seclusive. These girls were also seen as rough and awkward, deliberate, thoughtful, inflexible, idealistic but humble, and both self-distrusting and self-dissatisfied. Consistent with this picture, the terms that were very infrequently ascribed to the low 6 girls were sociable and worldly, cheerful and laughterful, high-strung and aggressive, adaptable and unemotional.

In their self-descriptions, the low 6 girls also endorsed the terms rough and arrogant, as well as the terms secretive, modest, and self-effacing, all of which are quite similar to the implications in the peer ratings. However, in addition they used rather frequently a term that the peer group avoided, aggressive, and added several similar terms including cynical, shrewd, hardhearted, arrogant, and rebellious. At some variance with the foregoing terms are the final two adjectives included in Black's findings, relaxed and cooperative. This group significantly avoided describing themselves as sentimental.

Anderson (1956) also noted the role of low 6 in the poor response of these subjects to counseling in a university counseling center.

High-Point 7's

Even in psychiatric populations, peaks on scale 7 are not particularly frequent. Black did not find any striking shifts over the adolescent and early years of maturity for the occurrence of peaks on this scale. Sundberg (1952) found relatively more of these peaks in acute outpatient groups of psychiatric patients than in hospitalized groups (see Appendix M). There is a striking absence of these patterns in the prison populations studied by Panton (1959; see Appendix M).

There are only a few adjectives in Black's findings on college women who had peak scores on scale 7. The peers of these girls typified them as kind, dependent, quiet, and trustful. Drake reported that counselors found a group of college counselees with peak scores on scale 7 to be unresponsive in the interview. The net effect of the operation of these personality traits seems to be that other people do not get to know these subjects very well. The list of terms that the peer judges in Black's study failed to endorse seems to reveal this same trend. The scale 7 peak women were not described as alert, individualistic, or aggressive. The terms friendly, enterprising, energetic, and independent were also omitted. Other items significantly considered to be uncharacteristic included clever, idealistic, self-centered, and impatient.

In their self-descriptions, however, these girls presented a more complete picture. They conceived of themselves as being gloomy, depressed, and emotional, with many physical complaints. They said they were dreamy, sentimental, softhearted, and indecisive. In addition, they viewed themselves as unpopular and dependent, irritable and suspicious, and absent-minded. They failed to endorse many terms in their self-descriptions as well. They did not see themselves as easygoing, independent, aggressive, or self-confident. Nor did they say they were alert or lively, worldly or adaptable, clear thinking, loyal, or show-offs.

According to Mello and Guthrie, the college counselees who had peak scores on scale 7 in their study were characterized by obsessive-compulsive ruminations and morbid introspective trends. The problems of these students were centered about poor study habits, poor personal relations, and difficulty with authority figures. They were very concerned about religious values and morality, and many had problems with homosexual impulses. As a group, these clients were the most seriously disturbed of the college counselees in the study. They showed strong resistances in therapy, developing considerable hostility toward the therapist and toward treatment itself. However, these counselees persisted in therapy longer than any other code group, their dependency increasing markedly with the number of interviews. Improvement came only slowly, with no dramatic remission of symptoms.

Medical patients with scale 7 as a peak score were characterized by Guthrie as prone to worry, anxious, fearful, and rigid. They presented medical problems that frequently centered about their hearts, with gastrointestinal and genitourinary difficulties also represented. However, the dramatic feature of these cases was their extreme concern about their medical difficulty; they required many return visits and repeated reassurances. Depression was present, but even in the 72 codes, it was less clearly manifested than was agitation and anxiety. Whatever their problem, they seemed as a group unable to modulate their reactions to the actual events, but rather characteristically overreacted.

It has also been reported that college students with 7 peaks were particularly conscientious in reporting for psychological experiments and gave an unusually high number of uncertain judgments in the course of such experiments on a discrimination task (Griffith, Upshaw, and Fowler, 1958; Griffith and Fowler, 1960).

72's

See also the 27's described above. Drake found that college counselees with this code pattern very frequently fell into problem groups characterized as tense and indecisive.

78's

Hathaway and Meehl (1951b) found that psychiatric cases with this code were rather evenly divided between neurotic and psychotic diagnoses. The neurotics were obsessive-compulsive, depressive, or, often, showed mixed forms, but few somatization patterns were included. The psychotic cases also ranged widely, although the manic forms were not represented. Depression and introversion were the dominant clinical features, together with worrying, irritability, nervousness, apathy, and social withdrawal.

Gilberstadt and Duker included a 78 prototype among their subgroups (see Chapter 3 for the defining characteristics of this pattern).

High-Point 8's

The data in Appendix M indicate that peak scores on scale 8 are quite rare in normal adult males and females, but are much more likely in younger subjects and in prison inmates. There is also an increase of these peaks in psychiatric samples, particularly hospitalized groups, and even in neurological patients. The relative infrequency of scale 8 peaks in the medical patients reported by Guthrie (see Tables 15 and 16 of Appendix M), even when compared with the low level for adults in general, is also striking.

The terms chosen by college-level peers to describe the high 8 girls in Black's study suggest the schizoid personality pattern present in the criterion group for this scale. That is, these girls were described as apathetic, serious, seclusive, and secretive. There is little to suggest any appreciable degree of disorganization in their behavior, however, since such terms as orderly, wise, clear-thinking, and adaptable seem to convey good control and integration. These girls were also described as worldly and sophisticated, but not apparently in the sense of snobbish, since they were also described as humble, peaceful, and grateful. In addition they were seen to be courageous and to have aesthetic interests, but to be undependable. The terms that were omitted to a significant degree in the ratings of the high-point 8 girls by their peers tend to support this same picture. The omissions include mature, self-confident, talkative, and sensitive.

In their self-descriptions, the girls in the Black study who had scale 8 peaks were quite self-derogatory and critical. They labeled themselves, similarly to their peers' ratings, as serious and as having aesthetic interests, but included conceited, boastful, and selfish. They also described themselves as hostile, rebellious, and pugnacious. They said they were eccentric and became easily bored. They also omitted the terms loyal and persevering from their self-descriptions to a significant degree.

Mello and Guthrie in their analysis of the records of college students seen in counseling found that the group who showed peak scores on scale 8 presented problems in peer relationships and group acceptance. Sexual preoccupation was frequent along with sexual confusion, nymphomanic tendencies, and bizarre fantasies. The students relied a great deal on daydreaming. In these young subjects the role of scale 8 does not appear to have the malignant qualities it takes on in older subjects; a frank psychosis was rarely shown by these counselees. They developed a positive transference quite readily, and tended to persist in treatment more than almost any other profile type (the exception being the scale 7 peaks) even though their response to treatment was quite variable.

Guthrie has also reported on a small subgroup of medical patients whose peak scores occurred on scale 8. As a group they did not show clear-cut physical symptoms, but rather presented a long history of vague complaints that had been treated by a variety of regimes. These histories strongly suggest long-standing, stabilized hypochondriacal trends.

In their psychological makeup Guthrie found the peak 8 group to be rather uniformly borderline psychotics, whose only psychotic manifestations were short-lived periods of confusion and disorientation. In the main, these subjects were able to attribute their problems to "trouble with their nerves," and they showed no evidence of deeper insight into their personality problems. Consequently response to treatment was quite poor, and over the course of time their particular complaints remained vague and gradually shifted without amelioration. They seemed to be sincerely seeking help from the physician, but did not benefit from the simple reassurance that usually helped neurotics. Although these patients were not violent, they were described as disagreeable and their home life was severely disrupted by the poor control they maintained over their hostility.

Drake often noted in college counselees with peak 8 profiles problems of "lack of knowledge" and of being "confused," while the peak 7 group was characterized by problems of "conflict."

81's

These cases are included in the 8123 pattern reported by Gilberstadt and Duker (see Chapter 3 for the defining characteristics of this pattern).

82's

Data on this configuration appear in the 28-82, 482-824 subgroups in the Marks and Seeman *Atlas* and in the 824 prototype reported by Gilberstadt and Duker. Both sets of patterns are defined in Chapter 3.

83's

See the code pattern in Marks and Seeman's *Atlas.*

84's

See the 824 note above.

86's

Both the Marks and Seeman and the Gilberstadt and Duker groups of code patterns include an 86 pattern. The definitions of each pattern are somewhat different (see Chapter 3 for the defining characteristics of each).

87's

See also the 78's above.

Halbower's Group IV. Halbower chose this code type for one of the four MMPI groups to serve as criterion cases for his actuarial approach to personality interpretation. This choice was determined in part by the frequency with which this pattern appears in psychiatric practice, but also by his desire to include some clearly psychotic group in his analysis. The criteria he chose for selecting cases for this code group consisted of the following: 87 high point in the profile (or 78 if 8 was within ten points of 7); 2, 4, or 6 the third highest scale; 4 higher than 1 and 3; 4 and 6 at a primed level; F at a primed level and highest of the validity scales; Pd-O higher than Pd-S; Pa-O higher than Pa-S (unless scale 6 was double primed); Hy-S less than a T score of 60.

Halbower found that 87's were described as tending to complain of worrying and nervousness, and as being introspective, ruminative, and overideational. Typically their personality difficulties were chronic, with long-standing feelings of inadequacy, inferiority, and insecurity. They were not seen to be self-reliant, independent, or particularly able to think for themselves, but rather to manifest passive dependence. They were unable to take a dominant or ascendant role in interactions with others. Socially they were lacking in poise and assurance, and they did not show in their histories evidence of even an average number of rewarding socialization experiences. These persons were not outgoing, optimistic, or euphoric, but rather dealt with their problems on an internalized basis. Somatic symptoms did not provide them with relief from their anxieties; in fact, they appeared to lack defenses which served in any efficient way to provide them with comfort or freedom from distress. They did not show ideational poverty, however, and their rich fantasies were frequently concerned with sexual problems. Their emotional difficulties frequently interfered with their judgment and they often appeared to lack common sense in everyday matters. Although these patients did not feel particularly defensive about admitting to their emotional problems and disturbances, they did not have a good prognosis for psychotherapy. They did not readily form stable, mature, or warm interpersonal relationships and did not integrate what they learned or profit from their own experiences.

89's

The 89 pattern appears in both the Marks and Seeman and the Gilberstadt and Duker lists of code patterns. They are somewhat different in their basic definitions (see Chapter 3 for the list of characteristics).

High-Point 9's

In the Minnesota normative samples, scale 9 is the most frequent peak score for both males and females, but it should be noted that scale 5 was not included in these tabulations. In the younger Minnesota subjects in the samples from the ninth-grade studies, Hathaway and Monachesi (1963; see Appendix M) included both scales 5 and 0 and still the peaks on scale 9 were the most prevalent for males and were second only to scale 4 in the female tabulations. At the college level, 9 peaks are the most frequent high point in women and run second only to scale 5 in men. In the various deviant populations reported in Appendix M, scale 9, while always contributing a substantial proportion of high points, does not compete for the highest ranks. Sutton (1952) found that for psychiatric groups the most frequent low point in the codes was on scale 9.

Ratings by Others. Black reported that the normal college women with peak scores on scale 9 were seen by their peers as enterprising, energetic, persevering, and idealistic. This high activity level does not appear to be well controlled, however, because these women were also judged to be awkward and infantile, boastful and show-offs, selfish, self-centered, and inflexible. Similarly in their omissions the peer raters reflected the same theme. They did not characterize the high 9 girls as mature, loyal, or popular. These girls had few aesthetic interests, nor did they impress others as honest or peaceable. The raters also omitted the terms unself-controlled and seclusive to a significant degree.

Mello and Guthrie found that the college counselees with peak scores on scale 9 did not often show a hypomanic picture in their presenting complaints when seeking help. They were most frequently concerned with personal relationships stemming from problems in the local college setting. The men often showed concern over homosexual tendencies while the women were more preoccupied with their aggressive impulses. These counselees also described themselves as rebelling against dominant parents. In the course of treatment the high 9 students were resistant and irregular in attendance, and frequently terminated their therapy very early. Mello and Guthrie reported that the resistances took the form of intellectualization, changing the subject, and repetition of their problems in a stereotyped manner. They did not become dependent on the therapist but remained guarded and hostile in their relations with him.

Drake made the general observation that when 9 is the peak score in college counselees, other traits are expressed in a more energetic fashion than when the scale is low.

Self-Ratings. The women that Black studied gave a long list of descriptive terms in the checklists they completed on themselves. While most of these terms are socially favorable and self-enhancing, a few of them are quite critical. They said they were jealous, aggressive, and flattering. They omitted using such terms as reliable, generous, and clear-thinking to a significant degree. They viewed themselves (as did their peers) as enterprising and energetic, to which they added such terms as enthusiastic, decisive, self-confident, and sociable in the sense of mixing well. Whereas the peers of these girls perceived them as quite immature, the high 9 girls saw themselves as polished, sophisticated, poised, and worldly. They said they were independent and individualistic, not conventional or dependent. They appeared to deny inner tensions and discomfort by endorsing such terms as relaxed, peaceable, and contented, and by omitting such terms as indecisive and sensitive. They described their temperament as affectionate, good-tempered, laughterful, and natural. They saw themselves as self-controlled and popular, curious, with aesthetic interests, but not quiet, shy, or seclusive. They said they were adaptable, versatile, courageous, practical, not unrealistic, and not given to partiality.

See also the 9 prototype in the Gilberstadt and Duker *Handbook* (the basic defining characteristics of this pattern are given in Chapter 3).

91's

Guthrie reported that patients seen by a physician in general practice who presented this code type were all in acute distress. The symptoms revolved about the gastrointestinal tract, with symptoms in the upper levels predominating, although spastic bowel was noteworthy too. Archibald (1955) also found this pattern frequent in men with headache syndromes. Guthrie said that the patients with this pattern were seldom in a hypomanic state, but they were tense, restless, and ambitious. When seen by the physician they were frustrated by failure to reach their high levels of aspiration. It was quite easy to demonstrate the relationship between their hypochondriacal problems and the situational difficulties they faced, but these patients were reluctant to accept psychogenic formulations of their symptoms.

92's

See also the 29's above. Although an apparent psychological contradiction in the traditional interpretation of manic and depressive conditions as opposing ends of a single personality process, this combination occurs with some frequency in psychiatric practice. The combination usually appears at a time when the manic mechanisms are no longer effective either in keeping the environmental pressures from overwhelming the patient or in distracting him from his mounting depression. The pattern reflects serious illness especially when scale 9 exceeds the primed level. Hathaway and Meehl (1951b) also noted the occurrence of this pattern in patients with organic deterioration of the brain.

93's

See also the 39's above. The normal college women with this code studied by Black were described in generally unflattering terms by their acquaintances. While the judges said these girls were sophisticated, they also labeled them dishonest, boastful, arrogant, show-offs, self-centered, suspicious, and flattering. These raters also omitted to a significant degree such terms as honest, loyal, natural, and popular. They did not describe the 93 girls as moody, partial, or having wide interests.

In the long list of adjectives checked by these girls in their self-ratings, it is not possible to find any more self-critical terms than flattering and aggressive. They did not seem to sense the reaction they evoked in others, for they described themselves as popular, sociable, loyal, generous, and grateful. Although they said they were polished and poised (matching perhaps the sophisticated rating their peers gave), they also said they were affectionate, good-tempered, and reasonable, with wide interests. They described themselves as enterprising and energetic, courageous and adventurous, cheerful and laughterful, alert and lively, and self-confident. In some contrast to the terms indicative of high energy level and easy involvement in various activities, these girls also described themselves as peaceable, orderly, and contented, and significantly omitted such terms as moody and easily bored. They included the terms adaptable and practical, while leaving out such adjectives as dreamy and unrealistic.

94's

See also the 49's above. Guthrie noted that this group when seen by an internist did not present a homogeneous complaint picture, but rather showed general effects of tension and fatigue. These medical difficulties frequently followed quite clearly upon overactive and frankly hypomanic periods. The 94's showed poor family adjustment and had problems centering around their sexual adjustment. They did not stay in treatment long and therefore could be treated only superficially.

96's

See the 96 code type in the Marks and Seeman *Atlas* (the defining characteristics of this pattern are provided in Chapter 3).

98's

Black studied the ratings of normal college women with this code and found them described in somewhat unflattering terms both by their peers and by themselves. Other girls saw these women as thoughtful, idealistic, and persevering, but also described them as self-centered and infantile, boastful and fickle, unemotional and self-dissatisfied. They omitted to a significant degree such terms as high-strung and courageous.

In their self-descriptions, the 98 women said they were polished, relaxed, and thoughtful. They omitted the terms sensitive, dependent, selfish, and worrying. They also described themselves as secretive, eccentric, gloomy, and inarticulate. Although they said that they were courageous, they omitted such terms as frank, reasonable, and clear-thinking. They also omitted the description likes drinking.

Hathaway and Meehl (1951b) indicated that the 98 combination was usually restricted in their samples to the psychiatric population and that it implies a more malignant hypomanic picture than the 94 combination. Guthrie also found this to be the case in his group of medical patients. His patients gave histories of having periods of hyperactivity and then seeking medical help as their depressions came on. Their behavior showed some variation, but schizoid features were not prominent. Guthrie also noted that the F-scale elevation varied with the severity of their condition.

Data on this pattern also appear in the 89-98 pattern in the Marks and Seeman *Atlas* (see Chapter 3 for the defining characteristics of this pattern).

Low-Point 9's

Black found several characteristics for normal college women with their lowest score on scale 9. The acquaintances of these girls described them as quiet, seclusive, modest, conventional, and humble. They also omitted to a significant degree the terms sociable and lively, talkative and aggressive, self-confident and self-controlled, adventurous, affectionate, and frivolous.

In their self-ratings, the low-point 9 women endorsed the terms good-tempered, narrow interests, and unpopular. More significantly, they omitted from their self-descriptions a long series of terms, mostly quite socially favorable and self-enhancing. Although they avoided such unflattering descriptions as show offs, self-distrusting, and suspicious, they also denied a number of more acceptable trends. They did not say they were lively, energetic, enterprising, or versatile. Nor did they endorse natural, popular, sociable, polished, practical, grateful, or self-denying. Neither did they describe themselves as laughterful, relaxed, talkative, aggressive, adventurous, or having wide interests.

Drake has observed in college counseling cases that low 9 seems to function as an inhibitor scale and that the low 9 counselees tend to be rather phlegmatic, with their behavior traits not well defined.

Sutton (1952) sought to find psychological uniformities running through the records of low-point 9 women who had been seen in the psychiatric service of the University of Minnesota Hospitals. After using a modified cluster search method (see the discussion in Volume II), she identified a modal profile that comprised the basic MMPI features of 101 females with low-point 9 records. Using this modal profile, she then selected a criterion group of eighteen women whose MMPI scores were very close to this standard. This select group had a mean profile with the total code 2*371″846′/59 F-KL?. In their presenting complaints, background history, and prognosis it was not possible to differentiate this group from a general run of female psychiatric inpatients. These women were depressed, severely neurotic and upset, tense and anxious. Although the potentiality of suicide is frequently noted in cases with profiles like this, the women with low points on scale 9 showed a marked reduction in rated suicidal risk. Although the group as a whole could not be differentiated from general female psychiatric inpatients, Sutton did find some significant differences between subgroups of women with this classic profile, separated on the basis of the height of the elevation of scale 9. The women with the lowest scores on scale 9 were judged to be either mixed psychoneurotic or reactive depressive in their psychiatric illness, while the women with higher scores on scale 9 were diagnosed as involutional melancholic to a significantly greater degree. Although both of these groups showed considerable improvement in the hospital, sometimes improving to a remarkable extent, the women with the lowest scores on scale 9 showed a better prognosis than those with high scores, both for recovery from the immediate upset and for long-range adjustment after returning to their families. Pearson (1950) also noted the favorable prognostic implications of low 9 scores in cases with involutional melancholia.

High-Point 0's

Scale 0 was not included in early code frequency tabulations sufficiently often to enable workers to gain either an appreciation of its occurrence in various populations or substantial empirical data on its important personality correlates. The tabulations provided in Appendix M are not sufficient to establish very many trends. Hathaway and Monachesi (1963; see Tables 5 and 6 in Appendix M) found it was at about the middle rank for ninth-grade boys and girls, occurring most frequently in combination with scales 7 and 8. Panton (1959; see Tables 17 and 18 in Appendix M) found scale 0 near the bottom rank in frequency of high points on records from male and female prison inmates. Goulding (1951) reported that scale 0 was the most frequent low point in codes from male college students. Welsh and Andersen (1948) found that for male psychiatric and neurological patients in a Veterans Administration hospital scale 0 was the high point in less than 3 percent of the cases while it was the low point in more than one-third of the profiles. As a high point, scale 0 was most frequently paired with scales 2, 7, and 8. Scale 0 peaks when they did occur were associated with diagnoses of some form of psychoneurosis.

The most extensive report of the relationship of scale 0 peaks to various personality features comes from the originator of the scale, Lewis E. Drake. Most of these observations have been summarized in *An MMPI Codebook for Counselors* prepared in collaboration with E. R. Oetting (1959). Only a few of the patterns summarized there have been abstracted here and the interested reader is urged to consult the full report for many additional configurations.

02's

Drake and Oetting report that several manifestations of social withdrawal and insecurity are frequent in the case records of men with this profile who sought help in a college counseling center. They appeared unhappy and tense, worried a great deal, and complained of insomnia. They were introverted and socially insecure, and lacked effective social skills, particularly with members of the opposite sex. Women in their study showed essentially the same presenting picture, with additional evidence of depression, lack of self-confidence, and (when scale 1 was the low point) feelings of physical inferiority.

07's

The men in the counselee group studied by Drake and Oetting presented a depressed picture in that they were described as unhappy, tense, confused, worrying a great deal, and suffering insomnia. They were shy in the interview and gave the impression of being generally introverted and insecure. They were often characterized as nonresponsive or nonverbal. They were also markedly indecisive and had several conflict areas centering around their home life and their relationships with their mothers and siblings, as well as their effectiveness in relating to members of the opposite sex.

College women with this pattern seen by Drake and Oetting did not generally show this complete picture. Their problems centered about social insecurity, self-consciousness, and lack of confidence. They too had difficulties in relationships with the opposite sex, and occasionally had feelings of physical inferiority. When this high-point pattern was combined with a low point on scale 5, the rest of the features noted above for males with this code type appeared in the female counselees as well. That is, these women appeared nervous and indecisive, worried and anxious, and were notably shy in the interview. They also complained of insomnia, headaches, and exhaustion.

08's

The counselees seen by Drake and Oetting with this code type showed some of the same features as the 07's, but the men did not demonstrate the social insecurity to the same extent. Rather they gave evidence of worries, confusion, and insomnia. They were also indecisive and unhappy. The women showed the more complete pattern of nervousness, social insecurity, shyness, and self-consciousness. They had many areas of conflict, significantly shifting from a mother conflict to one with the father. Recurring in many of the reports was the comment that these female counselees were nonrelators. The women had serious problems, particularly noted when scale 5 was the low point in this pattern, and they usually came back to the center for a number of interviews.

Low-Point 0's

Drake found no consistent characteristic in a large number of college counselees with this pattern except that as contrasted with the total group the low 0's tended not to follow through with counseling appointments. Conspicuously absent from this group were problems relating to indecisiveness, unhappiness, and poor rapport.

CHAPTER 8. Profile Interpretation

SEVERAL good introductory-level guides to the interpretation of the MMPI are now available (Carkhuff, Barnette, and McCall, 1965; Carson, 1969; Cuadra and Reed, 1954; Drake and Oetting, 1959; Good and Brantner, 1961) as well as the Lanyon *Handbook of Group Profiles* (1968) and the codebook résumés of correlates (Marks and Seeman, 1963; Gilberstadt and Duker, 1965; Gilberstadt, 1970) which furnish a great deal of interpretive material on MMPI profile patterns. This chapter will take up some of the persistent problems inherent in drawing psychological inferences from sets of test data and some of the safeguards needed when interpreting the MMPI protocol which may help to keep these biases to a minimum. It will then take up some computer-based approaches to test interpretation and present a representative printout from each of the available services providing such profile interpretations now. While these samples cannot provide a basis for any comparative evaluation of their respective accuracies or dependabilities, the reader will be able to judge the level of test inference employed, the range of material covered, and the kind of recipient for which each is intended.

Biases in Clinical Inferences from Test Profiles

A number of persistent difficulties in drawing accurate inferences from sets of scores such as those provided by MMPI profiles have raised serious doubts about the feasibility of carrying out this kind of personological appraisal (see Breger, 1968; Greenspoon and Gersten, 1967; Levine, 1968; and Levy, 1963). For some clinicians, these objections and difficulties are sufficiently compelling to force them to abandon testing altogether. For others, the decision is instead to restrict psychological assessment efforts to the evaluation of rather narrow referral problems rather than to attempt the broad psychodynamic interpretations that pose so many unresolvable issues. For still others, however, the decision is made to resort to various automated systems, particularly systems based upon computer methods, to get around some of the human limitations in the traditional psychodiagnostic approaches. The various MMPI interpretation services using automated systems that are currently available will be discussed below but first it is important to review some of the problems and biases that have been noted in the usual clinical interpretations of test data.

Sets of inferences from any behavioral sample are no more than samples of the behavior of individual clinicians. As samples of spontaneous behavior, personality interpretations may suffer from a variety of biases. One of the most serious kinds of bias stems from interpretative stereotypes. It is difficult to individualize the report, to make sure that the personality statements are closely matched to the particular patient or client under evaluation. One of the strongest stereotypes is the one that includes all the personality features having the highest frequency of occurrence in the population from which the subject comes. This is the safe report that says only what is true about almost all the clients of a given agency. Tallent (1958) characterized this report as the "Aunt Fanny" report: any statement in the report could be countered by the assertion "So is my Aunt Fanny. So what?" These statements are trivially true; they contribute nothing. The assessment procedure need not be carried out since these sorts of things are known before the new behavior samples provided by the tests are drawn.

Another kind of assertion about personality related to the trivially true form is the untestable statement that comes from some test and can be evaluated only by means of the test. For example, in the use of the Rorschach test, an Erlebnistyp is said to be coarctated if both extratensive and introversive tendencies are constricted, but coartative when these tendencies are merely weak but not necessarily constricted. This distinction is based solely on the test findings and leads to little difference in interpretation beyond some intratest relationships. To be useful, test inferences must carry clear and cogent import for behavior outside of the test situation, preferably within the domain of interest of the agency in which the assessment is being conducted. These test-bound statements, cloaked in esoteric jargon and giving the impression of omniscience, serve only as prestige or status supports for the clinician. There is the additional danger in their usage that when finally identified for their true worth, they may create an undesirable impression of charlatanism and flimflam.

Another strong stereotype in clinical evaluations may come from the tendency to ignore important differences among test subjects and give essentially the same interpretation to each client. Often these write-ups take on easily identified features in phraseology, defense preference, or diagnostic labeling. Tallent calls this stereotype the "trademarked" report. In this kind of report it is likely that along with the tendency to overlook differences in clients the clinician will project his own problems, defenses, and attributes into his case write-ups.

While the usual report in clinical psychology does not end up in the hands of the patient or client, in those situations where the clinician knows this will happen or is likely to happen, the "Barnum" effect may appear. Tallent took this label from a project carried out by D. G. Paterson (in M. L. Blum and Balinsky, 1951) in which a single standard report was given to a variety of businessmen as if it were an individualized résumé of Paterson's observations and findings. Since the report contained a few unfavorable implications it was not completely a whitewashing of the individual, but each such criticism was quickly covered by conciliatory statements so that the end effect was a document of blandishments and praise. Paterson found that people almost invariably accepted the report as an accurate and insightful description of their own personality. Sundberg (1955) has studied this kind of acceptance of faked reports more systematically. The danger from this kind of bias entering the psychological report is clear, and the psychologist cannot be limited to assertions that the test subject, or any other recipient of the report, would like to hear.

An even greater difficulty in keeping the psychological report balanced is reflected in what Tallent described as the "prosecuting-attorney" write-up. That is, rather than leaning backward in an attempt to make the description favorable, the clinician does the opposite, restricting the inferences to those that are negative and unfavorable. When the patient is unlikely to see the report and when the agency function is to evaluate personality disorders, many psychologists concentrate their efforts upon a description of the symptoms, the degree of distress and disruption, the breakdown of defenses, and the limitations and liabilities that they see in the client. This material may certainly be helpful in the evaluation of the person as he is at the time, and the extent to which he needs and deserves treatment or protection. However, efforts toward rehabilitation will have to be based upon existing assets, the goals set in terms of capacities, the treatment program geared to current strengths.

All these considerations emphasize the need for balance and breadth of coverage in the clinical report. The psychologist carrying out an assessment should realize that much of the personality material that he covers in a report can be, and probably will be, discovered by the therapist in the course of his detailed work with the patient. The assessment procedures are worth the time, energy, and expense that they demand primarily because they provide the same information with about the same degree of dependability in a short time before the costly and drawn-out treatment. If blind alleys can be foreseen, if problems can be anticipated and avoided, if proper precautions can be instituted early as a result of accurate and efficient initial assessment, then the diagnostician's efforts will be worthwhile.

In this discussion of stereotypes, it should be made clear that not all stereotypes are undesirable. When they fit the test subject, they may be very efficient and useful. The biases described above, of overgenerality, uniformity, and restricted coverage, may enter psychological reports however they are generated; conversely they may be avoided even when highly standardized techniques are used. To the extent that MMPI differences mirror both valid and useful differences in personality status of the test subjects, to that extent "recipes" based on these MMPI configurations will covary in essential details with the important differences in the clients and patients studied. (See Meehl, 1956.) The usefulness of such "recipes" has been established by empirical data. The methods used in such studies and some of the preliminary results are described in Volume II.

Present-day interpretations of the MMPI depend heavily upon the individual skill and experience of the psychologist. The material summarized in previous chapters is intended to help psychologists make more extensive and more dependable linkages between test data and personality inferences. Most inferences in a psychological report do not rely upon test data directly, however, and this fact should be kept in mind at all times. Various key conceptions may arise from a test pattern, or from a case-history item, or from a background characteristic; many related inferences are drawn subsequently not from the test or the biographical datum but from the general formulation of personality processes (see Spielberger, 1957). It should be remembered that substantial knowledge about general personality concepts is needed over and above a basic understanding of the MMPI and its research literature before meaningful and useful interpretations can be drawn from the test. It is one of the major goals of many research workers who use the MMPI to shorten the chain of inferences from objective test data to personality conclusions, to make the linkages more numerous and substantial.

The MMPI is generally administered and interpreted in a setting in which other data are also available and can be incorporated into the chain of reasoning that the clinician follows. Kostlan (1954) has shown that even experienced workers with the MMPI need additional information to make the most accurate inferences possible from the test data, primarily the material in a social case history. L. K. Sines (1957) carried out a similar study with many more patients, employing a Q-sort procedure rather than a checklist of inferences. He confirmed Kostlan's finding that the MMPI used alone was inferior to a combination of the test and interview data when evaluated against case descriptions provided by the patients' therapists, and inferior to the information supplied them by the interview alone. However, the MMPI always added valid information to the various combinations he studied, while certain devices (notably the Rorschach) decreased the validity of inferences drawn from some kinds of data. The most important finding that Sines obtained is probably the fact that the individual clinicians differed in their skill in utilizing different kinds of data. It is to be expected therefore that some clinicians cannot draw as accurate or insightful conclusions about patients from the MMPI as others can, or as accurate as they themselves can from other kinds of data on that type of case. (See K. B. Little and Shneidman, 1959; Golden, 1964.)

Below are suggestions for ways in which some of these biases and distortions may be reduced in interpreting MMPI protocols and errors kept to a minimum. It should be clear from the discussion above, however, that some of these difficulties will always be present in psychological assessments.

Suggestions for Profile Interpretation

Check on Clerical Accuracy. Anyone can make errors of omission or commission in handling the MMPI materials—in recording items, applying stencils, noting raw scores, transferring data to profiles, transforming to T scores, drawing psychographs, or coding score patterns. Some persons, because of lack of clerical aptitude or proper motivation, make consistently more errors in this series of steps than others. The interpreter should learn to check his own work and double-check what others have done for him. Unfamiliar profiles should always be scrutinized. A simple inspection of the correspondence between raw scores and T-score entries should be the first step in profile evaluation. Some incongruity may require tracing back even further through the scoring steps.

Evaluate the Validity-Scale Configuration. The validity-scale values should be compared with what is already known about the person. In view of the test subject's education, socioeconomic level, geographical origins, and occupational history, does he show a proper understanding of the test instructions, does he deal with most of the items, has he exaggerated his problems or covered them up more than would be expected for this kind of person? Is there evidence of other difficulties that are not suggested by available information? What can be expected on the profile of clinical scores from the validity-scale values alone? Many of these points have been covered in the discussion of these scales in Chapters 4 and 5 and should be reviewed if necessary.

Determine the Configuration of Clinical Scales. Although the peak score on the profile may not always be reliably different from some other scale value or may actually be tied with one or more scales, the high point or high-point pair is the most common means of describing the pattern of scores in the clinical profile. The peak score is always determinable from the Welsh code and is usually available in the Hathaway code. Is this pattern consistent with the validity-scale configuration? If the pattern is complex, does the pattern of the validity scales indicate that one subpeak is any more important than the others in the present symptomatic status of the subject? Has some special set to answer a particular way led to any systematic distortion of the profile?

Some evidence on the effects of age and sex of patients upon the distribution of peaks in MMPI codes has been provided by Aaronson (1958), who used the subjects collected by Hathaway and Meehl in the *Atlas* (1951a). He showed that men tended to get code peaks on scales 1 and 7 significantly more than women while the women earned an undue number of peaks on scales 3 and 6. Age differences appeared equally striking, younger patients getting scale peaks on 4 and 8 while older test subjects received more high points on scales 1 and 2. These influences should be taken into consideration in using the base rates of any agency or institution.

The tables in Appendix M show the relative frequencies of different peaks, subpeaks, and high-point pairs in different clinical and normal populations. If the configuration on the profile under study is compared with these tabulations, this will provide information on the typicalness of the configuration that the subject is presenting. Chapter 7 provides some basis for judging what configurations are sufficiently similar to a given pattern to be interchangeable with it for general interpretative purposes. Many workers also routinely establish the low point of the profile and compare the cross-point description (high and low scales) with the tabled frequencies of cross-points from different populations provided by Hathaway and Meehl (1951a). Is the pattern a familiar and internally consistent one? Is the profile one that is usually obtained from a person this age, this sex, this well educated? What are the kinds of deviations?

Some initial qualitative interpretations can be found for the major configurations summarized in Chapter 7. These descriptions will also probably depend upon the elevation and slope. Both scale-by-scale and configural data will probably prove to be useful in arriving at a full interpretation of the clinical profile.

Allow for Elevation and Slope. The features of slope and elevation were described and some of the diagnostic implications were discussed in Chapter 7. Slope is based largely upon the relationships between the neurotic- and psychotic-scale groups. Positive slope is generally related to emotional disorders in which the person has limited control, poor contact with reality, or even disorientation and confusion. This is particularly true when the profile is generally elevated as well. Negative slope is more characteristic of acute emotional upsets involving anxiety, poor morale, and physical symptoms without frankly psychotic distortions. The height of the general elevation in the profiles with negative slope corresponds to the magnitude of the discomfort and distress the person is experiencing. Profiles that have essentially flat or zero slope with moderate to high elevations indicate emotional reactions that have recently come to be called borderline states. In these reactions many psychotic symptoms can be detected in the patient although frank psychotic disorders are not readily discerned.

The profile characteristics reflected in slope measures or in some of the qualitative designations of patterns (diphasic, double-spike, etc.) depend upon many more features than merely the high-point pairs or the designations of high and low points. Many of these profile features have not been incorporated into explicit profile-patterning systems. They are communicated informally from clinician to clinician and lack empirical evidence of their effectiveness or dependability. Many of these configural values will eventually find a place in the test literature as research is designed, executed, and published.

Apply Special Indices and Scoring Templates. Throughout the foregoing material, and in Volume II, numerous special scales, indices, ratios, or item clusters are mentioned that may help to clarify some puzzling profile feature, answer some special referral question, or aid in the prediction of some special kind of behavior or achievement. The nature of these questions will vary extensively from one clinical setting to another. Routine application of certain of these measures may prove to be highly desirable. Some of the most promising scales have been provided with T scores from the Minnesota normative group; these scales are tabulated in Appendix F for each sex separately. Most of these procedures are so specialized, however, that they should be reserved for occasions when the need for them arises.

Blind Interpretation of the MMPI on a Research Case

Since the most meaningful use of the test can be made only in conjunction with other pertinent data, the method of "blind" interpretation in which all other data have been withheld is *not* the most useful way to utilize the test. It does not do justice to the test or to the tester. On the other hand, as indicated earlier, it may be of value to use blind interpretations either as a training device for those learning profile interpretations or as a method of establishing limitations on the different kinds of things that can be legitimately inferred from the profile itself. It is for these latter reasons that a profile will be taken up in which an essentially blind interpretation is attempted. It is to be hoped that the reader will by this means be made more sensitive to the interpretative features of the profile and will be able to adapt some of the general principles described to the particular kinds of problems that he has to deal with in his own use of the MMPI.

In Figure 8-1 is presented the MMPI profile obtained from a thirty-four-year-old professional man who was referred as part of a comprehensive diagnostic evaluation at a major midwestern psychiatric center. He was married, had twenty years of education, and was seen as an outpatient.

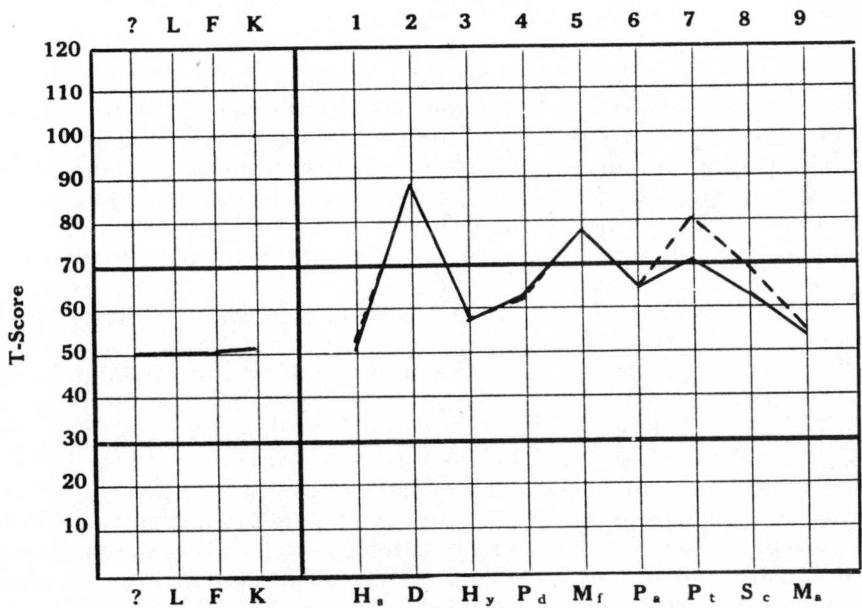

Figure 8-1. The uncorrected (solid line) and K-corrected (broken line) profiles of a thirty-four-year-old married professional man seen on an outpatient psychiatric referral. Uncorrected code = 2″57′0648–391/–?LF/. K-corrected code = 27″5′8064–391/–K?LF/.

Nothing else was known about this man at the time that the MMPI profile (without the answer sheet so that no additional scoring or item inspection was possible) was given to one of the authors of this volume (WGD) for a blind clinical interpretation. This experiment in blind interpretation of the MMPI profile was part of a larger study carried out by him in collaboration with P. S. Holzman and H. J. Schlesinger.

As can be seen in the report, each piece of identifying data available was also used in formulating the test inferences. Ordinarily a great deal more information of this kind is known; it can and should be utilized in tailoring the test-based indications to the particular case and the specific referral issues. A few of the test bases for the specific judgments are spelled out in the report but this material was not prepared specifically for tutorial purposes.

BLIND MMPI INTERPRETATION

Age: 34. Sex: M. Marital status: M. Education: 20 years. Status: Outpatient. Code: 27″5′80̲64–391/ –KLF/

Differential diagnostic issues: With this test pattern several alternative formulations must be considered. This man could be demonstrating a long-standing and severe obsessive-compulsive neurosis characterized by extreme dysphoria and suffering as well as crippling restrictions on his effectiveness and range of activities. The pattern is more consistent, however, with some acute disturbance. These reactions can stem from some depressive condition secondary to the loss of a loved one, to panic arising from facing new responsibilities, such as a promotion, new additions to the family, or a move to a new community, or, less likely, to some internal conflict over sexual adequacy or other masculine identification problems. Although he has probably always been shy and socially inhibited, the pattern does not strongly suggest any psychotic process at this time. Among the possible characterological disorders, the pattern is consistent to some extent with an alcoholic addiction or medication dependency. If this last alternative is supported by other findings, the difficulty is the sort that arises secondary to some chronic physical illness and would be fairly amenable to treatment; a marked character defect is not suggested. Among these various alternatives some reactive depression is the most likely possibility with favorable reaction to therapy to be anticipated.

Symptomatic status: All the indices of test-taking attitudes indicate that this man tried to comply fully with the instructions and describe himself as fully and completely as he was able. The usual defensiveness of a person with his educational background is not evident, suggesting that at this time he is being overly critical and rather hard on himself in these appraisals. Although this openness makes for easier evaluation of him, this same accessibility may reflect some loss of ego strength and ability at self-management. This would be one of several points of interest in future retesting of this man after treatment has been instituted.

At this time he appears to be highly tense, anxious, and agitated. He is markedly depressed and ruminative; some of his ideation may be frankly obsessive. He feels greatly overwhelmed and hopeless, with feelings of personal inadequacy and worthlessness. He is fearful of many things but particularly of loss of self-control, of failure to manage his affairs, and to protect and maintain his family. His worries and anxieties keep him from sleeping well and fatigue weighs heavily upon him. Although he does not appear to be a serious suicidal risk he is plagued by guilt and remorse, and finds his thoughts dwelling on death as one way in which his suffering could come to an end. Although he seems to have prided himself for many years on his independence and autonomy, he may have shown some childish emotional dependency during this period quite out of keeping with his usual self. This kind of breakdown has contributed to his guilt and self-depreciation. He appears to have good insight into the circumstances of his present adaptive difficulties and has been struggling to maintain control over his feelings and mood.

Prior history: This man is an idealist and perfectionist. In many matters he is rigid and stubborn. Although he can be hard on his family in demanding high ethical and moral behavior, he is even harder on himself. He is probably raising his own family in a way similar to his own background with strictness, excessive protectiveness, and emphasis upon duty and self-abnegation. He is apparently capable of love, compassion, and personal warmth, but often appears cold and aloof in withholding love for some violation of an ethical precept. When things go wrong, he is prone to blame himself, even for inadequacies in others. He takes his duties seriously and any new work demands constitute serious challenges to him to carry them out without help and without serious loss of efficiency. He is meticulous, precise, and often carps on minor details or side issues. In addition to a long-standing pattern of personal integrity and mature (perhaps overly mature) responsibility, he has some important conflicts over his sexual identification. He has some significant degree of feminine personality organization which makes full and adequate heterosexual expression difficult. These conflicts range beyond direct sexual potency or genital expression to include various expressions of dominance, self-assertiveness, or competitiveness.

He seems quite socially introverted and is probably seen by others as remote, bookish, and difficult to know. He is not a joiner or a participant in the usual round of social activities of his neighborhood or professional group. He is interested in his family and a few friends. His hobbies are likely to be solitary pursuits, such as collections, shopwork, or some artistic activity. These social patterns serve to keep to a minimum the challenges to his competencies and occasions upon which he would find himself put to the test in direct competition. Since he is not relying heavily upon self-deception or denial, it is out of keeping with his makeup to become heavily dependent upon drugs or alcohol or other crutches to bolster or preserve his self-esteem. Nor is he narcissistically or self-centeredly preoccupied with himself and his own satisfactions.

Treatment considerations: This man is sufficiently uncomfortable and distraught to have these tensions and anxieties interfere with psychotherapeutic efforts in the immediate future. If some psychopharmacological or physical treatment can be introduced to make him a little more comfortable and approachable, however, there are many features of the test pattern which indicate a favorable reaction to exploratory psychotherapy. In addition to the intellective ability suggested by his educational level, he appears to be reasonably integrated, able to care for and maintain himself, and to face his difficulties realistically. He is self-searching and introspective and can accept psychological explanations for his troubles. Although he has some concern at this time over the physiological signs of his anxiety and depression, he does not appear to be fixated upon physical symptoms or ill health. Although his depression is high enough now to produce some blocking or even retardation, if this is somewhat resolved he should have ready access to a great deal of his mental content and internal processes. He should also have the persistent self-discipline needed to work through a rather lengthy series of psychotherapeutic sessions.

The preceding report should be compared with what was learned about this patient from psychiatric interviews, previous medical records, physical examinations, and laboratory studies of him while he remained in the psychiatric center. His wife was also interviewed by a psychiatric social worker and the patient himself was administered a battery of individual tests and instruments that made up a routine psychological assessment battery in use in this center. The psychiatric résumé and the report of the psychological battery are both products of professional interchange and communication; although they are reported separately below they are not independent of one another. (Neither the staff psychologist nor the rest of the psychiatric team, however, knew the results of the MMPI administration.) Therefore, an additional report is presented in which another psychological staff member used the verbatim materials from the assessment battery to prepare a blind interpretation of the test results (less the MMPI). These three sources of information about the patient will serve to give the reader a general understanding of the man and his current difficulties and provide a framework within which to evaluate the accuracy of the blind MMPI interpretation and its contribution to the diagnostic formulation of this case.

PSYCHIATRIC RÉSUMÉ OF RESEARCH CASE

Male, age 34 — Outpatient

This ordained minister with five years of graduate study is currently teaching in religious education. He has a master's degree in religious education from an Ivy League school and has nearly completed his doctoral work. He has been married for ten years to a woman one year his senior. They have three sons, ages 5 to 9. Many items in his history are uncertain because of his marginal cooperation and premature departure from the center before the workup was fully complete.

The patient was born when his mother was in her early forties: "my pregnancy was a mistake—the discovery of my pregnancy was a catastrophe for her." He feels that she deeply resented the fact that he was not a girl, since a girl would not go away and leave her in her old age. His only sibling, a brother considerably older than the patient, was already breaking away from maternal controls at the time he was born. His brother is now a successful physician back in their hometown. His mother, now 76, is invalided in a rest home but still incurs the patient's anger and resentment. His father died over ten years ago at the age of 71. He considers his father to have been a "saint" for putting up with his mother's tirades and domineering behavior as patiently as he did.

This man sought an outpatient appointment on his own because weakness and pains in his legs and groin made walking any distance extremely difficult and he wanted "the best possible evaluation of his difficulties." He had already sought out medical and psychological treatment in the East and he arranged for reports from these workups to be sent to the center. In addition, he wrote a three-page personal statement enumerating ten points in his current situation and sent it ahead six weeks before his outpatient appointment. Most of the costs of the evaluation at the center were covered by the pension fund of the church organization.

The ten points in his personal statement focused upon his weakness and inability to walk more than a few hundred feet and elaborated upon his panic, as well as his efforts to get an accurate diagnosis and appropriate treatment. He also indicated feelings of numbness, dizziness, tension, discouragement over contradictory medical opinions, and failure to get any help. He entertained the possibility of a psychosomatic basis for his difficulties and had been seeing a clinical psychologist for treatment interviews during the spring. Less explicitly, the patient acknowledged "many burning problems which face me in regard to vocation, the church, personal identity problems, completion of graduate work, etc." He also indicated that "I have had moments of depression and deep concern with the future . . ." arising, he felt, from the medical studies taking so long and the time between weekly therapy sessions "weighed heavily upon me." He also noted how these difficulties added to his previous problems in personal identity, lack of security, fear of failure, and tension in entertaining visitors or in entering new situations. His wife also mentioned prominently his depression and general attitude that "he is existing merely to exist."

In the materials from the psychologist and the internist whom this patient had consulted, two other areas of difficulty were given special attention: difficulties in controlling homoerotic sexual impulses and a syphilitic infection incurred from one of these homosexual episodes about three years ago. Apparently the patient was inexperienced in either heterosexual or homosexual relations before his present marriage but many of his early sexual fantasies had centered upon his dressing up in his mother's clothing. At the time of his marriage, these fantasies shifted to the use of his wife's garments and he then began to engage in secret transvestite activities. Apparently, these activities gradually evolved into his leaving the house and soliciting homoerotic contacts while dressed in female clothing and wearing a wig. Several such excursions occurred during the spring of that year and on one of these occasions he was orally infected with syphilis while performing fellatio on one of these pickups. Early in the summer, he lost his position as associate pastor in a church and was offered a teaching post. Routine medical examinations required in this move brought the luetic infection to light but he does not appear to have sought full or proper treatment for the condition. He now refers to this episode as his having had "a touch of syphilis that produced a wakening of sorts." At this time he was finally able to tell his wife about his transvestism, his homosexual contacts, and his syphilitic infection. His wife seems to have been accepting of his sexual preferences and now enters into these sexual activities with him. She also has come to act out various sexual roles in which he suffers masochistic punishments. According to his report, the patient has not sought homosexual contacts since this time, although he acknowledged a strong desire for the sympathy and company of some other transvestite men who would be able to understand his needs and feelings. He also refrains from dressing up more often than every few months because he does not want to overtax his wife's patience.

The medical and neurological workup on this patient here revealed that his sensory functions were intact bilaterally but that several of his reflexes were more active on the left than on the right. He had difficulty standing or walking with his eyes closed, tending to deviate to the left. Loss of motor power to some extent in his left hand and wrist, with hypotonia in both his arms and legs. Atrophy and fasciculations in the tongue were noted, with loss of efficiency in rapid tongue manipulations. Mild paresis was found in the musculature of his neck and shoulders. In the light of this pattern of mild paresis, hyperreflexia, equilibratory ataxia, bilateral tongue atrophy and fasciculations, and hypotonia of the body and extremities, together with a history of positive blood serology, the diagnosis of neurosyphilis, meningiovascular form, was considered the most likely. Other syndromes also being considered were compression in the region of the foramen magnum from some craniovertebral disease or malformation. Additional X-ray and psychological studies were requested. A subsequent review of the findings from these additional studies led the neurologist to conclude: "I believe that the ailment which best explains his organic findings is meningiovascular syphilis." It was speculated that the penicillin courses given on two previous occasions may have merely served to reverse some of the laboratory indications of this disorder without reversing the clinical neurosyphilis. The original WAIS findings last spring yielded a 27-point discrepancy between the verbal IQ (125) and the performance IQ (98). Testing here with the W-B did not show such a large difference and only the Object Assembly subtest in the performance scale was suggestive of this degree of impairment, a score of 5. Administration of the neuropsychology battery did not reveal any gross intellective impairment indicative of cerebral pathology. Annual neurological reexaminations were strongly recommended to evaluate the further course of this patient's tertiary syphilis.

The choice of the ministry as a vocation was apparently dictated by this patient's mother rather than being a free decision by the patient himself. From the start he was assailed by anxieties over delivering sermons, meeting parishioners, and related duties in the church. The only enjoyable part of the work as associate pastor was his work with the young people in the congregation. The same ambivalences have developed over his studies in religious education and he is in deep conflict over the work of finishing his dissertation and final seminars. At first the teaching duties were a comfortable escape from the work with a congregation but recently this position has become strongly aversive as well: he is not kept busy enough, the work is still too unsettled and not sufficiently defined for him to get any sense of accomplishment out of it, and it currently has too much paper work. This fall, then, "I hated to go to my desk." He has tended to stay home and do his work there. However, he was able to take several trips during the summer and get to New England for a vacation. In August, when his wife went to join their boys at her parents' home and left him alone without a car, he became very angry with her for leaving him "stranded." During her absence he became more and more tense, restless, sleepless, and anxious.

Upon her return, he struck his wife once on the arm and told her she may as well take the boys and leave permanently because he was going to go to a state hospital. After this episode he initiated contact with the psychiatric center and arranged for the outpatient visit.

The patient was not fully cooperative during the workup, objecting particularly to the psychological examinations. (He did complete the MMPI, however.) His irritability was particularly noted, appearing when the interviewer or examiner would try to point out contradictions in his story or to test areas of denial. He was guarded and hyperalert throughout the examination. His great anxiety was apparent while his depression was somewhat more covert. Denial of all feeling or affect was maintained until he would suddenly lash out in irritation or anger. His anger toward his mother for what she had made him into and toward his wife for her having abandoned him during the summer were particularly noted. Thus, the patient's reality testing is seriously impaired at moments of pressure from strong, aggressive affect, at which time his previously rather weak capacity for reflection on himself completely disappears. Other attributes of ego strength, such as anxiety tolerance, impulse control, and gratifying sublimatory activity are all markedly deficient.

PSYCHOLOGICAL TEST REPORT

Tests Administered: Wechsler-Bellevue, Story Recall, Rorschach, BRL Sorting Test, Word Association Test, TAT, Bender VMG.

The patient stated in the early psychiatric interviews that he had received mixed medical opinions about weakness and pain in his legs and had decided to come to this psychiatric center for the best possible evaluation of his difficulty. In addition to his somatic difficulty he mentioned only dissatisfaction with his job as a source of psychic distress. His wife expressed considerable concern about depression, which he had not mentioned. He was very jovial during the testing and implied that he had little reason for such intensive psychiatric study. His manner of presenting himself was out of keeping with the fact that he had come halfway across the country for the two-week evaluation. Psychological testing was addressed initially to unraveling this disparity as a necessary step toward understanding the patient.

Often in the course of testing he made references to his liberal political views, his concerns for the rights of all men, and his life as a minister. These comments only hinted at the various reflections of grandiosity found in his test performance. His references to Jesus suggested a guiding fantasy of himself as a giver and healer. His contemptuous statements about a "flunky servant" and description of praise and punishment as "ways you deal with people or animals" suggested a sadistic sense of power and superiority. And his comments about a friend who had died in Selma, Alabama, his definition of hara-kiri as suicide done to further a cause, and his TAT story of Job, "a good man who suffered for no reason," add an element of martyrdom to his grandiose feelings. While he was superficially compliant throughout testing, there were numerous indications that he thought the rules of testing did not really apply to him. Frequently he set aside the tasks presented to him for the purpose of telling more about himself. Although he did not refuse to create percepts to the Rorschach stimuli, he arbitrarily delineated the areas of the inkblots to which he would respond—often responding negativistically by forming percepts out of the spaces around and within the inkblots rather than the inkblot areas themselves. Also, a majority of his responses were only weakly related to the formal properties of the stimuli since he made little effort to bring his fantasy into accord with the realities of the situation. Occasionally he grouped objects on the sorting test according to their usefulness to him. He indicated that he thought that sexual deprivation accompanying a woman's pregnancy would be an adequate reason for her husband to take a mistress. Thus, one would assume he is capable of disregarding society's conventions and other people's feelings in the same way he disregarded the implicit demands of testing. There were indications in the testing that he could be quite suspicious at times. He used the subtle shadings to delineate responses or parts of responses, though not frequently, and once spoke of the carvings of a totem pole which were present but could not quite be seen because they were hidden in the darkness of the interior of the inkblot.

There were a few hints of perverse sexual fantasy in the tests. These included two occurrences in which he either temporarily confused or reversed the sexual identity of TAT characters and one Rorschach percept of women's high-heeled shoes. The few manifestations of sexual disturbances in the tests suggest that his perverse sexual life is relatively nonconflictual for him. In contrast, there were numerous indications of a deep orally based disturbance. Even in the structured tests, his concerns that children may not be adequately cared for and his wish for a sense of inner fullness intruded into his answers. In addition, there was a Rorschach percept of a magic jar which one only had to rub to be granted one's wish, as well as several percepts of food and food-related objects. This imagery of oral fulfillment was matched by responses of vicious oral-aggressive animals. One would be inclined to see his grandiose image of himself as a giver and healer to be a reaction against a deeper sense of himself as a grasping, empty person. The omnipotence which is a part of the grandiosity seems to be also a derivative of fantasies of oral fulfillment emanating from a magic, all-gratifying object.

In most of his test performance he demonstrated a capacity for clear, well-organized thought. There were indications of compulsivity such as attempts to be overly precise in answers to questions or to group all the possible objects which might legitimately belong into a given category. His thinking was noticeably limited, however, in that he allowed himself little freedom of imagination. Thus, although he achieved a Superior IQ (verbal IQ 122–125, performance IQ 118–124, full-scale IQ 122–126), his Rorschach percepts were of pedestrian content (many insects, land areas, maps) and generally unembellished and poorly articulated. Also, his stories to TAT pictures were brief and frequently trite. On those tests more specifically designed to measure skills which are impaired by organic damage there were indications of mild, diffuse impairment. This seemed chronic and did not constitute a major element of his psychopathology.

In contrast to this picture of good thought organization and careful control, there occurred in the testing a few indications of formal thought disorder. Some of these were only hints of underlying pathology such as peculiar ways of phrasing statements (he said an eye and an ear are "sensory parts of the body") or unexpected temporary marked lapses in attention. Others, however, were quite severe. For example, in telling how an egg and a seed are alike his thinking was intruded by the notion that a seed must first die in order that a plant may live and grow. Also, in delineating one Rorschach percept of a sitting human he described arms, head, and lungs and only became aware of the peculiarity of seeing external structures and inner anatomy in such a relationship when the examiner asked how he could see the lungs from outside. Such a lapse of reality testing is severe and indicates a potential for temporary lapses into quite deviant thinking. It is likely that these would be associated primarily with ideas of grandiosity.

There were several indications in the test that he maintains a rigid and at best tenuous control over affects. He attempted to isolate affective experience from the rest of his life in order not to be overwhelmed by it. However, at times in spite of such attempts he is an unwilling host to angry affects which he cannot integrate into the rest of his experience. It seemed, from his pattern of handling affects and anxiety stimulated by the inkblots, that he would flee from situations of stress if free to do so. In addition, he denied the impact of the anxiety-stimulating inkblots by saying he did not respond to the textures of the shaded cards even after giving such textured images as animal hides. The impact was noticeable in his reactions as well as in the content of his responses. On the most heavily shaded inkblot he was unable to give a response for nearly a full minute. The denial of texture seemed so blatant it appeared that he could not admit any feelings of anxiety or vulnerability when he was experiencing them.

His most extreme denial was directed against depression. In this effort he even responded to the bright whiteness of the spaces within the inkblots and gave Rorschach percepts of frivolous Playboy bunnies. The denial was not adequate to stem the tide of despair. Even the faces of the Playboy bunnies took on the appearance of hollow-eyed sadness. Often he referred to the depressive blackness of the monochromatic cards, once describing a card as "foreboding." Some of his stories to TAT pictures were of people filled with sadness. When the examiner asked if such themes and responses reflected his own feelings he maintained that they did not—except that he occasionally became discouraged because of his somatic difficulties. He mentioned on another occasion that he had thought his family would be better off with him out of the way. This statement, in the context of his feelings of grand martyrdom and his current state of despair, has an ominous ring to it.

Summary: There were numerous indications that the patient maintains a grandiose sense of himself as an all-powerful healer and martyr. He seemed quite capable of disregarding rules and conventions as well as other people's feelings in his efforts to meet his own needs. The fact that there were few indications of sexual concerns or perversion in the tests suggested that his sexual deviations are relatively nonconflictual parts of his character. There were instead numerous indications of a deeper, orally based disturbance. There were a few indications of a formal thought disorder consistent with temporary lapses into quite deviant thinking. His control over affects is rigid and, at best, tenuous. His tolerance for frustration and anxiety seemed quite limited. He used extreme denial to ward off feelings of depression but was not successful. His feelings of martyrdom when coupled with the depression set the stage for a possible suicide.

BLIND TEST REPORT BASED ON THE ASSESSMENT BATTERY

Intellectual functioning: The patient's full-scale IQ is 122, his verbal IQ 122, and performance IQ 118, all approximately within the superior range of intelligence. The patterning of scores and the quality of his verbalizations suggest a compulsive personality organization that is under strain. He attempts to be precise and complete, but these efforts are coupled with considerable self-doubt. Conspicuous unproductive ruminative activity is present. He is concerned about the intactness of his memory, although there is no objective evidence for any memory impairment. There are signs of subtle confusion in his forced productivity. The confusion partly reflects a misfiring of obsessive meticulousness and overworked hairsplitting. This is discernible in a fuzziness in his thinking, particularly in abstracting. The confusion is also discernible in occasional word-finding difficulty and in word misusages (for example, "typographic" for "topographic"). He also shows an inappropriate redundancy in his speech (a "shore coast"). An occasional inappropriate fabulized combination on the Rorschach and some near-contamination responses add to the picture of periodic confusional periods. Although a prominent break with reality is not likely, for there is general intactness of intellectual functions, there probably are episodes of archaic, primitive experiences which are not particularly distressing to him. These may take the form of quasi-delusional preoccupations, inappropriately fixed ideas, or feeling too much external influence on him.

Defensive factors: The process of decompensation shows itself in weakened isolation and displacement defenses and in prominence of denial and projective defenses. Inferential reasoning is conspicuous although not extreme. Self-doubt, indecisiveness, and periods of unproductive rumination are likely. There is also a somatic concern, the significance of which is difficult to judge. On the object-assembly subtest of the Wechsler performance is strikingly impaired. The lowered score, however, does not reflect motor retardation, but rather impaired recognition of patterns having to do with body parts. The significance of the integrity of his body would seem to bear some investigating and probing. Some of the pattern recognition impairment on the object-assembly test can be attributed to thinking rigidity, and would therefore be consistent with the projective trends noted earlier. But there is some further evidence of pattern recognition difficulty in his reproduction of the Bender-Gestalt designs. The extreme drop of object assembly coupled with the subtle copying errors on the Bender Visual Motor Gestalt test would suggest a possible neurological involvement and therefore calls for further neurological examinations. Depressive moods taking the form of feelings of deprivation, an acute sense of loss and separation, a feeling of being hemmed in (reflecting the prominence of projection), all seem to be a part of the patient's experience. The depression seems to be confined to subjective experience and does not extend to a motor retardation as one would expect to see in clinical depressions. A reactive addictive potential is present.

Interpersonal relations: The patient's approach to people is cautious and tentative. There is little flexibility in his relationships and he seems constantly to be testing out what is expected of him. There is a noteworthy passive trend which he tries to deny to himself by forced rebelliousness and displays of independence. Anger, disdain, and contrariness are conspicuous, but these stem not from any conviction about causes and ideals.

They rather stem from a struggle against his passivity. He typically tries to fit his responses to his perceptions and expectations of the demands of people. Although he tries to appear courageous and outspoken, actually timidity and tentativeness are characteristic. Nevertheless, these struggles against passivity could lead him into battle with authority figures.

His sexual adjustment would appear to be disturbed. There is evidence of a strong homoerotic conflict. His aggressive impulses are handled by projection, resulting in a fear of external attacks. Loyalty to his wife reflects more expectation of his "duty" than strong bonds of affection. Aggressive impulses toward his children are probably close to consciousness. There is evidence of strong but fluctuating superego pressures—a sense of duty which is easily set aside, followed by remorse, shame, and self-loathing. Religious preoccupations are evident in his responses. Psychological-mindedness and reflectiveness are quite limited. One would judge him to be a poor candidate for expressive psychotherapy.

Diagnostic summary: The tests suggest a state of decompensation of obsessive-compulsive defenses with prominent projection of aggressive impulses and denial of passivity. A homoerotic conflict is significant. Feelings of depression may be a conspicuous complaint. There is suggestive evidence of some neurological involvement.

From the information in these reports there emerges a constellation of basic personological features and current emotional and organic disturbances. A bright, experienced religious educator who is socially ill at ease, obsessional, and insecure, with rigid standards of duty and obligation, is deeply conflicted about strong feminine identification, passivity and dependency, secret transvestite and homoerotic activities, as well as numerous professional and vocational dislocations. He had finally acted upon his homoerotic impulses and been infected with syphilis. He was apparently unable to face up to the full implications of this infection and get the proper series of treatment needed to avert the development of tertiary complications in the central nervous system. There is the distinct possibility that his pain, periodic mental confusion, walking difficulties, and some of the mental status characteristics may be attributable to this luetic process. When he discovered he had syphilis, however, he did find the courage to admit his sexual deviations and practices to his wife and work out a new accommodation with her. Their sexual relations from that time often took on role playing involving sex reversal with guilt and punishment themes. These new patterns are only engaged in at widely spaced intervals, however, and they do not seem to gratify all his sexual needs. He has had difficulty completing his graduate studies and the research to get his doctoral degree and he shows many other signs of vocational maladjustment. At the present time, he is anxious, deeply depressed, guilt-ridden, and possibly suicidal. He feels unworthy, unfulfilled, and obsessed with his many problems. He feels that his wife may abandon him and that he may be losing control and is facing possible psychiatric commitment.

How many of these salient features of this man were identified with the MMPI? How many of them are the kinds of things that the MMPI has been designed to evaluate? How adequate was the interpretation of the test data? Could the MMPI have been better utilized in a context of more information about the man and his present difficulties? These are some of the questions that must be raised in evaluating the clinical interpretation of a test like the MMPI and, by extension, must also be raised about some of the automated methods of profile interpretation. Although some suggestive leads can be obtained from examination of the interpretations provided on a single case (particularly a complicated and challenging case like this one) it should be obvious that little can be documented in this way about the general level of accuracy of the MMPI, the over-all suitability of blind interpretations on all kinds of clinical cases, or the comparative validity of different automated interpretive methods.

In this case, for example, the tertiary syphilis and any lesions it may have produced in the patient's central nervous system cannot reasonably be expected to be revealed in some aspect of the basic MMPI profile. On the other hand, the jovial cover which the patient presented over his serious depression is the kind of attribute which either the test pattern should reveal as a frequent correlate or the test interpreter should have been able to deduce from the data presented but which he failed to note. There was on balance a rather good congruence between the blind description of his presenting clinical status and the reported characteristics. The anxiety, depression, social introversion, guilt, and obsessive-compulsive trends were all noted, as was some struggle with passivity and femininity. His vocational dislocation and possible suicidal preoccupation were also noted. Not mentioned, in addition to his smiling depression, were the suspiciousness, the self-view of a martyr, and the grandiosity suggested in the psychological report from the routine test battery. There were some items that were clearly at odds in the two sets of interpretations: one, the extent to which the person was seen as struggling with and remorseful over his sexual transgressions or was relatively unaffected by these self-insights and impulses and, two, the degree of grandiosity or omnipotence which he was deemed to be manifesting in these activities.

There were also some general features of this man's longer ranging personality patterns which were reflected in the blind interpretation concerning his upbringing, social relationships, character, and religious commitments. Femininity, passivity, and inferiority feelings have apparently been basic features of his personality and self-concept over the years, as suggested by the MMPI interpretation. His reliance upon intellectualization, self-blame, and excessively high personal standards has also been noteworthy and was included in the blind interpretation. It is difficult to tell from the available evidence whether his martyr image has been a longstanding aspect of his relationships with others or is a recent (and ominously pathological trend in light of the possible paresis) development now as his career, family life, and health have all begun to disintegrate. From the MMPI evidence one would tend to believe the latter, from the staff psychologist's report the former.

From such comparisons, then, it is possible to see what kinds of material the MMPI may be suitable for and what kinds of clinical assessments must be obtained from other sources in a battery of intellective, personological, and neuropsychological instruments. It is also interesting to note that the two blind interpretations (the MMPI-based one and the reinterpretation of the data from the assessment battery) seem to be in closer agreement, at least in those areas in which the MMPI-based report ventured some opinions, than the two reports based upon the same test data. One crucial difference, in addition to the obvious one that the staff psychologist knew the referral issues and much of the background history of this man, is the opportunity to see the person and interact with him over an extended period for several hours on two different days. The personal impression formed in such a contact may be influenced, for better or worse, by the person's style to such an extent that it colors the interpretation of data, errors, slips, and other features of the patient's performance in a very pervasive way.

Comparison of Automated Interpretations of the Research Case

Computerization of the interpretive process involving psychometric data has proceeded rapidly in the last few years. Seen as a natural extension of the cookbook notion of clinical inference introduced by Meehl (1956) and the codebooks that rapidly followed Halbower's pioneering efforts (1955) at deriving accurate actuarial sets of descriptors for MMPI patterns, the computer-based interpretive services have already been able to alleviate some of the manpower shortages that have afflicted mental-health services in the last several decades. The available services differ importantly, however, one from another in the kinds of interpretations provided, the professional clients that they are intended to serve, and the costs that they involve. Their operations have also raised fundamental questions about validity, reliability, suitability, and even ethical safeguards and client protection. Some of these issues will be taken up below.

To furnish specific illustrations of the printouts of the various computer-based systems already in operation at this time, the authors sent the MMPI protocol (completed on the appropriate answer sheet for each service) on the research case that was described above to each installation as a routine referral. As noted in Chapter 3 in the discussion of machine scoring of the MMPI, some discrepancies were found in the raw scores on the basic MMPI scales that were reported back from these interpretive services. They will be noted below in the discussion of each service but it is clear that this kind of error can offset to some extent the inherent reliability of the subsequent interpretive steps of the computer program. As suggested by Fowler and Coyle (1968c), these discrepancies may arise in part because some scoring systems employ the answers given to one of the repeated items when it is first presented and others score the answer given to its second appearance. Any lack of consistency in the individual's performance on those sixteen items is bound to generate some disparities in the raw-score totals obtained by the different scoring approaches. These differences in the scoring stencils being used in the ordinary scoring steps do not seem to account for all the discrepancies that were encountered in this comparison, however, and it is interesting to note that Fowler and Coyle found apparent diurnal vagaries in some scoring services that they studied. Further disparities also arise in the printouts reported below in the transformation of raw scores to T scores. Since many of the computer rules are based upon absolute T-score values or upon coding of T-score patterns, these differences can also affect the content of the final printouts.

The automated systems now operating differ importantly in the level of the psychological analysis of the MMPI that is provided the user of the service. Thus, the pioneering computer-based system, the Mayo Clinic Automated MMPI Program, was designed by Pearson, Swenson, and Rome (see Pearson et al., 1965, 1967) to provide a psychiatric screening evaluation for a number of medical services in the medical center. It concentrates upon present symptomatology and emotional status with relatively little attention to aspects of the case that would be more central to the concerns of the psychiatrist or the psychotherapist. Within the range of interests of the psychiatrist or the clinical psychologist, as opposed to those outside the range of mental-health specialists, there are also recognizable levels in the details and analysis of the test data. Some services provide a general consultation report while others range much more widely in developing a rather comprehensive psychodynamic formulation and reconstruction of the client's personality. The latter presentation presumably would be most useful to a psychotherapist as he begins a rather extended regime of treatment with the individual. In the presentations below, therefore, we have divided the reports into screening level, consultative level, and psychodynamic formulation level printouts. In addition, there is the complicated question raised by Finney (1969) of a report prepared for the test subject himself. Several of the other services give a specific recommendation against showing the printouts to the client or patient. This question will be more fully discussed at the end of this chapter.

Screening-Level Reports. The Psychological Corporation, through the National Computer Systems of Minneapolis, Minnesota, provides a nationwide service of MMPI interpretation based upon the Mayo Clinic program which was formerly only available to patients and staff of the Mayo Clinic. The report on the research case described in the previous section which was received from the NCS computer is reproduced below. An identical report could be prepared by any trained clerk from the materials that are summarized in Marks and Seeman (1963), Appendixes E and F, once the MMPI protocol has been scored and the standard profile drawn. These materials are also given in Tables 2 and 3 of Pearson and Swenson (1967). There is, of course, an obvious advantage to any large-scale user of the MMPI in having the interpretive service provide these writeups with a minimum of human error and effort. In the report from the NCS service, a psychogram (oriented horizontally) is provided in which the computer prints a short bar at the appropriate level in each scale row. (The user can draw lines connecting these marks to generate a profile for the validity and the clinical scales.)

NCS (MAYO) MMPI ANALYSIS

Sex: Male. Education: 20. Age: 34. Marital Status: Married. Outpatient.
MMPI Code: 27″5′80̲64–391/ –K̲L̲F̲/

D 2 Severely depressed, worrying, indecisive, and pessimistic
Pt 7 Rigid and meticulous. Worrisome and apprehensive. Dissatisfied with social relationships. Probably very religious and moralistic
MfM 5 Probably sensitive and idealistic with high esthetic, cultural, and artistic interests
Sc 8 Tends toward abstract interests such as science, philosophy, and religion
Si 0 Probably retiring and shy in social situations
Pa 6 Sensitive. Alive to opinions of others
Pd 4 Independent or mildly nonconformist
Hy 3
Ma 9 Normal energy and activity level
Hs 1 Number of physical symptoms and concern about bodily functions fairly typical for clinic patients
Consider psychiatric evaluation

In this instance, the scale-by-scale designation of the patient's presenting picture appears to be quite accurate. There are few if any errors of commission; what is described is accurate as far as it goes. Most glaring, perhaps, is the absence of any indication of this man's serious sexual deviation. Perhaps some indication should have been included about his control, particularly the suicidal possibilities. Nevertheless, the severity of his depression is noted and the need for psychiatric attention is explicit. Also very appropriately, his lack of hypochondriacal trends is noted so that the internist or neurologist receiving such a report should have been strengthened in his determination to check out thoroughly any physical basis for the pains, weakness, and ambulatory difficulties which he reported. In the light of the paranoid trends noted by the staff psychologist above, perhaps the interpretation of the Pa level here is an underweighting of this trend (as was true in the blind interpretation of this record as well). It is interesting that some of the implications of the profile spelled out in this listing range beyond current symptomatic status.

In 1967, Hovey and Lewis published a profile analysis schema which resembles the hand-applied materials of the Mayo Clinic program that were cited above. That is, after the MMPI protocol has been scored and profiled a trained clerk can proceed through the Semiautomatic Interpretation tables and generate a report of the clinical implications of the profile by typing off appropriate entries from their library of statements. They propose that the schema be applied to records from male patients only and do not recommend that it be used in a completely routinized fashion. Rather, they suggest that the decisions about the alternative phrases from the library of statements be made by a trained clinician who is in the best position to note possible contradictions, grossly inappropriate judgments, or other material that is inapplicable to a particular case. Nevertheless, this set of procedures possesses many of the assets of a computer-based system in providing systematic coverage of possible interpretations, readily available memory storage, minimization of clinician trademark statements, and reduction of clinician time and energy expenditure. The result of applying the Hovey-Lewis system to the profile from our research case is reported below.

HOVEY-LEWIS: SEMIAUTOMATIC INTERPRETATION OF RESEARCH CASE

Male, age 34 Outpatient

The following personality traits have been shown to have some associations with MMPI profiles of the type produced by this examinee:

XV May have significant psychiatric problems
9 Shy, easy fatigability, somewhat withdrawn; over-critical of self, moody; somewhat sorrowful, unhappy; secretive
13 Obsessive trends; self-punishing, contains anger; very anxious and depressed, probable feelings of worthlessness and sinfulness, agitated
103 Dysphoric, worrying, pessimistic
107 Sensitive, tends to emphasize esthetic interests; dependent, submissive; seems to feel insecure over his own masculine role; tends to identify with females; rather strong feminine identification
109 Dissatisfied with social relationships; ruminative, may be preoccupied with religion; rigid
201 Relatively alert, responsible, cheerful; capable, relatively free from neurotic inhibitions and overevaluation of self and own problems; regarded as warm and wholesome; not overly concerned about adverse reactions of others; tactful, little concern about own health
332 Prone to worry
338 Conscientious
363 Tends to use imagination in problem solving

Comparison of the Hovey-Lewis product with the NCS printout reveals some striking similarities and a few important differences. They both tend to concentrate upon current emotional status; both in fact describe this man in quite similar terms. Both emphasize his need for psychiatric attention. Although the Hovey-Lewis material does not suggest homoerotic or transvestite difficulties directly, it is more emphatic and forceful in spelling out the femininity and personality inversion. It does not mention suicidal preoccupations either but many of the descriptors convey this kind of implication.

In its longer series of statements, the Hovey-Lewis schema tends to encounter the problem of internal contradictions. One instance arises here in statements 9, 13, and 103 where the subject is described in terms of depression and dysphoria while in statement 201 he is characterized as cheerful. There is, therefore, on the face of it a psychological contradiction; the report as it stands describes him both ways. In the recommended usage of these tables, the clinician at this point would have to exercise his judgment. He could, for example, exclude statement 201 and have the typist proceed to statements 201a, b, c, and d which constitute the rest of the paragraph. In this instance, however, he might decide to retain statement 201 with some appropriate modifying or qualifying disclaimer, such as "superficially," "to outward appearances," or "upon brief contact." If so, in this particular case, the report would have been accurate and would have avoided one of the notable omissions that was found in the blind MMPI interpretation reported earlier in the chapter.

Finney has been developing a computer-based interpretive system for a number of psychological devices (1966; 1967) including automatic processing of the MMPI. He now has this system operational in the Finney Institute for the Study of Human Behavior, Inc., in Lexington, Kentucky. The Finney-Auvenshine interpretive schema used in their psychodiagnostic consultation service is set up to deliver seven kinds of reports or interpretations at different levels of analysis or for different kinds of recipients (Finney, 1969; Karmel, 1970). One of these levels corresponds to the screening level being considered here, the report which they propose be used by physicians and surgeons. Their report on the research case is reproduced below.

FINNEY-AUVENSHINE: REPORT FOR PHYSICIANS AND SURGEONS

Male, age 34

This is a report for physicians and surgeons. It is sent only to fully qualified and licensed physicians.

This is a professional consultation by Dr. Joseph C. Finney, a psychiatrist and psychologist.

Analysis of this kind can be done from any of several psychological tests. In this case, the test answered and submitted for analysis was the Minnesota Multiphasic Personality Inventory

He does not give a consistently favorable nor a consistently unfavorable picture of himself. He tells us some good things and some bad things about himself.

He is a somewhat insecure person. He is a rather compliant person. He usually goes along with the rules, and he usually goes along with other people's wishes. He is a steady person. He uses self-control. He is cautious and careful. He has some tendency to make enemies. He becomes irritated, suspicious, and resentful at times.

At his best he is serious, quiet, peaceful, conscientious, well behaved, obedient, and sentimental.

He is not at all the sort of person that gets bodily symptoms to symbolize his emotional conflicts without organic cause.

He is not at all mentally ill: that is, not at all psychotic. He shows no tendency toward psychosis at all.

He is dependent in a passive way.

He is ethical enough. He generally deals fairly with people, and generally respects their rights well enough.

Diagnostic impression. Categorizing a patient with a diagnostic judgment must never be done from the results of psychological tests alone, nor from the reports of other laboratory tests alone. In making your diagnostic assessment of this patient, you will rely on the careful history that you have taken, and on the shrewd observations that you have made of the patient's behavior in the interview.

Insofar as we can judge from the analysis of the psychological testing alone, the diagnostic label most likely to fit the patient best is:

307. Situational stress reaction (adjustment reaction).

Other diagnostic labels that may be worth considering are as follows:

301.81 Personality trait disorder, neurotic personality trends, with elements of passive-aggressive personality, passive dependent type, and with obsessive-compulsive and depressive features.

301.0 Personality pattern disorder, paranoid personality.

300.4 Psychoneurosis, depressive reaction.

300.3 Psychoneurosis, obsessive-compulsive.

300.0 Psychoneurosis, anxiety reaction.

300.2 Psychoneurosis, phobic reaction.

318. No diagnosable psychological condition.

This report differs from the previous two in a number of ways. It is organized in paragraphic form and is compiled by assembling paragraphs rather than phrases. This format is quite characteristic of the remaining computerized reports presented in this chapter. This organization provides greater readability, interest, and familiarity since it makes the computer printout more like traditional psychodiagnostic reports but it simultaneously raises the risk of contradictions and even psychological nonsense to an important level. For the Finney-Auvenshine system, this paragraphic format provides opportunities for ingratiating statements to the recipients, for documenting the programmers' professional qualifications, and for a routine evaluation of the protocol validity of the MMPI record under consideration. This latter kind of warning is included in the NCS and Hovey-Lewis schema only when some special question of the validity-scale values is presented.

The content of this report is in general accord with the two other reports at this level; although it is longer it does not in fact cover very much more detail. It is noteworthy that it specifically disclaims the possibility of a psychotic process at this time in this man's case (although the paranoid trend is noted among the alternatives listed under the diagnostic impressions). Another noteworthy difference is the placement of the case into some category or other of the schema advanced by the revised *Diagnostic and Statistical Manual* (DSM-II) of the American Psychiatric Association. Finney, Smith, Skeeters, and Auvenshine (1970) present some supporting data on the relative accuracy of such diagnostic recommendations in the Finney-Auvenshine processing of MMPI records from a sample of recent admissions to a state hospital. Although the placement is sufficiently accurate to achieve statistically stable results in these comparisons between computer-based placement and staff diagnoses, the errors are sufficiently high at this time to make the inclusion of the disclaimer in their printout quite appropriate. One further note: it will be of interest to compare the content and format of the report for general practitioners to the coverage provided in reports for other professionals which are presented below on this same case.

Consultative-Level Reports. Somewhat more ambitious endeavors than the early screening or problem-identifying approaches to MMPI automated reports are the programs which generate consultative interpretations of the test profile in the sense of the term consultation as used by Tallent (1963) or the term interpretation as used by Levy (1963). The intent is to provide a more detailed analysis of the test data in professional language appropriate to a communication between colleagues. In other words, if a psychologist or psychiatrist who was relatively unfamiliar with MMPI patterns or interpretations were to present a test record to a professional who was more knowledgeable about these matters and ask him what he thought it might indicate about his client or patient, he would hope to receive, either orally or in writing, a coherent set of judgments about the test subject's personality and emotional status couched in terms with which he was generally familiar and focused upon particular differential diagnostic, therapeutic, or dispositional decisions. The printouts from these interpretive programs have been tailored to these ends with a relatively restricted range of recipients in view and rather specific decisions under consideration. These services have also been restricted to users with appropriate professional qualifications.

The Roche Psychiatric Service Institute of Nutley, New Jersey, established a routine interpretive service to provide reports of this level to psychiatrists and clinical psychologists in private practice. (Recently, this service has been made available to properly qualified physicians in general practice as well, and extensions to specific institutional populations and other mental-health agencies are being developed.) The basic interpretive program was developed by Fowler (Fowler, 1967, 1968, 1969a, 1969b; Fowler and Marlowe, 1968) primarily from extensive materials and investigations at the University of Alabama and the Computational Center at Redstone Arsenal.

In the work of developing the nonprofit Roche Psychiatric Service Institute operations, the staff sought clarification of a number of ethical and professional problems with the ethics committees of the American Psychological Association and the American Psychiatric Association. The resulting guidelines (Fowler, 1966a) have served a constructive purpose in all these rapidly developing operations and services. At issue, in addition to the professional qualifications of the subscribers who are eligible for such a test interpretation service, are matters of anonymity of the test subject, constant monitoring of quality control and elimination of errors in scoring and case identification, as well as continuing efforts to improve the usefulness and validity of the content of the printouts themselves.

Below is reproduced the report from the Roche Psychiatric Service Institute on the research case used in all the other sample reports. In addition to the materials presented here, the RPSI report includes a psychogram showing the profile of basic validity- and clinical-scale values on the case. The computer enters an X at the appropriate level in each scale column; the user may connect these points to generate the familiar MMPI profiles for the two sets of scores.

ROCHE PSYCHIATRIC SERVICE INSTITUTE MMPI REPORT

Age: 34 Male

The test results of this patient appeared to be valid. He seems to have made an effort to answer the items truthfully and to follow the instructions accurately. To some extent, this may be regarded as a favorable prognostic sign since it indicates that he is capable of following instructions and able to respond relevantly and truthfully to personal inquiry.

This patient shows a personality pattern which occurs frequently among persons who seek psychiatric treatment. Feelings of inadequacy, sexual conflict and rigidity are accompanied by a loss of efficiency, initiative and self-confidence. Insomnia is likely to occur along with chronic anxiety, fatigue, and tension. He may have suicidal thoughts. In the clinical picture, depression is a dominant feature. Psychiatric patients with this pattern are likely to be diagnosed as depressives or anxiety reactions. The basic characteristics are resistant to change and will tend to remain stable with time. Among medical patients with this pattern, a large number are seriously depressed, and others show some depression, along with fatigue and exhaustion. There are few spontaneous recoveries, although the intensity of the symptoms may be cyclic.

There are some unusual qualities in this patient's thinking which may represent an original or inventive orientation or perhaps some schizoid tendencies. Further information would be required to make this determination.

He shows undue sensitiveness and suspicion of those around him. He may tend to misinterpret the motivation of others, leading to difficulties in his interpersonal relationships.

He appears to be an idealistic, inner-directed person who may be seen as quite socially perceptive and sensitive to interpersonal interactions. His interest patterns are quite different from those of the average male. In a person with a broad educational and personal background this is to be expected, and may reflect such characteristics as self-awareness, concern with social issues, and an ability to communicate ideas clearly and effectively. In some men, however, the same interest pattern may reflect a rejection of masculinity accompanied by a relatively passive, effeminate, non-competitive personality.

This person may be hesitant to become involved in social relationships. He is sensitive, reserved, and somewhat uneasy, especially in new and unfamiliar situations. He may compensate by unusual conscientiousness in his work and other responsibilities.

Some aspects of this patient's test pattern are somewhat similar to those of psychiatric patients. Appropriate professional evaluation is recommended.

Note: Although not a substitute for the clinician's professional judgment and skill, the MMPI can be a useful adjunct in the diagnosis and management of emotional disorders. The report is for professional use only and should not be shown or released to the patient.

It is apparent that a report of this kind undertakes a more ambitious task than the reports discussed in the previous section. While the concentration is still upon clinical status, the content ranges more broadly over previous conditions and possible origins of the current problems. Each of the RSPI reports begins with a description of the protocol validity and the probable dependability of the test interpretations. Each also includes a

Roche Psychiatric Service Institute Scale Scores for MMPI

Scale	?	L	F	K	Hs	D	Hy	Pd	Mf	Pa	Pt	Sc	Ma	Si
Raw	1	4	3	13	5	33	21	19	35	13	25	19	16	42
K-C	1	4	3	13	12	33	21	24	35	13	38	32	19	42
T-C	OK	50	50	51	52	89	58	62	78	65	81	69	55	69

Scale	ES	MT	A	R	LB	CA	DY	DO	RE	PR	ST	CN	SO	SO-R
Raw	38	23	20	22	9	18	31	15	21	8	20	29	64	27
T-C	40	81	60	63	49	66	63	51	52	43	55	61	39	31

Critical Items

These test items, which were answered in the direction indicated, may require further investigation by the clinician. The clinician is cautioned, however, against overinterpretation of isolated responses.

182 I am afraid of losing my mind. (True)
74 I often wish I were a girl. (True)
133 I have never indulged in any unusual sex practices. (False)
179 I am worried about sex matters. (True)
302 I have never been in trouble because of my sex behavior. (False)

caution against either reliance exclusively upon such an assessment for the whole diagnostic workup or the casual handing-over of the report to the client or patient without preparing him for the content or language or without concern for the possible threat which such interpretations are likely to pose for him. In addition, the instructions and guides provided the users of this service contain additional injunctions and recommendations about the filing and storage of these reports after getting them back from RPSI.

The content of this report is quite accurate in what is stated about this particular case. It highlights his depressive state, his acute difficulties, and the long-standing social and sexual problems which he has faced over the years. Homoerotic practices and transvestite activities are not directly mentioned but the femininity, sexual conflicts, and dependency are probably made sufficiently explicit to alert the recipient to problems of this kind. It is interesting that the paranoid and schizoid features noted by the staff psychologist in his report are explicitly introduced in this report. The critical items (see Appendix G) which the RPSI report prints out routinely when endorsed in the significant direction by the test subject also help in this instance to focus the reader's attention on such problems. It is noteworthy that this interpretation specifically raises the question of suicidal preoccupations.

There are still many debatable questions inherent in the development and use of reports at this consultative level. If the subject's name is included on the answer sheet that is sent to the service for processing there is a possible risk, then or later, that the individual may be identified as a psychiatric patient or client of some other mental-health professional and subjected to slander, blackmail, or other unscrupulous treatment since the service usually retains the answer sheet. This is explicitly avoided in the

RPSI procedures since all transactions with the subscribers and their clients are carried out by means of code numbers. Although this probably eliminates the possibility of comparisons between various retests of the same client, this safeguard which RPSI has introduced seems to be an important component of ethical practice.

Another rather controversial issue involves the reporting of the content of the critical items and the direction of answering in the routine report. Many clinicians feel that it is impossible to tell what may have led a person to answer a given item in one particular way and that many different interpretations are possible of what the client was saying when he endorsed the item the way that he did. There is real danger that the interpretation that the clinician may put upon the answer is not isomorphic with the semantics of the client's interpretation. The caution included in the RPSI report, therefore, seems to be necessary. The clinical utility that such material may have seems well illustrated in this research case; it is to be hoped that in such routine use the general precautions will be observed and the risk of misinterpretations reduced to an acceptable level of error.

The RPSI report includes raw scores and T scores for a number of special clinical scales and research measures (see the listings in Appendix I of Volume II) in addition to the basic MMPI scales. These are all scaled on the basis of the Minnesota normal men and women. Recently, the report has also started to include the Welsh code for the profile pattern of the basic scales.

The staff of the RPSI have been publishing evaluations of the general utility and acceptability of this form of report based upon feedback from their users (Roche Laboratories, 1968; Webb, Miller, and Fowler, 1969, 1970) as well as upon descriptions of the kinds of clients being evaluated in this service (Webb, 1970a, 1970b). Validation of the content of such reports involves all the issues of validational research on personality tests, scales, and indices, plus the difficulties of semantic meaning and complexities of human communication. The program is under constant revision and review by the staff of RPSI and by its developer, Raymond D. Fowler.

A report of about the same level of analysis is available from the Institute of Clinical Analysis in Los Angeles, California, based upon a computerized program developed by Dunlop (1966). The research case was sent to the ICA for routine processing; the report is reproduced below.

INSTITUTE OF CLINICAL ANALYSIS

Male, age 34
Multiphasic Index (MI) = 101 = Moderate elevation
Probability of significant disturbance: 95%

Two separate and distinct methods of appraising emotional conflict are shown on scores above. Either score may suggest a disorder but clinical significance is greater when both scores are elevated.

MI interpretation: The MI, Multiphasic Index, reflects an emotional disorder of moderate to marked severity. There seems to be great difficulty maintaining autonomous function.

Summary: This person shows a significant degree of emotional disorder. The dynamics shown place this protocol in an uncertain diagnostic classification.

The subject is strongly signalling psychologic problems. Coping ability appears inadequate and defenses are down.

Validity: The patient presents a somewhat self-critical picture with a tendency to underestimate potential assets.

Personality description: A combination of depressive and obsessive reactions markedly interferes with performance. The subject usually cannot understand any reason for being plagued by these disorders. Manifestations include one or more of the following: unwanted thoughts, feelings or urges; vague physical complaints; incessant doubt and negativism; compulsive acts, sometimes associated with morbid gratification such as kleptomania, etc. Typically, these subjects complain of feeling miserable and often are preoccupied with religion, guilt and morals. Although exacting and rigid in certain respects, behavior may be contrastingly opposite in other areas. There is much inconsistency. Usually unable to escape mental ruminations, they show pervasive dissatisfaction, worry, apprehension, and inflexibility.

Suggestions to improve coping:

1. Therapy with subjects incapacitated by obsessional trends is notoriously difficult despite initial improvement. They require many return visits and repeated reassurances.

2. Encourage a re-evaluation of stringent morality in relation to modern concepts of normal channels of male and female aggression. There is a need to develop a greater feeling of spontaneity and individuality.

Special coping problems: Over-aggressiveness tends to offend an esthetic nature; sensitive, artistic, and intellective. There is considerable rejection of physical aggression.

Patient's positive traits are described as: sensitive, conscientious, permissive, peaceable, perfectionistic, self-reflective, and compliant toward authority.

Diagnostic impression (pattern resemblance to clinical cases): Obsessive-compulsive reaction.

Symptom review (critical item number marked by asterisk):

Anxiety: moderate autonomic concomitants.

Phobias and obsessions: phobias are moderately indicated.

Depression: a significant degree of depression is signalled.

Intropunitive: there is admission of some feelings of guilt, regret, or unworthiness.

Hostility: somewhat irritable or tense.

Hyperactivity: considerable agitated or restless. Mood swings. Euphoric episodes. Dysphoric episodes.

Sexual disturbance: the responses suggest further inquiry. See critical item section for specific items.

*74 I have often wished I were a girl. (True)

*133 I have never indulged in any unusual sex practices. (False)

*302 I have never been in trouble because of my sex behavior. (False)

Unusual thoughts and experiences:

*182 I am afraid of losing my mind. (True)

Dreams: frequently, recurrent.

Defense mechanisms: obsessive-compulsive.
Somatic expression: paraesthesia.

Computerized Technical Data Score Pages

The scores printed on this page are primarily used for research. Although the printed report interprets their numerous and complex combinations, the clinician may wish to study the nature of each score – for this purpose refer to the MMPI-ICA reference guide, which is available on request. The scores are listed in raw-score form unless specified as T scores.

Index or Scale		Score	Norm
AI	Anxiety index	127	50
IR	Internalization ratio	1.27	1.00
A-R	Anxiety-repression ratio		
	A factor – T score	60	45 to 54
	R factor – T score	63	45 to 54
Es	Ego strength – T score	40	60 or more
TR	Contradictory response	3	3 or less
F–K	Dissimulation index	–10	–12 to +8
Ds	Dissimulation scale	12	35 or less
Mp	Positive malingering	12	19 or less
Cn	Control	29	22 to 30
Ed	Ego defensiveness	40	45 to 65
FNF	Critical items	4	3 or less
At	Manifest anxiety	24	14 or less
Lb	Low back	9	10 or less
Rg	Rigidity defense	8	3 to 6
Dy	Manifest dependency	31	19 or less
Do	Social dominance	15	19 or more

Relative Elevation of Clinical Scales

Hs-1 low	D-2 marked	Hy-3 normal	Pd-4 mild
Mf-5 moderate	Pa-6 mild	Pt-7 moderate	Sc-8 mild
	Ma-9 normal	Si-0 moderate	

Obvious-Subtle Responses of Clinical Scales (T scores)

DO-91	HyO-60	PdO-67	PaO-49	MaO-60
DS-61	HyS-48	PdS-48	PaS-72	MaS-46

Note – Normal T-score range for obvious and subtle scales is usually considered between 40 and 60. Scores above or below this range increase probability of abnormal traits for the scale in question.

The report comes in a special cover which focuses the recipient's attention upon the test subject's name (no numerical coding is used), the recipient of the report, and one of the two global severity-of-disturbance measures that lead off this report, the Multiphasic Index. Although this MI has been mentioned in published materials, no indication of the component variables in this index has been provided for the general MMPI worker. Interpretive ranges for the MI are provided on the jacket of the ICA report. In addition, an analogy to the thermometer is carried out next to the table of MI values with the suggestion that the MI be used as a gauge to the test subject's emotional temperature. The probability of significant disturbance (based upon unspecified MMPI indicators) is also offered as another comparable gauge of global adjustment.

The inside of the report cover provides the user with a guide on how to use the report and the various scores and indices that are included. These are largely grouped together on the page of Computerized Technical Data and contain many of the same supplementary data included in the RPSI report. Most of these scores and indices are given in Chapter 3 or in Appendix I of Volume II. The report ends with a profile on which the T-score levels have been marked by X designations at the appropriate place in the scale columns; these can be connected by lines to form the usual two profiles for validity and clinical scales. The profile is unusual in that it marks out a silhouette of the normal range of deviation of T scores on each of the basic scales, in terms of their respective errors of measurement.

The content of this report is quite similar to the RPSI report; there are a few noteworthy differences, however. The test subject here is described as rather overcritical of himself while the RPSI report says he neither denies nor exaggerates about himself. The RPSI description would probably be most accurate about the meaning of such a configuration of the validity indicators for the general run of clinical cases; in this instance, however, the subject seems to be more self-critical than most men at his socioeconomic level (see the blind interpretation above). Presumably the phrase "morbid gratification" could be extended to cover this man's transvestite role playing and homoerotic promiscuity, but the femininity characteristic of this pattern is here interpreted largely in terms of masculine aggressiveness and assertiveness. In this regard, it is noteworthy that this ICA report offers the recipient some general suggestions about case management including advice that this man be brought to understand the more modern freedom about expression of aggression. In the light of his episode of striking his wife after she had returned from a visit with their children to her parents' home, such a recommendation may not be appropriate or constructive. Or perhaps it should be couched more in terms of self-acceptance than action.

Like the RPSI report, the ICA printout includes the content of the critical items which the test subject has endorsed. It is puzzling, however, that one of the critical items is missing in this list (no. 179); it is not one of the duplicated items so the omission cannot be explained by differences in item keying among the booklet numbers. In the ICA report, the content of the critical items is employed to call attention to or bolster particular trends that are interpreted from the profile rather than simply listing them for the user's own interpretive utilization.

The ICA report explicitly includes the advice not to show the report to the test subject but has not yet incorporated the protection provided by coding the subject's name so that only the clinician himself will know who is under study in this evaluation. Like the RPSI, the answer sheet for the MMPI is retained by ICA. The report is sent in duplicate in case the recipient wants to file the report in some more general case record as well as his own personal case file, or wants to send a copy of the report along with a referral to some specialist, therapist, or agency.

There are several versions of the Finney-Auvenshine printout which seem to be designed to provide a consultative level of interpretation. Although only one of them is directly comparable to the RPSI and ICA reports in terms of its intended recipients, all these reports are presented here to provide the reader with an opportunity to see some of the problems raised by the different professional backgrounds and qualifications of various potential recipients of computerized reports and their abilities to use the information and to understand the inherent limitations in this kind of clinical material.

In addition to a report for psychiatrists or clinical psychologists there are Finney-Auvenshine reports for counselors or case workers, for correctional counselors, and for industrial psychologists. Although this man is obviously the sort of person who is most likely to show up in the office of a psychiatrist or clinical psychologist in the course of dealing with his personal problems, it is not too wide a stretch of the imagination to believe that he might have appeared for vocational guidance or counseling somewhere and it is entirely possible, had he been arrested in female garb while engaged in homosexual activities in a public lavatory, that he might have been seen by a correctional counselor. What is not so easy to determine is whether he would have given this particular set of MMPI answers in each of those various testing settings. If not, the presenting picture would have been changed and the reports to these various professionals would have been altered in some possibly important ways. Nevertheless, had he completed the MMPI this way in his workup by these various mental-health workers and had they been subscribing to the Finney-Auvenshine service, they would have received the following descriptions of this man from this computerized program.

FINNEY-AUVENSHINE: SHORT REPORT FOR PSYCHIATRISTS AND CLINICAL PSYCHOLOGISTS

Male, age 34

This is a short clinical report for psychodiagnosis. It is sent only to psychiatrists and clinical psychologists. A more detailed form of report is also available, if you prefer.

This is a professional consultation by Dr. Joseph C. Finney, a psychiatrist and psychologist.

Analysis of this kind can be done from any of several psychological tests. In this case, the test answered and submitted for analysis was the Minnesota Multiphasic Personality Inventory.

He does not give a consistently favorable nor a consistently unfavorable picture of himself. He tells us some good things and some bad things about himself.

His personality makeup is not truly typical of patients seen by psychiatrists and clinical psychologists, but neither is it unusual for that group.

He is a compliant and unaggressive person. He generally goes along with what other people want, and does whatever the other people tell him he is supposed to do. He is known as an obedient and submissive person. If a conflict arises, he yields, and he gives in to the other party. He would rather give in than have a quarrel. He is undemanding and unaggressive.

He is one of those people that tend to view certain others as foes. Things that certain people do often seem to irritate him, annoy him, arouse his resentment, or make him angry. He may feel that the other party is doing wrong to him, treating him unjustly or unfairly. He sees the other party as an enemy.

He seems about as free from distress as the average person. In general, he does things to advance himself and not to defeat himself. He is fairly successful in life, and he is reasonably satisfied with the world.

He is fairly consistent and predictable. Yet he is moderately spontaneous and flexible, and he is not a rigid person.

At his best he is serious, quiet, peaceful, conscientious, well behaved, obedient, and sentimental.

But when a situation puts pressure on him, he is likely to worry and brood about things. He blames himself. He gets discouraged, unhappy, tense and tired, and he has trouble sleeping.

He is not at all mentally ill: that is, not at all psychotic. He shows no tendency toward psychosis at all.

He is ethical enough. He generally deals fairly with people, and generally respects their rights well enough.

Diagnostic impression. Categorizing a patient with a diagnostic judgment must never be done from the results of psychological tests alone, nor from the reports of other laboratory tests alone. In making your diagnostic assessment of this patient, you will rely on the careful history that you have taken, and on the shrewd observations that you have made of the patient's behavior in the interview.

Insofar as we can judge from the analysis of the psychological testing alone, the diagnostic label most likely to fit the patient best is:

307. Situational stress reaction (adjustment reaction).

Other diagnostic labels that may be worth considering are as follows:

301.81 Personality trait disorder, neurotic personality trends, with elements of passive-aggressive personality, passive dependent type, and with obsessive-compulsive and depressive features.

301.0 Personality pattern disorder, paranoid personality.

300.4 Psychoneurosis, depressive reaction.

300.3 Psychoneurosis, obsessive-compulsive.

300.0 Psychoneurosis, anxiety reaction.

300.2 Psychoneurosis, phobic reaction.

318. No diagnosable psychological condition.

He is not a candidate for intensive psychotherapy of the kind that aims at self-understanding.

He may be able to make use of social casework or counseling.

FINNEY-AUVENSHINE: REPORT FOR COUNSELORS AND CASEWORKERS

Male, age 34

This is a report for counselors and caseworkers.

This is a professional consultation by Joseph C. Finney and Charles Dwight Auvenshine, psychologists.

Analysis of this kind can be done from any of several psychological tests.

In this case, the test answered and submitted for analysis was the Minnesota Multiphasic Personality Inventory.

He does not give a consistently favorable nor a consistently unfavorable picture of himself. He tells us some good things and some bad things about himself.

He is a compliant and unaggressive person. He generally goes along with what other people want, and does whatever the other people tell him he is supposed to do. He is known as an obedient and submissive person. If a conflict arises, he yields, and he gives in to the other party. He would rather give in than have a quarrel. He is undemanding and unaggressive.

He is one of those people that tend to view certain others as foes. Things that certain people do often seem to irritate him, annoy him, arouse his resentment, or make him angry. He may feel that the other party is doing wrong to him unjustly or unfairly. He sees the other party as an enemy.

He seems about as free from distress as the average person. In general he does things to advance himself and not to defeat himself. He is fairly successful in life, and he is reasonably satisfied with the world.

He is fairly consistent and predictable. Yet he is moderately spontaneous and flexible, and he is not a rigid person.

At his best he is serious, quiet, peaceful, conscientious, well behaved, obedient, and sentimental.

He is the kind of person who sometimes trusts people too much and sometimes is too suspicious of people. He keeps alert for signs of what people are trying to do. He keeps searching for clues. As he screens his information, he can be highly sensitive to certain signs.

Unhappily, he may use the clues only to reinforce the beliefs that he already has. The problem is that he may be very sharp at seeing the things he's watching for, and may fail to see things he's not looking for. He can be keen and perceptive in identifying the clues that he sees, but because he loses appreciation of the context, he may get a slanted view of things.

He is dependent in a passive way.

In general, he is a person who does harm to himself, and does not do harm to other people. In other words, he is highly intrapunitive. If there is one thing that stands out about him it is this: he takes things out on himself much more than he takes things out on other people. This is something he needs to think about seriously. He is the sort of person who hates to hurt other people and would rather be hurt, himself. In his dealings with people, he keeps putting himself at a disadvantage. He lets people take advantage of him. And they do. Sometimes he may be seriously damaged by it, in one way or another. When trouble arises, he takes care not to let it hurt the other person. He lets it hurt him, instead, perhaps without knowing that he is causing his own troubles. In fairness to himself, he needs to call a halt to this business. He needs to decide what he wants from life; and then take realistic steps toward getting it.

He is ethical enough. He generally deals fairly with people, and generally respects their rights well enough.

Socially, he is somewhat introverted. He hesitates to speak out. He is cautious and shy with people. He is not very sociable. He may feel awkward in groups of people. His behavior is rather passive. He lets people influence him. He is rather hesitant and restrained, and not very sophisticated. He doesn't express himself very well. He is unsure what to do, and he keeps vacillating indecisively. He usually holds himself aloof from big parties and noisy crowds, especially those of a frankly pleasure-seeking aim, or those with public display of emotion, or with likelihood of rough behavior. With individuals he can relax, unbend, and find pleasure according to his own rules, but he is loath to do so in a crowd. He is not psychologically minded. He is simple in his approach to people. He takes people at their face value, without probing for hidden motives.

Let us consider how he stands in the personal qualities that have to do with success in the world of work.

Since he is 34 years old, he must already have chosen a career and worked in it. But if he is thinking of taking a new job, or of making some changes in his life work, it may be up to you, as his counselor, to help him consider how his personality jibes with the requirements of the various kinds of jobs that may be open to him.

He has good, normal ability to do work. He can do as well as any average, normal person in most kinds of work. He does well enough in the personal qualities that make for success at work. Of course, some kinds of working situations fit him better than others.

His strongest point, the one that can help him the most to succeed in his work, is his ability to keep his emotions from interfering with the teamwork that is needed in a competitive job. His approach to his work is realistic and practical. He harnesses his energies and directs his efforts to the task at hand, without letting personal resentments interfere. This is a real strength. He can do very well in a job that calls on him to control his personal feelings and focus his attention on the practical tasks of getting a job done by teamwork, in a competitive situation.

Another strong point that can help him in his work is his self-reliance in his work, and ability to use good judgment about it.

You will be wise to help him choose a line of work that calls on his strong points. In the right line of work, and in the right working conditions and setting, people will appreciate him for his best qualities.

One of his weak points, something that may handicap him in his work, is some lack of initiative, dominance, and leadership.

You will be wise to help him choose a line of work that doesn't demand so much along those lines.

He may be able to make use of social casework or counseling.

FINNEY-AUVENSHINE: REPORT FOR CORRECTIONAL COUNSELORS

Male, age 34

This is a report for correctional counselors, including probation and parole officers and caseworkers in correctional institutions.

This is a professional consultation by Joseph C. Finney and Charles Dwight Auvenshine, psychologists.

Analysis of this kind can be done from any of several psychological tests. In this case, the test answered and submitted for analysis was the Minnesota Multiphastic Personality Inventory.

He does not give a consistently favorable nor a consistently unfavorable picture of himself. He tells us some good things and some bad things about himself.

He is a compliant and unaggressive person. He generally goes along with what other people want, and does whatever the other people tell him he is supposed to do. He is known as an obedient and submissive person. If a conflict arises, he yields, and he gives in to the other party. He would rather give in than have a quarrel. He is undemanding and unaggressive.

He is one of those people that tend to view certain others as foes. Things that certain people do often seem to irritate him, annoy him, arouse his resentment, or make him angry. He may feel that the other party is doing wrong to him, treating him unjustly or unfairly. He sees the other party as an enemy.

He seems about as free from distress as the average person. In general he does things to advance himself and not to defeat himself. He is fairly successful in life, and he is reasonably satisfied with the world.

He is fairly consistent and predictable. Yet he is moderately spontaneous and flexible, and he is not a rigid person.

At his best he is serious, quiet, peaceful, conscientious, well behaved, obedient, and sentimental.

He is not very likely to escape.

He is unlikely to violate his parole.

In general, he is a person who does harm to himself, and does not do harm to other people. In other words, he is highly intrapunitive. If there is one thing that stands out about him it is this: he takes things out on himself much more than he takes things out on other people. This is something he needs to think about seriously. He is the sort of person who hates to hurt other people and would rather be hurt, himself. In his dealings with people, he keeps putting himself at a disadvantage. He lets people take advantage of him. And they do. Sometimes he may be seriously damaged by it, in one way or another. When trouble arises, he takes care not to let it hurt the other person. He lets it hurt him, instead, perhaps without knowing that he is causing his own troubles. In fairness to himself, he needs to call a halt to this business. He needs to decide what he wants from life; and then take realistic steps toward getting it.

He is ethical enough. He generally deals fairly with people, and generally respects their rights well enough.

Let us consider how he stands in the personal qualities that have to do with success in the world of work.

Since he is 34 years old, he must already have chosen a career and worked in it. But if he is thinking of taking a new job, or of making some changes in his life work, it may be up to you, as his counselor, to help him consider how his personality jibes with the requirements of the various kinds of jobs that may be open to him.

He has good, normal ability to do work. He can do as well as any average, normal person in most kinds of work.

His strongest point, the one that can help him the most to succeed in his work, is his ability to keep his emotions from interfering with the teamwork that is needed in a competitive job. This is a real strength. He can do very well in a job that calls on him to control his personal feelings and focus his attention on the practical tasks of getting a job done by teamwork, in a competitive situation.

You will be wise to help him choose a line of work that calls on his strong points. In the right line of work, and in the right working conditions and setting, people will appreciate him for his best qualities.

One of his weak points, something that may handicap him in his work, is some lack of initiative, dominance, and leadership.

You will be wise to help him choose a line of work that doesn't demand so much along those lines.

He may be able to make use of social casework or counseling.

If it is readily available, he may be given some form of group or individual counseling.

His counseling prediction score is 105.

FINNEY-AUVENSHINE: REPORT FOR INDUSTRIAL PSYCHOLOGISTS

Male, age 34

This is a report for industrial psychologists and personnel counselors.

This is a professional consultation by Joseph C. Finney and Charles Dwight Auvenshine, psychologists.

Analysis of this kind can be done from any of several psychological tests. In this case, the test answered and submitted for analysis was the Minnesota Multiphasic Personality Inventory.

He does not give a consistently favorable nor a consistently unfavorable picture of himself. He tells us some good things and some bad things about himself.

He is a somewhat insecure person. He is a rather compliant person. He usually goes along with the rules, and he usually goes along with other people's wishes. He is a steady person. He uses self-control. He is cautious and careful. He has some tendency to make enemies. He becomes irritated, suspicious, and resentful at times.

At his best he is serious, quiet, peaceful, conscientious, well behaved, obedient, and sentimental.

In general, he is a person who does harm to himself, and does not do harm to other people. In other words, he is highly intrapunitive. If there is one thing that stands out about him it is this: he takes things out on himself much more than he takes things out on other people. This is something he needs to think about seriously.

He is ethical enough. He generally deals fairly with people, and generally respects their rights well enough.

Socially, he is somewhat introverted. He hesitates to speak out. He is cautious and shy with people. He is not very sociable. He may feel awkward in groups of people. His behavior is rather passive. He lets people influence him. He is rather hesitant and restrained, and not very sophisticated. He doesn't express himself very well. He is unsure what to do, and he keeps vacillating indecisively. He usually holds himself aloof from big parties and noisy crowds, especially those of a frankly pleasure-seeking aim, or those with public display of emotion, or with likelihood of rough behavior. With individuals he can relax, unbend, and find pleasure according to his own rules, but he is loath to do so in a crowd. He is not psychologically minded. He is simple in his approach to people. He takes people at their face value, without probing for hidden motives.

Let us consider how he stands in the personal qualities that have to do with success in the world of work.

Since he is 34 years old, he must already have chosen a career and worked in it. But if he is thinking of taking a new job, or of making some changes in his life work, it may be up to you, as his counselor, to help him consider how his personality jibes with the requirements of the various kinds of jobs that may be open to him.

He has good, normal ability to do work. He can do as well as any average, normal person in most kinds of work. He does well enough in the personal qualities that make for success at work. Of course, some kinds of working situations fit him better than others.

His strongest point, the one that can help him the most to succeed in his work, is his ability to keep his emotions from interfering with the teamwork that is needed in a competitive job. His approach to his work is realistic and practical. He harnesses his energies and directs his efforts to the task at hand, without letting personal resentments interfere. This is a real strength. He can do very well in a job that calls on him to control his personal feelings and focus his attention on the practical tasks of getting a job done by teamwork, in a competitive situation.

Another strong point that can help him in his work is his self-reliance in his work, and ability to use good judgment about it.

You will be wise to help him choose a line of work that calls on his strong points. In the right line of work, and in the right working conditions and setting, people will appreciate him for his best qualities.

One of his weak points, something that may handicap him in his work, is some lack of initiative, dominance, and leadership. He is no better than average in leadership ability.

You will be wise to help him choose a line of work that doesn't demand so much along those lines.

The format for the Finney-Auvenshine reports is currently the familiar printout sheet of the standard computer printer-typewriter. Each report is preceded by a long list of scores and special indices (which have not been reproduced here). For the clinician who is familiar with the general profile and format of hand-processed MMPI, this Finney-Auvenshine material will be quite confusing. Although the raw scores for the basic scales are given in this list of scales (as well as Finney's special scales and numerous other supplementary measures) the corresponding T scores are given in normalized form based upon scale norms developed by Finney (1968). An additional problem in this case arose from numerous discrepancies between the Finney-Auvenshine scoring of the basic scales and the resulting raw-score values and the scores that were obtained for this research case from both hand-scoring and other machine-scoring services. If the recipients of these reports had tried to generate the usual MMPI profile from the given raw scores they would have been led to produce a test pattern that was a considerable departure from the pattern actually produced by this man. It is difficult to anticipate what a subscriber who is not experienced with the MMPI will be able to do with the technical material provided in these Finney-Auvenshine reports. Perhaps if all the cases in a given agency are processed by the Finney-Auvenshine system then the special norms and T-score transformations of this program can be used to build up local patterns and interpretive guides. Reliance upon such special scale values, however, has the effect of cutting the clinician off from the larger body of psychological research on the MMPI.

Perusal of these reports from the Finney-Auvenshine service shows a general similarity among the basic elements of the psychological formulation in each with specific departures for the particular interests and concerns of the different subscribers. These reports characterize this man as less emotionally upset and uncomfortable than the other interpretations of his MMPI have indicated and quite specifically rule out psychotic processes at this time. The paranoid trend does, however, seem to be noted but it is translated into a tendency to get annoyed, irritated, or angry with people, and to form enemies readily. The sexual difficulties are almost entirely bypassed in these reports and his femininity played down as merely some problem with passivity and a lack of assertiveness or ability to lead others. Contrary to the other interpretations also, he is considered to be free of rigidity in his personality makeup and dealings with others. This report does note his current dissatisfactions but seems to play down his depression and fails to mention suicidal concerns.

The report for the counseling psychologist introduces the very accurate description of this man's tendency to be his own worst enemy and to engender many of his own troubles. However, this line of interpretation seems to be spoiled or marred by one of the several internal contradictions which appear in these reports when in an earlier paragraph he is said not to be self-defeating. Other such contradictions center about his not being the sort of person who probes for hidden motives in others and yet is the kind of person who tends to misinterpret others' behavior and to see people as his enemies.

The special interpretive items for each specific subscriber are interpolated among paragraphs that are standard material for all these reports. The detail with which work-related material is developed would seem to make such reports quite useful for counselors or guidance workers with responsibilities for job placement or selection. There are very few special items for the correctional counselor, however, over and above the workup on vocational problems. A note on interpersonal relationships, combined with a prediction about tendencies toward escaping or violating his parole, seems to be all that is presented for this kind of subscriber. Perhaps some correctional workers could benefit from interpretive material on other prison classification problems, prison adjustment, sexual difficulties, drug problems, assaultiveness, and other aspects of adjustment within the institutional setting.

It is interesting to note the different ways in which the professional sources of these reports are identified to the different kinds of subscribers to this service. These authors have also seen fit to offer advice and guidance to the users in addition to the descriptions provided of the test subject.

Dynamic Formulation Report Level. Two reporting services offer routine interpretations of the MMPI which seem to go well beyond the level of a professional consultation on the case and provide very detailed analyses of the test subject's psychodynamics and personality structure. Some mental-health workers may find such a detailed level of analysis desirable and suitable for all their referrals but it is likely that most would find these reports to be too long, too discursive, or lacking in focus and direct relevance to the problems of case disposition or referral. There are also likely to be some clinicians who do not find the conceptualizations or terminology compatible with their own styles of formulating cases. Nevertheless, there will be many potential subscribers to such a service if it proves to be accurate, dependable, and reasonably prompt and efficient.

One example of this level of interpretation comes from the Finney-Auvenshine service already described in the previous two sections. The material on the research case for the psychodynamic report from the Finney-Auvenshine service is reproduced below.

FINNEY-AUVENSHINE: DETAILED PSYCHODYNAMIC REPORT FOR PSYCHIATRISTS AND CLINICAL PSYCHOLOGISTS

Male, age 34

This is a detailed clinical report for psychodiagnosis. It is sent only to psychiatrists and clinical psychologists. A shorter form of report is also available, if you prefer.

This is a professional consultation by Dr. Joseph C. Finney, a psychiatrist and psychologist.

Analysis of this kind can be done from any of several psychological tests. In this case, the test answered and submitted for analysis was the Minnesota Multiphasic Personality Inventory.

First, let us examine the evidence of validity and of the attitude with which he took the test.

He does not give a consistently favorable nor a consistently unfavorable picture of himself. He tells us some good things and some bad things about himself. He is an enterprising person who likes to put his best foot forward. Either he is warm and friendly, or he looks that way through trying to make a good impression. He tends to mark as false the neutral-sounding items that are frank in expressing feelings. He admits his faults willingly. He describes himself as an unenthusiastic person and avoids commitments, and is not overly devoted to duty.

Some of his answers are worth noting. Here is what he said:

133. False. By marking this one false, he tells us that he has sometimes taken part in some unusual sexual behavior.

177. False. By marking this one false, he denies that his mother was a good woman.

179. True. He says he worries about sex.

182. True. He says he is troubled by fears about losing his mind.

220. False. By marking this one false, he tells us that he did not love his mother.

302. False. By marking this one false, he lets us know that he has been in trouble from his sexual behavior.

It may be worthwhile to discuss those answers with him to find out what he meant by them.

His personality makeup is not truly typical of patients seen by psychiatrists and clinical psychologists, but neither is it unusual for that group.

He is a compliant and unaggressive person. He generally goes along with what other people want, and does whatever the other people tell him he is supposed to do. He is known as an obedient and submissive person. If a conflict arises, he yields, and he gives in to the other party. He would rather give in than have a quarrel. He is undemanding and unaggressive.

He is one of those people that tend to view certain others as foes. Things that certain people do, often seem to irritate him, annoy him, arouse his resentment, or make him angry. He may feel that the other party is doing wrong to him, treating him unjustly or unfairly. He sees the other party as an enemy.

He seems about as free from distress as the average person. In general he does things to advance himself and not to defeat himself. He is fairly successful in life, and he is reasonably satisfied with the world.

He is fairly consistent and predictable. Yet he is moderately spontaneous and flexible, and he is not a rigid person.

At his best he is serious, quiet, peaceful, conscientious, well behaved, obedient, and sentimental.

But when a situation puts pressure on him, he is likely to worry and brood about things. He blames himself. He gets discouraged, unhappy, tense and tired, and he has trouble sleeping.

He is the kind of person who sometimes trusts people too much and sometimes is too suspicious of people. He keeps alert for signs of what people are trying to do. He keeps searching for clues. As he screens his information, he can be highly sensitive to certain signs.

Unhappily, he may use the clues only to reinforce the beliefs that he already has. The problem is that he may be very sharp at seeing the things he's watching for, and may fail to see things he's not looking for. He can be keen and perceptive in identifying the clues that he sees, but because he loses appreciation of the context, he may get a slanted view of things.

He is not at all the sort of person that gets bodily symptoms to symbolize his emotional conflicts without organic cause.

Now what is the evidence for psychosis or mental illness?

He is not at all mentally ill: that is, not at all psychotic. He shows no tendency toward psychosis at all. He tends to get emotionally involved in issues and his thinking is not always realistic.

Next we consider his degree of basic trust and confidence, and the level of his self-esteem.

His attitude is rather pessimistic. He doesn't have much confidence in himself to make a success, nor confidence in others to do well by him. He expects poorly of the future. He is not a person that maintains an optimistic attitude by denying discouragement. His self-esteem is somewhat low, and he doesn't feel very proud of himself. He blames himself and feels guilty, and hence cripples himself into being methodical, conventional, passive, and narrow in interests.

He consistently fails to admit quite as much feeling of guilt, embarrassment, fear, and worry as he seems objectively to have. In other words, he seems to minimize those feelings a little. But he has no great amount of those feelings, anyhow. At present he may have some guilt feeling, but he denies it. Most of the time, he may have some guilt feeling, but he denies it. He shows moderate signs of guilt feeling. He is somewhat self-conscious, and concerned with what people think of him. He shows signs of having some fears or phobias. At present he may worry to some extent, but he denies it. Most of the time, he may worry to some extent, but he denies it. He is somewhat timid, worrying, indecisive, or neurotic. He seems to be worrying to some extent. He deals with anxiety by planning and worrying.

Now we turn our attention to problems of dependency.

He is neither clearly dependent nor clearly self-reliant. He is dependent in a passive way. In his inward feelings he is drawn to being somewhat passively dependent. Comparison of his dependency in action with his dependency urge shows that he strongly uses the defense of reaction formation against dependency.

Now, what about demandingness or oral aggression?

He is neither clearly demanding nor clearly undemanding.

Now we look for evidence of masochistic dependency and bitterness.

He does not seem especially bitter. If it is so, it is very slightly so. He seems to feel sorry for himself. To some extent, he is a dependent masochist, who does things so as to get people to disappoint him, reject him, or let him down. He shows no special tendency to get into trouble.

Now let's examine his anger or hostility and how he copes with it.

He is not a particularly hostile person. He is about like the average. He builds some resentment up within himself, but not much. Now let us see what he does with whatever hostility he has.

In general, he is a person who does harm to himself, and does not do harm to other people. In other words, he is highly intrapunitive. Though more can be said. If there is one thing that stands out about him it is this: he takes things out on himself much more than he takes things out on other people. This is something he needs to think about seriously. He is the sort of person who hates to hurt other people and would rather be hurt, himself. In his dealings with people, he keeps putting himself at a disadvantage. He lets people take advantage of him. And they do. Sometimes he may be seriously damaged by it, in one way or another. When trouble arises, he takes care not to let it hurt the other person. He lets it hurt him, instead, perhaps without knowing that he is causing his own troubles. In fairness to himself, he needs to call a halt to this business. He needs to decide what he wants from life; and then take realistic steps toward getting it.

He doesn't blame other people; or if he does so, it is less than the average person does. He doesn't take things out on other people at all. He likes to think of himself as broadminded and tolerant. He expects good of people. To some degree he gets his feelings easily hurt. He tends to classify people into allies and enemies. He tends to misjudge people's reactions to him. He tends to feel that he must be right. He makes some use of the defense of projection. No matter how he may feel, he tends to be somewhat meek, mild, and timid in dealing with people.

He tends to blame himself. And in certain ways, he takes things out on himself. He turns some hostility against himself. He is rather high-strung and moody. He gets distressed and discouraged when he can't control his impulses. He tries hard enough, but it doesn't seem to work very well. He readily and openly expresses some thoughts and feelings of discouragement. He appears somewhat discouraged and depressed. He turns some blame against himself unconsciously. That may burden him more than he knows. It may give him more feeling of discouragement than he is aware of.

Now, what can we say about his response to authorities?

Several measures show consistently that his response to authorities is one of submission. To some extent he does things so that people try to urge him, persuade him, or tell him what to do. He seems to like being told what to do. Openly, he is not rebellious.

Next we examine his compulsive character features.

He is neat, clean, and tidy. He is systematic, at least to an average degree, if not more. He is not a controlling person.

Now we must consider the hysterical personality features, including dissociation, repression, denial, conversion, unconscious acting-out, and some aspects of sexuality.

He shows some signs of dissociation and other hysterical processes. His normal and usual defense mechanism seems to be to make himself unaware of those impulses of his that would distress him if he were aware of them. He tends to make the worst of his troubles, and emphasizes his distress. He doesn't have conversion reactions. Because of some emotional problem, he may sometimes not do the sexual act very well.

Lastly, let us look at evidences of his identifications, ideals, and goals in life, and of the ways in which he meets his responsibilities as an adult.

He shows aesthetic interests. He may be effeminate. He may have some unmanly complaints.

He is ethical enough. He generally deals fairly with people, and generally respects their rights well enough.

All together, his conscience or ego ideal is of average strength, and his conduct for the most part is within normal limits. Nevertheless, he suffers guilt. He suffers more guilt than his deeds seem to account for. Maybe the guilt flows not so much from any deeds of his, as from forbidden wishes, perhaps unconscious ones. Maybe his conscience has unrealistic, puritanical, and perfectionistic standards. The guilt is a control mechanism that comes into play late and acts harshly and punitively. It may be that he goes through cycles of breaking rules, suffering guilt, and getting punished. The guilt is a source of his depression, blaming of himself, taking things out on himself, and getting people to disappoint him. Some goals of treatment are to reveal the guilt, to interpret the self-punishment, to reveal the unconscious forbidden wishes, to lessen the guilt and the self-punishment, to make the control mechanisms work more promptly and less harshly, and to interrupt the cycles, if such there be, and put an end to them.

Socially, he is somewhat introverted. He hesitates to speak out. He is cautious and shy with people. He is not very sociable. He may feel awkward in groups of people. His behavior is rather passive. He lets people influence him. He is rather hesitant and restrained, and not very sophisticated. He doesn't express himself very well. He is unsure what to do, and he keeps vacillating indecisively. He usually holds himself aloof from big parties and noisy crowds, especially those of a frankly pleasure-seeking aim, or those with public display of emotion, or with likelihood of rough behavior. With individuals he can relax, unbend, and find pleasure according to his own rules, but he is loath to do so in a crowd. He is not psychologically minded. He is simple in his approach to people. He takes people at their face value, without probing for hidden motives.

Let us consider how he stands in the personal qualities that have to do with success in the world of work.

Since he is 34 years old, he must already have chosen a career and worked in it. But if he is thinking of taking a new job, or of making some changes in his life work, it may be up to you, as his counselor, to help him consider how his personality jibes with the requirements of the various kinds of jobs that may be open to him.

He has good, normal ability to do work. He can do as well as any average, normal person in most kinds of work. He does well enough in the personal qualities that make for success at work. Of course, some kinds of working situations fit him better than others.

His strongest point, the one that can help him the most to succeed in his work, is his ability to keep his emotions from interfering with the teamwork that is needed in a competitive job. His approach to his work is realistic and practical. He harnesses his energies and directs his efforts to the task at hand, without letting personal resentments interfere. This is a real strength. He can do very well in a job that calls on him to control his personal feelings and focus his attention on the practical tasks of getting a job done by teamwork, in a competitive situation.

Another strong point that can help him in his work is his self-reliance in his work, and ability to use good judgment about it.

You will be wise to help him choose a line of work that calls on his strong points. In the right line of work, and in the right working conditions and setting, people will appreciate him for his best qualities.

One of his weak points, something that may handicap him in his work, is some lack of initiative, dominance, and leadership. He is no better than average in leadership abilities.

Another possible drawback, a point that may hamper him in his work, is some lack of willingness to conform to the customs and expectations of society. He does not do too badly in conforming to customs, but it is not a strong point with him. To a mild degree, he may be considered somewhat demanding or opinionated. He may be something of an individualist. The best job for him would not be one that depends strongly on dealing with the public.

You will be wise to help him choose a line of work that doesn't demand so much along those lines.

Diagnostic impression. Categorizing a patient with a diagnostic judgment must never be done from the results of psychological tests alone, nor from the reports of other laboratory tests alone. In making your diagnostic assessment of this patient, you will rely on the careful history that you have taken, and on the shrewd observations that you have made of the patient's behavior in the interview.

Insofar as we can judge from the analysis of the psychological testing alone, the diagnostic label most likely to fit the patient best is:

307. Situational stress reaction (adjustment reaction).

Other diagnostic labels that may be worth considering are as follows:

301.81 Personality trait disorder, neurotic personality trends, with elements of passive-aggressive personality, passive dependent type, and with obsessive-compulsive and depressive features.

301.0 Personality pattern disorder, paranoid personality.

300.4 Psychoneurosis, depressive reaction.

300.3 Psychoneurosis, obsessive-compulsive.

300.0 Psychoneurosis, anxiety reaction.

300.2 Psychoneurosis, phobic reaction.

318. No diagnosable psychological condition.

How would this person do in psychotherapy?

He is not a candidate for intensive psychotherapy of the kind that aims at self-understanding.

There is a problem in that the repression, which makes him unaware of the messages that he sends to people, is hard to penetrate. Most likely, if psychotherapy were tried, he would defend himself strongly against gaining insight or learning to label his motives. Even if psychotherapy were tried when he is anxious, he would be likely to ventilate his feelings and get reassurance and relief without learning much about himself.

Another side of his character is a problem. He wards self-criticism away and casts the blame on other people. Criticism of himself is too painful to bear.

He may be able to make use of social casework or counseling.

Summary. The statements that can be made most clearly about this person are as follows:

He is a sullen and passively resentful person. He sulks about things.

He doesn't take things out on other people at all.

By certain standards he shows a lack of warmth.

He blames himself and feels guilty, and hence cripples himself into being methodical, conventional, passive, and narrow in interests.

Almost all the different interpretive elements included in the previous reports have been incorporated into this dynamic formulation. They are presented in a matrix of supplementary or complementary interpretations which often serve to change their meaning and impact. As could perhaps be anticipated, then, the number of important internal contradictions arising within the report is appreciably increased. Particularly salient is the way in which guilt is analyzed and described in this man's current emotional adjustment; it is specifically minimized and then later taken up as a major feature of his clinical status. Here the cycle of acting out unacceptable impulses followed by periods of remorse and self-condemnation is developed in a way that seems highly accurate for this case but the material given in other parts of the report undercuts this excellent dynamic insight. Similarly, the masochistic trend is noted but then somewhat played down. The subject's sexual difficulties are specifically introduced in this report (the phraseology, however, appears to be awkward or strained) although they had been bypassed in the other reports given earlier. Two other developments are introduced here: the critical item content is given—in an augmented list of items (see Appendix G)—and treatment prognosis is offered. The influence of the special scales developed by Finney (1965a) to cover various psychoanalytic constructs can be readily discerned in the content of this extended psychodynamic report.

A similar kind of dynamic formulation appears to be the goal of the report from the Clinical Psychological Services, Inc., of Los Angeles, California. The service uses the interpretive program developed by Alex Caldwell, Ph.D. (see Caldwell, 1970a, 1970b). The report received from the routine processing of the research case is reproduced below.

CLINICAL PSYCHOLOGICAL SERVICES, INC.

Male, age 34
Education: 20 years

Test taking attitude: He was straightforward in answering the MMPI without being unduly defensive or self-critical. The profile appears valid.

Symptoms and personality characteristics: The profile indicates a moderate to severe disturbance. Tensions, worrying, self-doubts, and multiple fears and anxieties appear to seriously interfere with his life. In some related cases such symptoms as the blunting of affect, concreteness of thinking, morbid ruminations, and transitory ideas of reference suggested schizoid trends or chronic undifferentiated schizophrenic reactions despite preserved orientation and good general reality testing. Other patients were seen as having schizo-affective reactions or psychotic depressions as of the time of testing. Feelings of despondency, hopelessness, and guilt are suggested along with phobias and occasional thoughts about suicide. Indecisiveness and a pervasive loss of interest would relate to the depth of his ambivalences. Shy, introverted, and withdrawing, he appears quite uncomfortable socially, keeping others at a distance and fearing close involvement.

He appears overly sensitive, resentful, and easily hurt, sometimes reacting passively when others would show appropriate anger. When threatened, he could project and misinterpret the motives of others. His difficulties in expressing anger are apt to be a chronic personal handicap. Close relationships are apt to involve painful misunderstandings and repeated rejections. His responses suggest inquiry about difficulties over sexual activities and deviant behaviors in his sexual history. His balance of interests appears markedly feminine, passive, verbal, and esthetic. Serious self-doubts about male adequacy and disinterest in or rejection of masculine activities are suggested.

Typical family backgrounds involved rejection by one or sometimes both parents. Sometimes this was indirect, as by the illness or death of one parent and the resulting burdens on the other parent. Personal peculiarities often had provoked negative reactions from family members, including unfavorable comparisons to "superior" siblings or others in the family along with an excessive amount of teasing by siblings. Their interpersonal ineptness and difficulties in giving love resulted in repeated frustrations of their wishes for emotional closeness. They often studied and cultivated interests in obscure intellectual subjects such as religions and philosophies of life, typically ruminating about these with oddly personalized interpretations.

Diagnostic impression: The most typical diagnosis with this profile is of a chronic "endogenous" depression. In some cases this depression has been associated with chronic undifferentiated and schizo-affective schizophrenic reactions or with psychotic depressions.

Treatment considerations: The profile suggests a significant if not serious suicide risk. The treatment of similar patients has often included combinations of tranquilizers and antidepressants. These patients had only brief and limited responses to shock therapy, and the transient post-shock lifting of the depression was often followed by a flooding of intense anxieties, fears, and ruminations. His responses suggest a careful review of his sexual history.

Slowness to relate and immature emotional distortions are likely handicaps in psychotherapy. He is apt to have a resistively negative self-image with fixed and persistent self-criticisms despite his past accomplishments. These critical self-judgments are apt to be unrealistic but sufficiently integrated into the patient's identity so that they are slow to change. Many patients with this pattern were able to develop intellectual insights and introspections almost indefinitely with few or no apparent resulting changes in their behavior.

The profile predicts a gradual response to psychotherapy—especially if his depression is not of recent onset—but most similar patients have eventually made positive responses to treatment. One study reported relatively favorable responses by these patients to support from older, kindly, understanding, well-adjusted, and motherly female therapists. Difficulties brought on by his rigid internal standards and ideals are apt to be a major focus in treatment. Chronic difficulties in expressing anger and particularly his guilt over anger toward family members are apt to require an extended working through. Dissatisfaction with work achievement is a likely focus, especially if it involves the frustration or the possible giving up of his life ambitions. Overreactions to any physical, intellectual, and other handicaps are also likely points of focus in therapy. In some cases increasing self-assertiveness and integrated expressions of anger were seen as particularly meaningful signs of improvement.

Caldwell: MMPI Critical Items

Distress and Depression:
5 I am easily awakened by noise. (True)
86 I am certainly lacking in self-confidence. (True)
142 I certainly feel useless at times. (True)
182 I am afraid of losing my mind. (True)
259 I have difficulty in starting to do things. (True)
Guilt and Suicide:
None
Ideas of Reference, Persecution, and Delusions:
None
Peculiar Experiences and Hallucinations:
None
Sexual Difficulties:
74 I have often wished I were a girl. (True)
133 I have never indulged in any unusual sex practices. (False)
179 I am worried about sex matters. (True)
302 I have never been in trouble because of my sex behavior. (False)
Authority Problems:
None
Alcohol and Drugs:
None
Family Discord:
308 At times I have very much wanted to leave home. (True)
Somatic Concerns:
9 I am about as able to work as I ever was. (False)
189 I feel weak all over much of the time. (True)

The CPS report is accompanied by the familiar MMPI psychograph with the profile given in terms of the usual Minnesota adult T-score values.

Service is by return airmail like the other services described here. There is no provision yet for numerical coding of the test subject or recipient's identity. The format of the report is the familiar psychological report form.

This report includes an accurate and highly pertinent résumé of the clinical status of this man, highlighting his depression, anxiety, dysphoria, and guilt feelings. It deals explicitly with the suicidal preoccupations, the specific sexual problems, and the early forms of paranoid and other reality-distorting trends in his thinking. In addition, it quite accurately pinpoints aspects of his family life and early history. Little seems to be left out that is relevant to this man's case and little that is included appears to be very far off target.

The protocol validity is taken up directly. The CPS printout employs a somewhat augmented list of critical items and perhaps gives additional meaning to them in grouping them by general content. (They then seem to serve very much the same clinical interpretive purpose as the Harris-Lingoes subscales of the clinical scales; see Appendix I.) In addition, the report takes up in some detail treatment and management questions. It is interesting that the prognosis offered here is considerably more favorable than that given by the Finney-Auvenshine reports.

Computer Report for the Test Subject Himself. As noted at various times in the previous discussions, most services providing routine interpretive printouts for the MMPI include a specific admonition to the recipient not to turn the report over to the client or patient. These services intend only to provide a technical communication between professional colleagues. If the writers of the programs had to be also concerned about how the statements would be read and interpreted by the person under study, the content and format would probably have to be prepared in quite different ways. Although most of these reports have tried to avoid excessive reliance on technical jargon or special terminology, nevertheless they have had to use some professional-level concepts and descriptors. The reports would undoubtedly run considerably longer if all such terms were to be eliminated. This same need for brevity has also contributed to their being quite straightforward and abrupt; they provide little in the way of special explanation or background perspectives in their clinical assessments.

The Finney-Auvenshine service, however, has now made available a report specifically designed to be given to the test subject himself. Whether the case in this special comparison should be provided with this kind of feedback, of course, was not the concern here. Rather, it was of interest to find out what would have been the content of such a communication were the Finney-Auvenshine subject report to have been made available for this purpose. The report received from the Finney-Auvenshine service is reproduced below.

FINNEY-AUVENSHINE: REPORT FOR THE INDIVIDUAL HIMSELF

Male, age 34

This is a report written so that you can read about yourself and learn to understand yourself better. We send this report to your doctor or counselor.

He has read it before giving it to you, and he will discuss it with you. He will explain the parts that may not be clear to you.

Analysis of this kind can be done from any of several psychological tests. In this case, the test answered and submitted for analysis was the Minnesota Multiphasic Personality Inventory.

You have told us both good and bad things about yourself.

You are a somewhat insecure person. You are a rather compliant person. You usually go along with the rules, and you usually go along with other people's wishes. You are a steady person. You use self-control. You are cautious and careful. You have some tendency to make enemies. You become irritated, suspicious, and resentful at times.

At your best you are serious, quiet, peaceful, conscientious, well behaved, obedient, and sentimental.

You are the kind of person who sometimes trusts people too much and sometimes is too suspicious of people. You keep alert for signs of what people are trying to do. You keep searching for clues. As you screen your information, you can be highly sensitive to certain signs.

Unhappily, you may use the clues only to reinforce the beliefs that you already have. The problem is that you may be very sharp at seeing the things you're watching for, and may fail to see things you're not looking for. You can be keen and perceptive in identifying the clues that you see, but because you lose appreciation of the context, you may get a slanted view of things.

You are dependent in a passive way.

In general, you are a person who does harm to yourself, and does not do harm to other people. In other words, you are highly intrapunitive. If there is one thing that stands out about you it is this: you take things out on yourself much more than you take things out on other people. This is something you need to think about seriously. You are the sort of person who hates to hurt other people and would rather be hurt, yourself; in your dealings with people, you keep putting yourself at a disadvantage. You let people take advantage of you. And they do. Sometimes you may be seriously damaged by it, in one way or another. When trouble arises, you take care not to let it hurt the other person. You let it hurt you, instead, perhaps without knowing that you are causing your own troubles. In fairness to yourself, you need to call a halt to this business. You need to decide what you want from life; and then take realistic steps toward getting it.

One thing you need to think seriously about is that you are so full of anger, resentment, and unfriendliness. You resent people and treat them as your enemies when there is little or no reason for it. This can bring pain and grief onto you as well as onto other people. So the next time you feel angry or resentful, better stop and ask yourself, "What makes me feel this way? Do I really and truly have good reason to regard the other person as an enemy?"

You hate to admit being wrong. So when you suspect that you are wrong, you blame the other person, to avoid blaming yourself. You should keep an eye on yourself to stop yourself from doing so.

You are ethical enough. You generally deal fairly with people, and you generally respect their rights well enough.

Socially, you are somewhat introverted. You hesitate to speak out. You are cautious and shy with people. You are not very sociable. You may feel awkward in groups of people. Your behavior is rather passive. You let people influence you. You are rather hesitant and restrained, and not very sophisticated. You don't express yourself very well. You are unsure what to do, and you keep vacillating indecisively. You usually hold yourself aloof from big parties and noisy crowds, especially those of a frankly pleasure-seeking aim, or those with public display of emotion, or with likelihood of rough behavior. With individuals you can relax, unbend, and find pleasure according to your own rules, but you are loath to do so in a crowd. You are not psychologically minded. You are simple in your approach to people. You take people at their face value, without probing for hidden motives.

Let us consider how you stand in the personal qualities that have to do with success in the world of work.

Since you are 34 years old, you must have already chosen a career and worked in it. Let's consider how you fit in with different kinds of work.

You have good, normal ability to do work. You can do as well as any average, normal person at most kinds of work.

Your strongest point, the one that can help you the most to succeed in your work, is your ability to keep your emotions from interfering with the teamwork that is needed in a competitive job. This is a real strength. You can do very well in a job that calls on you to control your personal feelings and focus your attention on the practical tasks of getting a job done by teamwork, in a competitive situation.

Another strong point that can help you in your work is your self-reliance in your work, and ability to use good judgment about it.

You will be wise to choose a line of work that calls on your strong points. In the right line of work, and in the right working conditions and setting, people will appreciate you for your best qualities.

One of your weak points, something that may handicap you in your work, is some lack of initiative, dominance, and leadership.

It may be better to choose a line of work in which things of this kind don't matter much.

It is immediately clear how this material has been developed. Each of the paragraphs corresponds to interpretive elements appearing in the reports prepared at the consultative level of analysis. The sentences have been rephrased in the second person with relatively little additional editing. This direct transcription poses some special problems in communicating with the usual client. For example, one of the interpretations tells the test subject that he is dependent in a passive way. All by itself in this form the interpretation seems quite ambiguous and perhaps even threatening. Although it is noted at the beginning that the client's physician or psychologist will explain any parts that are not clear, this kind of flat assertion would seem to leave a heavy burden on the clinician to explain or illustrate this kind of psychological interpretation. It can also be seen that rather special technical terms survive this rewriting, such as intrapunitive, vacillating, and reinforce. Thus, there does not seem to have been any attempt to shift the vocabulary level from the professional communication to a more suitable language for the messages to be given to the client or patient. Some advice to the client, however, is introduced. It is difficult to know how effective or helpful such suggestions may be. One hopes that the advantages and disadvantages inherent in this kind of feedback to the test subject will be more thoroughly studied in empirical research on these important issues in the near future.

In this regard, the task of demonstrating the validity of psychological interpretations from the MMPI, whether produced by a computer-based system or by a trained clinician, appears formidable. There are several sources of difficulty in such an effort. The individual interpretive elements may each be appropriate to a substantial majority of cases with a particular MMPI profile; it is unlikely that even the most valid of these correlated personological or clinical items is correctly associated with every instance of the given pattern. Further, if there exists a large set of such elements for any particular pattern, these descriptors may covary among themselves in subclusters so that not all of them will be equally pertinent to a given case. The report, however, is submitted as a total package and must be read and applied in toto. If there are some coherent subpatterns among the descriptors, they may be lost in the format of the report, particularly in computer-based systems. The resulting communication may lack coherence, consistency, or internal logic if such contradictions or personological impossibilities are included. It is also likely that some of the descriptors have greater saliency or play a more central role in depicting an individual. If so, the value of the report may hinge more upon the validity of those central items than upon many less important ones which may be erroneous without detracting from the accuracy or value of the report. In evaluating the validity of such interpretations, therefore, it is quite possible for a large percentage of the material included to be accurate and applicable and yet have the report marred by a few extremely inappropriate items. Correspondingly, if the important items are correct, it is possible that the reader may find the report very appropriate even though a number of details in the descriptor set are misplaced or inapplicable. There is an obvious need for special studies of the proper research methods to apply to these questions and for a fund of accurate information about the level of validity now being achieved in clinical interpretations of the MMPI. In this research effort, putting the descriptors into the highly reproducible and readily modifiable format of a computer-based system would appear to be an essential first step in perfecting MMPI interpretive processes.

APPENDIXES

APPENDIX A Card-Form Scoring

The direction of scoring in the card form is given for each MMPI item (here listed by booklet number) when the item is answered True. The designation X indicates that the answer True is the minority, or deviant, response to that item, while the designation 0 indicates that True is the majority, or conforming, response. In the card form only the deviant, or X, replies are marked on the record blank in recording the test subject's answers; the 0 responses appear on the record blank as unfilled spaces. However, the standard scoring stencils designate both types of response. The indication in this list of the scoring direction for each item will facilitate the preparation of scoring stencils for the special scales given in Appendix I.

Card Form Scoring (X or 0) for True
Response to Each Item

Booklet No.	Direction for True	Booklet No.	Direction for True	Booklet No.	Direction for True	Booklet No.	Direction for True	Booklet No.	Direction for True
1....	0	26....	0	51....	0	76....	X	101....	0
2....	0	27....	X	52....	X	77....	0	102....	X
3....	0	28....	X	53....	X	78....	X	103....	0
4....	X	29....	X	54....	0	79....	0	104....	X
5....	X	30....	0	55....	0	80....	X	105....	0
6....	X	31....	X	56....	X	81....	X	106....	X
7....	0	32....	X	57....	0	82....	X	107....	0
8....	0	33....	X	58....	X	83....	0	108....	X
9....	0	34....	X	59....	X	84....	X	109....	X
10....	X	35....	X	60....	0	85....	X	110....	X
11....	X	36....	0	61....	X	86....	X	111....	0
12....	0	37....	0	62....	X	87....	X	112....	0
13....	X	38....	X	63....	0	88....	0	113....	0
14....	X	39....	X	64....	X	89....	X	114....	X
15....	0	40....	X	65....	0	90....	0	115....	0
16....	X	41....	X	66....	X	91....	0	116....	X
17....	0	42....	X	67....	X	92....	X	117....	X
18....	0	43....	X	68....	0	93....	X	118....	X
19....	X	44....	X	69....	X	94....	X	119....	0
20....	0	45....	0	70....	X	95....	0	120....	0
21....	X	46....	0	71....	0	96....	0	121....	X
22....	X	47....	X	72....	X	97....	X	122....	0
23....	X	48....	X	73....	X	98....	0	123....	X
24....	X	49....	X	74....	X	99....	0	124....	X
25....	X	50....	X	75....	0	100....	X	125....	X

No. Booklet	Direction for True	Booklet No.	Direction for True	Booklet No.	Direction for True	Booklet No.	Direction for True	Booklet No.	Direction for True
126....	X	176....	0	226....	X	276....	0	326....	X
127....	X	177....	0	227....	X	277....	X	327....	0
128....	0	178....	0	228....	0	278....	X	328....	X
129....	X	179....	X	229....	0	279....	X	329....	X
130....	0	180....	X	230....	0	280....	X	330....	0
131....	0	181....	X	231....	X	281....	0	331....	X
132....	X	182....	X	232....	X	282....	X	332....	X
133....	0	183....	X	233....	X	283....	X	333....	X
134....	0	184....	X	234....	X	284....	X	334....	X
135....	0	185....	0	235....	0	285....	0	335....	X
136....	X	186....	X	236....	X	286....	X	336....	X
137....	0	187....	0	237....	0	287....	0	337....	X
138....	X	188....	0	238....	X	288....	X	338....	X
139....	X	189....	X	239....	X	289....	0	339....	X
140....	X	190....	0	240....	X	290....	X	340....	X
141....	0	191....	X	241....	X	291....	X	341....	X
142....	X	192....	0	242....	0	292....	X	342....	X
143....	X	193....	0	243....	0	293....	X	343....	X
144....	X	194....	X	244....	X	294....	0	344....	X
145....	X	195....	0	245....	X	295....	X	345....	X
146....	X	196....	0	246....	X	296....	0	346....	X
147....	X	197....	X	247....	X	297....	X	347....	0
148....	X	198....	0	248....	X	298....	X	348....	0
149....	X	199....	0	249....	0	299....	X	349....	X
150....	0	200....	X	250....	X	300....	0	350....	X
151....	X	201....	X	251....	X	301....	X	351....	X
152....	0	202....	X	252....	X	302....	0	352....	X
153....	0	203....	X	253....	0	303....	X	353....	0
154....	0	204....	X	254....	0	304....	X	354....	X
155....	0	205....	X	255....	0	305....	X	355....	X
156....	X	206....	X	256....	X	306....	0	356....	X
157....	X	207....	0	257....	0	307....	X	357....	X
158....	X	208....	X	258....	0	308....	X	358....	X
159....	X	209....	X	259....	X	309....	0	359....	X
160....	X	210....	X	260....	X	310....	0	360....	X
161....	X	211....	X	261....	X	311....	X	361....	X
162....	X	212....	X	262....	0	312....	X	362....	X
163....	0	213....	X	263....	X	313....	X	363....	X
164....	0	214....	0	264....	0	314....	0	364....	X
165....	0	215....	X	265....	X	315....	X	365....	X
166....	X	216....	X	266....	X	316....	X	366....	X
167....	X	217....	X	267....	X	317....	X	367....	0
168....	X	218....	X	268....	0	318....	0	368....	X
169....	0	219....	X	269....	X	319....	X	369....	0
170....	0	220....	0	270....	0	320....	X	370....	0
171....	X	221....	0	271....	X	321....	X	371....	0
172....	X	222....	X	272....	0	322....	X	372....	0
173....	0	223....	X	273....	X	323....	X	373....	X
174....	0	224....	X	274....	0	324....	X	374....	X
175....	0	225....	0	275....	X	325....	X	375....	X

Booklet No.	Direction for True	Booklet No.	Direction for True	Booklet No.	Direction for True	Booklet No.	Direction for True	Booklet No.	Direction for True
376....	0	416....	X	456....	X	496....	0	536....	X
377....	X	417....	X	457....	X	497....	0	537....	X
378....	0	418....	X	458....	X	498....	0	538....	X
379....	0	419....	X	459....	X	499....	X	539....	0
380....	0	420....	X	460....	0	500....	X	540....	0
381....	X	421....	X	461....	0	501....	0	541....	X
382....	X	422....	X	462....	0	502....	0	542....	0
383....	X	423....	0	463....	X	503....	X	543....	X
384....	X	424....	X	464....	0	504....	X	544....	X
385....	X	425....	0	465....	X	505....	X	545....	X
386....	X	426....	X	466....	0	506....	X	546....	0
387....	0	427....	X	467....	X	507....	X	547....	0
388....	X	428....	0	468....	0	508....	0	548....	0
389....	X	429....	0	469....	X	509....	X	549....	X
390....	X	430....	0	470....	X	510....	X	550....	0
391....	0	431....	X	471....	X	511....	X	551....	X
392....	X	432....	X	472....	X	512....	X	552....	0
393....	0	433....	X	473....	X	513....	0	553....	X
394....	0	434....	X	474....	0	514....	X	554....	X
395....	X	435....	X	475....	X	515....	0	555....	X
396....	X	436....	0	476....	X	516....	0	556....	X
397....	X	437....	X	477....	X	517....	X	557....	X
398....	X	438....	X	478....	0	518....	X	558....	0
399....	0	439....	X	479....	0	519....	X	559....	X
400....	X	440....	0	480....	X	520....	0	560....	X
401....	0	441....	X	481....	X	521....	0	561....	0
402....	X	442....	0	482....	0	522....	0	562....	0
403....	0	443....	X	483....	0	523....	0	563....	0
404....	X	444....	0	484....	X	524....	0	564....	X
405....	0	445....	0	485....	X	525....	X	565....	X
406....	0	446....	X	486....	0	526....	X	566....	0
407....	0	447....	X	487....	X	527....	0		
408....	0	448....	X	488....	0	528....	0		
409....	0	449....	0	489....	X	529....	0		
410....	X	450....	0	490....	X	530....	X		
411....	X	451....	0	491....	0	531....	X		
412....	0	452....	X	492....	X	532....	0		
413....	X	453....	X	493....	0	533....	0		
414....	X	454....	X	494....	X	534....	0		
415....	0	455....	X	495....	0	535....	X		

APPENDIX B Basic Scale Membership and Scoring

The code numbers of the scales on which the item is scored if answered True are entered in the first column of this list; the code numbers of the scales on which the item is scored if answered False are entered in the second column. If the scale number appears in parentheses, the item is a zero entry on the card form key. Lower-case letters designate unscored items that are answered as True (t) or False (f) by the majority of Minnesota normals. The symbol ‡ indicates an item on scale 5 (Mf) that is scored in the opposite direction for females.

Scale Membership and Direction of Scoring for Each Item

Booklet No.[a]	True	False	Booklet No.	True	False
1		5	26		35
2		123	27	F6	
3		137	28		(5)
4	5		29	1	
5	2		30		LK23
6		(3)	31	F	
7		13	32 (328)	234780	
8 (318)		23478	33 (323)	48	(0)
9		123	34	F	
10	37		35 (331)	F468	
11	9		36		27
12		3	37 (302)		48
13 (290)	29		38 (311)	48	
14	F		39		(K2)
15 (314)	(678)	L	40	F8	
16 (315)	468		41	278	
17		F8	42	F4	
18		12	43	123	
19		(5)	44	3	
20 (310)		F48	45		L
21 (308)	489		46		2
22 (326)	6789		47	38	
23 (288)	F123		48	F	
24 (333)	468		49	F	
25	5	(0)	50	F	

[a] Both numbers are given for the sixteen items repeated in the booklet form.

Booklet No.	True	False
51		123
52	28	
53	F	
54		F
55		13
56	F	
57		20
58		(2)
59	9	
60		L
61	4	
62	1	
63		1
64	9	(2)
65		F8
66	F	
67	2470	
68		1
69	5‡	
70	5	
71		K3
72	1	
73	9	
74	5	
75		LF
76	378	
77	(5)	
78	5	
79		5
80		(25)
81		(5)
82	0	(4)
83		F
84	4	
85	F	
86	27	
87	5	
88		2
89		(K235)
90		L
91		40
92	5	
93		(36)
94	47	
95		2
96	(K)	4
97	89	

Booklet No.	True	False
98		2
99		50
100	9	
101		9
102	47	
103		138
104	28	
105		L9
106	47	
107		2346
108	1	
109	9	(36)
110	46	
111	(0)	69
112		F5
113		F
114	13	
115		F5
116		(5)
117	0	(56)
118	4	
119		890
120		L59
121	F68	
122		27
123	F6	
124	0	(K36)
125	1	
126	5	(0)
127	469	
128		3
129		(K3)
130	(2)	1
131		2
132	5	
133		5‡
134	(59)	K4
135		L
136		(3)
137		34
138	20	(K)
139	F	
140	5	
141		34
142	27	(K)
143	9	(0)
144		(5)
145		(2)

Booklet No.	True	False
146..........	F	
147..........	0	(3)
148..........		(K9)
149..........	5	
150..........		L
151..........	F6	
152..........		27
153..........		123
154..........		2
155..........		124
156..........	F89	
157..........	689	
158..........	26	
159..........	278	
160..........		(K23)
161..........	1	
162..........		(3)
163..........		13
164..........		F7
165..........		L
166..........		(9)
167..........	9	
168..........	F8	
169..........		F
170..........		K34
171..........	0	(K49)
172..........	0	(3)
173..........		4
174..........		3
175..........		13
176..........		5
177..........		F8
178..........		278
179..........	35‡8	
180..........	0	(K349)
181..........	9	
182..........	278	
183..........		(K4)
184..........	F	
185..........		F
186..........	3	
187..........	(5)	8
188..........		13
189..........	1237	
190..........		13
191..........		(2)
192..........		138
193..........	(2)	0
194..........	89	
195..........		L
196..........		F8
197..........	F	
198..........		5
199..........		F
200..........	F	
201..........	0	(34)
202..........	F68	
203..........	5	
204..........	5	
205..........	F	
206..........	F	
207..........		2
208..........		(20)
209..........	F	
210..........	F8	
211..........	F	
212..........	89	
213..........		(35)
214..........		5
215..........	F4	
216..........	4	
217..........	57	(K)
218..........	F	
219..........		(5)
220..........		F8
221..........		5
222..........	9	
223..........		(5)
224..........	4	
225..........		L
226..........	59	
227..........	F	
228..........	(9)	
229..........		50
230..........		13
231..........	5‡	(40)
232..........	9	
233..........	9	(2)
234..........		(K3)
235..........		4
236..........	20	
237..........		4
238..........	3789	
239..........	45	
240..........	9	

Booklet No.	True	False
241	8	(2)
242		2
243		13
244	4	
245	F4	
246	F	
247	F	
248		(24)
249		5
250	9	
251	89	
252	F	
253	(3)	
254		50
255		L
256	F	
257		F
258		F
259	28	
260		(5)
261	5	
262		50
263	9	(2)
264		5
265		(3)
266	789	
267	0	(K349)
268	(9)	6
269	F	
270		2
271	9	(2)
272		FK2
273	18	
274		13
275	F6	
276		F8
277	9	
278	50	
279	9	(3)
280		(5)
281		1680
282	58	
283		(5)
284	46	
285		L2
286	F	
287		4
288 (23)	F123	
289		349
290 (13)	29	
291	F68	
292	0	(3)
293	F6	
294		46
295	5	
296		K240
297	5‡8	
298	9	
299	56	
300		5
301	78	
302 (37)		48
303	8	
304	70	
305 (366)	678	
306		8
307	8	
308 (21)	489	
309		80
310 (20)		F48
311 (38)	48	
312	8	
313		(6)
314 (15)	(678)	L
315 (16)	468	
316	0	(K6)
317 (362)	67	
318 (8)		23478
319		(6)
320	8	
321	70	
322		(K8)
323 (33)	48	(0)
324	8	
325	8	
326 (22)	6789	
327		6
328 (32)	234780	
329		(7)
330		8
331 (35)	F468	
332	80	
333 (24)	468	
334	8	
335	8	

Booklet No.	True	False	Booklet No.	True	False
336	70		383	0	(K)
337	7		384		f
338	6		385		f
339	8		386		f
340	7		387	t	
341	68		388		f
342	70		389		f
343	7		390		f
344	7		391		0
345	8		392		f
346	7		393	t	
347		6	394	t	
348		6	395		f
349	78		396		f
350	8		397		(K)
351	7		398	0	(K)
352	78		399	t	
353		70	400		(0)
354	8		401	t	
355	8		402		f
356	78		403	t	
357	70		404		f
358	7		405	t	
359	7	(0)	406		K
360	78		407	t	
361	7		408	t	
362 (317)	67		409	t	
363	8		410		f
364	68		411	0	
365	6		412	t	
366 (305)	678		413		f
367	t		414		f
368		f	415		0
369	t		416		f
370	t		417		f
371		0	418		f
372	t		419		f
373		f	420		f
374		(K)	421		f
375		f	422		f
376	t		423	t	
377	0		424		f
378	t		425	t	
379	t		426		f
380	t		427	0	
381		f	428	t	
382		f	429	t	
			430	t	

Booklet No.	True	False	Booklet No.	True	False
431		f	478	t	
432		f	479		0
433		f	480		f
434		f	481		(0)
435		f	482		0
436	(0)		483	t	
437		f	484		f
438		f	485		f
439		f	486	t	
440		0	487	0	
441		f	488	t	
442	t		489		f
443		f	490		f
444	t		491	t	
445	t		492		f
446		(0)	493	t	
447		f	494		f
448		f	495	t	
449		0	496	t	
450		0	497	t	
451		0	498	t	
452		f	499		f
453		f	500		f
454		f	501	t	
455	0		502		K
456		f	503		f
457		f	504		f
458		f	505		(0)
459		f	506		f
460	t		507		f
461		K	508	t	
462		0	509		f
463		f	510		f
464	t		511		f
465		f	512		f
466	t		513	t	
467		f	514		f
468	t		515	t	
469		(0)	516	t	
470		f	517		f
471		f	518		f
472		f	519		f
473	0		520	t	
474	t		521		0
475		f	522	t	
476		f	523	t	
477		f	524	t	
			525		f

Appendix B — continued

Booklet No.	True	False	Booklet No.	True	False
526..........		f	546..........	t	
527..........	t		547..........		0
528..........	t		548..........	t	
529..........	t		549..........	0	
530..........		f	550..........	t	
531..........		f	551..........		f
532..........	t		552..........	t	
533..........	t		553..........		f
534..........	t		554..........		f
535..........		f	555..........		f
536..........		f	556..........		f
537..........		f	557..........		f
538..........		f	558..........	t	
539..........	t		559..........		f
540..........	t		560..........		f
541..........		f	561..........	t	
542..........	t		562..........	t	
543..........		f	563..........	t	
544..........		f	564..........	0	
545..........		f	565..........		f
			566..........	t	

APPENDIX C Item Conversion Tables

Table 1. Conversion from Card (Individual) to Booklet (Group) Form[a]

A	B	C	D	E	F	G	H	I	J
1-153	1-47	1-527	1-548	1-298	1-40	1-337	1-448	1-269	1-92
2-51	2-159	2-516	2-231	2-438	2-521	2-543	2-278	2-355	2-434
3-160	3-263	3-226	3-558	3-26	3-304	3-209	3-284	3-363	3-435
4-155	4-191	4-422	4-485	4-475	4-321	4-61	4-123	4-80	4-555
5-163	5-535	5-325	5-133	5-477	5-201	5-518	5-551	5-393	5-1
6-36	6-193	6-21*	6-199	6-437	6-371	6-338	6-293	6-218	6-559
7-412	7-34	7-237	7-101	7-250	7-170	7-104	7-275	7-85	7-219
8-242	8-130	8-421	8-206	8-456	8-171	8-413	8-291	8-252	8-557
9-299	9-55	9-247	9-369	9-28	9-172	9-202	9-348	9-83	9-512
10-190	10-230	10-282	10-95	10-410	10-317*	10-339	10-136	10-395	10-144
11-44	11-10	11-324	11-488	11-277	11-520	11-210	11-121	11-403	11-140
12-114	12-2	12-239	12-490	12-294	12-509	12-107	12-33*	12-84	12-132
13-108	13-424	13-220	13-373	13-376	13-368	13-439	13-349	13-102	13-544
14-161	14-533	14-177	14-491	14-478	14-222	14-372	14-151	14-394	14-556
15-23*	15-125	15-65	15-258	15-167	15-198	15-500	15-197	15-389	15-545
16-175	16-29	16-17	16-249	16-19	16-511	16-268	16-364	16-507	16-532
17-174	17-72	17-9	17-115	17-37*	17-384	17-386	17-200	17-382	17-513
18-154	18-18	18-322	18-98	18-479	18-303	18-296	18-400	18-402	18-78
19-156	19-14	19-443	19-483	19-453	19-498	19-100	19-73	19-409	19-203
20-194	20-63	20-564	20-387	20-276	20-502	20-266	20-350	20-531	20-554
21-251	21-542	21-370	21-53	21-286	21-504	21-238	21-184	21-481	21-433
22-22*	22-462	22-465	22-58	22-312	22-489	22-340	22-48	22-406	22-441
23-122	23-474	23-416	23-50	23-292	23-503	23-272	23-464	23-356	23-204
24-46	24-486	24-59	24-476	24-52	24-417	24-505	24-66	24-534	24-126
25-168	25-214	25-147	25-420	25-454	25-162	25-248	25-27	25-357	25-149
26-335	26-519	26-501	26-232	26-455	26-426	26-228	26-127	26-82	26-295
27-178	27-3	27-148	27-419	27-377	27-408	27-381	27-196	27-32*	27-566
28-560	28-43	28-461	28-471	28-391	28-404	28-399	28-351	28-415	28-561
29-508	29-442	29-257	29-56	29-449	29-444	29-234	29-499	29-411	29-283
30-334	30-152	30-493	30-118	30-450	30-469	30-134	30-360	30-244	30-562
31-274	31-5	31-233	31-445	31-181	31-336	31-39	31-287	31-397	31-300
32-188	32-211	32-495	32-38*	32-451	32-468	32-145	32-352	32-361	32-25
33-496	33-329	33-89	33-157	33-254	33-129	33-146	33-169	33-506	33-547
34-540	34-425	34-375	34-143	34-99	34-138	34-341	34-385	34-13*	34-4
35-185	35-31	35-173	35-111	35-229	35-305*	35-342	35-392	35-301	35-529
36-281	36-241	36-260	36-116	36-57	36-67	36-343	36-367	36-418	36-480
37-119	37-11	37-552	37-446	37-24*	37-407	37-64	37-525	37-142	37-463

Note: These two conversion tables were prepared by George S. Welsh and Patrick L. Sullivan (1952a).

[a] The items marked with an asterisk occur twice in the booklet form. The larger of the two booklet numbers for each of the repeated pairs is as follows: A15-288; A22-326; C6-308; C47-310; D32-311; E17-302; E37-333; F10-362; F35-366; F39-318; G53-331; G55-315; H12-323; I27-328; I34-290; J41-314.

Appendix C, Table 1 — continued

A	B	C	D	E	F	G	H	I	J
38-332	38-227	38-428	38-141	38-309	38-88	38-270	38-176	38-398	38-514
39-405	39-466	39-546	39-112	39-54	39-8*	39-467	39-539	39-86	39-458
40-189	40-279	40-429	40-447	40-306	40-517	40-213	40-522	40-264	40-74
41-330	41-460	41-164	41-432	41-207	41-487	41-346	41-401	41-549	41-15*
42-192	42-215	42-6	42-113	42-307	42-259	42-359	42-510	42-538	42-45
43-187	43-457	43-12	43-49	43-267	43-374	43-358	43-131	43-563	43-75
44-103	44-459	44-497	44-289	44-180	44-41	44-205	44-524	44-261	44-105
45-186	45-484	45-77	45-436	45-452	45-236	45-344	45-492	45-70	45-135
46-243	46-515	46-256	46-319	46-91	46-217	46-472	46-388	46-550	46-165
47-62	47-42	47-20*	47-280	47-440	47-396	47-97	47-166	47-423	47-195
48-273	48-137	48-208	48-71	48-240	48-379	48-139	48-553	48-536	48-225
49-541	49-216	49-430	49-271	49-262	49-76	49-380	49-365	49-81	49-255
50-68	50-212	50-69	50-117	50-94	50-106	50-109	50-494	50-221	50-285
51-528	51-235	51-179	51-183	51-378	51-158	51-345	51-473	51-223	51-30
52-523	52-224	52-320	52-93	52-383	52-79	52-347	52-353	52-537	52-60
53-530	53-245	53-297	53-316	53-265	53-390	53-35*	53-354	53-87	53-90
54-246	54-327	54-470	54-124	54-253	54-414	54-110	54-128	54-431	54-120
55-7	55-96	55-427	55-313	55-482	55-526	55-16*	55-182	55-565	55-150

Table 2. Conversion from Booklet (Group) to Card (Individual) Form[a]

1-J5	32*-I27	63-B20	94-E50	125-B15	156-A19	187-A43
2-B12	33*-H12	64-G37	95-D10	126-J24	157-D33	188-A32
3-B27	34-B7	65-C15	96-B55	127-H26	158-F51	189-A40
4-J34	35*-G53	66-H24	97-G47	128-H54	159-B2	190-A10
5-B31	36-A6	67-F36	98-D18	129-F33	160-A3	191-B4
6-C42	37*-E17	68-A50	99-E34	130-B8	161-A14	192-A42
7-A55	38*-D32	69-C50	100-G19	131-H43	162-F25	193-B6
8*-F39	39-G31	70-I45	101-D7	132-J12	163-A5	194-A20
9-C17	40-F1	71-D48	102-I13	133-D5	164-C41	195-J47
10-B11	41-F44	72-B17	103-A44	134-G30	165-J46	196-H27
11-B37	42-B47	73-H19	104-G7	135-J45	166-H47	197-H15
12-C43	43-B28	74-J40	105-J44	136-H10	167-E15	198-F15
13*-I34	44-A11	75-J43	106-F50	137-B48	168-A25	199-D6
14-B19	45-J42	76-F49	107-G12	138-F34	169-H33	200-H17
15*-J41	46-A24	77-C45	108-A13	139-G48	170-F7	201-F5
16*-G55	47-B1	78-J18	109-G50	140-J11	171-F8	202-G9
17-C16	48-H22	79-F52	110-G54	141-D38	172-F9	203-J19
18-B18	49-D43	80-I4	111-D35	142-I37	173-C35	204-J23
19-E16	50-D23	81-I49	112-D39	143-D34	174-A17	205-C44
20*-C47	51-A2	82-I26	113-D42	144-J10	175-A16	206-D8
21*-C6	52-E24	83-I9	114-A12	145-G32	176-H38	207-E41
22*-A22	53-D21	84-I12	115-D17	146-G33	177-C14	208-C48
23*-A15	54-E39	85-I7	116-D36	147-C25	178-A27	209-G3
24*-E37	55-B9	86-I39	117-D50	148-C27	179-C51	210-G11
25-J32	56-D29	87-I53	118-D30	149-J25	180-E44	211-B32
26-E3	57-E36	88-F38	119-A37	150-J55	181-E31	212-B50
27-H25	58-D22	89-C33	120-J54	151-H14	182-H55	213-G40
28-E9	59-C24	90-J53	121-H11	152-B30	183-D51	214-B25
29-B16	60-J52	91-E46	122-A23	153-A1	184-H21	215-B42
30-J51	61-C4	92-J1	123-H4	154-A18	185-A35	216-B49
31-B35	62-A47	93-D52	124-D54	155-A4	186-A45	217-F46

[a] The repeated pairs in the booklet form (marked with an asterisk) are 8 and 318; 13 and 290; 15 and 314; 16 and 315; 20 and 310; 21 and 308; 22 and 326; 23 and 288; 24 and 333; 32 and 328; 33 and 323; 35 and 331; 37 and 302; 38 and 311; 305 and 366; 317 and 362.

Appendix C, Table 2 – continued

218-I6	268-G16	318*-F39	368-F13	418-I36	468-F32	518-G5
219-J7	269-I1	319-D46	369-D9	419-D27	469-F30	519-B26
220-C13	270-G38	320-C52	370-C21	420-D25	470-C54	520-F11
221-I50	271-D49	321-F4	371-F6	421-C8	471-D28	521-F2
222-F14	272-G23	322-C18	372-G14	422-C4	472-G46	522-H40
223-I51	273-A48	323*-H12	373-D13	423-I47	473-H51	523-A52
224-B52	274-A31	324-C11	374-F43	424-B13	474-B23	524-H44
225-J48	275-H7	325-C5	375-C34	425-B34	475-E4	525-H37
226-C3	276-E20	326*-A22	376-E13	426-F26	476-D24	526-F55
227-B38	277-E11	327-B54	377-E27	427-C55	477-E5	527-C1
228-G26	278-H2	328*-I27	378-E51	428-C38	478-E14	528-A51
229-E35	279-B40	329-B33	379-F48	429-C40	479-E18	529-J35
230-B10	280-D47	330-A41	380-G49	430-C49	480-J36	530-A53
231-D2	281-A36	331*-G53	381-G27	431-I54	481-I21	531-I20
232-D26	282-C10	332-A38	382-I17	432-D41	482-E55	532-J16
233-C31	283-J29	333*-E37	383-E52	433-J21	483-D19	533-B14
234-G29	284-H3	334-A30	384-F17	434-J2	484-B45	534-I24
235-B51	285-J50	335-A26	385-H34	435-J3	485-D4	535-B5
236-F45	286-E21	336-F31	386-G17	436-D45	486-B24	536-I48
237-C7	287-H31	337-G1	387-D20	437-E6	487-F41	537-I52
238-G21	288*-A15	338-G6	388-H46	438-E2	488-D11	538-I42
239-C12	289-D44	339-G10	389-I15	439-G13	489-F22	539-H39
240-E48	290*-I34	340-G22	390-F53	440-E47	490-D12	540-A34
241-B36	291-H8	341-G34	391-E28	441-J22	491-D14	541-A49
242-A8	292-E23	342-G35	392-H35	442-B29	492-H45	542-B21
243-A46	293-H6	343-G36	393-I5	443-C19	493-C30	543-G2
244-I30	294-E12	344-G45	394-I14	444-F29	494-H50	544-J13
245-B53	295-J26	345-G51	395-I10	445-D31	495-C32	545-J15
246-A54	296-G18	346-G41	396-F47	446-D37	496-A33	546-C39
247-C9	297-C53	347-G52	397-I31	447-D40	497-C44	547-J33
248-G25	298-E1	348-H9	398-I38	448-H1	498-F19	548-D1
249-D16	299-A9	349-H13	399-G28	449-E29	499-H29	549-I41
250-E7	300-J31	350-H20	400-H18	450-E30	500-G15	550-I46
251-A21	301-I35	351-H28	401-H41	451-E32	501-C26	551-H5
252-I8	302*-E17	352-H32	402-I18	452-E45	502-F20	552-C37
253-E54	303-F18	353-H52	403-I11	453-E19	503-F23	553-H48
254-E33	304-F3	354-H53	404-F28	454-E25	504-F21	554-J20
255-J49	305*-F35	355-I2	405-A39	455-E26	505-G24	555-J4
256-C46	306-E40	356-I23	406-I22	456-E8	506-I33	556-J14
257-C29	307-E42	357-I25	407-F37	457-B43	507-I16	557-J8
258-D15	308*-C6	358-G43	408-F27	458-J39	508-A29	558-D3
259-F42	309-E38	359-G42	409-I19	459-B44	509-F12	559-J6
260-C36	310*-C47	360-H30	410-E10	460-B41	510-H42	560-A28
261-I44	311*-D32	361-I32	411-I29	461-C28	511-F16	561-J28
262-E49	312-E22	362*-F10	412-A7	462-B22	512-J9	562-J30
263-B3	313-D55	363-I3	413-G8	463-J37	513-J17	563-I43
264-I40	314*-J41	364-H16	414-F54	464-H23	514-J38	564-C20
265-E53	315*-G55	365-H49	415-I28	465-C22	515-B46	565-I55
266-C20	316-D53	366*-F35	416-C23	466-B39	516-C2	566-J27
267-E43	317*-F10	367-H36	417-F24	467-G39	517-F40	

Table 3. Conversion from Booklet (Group) Form to Form R[a]

367-400	387-479	407-407	427-378	447-447	467-467	487-393	507-507	527-527	547-397
368-406	388-481	408-408	428-428	448-448	468-468	488-488	508-508	528-528	548-548
369-411	389-482	409-409	429-429	449-382	469-388	489-489	509-509	529-529	549-398
370-415	390-487	410-410	430-430	450-383	470-470	490-490	510-510	530-530	550-550
371-367	391-371	411-376	431-431	451-384	471-471	491-491	511-511	531-531	551-551
372-427	392-502	412-412	432-432	452-452	472-472	492-492	512-512	532-532	552-552
373-436	393-505	413-413	433-433	453-453	473-389	493-493	513-513	533-533	553-553
374-368	394-521	414-414	434-434	454-454	474-474	494-494	514-514	534-534	554-554
375-440	395-547	415-377	435-435	455-385	475-475	495-495	515-515	535-535	555-555
376-446	396-549	416-416	436-379	456-456	476-476	496-496	516-516	536-536	556-556
377-369	397-372	417-417	437-437	457-457	477-477	497-497	517-517	537-537	557-557
378-449	398-373	418-418	438-438	458-458	478-478	498-498	518-518	538-538	558-558
379-450	399-564	419-419	439-439	459-459	479-390	499-499	519-519	539-539	559-559
380-451	400-374	420-420	440-380	460-460	480-480	500-500	520-520	540-540	560-560
381-455	401-401	421-421	441-441	461-386	481-391	501-501	521-396	541-541	561-561
382-461	402-402	422-422	442-442	462-387	482-392	502-394	522-522	542-542	562-562
383-370	403-403	423-423	443-443	463-463	483-483	503-503	523-523	543-543	563-563
384-462	404-404	424-424	444-444	464-464	484-484	504-504	524-524	544-544	564-399
385-469	405-405	425-425	445-445	465-465	485-485	505-395	525-525	545-545	565-565
386-473	406-375	426-426	446-381	466-466	486-486	506-506	526-526	546-546	566-566

[a]Item numbers for the booklet (group) form are listed consecutively, followed by the corresponding Form R item number. The order of the first 366 items is the same for both forms.

Table 4. Conversion from Form R to Booklet (Group) Form[a]

367-371	387-462	407-407	427-372	447-447	467-467	487-390	507-507	527-527	547-395
368-374	388-469	408-408	428-428	448-448	468-468	488-488	508-508	528-528	548-548
369-377	389-473	409-409	429-429	449-378	469-385	489-489	509-509	529-529	549-396
370-383	390-479	410-410	430-430	450-379	470-470	490-490	510-510	530-530	550-550
371-391	391-481	411-369	431-431	451-380	471-471	491-491	511-511	531-531	551-551
372-397	392-482	412-412	432-432	452-452	472-472	492-492	512-512	532-532	552-552
373-398	393-487	413-413	433-433	453-453	473-386	493-493	513-513	533-533	553-553
374-400	394-502	414-414	434-434	454-454	474-474	494-494	514-514	534-534	554-554
375-406	395-505	415-370	435-435	455-381	475-475	495-495	515-515	535-535	555-555
376-411	396-521	416-416	436-373	456-456	476-476	496-496	516-516	536-536	556-556
377-415	397-547	417-417	437-437	457-457	477-477	497-497	517-517	537-537	557-557
378-427	398-549	418-418	438-438	458-458	478-478	498-498	518-518	538-538	558-558
379-436	399-564	419-419	439-439	459-459	479-387	499-499	519-519	539-539	559-559
380-440	400-367	420-420	440-375	460-460	480-480	500-500	520-520	540-540	560-560
381-446	401-401	421-421	441-441	461-382	481-388	501-501	521-394	541-541	561-561
382-449	402-402	422-422	442-442	462-384	482-389	502-392	522-522	542-542	562-562
383-450	403-403	423-423	443-443	463-463	483-483	503-503	523-523	543-543	563-563
384-451	404-404	424-424	444-444	464-464	484-484	504-504	524-524	544-544	564-399
385-455	405-405	425-425	445-445	465-465	485-485	505-393	525-525	545-545	565-565
386-461	406-368	426-426	446-376	466-466	486-486	506-506	526-526	546-546	566-566

[a]Item numbers for Form R are listed consecutively, followed by the corresponding group-form item number. The order of the first 366 items is the same for both forms.

APPENDIX D An Alphabetical Listing of Items

Items Listed Alphabetically with Card and Booklet Form Numbers

Item [a]	Card No.	Booklet No.	Item	Card No.	Booklet No.
A large	D-3	558	Dirt	H-42	510
A minister	D-21	53	During one	D-32	38, 311
A person should	B-37	11	During the	A-1	153
A person shouldn't	E-8	456	Even	F-35	305, 366
A windstorm	H-35	392	Everything is	D-22	58
Almost every	H-30	360	Everything tastes	G-11	210
Any man	I-9	83	Evil	H-25	27
As a youngster	D-29	56	Except	B-39	466
At one	H-8	291	Horses	I-5	393
At parties	E-27	377	I almost never	B-33	329
At periods	F-43	374	I am a good	E-36	57
At times I am	G-23	272	I am a high-strung	I-33	506
At times I feel like picking	G-32	145	I am a special	D-24	476
At times I feel like smashing	G-31	39	I am about	C-17	9
At times I feel like swearing	J-51	30	I am afraid of being	H-48	553
At times I feel that	G-26	228	I am afraid of finding	H-50	494
At times I have a strong	G-47	97	I am afraid of losing	H-55	182
At times I have been	E-11	277	I am afraid of using	H-53	354
At times I have enjoyed	I-3	363	I am afraid to be alone	H-46	388
At times I have fits	A-22	22, 326	I am afraid when	H-47	166
At times I have very	C-6	21, 308	I am against	D-51	183
At times I have worn	I-19	409	I am almost	B-9	55
At times I hear	G-34	341	I am always	D-44	289
At times I think	I-36	418	I am an important	H-19	73
At times it	G-44	205	I am apt to hide	F-27	408
At times my	G-30	134	I am apt to pass . . . because	C-19	443
Bad	G-43	358	I am apt to pass . . . when	C-20	564
Children	D-6	199	I am apt to take	F-54	414
Christ	D-19	483	I am attracted	C-49	430
Criticism	F-34	138	I am bothered by acid	B-16	29
			I am bothered by people	H-1	448
			I am certainly	I-39	86

Note: This alphabetical list was prepared and published by J. A. Morris Kimber (1957). We are indebted to Dr. Kimber and to the publisher of the *Journal of Clinical Psychology* for permission to reproduce this material here.

[a] Only the first and as many additional words as are necessary to distinguish each item are given.

Item	Card No.	Booklet No.	Item	Card No.	Booklet No.
I am easily awakened	B-31	5	I believe my sins....	G-3	209
I am easily downed..	I-26	82	I believe that a......	B-43	457
I am easily embarrassed	F-4	321	I believe that my....	B-48	137
I am embarrassed....	C-55	427	I believe there is a Devil	D-16	249
I am entirely........	I-40	264	I believe there is a God	D-15	258
I am fascinated.....	G-46	472	I believe women.....	D-7	101
I am greatly........	A-28	560	I blush.............	A-51	528
I am happy.........	G-12	107	I brood	F-45	236
I am in just.........	A-2	51	I can be............	E-54	253
I am inclined.......	I-32	361	I can easily.........	I-1	269
I am liked..........	E-39	54	I can read..........	A-32	188
I am likely.........	E-23	292	I can remember......	I-21	481
I am made..........	H-37	525	I can sleep..........	B-32	211
I am more..........	F-10	317, 362	I can stand.........	J-16	532
I am neither........	A-4	155	I cannot do.........	F-40	517
I am never..........	E-21	286	I cannot keep.......	A-26	335
I am not afraid of fire	H-36	367	I cannot understand..	B-2	159
I am not afraid of mice	H-39	539	I certainly feel......	I-37	142
I am not afraid of picking	H-44	524	I commonly hear....	H-21	184
I am not afraid to handle	H-33	169	I commonly wonder..	H-10	136
I am not bothered....	B-14	533	I could.............	E-25	454
I am not easily......	G-28	399	I cry	F-51	158
I am not unusually....	F-6	371	I daydream.........	F-15	198
I am often afraid of..	J-36	480	I deserve...........	G-8	413
I am often afraid that	A-53	530	I dislike having......	E-22	312
I am often inclined..	D-40	447	I dislike to..........	J-9	512
I am often said......	G-27	381	I do many..........	E-50	94
I am often so annoyed	F-24	417	I do not always......	J-42	45
I am often sorry.....	F-32	468	I do not blame......	D-49	271
I am quite..........	E-26	455	I do not dread.......	A-7	412
I am so............	F-18	303	I do not have a......	H-38	176
I am sure I am......	H-3	284	I do not have spells..	B-6	193
I am sure I get......	G-55	16, 315	I do not like everyone	J-47	195
I am troubled by attacks	A-15	23, 288	I do not like to......	E-51	378
I am troubled by discomfort	B-17	72	I do not mind being..	E-46	91
I am usually........	F-37	407	I do not mind meeting	E-18	479
I am very careful....	J-14	556	I do not often......	A-36	281
I am very religious...	D-8	206	I do not read........	J-52	60
I am very seldom....	B-18	18	I do not tire........	A-5	163
I am very strongly...	C-50	69	I do not try to correct	F-29	444
I am worried........	C-51	179	I do not try to cover..	F-21	504
I believe I am a.....	G-9	202	I do not worry......	H-43	131
I believe I am being followed	H-4	123	I don't blame.......	E-7	250
I believe I am being plotted	H-11	121	I don't seem........	G-7	104
I believe I am no more	A-8	242	I dread	H-45	492
I believe in a life....	D-17	115	I dream frequently...	B-34	425
I believe in law......	D-42	113	I dream frequently about	B-36	241
I believe in the......	D-18	98	I drink.............	B-40	279
I believe my sense....	A-29	508	I easily	F-31	336
			I enjoy a race.......	D-36	116
			I enjoy children.....	E-20	276
			I enjoy detective.....	C-43	12
			I enjoy gambling....	D-37	446

Item	Card No.	Booklet No.
I enjoy many........	E-41	207
I enjoy reading......	C-45	77
I enjoy social.......	E-29	449
I enjoy stories.......	C-44	497
I enjoy the.........	E-30	450
I feel anxiety........	G-1	337
I feel hungry.......	B-13	424
I feel like giving.....	F-41	487
I feel like jumping...	I-55	565
I feel sure..........	D-13	373
I feel sympathetic....	F-22	489
I feel that I.........	D-33	157
I feel that it........	E-3	26
I feel tired.........	J-13	544
I feel unable........	F-17	384
I feel uneasy........	H-49	365
I feel weak.........	A-40	189
I find it hard to keep.	I-27	32, 328
I find it hard to make	E-44	180
I find it hard to set..	C-28	461
I forget...........	G-35	342
I frequently ask.....	I-14	394
I frequently find it...	D-39	112
I frequently find myself...........	F-46	217
I frequently have....	F-9	172
I frequently notice...	A-45	186
I get all...........	E-40	306
I get angry.........	J-43	75
I get anxious........	H-28	351
I get mad..........	G-29	234
I go..............	D-10	95
I gossip...........	J-48	225
I hardly ever feel....	A-50	68
I hardly ever notice..	B-10	230
I hate.............	C-21	370
I have a cough......	B-7	34
I have a daydream...	F-16	511
I have a good.......	B-12	2
I have a great.......	B-15	125
I have a habit.......	G-41	346
I have at times had..	F-26	426
I have at times stood.	C-31	233
I have been afraid...	H-32	352
I have been disappointed	C-12	239
I have been inspired..	D-26	232
I have been quite....	B-51	235
I have been told.....	B-38	227
I have certainly.....	G-6	338
I have diarrhea......	B-19	14
I have difficulty.....	F-42	259
I have felt..........	C-4	422
I have few..........	A-46	243
I have frequently....	I-16	507
I have had attacks...	A-20	194
I have had blank....	A-21	251
I have had no ... keeping	A-42	192
I have had no ... bowel	B-20	63
I have had no ... urine	B-22	462
I have had periods ... carried	A-19	156
I have had periods ... lost	B-29	442
I have had periods of days	F-44	41
I have had periods when	G-24	505
I have had some.....	D-25	420
I have had very......	H-12	33, 323
I have little.........	A-44	103
I have met..........	G-19	100
I have more.........	I-23	356
I have never been in love	C-11	324
I have never been in trouble (sex).....	E-17	37, 302
I have never been in trouble (law).....	E-12	294
I have never been made	E-14	478
I have never been paralyzed	A-41	330
I have never done....	D-35	111
I have never felt.....	A-3	160
I have never had a fainting	A-17	174
I have never had a fit	A-18	154
I have never had any black	B-21	542
I have never had any breaking	B-25	214
I have never indulged	D-5	133
I have never noticed	B-24	486
I have never seen a vision	H-23	464
I have never seen things	A-33	496
I have never vomited	B-8	130
I have nightmares...	B-35	31
I have no dread.....	H-52	353
I have no enemies...	G-52	347
I have no fear of spiders	H-40	522
I have no fear of water	H-41	401
I have no patience ...	D-14	491
I have no trouble	A-39	405
I have not lived	G-4	61
I have numbness.....	A-48	273

Item	Card No.	Booklet No.	Item	Card No.	Booklet No.
I have often been....	J-6	559	I like to keep........	G-17	386
I have often felt badly	F-53	390	I like to know.......	J-46	165
I have often felt guilty	G-5	518	I like to let..........	F-20	502
I have often felt that .	H-2	278	I like to poke........	E-45	452
I have often found...	F-30	469	I like to read about history	C-39	546
I have often had.....	C-24	59	I like to read about science	C-37	552
I have often lost.....	C-25	147	I like to read newspaper articles.....	C-42	6
I have often met.....	I-22	406	I like to read newspaper editorials....	C-38	428
I have often wished..	J-40	74	I like to study.......	C-41	164
I have one or more bad	B-44	459	I like to talk........	D-2	231
I have one or more faults	B-45	484	I like to visit........	H-27	196
I have periods in which	G-18	296	I liked "Alice in Wonderland"	J-26	295
I have periods of such	G-21	238	I liked school.......	C-35	173
I have reason.......	C-9	247	I love..............	E-28	391
I have several times given	I-25	357	I loved my father....	C-15	65
I have several times had	C-22	465	I loved my mother...	C-13	220
I have sometimes felt	I-31	397	I must............	H-29	499
I have sometimes stayed	F-13	368	I never attend.......	D-1	548
I have strange.......	H-13	349	I never worry.......	E-48	240
I have strong........	D-41	432	I often feel.........	G-51	345
I have the wanderlust	G-33	146	I often memorize....	G-39	467
I have to urinate.....	B-23	474	I often must.........	I-18	402
I have used alcohol excessively	B-42	215	I often think........	I-38	398
I have used alcohol moderately	B-41	460	I played...........	D-27	419
I have very few fears.	H-31	287	I practically.......	A-52	523
I have very few headaches	A-10	190	I pray.............	D-11	488
I have very few quarrels	B-55	96	I prefer to pass......	E-24	52
I hear	H-20	350	I prefer work.......	C-30	493
I know who.........	H-26	127	I read.............	D-12	490
I like adventure......	I-43	563	I readily become.....	G-15	500
I like collecting......	J-12	132	I refuse	E-42	307
I like dramatics.....	J-24	126	I resent...........	F-25	162
I like mannish.......	J-38	514	I see..............	H-24	66
I like mechanics.....	J-5	1	I seem to be.........	A-23	122
I like movie.........	J-27	566	I seem to make......	E-38	309
I like or have........	I-47	423	I seldom or never....	A-16	175
I like parties........	J-33	547	I seldom worry......	A-6	36
I like poetry	J-18	78	I should............	E-35	229
I like repairing......	I-46	550	I shrink............	I-41	549
I like science........	I-50	221	I sometimes feel.....	J-4	555
I like tall...........	J-22	441	I sometimes find.....	F-12	509
I like to attend......	C-40	429	I sometimes keep....	G-37	64
I like to be	E-33	254	I sometimes tease....	I-4	80
I like to cook........	J-11	140	I strongly..........	F-11	520
I like to flirt.........	C-48	208	I sweat............	B-3	263
I like to go..........	E-34	99	I tend to be interested	G-14	372
			I tend to be on my guard	H-9	348
			I think a great.......	D-48	71
			I think I would . . . forest	I-49	81

Appendix D — continued

Item	Card No.	Booklet No.
I think I would . . . building	J-7	219
I think I would . . . dressmaker	I-42	538
I think I would . . . librarian	J-34	4
I think Lincoln	J-17	513
I think most	D-52	93
I think nearly	D-53	316
I think that	A-9	299
I try to	E-47	440
I used to have	J-21	433
I used to keep	J-25	149
I used to like drop-the-handkerchief	I-45	70
I used to like hopscotch	J-37	463
I usually expect	C-29	257
I usually feel	F-38	88
I usually have	G-36	343
I usually "lay my cards . . ."	C-32	495
I usually work	C-26	501
I very much like horseback	J-28	561
I very much like hunting	I-51	223
I very seldom	F-48	379
I wake	B-27	3
I was a slow	C-36	260
I was fond	D-31	445
I wish I could be	F-36	67
I wish I could get	I-17	382
I wish I were not bothered	C-53	297
I wish I were not so	F-5	201
I work	I-34	13, 290
I worry over	C-18	322
I worry quite	I-54	431
I would certainly	E-10	410
I would like to be a florist	I-53	87
I would like to be a journalist	J-23	204
I would like to be a nurse	J-1	92
I would like to be a private	J-8	557
I would like to be a singer	J-32	25
I would like to be a soldier	J-10	144
I would like to be an auto	J-2	434
I would like to hunt	I-52	537
I would like to wear	J-35	529
I would rather	J-55	150
If given the chance I could	H-18	400
If given the chance I would	I-28	415
If I could	J-45	135
If I were a reporter . . . theater	J-19	203
If I were a reporter . . . sporting	J-29	283
If I were an artist . . . children	J-20	554
If I were an artist . . . flower	I-44	261
If I were in trouble	E-5	477
If people	G-53	35, 331
If several people	E-1	298
In a group	F-2	521
In my home	B-46	515
In school I found	F-3	304
In school I was	D-30	118
In school my marks	D-28	471
In walking	G-40	213
It bothers	C-23	416
It does not bother me particularly	I-6	218
It does not bother me that	E-49	262
It is all right	E-6	437
It is always	F-19	498
It is great	I-11	403
It is not	F-14	222
It is safer	E-53	265
It is unusual	F-23	503
It makes me angry	I-48	536
It makes me feel	I-29	411
It makes me impatient	C-27	148
It makes me nervous	G-13	439
It makes me uncomfortable	F-8	171
It takes	C-33	89
It would	D-43	49
It wouldn't	E-15	167
Life	I-35	301
Lightning	H-34	385
Many	C-52	320
Most any	F-1	40
Most nights	B-30	152
Most of the time I feel	F-49	76
Most of the time I wish	G-10	339
Most people are	D-50	117
Most people inwardly	D-46	319
Most people make	D-47	280
Most people will	D-54	124
Much of the time I feel	F-50	106

Item	Card No.	Booklet No.
Much of the time my head	A-11	44
My conduct	D-38	141
My daily	F-39	8, 318
My eyesight	A-31	274
My face	A-34	540
My family	B-47	42
My father	C-16	17
My feelings	F-52	79
My hands and	A-55	7
My hands have	A-43	187
My hardest	I-13	102
My hearing	A-35	185
My judgment	A-24	46
My memory	A-27	178
My mother or father	B-54	327
My mother was	C-14	177
My mouth	B-5	535
My neck	A-54	246
My parents and	B-53	245
My parents have	B-52	224
My people	B-50	212
My plans	I-15	389
My relatives	C-7	237
My sex	C-47	20, 310
My skin	A-49	541
My sleep	B-28	43
My soul	D-23	50
My speech	A-37	119
My table	J-54	120
My way	I-30	244
My worries	E-32	451
No one cares	I-8	252
No one seems	E-37	24, 333
Often, even	F-47	396
Often I can't	F-33	129
Often I cross	G-45	344
Often I feel	A-12	114
Once a week . . . very excited	G-20	266
Once a week without	B-1	47
Once in a while I feel	C-10	282
Once in a while I laugh	J-50	285
Once in a while I put	J-53	90
Once in a while I think	J-41	15, 314
One	C-8	421
Parts	A-47	62
Peculiar	A-30	334
People can	I-20	531
People generally	D-45	436
People have often	F-28	404
People often disappoint	E-52	383
People say	H-16	364
Policemen	E-13	376
Religion	D-9	369
Several times a week	G-2	543
Several times I	I-24	534
Sexual	C-54	470
Some of my family have habits	C-3	226
Some of my family have quick	C-2	516
Some people	G-50	109
Someone has been . . . influence	H-6	293
Someone has been . . . poison	H-14	151
Someone has been . . . rob me	H-15	197
Someone has control	H-7	275
Someone has it	G-54	110
Something exciting	G-16	268
Sometimes at elections	J-49	255
Sometimes I am strongly	I-7	85
Sometimes I am sure	H-5	551
Sometimes I become	G-22	340
Sometimes I enjoy	I-2	355
Sometimes I feel	G-48	139
Sometimes I have	J-15	545
Sometimes my voice	A-38	332
Sometimes some	G-42	359
Sometimes, when embarrassed	B-4	191
Sometimes when I	J-44	105
Sometimes without	G-25	248
The future is too	I-10	395
The future seems	F-55	526
The man who had	J-39	458
The man who provides	D-55	313
The members	C-1	527
The one	J-30	562
The only interesting	C-46	256
The only miracles	D-20	387
The sight	H-54	128
The things	C-5	325
The top	A-14	161
There are certain	E-2	438
There are persons	H-17	200
There is something . . . mind	A-25	168
There is something . . . sex	B-26	519
There is very	B-49	216
There never	J-31	300
There seems to be a fullness	A-13	108
There seems to be a lump	B-11	10
These days	I-12	84
Usually	J-3	435

Appendix D — continued

Item	Card No.	Booklet No.	Item	Card No.	Booklet No.
What	F-7	170	When I was a child, I belonged	D-34	143
When a man........	D-4	485	When I was a child, I didn't	E-19	453
When I am cornered..	E-4	475	When in a group.....	E-43	267
When I am feeling...	C-34	375	When someone does..	E-9	28
When I am with.....	H-22	48	When someone says..	G-49	380
When I get bored....	E-31	181	Whenever possible...	H-51	473
When I leave........	G-38	270	While in trains......	E-55	482
When I take	E-16	19			

APPENDIX E Key Word Index to Items

The following list of key words found among the component items of the MMPI was prepared by Aaronson and Rothman (1962). It is adapted here through the kind permission of these authors. The list contains those words or word units which serve to differentiate each item from all others in the test. The items in which these word units appear are listed by both card-form and booklet-form (see Appendix L) designations — the card-form designation is given first; the booklet-form number follows in parentheses. By means of this alphabetical listing it is possible to locate and verify any incompletely quoted item, to identify a reworded item (e.g., in simplified or interrogative form), or to compile a set of items with a given topical reference. If the full and precise wording of the item is available, it is more convenient to use the alphabetical listing of items provided in Appendix D.

Key Word Index

ability: I25 (357)
able: C17 (9); I9 (83). *See also* capable
accept: B45 (484)
acid: B16 (29)
act: G36 (343)
actions: F23 (503).
See also activities, behavior
active: C34 (375)
activities: A19 (156); A21 (251).
See also actions, behavior
admired: J30 (562)
admit: F25 (162)
advantage: D49 (124); D54 (271)
adventure: C44 (497); I43 (563)
advice: C27 (148); I14 (394)
affairs: E34 (99)
afraid: I1 (269); J36 (480).
See also fear, frighten
Africa: I52 (537)
afterlife: D16 (249). *See also* hereafter
afterwards: E50 (94)
again: I38 (398)
agent: D24 (476)
agree upon: E1 (298)
alcohol: B41 (215); B42 (460).
See also drink
alcoholic: B43 (457)
"Alice in Wonderland": J26 (295)
all over: A11 (44); A40 (47); B1 (189)
all right: A27 (178)
allow: D45 (436)
alone: E21 (286); E25 (350); H20 (388);
H46 (454); H48 (553)
amount (-ed, -ing) to: C31 (84);
I12 (233)
angered: G28 (399). *See also* mad
angry: I48 (75); J43 (536). *See also* mad
animals: H24 (66); H37 (80); I4 (218);
I6 (525)
annoy (-ing): C3 (226); F26 (426)
anxiety: G1 (337)
anxious: H28 (351). *See also* worry
anyone: C11 (324). *See also* someone
anything: F40 (517).
See also something, thing
appetite: B12 (2). *See also* hungry
approval: F23 (503)
argument (-s): C33 (82); D44 (89);
I26 (289)
arranged: I16 (507)
articles: C42 (6); I7 (85)
artist: I44 (261); J20 (554)

APPENDIX F T-Score Conversions for Supplementary MMPI Scales

T-Score Conversions

Raw Score	Males A	Males R	Males Es	Males Lb	Males Ca	Males Dy	Males Do	Males Re	Males Pr	Males St	Males Cn	Females A	Females R	Females Es	Females Lb	Females Ca	Females Dy	Females Do	Females Re	Females Pr	Females St	Females Cn
68			87											94								
67			86											92								
66			85											91								
65			83											89								
64			82											87								
63			80											86								
62			78											84								
61			77											83								
60			75											81								
59			74											80								
58			72											78								
57			70			91								76			84					
56			69			90								75			83					
55			67			89								73			82					
54			66			88								72			81					
53			64			87								70			80					
52			62			86								69			79					
51			61			85								67			78					
50			59			84					115			65			77					113
49			58			83					112			64			76					111
48			56			81					109			62			75					108
47			54			80					107			61			74					106
46			53			79					104			59			73					103
45			51			78					102			58			72					100
44			49			77					99			56			71					98
43			48			76					97			54			69					95
42			46			75					94			53			68					92
41			45			74					91			51			67					90
40		101	43			73					89		102	50			66					87
39	84	99	41			72					86	78	100	48			65					85
38	82	97	40			70					84	77	98	47			64					82
37	81	95	38			69					81	76	95	45			63					79
36	80	93	37		99	68					79	75	93	43		95	62					77

Appendix F—continued

Raw Score	Males											Females										
	A	R	Es	Lb	Ca	Dy	Do	Re	Pr	St	Cn	A	R	Es	Lb	Ca	Dy	Do	Re	Pr	St	Cn
35	79	91	35		98	67					76	74	91	42		93	61					74
34	77	89	33		96	66				86	73	73	88	41		91	60				86	72
33	76	86	32		94	65				84	71	71	86	39		89	59				84	69
32	75	84	30		92	64		78	88	82	68	70	84	37		87	58		78	88	82	66
31	74	82	29		90	63		76	86	80	66	69	81	36		85	57		75	86	80	64
30	72	80	27		88	62		74	84	78	63	68	79	34		84	56		72	84	78	61
29	71	78	25		86	61		71	82	75	61	67	76	32		82	55		70	82	75	58
28	70	76	24		84	59	87	69	80	73	58	66	74	31		80	54	87	67	80	73	56
27	69	74	22		83	58	85	66	78	71	55	64	72	29		78	53	85	64	78	71	53
26	67	72	20	120	81	57	82	64	76	69	53	63	69	28	120	76	51	82	62	76	69	51
25	66	70	19	116	79	56	79	62	75	66	50	62	67	26	116	74	50	79	59	75	66	48
24	65	68	17	112	77	55	76	59	73	64	48	61	65	24	112	72	49	76	57	73	64	45
23	64	66	16	108	75	54	73	57	71	62	45	60	62	23	108	71	48	73	54	71	62	43
22	62	63	14	104	73	53	70	54	69	60	43	58	60	21	104	69	47	70	51	69	60	40
21	61	61	12	99	71	52	68	52	67	58	40	57	58	20	99	67	46	68	49	67	58	38
20	60	59		95	69	51	65	50	65	55	38	56	55	18	95	65	45	65	46	65	55	35
19	59	57		91	68	50	62	47	63	53	35	55	53	17	91	63	44	62	43	63	53	32
18	57	55		87	66	48	59	45	62	51	32	54	51	15	87	61	43	59	41	62	51	30
17	56	53		83	64	47	56	42	60	49	30	53	48	14	83	60	42	56	38	60	49	27
16	55	51		78	62	46	53	40	58	46	27	51	46	12	78	58	41	53	35	58	46	25
15	54	49		74	60	45	51	37	56	44	25	50	44		74	56	40	51	33	56	44	22
14	52	47		70	58	44	48	35	54	42	22	49	41		70	54	39	48	30	54	42	19
13	51	45		66	56	43	45	33	52	40	20	48	39		66	52	38	45	28	52	40	17
12	50	43		62	55	42	42	30	51	38	17	47	36		62	50	37	42	25	51	38	14
11	49	40		57	53	41	39	28	49	35	14	46	34		57	49	36	39	22	49	35	11
10	47	38		53	51	40	37	25	47	33	12	44	32		53	47	35	37	20	47	33	9
9	46	36		49	49	39	34	23	45	31	9	43	29		49	45	34	34		45	31	6
8	45	34		45	47	37	31	21	43	29	7	42	27		45	43	32	31		43	29	4
7	44	32		41	45	36	28	18	41	27	4	41	25		41	41	31	28		41	27	1
6	42	30		36	43	35	25		39	24	2	40	22		36	39	30	25		39	24	
5	41	28		32	41	34	22		38	22		38	20		32	38	29	22		38	22	
4	40	26		28	40	33	20		36	20		37	18		28	36	28	20		36	20	
3	38	24		24	38	32			34	18		36	15		24	34	27			34	18	
2	37	22		20	36	31			32	15		35	13		20	32	26			32	15	
1	36	20			34	30			30	13		34	11			30	25			30	13	
0	35	17			32	29			28	11		33				28	24			28	11	

Hathaway and Briggs (1957).

APPENDIX G Critical Items

Each of the items in this list bears on some serious symptom, impulse, or experience to be checked in subsequent interviews with the patient or informants. Grayson (1951) recommends that these statements be used as "stop" items in screening patients for a psychiatric disorder.

Scale Membership and Direction of Scoring for Critical Items

Item No.	Item	Scale	Critical Direction
20 (310)	My sex life is satisfactory	F48	False
27	Evil spirits possess me at times	F6	True
33 (323)	I have had very peculiar and strange experiences	48 .... (0	True False)
37 (302)	I have never been in trouble because of my sex behavior	48	False
44	Much of the time my head seems to hurt all over	3	True
48	When I am with people I am bothered by hearing very queer things	F	True
66	I see things or animals or people around me that others do not see	F	True
69	I am very strongly attracted by members of my own sex	5	True
74	I have often wished I were a girl. (Or if you are a girl) I have never been sorry that I am a girl	5	True
85	Sometimes I am strongly attracted by the personal articles of others such as shoes, gloves, etc., so that I want to handle or steal them though I have no use for them	F	True
114	Often I feel as if there were a tight band about my head	13	True
121	I believe I am being plotted against	F68	True
123	I believe I am being followed	F6	True
133	I have never indulged in any unusual sex practices	5	False
139	Sometimes I feel as if I must injure either myself or someone else	F	True
146	I have the wanderlust and am never happy unless I am roaming or traveling about	F	True
151	Someone has been trying to poison me	F6	True
156	I have had periods in which I carried on activities without knowing later what I had been doing	F89	True
168	There is something wrong with my mind	F8	True

Note: These items are taken from a list prepared by L. I. Hellman.

Appendix G — continued

Item No.	Item	Scale	Critical Direction
179	I am worried about sex matters	358	True
182	I am afraid of losing my mind	278	True
184	I commonly hear voices without knowing where they come from	F	True
200	There are persons who are trying to steal my thoughts and ideas	F	True
202	I believe I am a condemned person	F68	True
205	At times it has been impossible for me to keep from stealing or shoplifting something	F	True
209	I believe my sins are unpardonable	F	True
215	I have used alcohol excessively	F4	True
251	I have had blank spells in which my activities were interrupted and I did not know what was going on around me	89	True
275	Someone has control over my mind	F6	True
291	At one or more times in my life I felt that someone was making me do things by hypnotizing me	F68	True
293	Someone has been trying to influence my mind	F6	True
334	Peculiar odors come to me at times	8	True
337	I feel anxiety about something or someone almost all the time	7	True
339	Most of the time I wish I were dead	8	True
345	I often feel as if things were not real	8	True
349	I have strange and peculiar thoughts	78	True
350	I hear strange things when I am alone	8	True
354	I am afraid of using a knife or anything very sharp or pointed	8	True

APPENDIX H T-Score Conversion Tables for the Basic Scales

T-score conversions are provided here (and scale composition data in Appendix I) for only the basic MMPI scales and their derivative subscales. Similar information on special scales will be found in Appendix F and in the appendix material in Volume II.

Table 1. Fractional Scores for Any Given Raw Score of K

Raw K	.5 K	.4 K	.2 K
30	15	12	6
29	15	12	6
28	14	11	6
27	14	11	5
26	13	10	5
25	13	10	5
24	12	10	5
23	12	9	5
22	11	9	4
21	11	8	4
20	10	8	4
19	10	8	4
18	9	7	4
17	9	7	3
16	8	6	3
15	8	6	3
14	7	6	3
13	7	5	3
12	6	5	2
11	6	4	2
10	5	4	2
9	5	4	2
8	4	3	2
7	4	3	1
6	3	2	1
5	3	2	1
4	2	2	1
3	2	1	1
2	1	1	0
1	1	1	0
0	0	0	0

Table 2. T-Score Conversions for Basic Scales with K Corrections for Minnesota Adults

	Males														Females														
Raw Score	?	L	F	K	1 (Hs) + .5 K	2 (D)	3 (Hy)	4 (Pd) + .4 K	5 (Mf)	6 (Pa)	7 (Pt) + 1 K	8 (Sc) + 1 K	9 (Ma) + .2 K	0 (Si)	?	L	F	K	1 (Hs) + .5 K	2 (D)	3 (Hy)	4 (Pd) + .4 K	5 (Mf)	6 (Pa)	7 (Pt) + 1 K	8 (Sc) + 1 K	9 (Ma) + .2 K	0 (Si)	Raw Score
60	58													87	58										107	107		87	60
59														86											106	106		86	59
58												119		85											104	104		85	58
57											120	117		84											102	103		84	57
56											118	115		83											101	101		83	56
55											116	113		82											99	100		82	55
54							118				114	111		81						117	112				98	98		81	54
53							116				112	109		80						115	110				96	97		80	53
52							115				110	107		79						113	109				94	95		79	52
51							113		110		107	105		78						111	107		20		93	94		78	51
50	56						111		108		105	103		77	56					109	105		22		91	92		77	50
49							109		106		103	101		76						107	103		24		89	91		76	49
48							107	119	104		101	99		75						105	101	119	26		88	89		75	48
47							106	116	102		99	97		74						103	100	116	28		86	87		74	47
46						120	104	114	100		97	96		73						102	98	114	30		84	86		73	46
45						118	102	111	98		95	94		72						100	96	111	32		83	84		72	45
44						116	100	109	96		93	92		71						98	94	109	34		81	83		71	44
43						113	98	107	94		91	90		70					111	96	93	107	37		79	81		70	43
42						111	96	104	92		89	88		69					109	94	91	104	39		78	80		69	42
41						108	95	102	90		87	86		68					107	92	89	102	41		76	78		68	41
40	53					106	93	100	88		85	84	108	67	53				105	90	87	100	43		74	77	108	67	40
39						104	91	97	86		83	82	106	66					103	88	86	97	45		73	75	106	66	39
38					118	101	89	95	84		81	80	103	65					101	86	84	95	47		71	74	103	65	38
37					116	99	87	93	82		79	78	101	64					99	84	82	93	49		69	72	101	64	37
36					113	96	86	90	80		77	76	98	63					97	82	80	90	51		68	71	98	63	36

35					111	94	84	88	78		75	74	96	62					95	80	79	88	53		66	69	96	62	35
34					108	92	82	86	76		73	73	93	61					93	78	77	86	55		65	67	93	61	34
33					106	89	80	83	74		71	71	91	60					91	76	75	83	57		63	66	91	60	33
32					103	87	78	81	73	120	69	69	88	58					89	75	73	81	59	120	61	64	88	58	32
31			110		100	84	76	79	71	117	66	67	86	56			110		87	73	72	79	61	117	60	63	86	56	31
30	50		108	83	98	82	75	76	69	114	64	65	83	55	50		108	83	85	71	70	76	63	114	58	61	83	55	30
29			106	81	95	80	73	74	67	111	62	63	81	54			106	81	82	69	68	74	66	111	56	60	81	54	29
28			104	79	93	77	71	71	65	108	60	61	78	53			104	79	80	67	66	71	68	108	55	58	78	53	28
27			102	77	90	75	69	69	63	105	58	59	75	52			102	77	78	65	64	69	70	105	53	57	75	52	27
26			100	75	88	72	67	67	61	102	56	57	73	51			100	75	76	63	63	67	72	102	51	55	73	51	26
25			98	74	85	70	65	64	59	100	54	55	70	50			98	74	74	61	61	64	74	100	50	54	70	50	25
24			96	72	82	68	64	62	57	97	52	53	68	49			96	72	72	59	59	62	76	97	48	52	68	49	24
23			94	70	80	65	62	60	55	94	50	51	65	48			94	70	70	57	57	60	78	94	46	51	65	48	23
22			92	68	77	63	60	57	53	91	48	50	63	47			92	68	68	55	56	57	80	91	45	49	63	47	22
21			90	66	75	60	58	55	51	88	46	48	60	46			90	66	66	53	54	55	82	88	43	47	60	46	21
20	47		88	64	72	58	56	53	49	85	44	46	58	45	47		88	64	64	51	52	53	84	85	41	46	58	45	20
19			86	62	70	56	55	50	47	82	42	44	55	44			86	62	62	49	50	50	86	82	40	44	55	44	19
18			84	61	67	53	53	48	45	79	40	42	53	43			84	61	60	47	49	48	88	79	38	43	53	43	18
17			82	59	65	51	51	46	43	76	38	40	50	42			82	59	58	46	47	46	90	76	36	41	50	42	17
16			80	57	62	48	49	43	41	73	36	38	48	41			80	57	56	44	45	43	92	73	35	40	48	41	16
15		86	78	55	59	46	47	41	39	70	34	36	45	40		86	78	55	54	42	43	41	95	70	33	38	45	40	15
14		83	76	53	57	44	45	39	37	67	32	34	43	39		83	76	53	52	40	42	39		67	32	37	43	39	14
13		80	73	51	54	41	44	36	35	65	30	32	40	38		80	73	51	50	38	40	36		65	30	35	40	38	13
12		76	70	49	52	39	42	34	34	62	28	30	38	37		76	70	49	48	36	38	34		62	28	34	38	37	12
11		73	68	48	49	36	40	32	32	59	26	28	35	36		73	68	48	46	34	36	32		59	27	32	35	36	11
10	44	70	66	46	47	34	38	29	30	56	23	26	33	35	44	70	66	46	44	32	34	29		56	25	31	33	35	10
9		66	64	44	44	32	36	27	28	53	21	25	30	34		66	64	44	42	30	33	27		53	23	29	30	34	9
8		63	62	42	41	29	35	24	26	50		23	28	33		63	62	42	39	28	31	24		50	22	27	28	33	8
7		60	60	40	39			22		47		21	26	32		60	60	40	37		29	22		47	20	26	26	32	7
6		56	58	38	36			20		44			23	30		56	58	38	35		27	20		44		24	23	30	6
5		53	55	36	34					41			21	29		53	55	36	33		26			41		23	21	29	5
4		50	53	35	31					38				28		50	53	35	31		24			38				28	4
3		46	50	33	29					35				27		46	50	33	29					35				27	3
2		44	48	31	26					33				26		44	48	31	27					33				26	2
1		40	46	29	23					30				25		40	46	29	25					30				25	1
0	41	36	44	27	21					27					41	36	44	27	23					27					0

Table 3. T-Score Conversions for Basic Scales with K Corrections for University of North Carolina Freshmen

	Males														Females														
Raw Score	?	L	F	K	1 (Hs) + .5 K	2 (D)	3 (Hy)	4 (Pd) + .4 K	5 (Mf)	6 (Pa)	7 (Pt) + 1 K	8 (Sc) + 1 K	9 (Ma) + .2 K	0 (Si)	?	L	F	K	1 (Hs) + .5 K	2 (D)	3 (Hy)	4 (Pd) + .4 K	5 (Mf)	6 (Pa)	7 (Pt) + 1 K	8 (Sc) + 1 K	9 (Ma) + .2 K	0 (Si)	Raw Score
70	62													101	62											114		96	70
69														100												113		95	69
68														99												111		94	68
67														98												110		93	67
66														97												108		92	66
65														95												107		91	65
64														94												105		90	64
63														93												104		89	63
62														92												102		87	62
61														91												101		86	61
60	58													90	58											99		85	60
59									119					89												98		84	59
58									117			119		88												96		83	58
57									115			117		86												95		82	57
56									113			115		85												93		81	56
55									111			113		84									21			92		80	55
54									109			111		83									22			90		79	54
53									107			109		82									23			89		78	53
52									105			107		81						120			25			87		77	52
51									103			105		80						118	119		26			86		76	51
50	56							116	101			103		79	56					116	117	120	28			84		75	50
49								113	99			101		78						114	114	118	29			83		74	49
48								111	97		99	99		76						112	112	115	30		85	81		73	48
47						120	120	109	95		97	97		75						109	110	113	32		83	80		71	47
46						118	118	106	93		95	95	118	74						107	107	110	33		81	78	115	70	46
45						116	115	104	91		93	93	116	73						105	105	108	35		80	77	112	69	45
44						113	113	102	89		91	91	113	72						103	103	105	36		78	75	110	68	44
43						111	110	100	87		89	89	110	71						101	100	103	37		76	74	107	67	43
42						109	108	97	85		87	87	108	70						99	98	100	39		74	72	105	66	42
41						106	105	95	83		85	85	105	69						96	96	98	40		72	71	103	65	41

40	53					104	103	93	81		83	83	103	68	53					94	93	96	41		70	69	100	64	40
39						102	101	90	79		80	81	100	66						92	91	93	43		69	68	98	63	39
38						99	98	88	77		78	79	97	65						90	89	91	44		67	66	95	62	38
37						97	96	86	75		76	77	95	64			119			88	86	88	46		65	65	93	61	37
36						94	93	83	73		74	75	92	63			117			86	84	86	47		63	63	90	60	36
35						92	91	81	71		72	73	90	62			115			84	82	83	48		61	62	88	59	35
34						90	88	79	69		70	71	87	61			113			81	79	81	50		60	60	86	58	34
33						87	86	77	67		68	69	84	60			111		105	79	77	79	51		58	59	83	57	33
32						85	83	74	65		66	67	82	59			109		102	77	75	76	53	119	56	57	81	55	32
31						83	81	72	63		64	65	79	57			107		99	75	72	74	54	115	54	56	78	54	31
30	50			82	119	80	78	70	61	120	62	63	77	56	50		105		97	73	70	71	55	112	52	54	76	53	30
29				80	116	78	76	67	59	117	60	61	74	55			102		94	71	68	69	57	109	50	53	73	52	29
28				78	112	76	73	65	57	114	58	59	71	54			100		91	68	65	66	58	106	49	51	71	51	28
27				76	108	73	71	63	55	110	55	57	69	53			98	117	88	66	63	64	60	102	47	50	69	50	27
26				74	105	71	69	60	53	107	53	55	66	52			96	112	86	64	61	62	61	99	45	48	66	49	26
25			120	72	101	69	66	58	51	104	51	53	64	51			94	106	83	62	58	59	62	96	43	47	64	48	25
24			117	70	97	66	64	56	49	100	49	51	61	50			92	100	80	60	56	57	64	93	41	45	61	47	24
23			114	67	94	64	61	53	47	97	47	49	58	49			90	94	78	58	54	54	65	89	40	44	59	46	23
22			110	65	90	61	59	51	45	94	45	47	56	47			87	88	75	55	51	52	66	86	38	42	57	45	22
21			107	63	86	59	56	49	43	91	43	45	53	46			85	82	72	53	49	49	68	83	36	41	54	44	21
20	47		104	61	83	57	54	47	41	87	41	43	51	45	47		83	77	70	51	47	47	69	80	34	39	52	43	20
19			100	59	79	54	51	44	39	84	39	41	48	44			81	71	67	49	44	44	71	76	32	38	49	42	19
18			97	57	75	52	49	42	37	80	37	39	45	43			79	65	64	47	42	42	72	73	30	36	47	41	18
17			94	55	72	50	46	40	35	77	35	37	43	42			77	59	62	45	40	40	73	70	29	35	44	39	17
16			90	53	68	47	44	37	33	74	33	35	40	41			75	53	59	42	37	37	75	67	27	33	42	38	16
15		113	87	50	64	45	41	35	31	70	31	33	38	40		119	73	47	56	40	35	35	76	63	25	32	40	37	15
14		108	83	48	61	43	39	33	29	67	28	31	35	39		113	70	41	54	38	33	32	78	60	23	30	37	36	14
13		102	80	46	57	40	37	30	27	64	26	29	32	37		107	68	36	51	36	30	30	79	57	21	29	35	35	13
12		96	77	44	53	38	34	28	25	60	24	27	30	36		101	66	30	48	34	28	27	80	54		27	32	34	12
11		91	73	42	50	36	32	26	23	57	22	25	27	35		96	64	24	45	32	26	25	82	50		26	30	33	11
10	44	85	70	40	46	33	29	24	21	54	20	23	25	34	44	90	62		43	30	24	23	83	47		24	27	32	10
9		79	67	38	42	31	27	21		50		21	22	33		84	60		40	27	21	20	84	44		23	25	31	9
8		74	63	36	39	28	24			47				32		78	58		37	25			86	41		22	23	30	8
7		68	60	34	35	26	22			44				31		72	56		35	23				37		20	20	29	7
6		63	56	31	31	24				40				30		66	53		32	21				34				28	6
5		57	53	29	28	21				37				28		60	51		29					31				27	5
4		51	50	27	24					34				27		55	49		27					28				26	4
3		46	46	25	20					30				26		49	47		24					24				25	3
2		40	43	23						27				25		43	45		21					21				23	2
1		34	40	21						24				24		37	43											22	1
0	41	29	36							20				23	41	31	41											21	0

Table 4. T-Score Conversions for Basic Scales with K Corrections for Minnesota Aged (Age 70 and Above)

	Males														Females														
Raw Score	?	L	F	K	1 (Hs) + .5 K	2 (D)	3 (Hy)	4 (Pd) + .4 K	5 (Mf)	6 (Pa)	7 (Pt) + 1 K	8 (Sc) + 1 K	9 (Ma) + .2 K	0 (Si)	?	L	F	K	1 (Hs) + .5 K	2 (D)	3 (Hy)	4 (Pd) + .4 K	5 (Mf)	6 (Pa)	7 (Pt) + 1 K	8 (Sc) + 1 K	9 (Ma) + .2 K	0 (Si)	Raw Score
70	62													107	62													105	70
69														106														103	69
68														105														102	68
67														103														101	67
66														102														100	66
65														101														98	65
64														99														97	64
63														98														96	63
62														97														94	62
61														95														93	61
60	58													94	58					119	118				109	119		92	60
59											119	119		93						117	117				108	117		91	59
58							119				117	117		91						115	115				106	116		89	58
57							117				115	116		90						113	113				104	114		88	57
56							115				113	114		89						111	111				102	112		87	56
55						119	114				111	112		87						109	110		20		100	110		85	55
54						117	112		120		109	110		86						108	108		22		99	108		84	54
53						115	110		118		107	108		85						106	106		24		97	106		83	53
52						113	108		116		105	106		83					119	104	104		26		95	104		82	52
51						111	107		114		103	104		82					117	102	103		28		93	102		80	51
50	56					109	105		111		101	102		81	56				115	100	101		30		91	100		79	50
49						107	103		109		99	100		79					113	98	99		32		89	98		78	49
48						105	101	120	107		97	98		78					111	97	97		34		88	96		76	48
47					119	103	99	118	105		95	97		77					109	95	96		36		86	95		75	47
46					117	101	98	115	103		93	95		75					108	93	94	119	38		84	93		74	46
45					115	99	96	112	100		91	93		74					106	91	92	116	40		82	91		73	45
44					113	97	94	110	98		89	91		73					104	89	90	114	42		80	89		71	44
43					111	95	92	108	96		87	89		71					102	87	88	111	44		78	87		70	43
42					109	93	91	105	94		85	87		70					100	86	87	109	46		77	85		69	42
41					107	91	89	102	92		83	85	120	69					98	84	85	106	48		75	83	120	67	41

40	53				105	89	87	100	89		81	83	117	67	53				96	82	83	104	50		73	81	118	66	40
39					103	87	85	98	87		79	81	115	66					94	80	81	101	52		71	79	115	65	39
38					101	85	83	95	85		77	79	112	65					93	78	80	99	54		69	77	112	63	38
37					99	83	81	92	83		75	77	109	64					91	76	78	96	56		68	75	109	62	37
36					96	81	80	90	80		73	76	106	62					89	75	76	94	58		66	74	106	61	36
35					94	79	78	88	78		71	74	103	61					87	73	74	91	60		64	72	103	60	35
34					92	77	77	85	76		69	72	100	60					85	71	73	89	62		62	70	101	58	34
33					90	75	75	82	74		67	70	97	58					83	69	71	86	65		60	68	98	57	33
32					88	73	73	80	72		65	68	94	57					81	67	69	84	68		58	66	95	56	32
31					86	71	71	78	69		63	66	92	56					79	65	67	81	70		57	64	92	54	31
30	50			80	84	69	69	75	67		61	64	89	54	50			87	77	64	66	79	72		55	62	90	53	30
29				78	82	67	67	72	65	118	59	62	86	53				85	76	62	64	76	74		53	60	87	52	29
28				76	80	65	66	70	63	115	57	60	83	52				83	74	60	62	74	76		51	58	84	51	28
27				74	78	63	64	68	61	111	55	58	80	50				80	72	58	60	71	78	118	49	56	81	49	27
26				72	76	61	62	65	58	108	54	57	77	49				78	70	56	58	69	80	115	47	54	79	48	26
25				70	74	59	60	62	56	105	52	55	74	48				76	68	54	57	66	82	111	46	52	76	47	25
24				68	71	57	59	60	54	101	50	53	71	46				74	66	53	55	64	84	107	44	51	73	45	24
23			119	66	69	55	57	58	52	98	48	51	69	45				72	64	51	53	61	86	104	42	49	70	44	23
22			116	64	67	53	55	55	50	94	46	49	66	44				69	62	49	51	59	88	100	40	47	68	43	22
21			112	62	65	51	53	52	47	91	44	47	63	42				67	61	47	50	56	90	96	38	45	65	42	21
20	47		108	60	63	49	52	50	45	88	42	45	60	41	47			65	59	45	48	54	92	93	36	43	62	40	20
19			105	58	61	47	50	48	43	85	40	43	57	40				63	57	43	46	51	94	89	35	41	59	39	19
18			101	56	59	45	48	45	41	82	38	41	54	38				60	55	42	44	49	96	85	33	39	57	38	18
17			97	54	57	43	46	42	39	78	36	39	51	37				58	53	40	43	46	98	82	31	37	54	36	17
16			94	52	55	41	44	40	36	75	34	37	48	36			119	56	51	38	41	44	100	78	29	35	51	35	16
15		94	90	50	53	39	43	38	34	72	32	36	45	34		96	113	54	49	36	39	41	102	74	27	33	48	34	15
14		90	86	48	51	37	41	35	32	68	30	34	43	33		91	108	52	47	34	37	39	104	71	26	31	46	33	14
13		86	83	46	49	35	39	32	30	65	28	32	40	32		87	102	49	45	32	36	36	106	67	24	30	43	31	13
12		82	79	44	46	33	37	30	28	62	26	30	37	30		82	97	47	44	31	34	34	108	63	22	28	40	30	12
11		78	75	43	44	31	36	28	25	59	24	28	34	29		78	91	45	42	29	32	31	110	60	20	26	38	29	11
10	44	73	72	41	42	29	34	25	23	55	22	26	31	28	44	73	85	43	40	27	30	29		56		24	35	27	10
9		69	68	39	40	27	32	22	21	52	20	24	28	26		69	80	40	38	25	29	26		52		22	32	26	9
8		65	64	37	38	25	31	20		49		22	25	25		64	74	38	36	23	27	24		48		20	29	25	8
7		61	61	35	36	23	28			45		20	22	24		60	69	36	34	21	25	21		45			27	24	7
6		57	57	33	34	21	27			42			20	22		55	63	34	32	20	23			41			24	22	6
5		53	53	31	32		25			39				21		51	58	31	30		21			37			21	21	5
4		49	50	29	30		23			36				20		46	52	29	28		20			34				20	4
3		45	46	27	28		21			32						42	47	27	27					30					3
2		40	42	25	26		20			29						37	41	25	25					26					2
1		36	39	23	24					26						33	35	23	23					23					1
0	41	32	35	21	21					22					41	28	30	20	21										0

Table 5. T-Score Conversions for Basic Scales without K Corrections

Raw Score	Males														Females														Raw Score
	?	L	F	K	1 (Hs)	2 (D)	3 (Hy)	4 (Pd)	5 (Mf)	6 (Pa)	7 (Pt)	8 (Sc)	9 (Ma)	0 (Si)	?	L	F	K	1 (Hs)	2 (D)	3 (Hy)	4 (Pd)	5 (Mf)	6 (Pa)	7 (Pt)	8 (Sc)	9 (Ma)	0 (Si)	
60	58													87	58													87	60
59												117		86												111		86	59
58												115		85												109		85	58
57												114		84												108		84	57
56												113		83												107		83	56
55												111		82												106		82	55
54							118					110		81						117	112					104		81	54
53							116					109		80						115	110					103		80	53
52							115					107		79						113	109					102		79	52
51							113		110			106		78						111	107		20			101		78	51
50	56						111		108			105		77	56					109	105		22			99		77	50
49							109		106			103		76						107	103		24			98		76	49
48							107		104		103	102		75						105	101		26		95	97		75	48
47							106		102		102	101		74						103	100		28		94	96		74	47
46						120	104		100		100	99		73						102	98		30		93	94		73	46
45						118	102		98		99	98		72						100	96		32		91	93		72	45
44						116	100		96		98	97		71						98	94		34		90	92		71	44
43						113	98		94		96	95		70						96	93	120	37		89	91		70	43
42						111	96		92		95	94		69						94	91	117	39		88	89		69	42
41						108	95	119	90		93	92		68						92	89	115	41		86	88		68	41
40	53					106	93	116	88		92	91		67	53					90	87	113	43		85	87		67	40
39						104	91	114	86		91	90	106	66						88	86	110	45		84	86	106	66	39
38						101	89	111	84		89	88	104	65						86	84	108	47		82	84	104	65	38
37						99	87	108	82		88	87	101	64						84	82	106	49		81	83	101	64	37
36						96	86	106	80		86	86	99	63						82	80	103	51		80	82	99	63	36

35						94	84	103	78		85	84	97	62
34						92	82	101	76		84	83	95	61
33					115	89	80	98	74		82	82	93	60
32					113	87	78	96	73	120	81	80	90	58
31			110		110	84	76	93	71	117	79	79	88	56
30	50		108	83	108	82	75	91	69	114	78	78	86	55
29			106	81	106	80	73	88	67	111	77	76	84	54
28			104	79	104	77	71	86	65	108	75	75	81	53
27			102	77	101	75	69	83	63	105	74	74	79	52
26			100	75	99	72	67	81	61	102	73	72	77	51
25			98	74	97	70	65	78	59	100	71	71	75	50
24			96	72	94	68	64	75	57	97	70	70	72	49
23			94	70	92	65	62	73	55	94	68	68	70	48
22			92	68	90	63	60	70	53	91	67	67	68	47
21			90	66	88	60	58	68	51	88	66	65	66	46
20	47		88	64	85	58	56	65	49	85	64	64	63	45
19			86	62	83	56	55	63	47	82	63	63	61	44
18			84	61	81	53	53	60	45	79	61	61	59	43
17			82	59	78	51	51	58	43	76	60	60	57	42
16			80	57	76	48	49	55	41	73	59	59	54	41
15		86	78	55	74	46	47	53	39	70	57	57	52	40
14		83	76	53	72	44	45	50	37	67	56	56	50	39
13		80	73	51	69	41	44	47	35	65	54	55	48	38
12		76	70	49	67	39	42	45	34	62	53	53	45	37
11		73	68	48	65	36	40	42	32	59	52	52	43	36
10	44	70	66	46	62	34	38	40	30	56	50	51	41	35
9		66	64	44	60	32	36	37	28	53	49	49	39	34
8		63	62	42	58	29	35	35	26	50	48	48	37	33
7		60	60	40	56			32		47	46	47	34	32
6		56	58	38	53			30		44	45	45	32	30
5		53	55	36	51			27		41	43	44	30	29
4		50	53	35	49			25		38	42	43	28	28
3		46	50	33	47			22		35	41	41	25	27
2		44	48	31	44			20		33	39	40	23	26
1		40	46	29	42					30	38	38		25
0	41	36	44	27	40					27	36	37		

					80	79	101	53		78	80	97	62	35
					78	77	99	55		77	79	95	61	34
				99	76	75	96	57		76	78	93	60	33
				97	75	73	94	59	120	75	77	90	58	32
		110		96	73	72	91	61	117	73	75	88	56	31
50		108	83	94	71	70	89	63	114	72	74	86	55	30
		106	81	92	69	68	87	66	111	71	73	84	54	29
		104	79	90	67	66	84	68	108	69	72	81	53	28
		102	77	88	65	64	82	70	105	68	70	79	52	27
		100	75	86	63	63	80	72	102	67	69	77	51	26
		98	74	84	61	61	77	74	100	65	68	75	50	25
		96	72	82	59	59	75	76	97	64	67	72	49	24
		94	70	80	57	57	73	78	94	63	65	70	48	23
		92	68	79	55	56	70	80	91	62	64	68	47	22
		90	66	77	53	54	68	82	88	60	63	66	46	21
47		88	64	75	51	52	65	84	85	59	62	63	45	20
		86	62	73	49	50	63	86	82	58	60	61	44	19
		84	61	71	47	49	61	88	79	56	59	59	43	18
		82	59	69	46	47	58	90	76	55	58	57	42	17
		80	57	67	44	45	56	92	73	54	57	54	41	16
	86	78	55	65	42	43	53	95	70	52	55	52	40	15
	83	76	53	63	40	42	51		67	51	54	50	39	14
	80	73	51	62	38	40	49		65	50	53	48	38	13
	76	70	49	60	36	38	47		62	49	52	45	37	12
	73	68	48	58	34	36	44		59	47	50	43	36	11
44	70	66	46	56	32	34	42		56	46	49	41	35	10
	66	64	44	54	30	33	40		53	45	48	39	34	9
	63	62	42	52	28	31	37		50	43	47	37	33	8
	60	60	40	50		29	35		47	42	45	34	32	7
	56	58	38	48		27	32		44	41	44	32	30	6
	53	55	36	46		26	30		41	39	43	30	29	5
	50	53	35	45		24	28		38	38	42	28	28	4
	46	50	33	43			25		35	37	40	25	27	3
	44	48	31	41			23		33	36	39	23	26	2
	40	46	29	39			21		30	34	38		25	1
41	36	44	27	37					27	33	37			0

Table 6. T-Score Conversions for Basic Scales without K Corrections for Minnesota Adolescents Age 14 and Below

	Males														Females														
Raw Score	?	L	F	K	1 (Hs)	2 (D)	3 (Hy)	4 (Pd)	5 (Mf)	6 (Pa)	7 (Pt)	8 (Sc)	9 (Ma)	0 (Si)	?	L	F	K	1 (Hs)	2 (D)	3 (Hy)	4 (Pd)	5 (Mf)	6 (Pa)	7 (Pt)	8 (Sc)	9 (Ma)	0 (Si)	Raw Score
78												116																	78
77												115																	77
76												114																	76
75												113																	75
74												112																	74
73												111																	73
72												110															120			72
71												108															119			71
70	62											107		106	62											118		102	70
69												106		104												117		101	69
68												105		103												115		100	68
67												104		102												114		99	67
66												103		100												113		97	66
65												102		99												112		96	65
64												101		98												110		95	64
63												100		96												109		94	63
62												99		95												108		92	62
61												98		93												107		91	61
60	58											97		92	58											106		90	60
59												96		91												104		88	59
58												95		89												103		87	58
57												93		88												102		86	57
56												92		87												101		85	56
55												91		85												99		83	55
54												90		84												98		82	54
53												89		83												97		81	53
52												88		81						120						96		80	52
51												87		80						118	120					95		78	51

50	56							119			86		79	56				116	118					93		77	50
49					119	120		117			85		77					114	115	119	20			92		76	49
48					117	118	120	114		96	84		76					112	113	117	22		97	91		75	48
47					115	115	118	112		95	83		75					110	111	115	24		96	90		73	47
46					112	113	116	109		93	82	105	73					108	109	113	26		94	88	113	72	46
45					110	111	113	107		92	81	103	72					106	106	111	29		93	87	110	71	45
44					108	109	111	105		91	80	101	70					104	104	109	31		92	86	108	69	44
43					106	107	109	102		89	78	100	69					102	102	107	33		90	85	106	68	43
42		119			103	104	106	100		88	77	98	68					99	100	104	35		89	84	104	67	42
41		117			101	102	104	98		86	76	96	66					97	98	102	37		87	82	102	66	41
40	53	115			99	100	102	95		85	75	94	65	53				95	95	100	40	115	86	81	100	64	40
39		113			97	98	100	93		84	74	92	64					93	93	98	42	113	84	80	98	63	39
38		111			95	95	97	91		82	73	90	62					91	91	96	44	110	83	79	96	62	38
37		109			92	93	95	88		81	72	88	61					89	89	94	46	108	82	77	94	61	37
36		107			90	91	93	86	120	80	71	86	60					87	86	92	48	106	80	76	91	59	36
35		105			88	89	90	83	117	78	70	84	58					85	84	89	51	104	79	75	89	58	35
34		103			86	87	88	81	114	77	69	82	57					83	82	87	53	102	77	74	87	57	34
33		101			83	84	86	79	112	75	68	80	56		119		118	80	80	85	55	99	76	73	85	56	33
32		99			81	82	83	76	109	74	67	78	54		116		116	78	78	83	57	97	74	71	83	54	32
31		97			79	80	81	74	106	73	66	76	53		114		113	76	75	81	59	95	73	70	81	53	31
30	50	95	85	123	77	78	79	72	104	71	65	74	51	50	111	87	111	74	73	79	62	93	72	69	79	52	30
29		93	83	120	75	75	76	69	101	70	63	72	50		109	85	109	72	71	76	64	91	70	68	77	51	29
28		91	81	117	72	73	74	67	98	69	62	70	49		106	82	106	70	69	74	66	89	69	67	75	49	28
27		89	79	114	70	71	72	65	95	67	61	68	47		104	80	104	68	66	72	68	86	67	65	72	48	27
26		87	76	111	68	69	69	62	93	66	60	66	46		101	78	101	66	64	70	70	84	66	64	70	47	26
25		85	74	108	66	67	67	60	90	65	59	64	45		99	76	99	64	62	68	73	82	64	63	68	45	25
24		83	72	105	63	64	65	57	87	63	58	62	43		96	73	96	62	60	66	75	80	63	62	66	44	24
23		81	70	102	61	62	62	55	84	62	57	60	42		94	71	94	59	58	64	77	78	62	60	64	43	23
22		79	68	99	59	60	60	53	82	60	56	58	41		91	69	91	57	55	61	79	75	60	59	62	42	22
21		77	66	96	57	58	58	50	79	59	55	56	40		89	67	89	55	53	59	81	73	59	58	60	40	21
20	47	75	64	93	55	56	56	48	76	58	54	54	38	47	86	65	86	53	51	57	84	71	57	57	58	39	20
19		73	62	90	52	53	53	46	74	56	53	52	37		84	62	84	51	49	55	86	69	56	56	56	38	19
18		71	60	87	50	51	51	43	71	55	52	50	35		81	60	81	49	46	53	88	67	54	54	54	37	18
17		70	58	84	48	49	49	41	68	54	51	49	34		79	58	79	47	44	51	90	65	53	53	51	35	17
16		68	56	82	46	47	46	38	65	52	50	47	33		76	56	76	45	42	49	92	62	52	52	49	34	16

Table 6. T-Score Conversions for Basic Scales without K Corrections for Minnesota Adolescents Age 14 and Below—continued

	Males														Females														
Raw Score	?	L	F	K	1 (Hs)	2 (D)	3 (Hy)	4 (Pd)	5 (Mf)	6 (Pa)	7 (Pt)	8 (Sc)	9 (Ma)	0 (Si)	?	L	F	K	1 (Hs)	2 (D)	3 (Hy)	4 (Pd)	5 (Mf)	6 (Pa)	7 (Pt)	8 (Sc)	9 (Ma)	0 (Si)	Raw Score
15		105	66	54	79	43	44	44	36	63	51	48	45	31		101	74	53	74	43	40	46	95	60	50	51	47	33	15
14		100	64	52	76	41	42	42	34	60	49	47	43	30		97	71	51	71	41	38	44	97	58	49	49	45	32	14
13		95	62	50	73	39	40	39	31	57	48	46	41	28		92	69	49	69	38	35	42	99	56	47	48	43	30	13
12		90	60	48	70	37	38	37	29	55	47	45	39	27		87	66	47	66	36	33	40	100	54	46	47	41	29	12
11		85	58	45	67	35	36	35	27	52	45	44	37	26		83	64	44	64	34	31	38	102	51	44	46	39	28	11
10	44	80	56	43	64	32	33	32	24	49	44	43	35	24	44	78	61	42	61	32	29	36	104	49	43	45	37	26	10
9		76	54	41	61	30	31	30	22	46	43	42	33	23		73	59	40	59	30	27	34	107	47	42	43	35	25	9
8		71	52	39	58	28	29	28	20	44	41	41	31	22		69	56	38	56	28	24	31	109	45	40	42	32	24	8
7		66	50	37	55	26	27	25		41	40	40	29	20		64	54	35	54	26	22	29	111	43	39	41	30	23	7
6		61	48	35	52	23	25	23		38	38	39	27			59	51	33	51	24	20	27	113	40	37	40	28	21	6
5		56	46	33	49	21	22	21		35	37	38	25			55	49	31	49	22		25	115	38	36	38	26	20	5
4		51	44	31	46		20			33	36	37	23			50	46	29	46	20		23	118	36	34	37	24		4
3		46	42	29	43					30	34	36	21			46	44	27	44			21	120	34	33	36	22		3
2		42	40	27	40					27	33	35				41	41	24	41					32	32	35	20		2
1		37	38	25	37					25	32	33				36	39	22	39					30	30	34			1
0	41	32	36	23	34					23	30	32			41	31	36		36					28	29	32			0

Table 7. T-Score Conversions for Basic Scales without K Corrections for Minnesota Adolescents Age 15

	Males														Females														
Raw Score	?	L	F	K	1 (Hs)	2 (D)	3 (Hy)	4 (Pd)	5 (Mf)	6 (Pa)	7 (Pt)	8 (Sc)	9 (Ma)	0 (Si)	?	L	F	K	1 (Hs)	2 (D)	3 (Hy)	4 (Pd)	5 (Mf)	6 (Pa)	7 (Pt)	8 (Sc)	9 (Ma)	0 (Si)	Raw Score
78												111														117			78
77												110														116			77
76												109														115			76
75												108														114			75
74												107														113			74
73												106														112			73
72												105														110			72
71												104														109			71
70	62											103		105	62											108		103	70
69												102		103												107		102	69
68												101		102												106		101	68
67												100		101												105		99	67
66												99		99												104		98	66
65												98		98												103		97	65
64												97		97												102		95	64
63												96		95												101		94	63
62												95		94												100		93	62
61												94		93												99		92	61
60	58											93		91	58											98		90	60
59												92		90												97		89	59
58												91		89												95		88	58
57												90		87												94		86	57
56												89		86												93		85	56

Table 7. T-Score Conversions for Basic Scales without K Corrections for Minnesota Adolescents Age 15—continued

	Males														Females														
Raw Score	?	L	F	K	1 (Hs)	2 (D)	3 (Hy)	4 (Pd)	5 (Mf)	6 (Pa)	7 (Pt)	8 (Sc)	9 (Ma)	0 (Si)	?	L	F	K	1 (Hs)	2 (D)	3 (Hy)	4 (Pd)	5 (Mf)	6 (Pa)	7 (Pt)	8 (Sc)	9 (Ma)	0 (Si)	Raw Score
55									120			88		85												92		84	55
54									118			87		83							120					91		82	54
53									116			86		82							118					90		81	53
52							120		114			85		81							115					89		80	52
51							118		112			84		79						119	113					88		79	51
50	56		120				116	118	110			83		78	56					116	111	118				87		77	50
49			119			120	114	116	108			82		77						114	109	115	20			86		76	49
48			117			117	112	114	106		98	81		75						112	107	113	22		94	85		75	48
47			115			115	110	111	104		96	80		74						110	105	111	24		93	84		73	47
46			114			113	108	109	101		95	79	103	73						108	103	109	26		91	83	104	72	46
45			112			111	106	107	99		93	78	101	71						106	101	107	28		90	82	102	71	45
44			110			108	104	105	97		92	77	99	70						103	99	105	30		89	80	100	70	44
43			108			106	102	103	95		90	76	97	69						101	97	103	32		87	79	98	68	43
42			107			104	100	101	93		89	75	95	67						99	95	101	34		86	78	96	67	42
41			105			101	98	99	91		88	74	93	66						97	93	99	36		85	77	95	66	41
40	53		103			99	96	96	89	111	86	73	91	64	53					95	91	97	38	114	83	76	93	64	40
39			102			97	94	94	87	109	85	72	89	63						93	89	95	40	112	82	75	91	63	39
38			100			95	91	92	85	106	83	71	87	62						90	87	92	42	110	80	74	89	62	38
37			98			92	89	90	83	104	82	70	86	60			120			88	85	90	45	108	79	73	87	61	37
36			97			90	87	88	81	102	81	69	84	59			118			86	83	88	47	106	78	72	85	59	36
35			95			88	85	86	79	100	79	68	82	58			116			84	81	86	49	103	76	71	83	58	35
34			93			86	83	84	76	98	78	67	80	56			114			82	79	84	51	101	75	70	82	57	34
33			92		114	83	81	81	74	96	76	66	78	55			111		110	80	76	82	53	99	74	69	80	55	33
32			90		112	81	79	79	72	94	75	65	76	54			109		108	78	74	80	55	97	72	68	78	54	32
31			88		109	79	77	77	70	92	73	64	74	52			107		106	75	72	78	57	95	71	66	76	53	31

30	50		87	85	107	77	75	75	68	90	72	63	72	51	50		104	86	104	73	70	76	59	93	70	65	74	52	30
29			85	83	105	74	73	73	66	88	71	62	70	50			102	84	102	71	68	74	61	90	68	64	72	50	29
28			83	81	102	72	71	71	64	86	69	61	68	48			100	82	99	69	66	71	63	88	67	63	70	49	28
27			82	78	100	70	69	69	62	83	68	60	66	47			98	80	97	67	64	69	65	86	66	62	69	48	27
26			80	76	98	67	67	66	60	81	66	59	65	46			95	77	95	65	62	67	67	84	64	61	67	46	26
25			78	74	95	65	65	64	58	79	65	58	63	44			93	75	93	62	60	65	69	82	63	60	65	45	25
24			77	72	93	63	63	62	56	77	64	57	61	43			91	73	90	60	58	63	71	79	62	59	63	44	24
23			75	70	91	61	61	60	53	75	62	56	59	42			89	71	88	58	56	61	73	77	60	58	61	42	23
22			73	68	88	58	59	58	51	73	61	55	57	40			86	69	86	56	54	59	75	75	59	57	59	41	22
21			72	66	86	56	57	56	49	71	59	54	55	39			84	67	84	54	52	57	77	73	58	56	57	40	21
20	47		70	64	84	54	54	54	47	69	58	53	53	38	47		82	64	81	52	50	55	79	71	56	55	56	39	20
19			68	62	81	52	52	52	45	67	56	52	51	36			79	62	79	49	48	53	82	68	55	54	54	37	19
18			67	60	79	49	50	49	43	65	55	51	49	35			77	60	77	47	46	51	84	66	53	53	52	36	18
17			65	58	76	47	48	47	41	63	54	50	47	34			75	58	75	45	44	48	86	64	52	51	50	35	17
16			63	55	74	45	46	45	39	60	52	49	45	32			73	56	72	43	42	46	88	62	51	50	48	33	16
15		98	62	53	72	43	44	43	37	58	51	48	43	31		96	70	53	70	41	39	44	90	60	49	49	46	32	15
14		93	60	51	69	40	42	41	35	56	49	47	42	30		92	68	51	68	39	37	42	92	58	48	48	44	31	14
13		89	58	49	67	38	40	39	33	54	48	46	40	28		88	66	49	66	37	35	40	94	55	47	47	42	30	13
12		85	57	47	65	36	38	37	31	52	46	45	38	27		83	63	47	64	34	33	38	96	53	45	46	41	28	12
11		80	55	45	62	33	36	34	28	50	45	44	36	25		79	61	45	61	32	31	36	98	51	44	45	39	27	11
10	44	76	53	43	60	31	34	32	26	48	44	43	34	24	44	75	59	42	59	30	29	34	100	49	43	44	37	26	10
9		72	52	41	58	29	32	30	24	46	42	42	32	23		70	57	40	57	28	27	32	101	47	41	43	35	24	9
8		67	50	39	55	27	30	28	22	44	41	41	30	21		66	54	38	55	26	25	30	103	44	40	42	33	23	8
7		63	48	37	53	24	28	26	20	42	39	40	28	20		62	52	36	52	24	23	27	105	42	39	41	31	22	7
6		59	46	34	51	22	26	24		40	38	39	26			58	50	34	50	21	21	25	107	40	37	40	29	21	6
5		55	45	32	48	20	24	22		37	37	38	24			53	47	32	48			23	109	38	36	39	28		5
4		50	43	30	46		22			35	35	37	22			49	45	29	46			21	111	36	35	37	26		4
3		46	41	28	44		20			33	34	36	21			45	43	27	43				113	33	33	36	24		3
2		42	40	26	41					31	32	35				40	41	25	41				115	31	32	35	22		2
1		37	38	24	39					29	31	34				36	38	23	39				118	29	31	34	20		1
0	41	32	37	22	36					27	29	33			41	31	36	21	37				120	26	29	32			0

Table 8. T-Score Conversions for Basic Scales without K Corrections for Minnesota Adolescents Age 16

	Males														Females														
Raw Score	?	L	F	K	1 (Hs)	2 (D)	3 (Hy)	4 (Pd)	5 (Mf)	6 (Pa)	7 (Pt)	8 (Sc)	9 (Ma)	0 (Si)	?	L	F	K	1 (Hs)	2 (D)	3 (Hy)	4 (Pd)	5 (Mf)	6 (Pa)	7 (Pt)	8 (Sc)	9 (Ma)	0 (Si)	Raw Score
78												116														114			78
77												115														113			77
76												114														112			76
75												112														111			75
74												111														110			74
73												110														109			73
72												109														108			72
71												108														107			71
70	62											107		107	62											106		98	70
69												106		106												105		96	69
68												105		105												104		95	68
67												104		103												103		94	67
66												103		102												102		93	66
65												102		100												101		91	65
64												101		99												100		90	64
63												99		98												99		89	63
62												98		96												98		88	62
61												97		95												97		86	61
60	58											96		93	58											95		85	60
59												95		92												94		84	59
58												94		90												93		83	58
57												93		89												92		82	57
56												92		88												91		80	56

55											91		86					120	119					90		79	55
54											90		85					118	117					89		78	54
53											89		83					116	115					88		77	53
52											88		82					114	113					87		75	52
51											86		81					112	111					86		74	51
50	56					120	118	119			85		79	56				110	109					85		73	50
49		120			119	117	116	117			84		78					108	107	119				84		72	49
48		118			116	115	114	114		99	83		76					106	105	116			91	83		70	48
47		117			114	113	112	112		98	82		75					104	103	114	20		90	82		69	47
46		115			112	111	110	110		96	81	109	73					102	101	112	22		89	81	115	68	46
45		113			110	109	107	107		95	80	107	72					100	99	110	24		87	80	113	67	45
44		112			107	106	105	105		93	79	105	71					98	97	108	27		86	79	111	65	44
43		110			105	104	103	103		92	78	103	69					96	95	106	29		85	78	109	64	43
42		108			103	102	101	100		90	77	100	68					94	93	103	31		83	77	106	63	42
41		106			101	100	99	98		89	76	98	66					92	91	101	34		82	75	104	62	41
40	53	105			98	98	97	95	92	87	75	96	65	53				89	89	99	36		81	74	102	60	40
39		103			96	96	95	93	91	86	74	94	63					87	87	97	38		79	73	100	59	39
38		101			94	93	92	91	89	85	72	92	62		120			85	85	95	40	120	78	72	98	58	38
37		99			92	91	90	88	88	83	71	90	61		118			83	83	92	43	118	77	71	95	57	37
36		98			89	89	88	86	86	82	70	88	59		116			81	81	90	45	115	75	70	93	55	36
35		96			87	87	86	84	85	80	69	85	58		113			79	79	88	47	112	74	69	91	54	35
34		94			85	85	84	81	83	79	68	83	56		111			77	77	86	50	110	73	68	89	53	34
33		92			83	82	82	79	82	77	67	81	55		109		112	75	75	84	52	107	71	67	86	52	33
32		91			80	80	79	76	80	76	66	79	54		107		109	73	73	82	54	105	70	66	84	51	32
31		89			78	78	77	74	79	74	65	77	52		104		107	71	71	79	57	102	69	65	82	49	31
30	50	87	88	118	76	76	75	72	77	73	64	75	51	50	102	88	105	69	69	77	59	99	67	64	80	48	30
29		86	85	115	74	74	73	69	76	71	63	73	49		100	85	102	67	67	75	61	97	66	63	77	47	29
28		84	83	112	71	71	71	67	74	70	62	70	48		98	83	100	65	65	73	64	94	65	62	75	46	28
27		82	81	109	69	69	69	65	73	68	61	68	46		95	81	98	63	63	71	66	92	64	61	73	44	27
26		80	79	107	67	67	66	62	71	67	59	66	45		93	79	95	61	61	68	68	89	62	60	71	43	26
25		79	76	104	65	65	64	60	70	65	58	64	44		91	77	93	59	59	66	70	87	61	59	68	42	25
24		77	74	101	63	63	62	57	68	64	57	62	42		89	74	91	57	57	64	73	84	60	58	66	41	24
23		75	72	98	60	61	60	55	67	62	56	60	41		86	72	88	55	56	62	75	81	58	56	64	39	23
22		73	70	95	58	58	58	53	66	61	55	58	39		84	70	86	53	54	60	77	79	57	55	62	38	22
21		72	67	93	56	56	56	50	64	59	54	55	38		82	68	84	51	52	57	80	76	56	54	59	37	21

Table 8. T-Score Conversions for Basic Scales without K Corrections for Minnesota Adolescents Age 16—continued

	Males														Females														
Raw Score	?	L	F	K	1 (Hs)	2 (D)	3 (Hy)	4 (Pd)	5 (Mf)	6 (Pa)	7 (Pt)	8 (Sc)	9 (Ma)	0 (Si)	?	L	F	K	1 (Hs)	2 (D)	3 (Hy)	4 (Pd)	5 (Mf)	6 (Pa)	7 (Pt)	8 (Sc)	9 (Ma)	0 (Si)	Raw Score
20	47		70	65	90	54	54	53	48	63	58	53	53	37	47		80	66	81	49	50	55	82	74	54	53	57	36	20
19			68	63	87	51	52	51	46	61	56	52	51	35			77	63	79	47	48	53	84	71	53	52	55	34	19
18			66	60	84	49	50	49	43	60	55	51	49	34			75	61	77	45	46	51	87	68	52	51	53	33	18
17			65	58	81	47	47	47	41	58	54	50	47	32			73	59	74	43	44	49	89	66	50	50	50	32	17
16			63	56	78	45	45	45	39	57	52	49	45	31			71	57	72	40	42	47	91	63	49	49	48	31	16
15		99	61	54	76	42	43	43	36	55	51	48	43	29		95	68	55	70	38	40	44	94	61	48	48	46	29	15
14		94	60	51	73	40	41	41	34	54	49	46	40	28		91	66	52	67	36	38	42	96	58	46	47	44	28	14
13		89	58	49	70	38	39	38	31	52	48	45	38	27		86	64	50	65	34	36	40	98	55	45	46	41	27	13
12		85	56	47	67	36	37	36	29	51	46	44	36	25		82	62	48	63	32	34	38	100	53	44	45	39	26	12
11		80	54	45	64	33	34	34	27	49	45	43	34	24		78	59	46	61	30	32	36	102	50	42	44	37	24	11
10	44	76	53	42	62	31	32	32	24	48	43	42	32	22	44	73	57	44	58	28	30	33	104	48	41	43	35	23	10
9		71	51	40	59	29	30	30	22	46	42	41	30	21		69	55	41	56	26	28	31	106	45	40	42	32	22	9
8		67	49	38	56	27	28	28	20	45	40	40	28	20		64	53	39	54	24	26	29	109	42	38	41	30	21	8
7		62	47	36	53	24	26	25		43	39	39	25			60	50	37	51	22	24	27	111	40	37	40	28	20	7
6		58	46	33	50	22	23	23		42	37	38	23			56	48	35	49	20	22	25	113	37	36	39	26		6
5		53	44	31	47	20	21	21		40	36	37	21			51	46	33	47		20	23	116	35	34	38	23		5
4		49	42	29	45					39	34	36				47	44	30	44			20	118	32	33	36	21		4
3		44	40	27	42					37	33	35				42	41	28	42				120	29	32	35			3
2		40	39	24	39					36	31	33				38	39	26	40					27	30	34			2
1		35	37	22	36					35	30	32				34	37	24	37					24	29	33			1
0	41	31	35	20	33					34	28	30			41	29	35	22	35					21	27	32			0

Table 9. T-Score Conversions for Basic Scales without K Corrections for Minnesota Adolescents Age 17

	Males														Females														
Raw Score	?	L	F	K	1 (Hs)	2 (D)	3 (Hy)	4 (Pd)	5 (Mf)	6 (Pa)	7 (Pt)	8 (Sc)	9 (Ma)	0 (Si)	?	L	F	K	1 (Hs)	2 (D)	3 (Hy)	4 (Pd)	5 (Mf)	6 (Pa)	7 (Pt)	8 (Sc)	9 (Ma)	0 (Si)	Raw Score
78												116														119			78
77												115														118			77
76												114														117			76
75												113														116			75
74												112														114			74
73												111														113			73
72												109														112			72
71												108														111			71
70	62											107		112	62											110		101	70
69												106		110												109		99	69
68												105		109												108		98	68
67												104		107												106		97	67
66												103		106												105		95	66
65												102		104												104		94	65
64												101		103												103		93	64
63												100		101												102		91	63
62												99		100												101		90	62
61												97		98												100		89	61
60	58											96		97	58											98		87	60
59												95		95												97		86	59
58												94		94												96		85	58
57						118						93		92												95		83	57
56						117	120					92		91							119					94		82	56

Table 9. T-Score Conversions for Basic Scales without K Corrections for Minnesota Adolescents Age 17—continued

Raw Score	Males														Females														Raw Score
	?	L	F	K	1 (Hs)	2 (D)	3 (Hy)	4 (Pd)	5 (Mf)	6 (Pa)	7 (Pt)	8 (Sc)	9 (Ma)	0 (Si)	?	L	F	K	1 (Hs)	2 (D)	3 (Hy)	4 (Pd)	5 (Mf)	6 (Pa)	7 (Pt)	8 (Sc)	9 (Ma)	0 (Si)	
55						115	118					91		89							117					93		81	55
54						113	116					90		88						120	115					92		79	54
53						112	114		120			89		86						118	113					90		78	53
52						110	112		118			88		85						116	111					89		77	52
51						108	110		116			86		83						114	109					88		75	51
50	56					106	108		114			85		82	56					112	107					87		74	50
49						104	107	119	111			84		80						110	105					86		73	49
48						102	105	117	109		101	83		79						108	103	118			95	85		71	48
47						101	103	114	107		99	82		77						105	101	116	20		94	84		70	47
46						99	101	112	105		98	81	109	76						103	99	114	22		93	82	114	69	46
45						97	99	110	103		96	80	107	74						101	97	111	24		91	81	112	67	45
44						95	97	108	100		95	79	105	73						99	95	109	27		90	80	110	66	44
43						93	95	105	98		93	78	103	71						97	93	107	29		88	79	108	65	43
42						92	93	103	96		92	77	101	70						95	91	104	31		87	78	106	63	42
41						90	91	101	94		90	75	99	68						93	89	102	33		85	77	104	62	41
40	53		119			88	89	98	92		89	74	96	67	53					90	87	100	36		84	76	101	61	40
39			117			86	87	96	90		87	73	94	65						88	85	98	38		82	74	99	59	39
38			115			84	86	94	87		86	72	92	64						86	83	95	40		81	73	97	58	38
37			113			83	84	91	85		84	71	90	62						84	81	93	42		79	72	95	57	37
36			110			81	82	89	83		82	70	88	61						82	79	91	44		78	71	93	55	36
35			108			79	80	87	81		81	69	86	59			118			80	77	88	47		77	70	91	54	35
34			106			77	78	85	79	120	79	68	84	58			116			78	75	86	49	119	75	69	89	53	34
33			104		118	75	76	82	77	117	78	67	82	56			113		107	75	73	84	51	116	74	68	86	51	33
32			102		115	73	74	80	74	114	76	66	79	55			111		105	73	71	81	53	113	72	66	84	50	32
31			100		113	72	72	78	72	111	75	64	77	53			109		103	71	69	79	56	110	71	65	82	49	31

30	50		97	86	110	70	70	75	70	108	73	63	75	52	50		106	94	100	69	67	77	58	108	69	64	80	47	30
29			95	84	108	68	68	73	68	105	72	62	73	50			104	91	98	67	65	74	60	105	68	63	78	46	29
28			93	82	105	66	67	71	66	102	70	61	71	49			101	89	96	65	63	72	62	102	66	62	76	45	28
27			91	80	103	64	65	69	63	99	69	60	69	47			99	86	93	62	61	70	65	99	65	61	73	43	27
26			89	78	100	63	63	66	61	96	67	59	67	45			96	84	91	60	59	67	67	96	63	60	71	42	26
25			87	75	98	61	61	64	59	93	65	58	65	44			94	81	89	58	57	65	69	93	62	58	69	41	25
24			84	73	95	59	59	62	57	90	64	57	62	42			91	79	87	56	55	63	71	90	60	57	67	39	24
23			82	71	93	57	57	59	55	87	62	56	60	41			89	76	84	54	53	61	74	87	59	56	65	38	23
22			80	69	90	55	55	57	53	84	61	55	58	39			86	74	82	52	51	58	76	84	58	55	63	37	22
21			78	67	88	54	53	55	50	81	59	53	56	38			84	71	80	50	49	56	78	82	56	54	60	35	21
20	47		76	64	85	52	51	52	48	78	58	52	54	36	47		81	69	77	47	47	54	80	79	55	53	58	34	20
19			73	62	83	50	49	50	46	75	56	51	52	35			79	66	75	45	45	51	83	76	53	52	56	33	19
18			71	60	80	48	48	48	44	72	55	50	50	33			77	64	73	43	43	49	85	73	52	50	54	31	18
17			69	58	78	46	46	46	42	70	53	49	48	32			74	61	71	41	41	47	87	70	50	49	52	30	17
16			67	56	75	44	44	43	40	67	52	48	45	30			72	59	68	39	39	44	89	67	49	48	50	29	16
15		93	65	53	73	43	42	41	37	64	50	47	43	29		91	69	56	66	37	37	42	92	64	47	47	47	27	15
14		88	63	51	70	41	40	39	35	61	48	46	41	27		87	67	54	64	35	35	40	94	61	46	46	45	26	14
13		84	60	49	68	39	38	36	33	58	47	45	39	26		83	64	51	61	32	33	37	96	59	44	45	43	25	13
12		80	58	47	65	37	36	34	31	55	45	44	37	24		79	62	49	59	30	31	35	98	56	43	44	41	23	12
11		76	56	45	63	35	34	32	29	52	44	43	35	23		74	59	46	57	28	29	33	100	53	42	43	39	22	11
10	44	72	54	42	60	34	32	29	26	49	42	41	33	21	44	70	57	44	55	26	27	31	102	50	40	41	37	21	10
9		68	52	40	58	32	30	27	24	46	41	40	31	20		66	54	41	52	24	25	28	104	47	39	40	34		9
8		63	50	38	55	30	29	25	22	43	39	39	28			62	52	38	50	22	23	26	106	44	37	39	32		8
7		59	47	36	53	28	27	23	20	40	38	38	26			58	49	36	48	20	21	24	108	41	36	38	30		7
6		55	45	34	50	26	25	20		37	36	37	24			54	47	33	45			21	111	38	34	37	28		6
5		51	43	31	48	24	23			34	35	36	22			49	45	31	43				113	35	33	36	26		5
4		47	41	29	45	23	21			31	33	35	20			45	42	28	41				115	33	31	35	24		4
3		43	39	27	43	21				28	32	34				41	40	26	38				117	30	30	33	22		3
2		38	36	25	40					25	30	33				37	37	23	36				120	27	28	32			2
1		34	34	23	38					22	28	32				33	35	21	34					24	27	31			1
0	41	30	32	20	35						27	31			41	28	32		31					21	25	29			0

Table 10. T-Score Conversions for Harris-Lingoes Subscales of Basic Scales for Minnesota Adults

Raw Score	D_1	D_2	D_3	D_4	D_5	Hy_1	Hy_2	Hy_3	Hy_4	Hy_5	Pd_1	Pd_2	Pd_3	Pd_{4A}	Pd_{4B}	Pa_1	Pa_2	Pa_3	Sc_{1A}	Sc_{1B}	Sc_{2A}	Sc_{2B}	Sc_{2C}	Sc_3	Ma_1	Ma_2	Ma_3	Ma_4	Raw Score
														Males															
32	122																												32
31	119																												31
30	117																												30
29	114																												29
28	111																												28
27	108																												27
26	105																												26
25	102																												25
24	99																												24
23	96																												23
22	93																												22
21	91																												21
20	88																		120					121					20
19	85																		116					117					19
18	82													95					111					113					18
17	79								106					91		117			107					109					17
16	76								102					88		113			103					105					16
15	73	103		114				104	98					84	93	108			99					101					15
14	70	98		109				100	94					81	89	104			94			115		97					14
13	67	92		104				95	91					77	85	99			90			110		93					13
12	65	87		100			79	91	87				68	74	81	95			86			105		89					12
11	62	81	104	95			75	87	83		103	92	64	70	77	90			82			99	112	85		102			11
10	59	76	98	90	92		71	83	79		98	86	60	66	74	86			77	118	103	94	106	81		95			10
9	56	70	91	85	87		66	79	75		92	80	56	63	70	82	95	76	73	109	97	88	99	77		87		89	9
8	53	65	84	80	82		62	74	71		86	74	52	59	66	77	88	71	69	101	91	83	93	73		80	77	83	8
7	50	59	77	75	76		58	70	67	82	80	67	48	56	62	73	81	66	65	92	85	77	86	69		73	71	77	7
6	47	54	70	70	71	64	54	66	63	75	74	61	44	52	58	68	75	61	60	83	78	72	80	65	81	66	65	71	6
5	44	48	63	65	65	59	50	62	59	68	69	55	40	49	54	64	68	56	56	74	72	66	73	60	74	59	59	65	5
4	41	43	56	60	60	53	46	57	55	60	63	49	35	45	51	59	62	51	52	66	66	61	67	56	67	52	53	58	4
3	39	37	49	55	54	47	42	53	51	53	57	43	31	42	47	55	55	46	48	57	60	55	60	52	59	45	47	52	3
2	36	32	42	50	49	42	38	49	47	46	51	37	27	38	43	50	49	41	44	48	53	50	54	48	52	38	42	46	2
1	33	26	35	45	44	36	34	45	43	39	45	30	23	35	39	46	42	36	39	39	47	45	47	44	45	31	36	40	1
0	30	21	29	40	38	31	30	41	39	31	39	24	19	31	35	41	36	31	35	31	41	39	41	40	37	24	30	34	0

Females

32	109																												32
31	106																												31
30	104																												30
29	101																												29
28	99																												28
27	96																												27
26	94																												26
25	91																												25
24	89																												24
23	86																												23
22	84																												22
21	81																												21
20	79																		117					118					20
19	76																		113					114					19
18	74													96					109					110					18
17	71								93					92		124			105					106					17
16	69								89					89		119			101					102					16
15	66	97		110				97	86					85	93	114			97					98					15
14	64	92		106				93	83					81	90	110			93			110		94					14
13	61	86		101				90	79					78	86	105			88			105		91					13
12	59	81		96			81	86	76				69	74	82	100			84			100		87					12
11	56	76	99	91			77	82	73		103	106	66	70	78	95			80			95	102	83		98			11
10	54	71	93	87	88		73	78	69		98	98	62	67	74	90			76	120	104	90	96	79		92			10
9	51	66	87	82	83		69	74	66		92	91	58	63	70	85	97	78	72	111	98	85	91	75		85		88	9
8	49	61	80	77	77		64	70	63		86	84	54	59	67	80	90	73	68	103	91	80	85	71		79	81	82	8
7	46	56	74	72	72		60	67	59	74	80	76	50	56	63	75	83	68	64	94	85	74	80	67		73	75	76	7
6	44	51	67	68	66	65	56	63	56	67	74	69	47	52	59	71	76	62	60	85	79	69	74	63	89	66	69	70	6
5	41	45	61	63	61	59	51	59	53	60	69	62	43	49	55	66	69	57	55	76	72	64	69	59	81	60	63	64	5
4	39	40	55	58	55	54	47	55	49	54	63	54	39	45	51	61	62	52	51	67	66	59	63	55	72	53	57	58	4
3	36	35	48	54	50	48	43	51	46	47	57	47	35	41	47	56	55	47	47	58	60	54	58	51	64	47	51	52	3
2	34	30	42	49	45	43	39	47	43	41	51	40	31	38	44	51	49	42	43	50	53	49	52	47	55	41	45	46	2
1	31	25	36	44	39	38	34	44	39	34	45	32	28	34	40	46	42	37	39	41	47	44	46	43	47	34	39	40	1
0	29	20	29	39	34	32	30	40	36	27	39	25	24	30	36	41	35	32	35	32	41	39	41	39	38	28	33	34	0

Table 11. T-Score Conversions for Wiener-Harmon Subtle-Obvious Subscales for Minnesota Adults

Raw Score	Males D-O	Males D-S	Males Hy-O	Males Hy-S	Males Pd-O	Males Pd-S	Males Pa-O	Males Pa-S	Males Ma-O	Males Ma-S	Females D-O	Females D-S	Females Hy-O	Females Hy-S	Females Pd-O	Females Pd-S	Females Pa-O	Females Pa-S	Females Ma-O	Females Ma-S	Raw Score
40											112										40
39	120										110										39
38	118										108										38
37	116										106										37
36	114										104										36
35	111										102										35
34	109										100										34
33	107										98										33
32	105		115								95		103								32
31	102		112								93		101								31
30	100		110								91		99								30
29	98		108								89		97								29
28	95		105	84	111						87		95	85	115						28
27	93		103	81	108						85		93	83	112						27
26	91		101	79	106						83		91	81	109						26
25	89		98	77	103						81		88	78	107						25
24	86		96	75	100						79		86	76	104						24
23	84		93	73	97		121		109	103	77		84	73	101				109	105	23
22	82		91	70	95	102	117		105	99	75		82	71	98	105			106	101	22
21	80		89	68	92	98	114		102	95	73		80	69	95	101			102	97	21
20	77	85	86	66	89	94	110		98	91	71	83	78	66	92	97	119		99	93	20
19	75	81	84	64	86	90	107		95	87	69	79	76	64	89	93	115		96	89	19
18	73	78	82	62	83	86	103		92	84	67	76	74	61	86	87	111		92	85	18
17	71	74	79	59	81	82	100	97	88	80	65	72	72	59	84	84	107	104	89	81	17
16	68	70	77	57	78	78	96	93	85	76	63	68	70	57	81	80	103	99	86	77	16
15	66	67	74	55	75	74	93	88	81	72	61	65	67	54	78	76	99	94	82	73	15
14	64	63	72	53	72	70	89	84	78	68	59	61	65	52	75	72	95	90	79	69	14
13	62	60	70	51	70	66	86	80	74	64	57	57	63	50	72	68	91	85	76	66	13
12	59	56	67	48	67	62	82	76	71	60	55	54	61	47	69	64	87	80	72	62	12
11	57	52	65	46	64	58	79	71	68	57	53	50	59	45	66	60	83	75	69	58	11

10	55	49	63	44	61	54	75	67	64	53	51	46	57	42	64	55	79	71	66	54	10
9	53	45	60	42	59	50	72	63	61	49	49	43	55	40	61	51	75	66	63	50	9
8	50	41	58	39	56	46	68	58	57	45	47	39	53	38	58	47	71	62	59	46	8
7	48	38	56	37	53	42	65	54	54	41	45	35	51	35	55	43	67	57	56	42	7
6	46	34	53	35	50	38	62	50	50	37	43	31	49	33	52	39	63	52	53	38	6
5	44	31	51	33	48	34	58	46	47	34	41	28	47	31	49	35	59	47	49	34	5
4	41	27	48	31	45	31	55	41	44	30	39	24	44	28	46	31	55	43	46	30	4
3	39	23	46	28	42	27	51	37	40	26	37	20	42	26	43	26	51	38	43	26	3
2	37	20	44	26	39	23	48	33	37	22	34	17	40	23	41	22	46	33	39	22	2
1	35	16	41	24	37	19	44	28	33	18	32	13	38	21	38	18	42	29	36	18	1
0	32	13	39	22	34	15	41	24	30	14	30	9	36	19	35	14	38	24	33	14	0

APPENDIX I Composition of the Basic Scales and Their Derivative Subscales

The items for each of the basic scales and for their derivative subscales, designated by their numbers in the standard booklet form, are listed below. The direction in which they are scored (True or False) is also indicated. By means of the data provided in the item conversion tables in Appendix C and the direction of answer data in Appendix A, keys for the card form with X and O designations can also be prepared from these item lists. (For T-score conversions, see Appendix H.) None of the special scales is included; data on these scales will be found in the appendix material in Volume II. Also included wherever available are the raw-score means and standard deviations for males and females in the original Minnesota normative sample. Since these cases were tested before the addition of a supplementary set of items to the MMPI pool (see the discussion in Chapter 1), these data are not available for the Mf scale and for some of the subscales.

L Scales

L. Lie. Hathaway and McKinley (1951). Total: 15 items

True	False							
none	15	30	45	60	75	90	105	120
	135	150	165	195	225	255	285	

Males: Mean, 4.24; S.D., 2.67. Females: Mean, 4.47; S.D., 2.57.

L″. Non-overlapping, purified L. Adams and Horn (1965). Total: 11 items

True	False										
none	15	30	45	60	75	90	150	165	195	225	285

Males: Mean, 2.61; S.D., 2.00. Females: Mean, 2.83; S.D., 1.92.

F Scales

F. Infrequency. Hathaway and McKinley (1951). Total: 64 items

True									False				
14	23	27	31	34	35	40	42	48	17	20	54	65	75
49	50	53	56	66	85	121	123	139	83	112	113	115	164
146	151	156	168	184	197	200	202	205	169	177	185	196	199
206	209	210	211	215	218	227	245	246	220	257	258	272	276
247	252	256	269	275	286	291	293						

Males: Mean, 4.87; S.D., 5.17. Females: Mean, 3.44; S.D., 2.86.

F″. Non-overlapping, purified F. Adams and Horn (1965). Total: 33 items

True

14 31 34 35 40 48 49 50 53 56 66 85
121 139 146 184 197 200 202 205 209 211 218 227
256 291

False

20 83 113 185 199 257 258

Males: Mean, 2.59; S.D., 2.99. Females: Mean, 1.69; S.D., 1.84.

K Scales

K. Correction. McKinley, Hathaway and Meehl (1948). Total: 30 items

True	False
96	30 39 71 89 124 129 134 138 142 148 160 170 171 180 183 217 234 267 272 296 316 322 374 383 397 398 406 461 502

Males: Mean, 13.21; S.D., 5.44. Females: Mean, 12.35; S.D., 5.07.

L_6. Preliminary correction. Meehl and Hathaway (1946). Total: 22 items

True	False
none	39 89 96 124 129 134 138 142 148 171 180 217 234 267 296 316 322 374 383 397 398 406

Males: Mean, 10.00; S.D., 4.81. Females: Mean, 8.97; S.D., 4.50.

K′. Pure correction. Welsh (1952b). Total: 19 items

True	False
96	30 89 124 138 142 160 170 171 180 217 267 374 397 398 406 461 482 502

Males: Mean, 8.40; S.D., 3.36. Females: Mean, 8.34; S.D., 3.20.

K″. Non-overlapping, purified K. Adams and Horn (1965). Total: 13 items

True	False
none	138 142 160 170 171 296 374 397 398 406 461 482 502

Males: Mean, 5.48; S.D., 2.44. Females: Mean, 5.44; S.D., 2.39.

Hs (1) Scales

Hs. Hypochondriasis. Hathaway and McKinley (1951). Total: 33 items

True

23 29 43 62 72 108 114 125 161 189 273

False

2 3 7 9 18 51 55 63 68 103 130 153
155 163 175 188 190 192 230 243 274 281

Males: Mean, 5.25; S.D., 4.85. Females: Mean, 7.18; S.D., 5.23.

Hs′. Pure hypochondriasis. Welsh (1952b). Total: 9 items

True	False
29 62 72 108 125 161	63 68 130

Males: Mean, 1.62; S.D., 1.77. Females: Mean, 1.75; S.D., 1.75.

Hs″. Non-overlapping, purified Hs. Adams and Horn (1965). Total: 27 items

True

23	29	43	62	72	108	114	125	161	189	273

False

2	9	51	55	63	68	103	153	155	175	188	190
192	230	243	274								

Males: Mean, 4.23; S.D., 3.98. Females: Mean, 5.52; S.D., 4.23.

D (2) Scales

D. Depression. Hathaway and McKinley (1942). Total: 60 items

True

5	13	23	32	41	43	52	67	86	104	130	138
142	158	159	182	189	193	236	259				

False

2	8	9	18	30	36	39	46	51	57	58	64
80	88	89	95	98	107	122	131	145	152	153	154
155	160	178	191	207	208	233	241	242	248	263	270
271	272	285	296								

Males: Mean, 18.20; S.D., 4.61. Females: Mean, 20.66; S.D., 5.24.

D′. Pure depression. Welsh (1952b). Total: 24 items

True

5	130	193

False

39	46	58	64	80	88	95	98	131	145	154	191
207	233	241	242	263	270	271	272	285			

Males: Mean, 10.29; S.D., 2.57. Females: Mean, 11.21; S.D., 2.42.

D″. Non-overlapping, purified D. Adams and Horn (1965). Total: 27 items

True

5	13	52	86	104	130	158	159	182	193	236	259

False

46	58	64	88	95	98	131	145	154	191	207	233
242	270	272									

Males: Mean, 8.56; S.D., 2.32. Females: Mean, 9.44; S.D., 2.68.

D-O. Depression, obvious. Wiener and Harmon (1946). Total: 40 items

True

23	32	41	43	52	67	86	104	138	142	158	159
182	189	236	259	290							

False

2	8	9	18	36	46	51	57	88	95	107	122
131	152	153	154	178	207	242	270	271	272	285	

Males: Mean, 7.84; S.D., 4.43. Females: Mean, 9.64; S.D., 4.92.

D-S. Depression, subtle. Wiener and Harmon (1946). Total: 20 items

True

5	130	193

False

30	39	58	64	80	89	98	145	155	160	191	208
233	241	248	263	296							

Males: Mean, 10.36; S.D., 2.77. Females: Mean, 11.03; S.D., 2.71.

D_1. Subjective depression. Harris and Lingoes (1955). Total: 32 items

True

32	41	43	52	67	86	104	138	142	158	159	182
189	236	259									

False

2	8	46	57	88	107	122	131	152	160	191	207
208	242	272	285	296							

Males: Mean, 6.97; S.D., 3.46. Females: Mean, 8.55; S.D., 3.98.

D_2. Psychomotor retardation. Harris and Lingoes (1955). Total: 15 items

True

41	52	182	259

False

8	30	39	57	64	89	95	145	207	208	233

Males: Mean, 5.33; S.D., 1.81. Females: Mean, 5.89; S.D., 1.95.

D_3. Physical malfunctioning. Harris and Lingoes (1955). Total: 11 items

True				False						
130	189	193	288	2	18	51	153	154	155	160

Males: Mean, 3.11; S.D., 1.45. Females: Mean, 3.27; S.D., 1.57.

D_4. Mental dullness. Harris and Lingoes (1955). Total: 15 items

True

32	41	86	104	159	182	259	290

False

8	9	46	88	122	178	207

Males: Mean, 2.00; S.D., 2.02. Females: Mean, 2.26; S.D., 2.11.

D_5. Brooding. Harris and Lingoes (1955). Total: 10 items

True								False	
41	67	104	138	142	158	182	236	88	107

Males: Mean, 2.20; S.D., 1.84. Females: Mean, 3.01; S.D., 1.84.

Hy (3) Scales

Hy. Conversion hysteria. McKinley and Hathaway (1944). Total: 60 items

True

10	23	32	43	44	47	76	114	179	186	189	238
253											

False

2	3	6	7	8	9	12	26	30	51	55	71
89	93	103	107	109	124	128	129	136	137	141	147
153	160	162	163	170	172	174	175	180	188	190	192
201	213	230	234	243	265	267	274	279	289	292	

Males: Mean, 17.44; S.D., 5.43. Females: Mean, 19.84; S.D., 5.48.

Hy′. Pure hysteria. Welsh (1952b). Total: 19 items

True

44	246	253

False

6	12	26	71	128	129	136	147	162	172	174	213
234	265	279	292								

Males: Mean, 7.98; S.D., 2.94. Females: Mean, 8.84; S.D., 2.70.

Hy″. Non-overlapping, purified Hy. Adams and Horn (1965). Total: 23 items

True

10 32 44 47 76 179 186 238 246

False

6 12 71 128 129 136 147 162 174 213 234 265 279 292

Males: Mean, 7.43; S.D., 2.37. Females: Mean, 8.50; S.D., 2.40.

Hy-O. Hysteria, obvious. Wiener and Harmon (1946). Total: 32 items

True

10 23 32 43 44 47 76 114 179 186 189 238

False

2 3 7 8 9 51 55 103 107 128 137 153 163 174 175 188 192 230 243 274

Males: Mean, 4.67; S.D., 4.22. Females: Mean, 6.66; S.D., 4.77.

Hy-S. Hysteria, subtle. Wiener and Harmon (1946). Total: 28 items

True: 253

False: 6 12 26 30 71 89 93 109 124 129 136 141 147 160 162 170 172 180 190 201 213 234 265 267 279 289 292

Males: Mean, 12.76; S.D., 4.53. Females: Mean, 13.18; S.D., 4.20.

Ad. Admission of symptoms. Little and Fisher (1958). Total: 32 items

True

10 23 32 43 44 47 76 114 179 186 189 238

False

2 3 7 8 9 55 103 107 128 137 153 160 163 174 175 188 190 192 230 243

Males: Mean, 4.91; S.D., 4.23. Females: Mean, 6.84; S.D., 4.91.

Dn. Denial of symptoms. Little and Fisher (1958). Total: 26 items

True: 253

False: 6 12 26 30 71 89 93 109 124 129 136 141 147 162 170 172 180 201 213 234 265 267 279 289 292

Males: Mean, 12.13; S.D., 4.52. Females: Mean, 12.45; S.D., 4.26.

Hy_1. Denial of social anxiety. Harris and Lingoes (1955). Total: 6 items

True: none

False: 141 172 180 201 267 292

Males: Mean, 3.47; S.D., 1.80. Females: Mean, 3.29; S.D., 1.86.

Hy_2. Need for affection. Harris and Lingoes (1955). Total: 12 items

True: 253

False: 26 71 89 93 109 124 136 162 234 265 289

Males: Mean, 4.93; S.D., 2.47. Females: Mean, 4.68; S.D., 2.33.

Hy_3. Lassitude-malaise. Harris and Lingoes (1955). Total: 15 items

True

32 43 76 189 238

False

2 3 8 9 51 107 137 153 160 163

Males: Mean, 2.24; S.D., 2.37. Females: Mean, 2.69; S.D., 2.61.

Hy4. Somatic complaints. Harris and Lingoes (1955). Total: 17 items

True

10 23 44 47 114 186

False

7 55 103 174 175 188 190 192 230 243 274

Males: Mean, 2.83; S.D., 2.51. Females: Mean, 4.24; S.D., 3.00.

Hy5. Inhibition of aggression. Harris and Lingoes (1955). Total: 7 items

True	False
none	6 12 30 128 129 147 170

Males: Mean, 2.56; S.D., 1.38. Females: Mean, 3.43; S.D., 1.50.

Pd (4) Scales

Pd. Psychopathic deviate. McKinley and Hathaway (1944). Total: 50 items

True

16 21 24 32 33 35 38 42 61 67 84 94
102 106 110 118 127 215 216 224 239 244 245 284

False

8 20 37 82 91 96 107 134 137 141 155 170
171 173 180 183 201 231 235 237 248 267 287 289
294 296

Males: Mean, 14.77; S.D., 3.98. Females: Mean, 13.98; S.D., 4.18.

Pd′. Pure psychopathic deviate. Welsh (1952b). Total: 18 items

True

42 61 84 118 215 216 224 239 244 245

False

82 96 134 173 183 235 237 287

Males: Mean, 5.27; S.D., 2.29. Females: Mean, 4.51; S.D., 2.19.

Pd″. Non-overlapping, purified Pd. Adams and Horn (1965). Total: 20 items

True

42 61 84 118 215 216 224 239 244 245

False

37 82 91 96 134 173 183 235 237 287

Males: Mean, 5.82; S.D., 2.35. Females: Mean, 5.35; S.D., 2.33.

Pd-O. Psychopathic deviate, obvious. Wiener and Harmon (1946). Total: 28 items

True

16 24 32 33 35 38 42 61 67 84 94 106
110 118 215 216 224 244 245 284

False

8 20 37 91 107 137 287 294

Males: Mean, 5.88; S.D., 3.62. Females: Mean, 5.30; S.D., 3.48.

Pd-S. Psychopathic deviate, subtle. Wiener and Harmon (1946). Total: 22 items

True

21 102 127 239

False

82 96 134 141 155 170 171 173 180 183 201 231
235 237 248 267 289 296

Males: Mean, 8.89; S.D., 2.51. Females: Mean, 8.68; S.D., 2.41.

Pd_1. Familial discord. Harris and Lingoes (1955). Total: 11 items

True						False				
21	42	212	216	224	245	96	137	235	237	527

Males: Mean, 1.81; S.D., 1.72. Females: Mean, 1.82; S.D., 1.72.

Pd_2. Authority problems. Harris and Lingoes (1955). Total: 11 items

True				False						
38	59	118	520	37	82	141	173	289	294	429

Males: Mean, 4.18; S.D., 1.62. Females: Mean, 3.39; S.D., 1.36.

Pd_3. Social imperturbability. Harris and Lingoes (1955). Total: 12 items

True				False							
64	479	520	521	82	141	171	180	201	267	304	352

Males: Mean, 7.61; S.D., 2.49. Females: Mean, 6.90; S.D., 2.64.

Pd_{4A}. Social alienation. Harris and Lingoes (1955). Total: 18 items

True

16 24 35 64 67 94 110 127 146 239 244 284
305 368 520

False

20 141 170

Males: Mean, 5.35; S.D., 2.83. Females: Mean, 5.41; S.D., 2.75.

Pd_{4B}. Self-alienation. Harris and Lingoes (1955). Total: 15 items

True

32 33 61 67 76 84 94 102 106 127 146 215
368

False

8 107

Males: Mean, 3.86; S.D., 2.61. Females: Mean, 3.66; S.D., 2.62.

Mf (5) Scales

Mf-m. Masculinity-femininity, male. Hathaway (1956b). Total: 60 items

True

4 25 69 70 74 77 78 87 92 126 132 134
140 149 179 187 203 204 217 226 231 239 261 278
282 295 297 299

False

1 19 26 28 79 80 81 89 99 112 115 116
117 120 133 144 176 198 213 214 219 221 223 229
249 254 260 262 264 280 283 300

Means and S.D.'s not available; see introductory note.

Mf-f. Masculinity-femininity, female. Hathaway (1956b). Total: 60 items

True

4 25 70 74 77 78 87 92 126 132 133 134
140 149 187 203 204 217 226 239 261 278 282 295
299

False

1 19 26 28 69 79 80 81 89 99 112 115
116 117 120 144 176 179 198 213 214 219 221 223
229 231 249 254 260 262 264 280 283 297 300

Means and S.D.'s not available; see introductory note.

Mf'. Pure masculinity-femininity. Welsh (1952b). Total: 40 items

True

4 25 69 70 74 77 78 87 92 126 132 140
149 187 203 204 261 295

False

1 19 28 79 81 112 115 116 133 144 176 198
214 219 221 223 249 260 264 280 283 300

Means and S.D.'s not available; see introductory note.

Mf_1. Personal and emotional sensitivity. Pepper and Strong (1958). Total: 15 items

True

134 217 226 239 278 282 299

False

79 99 176 198 214 254 262 264

Males: Mean, 4.71; S.D., 2.31. Females: Mean, 6.68; S.D., 2.35.

Mf_1''. Non-overlapping, purified Mf_1. Adams and Horn (1965). Total: 13 items

True

217 226 278 282 209

False

79 99 176 198 214 254 262 264

Males: Mean, 3.91; S.D., 2.06. Females: Mean, 5.85; S.D., 2.09.

Mf_2. Sexual identification. Pepper and Strong (1958). Total: 6 items

True

69 74 179 231 297

False

133

Males: Mean, 1.09; S.D., 1.02. Females: Mean, 0.88; S.D., 0.93. (Means and S.D.'s based on all items except 74.)

Mf_3. Altruism. Pepper and Strong (1958). Total: 9 items

True

none

False

19 26 28 80 89 112 117 120 280

Males: Mean, 4.00; S.D., 1.92. Females: Mean, 4.43; S.D., 1.84.

Mf_3''. Non-overlapping, purified Mf_3. Adams and Horn (1965). Total: 7 items

True

none

False

19 26 28 80 112 120 280

Males: Mean, 3.11; S.D., 1.52. Females: Mean, 3.54; S.D., 1.38.

Mf_4. Feminine occupational identification. Pepper and Strong (1958). Total: 17 items

True

4 25 70 77 78 87 92 126 132 140 149 203
204 261 295

False

260 300

Means and S.D.'s not available; see introductory note.

Mf_4''. Non-overlapping, purified Mf_4. Adams and Horn (1965). Total: 14 items

True

4 25 70 77 87 92 126 132 140 149 203 204
261 295

False

none

Means and S.D.'s not available; see introductory note.

Mf_5. Denial of masculine occupations. Pepper and Strong (1958). Total: 10 items

True

187

False

1 81 116 144 219 221 223 229 283

Means and S.D.'s not available; see introductory note.

Mf_5''. Non-overlapping, purified Mf_5. Adams and Horn (1965). Total: 8 items

True	False							
none	1	81	116	144	219	221	223	283

Means and S.D.'s not available; see introductory note.

Pa (6) Scales

Pa. Paranoia. Hathaway (1956b). Total: 40 items

True

15	16	22	24	27	35	110	121	123	127	151	157
158	202	275	284	291	293	299	305	317	338	341	364
365											

False

93	107	109	111	117	124	268	281	294	313	316	319
327	347	348									

Males: Mean, 8.73; S.D., 3.67. Females: Mean, 8.41; S.D., 3.17.

Pa'. Pure paranoia. Welsh (1952b). Total: 15 items

True

27	123	151	275	293	338	365

False

117	268	313	316	319	327	347	348

Males: Mean, 3.86; S.D., 2.27. Females: Mean, 3.41; S.D., 1.59.

Pa". Non-overlapping, purified Pa. Adams and Horn (1965). Total: 20 items

True

16	22	24	27	123	151	275	293	338	365

False

93	117	268	294	313	316	319	327	347	348

Males: Mean, 4.45; S.D., 2.24. Females: Mean, 4.00; S.D., 1.82.

Pa-O. Paranoia, obvious. Wiener and Harmon (1946). Total: 23 items

True

16	24	27	35	110	121	123	151	158	202	275	284
291	293	305	317	326	338	341	364				

False

281	294	347

Males: Mean, 2.68; S.D., 2.88. Females: Mean, 2.87; S.D., 2.48.

Pa-S. Paranoia, subtle. Wiener and Harmon (1946). Total: 17 items

True

15	127	157	299	365

False

93	107	109	111	117	124	268	313	316	319	327	348

Males: Mean, 6.05; S.D., 2.33. Females: Mean, 5.54; S.D., 2.13.

Pa_1. Persecutory ideas. Harris and Lingoes (1955). Total: 17 items

True

16	24	35	110	121	123	127	151	157	202	275	284
291	293	338	364								

False

347

Males: Mean, 1.97; S.D., 2.23. Females: Mean, 1.80; S.D., 2.05.

Pa_2. Poignancy. Harris and Lingoes (1955). Total: 9 items

True							False	
24	158	299	305	317	341	365	111	268

Males: Mean, 2.18; S.D., 1.53. Females: Mean, 2.21; S.D., 1.44.

Pa_3. Naiveté. Harris and Lingoes (1955). Total: 9 items

True	False							
314	93	109	117	124	313	316	319	348

Males: Mean, 3.79; S.D., 2.04. Females: Mean, 3.55; S.D., 1.97.

Pt (7) Scales

Pt. Psychasthenia. McKinley and Hathaway (1942). Total: 48 items

True											
10	15	22	32	41	67	76	86	94	102	106	142
159	182	189	217	238	266	301	304	305	317	321	336
337	340	342	343	344	346	349	351	352	356	357	358
359	360	361									

False								
3	8	36	122	152	164	178	329	353

Males: Mean, 10.92; S.D., 7.75. Females: Mean, 13.56; S.D., 8.06.

Pt′. Pure psychasthenia. Welsh (1952). Total: 12 items

True										False	
217	337	340	343	344	346	351	358	359	361	164	329

Males: Mean, 3.39; S.D., 2.53. Females: Mean, 4.62; S.D., 2.57.

Pt″. Non-overlapping, purified Pt. Adams and Horn (1965). Total: 25 items

True											
304	317	336	337	340	342	343	344	346	349	351	357
358	359	360	361								

False								
3	8	36	122	152	164	178	329	353

Males: Mean, 5.64; S.D., 4.14. Females: Mean, 7.34; S.D., 4.27.

Sc (8) Scales

Sc. Schizophrenia. Hathaway (1956b). Total: 78 items

True											
15	16	21	22	24	32	33	35	38	40	41	47
52	76	97	104	121	156	157	159	168	179	182	194
202	210	212	238	241	251	259	266	273	282	291	297
301	303	305	307	312	320	324	325	332	334	335	339
341	345	349	350	352	354	355	356	360	363	364	

False											
8	17	20	37	65	103	119	177	178	187	192	196
220	276	281	306	309	322	330					

Males: Mean, 10.56; S.D., 8.14. Females: Mean, 10.87; S.D., 8.03.

Sc′. Pure schizophrenia. Welsh (1952b). Total: 30 items

True											
40	168	210	241	282	297	303	307	312	320	324	325
334	335	339	345	350	354	355	363				

False									
17	65	177	187	196	220	276	306	323	330

Males: Mean, 4.39; S.D., 3.14. Females: Mean, 4.64; S.D., 2.97.

Sc″. Non-overlapping, purified Sc. Adams and Horn (1965). Total: 29 items

True

168 210 297 303 307 312 320 324 325 334 339 345
350 354 355 363

False

17 65 177 187 196 220 276 281 306 309 322 323
330

Males: Mean, 4.41; S.D., 2.72. Females: Mean, 4.57; S.D., 2.47.

Sc-s. Shortened schizophrenic scale. Clark and Danielson (1956). Total: 20 items

True

15 47 156 157 159 168 182 194 212 251 266 301
303 323 333 334 341 364

False

178 318

Males: Mean, 2.55; S.D., 2.41. Females: Mean, 2.40; S.D., 2.35.

Sc_{1A}. Social alienation. Harris and Lingoes (1955). Total: 21 items

True

16 21 24 35 52 121 157 212 241 282 305 312
324 325 352 364

False

65 220 276 306 309

Males: Mean, 3.53; S.D., 2.36. Females: Mean, 3.68; S.D., 2.43.

Sc_{1B}. Emotional alienation. Harris and Lingoes (1955). Total: 11 items

True

76 104 202 301 339 355 360 363

False

8 196 322

Males: Mean, 2.21; S.D., 1.15. Females: Mean, 2.04; S.D., 1.14.

Sc_{2A}. Lack of ego mastery, cognitive. Harris and Lingoes (1955). Total: 10 items

True

32 33 159 168 182 335 345 349 356

False

178

Males: Mean, 1.45; S.D., 1.60. Females: Mean, 1.46; S.D., 1.58.

Sc_{2B}. Lack of ego mastery, conative. Harris and Lingoes (1955). Total: 14 items

True

32 40 41 76 104 202 259 301 335 339 356

False

8 196 322

Males: Mean, 2.00; S.D., 1.83. Females: Mean, 2.17; S.D., 1.98.

Sc_{2C}. Lack of ego mastery, defective inhibition. Harris and Lingoes (1955). Total: 11 items

True

22 97 156 194 238 266 291 303 352 354 360

False

none

Males: Mean, 1.44; S.D., 1.53. Females: Mean, 1.64; S.D., 1.81.

Sc_3. Bizarre sensory experiences. Harris and Lingoes (1955). Total: 20 items

True

22 33 47 156 194 210 251 273 291 332 334 341
345 350

False

103 119 187 192 281 330

Males: Mean, 2.42; S.D., 2.47. Females: Mean, 2.72; S.D., 2.54.

Ma(9) Scales

Ma. Hypomania. McKinley and Hathaway (1944). Total: 46 items

True											
11	13	21	22	59	64	73	97	100	109	127	134
143	156	157	167	181	194	212	222	226	228	232	233
238	240	250	251	263	266	268	271	277	279	298	

False										
101	105	111	119	120	148	166	171	180	267	289

Males: Mean, 15.14; S.D., 4.36. Females: Mean, 14.26; S.D., 4.47.

Ma′. Pure hypomania. Welsh (1952b). Total: 27 items

True											
11	59	64	73	100	109	134	143	167	181	222	226
228	232	233	240	250	263	268	271	277	279	298	

False			
101	105	148	166

Males: Mean, 10.32; S.D., 3.39. Females: Mean, 9.58; S.D., 3.05.

Ma″. Non-overlapping, purified Ma. Adams and Horn (1965). Total: 25 items

True											
11	59	73	100	109	143	167	181	222	228	232	240
250	271	277	298								

False								
101	105	111	119	148	166	180	267	289

Males: Mean, 9.52; S.D., 2.71. Females: Mean, 8.44; S.D., 2.71.

Ma-O. Hypomania, obvious. Wiener and Harmon (1946). Total: 23 items

True											
13	22	59	73	97	100	156	157	167	194	212	226
238	250	251	263	266	277	279	298				

False	
111	119
120	

Males: Mean, 5.88; S.D., 2.92. Females: Mean, 5.22; S.D., 3.02.

Ma-S. Hypomania, subtle. Wiener and Harmon (1946). Total: 23 items

True											
11	21	64	109	127	134	143	181	222	228	232	233
240	268	271									

False							
101	105	148	166	171	180	267	289

Males: Mean, 9.27; S.D., 2.60. Females: Mean, 9.04; S.D., 2.55.

Ma_1. Amorality. Harris and Lingoes (1955). Total: 6 items

True				
143	250	271	277	298

False
289

Males: Mean, 1.73; S.D., 1.36. Females: Mean, 1.38; S.D., 1.17.

Ma_2. Psychomotor acceleration. Harris and Lingoes (1955). Total: 11 items

True								
13	97	100	134	181	228	238	266	268

False	
111	119

Males: Mean, 3.68; S.D., 1.42. Females: Mean, 3.45; S.D., 1.57.

Ma$_3$. Imperturbability. Harris and Lingoes (1955). Total: 8 items

True

167 222 240

False

105 148 171 180 267

Males: Mean, 3.43; S.D., 1.71. Females: Mean, 2.91; S.D., 1.66.

Ma$_4$. Ego inflation. Harris and Lingoes (1955). Total: 9 items

True

11 59 64 73 109 157 212 232 233

False

none

Males: Mean, 2.62; S.D., 1.63. Females: Mean, 2.71; S.D., 1.66.

Si(0) Scales

Si. Social introversion. Drake (1946). Total: 70 items

True

32 67 82 111 117 124 138 147 171 172 180 201
236 267 278 292 304 316 321 332 336 342 357 377
383 398 411 427 436 455 473 487 549 564

False

25 33 57 91 99 119 126 143 193 208 229 231
254 262 281 296 309 353 359 371 391 400 415 440
446 449 450 451 462 469 479 481 482 505 521 547

Males: Mean, 24.75; S.D., 7.99. Females: Mean, 29.16; S.D., 8.32. (Means and S.D.'s based on all items except 25, 126, 547, and 549.)

Si′. Pure social introversion. Welsh (1952b). Total: 50 items

True

82 117 124 147 171 172 180 201 267 278 292 316
377 383 398 411 427 436 455 473 487 549 564

False

25 33 99 126 143 193 229 254 262 359 371 391
400 415 440 446 449 450 451 462 469 479 481 482
505 521 547

Males: Mean, 18.40; S.D., 5.77. Females: Mean, 21.16; S.D., 6.01. (Means and S.D.'s based on all items except 25, 126, 547, and 549.)

Si″. Non-overlapping, purified Si. Adams and Horn (1965). Total: 28 items

True

124 172 201 377 383 411 427 436 455 473 487 549
564

False

33 229 391 400 415 440 446 449 450 462 469 479
505 521 547

Males: Mean, 10.39; S.D., 3.72. Females: Mean, 12.21; S.D., 3.93. (Means and S.D.'s based on all items except 547 and 549.)

Si-s. Short-form social introversion. Briggs and Tellegen (1967). Total: 42 items

True

32 67 82 111 117 124 138 147 171 172 180 201
236 267 278 292 304 316 321 332 336 342 357

False

25 33 57 91 99 119 126 143 193 208 229 231
254 262 281 296 309 353 359

Males: Mean, 14.89; S.D., 5.35. Females: Mean, 17.49; S.D., 5.54. (Means and S.D.'s based on all items except 25 and 126.)

APPENDIX J Rules for Profile Discrimination

Table 1. Meehl-Dahlstrom Rules

PROCEDURE

The following restrictions and warnings should be noted: If L ≥ 70, F ≥ 80, or ? ≥ 60,[a] these rules do not apply. The rules assume the diagnostic issue is between neurosis and psychosis. The digits 0 and 5 should either be deleted in recording the codes or ignored in applying the rules; for example, a 58′4 curve falls under Rule 9. "P" and "N" should be taken to mean *curve types*, not as mechanically diagnosing the *patient*. Cutting scores are based on equal base rates and will be increasingly nonoptimal for greater asymmetries in the population split. The calculations use K-corrected T scores, derived on males only.

The basic calculations should be recorded on the profile sheet for use. There are four computations:

1. Band Location: (Pt + Sc) − (Hs + D) = Beta

Band No.	*Beta Value*
1	−31 and less
2	−30 through −11
3	−10 through +6
4	+7 through +25
5	+26 and above

(It may be useful to circle the band number on the profile sheet so that it is not confused with other numbers.)

2. Delta = (Pd + Pa) − (Hs + Hy)
3. Hathaway Code
4. Welsh Index (compute only if the profile has no score ≥ 70):

$$IR = \frac{Hs + D + Pt}{Hy + Pd + Ma}$$

(Round off the numerator and denominator sums to two digits before dividing. If the third digit is 5, round downward.)

Apply the rules consecutively until the classification is reached. Classification is either "psychotic curve," "neurotic curve," or "indeterminate." "Indeterminate" is considered a classification; if a rule so classifies a profile, do *not* proceed to subsequent rules. Since most rules will not apply to a given profile, proceed in order until one is reached that does. If a rule applies but does not classify the curve as either "N," "P," or "I," it will instruct "Proceed," which means go on to the next rule which applies and so continue until a decision is made.

RULES

1. Elevation Rule: If 7 of the 8 clinical scores ≥ 80 and 5 of them ≥ 90, then call P, unless delta ≤ −15, then call I.

Appendix J, Table 1—continued

2. Manic Rule: Apply only if the code begins with 9 or $\underline{9}$ ($\underline{9}$ must be *first* if underlined!).
   A. Ma > (Hs and D and Hy) by 15 points or more, call P, unless one of the following conditions holds, in which case proceed:
      (1) D + Pt ≥ 115 *or*
      (2) Hs, D, Hy all ≥ 50.
   B. Ma not > all three of the neurotic triad by 15 points, proceed.
3. "Normal Profile" Rule: Apply only if none of the 8 clinical scores ≥ 70.
   A. All scores ≤ 55, call I.
   B. IR ≤ .90
      (1) Delta ≤ 0, call I.
      (2) Otherwise, call P.
   C. IR > .90
      (1) Delta ≤ −10, call N, unless code 4, 6, or 8; then call I.
      (2) Delta > −10
         (a) Both D and Hy ≥ (highest among Pd, Pa, Ma), call N.
         (b) Either D or Hy ≥ (highest among Pd, Pa, Ma), call I.
         (c) Neither D nor Hy ≥ (highest among Pd, Pa, Ma), call P.
4. "Fake Good" Rule: Apply if L ≥ 60.
   A. Band 3, 4, or 5, call P.
   B. Band 2, call I.
   C. Band 1, call N.
5. Psychotic Code Rule: Apply to primed codes only. If the first three digits of the code are among the four digits 4, 6, 8, and 9, and at least one is primed, call P.
6. Slope Rule: If each of the three scores Pa, Pt, and Sc is ≥ all of the three scores Hs, D, and Hy; and Pa or Sc or both ≥ 70, call P.
7. 4′ Rule: Apply if the code is 4′ or 4″ (or 4 . . .′ or 4 . . .″).
   A. Band 4 or 5 and delta ≥ 0, call P.
   B. Band 1 or 2 and delta negative, call N.
   C. Otherwise, call I.
8. 6′ Rule: Apply if code is 6′ or 6″ (or 6 . . .′ or 6 . . .″).
   A. Code 6″ or 6 . . .″ call P.
   B. Code 6′ or 6 . . .′ call P, unless
      (1) Band 1, call I, *or*
      (2) Delta ≤ +20 and (Pa − Pt) ≤ +10, call I.
9. 8′4 Rule: Apply if code 8′4 or 84′ or higher.
   A. Sc > Pt by 10 points or more, call P.
   B. Otherwise, proceed.
10. (Sc − Pt) Rule: Apply only if Sc ≥ 80.
    A. Sc > Pt by 10 or more points, unless delta ≤ −60, call P, *or*
    B. Pt ≤ both Pa and Sc, and Pa ≥ 70, call P.
    C. Otherwise, proceed.
11. (Pa − Pt) Rule: Apply if Pa ≥ Pt and Pa ≥ 70. Pa ≥ 70 and (Pa − Pt) ≥ 10, call P, unless Band 1, in which case proceed.
12. Band 1 Rule: Curve in Band 1. Call N, unless one of the following hold, in which case call I:
    A. F, Pd both ≥ 70, *or*
    B. Pd ≥ 65 and Pa ≤ 45, *or*
    C. Delta ≥ 0, *or*
    D. D ≥ 100 and (D − Ma) ≥ 60.
13. Band 2 Rule: Curve in Band 2. Call N, unless one of the following hold, in which case call I:
    A. D ≥ 100 and (D − Ma) ≥ 60, *or*
    B. Pa ≥ 75.
14. Band 3 Rule: Curve in Band 3.
    A. D ≥ 85
       (1) Pd > Hs by 10 points and Pd or Pa ≥ 70, call P.
       (2) 27 or $\underline{72}$ code, no other score ≥ 80, both Pd and Pa ≤ 70, call N.
       (3) Otherwise, call I.

B. D < 85
(1) F ≥ 70, call I.
(2) Code 4, 6, 8, or 9, call I.
(3) Delta ≥ −10, call I.
(4) Otherwise, call N.

15. Band 4 Rule: Curve in Band 4.
A. All three signs below present, call P:
(1) (Sc ≥ Pt) *and*
(2) Code 9 or 8 *and*
(3) Sc *or* Pd ≥ D.
B. None of three present, call N.
C. Otherwise, call I.

16. Band 5 Rule: Curve in Band 5.
A. D ≥ 75. Both signs below present, call P; otherwise, call I:
(1) Pd ≥ 75 and ≥ Hy *and*
(2) Sc ≥ Pt.
B. D < 75. All three signs below present, call N; otherwise, call I:
(1) Pt > Sc by ten points *and*
(2) Sc ≤ 80 *and*
(3) Pa ≤ 70.

SOURCE: Meehl and Dahlstrom (1960).
[a]Experience suggests that profiles with ? ≥ 60 can be handled by calling them "P" if they appear so under Rule 4 or by the usual application of the subsequent rules; otherwise call them "I" (i.e., "N" should not be diagnosed from such profiles).

Table 2a. Henrichs Rules for Males

PROCEDURE

These rules are derived from alterations and additions to the Meehl-Dahlstrom Neurotic-Psychotic Rules for the MMPI. If L ≥ 70, F ≥ 80, or ? ≥ 60, these rules do not apply. Digit 5 should be deleted in recording the codes, but recorded separately as it is employed under certain rules. "P," "N," and "Pd" should be taken to mean *curve types*, not *diagnoses*. The calculations employ K-corrected T scores. The four basic calculations should be recorded on the profile sheet.

1. Band Location: (Pt + Sc) − (Hs + D) = Beta

Band No.	*Beta Value*
1	−31 and less
2	−30 through −11
3	−10 through +6
4	+7 through +25
5	+26 and above

2. Delta = (Pd + Pa) − (Hs + Hy)
3. Welsh Code
4. Welsh Index (compute only if the profile has no score ≥ 70):

$$IR = \frac{Hs + D + Pt}{Hy + Pd + Ma}$$

(Round off the numerator and denominator sums to two digits before dividing. If the third digit is 5, round downward.)

Apply the rules consecutively until the classification is reached. Classification is either "P," "N," "Pd," or "I." Indeterminate (I) is a classification; if a rule so classifies a profile, do not proceed to subsequent rules. Since most rules will not apply to a given profile, proceed in order until one is reached that does. If a rule applies but does not classify the curve as either N, P, Pd, or I, it will instruct "Proceed," which means go on to the next rule which applies and continue until a decision is made.

RULES

1. Elevation Rule: If 7 of the 8 clinical scores ≥ 80 and 5 of them ≥ 90, then call P, unless delta ≤ −15, then call I.

2. Manic Rule: Apply only if the code begins with 9 or $\underline{9}$ ($\underline{9}$ must be first if underlined!).
   - A. Ma > (Hs and D and Hy) by 15 points or more, call P, unless one of the following conditions holds, in which case proceed:
     - (1) D + Pt ≥ 115, *or*
     - (2) Hs, D, Hy all ≥ 50, *or*
     - (3) Mf ≥ 65.
   - B. If the following conditions hold call Pd:
     - (1) (a) Curve in Band 3 and delta < 0, and
       - (b) Ma and Pd among first three scales, and
       - (c) Ma greater than next scale by 7 points; *or*
     - (2) Curve in Band 4 and delta ≥ 0.
   - C. Otherwise, proceed.
3. "Normal Profile" Rule: Apply only if none of the 8 clinical scores ≥ 70.
   - A. All scores ≤ 55, call I.
   - B. IR ≤ .90
     - (1) Delta ≤ 0, call I.
     - (2) If code 9, or 4 and 9 among first 3 scales, and delta > 0, call Pd.
     - (3) Otherwise, call P.
   - C. IR > .90
     - (1) If code 0, call Pd.
     - (2) Delta ≤ .10, call N, unless code 4, 6, or 8; then call I.
     - (3) Delta > −10
       - (a) Both D and Hy ≥ (highest among Pd, Pa, Ma), call N.
       - (b) Either D or Hy ≥ (highest among Pd, Pa, Ma), call I.
       - (c) Neither D nor Hy ≥ (highest among Pd, Pa, Ma), call P.
4. "Fake Good" Rule: Apply if L ≥ 60.
   - A. Band 3, 4, or 5, call P, unless curve in Band 3 or 4, delta ≥ 0 and 4′ code, in which case proceed.
   - B. Band 2, proceed.
   - C. Band 1, call N.
5. Psychotic Code Rule: Apply to primed codes only. If the first three digits of the code are among the four digits 4, 6, 8, and 9, and at least one is primed, call P.
6. Slope Rule: If each of the three scores Pa, Pt, and Sc is ≥ all of the three scores Hs, D, and Hy; and Pa or Sc or both ≥ 70, call P.
7. 4′ Rule: Apply if the code is 4′ or 4″ (or 4 . . .′, or 4 . . .″).
   - A. Band 4 or 5 and delta ≥ 0, call P, unless Band 4 and either Mf > Hy, or Hy ≥ 60, call Pd.
   - B. Band 1 or 2 and delta negative, call N.
   - C. Band 2 or 3 and delta ≥ 0, call Pd.
   - D. Otherwise, call I.
8. 6′ Rule: Apply if code is 6′ or 6″ (or 6 . . .′ or 6 . . .″).
   - A. Code 6″ or 6 . . .″, call P.
   - B. Code 6′ or 6 . . .′, call P, unless
     - (1) Band 1, call I.
     - (2) Delta ≤ +20 and (Pa − Pt) ≤ +10, call I.
9. 8′4 Rule: Apply if code 8′4 or 84′ or higher.
   - A. Sc > Pt by 10 points or more, call P.
   - B. Otherwise, proceed.
10. (Sc − Pt) Rule: Apply only if Sc ≥ 80.
    - A. Sc > Pt by 10 or more points, unless delta ≤ −60, call P, *or*
    - B. Pt ≤ both Pa and Sc, and Pa ≥ 70, call P.
    - C. Otherwise, proceed.
11. (Pa − Pt) Rule: Apply if Pa ≥ Pt and Pa ≥ 70. Pa ≥ 70 and (Pa − Pt) ≥ 10, call P, unless Band 1, in which case proceed.
12. Band 1 Rule: Curve in Band 1. Call N, unless one of the following hold, in which case call I:
    - A. F, Pd both ≥ 70, *or*
    - B. Pd ≥ 65 and Pa ≤ 45, *or*
    - C. Delta ≥ 0, *or*
    - D. D ≥ 100 and (D − Ma) ≥ 60.
13. Band 2 Rule: Curve in Band 2. Call N, unless one of the following hold, in which case call I:

A. D ≥ 100 and (D − Ma) ≥ 60, *or*
B. Pa ≥ 75.

14. Band 3 Rule: Curve in Band 3.
   A. D ≥ 85
      (1) Pd > Hs by 10 points and Pd or Pa ≥ 70, call P.
      (2) 27 or $\underline{72}$ code, no other score ≥ 80, both Pd and Pa ≤ 70, call N.
      (3) Otherwise, call I.
   B. D < 85
      (1) F ≥ 70, call I.
      (2) Code 4, 6, 8, or 9, call I.
      (3) Delta ≥ −10, call I.
      (4) Otherwise, call N.
15. Band 4 Rule: Curve in Band 4.
   A. All three signs below present, call P:
      (1) Sc ≥ Pt, *and*
      (2) Code 9 or 8, *and*
      (3) Sc *or* Pd ≥ D.
   B. None of three present, call N.
   C. Otherwise, call I.
16. Band 5 Rule: Curve in Band 5.
   A. D ≥ 75. Both signs below present, call P; otherwise, call I:
      (1) Pd ≥ 75 and ≥ Hy *and*
      (2) Sc ≥ Pt
   B. D < 75. All three signs below present, call N; otherwise, call I:
      (1) Pt > Sc by ten points, *and*
      (2) Sc ≤ 80, *and*
      (3) Pa ≤ 70.

SOURCE: Henrichs (1964).

Table 2b. Henrichs Rules for Females

PROCEDURE

See Table 2a for computational procedures.

RULES

1. Elevation Rule: If 7 of the 8 clinical scores ≥ 80 and 5 of them ≥ 90, then call P, unless delta ≤ −5, then call I.
2. Manic Rule: Apply only if the code begins with 9 or $\underline{9}$ ($\underline{9}$ must be first if underlined!).
   A. Ma > (Hs and D and Hy) by 15 points or more, call P, unless one of the following conditions holds, in which case proceed:
      (1) D + Pt ≥ 115, *or*
      (2) Hs, D, Hy all ≥ 50, *or*
      (3) Mf ≥ 65.
   B. If the following conditions hold, call Pd:
      (1) (a) Curve in Band 3 and delta < +10, *and*
          (b) Ma and Pd among first three scales; *or*
      (2) Curve in Band 4 and delta ≥ +10.
   C. Otherwise, proceed.
3. "Normal Profile" Rule: Apply only if none of the 8 clinical scores ≥ 70.
   A. All scores ≤ 55, call I.
   B. IR ≤ .90
      (1) Delta < +10, call I.
      (2) If code 4 or code 9, or 4 and 9 among first three scales, and delta ≥ +10, call Pd.
      (3) Otherwise, call P.
   C. IR > .90
      (1) If code 0, call Pd.

   (2) Delta ≤ 0, call N, unless code 4, 6, or 8; then call I.
   (3) Delta > 0
      (a) Both D and Hy $\geq$ (highest among Pd, Pa, Ma), call N.
      (b) Either D or Hy $\geq$ (highest among Pd, Pa, Ma), call I.
      (c) Neither D nor Hy $\geq$ (highest among Pd, Pa, Ma), call P.

4. "Fake Good" Rule: Apply if L ≥ 60.
   A. Band 3, 4, or 5, call P, unless curve in Band 3 or 4, delta $\geq +5$ and 4′ code, in which case proceed.
   B. Band 2, proceed.
   C. Band 1, call N.
5. Psychotic Code Rule: Apply to primed codes only. If the first three digits of the code are among the four digits 4, 6, 8, and 9, and at least one is primed, call P.
6. Slope Rule: If each of the three scores Pa, Pt, and Sc is $\geq$ all of the three scores Hs, D, and Hy; and Pa or Sc or both ≥ 70, call P.
7. 4′ Rule: Apply if the code is 4′ or 4″ (or 4 . . .′ or 4 . . .″).
   A. Band 4 or 5 and delta $\geq +10$, call P, unless Band 4 and either Mf $>$ Hy, or Hy ≥ 60, call Pd.
   B. Band 1 or 2 and delta negative, call N.
   C. Band 2 or 3 and delta $\geq +5$, call Pd.
   D. Otherwise, call I.
8. 6′ Rule: Apply if code is 6′ or 6″ (or 6 . . .′ or 6 . . .″).
   A. Code 6″ or 6 . . .″, call P.
   B. Code 6′ or 6 . . .′, call P, unless
      (1) Band 1, call I.
      (2) Delta $\leq +30$ and (Pa − Pt) $\leq +10$, call I.
9. 8′4 Rule: Apply if code 8′4 or 84′ or higher.
   A. Sc $>$ Pt by 10 points or more, call P.
   B. Otherwise, proceed.
10. (Sc − Pt) Rule: Apply only if Sc ≥ 80.
   A. Sc $>$ Pt by 10 or more points, unless delta ≤ -50, call P, *or*
   B. Pt $\leq$ both Pa and Sc, and Pa ≥ 70, call P.
   C. Otherwise, proceed.
11. (Pa − Pt) Rule: Apply if Pa $\geq$ Pt and Pa ≥ 70. Pa ≥ 70 and (Pa − Pt) ≥ 10, call P, unless Band 1, in which case proceed.
12. Band 1 Rule: Curve in Band 1. Call N, unless one of the following hold, in which case call I:
   A. F, Pd both ≥ 70, *or*
   B. Pd ≥ 65 and Pa ≤ 45, *or*
   C. Delta $\geq +10$, *or*
   D. D ≥ 100 and (D − Ma) ≥ 60.
13. Band 2 Rule: Curve in Band 2. Call N, unless one of the following hold, in which case call I:
   A. D ≥ 100 and (D − Ma) ≥ 60, *or*
   B. Pa ≥ 75.
14. Band 3 Rule: Curve in Band 3.
   A. D ≥ 85
      (1) Pd $>$ Hs by 10 points and Pd or Pa ≥ 70, call P.
      (2) 27 or 72 code, no other score ≥ 80, both Pd and Pa ≤ 70, call N.
      (3) Otherwise, call I.
   B. D < 85
      (1) F ≥ 70, call I.
      (2) Code 4, 6, 8, or 9, call I.
      (3) Delta ≥ 0, call I.
      (4) Otherwise, call N.
15. Band 4 Rule: Curve in Band 4.
   A. All three signs below present, call P:
      (1) Sc $\geq$ Pt, *and*
      (2) Code 9 or 8, *and*
      (3) Sc *or* Pd $\geq$ D.
   B. None of three present, call N, unless code O or O among first three scales and ≥ 70, then call I.
   C. Otherwise, call I.

Appendix J, Table 2b—continued

16. Band 5 Rule: Curve in Band 5.
    A. D ≥ 75. Both signs below present, call P; otherwise, call I:
        (1) Pd ≥ 75 and ≥ Hy *and*
        (2) Sc ≥ Pt.
    B. D < 75. All three signs below present, call N; otherwise, call I:
        (1) Pt > Sc by ten points, *and*
        (2) Sc ≤ 80, *and*
        (3) Pa ≤ 70.

SOURCE: Henrichs (1966).

Table 3. Kleinmuntz Rules

The MMPI should be scored on 16 scales: ?, L, F, K, Hs, D, Hy, Pd, Mf, Pa, Pt, Sc, Ma, Si, Es, and Mt. (The latter two scales usually do not appear on the conventional MMPI profile sheet; see Appendix I in Volume II for the composition of these scales.) K correction is assumed for scales Hs, Pd, Pt, Sc, and Ma. All scores except for scales Es and Mt are reported here as T scores; Es and Mt should be entered as raw-score values. Application of these rules without the aid of an electronic digital computer may be exceedingly cumbersome due to the pattern-analytic approach to the decision rules themselves.

The following calculations will be needed:

1. Hathaway Code
2. Band Location: (Pt + Sc) − (D + Hs) = Beta

Band No.	*Beta Value*
1	−31 and less
2	−30 through −11
3	−10 through +6
4	+7 through +25
5	+26 and above

3. Delta = (Pd + Pa) − (Hs + Hy)
4. Anxiety Index:

$$AI = \frac{Hs + D + Hy}{3} + (D + Pt) - (Hs + Hy)$$

5. Internalization Ratio:

$$IR = \frac{Hs + D + Pt}{Hy + Pd + Ma}$$

Note: Proceed to the next rule regardless of the maladjustment vs. adjustment decision. Since a tally must be kept of the number of rules that apply to an MMPI profile, the rule number must be notated.

Call Maladjusted if:

1. Four or more clinical scales ≥ 70 (Mt and Es excluded).
2. The first two scales of the Hathaway code are among the scales Pd or Pa or Sc and one of these ≥ 70. If Mf is one of the first two scales in the Hathaway code, then examine the first three scales.
3. Pa or Sc ≥ 70 and Pa or Pt or Sc ≥ Hs or D or Hy.
4. Pa ≥ 70, unless Mt ≤ 6 and K ≥ 65.
5. (Pa + Sc − 2·Pt) ≥ 20, if Pa or Sc ≥ 65 and if Pa and/or Sc ≥ Pt.
6. Pd ≥ 70 and
    A. Mt ≥ 15 (males).
    B. Mt ≥ 17 (females).
7. Pd ≥ 70 and
    A. Band 4 or 5 and delta ≥ 0, *or*
    B. Band 1 or 2 and delta ≤ 0.
8. Mt ≥ 23 and Es ≤ 50.
9. Mt ≥ 23 and Es ≤ 45.

10. Five or more scales ⩾ 65 and Pa or Sc ⩾ 65.
11. Male profile with Mf ⩾ 70 and Sc ⩾ 60 with Sc ⩾ Pt.
12. Sc ⩾ 70 and either Si or Pa ⩾ 60.
13. Es ⩽ 35.
14. IR ⩾ .90; delta ⩽ −10.
15. Sc is primary elevation (first in Hathaway code) and is ⩾ 65 and F ⩾ L and (not plus) K.
16. Band 2 profile.
17. Band 3 and IR ⩾ 1.00.
18. K ⩾ 50 and any scale except Es or Ma ⩾ 70.
19. Male profile and Mf ⩾ 65 and Pd ⩾ 63.
20. Sc ⩾ 60 and Si ⩾ 50 and AI ⩾ 60, unless the Ma scale ⩽ 65.
21. Sc ⩾ 60 and Si ⩾ 50 and Ma < 70 and AI ⩾ 50.
22. Pd ⩾ 63, and Hs ⩽ 48 and AI ⩾ 65.
23. Male profile and Pd ⩽ 54, Hs ⩾ 58, and Si ⩾ 44.
24. Hs ⩾ 58, Hy ⩽ 61.
25. Hy ⩽ 61 and Pd ⩾ 63; also hold for female profile if Pd is not the primary elevation.
26. Pa and Sc, > 60 if male; or > 65 if female.
27. (Hs + Hy − 2·D) ⩾ 10, Pa < 50, Pt ⩾ 50, and Mt ⩾ 10.
28. (Mt − Es) ⩾ 4.

Call Adjusted if:

29. Mt ⩽ 6.
30. All scales ⩽ 60 except Ma ⩽ 80 and Mt ⩽ 10.
31. D or Pt are primary elevations and D⩾ Hs and ⩾ Hy; and Pt ⩾ Pa and ⩾ Sc; and Es ⩾ 45.
32. Mt < 10.
33. Five scales between 40 and 60, and Es ⩾ 45.
34. (Hs + Hy − 2·D) ⩾ 20; and Pt < Pa ⩽ 70 *or* Mt ⩽ 10.
35. (Mt − Es) ⩽ 0, if female, ⩽ −20, if male, unless Rule 5 calls profile maladjusted.

Up to this point only tentative decisions have been made. The flow chart on p. 425 specifies the conditions for the final clinical decision. The decision is one of three: (a) Call Adjusted, (b) Call Maladjusted, or (c) Call Unclassified.

SOURCE: Kleinmuntz (1963).

Table 4. Rules for Applying the Buer Somatization Index

1. Mf ⩽ 43, with (Pa − Mf) ⩾ 7 and (K − F) < 5 (if true, not a somatizer; if false, go to 2).
2. Hs, Hy, Pt, and Sc all ⩾ 69, with K ⩽ 62 and Ma ⩽ 60 or D ⩾ 85 (if true, not a somatizer; if false, go to 3).
3. Pd ⩽ 50, D ⩽ 72, and Mf ⩽ 59, with F ⩽ 55 or Ma ⩽ 50 (if true, not a somatizer; if false, go to 4).
4. D ⩽ 48, with K ⩾ 65 or Si ⩾ 50 (if true, not a somatizer; if false, go to 5).
5. Hs and Hy ⩾ 40, with (Pa − Sc) < 100, Mf ⩾ 47, and D ⩽ 58 or (L − K) ⩾ 3 (if true, a somatizer; if false, go to 6).
6. Hs and Hy ⩾ 54 (if false, not a somatizer; if true, go to 7).
7. Sc ⩽ 60 or Pa ⩽ 50, with Mf ⩾ 55, L ⩽ 56, and Pa < 70 (if true, a somatizer; if false, go to 8).
8. D ⩾ 75, Pa ⩽ 70, L ⩽ 60, F ⩽ 64, with Si ⩽ 50 or Pa ⩽ 55 (if true, a somatizer; if false, go to 9).
9. Pa ⩾ 65 (if true, not a somatizer; if false, go to 10).
10. Pd < 60, Hy ⩾ 60, and Pa ⩾ 50 (if true, a somatizer; if false, go to 11).
11. Sc ⩾ 70 (if true, a somatizer; if false, go to 12).
12. (Hs + D + Hy + Pd)/4 ⩾ 65, with Mf ⩽ 55, L ⩽ 70, and Si ⩽ 60 (if true, a somatizer; if false, not a somatizer).

SOURCE: Buer (1958).

KLEINMUNTZ FLOW CHART

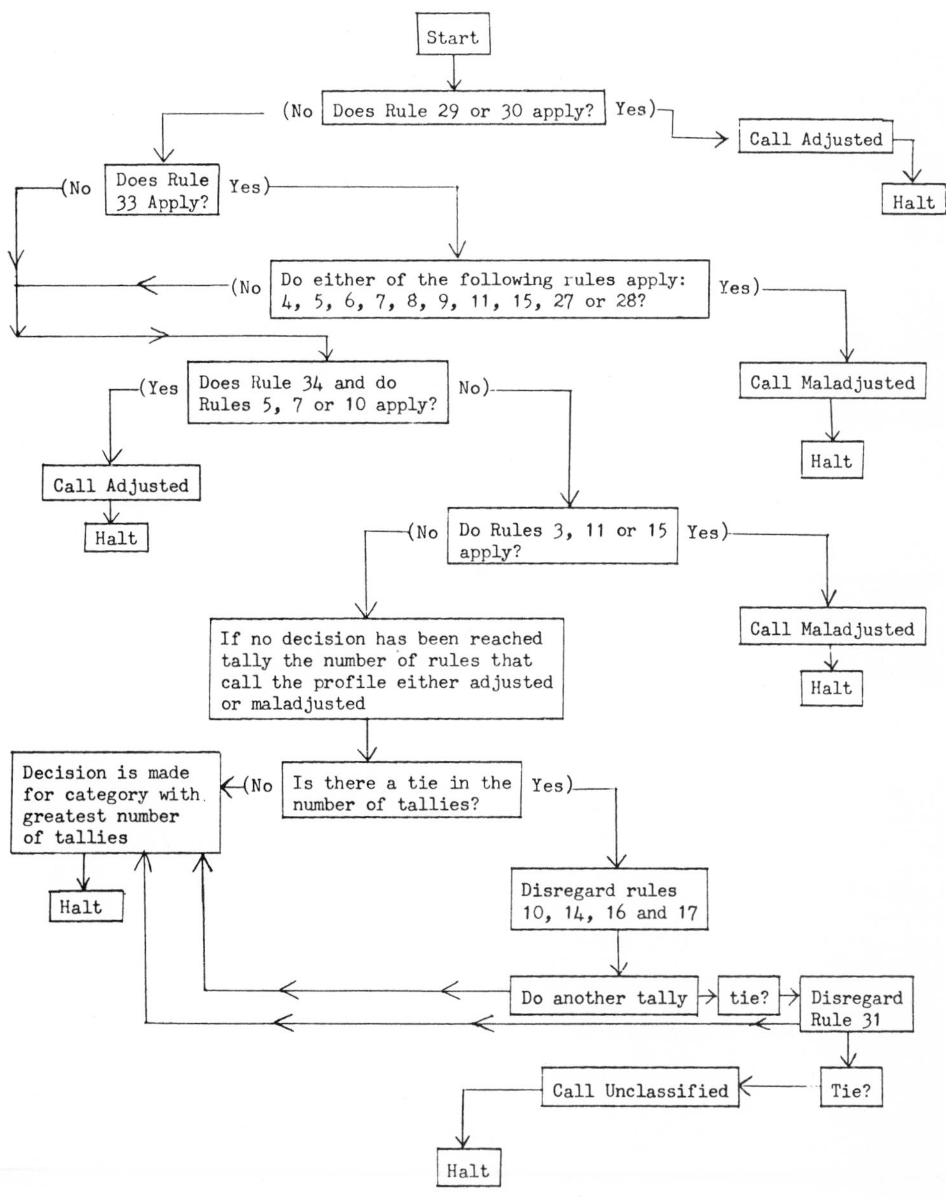

APPENDIX K Short-Form Tables

The following tables have been prepared for use with the regular booklet form. If only part of the booklet is covered by the test subject before he stops, an estimate can be made of the total raw score he would have earned on each scale from the prorated values provided. Since the items from the component scales are unevenly distributed throughout the booklet, the appropriate weights to be applied to each scale shift from one part of the test to the next. These prorating weights have been tabled for fifty-item increments; use the entries in the table which most closely correspond to the actual number of items that the subject answered.

To use these tables follow these steps: (1) score the answer sheet as if the subject had completed the test; (2) determine the point at which the test was stopped and locate the column heading in Table 1 which comes closest to this item total; (3) using the factor listed for the Cannot Say score in that column, multiply the number of items that the subject omitted before he reached the place where he stopped (not the total number of items unanswered) by this value and enter this product on the profile sheet in the Cannot Say column; (4) for each of the other raw scores to be prorated, consult the column in Table 2 which is indicated in Table 1 for each scale with the given number of completed items.

Example: The subject finished 260 items in the booklet before testing was stopped. He left nine items blank up to this point (and, of course, 304 items unanswered beyond this point). The following raw scores were found upon application of the scoring stencils to his incomplete answer sheet: L = 2, F = 8, K = 6, Hs = 12, D = 19, Hy = 18, Pd = 21, Mf = 4, Pa = 8, Pt = 11, Sc = 7, Ma = 10, Si = 15. To obtain the prorated raw scores for this subject, enter the column headed 250 in Table 1 since this is the closest value to the number of items to which he had responded (260) before stopping. For Cannot Say, the factor given in this column is 2.3. Multiplying 9 by 2.3 gives an estimate of 20.7 or 21 Cannot Say items for the whole test. According to Table 1, to obtain the value for the L score, one should use column G in Table 2 (that is, by item number 250 in the booklet, about nine-tenths of the L scale items have already been presented). Locating the obtained L raw score of 2 in the first column of Table 2 and reading the corresponding value in Column G, the prorated value of 2 is obtained. For the F score, column F in Table 2 must be used; a prorated value of 5 for the obtained value of 4 is given. Column D must be used for the prorated K raw score which gives a value of 10 for the obtained raw score of 6. If the rest of the scores are determined the following projected raw scores would be obtained: ? = 21, L = 2, F = 10, K = 10, Hs = 13, D = 24, Hy = 20, Pd = 23, Mf = 5, Pa = 20, Pt = 22, Sc = 18, Ma = 12, Si = 38. These values can then be transferred to a profile sheet and by means of the appropriate K-corrections and the regular T-score tables, a projected profile may be constructed.

Note that in Table 1 for item totals of 350 or more several scales have no letter designation. The raw scores for these scales do not require prorating.

Table 1. Conversion Factors for Prorating Raw Scores

Scale	Number of Items Completed 200	250	300	350	400	450	500
?.........	2.8	2.3	1.9	1.6	1.4	1.2	1.1
L........	F	G	H				
F........	D	F	H				
K........	C	D	E	F	G	G	H
1 (Hs)....	F	G	H				
2 (D).....	E	F	H				
3 (Hy)....	F	G	H				
4 (Pd)....	E	G	H				
5 (Mf)....	D	F	H				
6 (Pa)	B	B	D	G	H		
7 (Pt).....	C	C	C	F	H		
8 (Sc)	A	B	C	G	H		
9 (Ma)....	D	F	H				
0 (Si).....	A	B	C	D	E	F	G

Table 2. Prorated Raw Scores

Obtained Raw Score	Conversion Factor A (.3)	B (.4)	C (.5)	D (.6)	E (.7)	F (.8)	G (.9)	H (1.0)
78.........								78
77.........								77
76.........								76
75.........								75
74.........								74
73.........								73
72.........								72
71.........							78	71
70.........							77	70
69.........							76	69
68.........							75	68
67.........							74	67
66.........							73	66
65.........							72	65
64.........							70	64
63.........							69	63
62.........						78	68	62
61.........						76	67	61
60.........						75	66	60
59.........						74	65	59
58.........						72	64	58
57.........						71	63	57
56.........					78	70	62	56
55.........					77	69	60	55
54.........					76	68	59	54
53.........					74	66	58	53
52.........					73	65	57	52
51.........					71	64	56	51

Appendix K, Table 2—continued

Obtained Raw Score	A (.3)	B (.4)	C (.5)	D (.6)	E (.7)	F (.8)	G (.9)	H (1.0)
	Conversion Factor							
50					70	62	55	50
49					69	61	54	49
48					67	60	53	48
47					66	59	52	47
46				78	64	58	51	46
45				76	63	56	50	45
44				75	62	55	48	44
43				73	60	54	47	43
42				71	59	52	46	42
41			78	70	57	51	45	41
40			78	68	56	50	44	40
39			78	66	55	49	43	39
38			76	65	53	48	42	38
37			74	63	52	46	41	37
36			72	61	50	45	40	36
35			70	60	49	44	38	35
34			68	58	48	42	37	34
33			66	56	46	41	36	33
32		78	64	54	45	40	35	32
31		78	62	53	43	39	34	31
30		75	60	51	42	38	33	30
29		72	58	49	41	36	32	29
28		70	56	48	39	35	31	28
27		68	54	46	38	34	30	27
26	78	65	52	44	36	32	29	26
25	78	62	50	42	35	31	28	25
24	78	60	48	41	34	30	26	24
23	76	58	46	39	32	29	25	23
22	73	55	44	37	31	28	24	22
21	69	52	42	36	29	26	23	21
20	66	50	40	34	28	25	22	20
19	63	48	38	32	27	24	21	19
18	59	45	36	31	25	22	20	18
17	56	42	34	29	24	21	19	17
16	53	40	32	27	22	20	18	16
15	50	38	30	26	21	19	16	15
14	46	35	28	24	20	18	15	14
13	43	32	26	22	18	16	14	13
12	40	30	24	20	17	15	13	12
11	36	28	22	19	15	14	12	11
10	33	25	20	17	14	12	11	10
9	30	22	18	15	13	11	10	9
8	26	20	16	14	11	10	9	8
7	23	18	14	12	10	9	8	7
6	20	15	12	10	8	8	7	6
5	16	12	10	8	7	6	6	5
4	13	10	8	7	6	5	4	4
3	10	8	6	5	4	4	3	3
2	7	5	4	3	3	2	2	2
1	3	2	2	2	1	1	1	1

APPENDIX L List of MMPI Items

Below is a list of the statements in the order used in the Group Form booklet (see Appendix C for alternative numberings). Sixteen items in this list are duplicated for machine-scoring purposes; see Appendix B for identification of these items.

1. I like mechanics magazines.
2. I have a good appetite.
3. I wake up fresh and rested most mornings.
4. I think I would like the work of a librarian.
5. I am easily awakened by noise.
6. I like to read newspaper articles on crime.
7. My hands and feet are usually warm enough.
8. My daily life is full of things that keep me interested.
9. I am about as able to work as I ever was.
10. There seems to be a lump in my throat much of the time.
11. A person should try to understand his dreams and be guided by or take warning from them.
12. I enjoy detective or mystery stories.
13. I work under a great deal of tension.
14. I have diarrhea once a month or more.
15. Once in a while I think of things too bad to talk about.
16. I am sure I get a raw deal from life.
17. My father was a good man.
18. I am very seldom troubled by constipation.
19. When I take a new job, I like to be tipped off on who should be gotten next to.
20. My sex life is satisfactory.
21. At times I have very much wanted to leave home.
22. At times I have fits of laughing and crying that I cannot control.
23. I am troubled by attacks of nausea and vomiting.
24. No one seems to understand me.
25. I would like to be a singer.
26. I feel that it is certainly best to keep my mouth shut when I'm in trouble.
27. Evil spirits possess me at times.
28. When someone does me a wrong I feel I should pay him back if I can, just for the principle of the thing.
29. I am bothered by acid stomach several times a week.
30. At times I feel like swearing.
31. I have nightmares every few nights.
32. I find it hard to keep my mind on a task or job.
33. I have had very peculiar and strange experiences.
34. I have a cough most of the time.
35. If people had not had it in for me I would have been much more successful.
36. I seldom worry about my health.
37. I have never been in trouble because of my sex behavior.
38. During one period when I was a youngster I engaged in petty thievery.
39. At times I feel like smashing things.
40. Most any time I would rather sit and daydream than do anything else.
41. I have had periods of days, weeks, or months when I couldn't take care of things because I couldn't "get going."
42. My family does not like the work I have chosen (or the work I intend to choose for my life work).
43. My sleep is fitful and disturbed.
44. Much of the time my head seems to hurt all over.
45. I do not always tell the truth.
46. My judgment is better than it ever was.

47. Once a week or oftener I feel suddenly hot all over, without apparent cause.
48. When I am with people I am bothered by hearing very queer things.
49. It would be better if almost all laws were thrown away.
50. My soul sometimes leaves my body.
51. I am in just as good physical health as most of my friends.
52. I prefer to pass by school friends, or people I know but have not seen for a long time, unless they speak to me first.
53. A minister can cure disease by praying and putting his hand on your head.
54. I am liked by most people who know me.
55. I am almost never bothered by pains over the heart or in my chest.
56. As a youngster I was suspended from school one or more times for cutting up.
57. I am a good mixer.
58. Everything is turning out just like the prophets of the Bible said it would.
59. I have often had to take orders from someone who did not know as much as I did.
60. I do not read every editorial in the newspaper every day.
61. I have not lived the right kind of life.
62. Parts of my body often have feelings like burning, tingling, crawling, or like "going to sleep."
63. I have had no difficulty in starting or holding my bowel movement.
64. I sometimes keep on at a thing until others lose their patience with me.
65. I loved my father.
66. I see things or animals or people around me that others do not see.
67. I wish I could be as happy as others seem to be.
68. I hardly ever feel pain in the back of the neck.
69. I am very strongly attracted by members of my own sex.
70. I used to like drop-the-handkerchief.
71. I think a great many people exaggerate their misfortunes in order to gain the sympathy and help of others.
72. I am troubled by discomfort in the pit of my stomach every few days or oftener.
73. I am an important person.
74. I have often wished I were a girl. (Or if you are a girl) I have never been sorry that I am a girl.
75. I get angry sometimes.
76. Most of the time I feel blue.
77. I enjoy reading love stories.
78. I like poetry.
79. My feelings are not easily hurt.
80. I sometimes tease animals.
81. I think I would like the kind of work a forest ranger does.
82. I am easily downed in an argument.
83. Any man who is able and willing to work hard has a good chance of succeeding.
84. These days I find it hard not to give up hope of amounting to something.
85. Sometimes I am strongly attracted by the personal articles of others such as shoes, gloves, etc., so that I want to handle or steal them though I have no use for them.
86. I am certainly lacking in self-confidence.
87. I would like to be a florist.
88. I usually feel that life is worth while.
89. It takes a lot of argument to convince most people of the truth.
90. Once in a while I put off until tomorrow what I ought to do today.
91. I do not mind being made fun of.
92. I would like to be a nurse.
93. I think most people would lie to get ahead.
94. I do many things which I regret afterwards (I regret things more or more often than others seem to).
95. I go to church almost every week.
96. I have very few quarrels with members of my family.
97. At times I have a strong urge to do something harmful or shocking.
98. I believe in the second coming of Christ.
99. I like to go to parties and other affairs where there is lots of loud fun.
100. I have met problems so full of possibilities that I have been unable to make up my mind about them.
101. I believe women ought to have as much sexual freedom as men.
102. My hardest battles are with myself.
103. I have little or no trouble with my muscles twitching or jumping.
104. I don't seem to care what happens to me.
105. Sometimes when I am not feeling well I am cross.
106. Much of the time I feel as if I have done something wrong or evil.
107. I am happy most of the time.
108. There seems to be a fullness in my head or nose most of the time.
109. Some people are so bossy that I feel like doing the opposite of what they request, even though I know they are right.
110. Someone has it in for me.
111. I have never done anything dangerous for the thrill of it.

112. I frequently find it necessary to stand up for what I think is right.
113. I believe in law enforcement.
114. Often I feel as if there were a tight band about my head.
115. I believe in a life hereafter.
116. I enjoy a race or game better when I bet on it.
117. Most people are honest chiefly through fear of being caught.
118. In school I was sometimes sent to the principal for cutting up.
119. My speech is the same as always (not faster or slower, or slurring; no hoarseness).
120. My table manners are not quite as good at home as when I am out in company.
121. I believe I am being plotted against.
122. I seem to be about as capable and smart as most others around me.
123. I believe I am being followed.
124. Most people will use somewhat unfair means to gain profit or an advantage rather than to lose it.
125. I have a great deal of stomach trouble.
126. I like dramatics.
127. I know who is responsible for most of my troubles.
128. The sight of blood neither frightens me nor makes me sick.
129. Often I can't understand why I have been so cross and grouchy.
130. I have never vomited blood or coughed up blood.
131. I do not worry about catching diseases.
132. I like collecting flowers or growing house plants.
133. I have never indulged in any unusual sex practices.
134. At times my thoughts have raced ahead faster than I could speak them.
135. If I could get into a movie without paying and be sure I was not seen I would probably do it.
136. I commonly wonder what hidden reason another person may have for doing something nice for me.
137. I believe that my home life is as pleasant as that of most people I know.
138. Criticism or scolding hurts me terribly.
139. Sometimes I feel as if I must injure either myself or someone else.
140. I like to cook.
141. My conduct is largely controlled by the customs of those about me.
142. I certainly feel useless at times.
143. When I was a child, I belonged to a crowd or gang that tried to stick together through thick and thin.
144. I would like to be a soldier.
145. At times I feel like picking a fist fight with someone.
146. I have the wanderlust and am never happy unless I am roaming or traveling about.
147. I have often lost out on things because I couldn't make up my mind soon enough.
148. It makes me impatient to have people ask my advice or otherwise interrupt me when I am working on something important.
149. I used to keep a diary.
150. I would rather win than lose in a game.
151. Someone has been trying to poison me.
152. Most nights I go to sleep without thoughts or ideas bothering me.
153. During the past few years I have been well most of the time.
154. I have never had a fit or convulsion.
155. I am neither gaining nor losing weight.
156. I have had periods in which I carried on activities without knowing later what I had been doing.
157. I feel that I have often been punished without cause.
158. I cry easily.
159. I cannot understand what I read as well as I used to.
160. I have never felt better in my life than I do now.
161. The top of my head sometimes feels tender.
162. I resent having anyone take me in so cleverly that I have had to admit that it was one on me.
163. I do not tire quickly.
164. I like to study and read about things that I am working at.
165. I like to know some important people because it makes me feel important.
166. I am afraid when I look down from a high place.
167. It wouldn't make me nervous if any members of my family got into trouble with the law.
168. There is something wrong with my mind.
169. I am not afraid to handle money.
170. What others think of me does not bother me.
171. It makes me uncomfortable to put on a stunt at a party even when others are doing the same sort of things.
172. I frequently have to fight against showing that I am bashful.
173. I liked school.
174. I have never had a fainting spell.
175. I seldom or never have dizzy spells.
176. I do not have a great fear of snakes.
177. My mother was a good woman.
178. My memory seems to be all right.
179. I am worried about sex matters.

180. I find it hard to make talk when I meet new people.
181. When I get bored I like to stir up some excitement.
182. I am afraid of losing my mind.
183. I am against giving money to beggars.
184. I commonly hear voices without knowing where they come from.
185. My hearing is apparently as good as that of most people.
186. I frequently notice my hand shakes when I try to do something.
187. My hands have not become clumsy or awkward.
188. I can read a long while without tiring my eyes.
189. I feel weak all over much of the time.
190. I have very few headaches.
191. Sometimes, when embarrassed, I break out in a sweat which annoys me greatly.
192. I have had no difficulty in keeping my balance in walking.
193. I do not have spells of hay fever or asthma.
194. I have had attacks in which I could not control my movements or speech but in which I knew what was going on around me.
195. I do not like everyone I know.
196. I like to visit places where I have never been before.
197. Someone has been trying to rob me.
198. I daydream very little.
199. Children should be taught all the main facts of sex.
200. There are persons who are trying to steal my thoughts and ideas.
201. I wish I were not so shy.
202. I believe I am a condemned person.
203. If I were a reporter I would very much like to report news of the theater.
204. I would like to be a journalist.
205. At times it has been impossible for me to keep from stealing or shoplifting something.
206. I am very religious (more than most people).
207. I enjoy many different kinds of play and recreation.
208. I like to flirt.
209. I believe my sins are unpardonable.
210. Everything tastes the same.
211. I can sleep during the day but not at night.
212. My people treat me more like a child than a grown-up.
213. In walking I am very careful to step over sidewalk cracks.
214. I have never had any breaking out on my skin that has worried me.
215. I have used alcohol excessively.
216. There is very little love and companionship in my family as compared to other homes.
217. I frequently find myself worrying about something.
218. It does not bother me particularly to see animals suffer.
219. I think I would like the work of a building contractor.
220. I loved my mother.
221. I like science.
222. It is not hard for me to ask help from my friends even though I cannot return the favor.
223. I very much like hunting.
224. My parents have often objected to the kind of people I went around with.
225. I gossip a little at times.
226. Some of my family have habits that bother and annoy me very much.
227. I have been told that I walk during sleep.
228. At times I feel that I can make up my mind with unusually great ease.
229. I should like to belong to several clubs or lodges.
230. I hardly ever notice my heart pounding and I am seldom short of breath.
231. I like to talk about sex.
232. I have been inspired to a program of life based on duty which I have since carefully followed.
233. I have at times stood in the way of people who were trying to do something, not because it amounted to much but because of the principle of the thing.
234. I get mad easily and then get over it soon.
235. I have been quite independent and free from family rule.
236. I brood a great deal.
237. My relatives are nearly all in sympathy with me.
238. I have periods of such great restlessness that I cannot sit long in a chair.
239. I have been disappointed in love.
240. I never worry about my looks.
241. I dream frequently about things that are best kept to myself.
242. I believe I am no more nervous than most others.
243. I have few or no pains.
244. My way of doing things is apt to be misunderstood by others.
245. My parents and family find more fault with me than they should.
246. My neck spots with red often.
247. I have reason for feeling jealous of one or more members of my family.
248. Sometimes without any reason or even when things are going wrong I feel excitedly happy, "on top of the world."

249. I believe there is a Devil and a Hell in afterlife.
250. I don't blame anyone for trying to grab everything he can get in this world.
251. I have had blank spells in which my activities were interrupted and I did not know what was going on around me.
252. No one cares much what happens to you.
253. I can be friendly with people who do things which I consider wrong.
254. I like to be with a crowd who play jokes on one another.
255. Sometimes at elections I vote for men about whom I know very little.
256. The only interesting part of newspapers is the "funnies."
257. I usually expect to succeed in things I do.
258. I believe there is a God.
259. I have difficulty in starting to do things.
260. I was a slow learner in school.
261. If I were an artist I would like to draw flowers.
262. It does not bother me that I am not better looking.
263. I sweat very easily even on cool days.
264. I am entirely self-confident.
265. It is safer to trust nobody.
266. Once a week or oftener I become very excited.
267. When in a group of people I have trouble thinking of the right things to talk about.
268. Something exciting will almost always pull me out of it when I am feeling low.
269. I can easily make other people afraid of me, and sometimes do for the fun of it.
270. When I leave home I do not worry about whether the door is locked and the windows closed.
271. I do not blame a person for taking advantage of someone who lays himself open to it.
272. At times I am full of energy.
273. I have numbness in one or more regions of my skin.
274. My eyesight is as good as it has been for years.
275. Someone has control over my mind.
276. I enjoy children.
277. At times I have been so entertained by the cleverness of a crook that I have hoped he would get by with it.
278. I have often felt that strangers were looking at me critically.
279. I drink an unusually large amount of water every day.
280. Most people make friends because friends are likely to be useful to them.
281. I do not often notice my ears ringing or buzzing.
282. Once in a while I feel hate toward members of my family whom I usually love.
283. If I were a reporter I would very much like to report sporting news.
284. I am sure I am being talked about.
285. Once in a while I laugh at a dirty joke.
286. I am never happier than when alone.
287. I have very few fears compared to my friends.
288. I am troubled by attacks of nausea and vomiting.
289. I am always disgusted with the law when a criminal is freed through the arguments of a smart lawyer.
290. I work under a great deal of tension.
291. At one or more times in my life I felt that someone was making me do things by hypnotizing me.
292. I am likely not to speak to people until they speak to me.
293. Someone has been trying to influence my mind.
294. I have never been in trouble with the law.
295. I liked "Alice in Wonderland" by Lewis Carroll.
296. I have periods in which I feel unusually cheerful without any special reason.
297. I wish I were not bothered by thoughts about sex.
298. If several people find themselves in trouble, the best thing for them to do is to agree upon a story and stick to it.
299. I think that I feel more intensely than most people do.
300. There never was a time in my life when I liked to play with dolls.
301. Life is a strain for me much of the time.
302. I have never been in trouble because of my sex behavior.
303. I am so touchy on some subjects that I can't talk about them.
304. In school I found it very hard to talk before the class.
305. Even when I am with people I feel lonely much of the time.
306. I get all the sympathy I should.
307. I refuse to play some games because I am not good at them.
308. At times I have very much wanted to leave home.
309. I seem to make friends about as quickly as others do.
310. My sex life is satisfactory.
311. During one period when I was a youngster I engaged in petty thievery.
312. I dislike having people about me.
313. The man who provides temptation by leaving valuable property unprotected is about as much to blame for its theft as the one who steals it.

314. Once in a while I think of things too bad to talk about.
315. I am sure I get a raw deal from life.
316. I think nearly anyone would tell a lie to keep out of trouble.
317. I am more sensitive than most other people.
318. My daily life is full of things that keep me interested.
319. Most people inwardly dislike putting themselves out to help other people.
320. Many of my dreams are about sex matters.
321. I am easily embarrassed.
322. I worry over money and business.
323. I have had very peculiar and strange experiences.
324. I have never been in love with anyone.
325. The things that some of my family have done have frightened me.
326. At times I have fits of laughing and crying that I cannot control.
327. My mother or father often made me obey even when I thought that it was unreasonable.
328. I find it hard to keep my mind on a task or job.
329. I almost never dream.
330. I have never been paralyzed or had any unusual weakness of any of my muscles.
331. If people had not had it in for me I would have been much more successful.
332. Sometimes my voice leaves me or changes even though I have no cold.
333. No one seems to understand me.
334. Peculiar odors come to me at times.
335. I cannot keep my mind on one thing.
336. I easily become impatient with people.
337. I feel anxiety about something or someone almost all the time.
338. I have certainly had more than my share of things to worry about.
339. Most of the time I wish I were dead.
340. Sometimes I become so excited that I find it hard to get to sleep.
341. At times I hear so well it bothers me.
342. I forget right away what people say to me.
343. I usually have to stop and think before I act even in trifling matters.
344. Often I cross the street in order not to meet someone I see.
345. I often feel as if things were not real.
346. I have a habit of counting things that are not important such as bulbs on electric signs, and so forth.
347. I have no enemies who really wish to harm me.
348. I tend to be on my guard with people who are somewhat more friendly than I had expected.
349. I have strange and peculiar thoughts.
350. I hear strange things when I am alone.
351. I get anxious and upset when I have to make a short trip away from home.
352. I have been afraid of things or people that I knew could not hurt me.
353. I have no dread of going into a room by myself where other people have already gathered and are talking.
354. I am afraid of using a knife or anything very sharp or pointed.
355. Sometimes I enjoy hurting persons I love.
356. I have more trouble concentrating than others seem to have.
357. I have several times given up doing a thing because I thought too little of my ability.
358. Bad words, often terrible words, come into my mind and I cannot get rid of them.
359. Sometimes some unimportant thought will run through my mind and bother me for days.
360. Almost every day something happens to frighten me.
361. I am inclined to take things hard.
362. I am more sensitive than most other people.
363. At times I have enjoyed being hurt by someone I loved.
364. People say insulting and vulgar things about me.
365. I feel uneasy indoors.
366. Even when I am with people I feel lonely much of the time.
367. I am not afraid of fire.
368. I have sometimes stayed away from another person because I feared doing or saying something that I might regret afterwards.
369. Religion gives me no worry.
370. I hate to have to rush when working.
371. I am not unusually self-conscious.
372. I tend to be interested in several different hobbies rather than to stick to one of them for a long time.
373. I feel sure that there is only one true religion.
374. At periods my mind seems to work more slowly than usual.
375. When I am feeling very happy and active, someone who is blue or low will spoil it all.
376. Policemen are usually honest.
377. At parties I am more likely to sit by myself or with just one other person than to join in with the crowd.
378. I do not like to see women smoke.
379. I very seldom have spells of the blues.
380. When someone says silly or ignorant things about something I know about, I try to set him right.

381. I am often said to be hotheaded.
382. I wish I could get over worrying about things I have said that may have injured other people's feelings.
383. People often disappoint me.
384. I feel unable to tell anyone all about myself.
385. Lightning is one of my fears.
386. I like to keep people guessing what I'm going to do next.
387. The only miracles I know of are simply tricks that people play on one another.
388. I am afraid to be alone in the dark.
389. My plans have frequently seemed so full of difficulties that I have had to give them up.
390. I have often felt badly over being misunderstood when trying to keep someone from making a mistake.
391. I love to go to dances.
392. A windstorm terrifies me.
393. Horses that don't pull should be beaten or kicked.
394. I frequently ask people for advice.
395. The future is too uncertain for a person to make serious plans.
396. Often, even though everything is going fine for me, I feel that I don't care about anything.
397. I have sometimes felt that difficulties were piling up so high that I could not overcome them.
398. I often think, "I wish I were a child again."
399. I am not easily angered.
400. If given the chance I could do some things that would be of great benefit to the world.
401. I have no fear of water.
402. I often must sleep over a matter before I decide what to do.
403. It is great to be living in these times when so much is going on.
404. People have often misunderstood my intentions when I was trying to put them right and be helpful.
405. I have no trouble swallowing.
406. I have often met people who were supposed to be experts who were no better than I.
407. I am usually calm and not easily upset.
408. I am apt to hide my feelings in some things, to the point that people may hurt me without their knowing about it.
409. At times I have worn myself out by undertaking too much.
410. I would certainly enjoy beating a crook at his own game.
411. It makes me feel like a failure when I hear of the success of someone I know well.
412. I do not dread seeing a doctor about a sickness or injury.
413. I deserve severe punishment for my sins.
414. I am apt to take disappointments so keenly that I can't put them out of my mind.
415. If given the chance I would make a good leader of people.
416. It bothers me to have someone watch me at work even though I know I can do it well.
417. I am often so annoyed when someone tries to get ahead of me in a line of people that I speak to him about it.
418. At times I think I am no good at all.
419. I played hooky from school quite often as a youngster.
420. I have had some very unusual religious experiences.
421. One or more members of my family is very nervous.
422. I have felt embarrassed over the type of work that one or more members of my family have done.
423. I like or have liked fishing very much.
424. I feel hungry almost all the time.
425. I dream frequently.
426. I have at times had to be rough with people who were rude or annoying.
427. I am embarrassed by dirty stories.
428. I like to read newspaper editorials.
429. I like to attend lectures on serious subjects.
430. I am attracted by members of the opposite sex.
431. I worry quite a bit over possible misfortunes.
432. I have strong political opinions.
433. I used to have imaginary companions.
434. I would like to be an auto racer.
435. Usually I would prefer to work with women.
436. People generally demand more respect for their own rights than they are willing to allow for others.
437. It is all right to get around the law if you don't actually break it.
438. There are certain people whom I dislike so much that I am inwardly pleased when they are catching it for something they have done.
439. It makes me nervous to have to wait.
440. I try to remember good stories to pass them on to other people.
441. I like tall women.
442. I have had periods in which I lost sleep over worry.
443. I am apt to pass up something I want to do because others feel that I am not going about it in the right way.
444. I do not try to correct people who express an ignorant belief.

445. I was fond of excitement when I was young (or in childhood).
446. I enjoy gambling for small stakes.
447. I am often inclined to go out of my way to win a point with someone who has opposed me.
448. I am bothered by people outside, on streetcars, in stores, etc., watching me.
449. I enjoy social gatherings just to be with people.
450. I enjoy the excitement of a crowd.
451. My worries seem to disappear when I get into a crowd of lively friends.
452. I like to poke fun at people.
453. When I was a child I didn't care to be a member of a crowd or gang.
454. I could be happy living all alone in a cabin in the woods or mountains.
455. I am quite often not in on the gossip and talk of the group I belong to.
456. A person shouldn't be punished for breaking a law that he thinks is unreasonable.
457. I believe that a person should never taste an alcoholic drink.
458. The man who had most to do with me when I was a child (such as my father, stepfather, etc.) was very strict with me.
459. I have one or more bad habits which are so strong that it is no use in fighting against them.
460. I have used alcohol moderately (or not at all).
461. I find it hard to set aside a task that I have undertaken, even for a short time.
462. I have had no difficulty starting or holding my urine.
463. I used to like hopscotch.
464. I have never seen a vision.
465. I have several times had a change of heart about my life work.
466. Except by a doctor's orders I never take drugs or sleeping powders.
467. I often memorize numbers that are not important (such as automobile licenses, etc.).
468. I am often sorry because I am so cross and grouchy.
469. I have often found people jealous of my good ideas, just because they had not thought of them first.
470. Sexual things disgust me.
471. In school my marks in deportment were quite regularly bad.
472. I am fascinated by fire.
473. Whenever possible I avoid being in a crowd.
474. I have to urinate no more often than others.
475. When I am cornered I tell that portion of the truth which is not likely to hurt me.
476. I am a special agent of God.
477. If I were in trouble with several friends who were equally to blame, I would rather take the whole blame than to give them away.
478. I have never been made especially nervous over trouble that any members of my family have gotten into.
479. I do not mind meeting strangers.
480. I am often afraid of the dark.
481. I can remember "playing sick" to get out of something.
482. While in trains, busses, etc., I often talk to strangers.
483. Christ performed miracles such as changing water into wine.
484. I have one or more faults which are so big that it seems better to accept them and try to control them rather than to try to get rid of them.
485. When a man is with a woman he is usually thinking about things related to her sex.
486. I have never noticed any blood in my urine.
487. I feel like giving up quickly when things go wrong.
488. I pray several times every week.
489. I feel sympathetic towards people who tend to hang on to their griefs and troubles.
490. I read in the Bible several times a week.
491. I have no patience with people who believe there is only one true religion.
492. I dread the thought of an earthquake.
493. I prefer work which requires close attention, to work which allows me to be careless.
494. I am afraid of finding myself in a closet or small closed place.
495. I usually "lay my cards on the table" with people that I am trying to correct or improve.
496. I have never seen things doubled (that is, an object never looks like two objects to me without my being able to make it look like one object).
497. I enjoy stories of adventure.
498. It is always a good thing to be frank.
499. I must admit that I have at times been worried beyond reason over something that really did not matter.
500. I readily become one hundred per cent sold on a good idea.
501. I usually work things out for myself rather than get someone to show me how.
502. I like to let people know where I stand on things.
503. It is unusual for me to express strong

approval or disapproval of the actions of others.
504. I do not try to cover up my poor opinion or pity of a person so that he won't know how I feel.
505. I have had periods when I felt so full of pep that sleep did not seem necessary for days at a time.
506. I am a high-strung person.
507. I have frequently worked under people who seem to have things arranged so that they get credit for good work but are able to pass off mistakes onto those under them.
508. I believe my sense of smell is as good as other people's.
509. I sometimes find it hard to stick up for my rights because I am so reserved.
510. Dirt frightens or disgusts me.
511. I have a daydream life about which I do not tell other people.
512. I dislike to take a bath.
513. I think Lincoln was greater than Washington.
514. I like mannish women.
515. In my home we have always had the ordinary necessities (such as enough food, clothing, etc.).
516. Some of my family have quick tempers.
517. I cannot do anything well.
518. I have often felt guilty because I have pretended to feel more sorry about something than I really was.
519. There is something wrong with my sex organs.
520. I strongly defend my own opinions as a rule.
521. In a group of people I would not be embarrassed to be called upon to start a discussion or give an opinion about something I know well.
522. I have no fear of spiders.
523. I practically never blush.
524. I am not afraid of picking up a disease or germs from door knobs.
525. I am made nervous by certain animals.
526. The future seems hopeless to me.
527. The members of my family and my close relatives get along quite well.
528. I blush no more often than others.
529. I would like to wear expensive clothes.
530. I am often afraid that I am going to blush.
531. People can pretty easily change me even though I thought that my mind was already made up on a subject.
532. I can stand as much pain as others can.
533. I am not bothered by a great deal of belching of gas from my stomach.
534. Several times I have been the last to give up trying to do a thing.
535. My mouth feels dry almost all the time.
536. It makes me angry to have people hurry me.
537. I would like to hunt lions in Africa.
538. I think I would like the work of a dressmaker.
539. I am not afraid of mice.
540. My face has never been paralyzed.
541. My skin seems to be unusually sensitive to touch.
542. I have never had any black, tarry-looking bowel movements.
543. Several times a week I feel as if something dreadful is about to happen.
544. I feel tired a good deal of the time.
545. Sometimes I have the same dream over and over.
546. I like to read about history.
547. I like parties and socials.
548. I never attend a sexy show if I can avoid it.
549. I shrink from facing a crisis or difficulty.
550. I like repairing a door latch.
551. Sometimes I am sure that other people can tell what I am thinking.
552. I like to read about science.
553. I am afraid of being alone in a wide-open place.
554. If I were an artist I would like to draw children.
555. I sometimes feel that I am about to go to pieces.
556. I am very careful about my manner of dress.
557. I would like to be a private secretary.
558. A large number of people are guilty of bad sexual conduct.
559. I have often been frightened in the middle of the night.
560. I am greatly bothered by forgetting where I put things.
561. I very much like horseback riding.
562. The one to whom I was most attached and whom I most admired as a child was a woman. (Mother, sister, aunt, or other woman.)
563. I like adventure stories better than romantic stories.
564. I am apt to pass up something I want to do when others feel that it isn't worth doing.
565. I feel like jumping off when I am on a high place.
566. I like movie love scenes.

APPENDIX M # Frequencies of Two-Point Codes

Table 1. Percentage of Codes from Male Minnesota Normal Adults (N = 258) in Which Each Pair of High Points Occurs

Second Point	High Point 1	2	3	4	6	7	8	9	Second Point Total
1	(1.2) [a]	0.8	1.6	0.4	0.4	1.2	1.2		5.6
2	2.7	(1.9)	0.8	0.8	1.6	1.2	0.8	0.4	8.3
3	3.5	1.2	(1.9)	3.5	0.4	0.4		0.8	9.8
4	0.4	0.4	1.2	(2.7)	2.3		1.2	4.3	9.8
6		0.8			(1.2)		0.8	0.8	2.4
7	0.4	0.8		0.4	0.8	(1.6)	0.4	1.2	4.0
8	1.6		1.2	1.9	0.4	1.2	(0.4)	0.8	7.1
9	0.8	0.8	0.4	1.9	0.8	1.2	0.4	(9.3)	6.3
High point total	10.6	6.7	7.1	11.6	7.9	6.8	5.2	17.6	73.5 [b]

SOURCE: Hathaway and Meehl (1951a).

[a] The percentage of codes without a second point in the Hathaway system is given in parentheses in the diagonal cells.

[b] 23.6 percent were – codes (no high point) in the Hathaway system; 3.9 percent had an indeterminate high point.

Table 2. Percentage of Codes from Female Minnesota Normal Adults (N = 360) in Which Each Pair of High Points Occurs

Second Point	High Point 1	2	3	4	6	7	8	9	Second Point Total
1	(0.6) [a]	2.5	3.1		0.3	0.6	0.6	0.8	7.9
2	1.1	(2.5)	0.6	0.6	0.8	1.7	0.6	0.3	5.7
3	3.9	1.7	(1.4)	1.1		0.6	0.6	0.6	8.5
4	1.7	1.1	0.8	(3.6)	0.6	0.3	0.8	2.2	7.5
6		0.8	0.6	1.1	(2.8)	0.6	0.6	0.6	4.3
7	1.1	3.3	0.6	0.6	0.6	(1.1)	1.1	0.3	7.6
8		0.3	0.6	0.3	1.1	1.4	(0.8)	0.8	4.5
9	0.3	0.3		1.1	1.1	0.3	1.1	(7.5)	4.2
High point total	8.7	12.5	7.7	8.4	7.3	6.6	6.2	13.1	70.5 [b]

SOURCE: Hathaway and Meehl (1951a).

[a] The percentage of codes without a second point in the Hathaway system is given in parentheses in the diagonal cells.

[b] 25.8 percent were – codes (no high point) in the Hathaway system; 4.4 percent had an indeterminate high point.

Table 3. Percentage of Codes from Male Midwestern Normal Adults (N = 136) in Which Each Pair of High Points Occurs

Second Point	High Point 1	2	3	4	5	6	7	8	9	Second Point Total
1		0.7	2.2		0.7					3.6
2	1.5		2.2	2.9	5.9	0.7	1.5		1.5	16.2
3		3.7		3.7	8.8	0.7	0.7		1.5	19.1
4	1.5		5.1		1.5		0.7		4.4	13.2
5		2.2	3.7	1.5		1.5	0.7	1.5	2.9	14.0
6		0.7	0.7	2.2	2.2				2.2	8.0
7		1.5	0.7	1.5	1.5	0.7				5.9
8			1.5	1.5	2.2				1.5	6.7
9		1.5	0.7	4.4	5.1		0.7	0.7		13.1
High point total	3.0	10.3	16.8	17.7	27.9	3.6	4.3	2.2	14.0	99.8

SOURCE: Goodstein and Dahlstrom (1956).

Table 4. Percentage of Codes from Female Midwestern Normal Adults (N = 136) in Which Each Pair of High Points Occurs

Second Point	High Point 1	2	3	4	5	6	7	8	9	Second Point Total
1		1.5	5.1	0.7	1.5	0.7		1.5		11.0
2	0.7		2.2	0.7		0.7	2.9		0.7	7.9
3	2.9	2.2		5.1	1.5	5.1	2.2	0.7	0.7	20.4
4		2.9	4.4		2.9	2.2				12.4
5		2.9	4.4	2.2					0.7	10.2
6		1.5	5.9	1.5				0.7	0.7	10.3
7		2.9	1.5	0.7		0.7		2.2	0.7	8.7
8		0.7	1.5	2.9		1.5			0.7	7.3
9		0.7	2.2	4.4		2.2	0.7	0.7		10.9
High point total	3.6	15.3	27.2	18.2	5.9	13.1	5.8	5.8	4.2	99.1

SOURCE: Goodstein and Dahlstrom (1956).

Table 5. Percentage of Codes from Male Minnesota Ninth-Grade Students (N = 4,944) in Which Each Pair of High Points Occurs

Second Point	High Point 1	2	3	4	5	6	7	8	9	0	Second Point Total
1	(–) [a]	0.2	0.3	0.8		0.1	0.1	0.8	0.3	0.1	2.7
2	0.1	(0.3)	0.2	1.3	0.4	0.2	0.5	0.7	0.3	0.8	4.5
3	0.4	0.2	(0.3)	2.0	0.3	0.3	0.3	0.4	0.8	0.1	4.8
4	0.3	0.8	0.7	(1.0)	0.8	0.9	1.0	3.0	5.1	0.6	13.2
5		0.2	0.2	0.9	(0.4)	0.5	0.3	0.5	1.3	0.7	4.6
6	0.1	0.2	0.3	1.9	0.6	(0.4)	0.5	1.9	1.9	0.7	8.1
7	0.2	0.5	0.3	1.9	0.4	0.4	(0.2)	5.4	1.8	1.2	12.1
8	0.4	0.5	0.2	3.7	0.6	1.2	2.8	(0.2)	6.3	1.2	16.9
9	0.2	0.3	0.2	4.1	0.6	1.0	0.9	4.4	(2.1)	0.8	12.5
0	0.2	0.9	0.1	0.7	0.5	0.7	1.1	1.3	1.2	(1.2)	6.7
High point total .	1.9	4.1	2.8	18.3	4.6	5.7	7.7	18.6	21.1	7.4	92.2 [b]

SOURCE: Hathaway and Monachesi (1963).

[a] The percentage of codes without a second point in the Hathaway system is given in parentheses in the diagonal cells.

[b] 1.6 percent were – codes (no high point) in the Hathaway system; 6.3 percent had an indeterminate high point.

Table 6. Percentage of Codes from Female Minnesota Ninth-Grade Students (N = 5,207) in Which Each Pair of High Points Occurs

Second Point	High Point 1	2	3	4	5	6	7	8	9	0	Second Point Total
1 ……	(—)[a]		0.3	0.3	0.1		0.1	0.2	0.1	0.1	1.2
2 ……	0.1	(0.1)	0.2	0.7	0.3	0.2	0.2	0.2	0.1	0.9	2.9
3 ……	0.1	0.2	(0.3)	2.2	0.4	0.5	0.2	0.4	0.5	0.3	4.8
4 ……	0.1	0.2	1.2	(0.9)	2.1	1.8	0.7	1.4	4.1	1.3	12.9
5 ……	0.1	0.1	0.3	2.1	(2.1)	0.6	0.4	0.9	2.7	2.1	9.3
6 ……		0.1	0.4	2.8	0.9	(0.5)	0.6	1.5	2.1	1.5	9.9
7 ……		0.1	0.3	2.1	0.7	1.1	(0.3)	2.3	1.5	2.1	10.2
8 ……	0.1	0.2	0.5	3.4	1.4	1.8	1.6	(0.2)	4.4	1.7	15.1
9 ……			0.3	3.9	2.2	1.3	0.5	2.0	(0.9)	0.7	10.9
0 ……	0.1	0.5	0.1	1.4	2.0	1.3	0.8	1.1	1.0	(1.4)	8.3
High point total .	0.6	1.5	3.9	19.8	12.2	9.1	5.4	10.2	17.4	12.1	92.2[b]

SOURCE: Hathaway and Monachesi (1963).

[a] The percentage of codes without a second point in the Hathaway system is given in parentheses in the diagonal cells.

[b] 1.6 percent were – codes (no high point) in the Hathaway system; 7.0 percent had an indeterminate high point.

Table 7. Percentage of Codes from Male North Carolina Freshmen (N = 1,537) in Which Each Pair of High Points Occurs

Second Point	High Point 1	2	3	4	5	6	7	8	9	0	Second Point Total
1 …..			0.4	0.4	0.6	0.1			0.4		1.9
2 …..	0.1		0.4	0.6	1.9	0.3	1.0	0.4	0.3	0.8	5.8
3 …..	0.5	0.3		3.0	3.2	0.8	0.6	0.4	2.5	0.1	11.4
4 …..	0.2	0.6	1.9		2.8	0.8	0.9	1.0	6.4	0.1	14.7
5 …..	0.2	0.8	1.5	2.4		1.0	1.7	0.6	5.9	1.0	15.1
6 …..	0.1	0.2	0.7	1.5	2.9		1.2	0.3	1.9	0.5	9.3
7 …..	0.1	1.2	0.5	1.0	3.4	0.6		2.5	2.7	0.8	12.8
8 …..	0.2	0.3	0.9	2.2	1.8	0.5	3.0		3.8	0.1	12.8
9 …..	0.2	0.3	0.7	3.1	5.0	0.5	1.5	1.4		0.2	12.9
0 …..		0.4		0.2	1.6	0.1	0.7	0.4	0.3		3.7
High point total	1.6	4.1	7.0	14.4	23.2	4.7	10.6	7.0	24.2	3.6	100.4

SOURCE: Dahlstrom and Reifler (1970).

Table 8. Percentage of Codes from Female North Carolina Freshmen (N = 129) in Which Each Pair of High Points Occurs

Second Point	High Point 1	2	3	4	5	6	7	8	9	0	Second Point Total
1			1.5		0.4	0.4					2.3
2					0.8		1.2			2.7	4.7
3	0.8	0.4		2.6	1.5	4.5	2.3	0.8	3.1	0.8	16.8
4		1.2	0.8		2.3	1.2	0.8	1.2	2.3	0.8	10.6
5			0.4	1.5		0.8	0.8	0.4	0.8	1.2	5.9
6			0.8	2.7	2.7		3.1	1.9	6.9	4.6	22.7
7					1.2	0.8		1.2	1.9	0.8	5.9
8		0.8	0.4	1.2	1.9	1.2			2.3	2.3	10.1
9				3.9	3.5	3.9	0.8			1.5	13.6
0				0.8	4.2	0.8	0.8	0.8	0.8		8.2
High point total	0.8	2.4	3.9	12.7	18.5	13.6	9.8	6.3	18.1	14.7	100.8

SOURCE: Dahlstrom and Reifler (1970).

Table 9. Percentage of Codes from Male Minnesota Psychiatric Patients (N = 710) in Which Each Pair of High Points Occurs

Second Point	High Point 1	2	3	4	6	7	8	9	Second Point Total
1	(—) [a]	6.6	2.7	0.7		0.6	1.1	0.6	12.3
2	3.8	(0.3)	1.3	4.1	0.8	3.8	1.7	1.0	16.5
3	6.1	3.8	(0.4)	2.4	0.1		0.4	0.8	13.6
4	1.4	2.4	0.6	(0.7)	0.7	0.6	1.8	1.7	9.2
6	0.1	1.1	0.1	1.5	(—)	0.4	1.1	0.4	4.7
7	0.6	9.9	0.1	1.4	0.4	(—)	3.2	0.1	15.7
8	1.3	2.0	0.4	4.6	1.0	2.4	(—)	2.1	13.8
9	0.8	0.3	0.3	3.0	0.4	0.3	1.5	(1.1)	6.6
High point total ...	14.1	26.4	5.9	18.4	3.4	8.1	10.8	7.8	94.9 [b]

SOURCE: Hathaway and Meehl (1951a.)

[a] The percentage of codes without a second point in the Hathaway system is given in parentheses in the diagonal cells.

[b] 1.8 percent were — codes (no high point) in the Hathaway system; 3.0 percent had an indeterminate high point.

Table 10. Percentage of Codes from Female Minnesota Psychiatric Patients (N = 1,053) in Which Each Pair of High Points Occurs

Second Point	High Point 1	2	3	4	6	7	8	9	Second Point Total
1	(0.2) [a]	3.5	7.8	0.9	0.5	0.1	0.7	0.4	13.9
2	1.7	(0.8)	3.2	2.4	1.3	2.0	2.0	0.3	12.9
3	7.1	5.3	(0.2)	2.3	0.9	0.3	0.6	0.7	17.2
4	0.5	2.1	1.9	(0.4)	1.3	0.2	1.3	2.6	9.9
6	0.4	2.0	0.5	2.5	(0.3)	0.4	1.7	1.5	9.0
7	0.1	8.1	0.6	0.7	0.7	(0.1)	1.9	0.5	12.6
8	0.2	2.4	0.7	2.7	1.7	1.1	(0.1)	1.7	10.5
9	0.2	0.3	0.7	1.7	0.4		0.8	(0.7)	4.1
High point total	10.4	24.5	15.6	13.6	7.1	4.2	9.1	8.4	92.9 [b]

SOURCE: Hathaway and Meehl (1951a).

[a] The percentage of codes without a second point in the Hathaway system is given in parentheses in the diagonal cells.

[b] 1.7 percent were – codes (no high point) in the Hathaway system; 6.1 percent had an indeterminate high point.

Table 11. Percentage of Codes from Male Minnesota Psychiatric Outpatients (N = 58) in Which Each Pair of High Points Occurs

Second Point	High Point 1	2	3	4	6	7	8	9	Second Point Total
1		12.9	2.6	1.7	1.7	0.9	0.9		20.7
2	9.5	(2.6) [a]	0.9	2.6		5.2			18.2
3	2.6	6.0		1.7		0.9	0.9	0.9	13.0
4					0.9	2.6		0.9	4.4
6				2.6					2.6
7		8.6					5.2	0.9	14.7
8		6.0	2.6	3.4		3.4		3.4	18.8
9			0.9			0.9	0.9	(3.4)	2.7
High point total	12.1	36.1	7.0	12.0	2.6	13.9	7.9	9.5	101.1

SOURCE: Sundberg (1952).

[a] The percentage of codes without a second point in the Hathaway system is given in parentheses in diagonal cells.

Table 12. Percentage of Codes from Female Minnesota Psychiatric Outpatients (N = 108) in Which Each Pair of High Points Occurs

Second Point	High Point 1	2	3	4	6	7	8	9	Second Point Total
1		2.8	4.6	1.9			1.4		10.7
2	2.8		1.4	3.7	1.9	4.6	0.9	0.5	15.8
3	8.8	5.1		4.6		0.5	0.5	1.4	20.9
4		4.2	2.8		3.2	0.9	2.3	0.9	14.3
6		4.7	3.7	2.3			0.9		11.6
7		1.9		1.4	0.9		3.2		7.4
8		1.9	0.5	4.6		4.2		0.9	12.1
9	0.9		0.5	3.7			0.5	(0.9) [a]	5.6
High point total	12.5	20.6	13.5	22.2	6.0	10.2	9.7	4.6	99.3 [b]

SOURCE: Sundberg (1952).

[a] The percentage of codes without a second point in the Hathaway system is given in parentheses in the diagonal cell.

[b] 0.9 percent were – codes (no high point) in the Hathaway system.

Table 13. Percentage of Codes from Male Minnesota Neurologic Inpatients (N = 202) in Which Each Pair of High Points Occurs

Second Point	High Point 1	2	3	4	6	7	8	9	Second Point Total
1	(1.0) [a]	7.1	3.0	0.2	0.2	0.5	2.5	1.7	15.2
2	5.0	(1.0)	1.5	0.9	0.5	2.5	4.0	1.0	15.4
3	10.4	2.2	(0.5)	1.2	0.2	0.7	0.2	0.2	15.1
4	0.9	3.2	1.9	(0.5)		0.5	1.0	3.5	11.0
6		2.7	0.2	1.0	(–)	1.0	1.7	1.7	8.3
7	1.0	5.4	0.7	0.5	0.2	(0.5)	2.4	0.5	10.7
8	0.7	3.5	1.2	2.0	0.2	1.7	(–)	2.7	12.0
9	0.5	0.7	0.4	1.0			1.9	(0.5)	4.5
High point total ...	19.5	25.8	9.4	7.3	1.3	7.4	13.7	11.8	96.2 [b]

SOURCE: Brantner (1957).

[a] The percentage of codes without a second point in the Hathaway system is given in parentheses in the diagonal cells.

[b] 1.0 percent were – codes (no high point) in the Hathaway system; 2.8 percent had an indeterminate high point.

Table 14. Percentage of Codes from Female Minnesota Neurologic Inpatients (N = 206) in Which Each Pair of High Points Occurs

Second Point	High Point 1	2	3	4	6	7	8	9	Second Point Total
1	(0.5) [a]	7.1	10.3			0.7	0.5	1.7	20.3
2	3.2	(2.4)	2.9	0.7	1.0	2.0	0.2	0.4	10.4
3	8.8	4.6	(1.9)	2.4		0.2	0.4	1.9	18.3
4	0.2	0.5	2.6	(1.0)		0.5	0.2	1.0	5.0
6	1.5	0.2	0.2	0.9	(0.5)	0.2	2.1	0.7	5.8
7		2.6	0.2		0.2	(–)	2.7		5.7
8	1.2	1.2	2.0	1.9	1.4	0.7	(–)	3.0	11.4
9	0.5	0.2	1.5	1.5	0.4	0.7	0.7	(1.9)	5.5
High point total ...	15.9	18.8	21.6	8.4	3.5	5.0	6.8	10.6	90.6 [b]

SOURCE: Brantner (1957).

[a] The percentage of codes without a second point in the Hathaway system is given in parentheses in the diagonal cells.

[b] 1.9 percent were – codes (no high point) in the Hathaway system; 7.5 percent had an indeterminate high point.

Table 15. Percentage of Codes from Male Medical Outpatients (N = 365) in Which Each Pair of High Points Occurs

Second Point	High Point 1	2	3	4	6	7	8	9	Second Point Total
1	(0.3) [a]	9.9	6.0	0.5		1.1		1.4	18.9
2	9.3	(1.6)	6.0	1.4	0.3	0.8	0.8	0.5	19.1
3	7.7	13.4	(1.9)	1.6	0.5			1.4	24.6
4	0.8	1.9	2.5	(–)	0.5	0.3		0.8	6.8
6	0.3	0.8	2.5	0.5	(0.3)	0.3	0.3	1.4	6.1
7	1.1	6.3			0.3	(0.3)	0.5	0.8	9.0
8	0.5	0.5		0.5	0.5	0.5	(–)	0.8	3.3
9	1.4	1.1	2.2	1.4		0.3		(1.1)	6.4
High point total ...	21.4	35.5	21.1	5.9	2.4	3.6	1.6	8.2	99.7

SOURCE: Guthrie (1949).

[a] The percentage of codes without a second point in the Hathaway system is given in parentheses in the diagonal cells.

Table 16. Percentage of Codes from Female Medical Outpatients (N = 739) in Which Each Pair of High Points Occurs

Second Point	High Point 1	2	3	4	6	7	8	9	Second Point Total
1	(–) [a]	3.8	12.2	0.8	0.7	0.3		0.7	18.5
2	2.6	(1.1)	9.1	1.6	1.1	1.2		0.1	15.7
3	4.3	12.3	(4.5)	1.9	1.9	0.1		0.7	21.2
4	0.1	2.4	4.9	(0.1)	0.5		0.5	1.1	9.5
6	0.4	2.2	5.4	1.9	(0.7)	0.3	0.3	0.1	10.6
7	0.9	4.3	1.4	0.8	0.3	(–)	1.2	0.3	9.2
8	0.1	0.7	1.5	1.1	0.7	0.1	(–)	0.1	4.3
9	0.1	0.5	2.3	0.5	0.4		0.3	(0.4)	4.1
High point total ...	8.5	27.3	41.3	8.7	6.3	2.0	2.3	3.5	99.9

SOURCE: Guthrie (1949).

[a] The percentage of codes without a second point in the Hathaway system is given in parentheses in the diagonal cells.

Table 17. Percentage of Codes from Male North Carolina Prison Inmates (N = 2,551) in Which Each Pair of High Points Occurs

Second Point	High Point 1	2	3	4	5	6	7	8	9	0	Second Point Total
1		1.8	0.6	3.4		0.4	0.2	2.8	0.4	0.1	9.7
2	3.7		0.3	7.3	0.2	0.4	0.4	3.2	0.4	0.3	16.2
3	2.2	0.8		3.4	0.2	0.1	0.1	0.2	0.4		7.4
4	2.4	3.4	0.7		0.7	0.9	0.9	3.4	4.4	0.2	17.0
5	0.2	0.4		1.2		0.2		0.2	0.6		2.8
6	0.5	0.5	0.2	3.1	0.2		0.2	6.9	0.7	0.1	12.4
7	0.3	0.7	0.1	2.5	0.2	0.5		4.9	0.5	0.1	9.8
8	1.2	1.2		3.4	0.2	1.9	1.3		1.0		10.2
9	0.5	0.3	0.1	7.4	0.4	0.6	0.4	2.8		0.2	12.7
0	0.1	0.6		0.5	0.2	0.1	0.1		0.2		1.8
High point total	11.1	9.7	2.0	32.2	2.3	5.1	3.6	24.4	8.6	1.0	100.0

SOURCE: Panton (1959).

Table 18. Percentage of Codes from Female North Carolina Prison Inmates (N = 446) in Which Each Pair of High Points Occurs

Second Point	High Point 1	2	3	4	5	6	7	8	9	0	Second Point Total
1		0.2	0.9	2.2	0.4		0.2	0.7	0.2	0.2	5.0
2	0.4			4.9	0.4	0.4		0.7	0.2	0.4	7.4
3	1.3	0.2		1.3	0.2	0.7			0.7		4.4
4	0.9	2.2	1.8		1.3	4.7	1.1	3.6	2.7	1.1	19.4
5	0.4	0.2	0.2	2.2		1.1		0.9	0.2	0.7	5.9
6	0.4	0.4	0.2	10.8	1.3			5.6	2.2	0.4	21.3
7		0.4		0.4	0.2	0.7		0.4	0.7	0.2	3.0
8	0.4	0.4	0.4	3.8	0.7	3.6	0.2		1.8	0.2	11.5
9	0.2		0.2	5.2	1.1	2.5		3.6		0.4	13.2
0	0.2	1.1	0.2	2.9	0.4	0.9		0.7	1.1		7.5
High point total	4.2	5.1	3.9	33.7	6.0	14.6	1.5	16.2	9.8	3.6	98.6

SOURCE: Panton (1959).

Table 19. Percentage of Codes from Male North Carolina Youthful Offenders (N = 183) in Which Each Pair of High Points Occurs

Second Point	High Point 1	2	3	4	5	6	7	8	9	0	Second Point Total
1				1.1				0.5		0.5	2.1
2	0.5			10.9			2.7				14.1
3	0.5	0.5		2.7			1.1		1.6		6.4
4	1.1	2.7			1.1	2.2	0.5	1.1	10.9	0.5	20.1
5		0.5		2.7					2.2		5.4
6				2.7				1.6	1.1		5.4
7				6.0		0.5		4.9			11.4
8		0.5		6.0		1.1	1.6		4.4		13.6
9	0.5			13.7	0.5	0.5	1.1	1.1			17.4
0		0.5		2.2				0.5			3.2
High point total	2.6	4.7	0.0	48.0	1.6	4.3	7.0	9.7	20.2	1.0	99.1

SOURCE: McMahon (1970).

Table 20. Percentage of Codes from Male Military Prisoners (N = 2,126) in Which Each Pair of High Points Occurs

Second Point	High Point 1	2	3	4	5	6	7	8	9	0	Second Point Total
1		1.1	1.0	2.2	0.1	0.1	0.2	0.6	0.9	0.1	6.3
2	0.7		0.5	6.8	0.2	0.3	1.5	0.9	1.1	0.5	12.5
3	1.4	1.3		6.1	0.4	0.3	0.2	0.1	1.3	0.1	11.2
4	0.7	3.3	2.0		1.2	1.0	0.9	2.0	10.3	0.2	21.6
5	0.1	0.5	0.2	1.7		0.1	0.1	0.1	1.2	0.1	4.1
6	0.1	0.4	0.3	3.8	0.2		0.2	0.8	1.0	0.2	7.0
7	0.2	1.6	0.2	2.7	0.3	0.3		2.5	0.7	0.4	8.9
8	0.3	0.9	0.2	4.9	0.3	0.9	1.1		2.7		11.3
9	0.4	0.5	0.6	12.3	0.5	0.4	0.7	2.0		0.1	17.7
0	0.1	0.7	0.1	0.9		0.1	0.2	0.3	0.3		2.7
High point total	4.0	10.3	5.1	41.4	3.2	3.5	5.1	9.3	19.5	1.7	99.1

SOURCE: Brodsky (1967).

Table 21. Percentage of Codes from White Male VA Patients (N = 100) in Which Each Pair of High Points Occurs

Second Point	High Point 1	2	3	4	5	6	7	8	9	Second Point Total
1		8.0	4.0		2.0		1.0		2.0	17.0
2	11.0		1.0	2.0			2.0	1.0		17.0
3	11.0	3.0		1.0	1.0			1.0		17.0
4	2.0	4.0			4.0			1.0		11.0
5	1.0	2.0		1.0						4.0
6			1.0		1.0			1.0	1.0	4.0
7	3.0	12.0	1.0					1.0		17.0
8		2.0		1.0	3.0		2.0			8.0
9	2.0	1.0		1.0				1.0		5.0
High point total	30.0	32.0	7.0	6.0	11.0	0.0	5.0	6.0	3.0	100.0

SOURCE: Miller, Knapp, and Daniels (1968).

Table 22. Percentage of Codes from Negro Male VA Patients (N = 100) in Which Each Pair of High Points Occurs

Second Point	High Point 1	2	3	4	5	6	7	8	9	Second Point Total
1		10.0	8.0	1.0			1.0	7.0	1.0	28.0
2	8.0		1.0	1.0				5.0	1.0	16.0
3	8.0	5.0		1.0						14.0
4	3.0	5.0					1.0	1.0		10.0
5	1.0	2.0								3.0
6				1.0	1.0			1.0		3.0
7	1.0	7.0						3.0	1.0	12.0
8	7.0	2.0		1.0					1.0	11.0
9			2.0					1.0		3.0
High point total	28.0	31.0	11.0	5.0	1.0	0.0	2.0	18.0	4.0	100.0

SOURCE: Miller, Knapp, and Daniels (1968).

Table 23. Percentage of Codes from Male North Carolina Physicians (N = 114) in Which Each Pair of High Points Occurs

Second Point	High Point 1	2	3	4	5	6	7	8	9	0	Second Point Total
1		1.8	0.9	1.8	0.9		0.9		0.9		7.2
2			0.9	1.8	3.5	0.9					7.1
3	0.9	3.5		2.6	2.6	2.6	0.9		1.8		14.9
4		0.9	3.5		1.8				6.1		12.3
5	0.9	5.3	1.8	1.8		1.8		0.9	7.0	3.5	23.0
6			2.6	2.6	3.5				1.8		10.5
7		0.9	1.8		3.5				0.9		7.1
8			2.6	0.9							3.5
9			3.5	1.8	6.1	0.9					12.3
0		0.9			0.9				0.9		2.7
High point total	1.8	13.3	17.6	13.3	22.8	6.2	1.8	0.9	19.4	3.5	100.6

SOURCE: Dahlstrom and Spain (1958).

APPENDIX N MMPI Forms

On the following pages are reproduced these forms:

Front of card-form recording blank (reduced from 8½″ x 11″)

IBM 805 answer sheet (reduced from 8½″ x 11″)

IBM 1230 answer sheet (reduced from 8½″ x 11″)

Print area of the IBM 1230 answer sheet (reduced from 8½″ x 11″)

Form R answer sheet (reduced from 9½″ x 11¼″)

Hankes group-form answer sheet (reduced from 8½″ x 11″)

Left half of profile form (the entire sheet is 8½″ x 11″)

Note: A similar form is used for females

A	B	C	D	E	F	G	H	I	J	
1 ___	1 ___	1 ___	1 ___	1 ___	1 ___	1 ___	1 ___	1 ___	1 ___	
2 ___	2 ___	2 ___	2 ___	2 ___	2 ___	2 ___	2 ___	2 ___	2 ___	RAW SCORES
3 ___	3 ___	3 ___	3 ___	3 ___	3 ___	3 ___	3 ___	3 ___	3 ___	
4 ___	4 ___	4 ___	4 ___	4 ___	4 ___	4 ___	4 ___	4 ___	4 ___	
5 ___	5 ___	5 ___	5 ___	5 ___	5 ___	5 ___	5 ___	5 ___	5 ___	
6 ___	6 ___	6 ___	6 ___	6 ___	6 ___	6 ___	6 ___	6 ___	6 ___	
7 ___	7 ___	7 ___	7 ___	7 ___	7 ___	7 ___	7 ___	7 ___	7 ___	___ ?
8 ___	8 ___	8 ___	8 ___	8 ___	8 ___	8 ___	8 ___	8 ___	8 ___	
9 ___	9 ___	9 ___	9 ___	9 ___	9 ___	9 ___	9 ___	9 ___	9 ___	
10 ___	10 ___	10 ___	10 ___	10 ___	10 ___	10 ___	10 ___	10 ___	10 ___	___ L
11 ___	11 ___	11 ___	11 ___	11 ___	11 ___	11 ___	11 ___	11 ___	11 ___	
12 ___	12 ___	12 ___	12 ___	12 ___	12 ___	12 ___	12 ___	12 ___	12 ___	___ F
13 ___	13 ___	13 ___	13 ___	13 ___	13 ___	13 ___	13 ___	13 ___	13 ___	
14 ___	14 ___	14 ___	14 ___	14 ___	14 ___	14 ___	14 ___	14 ___	14 ___	
15 ___	15 ___	15 ___	15 ___	15 ___	15 ___	15 ___	15 ___	15 ___	15 ___	___ $H\text{-}C_H$
16 ___	16 ___	16 ___	16 ___	16 ___	16 ___	16 ___	16 ___	16 ___	16 ___	
17 ___	17 ___	17 ___	17 ___	17 ___	17 ___	17 ___	17 ___	17 ___	17 ___	
18 ___	18 ___	18 ___	18 ___	18 ___	18 ___	18 ___	18 ___	18 ___	18 ___	___ D
19 ___	19 ___	19 ___	19 ___	19 ___	19 ___	19 ___	19 ___	19 ___	19 ___	
20 ___	20 ___	20 ___	20 ___	20 ___	20 ___	20 ___	20 ___	20 ___	20 ___	___ H_y
21 ___	21 ___	21 ___	21 ___	21 ___	21 ___	21 ___	21 ___	21 ___	21 ___	
22 ___	22 ___	22 ___	22 ___	22 ___	22 ___	22 ___	22 ___	22 ___	22 ___	
23 ___	23 ___	23 ___	23 ___	23 ___	23 ___	23 ___	23 ___	23 ___	23 ___	___ P_d
24 ___	24 ___	24 ___	24 ___	24 ___	24 ___	24 ___	24 ___	24 ___	24 ___	
25 ___	25 ___	25 ___	25 ___	25 ___	25 ___	25 ___	25 ___	25 ___	25 ___	
26 ___	26 ___	26 ___	26 ___	26 ___	26 ___	26 ___	26 ___	26 ___	26 ___	___ M_f
27 ___	27 ___	27 ___	27 ___	27 ___	27 ___	27 ___	27 ___	27 ___	27 ___	
28 ___	28 ___	28 ___	28 ___	28 ___	28 ___	28 ___	28 ___	28 ___	28 ___	
29 ___	29 ___	29 ___	29 ___	29 ___	29 ___	29 ___	29 ___	29 ___	29 ___	___ P_a
30 ___	30 ___	30 ___	30 ___	30 ___	30 ___	30 ___	30 ___	30 ___	30 ___	
31 ___	31 ___	31 ___	31 ___	31 ___	31 ___	31 ___	31 ___	31 ___	31 ___	___ P_t
32 ___	32 ___	32 ___	32 ___	32 ___	32 ___	32 ___	32 ___	32 ___	32 ___	
33 ___	33 ___	33 ___	33 ___	33 ___	33 ___	33 ___	33 ___	33 ___	33 ___	
34 ___	34 ___	34 ___	34 ___	34 ___	34 ___	34 ___	34 ___	34 ___	34 ___	___
35 ___	35 ___	35 ___	35 ___	35 ___	35 ___	35 ___	35 ___	35 ___	35 ___	
36 ___	36 ___	36 ___	36 ___	36 ___	36 ___	36 ___	36 ___	36 ___	36 ___	
37 ___	37 ___	37 ___	37 ___	37 ___	37 ___	37 ___	37 ___	37 ___	37 ___	___
38 ___	38 ___	38 ___	38 ___	38 ___	38 ___	38 ___	38 ___	38 ___	38 ___	
39 ___	39 ___	39 ___	39 ___	39 ___	39 ___	39 ___	39 ___	39 ___	39 ___	
40 ___	40 ___	40 ___	40 ___	40 ___	40 ___	40 ___	40 ___	40 ___	40 ___	___
41 ___	41 ___	41 ___	41 ___	41 ___	41 ___	41 ___	41 ___	41 ___	41 ___	
42 ___	42 ___	42 ___	42 ___	42 ___	42 ___	42 ___	42 ___	42 ___	42 ___	___
43 ___	43 ___	43 ___	43 ___	43 ___	43 ___	43 ___	43 ___	43 ___	43 ___	
44 ___	44 ___	44 ___	44 ___	44 ___	44 ___	44 ___	44 ___	44 ___	44 ___	
45 ___	45 ___	45 ___	45 ___	45 ___	45 ___	45 ___	45 ___	45 ___	45 ___	___
46 ___	46 ___	46 ___	46 ___	46 ___	46 ___	46 ___	46 ___	46 ___	46 ___	
47 ___	47 ___	47 ___	47 ___	47 ___	47 ___	47 ___	47 ___	47 ___	47 ___	
48 ___	48 ___	48 ___	48 ___	48 ___	48 ___	48 ___	48 ___	48 ___	48 ___	___
49 ___	49 ___	49 ___	49 ___	49 ___	49 ___	49 ___	49 ___	49 ___	49 ___	
50 ___	50 ___	50 ___	50 ___	50 ___	50 ___	50 ___	50 ___	50 ___	50 ___	
51 ___	51 ___	51 ___	51 ___	51 ___	51 ___	51 ___	51 ___	51 ___	51 ___	
52 ___	52 ___	52 ___	52 ___	52 ___	52 ___	52 ___	52 ___	52 ___	52 ___	
53 ___	53 ___	53 ___	53 ___	53 ___	53 ___	53 ___	53 ___	53 ___	53 ___	
54 ___	54 ___	54 ___	54 ___	54 ___	54 ___	54 ___	54 ___	54 ___	54 ___	
55 ___	55 ___	55 ___	55 ___	55 ___	55 ___	55 ___	55 ___	55 ___	55 ___	
A	B	C	D	E	F	G	H	I	J	

THE MINNESOTA MULTIPHASIC PERSONALITY INVENTORY

Hathaway and McKinley

Published by The Psychological Corporation, New York.

K ___ + ___ Hs = ___ Pa ___ + ___ = ___ Si ___ + ___ = ___
F = ___ Hy = ___ Pt ___ + ___ = ___ ? = ___
Hs = ___ Pd = ___ Sc ___ + ___ = ___ L = ___
D = ___ Mf = ___ Ma ___ + ___ = ___

SCORES

NAME ___ LAST FIRST MIDDLE
DATE OF BIRTH ___ AGE ___ SEX ___ M OR F
DATE OF TESTING ___

T F	T F	T F	T F	T F	T F	T F	T F	T F	T F
1	31	61	91	121	151	181	211	241	271
2	32	62	92	122	152	182	212	242	272
3	33	63	93	123	153	183	213	243	273
4	34	64	94	124	154	184	214	244	274
5	35	65	95	125	155	185	215	245	275
6	36	66	96	126	156	186	216	246	276
7	37	67	97	127	157	187	217	247	277
8	38	68	98	128	158	188	218	248	278
9	39	69	99	129	159	189	219	249	279
10	40	70	100	130	160	190	220	250	280
11	41	71	101	131	161	191	221	251	281
12	42	72	102	132	162	192	222	252	282
13	43	73	103	133	163	193	223	253	283
14	44	74	104	134	164	194	224	254	284
15	45	75	105	135	165	195	225	255	285

BE SURE YOUR MARKS ARE HEAVY AND BLACK.
ERASE COMPLETELY ANY ANSWER YOU WISH TO CHANGE.

T F	T F	T F	T F	T F	T F	T F	T F	T F	T F
16	46	76	106	136	166	196	226	256	286
17	47	77	107	137	167	197	227	257	287
18	48	78	108	138	168	198	228	258	288
19	49	79	109	139	169	199	229	259	289
20	50	80	110	140	170	200	230	260	290
21	51	81	111	141	171	201	231	261	291
22	52	82	112	142	172	202	232	262	292
23	53	83	113	143	173	203	233	263	293
24	54	84	114	144	174	204	234	264	294
25	55	85	115	145	175	205	235	265	295
26	56	86	116	146	176	206	236	266	296
27	57	87	117	147	177	207	237	267	297
28	58	88	118	148	178	208	238	268	298
29	59	89	119	149	179	209	239	269	299
30	60	90	120	150	180	210	240	270	300

65-153AS PRINTED IN U. S. A. IBM FORM I. T. S. 1100 A 7421

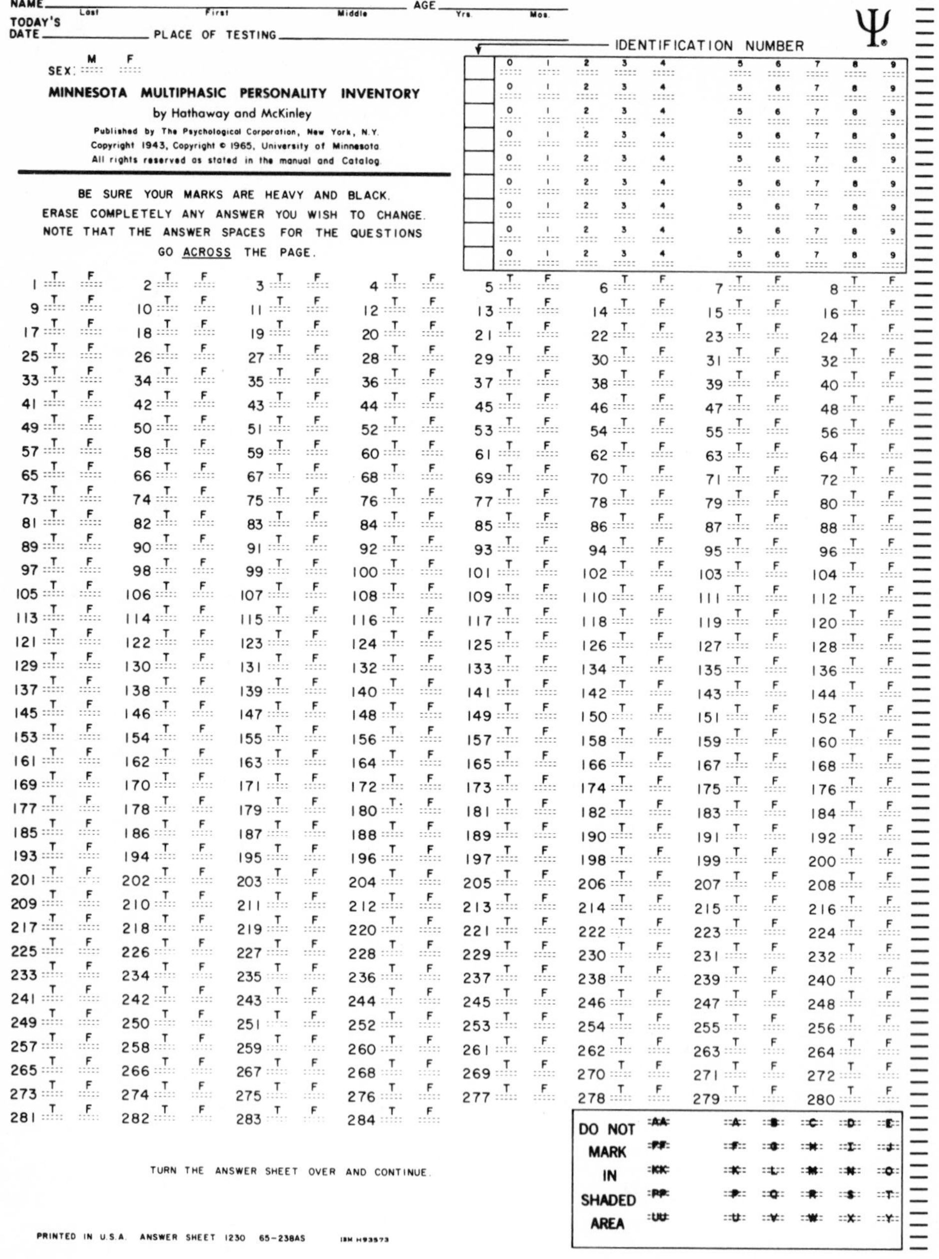

NAME ______ Last ______ First ______ Middle ______ AGE ______ Yrs. ______ Mos.

TODAY'S DATE ______ PLACE OF TESTING ______

SEX: M F

MINNESOTA MULTIPHASIC PERSONALITY INVENTORY

by Hathaway and McKinley

Published by The Psychological Corporation, New York, N.Y.

Ψ

IDENTIFICATION NUMBER

	0	1	2	3	4	5	6	7	8	9
	0	1	2	3	4	5	6	7	8	9
	0	1	2	3	4	5	6	7	8	9
	0	1	2	3	4	5	6	7	8	9
	0	1	2	3	4	5	6	7	8	9
	0	1	2	3	4	5	6	7	8	9
	0	1	2	3	4	5	6	7	8	9
	0	1	2	3	4	5	6	7	8	9
	0	1	2	3	4	5	6	7	8	9

BE SURE YOUR MARKS ARE HEAVY AND BLACK.
ERASE COMPLETELY ANY ANSWER YOU WISH TO CHANGE.
NOTE THAT THE ANSWER SPACES FOR THE QUESTIONS
GO ACROSS THE PAGE.

1 T F	2 T F	3 T F	4 T F	5 T F	6 T F	7 T F	8 T F
9 T F	10 T F	11 T F	12 T F	13 T F	14 T F	15 T F	16 T F
17 T F	18 T F	19 T F	20 T F	21 T F	22 T F	23 T F	24 T F
25 T F	26 T F	27 T F	28 T F	29 T F	30 T F	31 T F	32 T F
33 T F	34 T F	35 T F	36 T F	37 T F	38 T F	39 T F	40 T F
41 T F	42 T F	43 T F	44 T F	45 T F	46 T F	47 T F	48 T F
49 T F	50 T F	51 T F	52 T F	53 T F	54 T F	55 T F	56 T F
57 T F	58 T F	59 T F	60 T F	61 T F	62 T F	63 T F	64 T F
65 T F	66 T F	67 T F	68 T F	69 T F	70 T F	71 T F	72 T F
73 T F	74 T F	75 T F	76 T F	77 T F	78 T F	79 T F	80 T F
81 T F	82 T F	83 T F	84 T F	85 T F	86 T F	87 T F	88 T F
89 T F	90 T F	91 T F	92 T F	93 T F	94 T F	95 T F	96 T F
97 T F	98 T F	99 T F	100 T F	101 T F	102 T F	103 T F	104 T F
105 T F	106 T F	107 T F	108 T F	109 T F	110 T F	111 T F	112 T F
113 T F	114 T F	115 T F	116 T F	117 T F	118 T F	119 T F	120 T F
121 T F	122 T F	123 T F	124 T F	125 T F	126 T F	127 T F	128 T F
129 T F	130 T F	131 T F	132 T F	133 T F	134 T F	135 T F	136 T F
137 T F	138 T F	139 T F	140 T F	141 T F	142 T F	143 T F	144 T F
145 T F	146 T F	147 T F	148 T F	149 T F	150 T F	151 T F	152 T F
153 T F	154 T F	155 T F	156 T F	157 T F	158 T F	159 T F	160 T F
161 T F	162 T F	163 T F	164 T F	165 T F	166 T F	167 T F	168 T F
169 T F	170 T F	171 T F	172 T F	173 T F	174 T F	175 T F	176 T F
177 T F	178 T F	179 T F	180 T F	181 T F	182 T F	183 T F	184 T F
185 T F	186 T F	187 T F	188 T F	189 T F	190 T F	191 T F	192 T F
193 T F	194 T F	195 T F	196 T F	197 T F	198 T F	199 T F	200 T F
201 T F	202 T F	203 T F	204 T F	205 T F	206 T F	207 T F	208 T F
209 T F	210 T F	211 T F	212 T F	213 T F	214 T F	215 T F	216 T F
217 T F	218 T F	219 T F	220 T F	221 T F	222 T F	223 T F	224 T F
225 T F	226 T F	227 T F	228 T F	229 T F	230 T F	231 T F	232 T F
233 T F	234 T F	235 T F	236 T F	237 T F	238 T F	239 T F	240 T F
241 T F	242 T F	243 T F	244 T F	245 T F	246 T F	247 T F	248 T F
249 T F	250 T F	251 T F	252 T F	253 T F	254 T F	255 T F	256 T F
257 T F	258 T F	259 T F	260 T F	261 T F	262 T F	263 T F	264 T F
265 T F	266 T F	267 T F	268 T F	269 T F	270 T F	271 T F	272 T F
273 T F	274 T F	275 T F	276 T F	277 T F	278 T F	279 T F	280 T F
281 T F	282 T F	283 T F	284 T F				

DO NOT MARK IN SHADED AREA						
	AA	A	B	C	D	E
	FF	F	G	H	I	J
	KK	K	L	M	N	O
	PP	P	Q	R	S	T
	UU	U	V	W	X	Y

TURN THE ANSWER SHEET OVER AND CONTINUE.

PRINTED IN U.S.A. ANSWER SHEET 1230 65-238AS IBM H93573

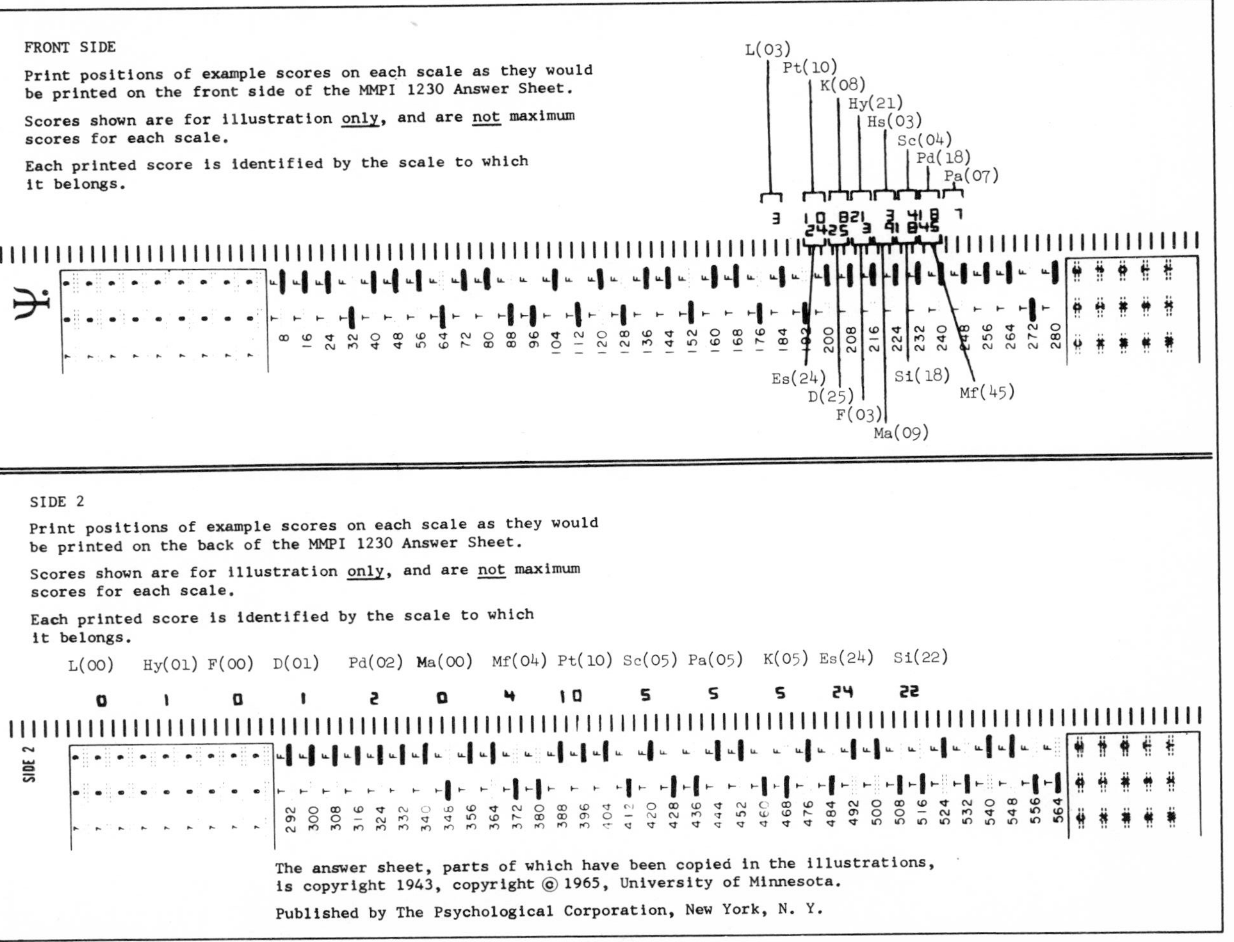
FRONT SIDE
Print positions of example scores on each scale as they would be printed on the front side of the MMPI 1230 Answer Sheet.
Scores shown are for illustration only, and are not maximum scores for each scale.
Each printed score is identified by the scale to which it belongs.
L(03) Pt(10) K(08) Hy(21) Hs(03) Sc(04) Pd(18) Pa(07)
Es(24) D(25) F(03) Ma(09) Si(18) Mf(45)
SIDE 2
Print positions of example scores on each scale as they would be printed on the back of the MMPI 1230 Answer Sheet.
Scores shown are for illustration only, and are not maximum scores for each scale.
Each printed score is identified by the scale to which it belongs.
L(00) Hy(01) F(00) D(01) Pd(02) Ma(00) Mf(04) Pt(10) Sc(05) Pa(05) K(05) Es(24) Si(22)
0 1 0 1 2 0 4 10 5 5 5 24 22
SIDE 2
The answer sheet, parts of which have been copied in the illustrations, is copyright 1943, copyright © 1965, University of Minnesota.
Published by The Psychological Corporation, New York, N. Y.

NCS Answer Sheet for MINNESOTA MULTIPHASIC PERSONALITY INVENTORY FORM-R

Starke R. Hathaway
J. Charnley McKinley

DIRECTIONS FOR USING NAME GRID

Print your name in the boxes above the columns of letters. Print your last name first. Skip a box, then print as much of your first name as possible. Below each box blacken the circle that is lettered the same as the letter in the box. Blacken the blank circle for spaces.

Age	Do not write below unless told to.	FOR N.C.S. USE ONLY

SEX — MALE ○ FEMALE ○

Scored By: NATIONAL COMPUTER SYSTEMS, 1015 So. 6th, Minneapolis, Minn.
Printed in U.S.A.
Published By THE PSYCHOLOGICAL CORPORATION, NEW YORK, N. Y.
67 204 AS

NAME (Please Print)

SCHOOL OR AGENCY

ADDRESS

AGE

SEX

SCHOOL YR.

OCCUPATION

NO.

T / F	1	2	3	4	5	6	7	8	9	10	11	12	13	14	15	16	17	18	19	20	21	22	23	24	25	26	27	28	29	30
T / F	31	32	33	34	35	36	37	38	39	40	41	42	43	44	45	46	47	48	49	50	51	52	53	54	55	56	57	58	59	60
T / F	61	62	63	64	65	66	67	68	69	70	71	72	73	74	75	76	77	78	79	80	81	82	83	84	85	86	87	88	89	90
T / F	91	92	93	94	95	96	97	98	99	100	101	102	103	104	105	106	107	108	109	110	111	112	113	114	115	116	117	118	119	120
T / F	121	122	123	124	125	126	127	128	129	130	131	132	133	134	135	136	137	138	139	140	141	142	143	144	145	146	147	148	149	150
T / F	151	152	153	154	155	156	157	158	159	160	161	162	163	164	165	166	167	168	169	170	171	172	173	174	175	176	177	178	179	180
T / F	181	182	183	184	185	186	187	188	189	190	191	192	193	194	195	196	197	198	199	200	201	202	203	204	205	206	207	208	209	210
T / F	211	212	213	214	215	216	217	218	219	220	221	222	223	224	225	226	227	228	229	230	231	232	233	234	235	236	237	238	239	240
T / F	241	242	243	244	245	246	247	248	249	250	251	252	253	254	255	256	257	258	259	260	261	262	263	264	265	266	267	268	269	270
T / F	271	272	273	274	275	276	277	278	279	280	281	282	283	284	285	286	287	288	289	290	291	292	293	294	295	296	297	298	299	300
T / F	301	302	303	304	305	306	307	308	309	310	311	312	313	314	315	316	317	318	319	320	321	322	323	324	325	326	327	328	329	330
T / F	331	332	333	334	335	336	337	338	339	340	341	342	343	344	345	346	347	348	349	350	351	352	353	354	355	356	357	358	359	360
T / F	361	362	363	364	365	366	367	368	369	370	371	372	373	374	375	376	377	378	379	380	381	382	383	384	385	386	387	388	389	390
T / F	391	392	393	394	395	396	397	398	399	400	401	402	403	404	405	406	407	408	409	410	411	412	413	414	415	416	417	418	419	420
T / F	421	422	423	424	425	426	427	428	429	430	431	432	433	434	435	436	437	438	439	440	441	442	443	444	445	446	447	448	449	450
T / F	451	452	453	454	455	456	457	458	459	460	461	462	463	464	465	466	467	468	469	470	471	472	473	474	475	476	477	478	479	480
T / F	481	482	483	484	485	486	487	488	489	490	491	492	493	494	495	496	497	498	499	500	501	502	503	504	505	506	507	508	509	510
T / F	511	512	513	514	515	516	517	518	519	520	521	522	523	524	525	526	527	528	529	530	531	532	533	534	535	536	537	538	539	540
T / F	541	542	543	544	545	546	547	548	549	550	551	552	553	554	555	556	557	558	559	560	561	562	563	564	565	566				

Hankes Answer Sheet for use with the

MINNESOTA MULTIPHASIC PERSONALITY INVENTORY

(Group Form Booklet)

Starke R. Hathaway, Ph. D. and J. Charnley McKinley, M.D.

Printed in the U.S.A. 2-62

Published by The Psychological Corporation, New York 17 N. Y.

See other side for instructions

Form No. P-EN

The Minnesota Multiphasic Personality Inventory

Starke R. Hathaway and J. Charnley McKinley

Scorer's Initials____________

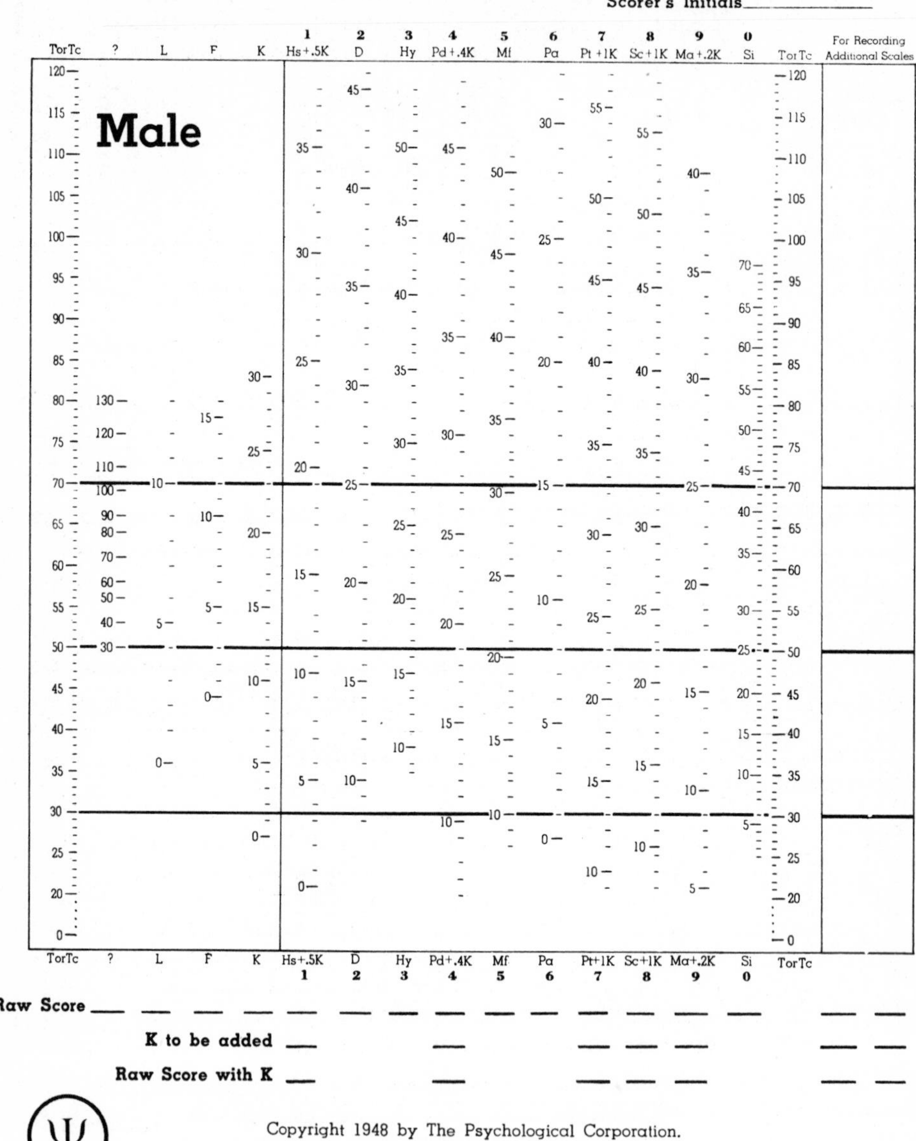

Raw Score ___ ___ ___ ___ ___ ___ ___ ___ ___ ___ ___ ___ ___ ___ ___ ___ ___

K to be added ___ ___ ___ ___ ___ ___ ___

Raw Score with K ___ ___ ___ ___ ___ ___ ___

The Psychological Corporation, 304 East 45th Street, New York, N. Y. 10017

Printed in U.S.A.

65-313S

APPENDIX O Addresses of Scoring Services and Interpretation Services

Clinical Psychological Services, Inc., 1722 Westwood Boulevard, Suite 205, Los Angeles, California 90024.

Finney-Auvenshine Project, Department of Educational Psychology, University of Kentucky, Lexington, Kentucky 40506.

Institute of Clinical Analysis, 1000 East Broadway, Glendale, California 91205.

National Computer Systems, Inc., 4401 West 76th Street, Minneapolis, Minnesota 55435.

The Psychological Corporation, 304 East 45th Street, New York, New York 10017.

Roche Psychiatric Service Institute, Roche Laboratories, Hoffmann-La Roche, Inc., Nutley, New Jersey 07110.

TESTSCOR, 2312 Snelling Avenue, Minneapolis, Minnesota 55404.

BIBLIOGRAPHY AND INDEX

Bibliography

Listed below are those references cited in this volume. A more complete MMPI bibliography will be found in Volume II.

Aaronson, B. S. Age and sex influence on MMPI profile peak distributions in an abnormal population. *Journal of Consulting Psychology,* 1958, 22, 203–206.

———. Hypochondriasis and somatic seizure auras. *Journal of Clinical Psychology,* 1959, 15, 450–451.

———, and I. Rothman. A key-word index to the items of the MMPI. *Journal of Psychological Studies,* 1962, 13, 121–151.

Adams, D. K., and J. L. Horn. Nonoverlapping keys for the MMPI scales. *Journal of Consulting Psychology,* 1965, 29, 284.

Alex, C. *How to beat personality tests.* New York: ARC Books, 1965.

Altrocchi, J. Interpersonal perceptions of repressors and sensitizers and component analysis of assumed dissimilarity scores. *Journal of Abnormal and Social Psychology,* 1961, 62, 528–534.

———, and Hilda D. Perlitsh. Patterns of ego control and expression of hostility. Unpublished materials, 1963.

———, O. A. Parsons, and Hilda Dickoff. Changes in self-ideal discrepancy in repressors and sensitizers. *Journal of Abnormal and Social Psychology,* 1960, 61, 67–72.

———, S. Shrauger, and Mary Anne McLeod. Attribution of hostility to self and others by expressors, sensitizers, and repressors. *Journal of Clinical Psychology,* 1964, 20, 223.

Altus, W. D. The adjustment of army illiterates. *Psychological Bulletin,* 1945, 42, 461–476.

———. Adjustment items which differentiate between psychiatric categories of military general prisoners. *Journal of General Psychology,* 1953, 49, 293–301.

———, and H. M. Bell. The validity of certain measures of maladjustment in an army special training center. *Psychological Bulletin,* 1945, 42, 98–103.

———, and H. M. Bell. An analysis of four orally administered measures of adjustment. *Educational and Psychological Measurement,* 1947, 7, 101–115.

Anderson, Helen J. Validity of a paper and pencil form of the MMPI Pd scale. M.A. thesis, Brooklyn College, 1948.

Anderson, W. The MMPI: low Pa scores. *Journal of Counseling Psychology,* 1956, 3, 226–228.

Angers, W. P. Guidelines for counselors for MMPI interpretation. *Catholic Counselor,* 1963, 7, 120–124.

Anthony, N. C. Comparison of clients' standard, exaggerated, and matching MMPI profiles. *Journal of Consulting and Clinical Psychology,* 1971, 36, 100–103.

Archibald, H. C. Referred pain in headache. *California Medicine,* 1955, 82, 186–187.

Armentrout, J. A., and D. L. Rouzer. Utility of the Mini-Mult with delinquents. *Journal of Consulting and Clinical Psychology,* 1970, 34, 450.

Astin, A. W. A factor study of the MMPI psychopathic deviate scale. *Journal of Consulting Psychology,* 1959, 23, 550–554.

———. A note on the MMPI psychopathic deviate scale. *Educational and Psychological Measurement,* 1961, 21, 895–897.

Aumack, L. Misconceptions concerning the interpretation of subgroup variations within normative data. *Journal of Psychology,* 1954, 38, 79–82.

Baldry, A. I., and I. G. Sarason. Test anxiety, preliminary instructions, and responses to personality inventories. *Journal of Clinical Psychology*, 1968, 24, 67.

Ball, J. C., and Donna Carroll. Analysis of MMPI Cannot Say scores in an adolescent population. *Journal of Clinical Psychology*, 1960, 16, 30–31.

Barker, H. R., R. D. Fowler, and L. P. Peterson. Factor analytic structure of the short form MMPI in a Veterans Administration hospital population. *Journal of Clinical Psychology*, 1971, 27, 228–233.

Barron, F. An ego-strength scale which predicts response to psychotherapy. *Journal of Consulting Psychology*, 1953, 17, 327–333.

Bashaw, W. L. A comparison of MMPI profiles and validity scale scores obtained by normal and slide-projected administration. *Multivariate Behavioral Research*, 1967, 2, 241–249.

Bauernfeind, R. H. Are sex norms necessary? *Journal of Counseling Psychology*, 1956, 3, 57–63.

Baughman, E. E., and W. G. Dahlstrom. *Negro and white children: a psychological study in the rural South*. New York: Academic Press, 1968.

Beall, H. S., and J. H. Panton. Development of a prison adjustment scale (PAS) for the MMPI. Unpublished manuscript, Central Prison, Raleigh, N.C., 1957.

Beaver, Alma P. Personality factors in choice of nursing. *Journal of Applied Psychology*, 1953, 37, 374–379.

Bechtoldt, H. P. Response defined anxiety and MMPI variables. *Proceedings of the Iowa Academy of Science*, 1953, 60, 495–499.

Benarick, S. J., G. M. Guthrie, and W. U. Snyder. An interpretative aid for the Sc scale of the MMPI. *Journal of Consulting Psychology*, 1951, 15, 142–144.

Bendig, A. W. The development of a short form of the manifest anxiety scale. *Journal of Consulting Psychology*, 1956, 20, 384.

Berdie, R. F., and W. L. Layton. *Minnesota counseling inventory manual*. New York: Psychological Corporation, 1957.

Berg, I. A. Response bias and personality: the deviation hypothesis. *Journal of Psychology*, 1955, 40, 61–72.

———. Deviant responses and deviant people: the formulation of the deviation hypothesis. *Journal of Counseling Psychology*, 1957, 4, 154–161.

Berger, E. M. Relationships among expressed acceptance of self, expressed acceptance of others, and the MMPI. *American Psychologist*, 1953, 8, 320–321.

———. Relationships among acceptance of self, acceptance of others, and MMPI scores. *Journal of Counseling Psychology*, 1955, 2, 279–283.

Bier, W. C. A comparative study of a seminary group and four other groups on the MMPI. *Studies in Psychology and Psychiatry, Catholic University of America*, 1948, 7, 1–107. (Also reprinted in part in Welsh and Dahlstrom, *Basic readings*.)

———. Modified version of the MMPI (with norms) for use with religious groups. Unpublished materials, 1965.

Bird, C. MMPI patterns under instructions to deliberately fake various psychiatric syndromes. Unpublished materials, University of Minnesota, 1948.

Black, J. D. The interpretation of MMPI profiles of college women. Ph.D. dissertation, University of Minnesota, 1953. (Printed in part in Welsh and Dahlstrom, *Basic readings*.)

———. A study of the efficiency of the MMPI for screening college women. *American Psychologist*, 1954, 9, 562.

Blazer, J. A. MMPI interpretation in outline: I. The ? scale. *Psychology*, 1965, 2(2), 23–24. (a)

———. MMPI interpretation in outline: II. The L scale. *Psychology*, 1965, 2(3), 2–7. (b)

———. MMPI interpretation in outline: III. The F scale. *Psychology*, 1965, 2(4), 2–9. (c)

———. MMPI interpretation in outline: IV. The K scale. *Psychology*, 1966, 3(2), 4–11.

Block, J. *The Q-sort method in personality assessment and psychiatric research*. Springfield, Ill.: Thomas, 1961.

———. *The challenge of response sets: unconfounding meaning, acquiescence, and social desirability in the MMPI*. New York: Appleton-Century-Crofts, 1965.

———, and D. Bailey. Q-sort item analyses of a number of MMPI scales. Officer Education Research Laboratory, Technical Memorandum, OERL-TM-55-7, May 1955.

Blum, M. L., and B. Balinsky. *Counseling and psychology*. New York: Prentice-Hall, 1951.

Blumberg, S. MMPI F scale as an indicator of severity of psychopathology. *Journal of Clinical Psychology*, 1967, 23, 96–99.

Boe, E. E., and W. S. Kogan. Effect of social desirability instructions on several MMPI measures of social desirability. *Journal of Consulting Psychology*, 1964, 28, 248–251.

Braaten, D. Kooky personality test. *Washington Star,* June 8, 1965.

Braginsky, B. M., Dorothea D. Braginsky, and K. Ring. *Methods of madness: the mental hospital as a last resort.* New York: Holt, Rinehart and Winston, 1969.

Branca, A. A., and E. E. Podolnick. Normal, hypnotically induced, and feigned anxiety as reflected in and detected by the MMPI. *Journal of Consulting Psychology,* 1961, 25, 165–170.

Brantner, J. P. MMPI high-point codes of neurological inpatients in a university hospital. Unpublished materials, 1957.

———. Homeless men: a psychological and medical survey. Ph.D. dissertation, University of Minnesota, 1958.

Brayfield, A. H., ed. Special issue: testing and public policy. *American Psychologist,* 1965, 20, 857–1005.

Breger, L. Psychological testing: treatment and research implications. *Journal of Consulting and Clinical Psychology,* 1968, 32, 176–181.

Briggs, P. F., and A. Tellegen. An abbreviation of the social introversion scale for 373-item MMPI. *Journal of Clinical Psychology,* 1967, 23, 189–191.

Brodsky, S. L. *Collected papers in prison psychology.* Council for Research and Evaluation Project 6-66, U.S. Disciplinary Barracks, Fort Leavenworth, Kansas, 1967.

Brown, M. N. Evaluating and scoring the Minnesota Multiphasic "Cannot Say" items. *Journal of Clinical Psychology,* 1950, 6, 180–184.

Brown, R. A., and L. D. Goodstein. Adjective check list correlates of extreme scores on the MMPI depression scale. *Journal of Clinical Psychology,* 1962, 18, 477–481.

Brozek, J. Personality of young and middle-aged normal men: item analysis of a psychosomatic inventory. *Journal of Gerontology,* 1952, 7, 410–418.

———. Personality changes with age: an item analysis of the MMPI. *Journal of Gerontology,* 1955, 10, 194–206.

———, and B. C. Schiele. Clinical significance of the Minnesota Multiphasic F scale evaluated in experimental neurosis. *American Journal of Psychiatry,* 1948, 105, 259–266.

Buechley, R., and H. Ball. A new test of "validity" for the group MMPI. *Journal of Consulting Psychology,* 1952, 16, 299–301.

Buer, C. F. An MMPI configural index for determination of somatization. Ph.D. dissertation, University of Minnesota, 1958.

Burton, A., and C. J. Bright. Adaptation of the MMPI for group administration and rapid scoring. *Journal of Consulting Psychology,* 1946, 10, 99–103.

Butcher, J. N. Manifest aggression: MMPI correlates in normal boys. *Journal of Consulting Psychology,* 1965, 29, 446–454. (Also in *Dissertation Abstracts,* 1965, 25, 6755–6756.)

———, ed. *MMPI: research developments and clinical applications.* New York: McGraw-Hill, 1969.

———, and A. Tellegen. Objections to MMPI items. *Journal of Consulting Psychology,* 1966, 30, 527–534.

Buttiglieri, M. W. Driver accidents and the neuropsychiatric patient. Institute of Transportation and Traffic Engineering Report No. 69-33 (UCLA), 1969. (Also in *Journal of Consulting and Clinical Psychology,* 1969, 33, 381.)

Byrne, D. The repression-sensitization scale: rationale, reliability, and validity. *Journal of Personality,* 1961, 29, 334–349.

Caldwell, A. B. Automated personality test interpretation as a resource for rapid patient evaluation. Paper read at the tenth IBM Medical Symposium, Poughkeepsie, N.Y., June 1970. (a)

———. Recent advances in automated interpretation of the MMPI. Paper read at the Fifth Annual Symposium on Recent Developments in the Use of the MMPI, Mexico City, February 1970. (b)

Canter, A. The efficacy of a short form of the MMPI to evaluate depression and morale loss. *Journal of Consulting Psychology,* 1960, 24, 14–17.

Cantor, J. M. Syndromes found in psychiatric populations selected for certain MMPI code endings. Ph.D. dissertation, University of Minnesota, 1952. (Also in *Dissertation Abstracts,* 1952, 12, 394.)

Capwell, Dora F. Personality patterns of adolescent girls: I. Girls who show improvement in IQ. *Journal of Applied Psychology,* 1945, 29, 212–228. (a)

———. Personality patterns of adolescent girls: II. Delinquents and non-delinquents. *Journal of Applied Psychology,* 1945, 29, 289–297. (b)

Carkhuff, R. R., L. Barnett, and J. N. McCall. *The counselor's handbook: scale and profile interpretation of the MMPI.* Urbana, Ill.: R. W. Parkinson and Associates, 1965.

Carr, J. E., C. N. Brownsberger, and R. C. Rutherford. Characteristics of symptom-matched psychogenic and "real" pain patients on the MMPI. *Proceedings of the 74th Annual Convention of the APA*, 1966, 1, 215–216.
Carson, R. C. Interpretative manual to the MMPI. In J. N. Butcher, ed. *MMPI: research developments and clinical applications*. New York: McGraw-Hill, 1969.
Charen, S. A note on the use of a paper-and-pencil form of the MMPI Hs scale for hospital use. *Journal of Consulting Psychology*, 1954, 18, 344.
Choynowski, M. The usefulness of the Fisher linear discriminant function in clinical diagnosis with the MMPI. *Przeglad Psychologiczny* (Poznan, Poland), 1966, 11, 98–114.
Clark, G. C., and R. M. Allen. Item analysis aid for the MMPI. *Journal of Consulting Psychology*, 1951, 15, 262.
Clark, J. H. Clinical use of the Altus thirty-six point adjustment test in screening army AWOL's. *Journal of Consulting Psychology*, 1948, 12, 276–279.
———. Additional applications of the Altus thirty-six point adjustment test as a screening instrument. *Journal of General Psychology*, 1949, 40, 261–265. (a)
———. The adjustment of army AWOL's. *Journal of Abnormal and Social Psychology*, 1949, 44, 394–401. (b)
———, and J. R. Danielson. A shortened schizophrenic scale for use in rapid screening. *Journal of Social Psychology*, 1956, 43, 187–190.
Cochrane, C. M., A. J. Prange, and D. W. Abse. Reserpine-produced changes in the direction of aggressive drives. *Proceedings of the Third World Congress of Psychiatry*, 1963, 3, 370–373.
Cofer, C. N., June E. Chance, and A. J. Judson. A study of malingering on the MMPI. *Journal of Psychology*, 1949, 27, 491–499.
Collier, Mary E. (Jeffrey). Some factors influencing answers on the Multiphasic K scale. Ph.D. dissertation, University of Minnesota, 1946.
Comrey, A. L. A factor analysis of items on the MMPI hypochondriasis scale. *Educational and Psychological Measurement*, 1957, 17, 568–577. (a)
———. A factor analysis of items on the MMPI depression scale. *Educational and Psychological Measurement*, 1957, 17, 578–585. (b)
———. A factor analysis of items on the MMPI hysteria scale. *Educational and Psychological Measurement*, 1957, 17, 586–592. (c)
———. A factor analysis of items on the F scale of the MMPI. *Educational and Psychological Measurement*, 1958, 18, 621–632. (a)
———. A factor analysis of items on the K scale of the MMPI. *Educational and Psychological Measurement*, 1958, 18, 633–639. (b)
———. A factor analysis of items on the MMPI psychopathic deviate scale. *Educational and Psychological Measurement*, 1958, 18, 91–98. (c)
———. A factor analysis of items on the MMPI paranoia scale. *Educational and Psychological Measurement*, 1958, 18, 99–107. (d)
———. A factor analysis of items on the MMPI psychasthenia scale. *Educational and Psychological Measurement*, 1958, 18, 293–300. (e)
———. A factor analysis of items on the MMPI hypomania scale. *Educational and Psychological Measurement*, 1958, 18, 313–323. (f)
———, and W. M. Marggraff. A factor analysis of items on the MMPI schizophrenia scale. *Educational and Psychological Measurement*, 1958, 18, 301–311.
Cone, J. D. A note on Marks' and Seeman's rules for actuarially classifying psychiatric patients. *Journal of Clinical Psychology*, 1966, 22, 270.
Cooke, Jane K. Clinicians' decisions as a basis for deriving actuarial formulae. *Journal of Clinical Psychology*, 1967, 23, 232–233. (a)
———. MMPI in actuarial diagnosis of psychological disturbance among college males. *Journal of Counseling Psychology*, 1967, 14, 474–477. (b)
Corsini, R. J. A time and motion study of hand scoring the individual MMPI. *Journal of Consulting Psychology*, 1949, 13, 62–63.
Costa, L. D., P. London, and E. Levita. A modification of the F scale of the MMPI. *Psychological Reports*, 1963, 12, 427–433.
Cottle, W. C. Card versus booklet forms of the MMPI. *Journal of Applied Psychology*, 1950, 34, 255–259.
———, and J. O. Powell. The effect of random answers to the MMPI. *Educational and Psychological Measurement*, 1951, 11, 224–227.
Coyle, F. A., and R. F. Heap. Interpreting the MMPI L scale. *Psychological Reports*, 1965, 17, 722.

Cronbach, L. J. Further evidence on response sets and test design. *Educational and Psychological Measurement,* 1950, 10, 3–31.

Crook, G. H. The measurement of personal characteristics: are available tests of personality of use in the army? Adjutant General's Office, Personnel Research Section, Report No. 669, 1944.

Cuadra, C. A., and C. F. Reed. *An introduction to the MMPI.* Downey, Ill.: Veterans Administration Hospital, 1954.

Dahlstrom, W. G. Invasion of privacy: how legitimate is the current concern over this issue? In J. N. Butcher, ed. *MMPI: research developments and clinical applications.* New York: McGraw-Hill, 1969. (a)

———. Recurrent issues in the development of the MMPI. In J. N. Butcher, ed. *MMPI: research developments and clinical applications.* New York: McGraw-Hill, 1969. (b)

———, and J. N. Butcher. Comparability of the taped and booklet versions of the MMPI. Unpublished manuscript, 1964.

———, and C. B. Reifler. MMPI code patterns for entering freshmen. Unpublished materials, 1970.

———, and R. S. Spain. Personality correlates of rated efficiency in the practice of medicine. Unpublished manuscript, 1958.

———, and H. J. Wahler. The application of discriminant function techniques to problems of psychiatric classification. *American Psychologist,* 1955, 10, 478.

———, and G. S. Welsh. *An MMPI handbook: a guide to use in clinical practice and research.* Minneapolis: University of Minnesota Press, 1960.

Davis, C. E. The MMPI: a new method of scoring and analysis. *Journal of Clinical Psychology,* 1947, 3, 298–301.

Dean, R. B., and H. Richardson. Analysis of MMPI profiles of forty college-educated overt male homosexuals. *Journal of Consulting Psychology,* 1964, 28, 483–486.

———, and H. Richardson. On MMPI high-point codes of homosexual versus heterosexual males. *Journal of Consulting Psychology,* 1966, 30, 558–560.

Dean, S. I. Adjustment testing and personality factors of the blind. *Journal of Consulting Psychology,* 1957, 21, 171–177.

Dempsey, P. A unidimensional depression scale for the MMPI. *Journal of Consulting Psychology,* 1964, 28, 364–370.

———. Depression or social desirability: comments on Edwards' appraisal of the D_{30} scale. *Journal of Consulting Psychology,* 1965, 29, 274–276.

Dies, R. R. Detection of simulated MMPI records using the desirability (Dy) scales. *Journal of Clinical Psychology,* 1968, 24, 335–337.

Drake, L. E. A social I. E. scale for the MMPI. *Journal of Applied Psychology,* 1946, 30, 51–54. (Also reprinted in Welsh and Dahlstrom, *Basic readings.*)

———. A method for machine scoring the card form of the MMPI. *Journal of Educational Research,* 1947, 41, 139–141.

———. MMPI profiles and interview behavior. *Journal of Counseling Psychology,* 1954, 1, 92–95. (Also reprinted in Welsh and Dahlstrom, *Basic readings.*)

———. Interpretation of MMPI profiles in counseling male clients. *Journal of Counseling Psychology,* 1956, 3, 83–88.

———, and E. R. Oetting. *An MMPI codebook for counselors.* Minneapolis: University of Minnesota Press, 1959.

———, and W. B. Thiede. Further validation of the social I. E. scale for the MMPI. *Journal of Educational Research,* 1948, 41, 551–556. (Also reprinted in Welsh and Dahlstrom, *Basic readings.*)

Drasgow, J., and W. L. Barnette. F–K in a motivated group. *Journal of Consulting Psychology,* 1957, 21, 399–401.

Duker, Jan. The utility of the MMPI Atlas in the derivation of personality descriptions. Ph.D. dissertation, University of Minnesota, 1958. (Also in *Dissertation Abstracts,* 1959, 19, 3021.)

Dunlop, E. *Essentials of the automated MMPI.* Glendale, Calif.: Institute of Clinical Analysis, 1966.

Dustin, D. S. *How psychologists do research: the example of anxiety.* Englewood Cliffs, N.J.: Prentice-Hall, 1969.

Eaddy, M. L. An investigation of the Cannot Say scale of the group MMPI. Ph.D. dissertation, University of Florida (Gainesville), 1962. (Also in *Dissertation Abstracts,* 1962, 23, 1070–1071.)

Edwards, A. L. The relationship between the judged desirability of a trait and the probability that the trait will be endorsed. *Journal of Applied Psychology,* 1953, 37, 90–93.

———. *The social desirability variable in personality assessment and research.* New York: Dryden, 1957.

———, and J. A. Walsh. A factor analysis of ? scores. *Journal of Abnormal and Social Psychology,* 1964, 69, 559–563.

Eichman, W. J. Discrimination of female schizophrenics with configural analysis of the MMPI profile. *Journal of Consulting Psychology,* 1959, 23, 442–447.

———. Replicated factors on the MMPI with female NP patients. *Journal of Consulting Psychology,* 1961, 25, 55–60.

———. Factored scales for the MMPI: a clinical and statistical manual. *Journal of Clinical Psychology,* 1962, 18, 363–395.

———. Personality correlates of MMPI factor scale patterns. Unpublished materials, 1970.

Eisenberg, P. Minnesota T-S-E Inventory: a review. In O.K. Buros, ed. *The third mental measurements yearbook.* New Brunswick, N.J.: Rutgers University Press, 1949.

Ellis, A. The validity of personality questionnaires. *Psychological Bulletin,* 1946, 43, 385–440.

Endicott, N. A., and Jean Endicott. Objective measures of somatic preoccupation. *Journal of Nervous and Mental Disease,* 1963, 137, 427–437.

———, and S. Jortner. Objective measures of depression. *Archives of General Psychiatry,* 1966, 15, 249–255.

———, and S. Jortner. Correlates of somatic concern derived from psychological tests. *Journal of Nervous and Mental Disease,* 1967, 144, 133–138.

———, S. Jortner, and Eileen Abramoff. Objective measures of suspiciousness. *Journal of Abnormal Psychology,* 1969, 74, 26–32.

Engberg, E. *The spy in the corporate structure and the right to privacy.* Cleveland: World Publishing Co., 1967.

Eriksen, C. W., and A. Davids. The meaning and clinical validity of the Taylor anxiety scale and the hysteria-psychasthenia scales from the MMPI. *Journal of Abnormal and Social Psychology,* 1955, 50, 135–137.

Evans, Catharine, and T. R. McConnell. A new measure of introversion-extroversion. *Journal of Psychology,* 1941, 12, 111–124.

Exner, J. E., E. McDowell, Joan Pabst, W. Stackman, and L. Kirk. On the detection of willful falsifications in the MMPI. *Journal of Consulting Psychology,* 1963, 27, 91–94.

Farber, I. E., ed. *Biographical inventory (A, R, Ho, F, L, and K-scales).* Iowa City: Department of Psychology, State University of Iowa, 1952.

Feldman, M. J. The use of the MMPI profile for prognosis and evaluation of shock therapy. *Journal of Consulting Psychology,* 1952, 16, 376–382. (Also reprinted in Welsh and Dahlstrom, *Basic readings.*)

Ferguson, R. G. A useful adjunct to the MMPI scoring and analysis. *Journal of Clinical Psychology,* 1946, 2, 248–253.

Finney, J. C. Development of a new set of MMPI scales. *Psychological Reports,* 1965, 17, 707–713. (a)

———. Effects of response sets on new and old MMPI scales. *Psychological Reports,* 1965, 17, 907–915. (b)

———. Programmed interpretation of MMPI and CPI. *Archives of General Psychiatry,* 1966, 15, 75–81.

———. Methodological problems in programmed composition of psychological test reports. *Behavioral Science,* 1967, 12, 142–152.

———. Normative data on some MMPI scales. *Psychological Reports,* 1968, 23, 219–229.

———. *Manual for psychiatrists and psychologists: psychodiagnostic consultation service, Finney Institute for the Study of Human Behavior.* Lexington, Ky.: Finney Institute for the Study of Human Behavior, 1969.

———, D. F. Smith, D. E. Skeeters, and C. D. Auvenshine. Validation of computer diagnosis in psychiatry. Unpublished manuscript, 1970.

Fiske, D. W. Subject reactions to inventory format and content. *Proceedings of the 77th Annual Convention of the APA,* 1969, 4, 137–138.

Fitts, W. H. *Manual of Tennessee Self Concept Scale.* Nashville: Mental Health Department, 1965.

Fordyce, W. E. Social desirability in the MMPI. *Journal of Consulting Psychology,* 1956, 20, 171–175.

Forsyth, R. P., and Sandra F. Smith. MMPI related behavior in a student nurse group. *Journal of Clinical Psychology,* 1967, 23, 224–229.

Foster, Violet H., and H. H. Goddard. The Ohio literacy test. *Pedagogical Seminary*, 1924, 31, 340–351.

Fowler, R. D. Ethical principles of the Roche Psychiatric Service Institute regarding computer-based MMPI reports to professional clients. Mimeographed materials, 1966. (a)

———. *The MMPI notebook: a guide to the clinical use of the automated MMPI*. Nutley, N.J.: Roche Psychiatric Service Institute, 1966. (b)

———. Computer interpretation of personality tests: the automated psychologist. *Comprehensive Psychiatry*, 1967, 8, 455–467.

———. MMPI computer interpretation for college counseling. *Journal of Psychology*, 1968, 69, 201–207.

———. Automated interpretation of personality test data. In J. N. Butcher, ed. *MMPI: research developments and clinical applications*. New York: McGraw-Hill, 1969. (a)

———. The current status of computer interpretation of psychological tests. *American Journal of Psychiatry*, 1969, 125, 21–27. (b)

———, and Elizabeth B. Athey. A cross-validation of Gilberstadt and Duker's 1-2-3-4 profile type. *Journal of Clinical Psychology*, 1971, 27, 238–240.

———, and F. A. Coyle. A comparison of two MMPI actuarial systems used in classifying an alcoholic out-patient population. *Journal of Clinical Psychology*, 1968, 24, 434–435. (a)

———, and F. A. Coyle. Overlap as a problem in Atlas classification of MMPI profiles. *Journal of Clinical Psychology*, 1968, 24, 435. (b)

———, and F. A. Coyle. Scoring error on the MMPI. *Journal of Clinical Psychology*, 1968, 24, 68–69. (c)

———, and G. H. Marlowe. A computer program for personality analysis. *Behavioral Science*, 1968, 13, 413–416.

Fox, J. *Patterns of stimulus-avoidance on the MMPI*. Patton State Hospital, Patton, California, 1964.

Franks, C. MMPI interpretive rules. Unpublished materials, 1965.

French, J. W. Minnesota T-S-E Inventory: a review. In O. K. Buros, ed. *The third mental measurements yearbook*. New Brunswick, N.J.: Rutgers University Press, 1949.

Friberg, R. R. Measures of homosexuality: cross-validation of two MMPI scales and implications for usage. *Journal of Consulting Psychology*, 1967, 31, 88–91.

Fricke, B. G. Conversion hysterics and the MMPI. *Journal of Clinical Psychology*, 1956, 12, 322–326.

———. A response bias (B) scale for the MMPI. *Journal of Counseling Psychology*, 1957, 4, 149–153.

Fulkerson, S. C. An acquiescence key for the MMPI. *USAF School of Aviation Medicine Reports*, 1958, No. 58-71.

Gallagher, J. J. MMPI changes concomitant with client-centered therapy. *Journal of Consulting Psychology*, 1953, 17, 334–338. (Also reprinted in Welsh and Dahlstrom, *Basic readings*.)

Gauron, E., R. Severson, and R. Englehart. MMPI F scores and psychiatric diagnosis. *Journal of Consulting Psychology*, 1962, 26, 488.

Ghiselli, E. D. The prediction of predictability. *Educational and Psychological Measurement*, 1960, 20, 3–8.

Giedt, F. H., and L. Downing. An extraversion scale for the MMPI. *Journal of Clinical Psychology*, 1961, 17, 156–159.

Gilberstadt, H. An exploratory investigation of the Hathaway-Meehl method of MMPI profile analysis with psychiatric clinical data. Ph.D. dissertation, University of Minnesota, 1952. (Also in *Dissertation Abstracts*, 1953, 13, 256–257.)

———. A modal MMPI profile type in neurodermatitis. *Psychosomatic Medicine*, 1962, 24, 471–476.

———. Construction and application of MMPI cookbooks. In J. N. Butcher, ed. *MMPI: research developments and clinical applications*. New York: McGraw-Hill, 1969.

———. *Comprehensive MMPI code book for males*. Minneapolis: MMPI Research Laboratory, Veterans Administration Hospital, Report 1B 11-5, 1970.

———, and Jan Duker. Case history correlates of three MMPI profile types. *Journal of Consulting Psychology*, 1960, 24, 361–367.

———, and Jan Duker. *A handbook for clinical and actuarial MMPI interpretation*. Philadelphia: W. B. Saunders Co., 1965.

———, and Maruta Jancis. "Organic" vs. "functional" diagnoses from 1-3 MMPI profiles. *Journal of Clinical Psychology*, 1967, 23, 480–483.

Gilbert, Jeanne G., and D. N. Lombardi. Personality characteristics of young male narcotic addicts. *Journal of Consulting Psychology*, 1967, 31, 536–538.

+ Gilliland, A. R., and R. Colgin. Norms, reliability, and forms of the MMPI. *Journal of Consulting Psychology*, 1951, 15, 435–438.

Glasscock, E. M. An investigation of the value of the MMPI as a prognostic instrument. Ph.D. dissertation, Washington University, 1954. (Also in *Dissertation Abstracts*, 1955, 15, 874–875.)

Glenn, R. A study of personality patterns of male defective delinquents as indicated by the MMPI. M.A. thesis, Pennsylvania State University, 1949.

Gocka, E. F., and H. W. Burk. MMPI test-taking time and social desirability. *Journal of Clinical Psychology*, 1963, 19, 111–113.

———, and Hildegund Holloway. A composite MMPI introversion-extraversion scale. *Journal of Clinical Psychology*, 1962, 18, 474–477.

Goldberg, L. R. Diagnosticians vs. diagnostic signs: the diagnosis of psychosis vs. neurosis from the MMPI. *Psychological Monographs*, 1965, 79 (9; whole no. 602), 1–28.

———. The search for configural relationships in personality assessment: the diagnosis of psychosis vs. neurosis from the MMPI. *Multivariate Behavioral Research*, 1969, 4, 523–536.

———, and R. R. Jones. The reliability of reliability: the generality and correlates of intra-individual consistency in responses to structured personality inventories. *Oregon Research Institute Research Monographs*, 1969, 9, no. 2.

———, and L. G. Rorer. Test-retest item statistics for original and reversed MMPI items. *Oregon Research Institute Research Monographs*, 1963, 3, no. 1.

———, and L. G. Rorer. Test-retest item statistics. *Psychological Reports*, 1964, 15, 413–414.

Golden, M. Some effects of combining psychological tests on clinical inferences. *Journal of Consulting Psychology*, 1964, 28, 440–446.

Goldman, L. *Using tests in counseling*. New York: Appleton-Century-Crofts, 1961.

Goldstein, S. G., J. D. Linden, and T. T. Baker. 7094 template programs for scoring dichotomous response format tests with special reference to the MMPI. *Educational and Psychological Measurement*, 1967, 27, 719–721.

Good, Patricia K.-E., and J. P. Brantner. *The physician's guide to the MMPI*. Minneapolis: University of Minnesota Press, 1961.

Goodenough, Florence L. *Mental testing: its history, principles, and applications*. New York: Rinehart, 1949.

Goodstein, L. D. Regional differences in MMPI responses among male college students. *Journal of Consulting Psychology*, 1954, 18, 437–441. (Also reprinted in Welsh and Dahlstrom, *Basic readings*.)

———, and W. G. Dahlstrom. MMPI differences between parents of stuttering and non-stuttering children. *Journal of Consulting Psychology*, 1956, 20, 365–370.

Gordon, J. E. A communication: snooping and testing. *New Republic*, January 9, 1965, pp. 28–30.

Goss, A., and T. E. Morosko. Alcoholism and clinical symptoms. *Journal of Abnormal Psychology*, 1969, 74, 682–684.

Gough, H. G. Diagnostic patterns on the MMPI. *Journal of Clinical Psychology*, 1946, 2, 23–37. (Also reprinted in Welsh and Dahlstrom, *Basic readings*.)

———. Simulated patterns on the MMPI. *Journal of Abnormal and Social Psychology*, 1947, 42, 215–225.

———. The F minus K dissimulation index for the MMPI. *Journal of Consulting Psychology*, 1950, 14, 408–413. (Also reprinted in Welsh and Dahlstrom, *Basic readings*.)

———. On making a good impression. *Journal of Educational Research*, 1952, 46, 33–42.

———. Tests of personality: questionnaires. A. MMPI. In A. Weider, ed. *Contributions toward medical psychology: theory and psychodiagnostic methods*, vol. II. New York: Ronald Press, 1953.

———. Some common misconceptions about neuroticism. *Journal of Consulting Psychology*, 1954, 18, 287–292. (Also reprinted in Welsh and Dahlstrom, *Basic readings*.)

———. *Reference handbook for the Gough adjective check list*. Berkeley: Institute for Personality Assessment and Research, University of California, 1955.

———. *California psychological inventory manual*. Palo Alto, Calif.: Consulting Psychologists Press, 1957.

———. *Bibliography of reports on the CPI through March, 1963, indexed for easy reference*. Palo Alto, Calif.: Consulting Psychologists Press, 1963.

———. Personal communication. Cited in L. R. Goldberg. Diagnosticians vs. diagnostic signs: the diagnosis of psychosis vs. neurosis from the MMPI. *Psychological Monographs*, 1965, 79 (9; whole no. 602), 1–28.

———, and A. B. Heilbrun. *The adjective check list manual*. Palo Alto, Calif.: Consulting Psychologists Press, 1965.

———, M. G. McKee, and R. J. Yandell. Adjective check list analyses of a number of selected psychometric and assessment variables. Officer Education Research Laboratory, Technical Memorandum, OERL-TM-55-10, 1955.

Goulding, C. W. A study of the distribution of MMPI profiles in a college population. M.A. thesis, University of Minnesota, 1951.

Gowan, J. C. Relation of the K scale of the MMPI to teaching personality. *California Journal of Educational Research*, 1955, 6, 208–212.

Graham, J. R. The relationship between response bias and "Cannot Say" responses on the MMPI. M.A. thesis, University of North Carolina, 1963.

———, H. E. Schroeder, and R. S. Lilly. Factor analysis of items on the social introversion and masculinity-femininity scales of the MMPI. *Journal of Clinical Psychology*, 1971, 27, 367–370.

Grant, H. A rapid personality evaluation based on the MMPI and the Cornell Selectee Index. *American Journal of Psychiatry*, 1946, 103, 33–41.

Gravitz, M. A. Frequency and content of test items normally omitted from MMPI scales. *Journal of Consulting Psychology*, 1967, 31, 642. (a)

———. A new computerized method for the fully automated printout of MMPI graphic profiles. *Journal of Clinical Psychology*, 1967, 23, 101–102. (b)

———. Normative findings for the frequency of MMPI critical items. *Journal of Clinical Psychology*, 1968, 24, 220.

———. Validity implications of normal adult MMPI "L" scale endorsement. *Journal of Clinical Psychology*, 1970, 26, 497–499.

———, and N. W. Davis. High speed electronic computer scoring and analysis of the MMPI. *American Psychologist*, 1965, 20, 516. (a)

———, and N. W. Davis. Procedures and problems in computer analysis of the MMPI. *Journal of Psychology*, 1965, 61, 171–176. (b)

Grayson, H. M. *A psychological admissions testing program and manual*. Los Angeles: Veterans Administration Center, Neuropsychiatric Hospital, 1951.

———, and L. B. Olinger. Simulation of "normalcy" by psychiatric patients on the MMPI. *Journal of Consulting Psychology*, 1957, 21, 73–77.

Greene, E. B. Medical reports and selected MMPI items among employed adults. *American Psychologist*, 1954, 9, 384.

Greenspoon, J., and C. D. Gersten. A new look at psychological testing: psychological testing from the standpoint of a behaviorist. *American Psychologist*, 1967, 22, 848–853.

Griffith, A. V., and R. D. Fowler. Psychasthenic and hypomanic scales of the MMPI and reaction to authority. *Journal of Counseling Psychology*, 1960, 7, 146–147.

———, H. S. Upshaw, and R. D. Fowler. The psychasthenic and hypomanic scales of the MMPI and uncertainty in judgments. *Journal of Clinical Psychology*, 1958, 14, 385–386.

Gross, L. R. MMPI L-F-K relationships with criteria of behavioral disturbance and social adjustment in a schizophrenic population. *Journal of Consulting Psychology*, 1959, 23, 319–323.

Gross, M. *The brain watchers*. New York: Random House, 1962.

Guilford, J. P. *Psychometric methods*. New York: McGraw-Hill, 1936.

———, and Ruth B. Guilford. Personality factors S, E, and M, and their measurement. *Journal of Psychology*, 1936, 2, 109–127.

———, and Ruth B. Guilford. Personality factors D, R, T, and A. *Journal of Abnormal and Social Psychology*, 1939, 34, 21–36.

Gulde, C. J., and H. L. Roy. A note on the scoring of the MMPI. *Journal of Consulting Psychology*, 1947, 11, 221–222.

Guthrie, G. M. A study of the personality characteristics associated with the disorders encountered by an internist. Ph.D. dissertation, University of Minnesota, 1949.

Gynther, M. D. The clinical utility of "invalid" MMPI F scores. *Journal of Consulting Psychology*, 1961, 25, 540–542.

———, and Patricia J. Brilliant. The MMPI K+ profile: a reexamination. *Journal of Consulting and Clinical Psychology*, 1968, 32, 616–617.

———, and T. P. Petzel. Differential endorsement of MMPI F scale items by psychotics

and behavior disorders. *Journal of Clinical Psychology*, 1967, 23, 185–188.
———, and A. M. Shimkunas. Age, intelligence, and MMPI F scores. *Journal of Consulting Psychology*, 1965, 29, 383–388. (a)
———, and A. M. Shimkunas. More data on MMPI F> 16 scores. *Journal of Clinical Psychology*, 1965, 21, 275–277. (b)
Haertzen, C. A., and H. E. Hill. Assessing subjective effects of drugs: an index of carelessness and confusion for use with the Addiction Research Center Inventory (ARCI). *Journal of Clinical Psychology*, 1963, 19, 407–412.
Halbower, C. C. A comparison of actuarial versus clinical prediction to classes discriminated by MMPI. Ph.D. dissertation, University of Minnesota, 1955. (Also in *Dissertation Abstracts*, 1955, 15, 1115.)
Hanes, B. Reading ease and MMPI results. *Journal of Clinical Psychology*, 1953, 9, 83–85.
Hanley, C. Social desirability and responses to items from three MMPI scales: D, Sc, and K. *Journal of Applied Psychology*, 1956, 40, 324–328.
———. Deriving a measure of test-taking defensiveness. *Journal of Consulting Psychology*, 1957, 21, 391–397.
———. Social desirability and response bias in the MMPI. *Journal of Consulting Psychology*, 1961, 25, 13–20.
———. The "difficulty" of a personality inventory item. *Educational and Psychological Measurement*, 1962, 22, 577–584.
Hanvik, L. J. MMPI profiles in patients with low-back pain. *Journal of Consulting Psychology*, 1951, 15, 350–353. (Also reprinted in Welsh and Dahlstrom, *Basic readings*.)
Harding, G. F., W. C. Holz, and A. D. Kawakami. The differentiation of schizophrenic and superficially similar reactions. *Journal of Clinical Psychology*, 1958, 14, 147–149.
Harris, J. G., and J. C. Baxter. Ambiguity in the MMPI. *Journal of Consulting Psychology*, 1965, 29, 112–118.
Harris, R. E., and J. C. Lingoes. Subscales for the MMPI: an aid to profile interpretation. Mimeographed materials. Department of Psychiatry, University of California, 1955. (Corrected version, 1968.)
Hartshorne, H., and M. A. May. *Studies in the nature of character: I. Studies in deceit*. New York: Macmillan, 1928.
———, M. A. May, and F. K. Shuttleworth. *Studies in the nature of character: III. Studies in the organization of character*. New York: Macmillan, 1930.
Hastings, D. W., S. R. Hathaway, R. M. Amberg, and Lucy Balian. Early objective personality evaluation in medical diagnosis. *University of Minnesota Medical Bulletin*, 1957, 28, 1–12.
Hathaway, S. R. The Multiphasic Personality Inventory. *Modern Hospital*, 1946, 66, 65–67.
———. A coding system for MMPI profiles. *Journal of Consulting Psychology*, 1947, 11, 334–337. (Also reprinted in Welsh and Dahlstrom, *Basic readings*.)
———. IBM scoring procedures for the card form of the MMPI. Unpublished materials, 1956. (a)
———. Scales 5 (masculinity-femininity), 6 (paranoia), and 8 (schizophrenia). In G. S. Welsh and W. G. Dahlstrom, eds. *Basic readings on the MMPI in psychology and medicine*. Minneapolis: University of Minnesota Press, 1956. (b)
———. Foreword. In W. G. Dahlstrom and G. S. Welsh. *An MMPI handbook: a guide to use in clinical practice and research*. Minneapolis: University of Minnesota Press, 1960.
———. MMPI: professional use by professional people. *American Psychologist*, 1964, 19, 204–210.
———. Personality inventories. In B. B. Wolman, ed. *Handbook of clinical psychology*. New York: McGraw-Hill, 1965.
———. Where have we gone wrong? The mystery of the missing progress. Paper given at the Fourth Annual Symposium on the Recent Developments in the Use of the MMPI. University of Minnesota, April 1969.
———, and P. F. Briggs. Some normative data on new MMPI scales. *Journal of Clinical Psychology*, 1957, 13, 364–368.
———, and J. C. McKinley. A multiphasic personality schedule (Minnesota): I. Construction of the schedule. *Journal of Psychology*, 1940, 10, 249–254. (Also reprinted in Welsh and Dahlstrom, *Basic readings*.) (a)
———, and J. C. McKinley. The measurement of symptomatic depression with the Minnesota Multiphasic Personality Schedule. *Psychological Bulletin*, 1940, 37, 425. (b)
———, and J. C. McKinley. A multiphasic personality schedule (Minnesota): III. The measurement of symptomatic depression. *Journal of Psychology*, 1942, 14, 73–84. (Also re-

printed in Welsh and Dahlstrom, *Basic readings*.)
———, and J. C. McKinley. *The Minnesota Multiphasic Personality Schedule*. Minneapolis: University of Minnesota Press, 1943.
———, and J. C. McKinley. *The Minnesota Multiphasic Personality Inventory Manual*. New York: Psychological Corporation, 1951, 1967.
———, and P. E. Meehl. *An atlas for the clinical use of the MMPI*. Minneapolis: University of Minnesota Press, 1951. (a)
———, and P. E. Meehl. The MMPI. In *Military clinical psychology*. Department of the Army, Technical Manual, TM 8-242; Department of the Air Force Manual, AFM 160-45, 1951. (Also reprinted in Welsh and Dahlstrom, *Basic readings*.) (b)
———, and P. E. Meehl. Adjective check list correlates of MMPI scores. Unpublished materials, 1952.
———, and E. D. Monachesi, eds. *Analyzing and predicting juvenile delinquency with the MMPI*. Minneapolis: University of Minnesota Press, 1953.
———, and E. D. Monachesi. The personalities of predelinquent boys. *Journal of Criminal Law, Criminology, and Police Science*, 1957, 48, 149–163.
———, and E. D. Monachesi. *An atlas of juvenile MMPI profiles*. Minneapolis: University of Minnesota Press, 1961.
———, and E. D. Monachesi. *Adolescent personality and behavior: MMPI patterns of normal, delinquent, dropout, and other outcomes*. Minneapolis: University of Minnesota Press, 1963.
Heilbrun, A. B. The psychological significance of the MMPI K scale in a normal population. *Journal of Consulting Psychology*, 1961, 25, 486–491.
———. Revision of the MMPI K correction procedure for improved detection of maladjustment in a normal college population. *Journal of Consulting Psychology*, 1963, 27, 161–165.
Heineman, C. E. A forced-choice form of the Taylor anxiety scale. *Journal of Consulting Psychology*, 1953, 17, 447–454. (Also in *Dissertation Abstracts*, 1952, 12, 584–585.)
Heist, P. A., T. R. McConnell, H. D. Webster, and G. D. Yonge. *Omnibus Personality Inventory manual*. New York: Psychological Corporation, 1960.
Henrichs, T. Objective configural rules for discriminating MMPI profiles in a psychiatric population. *Journal of Clinical Psychology*, 1964, 20, 157–159.
———. A note on the extension of MMPI configural rules. *Journal of Clinical Psychology*, 1966, 22, 51–52.
Himelstein, P., and B. Lubin. Relationship of the MMPI K scale and a measure of self-disclosure in a normal population. *Psychological Reports*, 1966, 19, 166.
Holzberg, J. D., and S. Alessi. Reliability of the shortened MMPI. *Journal of Consulting Psychology*, 1949, 13, 288–292.
Houk, T. W. MMPI in diagnosis of psychoneuroses. *Northwest Medicine*, 1946, 45, 248–252.
Hovey, H. B. Detection of circumvention in the MMPI. *Journal of Clinical Psychology*, 1948, 4, 97.
———. Somatization and other neurotic reactions and MMPI profiles. *Journal of Clinical Psychology*, 1949, 5, 153–156. (Also reprinted in Welsh and Dahlstrom, *Basic readings*.)
———. MMPI profiles and personality characteristics. *Journal of Consulting Psychology*, 1953, 17, 142–146. (Also reprinted in Welsh and Dahlstrom, *Basic readings*.)
———. MMPI aberration potentials in a non-clinical group. *Journal of Social Psychology*, 1954, 40, 299–307. (Also reprinted in Welsh and Dahlstrom, *Basic readings*.)
———. Correction of MMPI profiles for excessive item omissions. Unpublished materials, 1958.
———, and E. G. Lewis. Semi-automatic interpretation of the MMPI. *Journal of Clinical Psychology*, 1967, 23, 123–134.
Huff, F. W. Use of actuarial descriptions of personality in a mental hospital. *Psychological Reports*, 1965, 17, 224.
Hunt, H. F. The effect of deliberate deception on MMPI performance. *Journal of Consulting Psychology*, 1948, 12, 396–402.
———, A. Carp, W. A. Cass, C. L. Winder, and R. E. Kantor. A study of the differential diagnostic efficiency of the MMPI. *Journal of Consulting Psychology*, 1948, 12, 331–336.
Hurwitz, J. I., and D. Lelos. A multilevel interpersonal profile of employed alcoholics. *Quarterly Journal of Studies of Alcohol*, 1968, 29, 64–75.
IPAR staff. *Special composite personality inventory*. Berkeley: University of California Press, 1952.
Jackson, D. N., and S. Messick. Content and style in personality assessment. *Psychological*

Bulletin, 1958, 55, 243–252.

———, and S. Messick. Acquiescence and desirability as response determinants on the MMPI. *Educational and Psychological Measurement*, 1961, 21, 771–790.

———, and S. Messick. Response styles and the assessment of psychopathology. In S. Messick and J. Ross, eds. *Measurement in personality and cognition.* New York: Wiley and Sons, 1962. (a)

———, and S. Messick. Response styles on the MMPI: comparison of clinical and normal samples. *Journal of Abnormal and Social Psychology*, 1962, 65, 285–299. (b)

Jacobs, A., and S. Leventer. Response to personality inventories with situational stress. *Journal of Abnormal and Social Psychology*, 1955, 51, 449–451.

Jastak, J., S. Bijou, and Sarah Jastak. *Wide Range Achievement Test: manual.* New York; Psychological Corporation, 1965.

Jenkins, W. L. The MMPI applied to the problem of prognosis in schizophrenia. Ph.D. dissertation, University of Minnesota, 1952.

Jennings, G., L. Goldberg, and A. Powell. Experimental MMPI verbal form. Unpublished materials, Cherry Hospital, Goldsboro, N.C., 1969.

Johnson, M. H., and D. S. Holmes. An attempt to develop a process-reactive scale for the MMPI. *Journal of Clinical Psychology*, 1967, 23, 191.

Johnson, R. H., and G. L. Bond. Reading ease of commonly used tests. *Journal of Applied Psychology*, 1950, 34, 319–324.

Jorgensen, C. A short form of the MMPI. *Australian Journal of Psychology*, 1958, 341–350.

Jung, C. G. *Psychological types, or the psychology of individuation.* New York: Harcourt, Brace, 1923.

Kamman, G. R. Psychosomatic diagnosis. *Journal-Lancet*, 1947, 67, 102–107.

———, and C. Kram. Value of psychometric examinations in medical diagnosis and treatment. *Journal of the American Medical Association*, 1955, 158, 555–560.

Kanun, Clara, and E. D. Monachesi. Delinquency and the validating scales of the MMPI. *Journal of Criminal Law, Criminology, and Police Science*, 1960, 50, 525–534.

Karmel, L. J. *Measurement and evaluation in the schools.* New York: Macmillan, 1970.

Kausler, D. H., E. P. Trapp, and C. L. Brewer. Time score as a criterion measure on the Taylor manifest anxiety scale. *Journal of Clinical Psychology*, 1959, 15, 51–54.

Kazan, A. T., and I. M. Sheinberg. Clinical note on the significance of the validity score (F) in the MMPI. *American Journal of Psychiatry*, 1945, 102, 181–183.

Kent, Grace H. *Series of emergency scales.* New York: Psychological Corporation, 1946.

Kimber, J. A. M. An alphabetical list of MMPI items. *Journal of Clinical Psychology*, 1957, 13, 197–202.

Kincannon, J. C. Prediction of the standard MMPI scale scores from 71 items: the Mini-Mult. *Journal of Consulting and Clinical Psychology*, 1968, 32, 319–325.

King, F. W. The MMPI F scale as a predictor of lack of adaptation to college. *Journal of the American College Health Association*, 1967, 15, 261–269.

King, G. F., and M. Schiller. A research note on the K scale of the MMPI and "defensiveness." *Journal of Clinical Psychology*, 1959, 15, 305–306.

Kleinmuntz, B. MMPI decision rules for the identification of college maladjustment: a digital computer approach. *Psychological Monographs*, 1963, 77 (14; whole no. 577), 1–22.

———, ed. *Clinical information processing by computer.* New York: Holt, Rinehart and Winston, 1969.

———, and L. B. Alexander. Computer program for the Meehl-Dahlstrom MMPI profile rules. *Educational and Psychological Measurement*, 1962, 22, 193–199.

Klopfer, W. G. A cross validation of Leary's "public" communication level. *Journal of Clinical Psychology*, 1961, 17, 321–322.

Kostlan, A. A method for the empirical study of psychodiagnosis. *Journal of Consulting Psychology*, 1954, 18, 83–88.

Krippner, S. The identification of male homosexuality with the MMPI. *Journal of Clinical Psychology*, 1964, 20, 159–161.

Krise, E. M. A short method of scoring the MMPI. *Journal of Clinical Psychology*, 1947, 3, 386–392.

———. A common error in scoring the MMPI. *Journal of Clinical Psychology*, 1949, 5, 180–181.

Krug, R. S. MMPI response inconsistency of brain damaged individuals. *Journal of Clinical Psychology*, 1967, 23, 366.

L'Abate, L. MMPI scatter as a single index of maladjustment. *Journal of Clinical Psychology*, 1962, 18, 142–143.

LaForge, R. Interpersonal domains or interpersonal levels? A validation of Leary's "MMPI Level I indices." *American Psychologist*, 1963, 18, 592.

Lair, C. V., and E. P. Trapp. The differential diagnostic value of MMPI with somatically disturbed patients. *Journal of Clinical Psychology*, 1962, 18, 146–147.

Lanyon, R. I. Simulation of normal and psychopathic MMPI personality patterns. *Journal of Consulting Psychology*, 1967, 31, 94–97.

———. *A handbook of MMPI group profiles*. Minneapolis: University of Minnesota Press, 1968.

Lauber, Margaret, and W. G. Dahlstrom. MMPI findings in the rehabilitation of delinquent girls. In S. R. Hathaway and E. D. Monachesi, eds. *Analyzing and predicting juvenile delinquency with the MMPI*. Minneapolis: University of Minnesota Press, 1953.

Layton, W. L. The variability of individuals' scores upon successive testings on the MMPI. *Educational and Psychological Measurement*, 1954, 14, 634–640.

Leary, T. *Interpersonal diagnosis of personality: a functional theory and methodology for personality evaluation*. New York: Ronald Press, 1957.

Leath, J. R., and R. Pricer. Reliability of the MMPI tape form with institutionalized epileptics of average intelligence. Unpublished manuscript, 1968.

Levine, D. Why and when to test: the social context of psychological testing. In A. I. Rabin, ed. *Projective techniques in personality assessment: a modern introduction*. New York: Springer, 1968.

Levy, L. H. *Psychological interpretation*. New York: Holt, Rinehart and Winston, 1963.

Ligon, E. M. The administration of group tests. *Educational and Psychological Measurement*, 1942, 2, 387–399.

Lindquist, E. F., ed. *Educational measurement*. Washington, D.C.: American Council on Education, 1951.

Little, J. W. An analysis of the MMPI. M.A. thesis, University of North Carolina, 1949.

Little, K. B., and J. Fisher. Two new experimental scales of the MMPI. *Journal of Consulting Psychology*, 1958, 22, 305–306.

———, and E. S. Shneidman. Congruencies among interpretations of psychological test and anamnestic data. *Psychological Monographs*, 1959, 73 (6; whole no. 476).

Lorr, M. A test of seven MMPI factors. *Multivariate Behavioral Research*, 1968, 3, 151–156.

Lovell, V. R. Personal communication. Cited in L. R. Goldberg. Diagnosticians vs. diagnostic signs: the diagnosis of psychosis vs. neurosis from the MMPI. *Psychological Monographs*, 1965, 79 (9; whole no. 602), 1–28.

Lushene, R. E. Factor structure of the MMPI item pool. M.A. thesis, Florida State University, 1967.

McAree, C. P., R. A. Steffenhagen, and L. S. Zheutlin. Personality factors in college drug users. *International Journal of Social Psychiatry*, 1969, 15, 102–106.

MacDonald, G. L. A study of the shortened group and individual forms of the MMPI. *Journal of Clinical Psychology*, 1952, 8, 309–311. (a)

———. Effect of test-retest interval and item arrangement on the shortened forms of the MMPI. *Journal of Clinical Psychology*, 1952, 8, 408–410. (b)

McDonald, R. L. Ego control patterns and attribution of hostility to self, parents, and others. *Perceptual and Motor Skills*, 1965, 21, 340–348.

———. Leary's overt interpersonal behavior: a validation attempt. *Journal of Social Psychology*, 1968, 74, 259–264.

McKegney, F. P. An item analysis of the MMPI F scale in juvenile delinquents. *Journal of Clinical Psychology*, 1965, 21, 201–205.

McKinley, J. C., and S. R. Hathaway. A multiphasic personality schedule (Minnesota): II. A differential study of hypochondriasis. *Journal of Psychology*, 1940, 10, 255–268. (Also reprinted in Welsh and Dahlstrom, *Basic readings*.)

———, and S. R. Hathaway. A multiphasic personality schedule (Minnesota): IV. Psychasthenia. *Journal of Applied Psychology*, 1942, 26, 614–624. (Also reprinted in Welsh and Dahlstrom, *Basic readings*.)

———, and S. R. Hathaway. The MMPI: V. Hysteria, hypomania and psychopathic deviate. *Journal of Applied Psychology*, 1944, 28, 153–174. (Also reprinted in Welsh and Dahlstrom, *Basic readings*.)

———, S. R. Hathaway, and P. E. Meehl. The MMPI: VI. The K scale. *Journal of Consulting Psychology*, 1948, 12, 20–31. (Also reprinted in Welsh and Dahlstrom, *Basic readings*.)

MacLean, A. G., A. T. Tait, and C. D. Catterall. The F minus K index on the MMPI. *Journal of Applied Psychology*, 1953, 37, 315–316.

McMahon, R. MMPI profiles from a sample of North Carolina youth offenders. Unpublished materials, 1970.

McQuary, J. P., and W. E. Truax. A comparison of the group and individual forms of the MMPI. *Journal of Educational Research*, 1952, 45, 609–614.

Mack, J. L. The MMPI and recidivism. *Journal of Abnormal Psychology*, 1969, 74, 612–614.

Manosevitz, M. Item analyses of the MMPI Mf scale using homosexual and heterosexual males. *Journal of Consulting and Clinical Psychology*, 1970, 35, 395–399.

Manson, M. P. A psychometric differentiation of alcoholics from nonalcoholics. *Quarterly Journal of Studies of Alcohol*, 1948, 9, 175–206.

———, and H. M. Grayson. Keysort method of scoring the MMPI. *Journal of Applied Psychology*, 1946, 30, 509–516.

Marks, P. A., and P. F. Briggs. Adolescent norm tables for the MMPI. Unpublished materials, 1967.

———, and W. Seeman. *The actuarial description of personality: an atlas for use with the MMPI*. Baltimore: Williams and Wilkins, 1963.

Marsh, J. T., Jassamine Hilliard, and R. Liechti. A sexual deviation scale for the MMPI. *Journal of Consulting Psychology*, 1955, 19, 55–59.

May, J. R. The effects of pacing on MMPI performance. Unpublished manuscript, 1968.

Meehl, P. E. An investigation of a general normality or control factor in personality testing. *Psychological Monographs*, 1945, 4 (whole no. 274).

———. Profile analysis of the MMPI in differential diagnosis. *Journal of Applied Psychology*, 1946, 30, 517–524. (Also reprinted in Welsh and Dahlstrom, *Basic readings*.)

———. Configural scoring. *Journal of Consulting Psychology*, 1950, 14, 165–171. (Also reprinted in Welsh and Dahlstrom, *Basic readings*.)

———. *Research results for counselors*. St. Paul, Minn.: State Department of Education, 1951.

———. Wanted–a good cookbook. Presidential address, Midwestern Psychological Association, Chicago, April 1955. *American Psychologist*, 1956, 11, 263–272.

———. Comments on the invasion of privacy issue. In J. N. Butcher, ed. *MMPI: research developments and clinical applications*. New York: McGraw-Hill, 1969.

———, and W. G. Dahlstrom. Objective configural rules for discriminating psychotic from neurotic MMPI profiles. *Journal of Consulting Psychology*, 1960, 24, 375–387.

———, and S. R. Hathaway. The K factor as a suppressor variable in the MMPI. *Journal of Applied Psychology*, 1946, 30, 525–564. (Also reprinted in Welsh and Dahlstrom, *Basic readings*.)

Mees, H. L. Preliminary steps in the construction of factor scales for the MMPI. Ph.D. dissertation, University of Washington, 1959. (Also in *Dissertation Abstracts*, 1960, 20, 2905.)

Mehlman, B., and M. E. Rand. Face validity of the MMPI. *Journal of General Psychology*, 1960, 63, 171–178.

Mello, Nancy K., and G. M. Guthrie. MMPI profiles and behavior in counseling. *Journal of Counseling Psychology*, 1958, 5, 125–129.

Miller, Christine, Sarah C. Knapp, and Clara W. Daniels. MMPI study of Negro mental hygiene clinic patients. *Journal of Abnormal Psychology*, 1968, 73, 168–173.

Miller, J. P., Suzanne E. Bohn, Joanne B. Gilden, and E. Stevens. Anxiety as a function of taking the MMPI. *Journal of Consulting and Clinical Psychology*, 1968, 32, 120–124.

Miller, W. G., and T. E. Hannum. Characteristics of homosexually involved incarcerated females. *Journal of Consulting Psychology*, 1963, 27, 277.

Mills, W. W. MMPI profile pattern and scale stability throughout four years of college attendance. Ph.D. dissertation, University of Minnesota, 1954. (Also in *Dissertation Abstracts*, 1954, 14, 1259.)

Modlin, H. C. A study of the MMPI in clinical practice with notes on the Cornell Index. *American Journal of Psychiatry*, 1947, 103, 758–769. (Also reprinted in Welsh and Dahlstrom, *Basic readings*.)

Morf, M. E., and D. N. Jackson. An analysis of two response styles: true responding and item endorsement. Department of Psychology, University of Western Ontario Research Bulletin No. 98, November 1969.

Morgan, W. P. Selected physiological and psychomotor correlates of depression in psychiatric patients. *Research Quarterly of the American Association of Health and Physical Education*, 1968, 39, 1037–1043.

Morton, Mary A. The army adaptation of the MMPI. *American Psychologist*, 1948, 3, 271–272.

Mosher, D. L. Some characteristics of high and low frequency "Cannot Say" items on the

MMPI. *Journal of Consulting Psychology,* 1966, 30, 177.
Mucha, T. F., and R. F. Reinhart. Conversion reactions in student aviators. *American Journal of Psychiatry,* 1970, 127, 493–497.
Mullen, F. A. The MMPI: an extension of the Davis scoring method. *Journal of Clinical Psychology,* 1948, 4, 86–88.
Murphree, H. B., M. J. Karabelas, and L. L. Bryan. Scores of inmates of a federal penitentiary on two scales of the MMPI. *Journal of Clinical Psychology,* 1962, 18, 137–139.
Murray, J. B. The Mf scale of the MMPI for college students. *Journal of Clinical Psychology,* 1963, 19, 113–115.
———, M. Judith Munley, and T. E. Gilbart. The Pd scale of the MMPI for college students. *Journal of Clinical Psychology,* 1965, 21, 48–51.
Nakamura, C. Y. Validity of K scale (MMPI) in college counseling. *Journal of Counseling Psychology,* 1960, 7, 108–115.
Navran, L. A short method of scoring the MMPI. Mimeographed. Palo Alto, Calif.: Veterans Administration, Neuropsychiatric Hospital, 1950.
Nelson, S. E. The development of an indirect, objective measure of social status and its relationship to certain psychiatric syndromes. Ph.D. dissertation, University of Minnesota, 1952.
O'Connor, J. P., and E. C. Stefic. Some patterns of hypochondriasis. *Educational and Psychological Measurement,* 1959, 19, 363–371.
———, E. C. Stefic, and C. J. Gresock. Some patterns of depression. *Journal of Clinical Psychology,* 1957, 13, 122–125.
Oliver, W. A., and D. L. Mosher. Psychopathology and guilt in heterosexual and subgroups of homosexual reformatory inmates. *Journal of Abnormal Psychology,* 1968, 73, 323–329.
Olson, G. W. The Hastings short form of the group MMPI. *Journal of Clinical Psychology,* 1954, 10, 386–388.
Osborne, D. A moderator variable approach to MMPI validity. *Journal of Clinical Psychology,* 1970, 26, 486–490.
Overall, J. E., L. E. Hollister, A. D. Pokorney, J. F. Casey, and G. Katz. Drug therapy in depressions, controlled evaluation of imipramine, isocarboxazid, dextro-amphetamine-amobarbital and placebo. *Clinical Pharmacology and Therapeutics,* 1962, 3, 16–22.
Panton, J. H. Predicting prison adjustment with the MMPI. *Journal of Clinical Psychology,* 1958, 14, 308–312.
———. MMPI high-point codes on samples of male and female prison inmates. Unpublished materials, 1959.
———. A new MMPI scale for the identification of homosexuality. *Journal of Clinical Psychology,* 1960, 16, 17–21.
———. The MMPI: oral interrogative form. Unpublished materials, Reception Center, Central Prison, Raleigh, N.C., 1969.
Paterson, D. G., Gwendolen G. Schneidler, and J. S. Carlson. *Minnesota occupational rating scales, revised.* University of Minnesota Mechanical Abilities Research Project, 1936.
Pauker, J. D. MMPI profile stability in a psychiatric, inpatient population. *Journal of Clinical Psychology,* 1965, 21, 281–282.
———. Stability of MMPI profiles of female psychiatric inpatients. *Journal of Clinical Psychology,* 1966, 22, 209–212. (a)
———. Identification of MMPI profile types in a female, inpatient, psychiatric setting using the Marks and Seeman rules. *Journal of Consulting Psychology,* 1966, 30, 90. (b)
Payne, F. D., and J. S. Wiggins. Effects of rule relaxation and system combination on classification rates in two MMPI "cookbook" systems. *Journal of Consulting and Clinical Psychology,* 1968, 32, 734–736.
Pearson, J. S. Prediction of the response of schizophrenic patients to electroconvulsive therapy. *Journal of Clinical Psychology,* 1950, 6, 285–287. (Also reprinted in Welsh and Dahlstrom, *Basic readings.*)
———, H. P. Rome, W. M. Swenson, P. Mataya, and T. L. Brannick. Development of a computer system for scoring and interpretation of MMPI's in a medical clinic. *Annals of the New York Academy of Sciences,* 1965, 126, 684–692.
———, and W. M. Swenson. *A user's guide to the Mayo Clinic automated MMPI program.* New York: Psychological Corporation, 1967.
Pepper, L. J. The MMPI: initial test predictors of retest changes. Ph.D. dissertation, University of North Carolina, 1964.
———, and P. N. Strong. Judgmental subscales for the Mf scale of the MMPI. Unpublished materials, 1958.

Perkins, Julia E., and L. R. Goldberg. Contextual effects on the MMPI. *Journal of Consulting Psychology*, 1964, 28, 133–140.

Persons, R. W., and P. A. Marks. The violent 4-3 MMPI personality type. *Journal of Consulting and Clinical Psychology*, 1971, 36, 189–196.

Peterson, D. R. The diagnosis of subclinical schizophrenia. *Journal of Consulting Psychology*, 1954, 18, 198–200. (Also reprinted in Welsh and Dahlstrom, *Basic readings.*)

Phillips, C. E. Measuring power of spouse. *Sociology and Social Research*, 1967, 52, 35–49.

Pierce-Jones, J. The readability of certain standard tests. *California Journal of Educational Research*, 1954, 5, 80–82.

Pinneau, S. R., and A. Milton. The ecological veracity of the self report. *Journal of Genetic Psychology*, 1958, 93, 249–276.

Plutchik, R. *The emotions: facts, theories and a new model.* New York: Random House, 1962.

Pothast, M. D. A personality study of two types of murderers. Ph.D. dissertation, Michigan State University, 1956. (Also in *Dissertation Abstracts*, 1957, 17, 898–899.)

Potter, C. S. A method of using the MMPI with the blind. In Wilma Donahue and D. Dabelstein, eds. *Psychological diagnosis and counseling of the adult blind: selected papers from the proceedings of the University of Michigan Conference for the Blind (1947).* New York: American Foundation for the Blind, 1950.

Rankin, R. J. Analysis of items perceived as objectionable in the MMPI. *Perceptual and Motor Skills*, 1968, 27, 627–633.

Rapaport, G. M. "Ideal self" instructions, MMPI profile changes, and the prediction of clinical improvement. *Journal of Consulting Psychology*, 1958, 22, 459–463.

Reese, Phyllis M., J. T. Webb, and J. D. Foulks. A comparison of oral and booklet forms of the MMPI for psychiatric inpatients. *Journal of Clinical Psychology*, 1968, 24, 436–437.

Rempel, P. B. The use of multivariate statistical analysis of MMPI scores in the classification of delinquent and nondelinquent high school boys. *Journal of Consulting Psychology*, 1958, 22, 17–23.

———. Analysis of MMPI data for classification purposes by multivariate statistical techniques. *Journal of Experimental Education*, 1960, 28, 219–228.

Renaud, H. R. Clinical correlates of the masculinity-femininity scale of the MMPI. Ph.D. dissertation, University of California, 1950.

Rice, D. G. Rorschach responses and aggressive characteristics of MMPI F > 16 scorers. *Journal of Projective Techniques*, 1968, 32, 253–261.

Ridgeway, J. The snoops: private lives and public service. *New Republic*, December 19, 1964.

Roche Laboratories Staff. The computer now aids private practice. *Roche Report: Frontiers of Clinical Psychiatry*, 1968, 5, no. 15.

Rogers, A. H., and T. M. Walsh. Defensiveness and unwitting self-evaluation. *Journal of Clinical Psychology*, 1959, 15, 302–304.

Rorer, L. G. The function of item content in MMPI responses. Ph.D. dissertation, University of Minnesota, 1963. (Also in *Dissertation Abstracts*, 1963, 24, 2566.)

Rosanoff, A. J. *Manual of psychiatry* (7th ed.). New York: Wiley, 1938.

Rosen, A. Reliability of MMPI scales. *American Psychologist*, 1952, 7, 341.

———. Test-retest stability of MMPI scales for a psychiatric population. *Journal of Consulting Psychology*, 1953, 17, 217–221.

Rosman, R. R., S. M. Barry, and P. J. Gibeau. Problems in Atlas classification of MMPI profiles. *Journal of Clinical Psychology*, 1966, 22, 308–310.

Rozynko, V. V. MMPI internalization-externalization scale number 3. American Lake, Wash.: Research Service, Veterans Administration Hospital, 1959.

Ruesch, J., and K. M. Bowman. Prolonged post-traumatic syndromes following head injury. *American Journal of Psychiatry*, 1945, 102, 145–163.

Sanford, R. N., H. Webster, and M. Freedman. Impulse expression as a variable of personality. *Psychological Monographs*, 1957, 71 (11; whole no. 440).

Saunders, D. R. Moderator variables in prediction. *Educational and Psychological Measurement*, 1956, 16, 209–222.

Schiele, B. C., A. B. Baker, and S. R. Hathaway. The MMPI. *Journal-Lancet*, 1943, 63, 292-297.

Schiele, B. C., and J. Brozek. "Experimental neurosis" resulting from semistarvation in man. *Psychosomatic Medicine*, 1948, 10, 31–50. (Also reprinted in Welsh and Dahlstrom, *Basic readings.*)

Schmidt, H. O. Notes on the MMPI: the K factor. *Journal of Consulting Psychology*, 1948, 12, 337–342.

Schneck, J. M. Clinical evaluation of the F scale on the MMPI. *American Journal of Psychiatry,* 1948, 104, 440–442.

Schofield, W. Changes in responses to the MMPI following certain therapies. *Psychological Monographs,* 1950, 64 (5; whole no. 311). (Also reprinted in part in Welsh and Dahlstrom, *Basic readings.*)

———. A further study of the effects of therapies on MMPI responses. *Journal of Abnormal and Social Psychology,* 1953, 48, 67–77. (Also reprinted in part in Welsh and Dahlstrom, *Basic readings.*)

———. Clinical and counseling psychology: some perspectives. *American Psychologist,* 1966, 21, 122–131.

Seeman, W. "Subtlety" in structured personality tests. *Journal of Consulting Psychology,* 1952, 16, 278–283. (Also reprinted in Welsh and Dahlstrom, *Basic readings.*)

———. Concept of "subtlety" in structured psychiatric and personality tests: an experimental approach. *Journal of Abnormal and Social Psychology,* 1953, 48, 239–247. (Also reprinted in Welsh and Dahlstrom, *Basic readings.*)

Shaffer, J. W. A new acquiescence scale for the MMPI. *Journal of Clinical Psychology,* 1963, 19, 412–415.

———, Kay Y. Ota, and T. E. Hanlon. The comparative validity of several MMPI indices of severity of psychopathology. *Journal of Clinical Psychology,* 1964, 22, 467–473.

Sheppard, C., Diane Fiorentino, Lois Collins, and S. Merlis. Comparison of emotion profiles as defined by two additional MMPI profile types in male narcotic addicts. *Journal of Clinical Psychology,* 1969, 25, 186–188.

Sheppard, C., Diane Fiorentino, and S. Merlis. Affective differential-comparison of emotion profiles gained from clinical judgment and patient self-report. *Psychological Reports,* 1968, 22, 809–814.

Shinohara, M., and R. L. Jenkins. MMPI study of three types of delinquents. *Journal of Clinical Psychology,* 1967, 23, 156–163.

Shipman, W. G. A one-page scale of anxiety and depression. *Psychological Reports,* 1963, 13, 289–290.

Shneidman, E. S. A short method of scoring the MMPI. *Journal of Consulting Psychology,* 1946, 10, 143–145.

Shultz, T. D., P. J. Gibeau, and S. M. Barry. Utility of MMPI "cookbooks." *Journal of Clinical Psychology,* 1968, 24, 430–433.

Silver, R. J., and L. K. Sines. Diagnostic efficiency of the MMPI with and without the K correction. *Journal of Clinical Psychology,* 1962, 18, 312–314.

Simia, R. A., and A. O. di Loreto. Comparability of oral and booklet forms of the MMPI. Unpublished manuscript, 1970. (Based on M.A. thesis of R. A. Simia, 1969.)

Simmons, D. D. Invasion of privacy and judged benefit of personality-test inquiry. *Journal of General Psychology,* 1968, 79, 177–181.

Sines, J. O. Actuarial methods in personality assessment. In B. Maher, ed. *Progress in experimental personality research.* New York: Academic Press, 1966.

Sines, L. K. An experimental investigation of the relative contribution to clinical diagnosis and personality description of various kinds of pertinent data. Ph.D. dissertation, University of Minnesota, 1957. (Also in *Dissertation Abstracts,* 1957, 17, 2067.)

———, and R. J. Silver. An index of psychopathology (Ip) derived from clinicians' judgments of MMPI profiles. *Journal of Clinical Psychology,* 1963, 19, 324–326.

Singer, M. I. Comparison of indicators of homosexuality on the MMPI. *Journal of Consulting and Clinical Psychology,* 1970, 34, 15–18.

Sivanich, G. Test-retest changes during the course of hospitalization among some frequently occurring MMPI profiles. Ph.D. dissertation, University of Minnesota, 1960.

Skovron, M. The Mini-Mult: its meaningfulness as related to a profile classification system. M.A. thesis, University of Dayton, 1969.

Smart, R. G., and Dianne Fejer. Illicit LSD users: their social backgrounds, drug use and psychopathology. *Journal of Health and Social Behavior,* 1969, 10, 297–308.

———, and Dianne Jones. Illicit drug users: their personality characteristics and psychopathology. *Journal of Consulting and Clinical Psychology,* 1970, 75, 286–292.

Smith, E. E. Defensiveness, insight, and the K scale. *Journal of Consulting Psychology,* 1959, 23, 275–277.

Smith, J., and R. I. Lanyon. Prediction of juvenile probation violators. *Journal of Consulting and Clinical Psychology,* 1968, 32, 54–58.

Smith, L. D. The "beats" and Bohemia: positive social deviance or a problem in collective disturbance? In S. C. Plog and R. B. Edgerton, eds. *Changing perspectives in mental illness.* New York: Holt, Rinehart and Winston, 1969.

Snoke, Mary, and N. Ziesner. Relationship between subtle-obvious keys and K scale of the MMPI. Advisement Bulletin No. 6, Regional Veterans Administration Office, Minneapolis, 1946.

Spielberger, C. D. Personality processes reflected in the MMPI. *American Psychologist,* 1957, 12, 574.

Stanton, J. M. Group personality profile related to aspects of antisocial behavior. *Journal of Criminal Law, Criminology, and Police Science,* 1956, 47, 340–349.

Stein, K. B. The TSC scales: the outcome of a cluster analysis of the 550 MMPI items. In P. McReynolds, ed. *Advances in psychological assessment,* vol. I. Palo Alto, Calif.: Science and Behavior Books, 1968.

Stone, D. R., and L. L. West. "First day" orientation testing with the MMPI contrasted with a re-test. *Journal of Educational Research,* 1955, 49, 621–624.

Stone, F. Beth, and V. N. Rowley. MMPI differences between emotionally disturbed and delinquent adolescent boys. *Journal of Clinical Psychology,* 1962, 18, 481–484.

———, and V. N. Rowley. MMPI differences between emotionally disturbed and delinquent adolescent girls. *Journal of Clinical Psychology,* 1963, 19, 227–230.

———, V. N. Rowley, and J. C. MacQueen. Using the MMPI with adolescents who have somatic symptoms. *Psychological Reports,* 1966, 18, 139–147.

Stone, L. A. Social desirability and order of item presentation in the MMPI. *Psychological Reports,* 1965, 17, 518.

———, and A. Margoshes. Verbal embellishment responses on the MMPI. *Journal of Clinical Psychology,* 1965, 21, 278–279.

Sullivan, P. L., and G. S. Welsh. A technique for objective configural analysis of MMPI profiles. *Journal of Consulting Psychology,* 1952, 16, 383–388. (Also reprinted in Welsh and Dahlstrom, *Basic readings.*)

Sundberg, N. D. MMPI codes of University Hospital out-patients seen for intake interviews (10/51–6/52). Mimeographed. Minneapolis: University of Minnesota, 1952.

———. The acceptability of "fake" versus "bona fide" personality test interpretations. *Journal of Abnormal and Social Psychology,* 1955, 50, 145–147.

Super, D. E. *Appraising vocational fitness by means of psychological tests.* New York: Harper, 1949.

Sutton, Mary L. Profile patterning and descriptive correlates of patients having low scores on scale 9 of the MMPI. Ph.D. dissertation, University of Minnesota, 1952. (Also in *Dissertation Abstracts,* 1952, 12, 786.)

Sweetland, A., and H. Quay. A note on the K scale of the MMPI. *Journal of Consulting Psychology,* 1953, 17, 314–316.

Swenson, W. M. Structured personality testing in the aged: an MMPI study of theorontic population. *Journal of Clinical Psychology,* 1961, 17, 302–304.

Tallent, N. On individualizing the psychologist's clinical evaluation. *Journal of Clinical Psychology,* 1958, 14, 243–244.

———. *Clinical psychological consultation.* Englewood Cliffs, N.J.: Prentice-Hall, 1963.

Tamkin, A. S., and I. W. Scherer. What is measured by the "Cannot Say" scale of the group MMPI? *Journal of Consulting Psychology,* 1957, 21, 370–371.

Taulbee, E. S. Relationship between certain personality variables and continuation in psychotherapy. *Journal of Consulting Psychology,* 1958, 22, 83–89.

———, and B. D. Sisson. Configurational analysis of MMPI profiles of psychiatric groups. *Journal of Consulting Psychology,* 1957, 21, 413–417.

Taylor, Janet A. A personality scale of manifest anxiety. *Journal of Abnormal and Social Psychology,* 1953, 48, 285–290.

Terman, L. M., and Catharine C. Miles. *Sex and personality: studies in masculinity and femininity.* New York: McGraw-Hill, 1936.

Terman, L. M., and Catharine C. Miles. *Manual of information and directions for use of Attitude-Interest Analysis Test.* New York: McGraw-Hill, 1938.

Tryon, R. C. Unrestricted cluster and factor analysis, with application to the MMPI and Holzinger-Harman problems. *Multivariate Behavioral Research,* 1966, 1, 229–244.

———. Person-clusters on intellectual abilities and on MMPI attributes. *Multivariate Behavioral Research,* 1967, 2, 5–34.

Tsubouchi, K., and R. L. Jenkins. Three types of delinquents: their performance on MMPI and PCR. *Journal of Clinical Psychology,* 1969, 25, 353–358.

Tuthill, E. W., J. E. Overall, and L. E. Hollister. Subjective correlates of clinically manifested anxiety and depression. *Psychological Reports,* 1967, 20, 535–542.

Ungerleider, J. T., D. D. Fisher, Marielle Fuller, and A. Caldwell. The "bad trip": the etiology of the adverse LSD reaction. *American Journal of Psychiatry*, 1968, 124, 1483–1490.

U.S. Army. *Multiphasic personality inventory manual.* Adjutant General's Office, War Department, TC-M3, 1944.

Urmer, A. H., H. O. Black, and L. V. Wendland. A comparison of taped and booklet forms of the MMPI. *Journal of Clinical Psychology*, 1960, 16, 33–34.

Vaughan, R. P. The effect of stress on the MMPI scales K and D. *Journal of Clinical Psychology*, 1963, 19, 432.

Vestre, N. D., and W. G. Klett. Classification of MMPI profiles using the Gilberstadt-Duker rules. *Journal of Clinical Psychology*, 1969, 25, 284–286.

Voas, R. B. Correlates of reading speed and the time required to complete personality inventories. U.S. Navy School of Aviation Medicine, Research Report, No. 16, 1956.

———. Personality correlates of reading speed and the time required to complete questionnaires. *Psychological Reports*, 1957, 3, 177–182.

Walch, A. E., and R. A. Schneider. The MMPI: an evaluation of its use in private practice. *Minnesota Medicine*, 1947, 30, 753–758.

Walker, C. E. The effect of eliminating offensive items on the reliability and validity of the MMPI. *Journal of Clinical Psychology*, 1967, 23, 363–366.

———, and J. Ward. Characteristics of offensive MMPI items and the consequences of instructions to the subject to omit such items. *American Psychologist*, 1968, 23, 618.

Waller, Patricia F., D. W. Reinfurt, C. B. Reifler, and G. G. Koch. *Motorcycles versus automobiles: how do their owners differ?* Chapel Hill: University of North Carolina Highway Safety Research Center, 1969.

Warner, W. L., Marcia Meeker, and K. Eells. *Social class in the United States.* Chicago: Science Research Associates, 1949.

Watman, W. A. The relationship between acting-out behavior and some psychological test indices in a prison population. *Journal of Clinical Psychology*, 1966, 22, 279–280.

Watson, C. G. Construction of MMPI scales to differentiate chronic schizophrenic and brain-damaged men. Unpublished manuscript, 1968.

———. An attempt to develop a useful process-reactive scale for the MMPI. *Journal of Clinical Psychology*, 1969, 25, 194–196.

———, and R. W. Thomas. MMPI profiles of brain-damaged and schizophrenic patients. *Perceptual and Motor Skills*, 1968, 27, 567–573.

Webb, J. T. Difference in patient populations of private practice psychologists and private practice psychiatrists. *American Psychologist*, 1970, 25, 860. (a)

———. Regional and sex differences in MMPI scale high-point frequencies of psychiatric patients. *American Psychologist*, 1970, 25, 809. (b)

———, M. L. Miller, and R. D. Fowler. Validation of a computerized MMPI interpretation system. *Proceedings of the 77th Annual Convention of the APA*, 1969, 4, 523–524.

———, M. L. Miller, and R. D. Fowler. Extending professional time: a computerized MMPI interpretation service. *Journal of Clinical Psychology*, 1970, 26, 210–214.

Wechsler, D. *The measurement and appraisal of adult intelligence.* Baltimore: Williams and Wilkins, 1958.

Weigel, R. G., and Maryann Phillips. An evaluation of MMPI scoring accuracy by two national scoring agencies. *Journal of Clinical Psychology*, 1967, 23, 102–103.

Weisgerber, C. A. Norms for the MMPI with student nurses. *Journal of Clinical Psychology*, 1954, 10, 192–194.

———. Comparison of normalized and linear T scores in the MMPI. *Journal of Clinical Psychology*, 1965, 21, 412–415.

Weiss, R. L., and R. H. Moos. Response biases in the MMPI: a sequential analysis. *Psychological Bulletin*, 1965, 63, 403–409.

Welsh, G. S. An extension of Hathaway's MMPI profile coding system. *Journal of Consulting Psychology*, 1948, 12, 343–344. (Also reprinted in Welsh and Dahlstrom, *Basic readings.*)

———. Some practical uses of MMPI profile coding. *Journal of Consulting Psychology*, 1951, 15, 82–84. (Also reprinted in Welsh and Dahlstrom, *Basic readings.*)

———. An anxiety index and an internalization ratio for the MMPI. *Journal of Consulting Psychology*, 1952, 16, 65–72. (Also reprinted in Welsh and Dahlstrom, *Basic readings.*) (a)

———. A factor study of the MMPI using scales with item overlap eliminated. *American Psychologist*, 1952, 7, 341. (b)

———. A comparison of original and extended methods of coding. In G. S. Welsh and W. G. Dahlstrom, eds. *Basic readings on the MMPI in psychology and medicine*. Minneapolis: University of Minnesota Press, 1956. (a)

———. Factor dimensions A and R. In G. S. Welsh and W. G. Dahlstrom, eds. *Basic readings on the MMPI in psychology and medicine*. Minneapolis: University of Minnesota Press, 1956. (b)

———. Intercorrelations amongst validity and clinical scales on the MMPI. Unpublished materials, 1956. (c)

———. MMPI profiles and factor scales A and R. *Journal of Clinical Psychology*, 1965, 21, 43–47.

———, and A. L. Andersen. The correlation of Si with other scales. Unpublished manuscript, 1948.

———, and W. G. Dahlstrom, eds. *Basic readings on the MMPI in psychology and medicine*. Minneapolis: University of Minnesota Press, 1956.

———, and P. L. Sullivan. Booklet-card, card-booklet item conversion tables for MMPI. *Psychological Abstracts*, 1952, 26, 652. (a)

———, and P. L. Sullivan. MMPI configurations in passive-aggressive personality problems. Unpublished materials, 1952. (b)

Westin, A. F. *Privacy and freedom*. New York: Atheneum, 1967.

Wheeler, W. M., K. B. Little, and G. F. J. Lehner. The internal structure of the MMPI. *Journal of Consulting Psychology*, 1951, 15, 134–141. (Also reprinted in Welsh and Dahlstrom, *Basic readings*.)

White, A. A. Evaluation of psychogenic symptoms in general medicine. *Journal of the American Medical Association*, 1951, 147, 1521–1526.

Whyte, W. H. *The organization man*. New York: Doubleday, 1956.

Wiener, D. N. Differences between the individual and group forms of the MMPI. *Journal of Consulting Psychology*, 1947, 11, 104–106.

———. MMPI K-correction results for non-institutionalized neuropsychiatric cases. *Minnesota Counselor*, 1948, 3, 12–13. (a)

———. Selecting salesmen with subtle-obvious keys for the MMPI. *American Psychologist*, 1948, 3, 364. (b)

———. A control factor in social adjustment. *Journal of Abnormal and Social Psychology*, 1951, 46, 3–8.

———, and L. R. Harmon. Subtle and obvious keys for the MMPI: their development. Advisement Bulletin No. 16, Regional Veterans Administration Office, Minneapolis, 1946.

Wiggins, J. S. Interrelationships among MMPI measures of dissimulation under standard and social desirability instructions. *Journal of Consulting Psychology*, 1959, 23, 419–427.

———. Strategic, method, and stylistic variance in the MMPI. *Psychological Bulletin*, 1962, 59, 224–242.

———, and Judith Vollmar. The content of the MMPI. *Journal of Clinical Psychology*, 1959, 15, 45–47.

Wilcox, G. T. Note on a rapid scoring procedure for the card form of the MMPI. *Journal of Clinical Psychology*, 1958, 14, 85.

Wilcox, R., and A. Krasnoff. Influence of test-taking attitudes on personality inventory scores. *Journal of Consulting Psychology*, 1967, 31, 188–194.

Wilson, D. L. Interpretive hypotheses for the MMPI in a Veterans Administration setting. Pre-doctoral clinical paper, University of North Carolina, 1965.

Windle, C. Test-retest effect on personality questionnaires. *Educational and Psychological Measurement*, 1954, 14, 617–633.

———. The relationships among five MMPI "anxiety" indices. *Journal of Consulting Psychology*, 1955, 19, 61–63.

Wolf, S., W. R. Freinek, and J. W. Shaffer. Comparability of complete oral and booklet forms of the MMPI. *Journal of Clinical Psychology*, 1964, 20, 375–378.

Woodworth, D. G., F. Barron, and D. W. MacKinnon. An analysis of life history interviewer's ratings for 100 air force captains. Air Force Personnel and Training Research Center, Research Report, AFPTRC-TN-57-129, 1957.

Yonge, G. D. Certain consequences of applying the K factor to MMPI scores. *Educational and Psychological Measurement*, 1966, 26, 887–893.

Young, R. C. Effects of differential instruction on the MMPI's of state hospital patients. *Proceedings of the 73rd Annual Convention of the APA*, 1965, 281–282.

Zucker, R. A., and M. Manosevitz. MMPI patterns of overt male homosexuals: reinterpretation and comment on Dean and Richardson's study. *Journal of Consulting Psychology*, 1966, 30, 555–557.

Zuckerman, M., H. Persky, K. M. Eckman, and T. R. Hopkins. A multitrait multimethod measurement approach to the traits (or states) of anxiety, depression and hostility. *Journal of Projective Techniques and Personality Assessment*, 1967, 31, 39–48.

Zung, W. W. Factors influencing the self-rating depression scale. *Archives of General Psychiatry*, 1967, 16, 543–547.

———, C. B. Richards, and M. J. Short. Self-rating depression scale in an outpatient clinic: further validation of the SDS. *Archives of General Psychiatry*, 1965, 13, 508–515.

Index